The College WRITER

A Guide to Thinking, Writing, and Researching

Sixth Edition

Australia • Brazil • Mexico • Singapore • United Kingdom • United States

John Van Rys
Redeemer University College

Verne Meyer
Dordt College

Randall VanderMey
Westmont College

Pat Sebranek

***The College Writer: A Guide to Thinking, Writing, and Researching,* Sixth Edition**

John Van Rys, Verne Meyer, Randall VanderMey, and Pat Sebranek

Product Director: Monica Eckman

Product Manager: Laura Ross

Content Developer: Kate Scheinman, Leslie Taggart

Associate Content Developer: Claire Branman

Product Assistant: Shelby Nathanson

Marketing Manager: Kina Lara

Content Project Manager: Aimee Bear

Art Director: Marissa Falco

Manufacturing Planner: Betsy Donaghey

IP Analyst: Ann Hoffmann

IP Project Manager: Kathryn Kucharek

Production Service: Thoughtful Learning

Compositor: Thoughtful Learning

Text and Cover Designer: Thoughtful Learning

Cover Image: Vadim Sadovski/Shutterstock.com; riggsby/Shutterstock.com

Printed in the United States of America

Print Number: 02 Print Year: 2017

Library of Congress Control Number: 2016950501

Student edition: ISBN: 978-1-305-95806-7

Loose-leaf edition: ISBN: 978-1-305-95909-5

Cengage Learning
20 Channel Center Street
Boston, MA 02210
USA

Brief Contents

Contents

Online Bonus Chapters

III. Research and Writing

IV. Handbook

Thematic Table of Contents for Readings

Character and Conscience

Community and Culture

Disease, Death, and Coping

Diversity and Equity

Education and Learning

Environment and Nature

Ethics and Ideology

Ethnicity and Identity

Family and Friends

Fashion and Lifestyle

Gender and Integrity

Humor and Humanity

Language and Literature

Memory and Tradition

Science and Health

Terror and Our Time

Work and Play

Preface

Combining streamlined instruction in the writing process with outstanding accessibility, the sixth edition of *The College Writer* is a fully updated four-in-one text with a rhetoric, a reader, a research guide, and a handbook for students at any skill level. Throughout the text, numerous student and professional writing samples highlight important features of academic writing—from voice to documentation—and offer guidance for students' own papers. The sixth edition features fully refreshed sample essays, stronger instruction in argumentative writing, revamped activities and projects, and MLA 8th edition updates.

New Features

- **Thirty NEW sample essays,** 12 student and 18 professional, offer students fresh perspectives on relevant, current topics—from human empathy for whales to groupthink to cyberbullying. Perfect for discussion, these essays will also inspire students' own writing. New professional writers include such well-knowns as Susan Sontag, Amy Tan, Atul Gawande, Malcolm Gladwell, Ernest Hemingway, and David Brooks, along with Melissa Pritchard, Reshma Memon Yaqub, Brian Phillips, Maria Konnikova, Susan Cain, and James Kilmore. New student writers tackle topics such as family violence, cultural identity, face blindness, e-waste, and privacy in a surveillance age.
- **ENHANCED Chapter 17, "Strategies for Argumentation and Persuasion," and the NEW Chapter 18, "Arguing for Positions, Actions, and Solutions,"** strengthen instruction in argumentative writing. Chapter 17 now includes attention to the contrast between Toulmin and Rogerian approaches to argument, along with a sample argument by Malcolm Gladwell and a fallacy-focused essay by philosopher Kathleen Dean Moore. Chapter 18 integrates and streamlines instruction in forms of argumentative writing that had previously been somewhat artificially separated into chapters on taking a position, calling for action, and solving problems. At the same time, this new chapter offers more instruction on the principles involved in forms of argumentative writing, along with new sample essays that cluster around campus controversies, environmental challenges, and social institutions (including the family).
- **NEW activities and projects** help students fully engage readings, complete their own writing, and extend their learning through critical thinking. After each sample essay, "Reading for Better Writing" questions now ask students to *connect* the reading to their own lives and experiences, show *comprehension* of the content, study *writing strategies* within the piece, and brainstorm related topics and approaches for their own projects. End-of-chapter activities now extend students' learning through critical-thinking applications such as *Photo Op, Wise Words, Living Today, Public Texts, Writing Reset,* and *Major Work.*

- **NEW and ENHANCED instruction in principles of academic writing** helps students to more effectively produce thoughtful, energetic, college-level prose. A new diagram of the writing process (Figure 2.2 on page 26) does justice to the recursive nature of writing, while more attention to thesis development (page 46) and an introduction to academic writing moves (pages 64–66) shows students how to strengthen, develop, and expand their ideas. A new overview of the rhetorical modes (pages 140–141) underscores how writers draw upon and integrate thinking patterns in their work. New attention to eliminating wordiness (page 102) and striving for plain English (page 105) helps students write clear, concise prose. And to reinforce new instruction, students will find tips on reviewing instructor feedback on writing (page 113).
- **Fully UPDATED MLA Documentation (8th edition)** gives students the instruction they need to understand the major changes to the MLA system and to implement those changes through correct and effective documentation of their research. The new system is introduced through an easy-reference quick guide, presented through clear examples, and modeled in new student essays.
- **REORGANIZED chapters in the Reader and the Handbook** offer a more logical progression in concepts for instructors and students. In the Reader, the analytical modes follow a sequence from lesser to greater thinking complexity: definition, classification, process, comparison-contrast, and cause-effect. In the Handbook, instruction now begins with the foundational matters of parts of speech and sentence structure before moving on to sentence errors, punctuation, mechanics, and usage.

Key Features

- ***The College Writer* provides students with a concise yet complete overview of the writing process.** The text's unique "at-a-glance" visual format presents each major concept in a one- or two-page spread, with examples illustrating explanations, and then the opportunity for hands-on practice, with writing assignments or practice exercises.
- **Consistent attention to the rhetorical situation**—writer, reader, message, medium, and context—gives students a tool to analyze the works of others and create their own works. Chapter 1, for instance, begins with an illustration of the rhetorical situation and extended tips for reading actively.
- **"Learning Objectives" at the beginning of each chapter help students focus on key learning points;** main headings throughout the chapter reinforce those points; and "Learning-Objective Checklists" at the end of the chapter enable students to track their performance.
- **"Common Traits of College Writing," introduced in chapter 2 and then underlying much of the instruction in the text, help students understand and achieve college-level writing.** These traits are also in sync with the "WPA Outcomes Statement for First-Year Composition."

- **Emphasis on thesis and outline creation encourages students to organize their thinking as they write.**
- **High-interest academic writings from students and professionals help writers understand and create a scholarly tone.** Throughout the text, the authors offer examples of writing for different disciplines as well as in different work contexts.
- **"Writing with Sources" boxes, integrated into the writing-process chapters, show students how attention to research-related issues might help them at a given step in the writing process.**
- **Each chapter includes projects or activities that may be completed individually or in groups.** That way, the text is a flexible tool for cultivating individual skills and facilitating collaborative learning.
- **Chapter 16, "Reading Literature: A Case Study in Analysis," addresses literary analysis as a form of analytical writing that utilizes many of the principles and practices addressed in the analytical writing chapters (11-15).** In that way, the chapter consolidates and illustrates that instruction, showing how writers draw upon several analytical modes to answer their questions about poems, short stories, and even films. The chapter also includes the poem and short story analyzed by student writers.
- **The Research section gives students all the tools they need to do twenty-first century research,** including working with digital databases; understanding the differences between primary, secondary, and tertiary sources; working effectively with sources, while avoiding plagiarism; learning to evaluate diverse sources; and documenting their research in MLA or APA format.
- **The Handbook covers key points of grammar, sentence structure, sentence errors, punctuation, mechanics, and usage, as well as multilingual and ESL guidelines.** These topics are reinforced by exercises available both in the text and online via MindTap.
- **Charts, graphs, and photos help visual learners grasp concepts and cultivate visual literacy in all students.** These elements range from the high-interest chapter-opening photos with a "Visually Speaking" prompt to "Photo Op" activities at the end of many chapters, critical-thinking through viewing examples in chapter 1, and graphic organizers in chapter 3.
- **Color-coded cut-out tabs make it easy to flip to any of the four sections of the book.**
- **The entire text is available as a multimedia eBook, featuring audio, video, exercises, models, and web links.**
- **Chapters on "Writing for the Web," "Taking Tests," "Writing for the Workplace," and "Preparing Oral Presentations"** are listed in the Table of Contents and are available online in MindTap.

New to This Edition

New Sample Essays: Thirty new sample essays include works by professionals such as Susan Sontag, Amy Tan, Atul Gawanda, Malcolm Gladwell, Ernest Hemingway, David Brooks, Melissa Pritchard, Reshma Memon Yaqub, Brian Phillips, and Maria Konnikova.

214 Reader: Strategies and Samples

Analyzing Medical Procedures

"No Risky Chances" is an essay excerpted from the book, *Being Mortal: Medicine and What Matters in the End*. In both texts, author and physician Dr. Atul Gawande critiques traditional procedures used by physicians to care for patients during their last stages of life. "Lacking a coherent view of how people might live successfully all the way to the very end," he says, "we have allowed our fates to be controlled by medicine, technology, and strangers."

No Risky Chances:
The conversation that matters most.

I learned about a lot of things in medical school, but mortality wasn't one of them. Although I was given a dry, leathery corpse to dissect in anatomy class in my first term, our textbooks contained almost nothing about aging or frailty or dying. The purpose of medical schooling was to teach how to save lives, not how to tend to their demise.

I had never seen anyone die before I became a doctor, and when I did, it came as 2
a shock. I'd seen multiple family members—my wife, my parents, and my children—go through serious, life-threatening illnesses, but medicine had always pulled them through. I knew theoretically that my patients could die, of course, but every actual instance seemed like a violation, as if the rules I thought we were playing by were broken.

Dying and death confront every new doctor and nurse. The first times, some cry. Some shut down. Some hardly notice. When I saw ... to weep. But I had recurring nightmares in which ... house—even in my bed.

I felt as if I'd failed. But death, of course, is n... may be the enemy, but it is also the natural order ... abstractly, but I didn't know them concretely—th... everyone but also for this person right in front of ... for.

You don't have to spend much time with the ... to see how often medicine fails the people it is sup... our lives are given over to treatments that addle o... sliver's chance of benefit. These days are spent in i... intensive-care units—where regimented, anonym... things that matter to us in life.

As recently as 1945, most deaths occurred in ... percent did. Lacking a coherent view of how peop...

Chapter 11 | Definition 183

Illustrating a Term

Amy Tan is an award-winning writer whose many books include *The Joy Luck Club, The Kitchen God's Wife, The Bonesetter's Daughter,* and *The Valley of Amazement*. When asked to respond to the writing prompt "confession," she relayed the following personal experience that concludes with an urgent confession.

Confession

"My mother had a very difficult childhood, having seen her own mother kill herself. So she didn't always know how to be the nurturing mother that we all expect we should have." —Amy Tan 1

My mother has Alzheimer's disease. Often her thoughts reach back like the 2
winter tide, exposing the wreckage of a former shore. Often she's mired in 1968, the year my older brother and father died. This was also the year that she took me and my younger brother across an ocean to Switzerland, a place so preposterously different that she knew she had to give up grieving simply to survive. That year, she remembers, she was very, very sad. I too remember. I was sixteen then, and I recall a late-night hour when my mother and I were arguing in a chalet, that tinder box of emotions where we lived.

She had pushed me into the small bedroom we shared, and as she slapped me 3
about the head, I backed into a corner, to a room that looked out upon the lake, the Alps, the beautiful outside world. My mother was furious because I had a boyfriend. She said he was a drug addict, a bad man who would use me for sex and throw me away like leftover garbage. "Stop seeing him!" she ordered. I shook my head. The more she beat me, the more implacable I became, and this in turn fueled her outrage. "You didn't love your daddy or Peter! When they die you not even sad." I kept my face to the window, unmoved. What does she know about sad? She sobbed and beat her chest. "I'd rather kill myself first than see you destroy your life!" Suicide. How many times had she threatened that before? "I wish you the one die! Not Peter, not Daddy." She had just confirmed what I had always suspected. Now she flew at me with her fists. "I rather kill you! I rather see you die!" And then perhaps horrified by what she had just said, she fled the room.

Thank God that was over. Suddenly she was back. She slammed shut the door, 4
latched it, then locked it with a key. I saw the flash of a meat cleaver just before she pushed me to the wall and brought the blade's edge to within an inch from my throat. Her eyes were like a wild animal's, shiny, fixated on the kill. In an excited voice she said she was going to kill me first, then my younger brother, then herself, the whole

Enhanced, Streamlined Instruction in Argumentation and Persuasion: Chapter 17, "Strategies for Argumentation and Persuasion," now includes attention to the contrast between Toulmin and Rogerian approaches to argument, along with sample arguments by Kathleen Dean Moore and Malcolm Gladwell. **Chapter 18, "Arguing for Positions, Actions, and Solutions,"** integrates instruction in three forms of argumentative writing.

Structuring Arguments

The shape of an argument often emerges organically as you think about and research an issue. While you have a lot of freedom about how to shape arguments, two patterns have become popular methods of doing so: Toulmin and Rogerian. In what follows, you will find a brief introduction to each method. Use these introductions to guide your choices for specific arguments.

Understand Toulmin Argumentation

Made popular by British philosopher Stephen Toulmin in his book *The Uses of Argument* (1958), this method lends structure to the way people naturally make arguments. Not exactly formal logic, this pattern offers a practical approach that allows writers and their readers to wrestle over debatable issues through sound thinking. Toulmin's elements do not map out a strict sequence of elements, but writers may draw upon the elements to unfold their thinking within a paragraph or for an entire essay. Many of these elements are addressed more fully later in this chapter (pages 315–322), but here is an overview:

- **Claims** The debatable statement the writer aims to prove or support.

  > Planting trees is a practical step to fight climate change.

- **Qualifiers** Any limits the writer puts on claims in order to make those claims more reasonable, precise, and honest.

  > *Although it is a small step*, planting trees is *one* practical way that *many* people can fight climate change.

- **Support** The reasoning that the writer offers to explain and defend the claim; the evidence that the writer offers to back up the reasoning and thereby ground the claim (various forms of data, information, experience, narratives, authority, and so on).

  > According to the UN, "Deforestation causes 12-18 percent of the world's carbon emission, almost equal to all the CO2 emissions from the global transport sector."

- **Warrants** The logical glue that holds together claims, reasons, and evidence; the assumptions, principles, and values (sometimes unstated), that lie behind the writer's reasoning.

  > Stopping climate change is more important than the economic benefits of deforestation.

- **Backing** When warrants aren't shared or understood by readers, the special reasoning and evidence writers offer to convince readers to accept those principles.

  > Recent research has determined that the 32 million acres of forest lost each year make a significant contribution to global warming.

- **Conditions of Rebuttal** The writer's anticipation of and response to possible objections; his or her sense of other perspectives and positions.

  > Economies dependent on deforestation can take a number of steps toward sustainable practices.

Enriching Questions, Activities, and Projects: After each sample essay, "Reading for Better Writing" questions ask students to *connect* the reading to their own life, show *comprehension* of the content, study *writing strategies* within the piece, and brainstorm related topics and approaches for their own *project*. End-of-chapter activities extend students' learning through critical-thinking applications such as *Photo Op, Wise Words, Living Today, Public Texts, Writing Reset,* and *Major Work.*

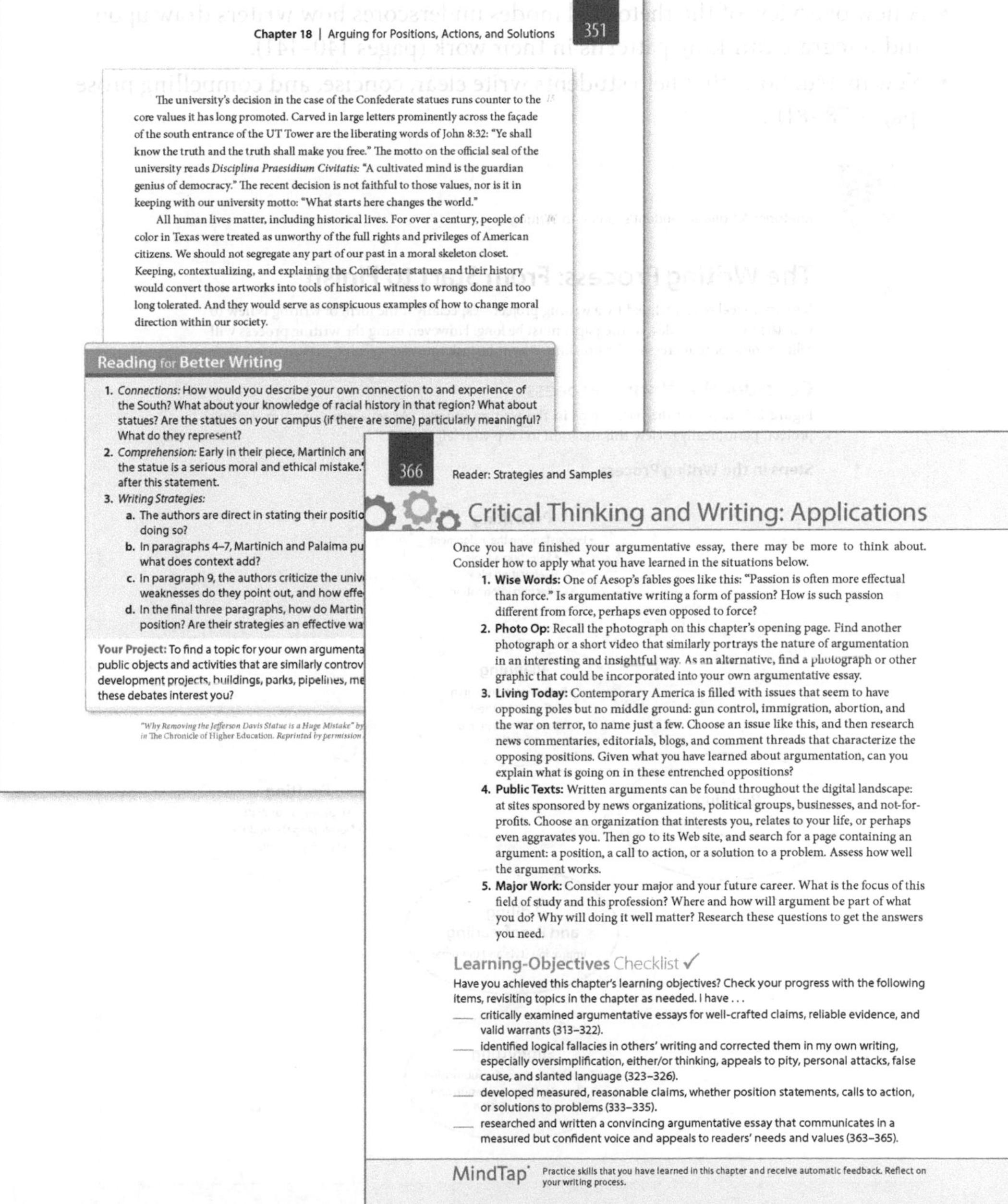

Chapter 18 | Arguing for Positions, Actions, and Solutions 351

The university's decision in the case of the Confederate statues runs counter to the core values it has long promoted. Carved in large letters prominently across the façade of the south entrance of the UT Tower are the liberating words of John 8:32: "Ye shall know the truth and the truth shall make you free." The motto on the official seal of the university reads *Disciplina Praesidium Civitatis*: "A cultivated mind is the guardian genius of democracy." The recent decision is not faithful to those values, nor is it in keeping with our university motto: "What starts here changes the world."

All human lives matter, including historical lives. For over a century, people of color in Texas were treated as unworthy of the full rights and privileges of American citizens. We should not segregate any part of our past in a moral skeleton closet. Keeping, contextualizing, and explaining the Confederate statues and their history would convert those artworks into tools of historical witness to wrongs done and too long tolerated. And they would serve as conspicuous examples of how to change moral direction within our society.

Reading for Better Writing

1. *Connections:* How would you describe your own connection to and experience of the South? What about your knowledge of racial history in that region? What about statues? Are the statues on your campus (if there are some) particularly meaningful? What do they represent?
2. *Comprehension:* Early in their piece, Martinich an the statue is a serious moral and ethical mistake. after this statement.
3. *Writing Strategies:*
   a. The authors are direct in stating their positio doing so?
   b. In paragraphs 4–7, Martinich and Palaima pu what does context add?
   c. In paragraph 9, the authors criticize the univ weaknesses do they point out, and how effe
   d. In the final three paragraphs, how do Martin position? Are their strategies an effective wa

Your Project: To find a topic for your own argumenta public objects and activities that are similarly controv development projects, buildings, parks, pipelines, me these debates interest you?

"Why Removing the Jefferson Davis Statue is a Huge Mistake" by in The Chronicle of Higher Education. Reprinted by permission

366 Reader: Strategies and Samples

Critical Thinking and Writing: Applications

Once you have finished your argumentative essay, there may be more to think about. Consider how to apply what you have learned in the situations below.

1. **Wise Words:** One of Aesop's fables goes like this: "Passion is often more effectual than force." Is argumentative writing a form of passion? How is such passion different from force, perhaps even opposed to force?
2. **Photo Op:** Recall the photograph on this chapter's opening page. Find another photograph or a short video that similarly portrays the nature of argumentation in an interesting and insightful way. As an alternative, find a photograph or other graphic that could be incorporated into your own argumentative essay.
3. **Living Today:** Contemporary America is filled with issues that seem to have opposing poles but no middle ground: gun control, immigration, abortion, and the war on terror, to name just a few. Choose an issue like this, and then research news commentaries, editorials, blogs, and comment threads that characterize the opposing positions. Given what you have learned about argumentation, can you explain what is going on in these entrenched oppositions?
4. **Public Texts:** Written arguments can be found throughout the digital landscape: at sites sponsored by news organizations, political groups, businesses, and not-for-profits. Choose an organization that interests you, relates to your life, or perhaps even aggravates you. Then go to its Web site, and search for a page containing an argument: a position, a call to action, or a solution to a problem. Assess how well the argument works.
5. **Major Work:** Consider your major and your future career. What is the focus of this field of study and this profession? Where and how will argument be part of what you do? Why will doing it well matter? Research these questions to get the answers you need.

Learning-Objectives Checklist ✓

Have you achieved this chapter's learning objectives? Check your progress with the following items, revisiting topics in the chapter as needed. I have . . .

___ critically examined argumentative essays for well-crafted claims, reliable evidence, and valid warrants (313–322).
___ identified logical fallacies in others' writing and corrected them in my own writing, especially oversimplification, either/or thinking, appeals to pity, personal attacks, false cause, and slanted language (323–326).
___ developed measured, reasonable claims, whether position statements, calls to action, or solutions to problems (333–335).
___ researched and written a convincing argumentative essay that communicates in a measured but confident voice and appeals to readers' needs and values (363–365).

MindTap® Practice skills that you have learned in this chapter and receive automatic feedback. Reflect on your writing process.

Enhanced Instruction in the Principles of Academic Writing: The following new elements help students to more effectively produce thoughtful, energetic, college-level prose:

- A new diagram of the writing process illustrating the recursive nature of writing (Figure 2.2 on page 26).
- Expanded instruction on thesis development (page 46).
- An introduction to academic writing moves (pages 64–66) showing students how to strengthen, develop, and expand their ideas.
- A new overview of the rhetorical modes underscores how writers draw upon and integrate thinking patterns in their work (pages 140–141).
- New instructions that help students write clear, concise, and compelling prose (pages 78–81).

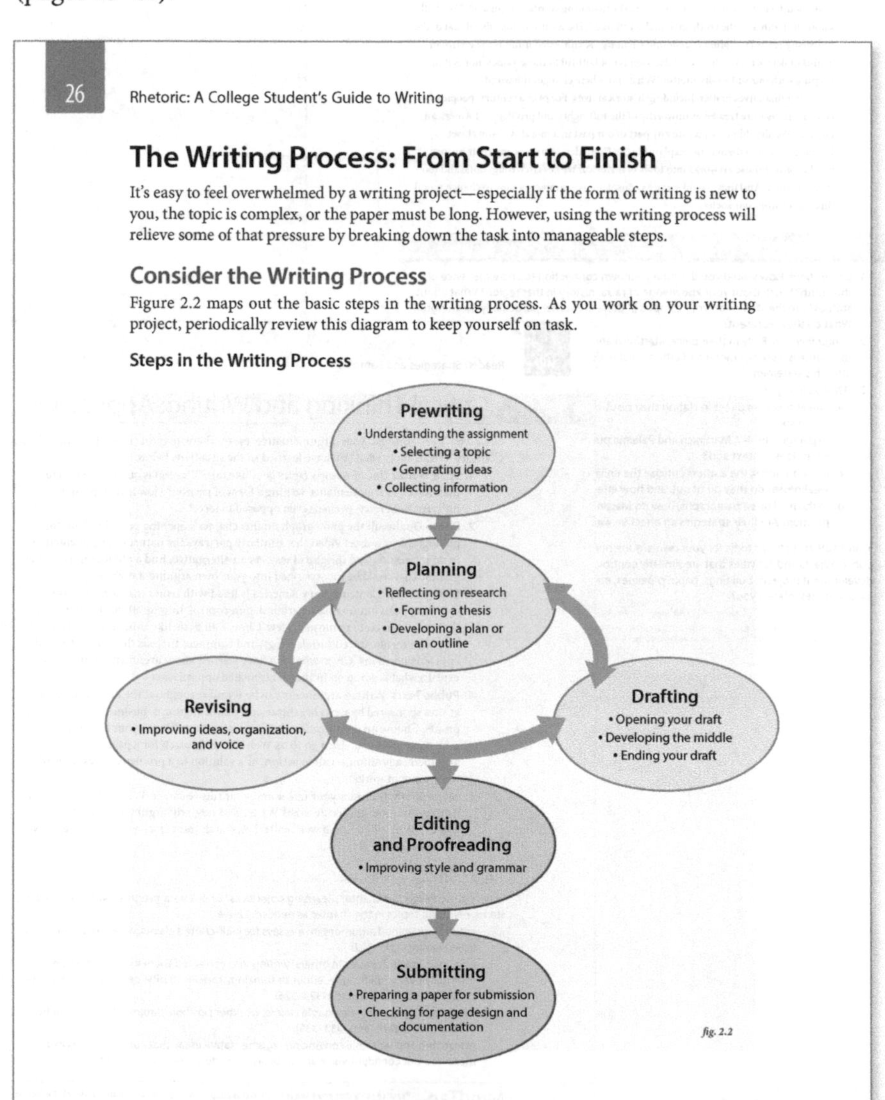

Updated Chapter 23 Instructions on MLA Documentation and Style (8th edition): Clear instructions and illustrations help students understand and use the current MLA system for documenting research writing. The new system is introduced through an easy-reference quick guide, presented through clear examples, and modeled in new student essays.

476 Research and Writing

Guidelines for Works-Cited Entries

The works-cited section lists only those sources that you have cited in your paper. For guidelines on formatting your works-cited list, see pages 487–488, as well as the sample works-cited list on pages 501–502. In what follows, you will first find a template for works-cited entries, showing the essential pattern to follow. After the template, you will find guidelines for constructing any entry by drawing upon the nine core elements of source identification and arranging those elements in the order listed.

Works-Cited Template

Every works-cited entry will include some or all of nine elements, formatted and punctuated in the manner indicated.

Author. Title of Source [normally italicized or in quotation marks]. *Title of Container,* Other Contributors, Version, Number, Publisher, Publication Date, Location.

Works-Cited Components

The following table provides you with guidelines for presenting each of the nine main components of works-cited entries. Review both the instructions and examples to understand the logic of each element.

1. **The Author** is the person, people, or organization that created the source. Note that for online sources, pseudonyms and handles may be used. In general, omit titles and degrees from names, but present the name accurately from the source. Follow the author with a period.
   - **One author:** Invert the author's name.
   - **Two authors:** Follow the order given in the source. Invert the first author's name, but put the second in traditional order. Separate the authors' names with a comma.
   - **Three or more authors:** Name only the first author listed, followed by *et al.* (meaning *and others).*
   - **Other contributors:** If appropriate, you may put another contributor in this first position to emphasize the focus in your writing: an editor, a director, a performer, and so on. Spell out the role after the name and a comma.

Jacob, Mira.

King, Martin Luther, Jr.
@PiradorUSA.

Environmental Protection Agency.

Pratchett, Terry, and Neil Gaiman.

Raabe, William A., et al.

Dunham, Lena, performer.

Reorganized Chapters in the Reader and the Handbook: The new organization offers a more logical progression of instruction. In the Reader, the analytical modes (chapters 10-15) follow a sequence from lesser to greater thinking complexity: definition, classification, process, comparison-contrast, and cause-effect. Also in chapter 18, three forms (arguing for positions, actions, and solutions) are integrated and enhanced.

In the Handbook, instruction now begins with the foundational matters of parts of speech and sentence structure before moving on to sentence errors, punctuation, mechanics, and usage.

Part II Reader: Strategies and Samples

9. Forms of College Writing
10. Narration, Description, and Reflection
11. Definition
12. Classification
13. Process
14. Comparison and Contrast
15. Cause and Effect
16. Analyzing Literature: A Case Study
17. Strategies for Argumentation and Persuasion
18. Arguing for Positions, Actions, and Solutions

Part IV Handbook

25. Understanding Grammar
26. Constructing Sentences
27. Avoiding Sentence Errors
28. Marking Punctuation
29. Checking Mechanics
30. Using the Right Word
31. Multilingual and ESL Guidelines

MindTap

MindTap® English for Van Rys/Meyer/VanderMey/Sebranek's *The College Writer,* 6th edition engages your students to become better thinkers, communicators, and writers by blending your course materials with content that supports every aspect of the writing process.

- Interactive activities on grammar and mechanics promote application in student writing.
- An easy-to-use paper management system helps prevent plagiarism and allows for electronic submission, grading, and peer review.
- A vast database of scholarly sources with video tutorials and examples supports every step of the research process.
- Professional tutoring guides students from rough drafts to polished writing.
- Visual analytics track student progress and engagement.
- Seamless integration into your campus learning management system keeps all your course materials in one place.
- MindTap lets you compose your course, your way.

MindTap® English now comes equipped with the diagnostic-guided JUST IN TIME PLUS learning module for foundational concepts and embedded course support. The module features scaffolded video tutorials, instructional text content, and auto-graded activities designed to address each student's specific needs for practice and support to succeed in college-level composition courses.

Instructor's Resources

The instructor's manual provides teaching suggestions, suggested answers to exercises, and a sample course syllabus to assist instructors in teaching the course. The instructor's manual and other resources for teaching can be accessed in MindTap.

Acknowledgements

The authors express their gratitude to the following reviewers of the *The College Writer,* 6th Edition.

Marsha Anderson-Hudson, *Wharton County Junior College*
Lauryn Angel, *Collin College*
Julie Baker, *Northeastern University*
Jacqueline A. Bollinger, *Erie Community College*
Elizabeth Bookser Barkley, *Mount St. Joseph University*
David Carpenter, *University of Arkansas Community College at Batesville*
James Celestino, *Salt Lake Community College*
Theron Coleman, *Baltimore City Community College*
Michael Conver, *Cornerstone University*
Judith Cortelloni, *Lincoln College*
Patricia Coward, *Canisius College*
Jean Dean, *Milwaukee Area Technical College*
Mackinzee Escamilla, *South Plains College*
Ulanda Forbess, *North Lake College*
Jill Goad, *Shorter University*
Jerri Harwell, *Salt Lake Community College*
Suzanne Hess, *Florida State College at Jacksonville*
Michael Hricik, *Westmoreland County Community College*
Tehmina Khan, *South Coast College*
Paul Long, *Baltimore City Community College*
Kelly B. McCalla, *Riverland Community College*
Nell Morningstar, *IPR*
Katrina Neckuty-Fodness, *Globe University*
Starr Nordgren, *McHenry County College*
Julianne Palma, *Monroe Community College*
Alexandria Piland, *Central New Mexico Community College*
Karrie Preasmyer, *Vanguard University*
Sharon Prince, *Wharton County Junior College*
Chyrel Remmers, *Central Community College*
Dr. Jim Richey, *Tyler Junior College*
Justin Senter, *Northeastern University*
Marian Smith, *Chippewa Valley Technical College*
Eric Stalions, Martin Methodist College
Jennifer Stefaniak, *Springfield Technical Community College*
Grazia Svokos, *Northeastern CPS*
Tom Vollman, *Milwaukee Area Technical College*
Rosanna Walker, *Southwestern College*
Audrey A. Wick, *Blinn College*
Joseph A. Wolcott, *Erie Community College*

I. Rhetoric:
A College Student's Guide to Writing

Chapter 1

Critical Thinking Through Reading, Viewing, and Writing

MindTap

Understand the goals of the chapter and complete a warm-up activity online.

Every day, we encounter words and images; often, we create them for others to read and view. Exchanging these messages constitutes communication, a complex process that involves several variables: the writer/designer, the message and the medium used, the reader/viewer, and the context.

In college, such communication—whether in reading articles, viewing films, or writing essays—requires critical thinking. Such thinking puts ideas in context, makes connections between them, and tests their meaning and logic. This chapter provides strategies that will help you think critically as you read, view, and write.

Learning Objectives

By working through this chapter, you will be able to

- actively read different written texts.
- produce personal responses to texts.
- objectively summarize texts.
- actively view, analyze, and critique visual images.
- implement strategies to think critically about topics.
- practice modes of thinking through writing.

Visually Speaking Figure 1.1 shows people viewing art in a museum. Look closely at the image: how would you describe what these people are doing? What thinking practices does such viewing involve? Consider, as well, other types of images. What viewing do you do, for what reasons, and using what brain power?

Adriano Castelli / Shutterstock.com

fig. 1.1

Critical Thinking Through Reading

Critical reading involves a kind of mental dialogue with the text. To initiate that dialogue, engage the text smartly by using strategies like these: reading actively, mapping the text, outlining it, responding to it, summarizing it, and evaluating it.

Read Actively

Active reading is reading that is mentally alert. Practically speaking, you can read actively by following techniques like these.

- **Remove distractions.** Engaged reading requires that you disengage from all distractions such as your cell phone, Facebook, or TV.
- **Take your time.** Read in stretches of about 45 minutes, followed by short breaks. And when you break, think about what you read, what might come next, and why.
- **Assess the rhetorical situation.** Where and when was this text written and published? Who is the author, and why did he or she write the piece? What are the writer's qualifications to address this topic? Why are you reading it?
- **Preview, read, review.** Start by previewing the text: scan the title, opening and closing paragraphs, headings, topic sentences, and graphics. Next, read the text carefully, asking questions such as "What does this mean?" and "Why is this important?" Finally, review what you have learned and what questions remain unanswered.
- **Read aloud.** Do so for especially difficult parts of the text.
- **Write while reading.** Take notes, especially when working on research projects. Annotate the text by highlighting main points, writing a "?" beside puzzling parts, or jotting key insights in the margin.

Sample Text

The following article was written by Dan Heath and was first published in the June 2, 2010 edition of *Fast Company*. Read the essay, using the active reading tips above and answering the questions that follow.

Why Change Is So Hard: Self-Control Is Exhaustible

You hear something a lot about change: People won't change because they're too lazy. Well, I'm here to stick up for the lazy people. In fact, I want to argue that what looks like laziness is actually exhaustion. The proof comes from a psychology study that is absolutely fascinating. 1

The Study

So picture this: Students come into a lab. It smells amazing—someone has just baked chocolate-chip cookies. On a table in front of them, there are two bowls. One has the fresh-baked cookies. The other has a bunch of radishes. Some of the students are asked to eat some cookies but no radishes. Others are told to eat radishes but no cookies, and while 2 they sit there, nibbling on rabbit food, the researchers leave the room—which is intended to tempt them and is frankly kind of sadistic. But in the study none of the radish-eaters slipped—they showed admirable self-control. And meanwhile, it probably goes without saying that the people gorging on cookies didn't experience much temptation.

Then, the two groups are asked to do a second, seemingly unrelated task—basically a 3
kind of logic puzzle where they have to trace out a complicated geometric pattern without raising their pencils. Unbeknownst to the group, the puzzle can't be solved. The scientists are curious how long individuals will persist at a difficult task. So the cookie-eaters try again and again, for an average of 19 minutes, before they give up. But the radish-eaters—they only last an average of 8 minutes. What gives?

The Results

The answer may surprise you: The radish-eaters ran out of self-control. Psychologists 4
have discovered that self-control is an exhaustible resource. And I don't mean self-control only in the sense of turning down cookies or alcohol; I mean a broader sense of self-supervision—any time you're paying close attention to your actions, like when you're having a tough conversation or trying to stay focused on a paper you're writing. This helps to explain why, after a long hard day at the office, we're more likely to snap at our spouses or have one drink too many—we've depleted our self-control.

And here's why this matters for change: In almost all change situations, you're 5
substituting new, unfamiliar behaviors for old, comfortable ones, and that burns self-control. Let's say I present a new morning routine to you that specifies how you'll shower and brush your teeth. You'll understand it and you might even agree with my process. But to pull it off, you'll have to supervise yourself very carefully. Every fiber of your being will want to go back to the old way of doing things. Inevitably, you'll slip. And if I were uncharitable, I'd see you going back to the old way and I'd say, "You're so lazy. Why can't you just change?"

This brings us back to the point I promised I'd make: That what looks like laziness is 6
often exhaustion. Change wears people out—even well-intentioned people will simply run out of fuel.

Reading for Better Writing

1. *Connections:* Think about your own life. Which activities require you to exert a great deal of self-control? How might this article help you with those struggles?
2. *Comprehension:* In a single sentence, what is the thesis of this essay? How does that thesis grow out of the findings of the psychology study that the essay discusses? Summarize those findings.
3. *Reading Strategies:* Which active-reading practices did you follow when reading this essay? Which ones helped you understand and engage the essay fully? Compare your notes and annotations with a classmate's.

Your Project: Dan Heath's essay explains the results of a research study. For your own writing, consider finding a research report on a topic that interests you. Then use the active reading strategies in this chapter to write an essay like Heath's.

Map the Text

If you are visually oriented, you may understand a text best by mapping out its important parts. One way to do so is by "clustering." Start by naming the main topic in an oval at the center of the page. Then branch out using lines and "balloons," where each balloon contains a word or phrase for one major subtopic. Branch out in further layers of balloons to show even more subpoints, as in Figure 1.2. If you wish, add graphics, arrows, drawings—anything that helps you visualize the relationships among ideas.

fig. 1.2

Outline the Text

Outlining is the traditional way of showing all the major parts, points, and subpoints in a text. An outline uses parallel structure to show main points and subordinate points. See pages 49–52 for more on outlines.

Sample Outline for "Why Change Is So Hard: Self-Control Is Exhaustible"

1. Introduction: Change is hard not because of laziness but because of exhaustion.
2. A study tests self-control.
   - **a.** Some students must eat only cookies—using little self-control.
   - **b.** Some students must eat only radishes—using much self-control.
   - **c.** Both sets of students have to trace a pattern without lifting the pencil—an unsolvable puzzle.
     - Cookie-only students last an average of 19 minutes before quitting.
     - Radish-only students last an average of 8 minutes before quitting.
3. Results show that self-control is exhaustible.
   - **a.** Avoiding temptation and working in a hard, focused way require self-control.
   - **b.** Change requires self-control.
   - **c.** Failure to change often results from exhaustion of self-control.

Evaluate the Text

Critical reading does not mean disproving the text or disapproving of it. It means thoughtfully inspecting, weighing, and evaluating the writer's ideas. To strengthen your reading skills, learn to evaluate texts using the following criteria.

1. **Judge the reading's credibility.** Where was it published? How reliable is the author? How current is the information? How accurate and complete does it seem to be? In addition, consider the author's tone of voice, attitude, and apparent biases.

   Discussion: Dan Heath, the author of "Why Change Is So Hard" is a *New York Times* best-selling author, a consultant to the Aspen Institute, and a monthly columnist for *Fast Company*. How do these credentials affect your reading of the article? How does the article itself build or break credibility?

2. **Put the reading in a larger context.** How do the text's ideas match what you know from other sources? Which details of background, history, and social context help you understand this text's perspective? How have things changed or remained the same since the text's publication? Which allusions (references to people, events, and so on) does the writer use? Why?

   Discussion: "Why Change Is So Hard" centers around a single psychological study and draws from it specific conclusions about self-control. What other studies have attempted to track self-control? Is this a new subdiscipline in psychological research, or a well-established one?

3. **Evaluate the reasoning and support.** Is the reasoning clear and logical? Are the examples and other supporting details appropriate and enlightening? Are inferences (what the text implies) consistent with the tone and message? (Look especially for hidden logic and irony that undercut what is said explicitly.)

   Discussion: In "Why Change Is So Hard," Heath identifies exhaustion of self-control as the reason for the difference between the performance of the two test groups. What other explanations could there be for the difference in performance between the two groups of subjects? Is Heath's reasoning sound and convincing?

4. **Reflect on how the reading challenges you.** Which of your beliefs and values does the reading call into question? What discomfort does it create? Does your own perspective skew your evaluation?

   Discussion: What self-control issues have you faced? What might this article have to say about those who work two jobs, run single-parent households, serve extended terms in war zones, or otherwise must exert superhuman levels of self-control? What social changes could help keep people from "snapping"?

fyi For additional help evaluating texts, see pages 384–387. For information on detecting logical fallacies, which weaken writers' arguments, see pages 323–326.

Responding to a Text

In a sense, when you read a text, you enter into a dialogue with it. Your response expresses your turn in the dialogue. Such a response can take varied forms, from a journal entry to a blog to a posting in an online-comments forum.

Guidelines for Response Writing

On the surface, responding to a text seems perfectly natural—just let it happen. But it can be a bit more complicated. A written response typically is not the same as a private diary entry but is instead shared with other readers, who may be in your class or elsewhere, including online. To develop a fitting response, keep in mind common expectations for this kind of writing, as well as your instructor's requirements, if the response is for a course:

1. **Be honest.** Although you want to remain sensitive to the context in which you will share your response, be bold enough to be honest about your reaction to the text—what it makes you think, feel, and question. To that end, a response usually allows you to express yourself directly using the pronoun "I."
2. **Be fluid.** Let the flow of your thoughts guide you in what you write. Don't stop to worry about grammar, punctuation, mechanics, and spelling. These can be quickly cleaned up before you share or submit your response.
3. **Be reflective.** Generally, the goal of a response is to offer thoughtful reflection as opposed to knee-jerk reaction. Show, then, that you are engaging the text's ideas, relating them to your own experience, looking both inward and outward. Avoid a shallow reaction that comes from skimming the text or misreading it.
4. **Be selective.** By nature, a response must limit its focus; it cannot exhaust all your reactions to the text. So zero in on one or two elements of your response, and run with those to see where they take you in your dialogue with the text.

Sample Response

Here is part of a student's response to Dan Heath's "Why Change Is So Hard" on pages 4–5. Note the informality and explanatory tone.

Heath's report of the psychological experiment is very vivid, referring to the smell of chocolate-chip cookies and hungry students "gorging" on them. He uses the term "sadistic" to refer to making the radish-eaters sit and watch this go on. I wonder if this mild torment plays into the student's readiness to give up on the later test. If I'd been rewarded with cookies, I'd feel indebted to the testers and would stick with it longer. If I'd been punished with radishes, I might give up sooner just to spite the testers.

Now that I think of it, the digestion of all that sugar and fat in the cookies, as opposed to the digestion of roughage from the radishes, might also affect concentration and performance. Maybe the sugar "high" gives students the focus to keep going?

Summarizing a Text

Writing a summary disciplines you by making you pull only essentials from a reading—the main points, the thread of the argument. By doing so, you create a brief record of the text's contents and exercise your ability to comprehend, analyze, and synthesize.

Guidelines for Summary Writing

Writing a summary requires sifting out the least important points, sorting the essential ones to show their relationships, and stating those points in your own words. Follow these guidelines:

1. **Skim first; then read closely.** First, get a sense of the whole, including the main idea and strategies for support. Then read carefully, taking notes as you do.
2. **Capture the text's argument.** Review your notes and annotations, looking for main points and clear connections. State these briefly and clearly, in your own words. Include only what is essential, excluding most examples and details. Don't say simply that the text talks about its subject; tell what it says about that subject.
3. **Test your summary.** Aim to objectively provide the heart of the text; avoid interjecting your own opinions and presence as a writer. Don't confuse an objective summary of a text with a response to it (shown on the previous page). Check your summary against the original text for accuracy and consistency.

Sample Summary

Below is a student's summary of Dan Heath's "Why Change Is So Hard," on pages 4–5. Note how the summary writer includes only main points and phrases them in her own words. She departs from the precise order of details, but records them accurately.

> In the article "Why Change Is So Hard," Dan Heath argues that people who have trouble changing are not lazy, but have simply exhausted their self-control. Heath refers to a study in which one group of students was asked to eat cookies and not radishes, while another group in the same room was asked to eat radishes and not cookies. Afterward, both groups of students were asked to trace an endless geometric design without lifting their pencils. The cookie-only group traced on average 19 minutes before giving up, but the radish-only group traced on average only 8 minutes. They had already used up their self-control. Heath says that any behavioral change requires self-control, an exhaustible resource. Reverting to old behavior is what happens due not to laziness but to exhaustion.

INSIGHT Writing formal summaries—whether as part of literature reviews or as abstracts—is an important skill, especially in the social and natural sciences.

Critical Thinking Through Viewing

Images are created to communicate, just as words are. Most images in everyday life are made to communicate very quickly—magazine covers, ads, signs, movie trailers, and so forth. Other images require contemplation, such as the *Mona Lisa*. When you view an image, view actively and critically.

Actively View Images

Survey the image. See the image as a whole so that you can absorb its overall idea. Look for the image's focal point—what your eye is drawn to. Also consider the relationship between the image's foreground and background, its left content and right content, and its various colors.

Inspect the image. Let your sight touch every part of the image, as if you were reading Braille. Hints of its meaning may lurk in the tiny details as well as in the relationship between the image's parts.

Question the image. Think in terms of each part of the rhetorical situation.

- **Designer:** Who created the image? Why did the person create it?
- **Message:** What is the subject of the image? What is the purpose?
- **Medium:** How was the image originally shown? How is it currently shown?
- **Viewer:** Who is the intended viewer? Why are you viewing the image?
- **Context:** When and where did the image first appear? When and where does it appear now? How does the image relate to its context?

Understand the purpose. Different images have different purposes. Ask yourself, "What is this image meant to do?" and then decide on an appropriate response.

- **Arouse curiosity?** Open your imagination, but stay on guard.
- **Entertain?** Look for the pleasure or the joke, but be wary of excess or of ethically questionable material in the image.
- **Inform or educate?** Search for key instructions, noting what's left out.
- **Illustrate?** Relate the image to the words or concept being illustrated: Does the image clarify or distort the meaning?
- **Persuade?** Examine how the image appeals to the viewer's needs, from safety and satisfaction to self-worth. Are the appeals manipulative, clichéd, or fallacious? Do they play on emotions to bypass reason?
- **Summarize?** Look for the essential message in the image: Does that main idea correspond with the written text?

MOLDOVA 3L

catwalker / Shutterstock.com

View an Image

Chris Krenzke / Thoughtful Learning

The use of *minors* as *miners* is no *minor* problem. *fig. 1.3*

Discussion

Figure 1.3 by Chris Krenzke and the caption by Verne Meyer effectively combine humor with instruction. Originally published in a high school writing handbook, the image's aim is to teach students about a specific word-usage problem while also entertaining them. The image is line art in the "comic" genre, using a humorous scene to convey a serious message. Here are some thoughts on how you might actively view this image:

1. **Survey.** The image tells a story of heavily burdened children working under the demanding supervision of an authoritarian male. That story moves from left to right, from breaking rocks to loading rocks to carrying rocks toward a likely distant destination, the destination pointed to by the man. The black-and-white medium accentuates the starkness.
2. **Inspect.** In terms of the illustration's details, each figure is striking. The individual children share a thinness in their bodies and a strain in their faces. The four children in the line are pictured as beasts of burden bent over by bags that dwarf them. The repetition of figures emphasizes the trudging repetition of their work, and each child in line is pressed farther toward the ground. As for the man, his back is straight and his posture tall. His enormous chin, large nose, overly long but skinny arm, and sharply pointed finger suggest a negative authority. His stubbly face and his caveman clothing add to this figure's prehistoric character.
3. **Question.** Who is the artist Chris Krenzke? When did he first create this image? In what book was it published? When? Why did Krenzke use this caveman style? Who or what do "minors," "miners," and "minor" refer to in the illustration?
4. **Relate.** The connection between the sentence and the image becomes clear when the viewer realizes that "minors" are children not of a legal age to work, "miners" refers to an occupation, and "minor" means insignificant. But the image prompts other connections: the history of horrific child-labor practices during the Industrial Revolution as well as continuing child-labor issues in today's global economy. With these allusions, Krenzke succeeds in deepening the instruction offered by his art.

Interpreting an Image

Interpreting an image follows naturally from viewing or "reading" the image. Interpreting means figuring out what the image or design is meant to do, say, or show. Interpreting requires you to think more deeply about each element of the rhetorical situation shown in Figure 1.4, and about possible complications with each element.

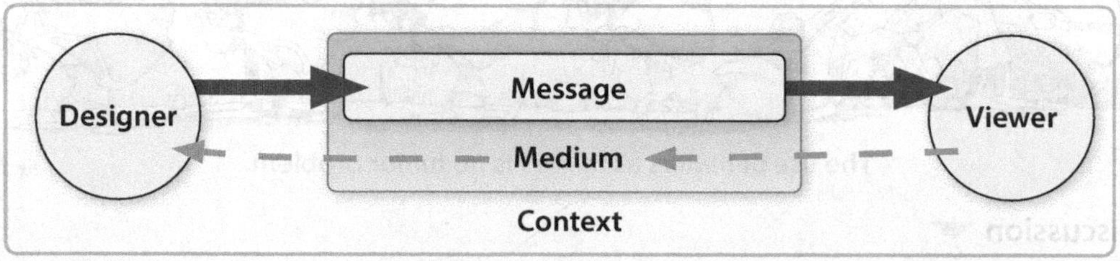

fig. 1.4

- **Designer:** Who created the image—a photographer, a painter, a Web designer, an eyewitness using a smartphone? Why did the person create it? What other people might have been involved—editors, patrons?

  Complications: The designer might be unknown or a group.

- **Message:** What is the subject of the image? How is the subject portrayed? What is the main purpose of the image—to entertain, inform, persuade, entice, or shock?

  Complications: The message might be mixed, implied, ironic, unwelcome, or distorted. The subject might be vague, unfamiliar, complex, or disturbing.

- **Medium:** What is the image—a painting, a cartoon panel, a photo? How might the image have been modified over time? What visual language has the sender used?

  Complications: The medium might be unusual or unfamiliar, or more than one medium may be involved. The visual languages might be literal, stylized, numeric, symbolic, and so on.

- **Viewer:** Whom was the image made for? Are you part of the intended audience? What is your relationship with the designer? Do you agree with the message? How comfortable are you with the medium? What is your overall response to the image?

  Complications: You might be uninterested in, unfamiliar with, or biased toward the message.

- **Context:** What was the context in which the image was first presented? What context surrounds the image now? Does the image fit its context or fight it?

  Complications: The context might be disconnected, ironic, changing, or multilayered.

INSIGHT Like words, visuals can be clichés—trite, misleading, or worn-out expressions of concepts or ideas. For example, TV ads for weight-loss drugs commonly picture scantily clad, fit young people, deceptively linking use of the drug to beauty, youth, and sex.

Interpret an Image

fig. 1.5

Ketevan Kardava / Contributor / Getty Images News

Discussion

Figure 1.5 shows two women in the Brussels Airport after terrorist bombings on March 22, 2016. The image's power is found in the connections and contrasts between the women, within the airport setting. It shows a tiled wall and floor, scattered luggage, and airport seating that is metallic, angular, and likely plastic—a somewhat cold, contemporary, and uncomfortable scene. A chalky dust covers everything, an echo of other attacks. The woman on the right (flight attendant Nidhi Chaphekar) sits prone across two seats, her hands gripping the chairs and her right foot hovering over the floor. Her disheveled dress, the dust and blood, and above all her pained, dazed facial expression—looking directly at the camera—show her vulnerability and symbolize terrorism's effects on the innocent. The unidentified woman on the left is striking for different reasons. She is seated facing forward and turned slightly to her right, emphasizing the isolation of each woman. The second woman's right hand and sleeve are bloodied and her left hand hidden behind her neck as she leans forward and speaks into her cell phone: this, too, shows the impact of terrorism today as the woman instantly connects with friends, loved ones, and possibly authorities moments after the attack.

Designer: Photographed by Ketevan Kardava; supplied to the Associated Press by Georgian Public Broadcaster.
Message: Two women recover from the March 22, 2016, terrorist attack on the Brussels Airport. The focus is the attack's personal, traumatic impact.
Medium: Digital color photograph
Viewer: The original intended viewers were people reading newspaper, magazine, and online stories about the attacks.
Context: This photograph was part of a large number provided by the Associated Press for news organizations after the Brussels attacks, which followed the Paris attacks of November 13, 2015, and preceded a similar terrorist attack in Lahore, Pakistan, on March 27, 2016.

Evaluating an Image

As a critical thinker, you must do more than understand and interpret an image you encounter: You must assess its quality, truthfulness, and value. In other words, you must evaluate it. When you have done that well, you can fairly say you have thought it through. The following questions will guide your assessment.

Consider the Purpose

What purpose does the visual image best seem to serve?

- **Ornamentation:** Makes the page more pleasing to the eye
- **Illustration:** Supports points made in the accompanying text
- **Revelation:** Gives an inside look at something or presents new data
- **Explanation:** Uses imagery or graphics to clarify a complex subject
- **Instruction:** Guides the viewer through a complex process
- **Persuasion:** Influences feelings or beliefs
- **Entertainment:** Amuses the viewer

Evaluate the Quality

Essentially, how good is the image?

- **Is the image done with skill?** A map, for example, should be accurately and attractively drawn, should use color effectively, and should be complete enough to serve its purpose.
- **Does the image measure up to standards of quality?**
- **Is it backed by authority?** Does the designer have a good reputation? Does the publication or institution have good credentials?
- **How does the image compare to other images like it?** Are clearer or more accurate images available?
- **What are its shortcomings?** Are there gaps in its coverage? Does it twist the evidence? Does it convey clichéd or fallacious information? (See pages 323–326 for a discussion of logical fallacies.)
- **Could you think of a better way to approach the image's subject?** If you were to produce the visual, what might you improve?

Determine the Value

What is the image's tangible and intangible worth? Its benefits and drawbacks?

- **Is the visual worth viewing?** Does it enrich the document by clarifying or otherwise enhancing its message?
- **Does the visual appeal to you?** Listen to authorities and peers, but also consider your own perspective.

Evaluate an Image

National Archives, London, Great Britain

fig. 1.6

Discussion

Evaluating an image such as the WWII poster in Figure 1.6 aimed at U.S. servicemen reveals its strong stereotypes of both men and women, stereotypes related to the historical period. As with all images, evaluation begins with understanding and interpreting the poster.

In the poster's center is a woman in evening dress, her hair done up, wearing jewels and a corsage. She is seated, at ease, looking at us. Perhaps she represents beauty, both sensual attractiveness and sophistication. The colors used to present her are pale and muted, except for her blue eyes and red lips.

Surrounding the woman are three men, individually dressed in the uniforms of Army, Air Force, and Navy. Drinking and smoking, the men seem to be competing for her attention.

The poster implies that all service personnel were male, which was not true even in WWII, when WACs and WAVEs served in the armed forces. It cautions that these male members of the armed forces should be wary in seemingly innocent social situations, since even a beautiful woman, whom popular stereotypes of the day characterized as "dumb," might not be what she appears. Such a woman might, in fact, be a spy—an idea perhaps inspired by the famous case of WWI spy Mata Hari. The statement that "careless talk costs lives" is a version of another common phrase from the period: "Loose lips sink ships."

Evaluating this poster involves considering its original context while assessing it from our current perspective. In the heat of WWII, this poster could be considered a fair piece of military persuasion. Today, however, what is striking are the gender stereotypes at work in both image and words. Not only are service personnel today both male and female, in every branch of the armed forces, but they fulfill the same roles, including combat positions. With respect to the men, the image implies that in social situations (which are assumed to include smoking and drinking), they are untrustworthy and apt to boast or compete in the presence of an attractive woman. With respect to women, the image both denounces and warns, implying that women, especially attractive women, are cunning and dangerous. Today, such stereotypes press us to question the quality, truthfulness, and value of the image.

Critical Thinking Through Writing

In college, your writing often must show your ability to think critically about topics and issues by analyzing complex processes, synthesizing distinct concepts, weighing the value of opposing perspectives, and practicing new applications of existing principles. The following tips can help you.

Develop Sound Critical-Thinking Habits

Like everything worthwhile, improving your critical-thinking skills takes time and practice. But cultivating the habits below will pay off in sound, thoughtful writing.

1. **Be curious.** Ask "Why?" Cultivate your ability to wonder; question what you see, hear, and read—both inside and outside the classroom.
2. **Be creative.** Don't settle for obvious answers. Look at things in a fresh way, asking "what-if" questions such as "What if Ophelia didn't die in *Hamlet*?"
3. **Be open to new ideas.** Approach thinking as you would approach a road trip—looking for the unexpected and musing over mysteries.
4. **Value others' points of view.** Look at issues from another person's perspective and weigh that against your own. Honestly examine how the core of her or his perspective compares to the core of your perspective, and how each basis for thought might lead to different conclusions.
5. **Get involved.** Read books, journals, and newspapers. Watch documentaries. Join book clubs, film clubs, or political and social-action activities.
6. **Focus.** Sharpen your concentration, looking for details that distinguish a topic and reveal key questions related to its nature, function, and impact.
7. **Be rational.** Choose logical thinking patterns like those discussed in this chapter, and then work through the steps to deepen your understanding of a topic.
8. **Make connections.** Use writing to explore how and why topics or issues are related. Use comparisons to identify and name these relationships.
9. **Tolerate ambiguity.** Respectfully analyze issues not readily resolved—and acknowledge when your position requires further research or thought.
10. **Test the evidence.** Be properly skeptical about all claims (see pages 318–319). Look for corroboration (or verification) in other sources.
11. **Develop research-based conclusions.** Focus on understanding issues, assessing their history, development, function, and impact. During the process, gather details that lead to and support a reasonable conclusion.
12. **Assess results.** Consider each paper you complete to be a benchmark that reflects your progress in developing your thinking and writing skills. Save your papers for periodic analyses of your progress and revision of the writing.

Ask Probing Questions

Every field uses questions to trigger critical thinking. For example, scientific questions generate hypotheses, sociological questions lead to studies, mathematical questions call for proofs, and literary criticism questions call for interpretations. A good question opens up a problem and guides you all the way to its solution. But not all questions are created equal. Consider the differences:

- **"Rhetorical" questions** aren't meant to be answered. They're asked for effect.
  Example: Who would want to be caught in an earthquake?
- **Closed questions** seek a limited response and can be answered with "yes," "no," or a simple fact.
  Example: Would I feel an earthquake measuring 3.0 on the Richter scale?
- **Open questions** invite brainstorming and discussion.
  Example: How might a major earthquake affect this urban area?
- **Theoretical questions** call for organization and explanation of an entire field of knowledge.
  Example: What might cause a sudden fracturing of Earth's crust along fault lines?

To improve the critical thinking in your writing, ask better questions. The strategies below will help you think freely, respond to reading, study for a test, or collect your thoughts for an essay.

☑ **Ask open questions.** Closed questions sometimes choke off thinking. Use open questions to trigger a flow of ideas.

☑ **Ask "educated" questions.** Compare these questions: (A) What's wrong with television? (B) Does the 16.3 percent rise in televised acts of violence during the past three years signal a rising tolerance for violence in the viewing audience? You have a better chance of expanding the "educated" question—question B—into an essay because the question is clearer and suggests debatable issues.

☑ **Keep a question journal.** Divide a blank notebook page or split a computer screen. On one side, write any questions that come to mind regarding the topic that you want to explore. On the other side, write down answers and any thoughts that flow from them.

☑ **Write Q & A drafts.** To write a thoughtful first draft, write quickly, then look it over. Turn the main idea into a question and write again, answering your question. For example, if your main idea is that TV viewers watch far more violence than they did ten years ago, ask *Which viewers? Why?* and *What's the result?* Go on that way until you find a key idea to serve as the main point of your next draft.

fyi For more help with critical thinking skills such as making and supporting claims, recognizing logical fallacies, and dealing with opposition, see "Strategies for Argumentation and Persuasion," pages 309–330.

Practice Inductive and Deductive Logic

Questions invite thinking; reasoning responds to that challenge in an organized way. Will the organization of your thoughts be inductive or deductive? Inductive logic reasons from specific information toward general conclusions. Deductive logic reasons from general principles toward specific applications. Notice in Figure 1.7 that inductive reasoning starts with specific details or observations (as shown at the base) and then moves "up" to broader ideas and then to a concluding generalization. In contrast, deduction starts with general principles at the top and works down, applying the principles to explain particular instances.

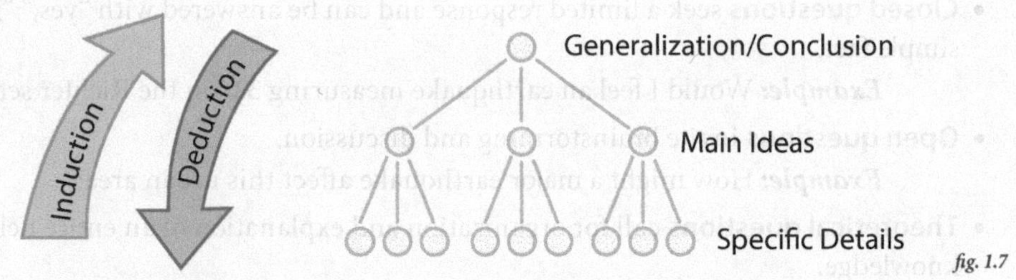

fig. 1.7

Sentences, paragraphs, and essays can be organized either inductively or deductively. Use induction to postpone your conclusions. Use deduction for logical clarity, directness, and strength, or to apply what is already agreed on to what is still under dispute. Narrative or personal essays tend toward inductive organization, whereas analytical essays typically use both induction and deduction.

Example: Read the excerpt from "Familiar Strangers." (The full essay is on pages 254–258.) Note how the first paragraph builds through narrative details to a conclusion, whereas the second paragraph names a concept and then explores through details its meaning.

Induction: specific details to conclusion

Dr. Smith stood beside a fellow neurobiologist on the campus of Washington University in St. Louis. While engrossed in conversation, Smith noticed from the corner of his eye an undergraduate walking in their direction. At first he thought nothing of it, but as she approached, it dawned on him that she was looking directly at him. "Strange," he thought. He tried to ignore her and continue his conversation, but when she was about 20 feet away he heard her laugh. Upon hearing the sound, the unfamiliar undergraduate who had been staring so intently at him morphed into his daughter. Smith had been unable to recognize her. *1*

Deduction: general concept explained through specifics

Dr. Smith suffers from a unique condition known as *prosopagnosia*, or face blindness. Historically, most documented cases have been due to brain damage suffered after maturity from head trauma, stroke, or degenerative diseases. Recently, however, studies have demonstrated that many more people suffer from prosopagnosia without experiencing neurological damage (Avidan, Hasson, Malach, & Behrmann, 2005). Smith suffers from this form of face blindness, known as congenital prosopagnosia. Although he spent the vast majority of his life unaware of his condition, Dr. Smith, now 54 years old, acknowledges that it all makes sense in retrospect. *2*

Practicing Modes of Thinking in Your Writing

In your various writing assignments, you will need to practice specific modes of thinking. The following table maps out these modes (from elementary to complex) and the tasks each requires. The more complex modes are then fleshed out on the following pages.

When you are asked to . . .	be ready to . . .
Know define, identify, list, match, memorize, name, recall, recognize	**Call to mind what you have learned** • Recall information • List details • Define key terms • Identify main points
Understand comprehend, connect, explain, grasp, interpret, restate, summarize	**Show what you have learned** • Connect related examples • Summarize important details • Explain how something works • Interpret what something means
Analyze characterize, classify, compare, contrast, divide, examine	**Break down information** • Divide a whole into its parts • Group things into categories • Analyze causes and effects • Examine similarities and differences
Synthesize assemble, combine, construct, formulate, imagine, invent, link	**Shape information into a new form** • Bring together a body of evidence • Blend the old with the new • Predict or hypothesize • Construct a new way of looking at something
Evaluate assess, check, critique, judge, measure, monitor, rank, rate	**Determine the worth of information** • Point out a subject's strengths and weaknesses • Evaluate its clarity, accuracy, logic, value, and so on • Convince others of its value/worth
Apply anticipate, choose, generate, propose, select	**Use what you have learned** • Propose a better way of doing something • Generate a plan of action • Offer solutions to a problem

Think by Using Analysis

The word *analyze* literally means "to loosen or undo." When you analyze something, you break it down into parts and examine each part separately. You classify information, compare objects, trace a process, or explain causes.

As you analyze, think about the analysis questions that follow. Note that each type of thinking answers certain kinds of questions. Remember, too, that thinking tasks often require two or more kinds of analysis that support one another.

Composition: What elements does it contain? What is not part of it?

Categories: How are things grouped, divided, or classified?

Structures: What are the parts or elements? How are they related?

Comparisons/ contrasts: How are things similar? How are they different?

Causes/effects: Why did this happen? What are the results?

Processes: How does it work or happen? What are the stages?

Example: Read through the following passage, from "Wayward Cells." In the full essay on pages 212–213, student writer Kerri Mertz explains the process by which healthy body cells become cancerous cells. Note how in this excerpt, the writer develops an overall analysis based on a process but also uses compare-contrast and cause-effect thinking within that structure, as well as informal definition.

The writer explains a cellular process and contrasts healthy and cancerous versions.

1 Most healthy cells reproduce rather quickly, but their reproduction rate is controlled. For example, your blood cells completely die off and replace themselves within a matter of weeks, but existing cells make only as many new cells as the body needs. The DNA codes in healthy cells tell them how many new cells to produce. However, cancer cells don't have this control, so they reproduce quickly with no stopping point, a characteristic called "autonomy" (Braun 3). What's more, all their "offspring" have the same qualities as their messed-up parent, and the resulting overpopulation produces growths called tumors.

The writer explains the three harmful effects of tumor cells (the cause).

2 Tumor cells can hurt the body in a number of ways. First, a tumor can grow so big that it takes up space needed by other organs. Second, some cells may detach from the original tumor and spread throughout the body, creating new tumors elsewhere. This happens with lymphatic cancer—a cancer that's hard to control because it spreads so quickly. A third way that tumor cells can hurt the body is by doing work not called for in their DNA. For example, a gland cell's DNA code may tell the cell to produce a necessary hormone in the endocrine system. However, if cancer damages or distorts that code, sick cells may produce more of the hormone than the body can use—or even tolerate (Braun 4). Cancer cells seem to have minds of their own, and this is why cancer is such a serious disease.

Examples illustrate the analysis.

Think by Using Synthesis

Synthesis is the opposite of analysis. Whereas analysis breaks things down into parts, synthesis combines elements into a new whole. In your writing, when you pull together things that are normally separate, you are synthesizing. Common ways of synthesizing include predicting, inventing, redesigning, and imagining a whole new way of looking at something.

Working with synthesis involves both reason and imagination. Start by looking closely at two or more items that you want to synthesize, and then think of fresh ways they can be related. Don't be afraid to see your subjects in a new way. In other words, think "sideways" rather than straight ahead. Ask the following questions:

Applying: What can I do with both? What will be the outcome?
Bridging: How can I build a connection between the two?
Combining: How can I connect, associate, or blend the two?
Conflicting: Which is good, better, or best? What strength does each offer the other?
Inventing: What parts could these two play in a drama?
Proposing: What do I suggest doing with both?
Sequencing: Which comes first? Is one an extension of the other?
Projecting: Based on current information, what is the best forecast for what will happen in the near future or the long term?

Example: Read through the following passage, from "In Africa, AIDS Has a Woman's Face," by former United Nations Secretary-General Kofi Annan (see pages 352–354). In the full article, Annan argues that resolving the AIDS crisis in Africa must begin by saving the familial, social, and economic backbones of African cultures—women. In the following passage, Annan synthesizes his discussion by projecting what is necessary for successful solutions.

Pulling together his discussion of the twin tragedies of AIDS and famine in Africa, the writer calls for imaginative, multifaceted solutions.

Because this crisis is different from past famines, we must look beyond relief measures of the past. Merely shipping in food is not enough. Our effort will have to combine food assistance and new approaches to farming with treatment and prevention of H.I.V. and AIDS. It will require creating early-warning and analysis systems that monitor both H.I.V. infection rates and famine indicators. It will require new agricultural techniques, appropriate to a depleted work force. It will require a renewed effort to wipe out H.I.V.-related stigma and silence. 1

It will require innovative, large-scale ways to care for orphans, with specific measures that enable children in AIDS-affected communities to stay in school. Education and prevention are still the most powerful weapons against the spread of H.I.V. Above all, this new international effort must put women at the center of our strategy to fight AIDS. 2

Think by Using Evaluation

Movies, proposals, arguments—anything can be evaluated. Evaluation measures the value or worth of things. For example, when you express your judgment about an issue or discuss the weak and strong points of what someone else has said, you are evaluating. Many kinds of writing are evaluative.

To evaluate a topic, start by learning as much about it as possible. Then consider which criteria or standards are appropriate. Next, judge how the topic measures up based on those criteria. Support your judgment with concrete details, examples, illustrations, and comparisons. Ask questions like these:

Aspects: What elements of the topic will I evaluate?
Vantage point: What are my experience and my point of view?
Criteria: On which standards will I base my judgment?
Assessment: How does the topic measure up by those standards?
Comparison: How does it compare to and contrast with similar things?
Recommendation: Based on my evaluation, what do I advise?

Example: The following passage is taken from David Blankenhorn's "Fatherless America," on pages 358–362. In the full essay, Blankenhorn examines the causes and effects of the increased fatherlessness within U.S. families—that is, the absence of fathers in many homes. In the following excerpt, he assesses the failures of a society that is losing a healthy sense of fatherhood.

The writer establishes a criterion for evaluating a culture's fatherhood models and practices.

1 . . . Margaret Mead and others have observed that the supreme test of any civilization is whether it can socialize men by teaching them to be fathers—creating a culture in which men acknowledge their paternity and willingly nurture their offspring. Indeed, if we can equate the essence of the antisocial male with violence, we can equate the essence of the socialized male with being a good father. Thus, at the center of our most important cultural imperative, we find the fatherhood script: the story that describes what it ought to mean for a man to have a child. . . .

After exploring this criterion in depth (not shown), the writer measures U.S. culture and assesses its failures with respect to fatherhood.

2 The stakes on this issue could hardly be higher. Our society's conspicuous failure to sustain or create compelling norms of fatherhood amounts to a social and personal disaster. Today's story of fatherhood features one-dimensional characters, an unbelievable plot, and an unhappy ending. It reveals in our society both a failure of collective memory and a collapse of moral imagination. It undermines families, neglects children, causes or aggravates our worst social problems, and makes individual adult happiness—both male and female—harder to achieve.

3 Ultimately, this failure reflects nothing less than a culture gone awry: a culture increasingly unable to establish the boundaries, erect the sign-posts, and fashion the stories that can harmonize individual happiness with collective well-being. In short, it reflects a culture that increasingly fails to "enculture" individual men and women, mothers and fathers.

Think by Using Application

Thinking by using application defines the practical implications of something. It involves using what you know to demonstrate, show, relate, or extend ideas in view of their outcomes. For example, using what you have learned about the ecology of forest fires to examine the effects of a particular fire—that's application in action.

Applying involves moving from ideas to possible action. First, understand the information you have. Second, relate this information to a given situation. Third, select those facts and details that clarify and support the application. Fourth, test the application to see whether it has been reasonable.

When applying ideas, let questions like these guide your writing:

Purpose: What is something designed to be or do?
Benefits: What would this idea make clearer, better, or more complete?
Solutions: What problems are solved by application of this idea?
Outcomes: What results can be expected? Where could we go from there?

Example: Read the following paragraphs from Maria Konnikova's "How the Internet Has Changed Bullying" (pages 244–247). In her essay, Konnikova compares traditional and digital bullying, based on current research into the phenomenon. In this passage, she applies her conclusions about the nature and causes of bullying in a discussion of possible solutions, with cultivating self-awareness as the key concept.

Using the word "self-awareness," the writer introduces a key principle that she then applies to children and adults as bullies.

1 In children, it's possible to instill self-awareness about bullying through schoolwide interventions. Catherine Bradshaw, a psychologist and associate dean at the University of Virginia who studies bullying prevention, has found that the most effective approaches are multilayered and include training, behavior-modification guidelines, and systems for detailed data collection. (More, in other words, than a stray assembly or distributed book.) Unfortunately, the equivalent for adults can be hard to find. Many adult bullies hide behind the idea that bullying happens only among children. They conceive of themselves as adults who know better and are offering their hard-earned wisdom to others. The Internet makes that sort of certainty easier to attain: looking at their screens, adult bullies rarely see the impact of their words and actions. Instead, they comfortably bask in self-righteous glory. The U.K. study from 2012 found that online bystanders, too, are disengaged. Observing the actions of cyberbullies, they were less concerned than when they watched in-person bullying.

She applies the concept to the Internet, calling readers to act in a way that implements the concept.

2 In short, the picture that's emerged suggests that the Internet has made bullying both harder to escape and harder to identify. It has also, perhaps, made bullies out of some of us who would otherwise not be. We are immersed in an online world in which consequences often go unseen—and that has made it easier to deceive ourselves about what we are doing. The first step to preventing bullying among adults, therefore, might be simple: introspection.

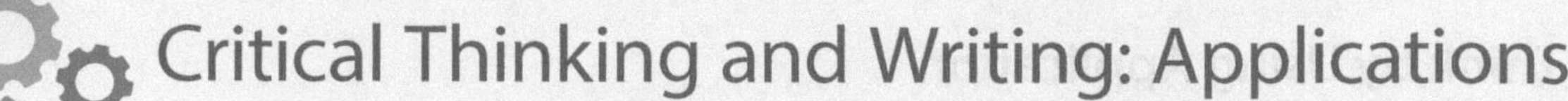

Critical Thinking and Writing: Applications

Apply what you have learned about critical thinking through reading, viewing, and writing by completing these activities.

1. **Wise Words:** Northrop Frye has argued that "[n]obody is capable of free speech unless he knows how to use language, and such knowledge is not a gift: It has to be learned and worked at." How does Frye's claim relate to the discussions of critical reading, viewing, and writing in this chapter?
2. **Public Texts:** Close reading is required to make sense of many texts. Find a story, article, or report related to an issue that you find important. Then use the critical reading strategies on pages 4–7 to understand, analyze, and evaluate the text.
3. **Photo Op:** From the photo on the opening page (Figure 1.1) to the images on pages 11–15 (Figures 1.3, 1.5, and 1.6), this chapter offers instruction in critical viewing. Find a striking image related to an important news event of the past week. Using the instruction in this chapter, carefully view, interpret, and evaluate the image.
4. **Living Today:** With what recreational activities, games, and hobbies are you thoroughly familiar? Choose one, and then practice thinking inductively and deductively (page 18) about that topic, drafting a paragraph for each.
5. **Major Work:** Consider your major and your future career. What is the focus of this field of study and this profession? What critical reading, viewing, and writing skills are required and valued in this area? Research these questions, as needed.

Learning-Objectives Checklist ✓

Have you achieved this chapter's learning objectives? Check your progress with the following items, revisiting topics in the chapter as needed. I have . . .

____ read texts actively by assessing their rhetorical situation (writer, message, medium, reader, context), and practicing techniques such as preview, read, review (4–5).

____ read texts actively through note-taking, annotating, mapping, and outlining (6–7).

____ responded to written texts in an honest, fluid, reflective, and selective way (8).

____ objectively summarized texts in my own words, distinguishing main arguments and key supporting points from secondary content (9).

____ viewed images actively by surveying and inspecting them (10–11).

____ carefully interpreted images by deeply analyzing the rhetorical situation and its complications—designer, message, medium, viewer, and context (12–13).

____ critiqued visual images by assessing their purpose, value, and quality (14–15).

____ thought critically about topics by practicing sound thinking habits, asking probing questions, and using inductive and deductive patterns strategically (16–18).

____ produced writing that practices modes of thinking such as analysis, synthesis, evaluation, and application (19–23).

MindTap® Practice skills that you have learned in this chapter and receive automatic feedback. Reflect on your writing process.

Chapter 2

Beginning the Writing Process

The blank page or screen can be daunting for any writer. That's because writing doesn't go from nothing to a masterpiece in one step. Writing is a process, much like painting.

The aim of the writing process is discovery—along the way and in the finished text, both for the writer and for the reader. As Peter Stillman argues, "Writing is the most powerful means of discovery available to all of us throughout life." Discovery happens when you give ample time to each step, and when you follow strategies that encourage your thinking to deepen and your writing to sharpen.

This chapter introduces the writing process and then focuses on getting started on any writing project through prewriting strategies. As with many things in life, completing the first step right sets you up to succeed on the whole journey.

Visually Speaking Painting is the process of converting infinite possibilities into a single image. How is writing similar? How is it different? What is the starting point for painting? For writing? Consider these questions as you examine Figure 2.1.

MindTap®

Understand the goals of the chapter and complete a warm-up activity online.

Learning Objectives

By working through this chapter, you will be able to

- outline the writing process and decide how to follow it for different projects.
- analyze the rhetorical situation behind writing tasks.
- summarize seven traits of strong, college-level writing.
- interpret the nature and requirements of specific writing assignments.
- generate and choose topics for writing projects.
- collect, track, and examine information for writing projects.

Chamille White / Shutterstock.com

fig. 2.1

The Writing Process: From Start to Finish

It's easy to feel overwhelmed by a writing project—especially if the form of writing is new to you, the topic is complex, or the paper must be long. However, using the writing process will relieve some of that pressure by breaking down the task into manageable steps.

Consider the Writing Process

Figure 2.2 maps out the basic steps in the writing process. As you work on your writing project, periodically review this diagram to keep yourself on task.

Steps in the Writing Process

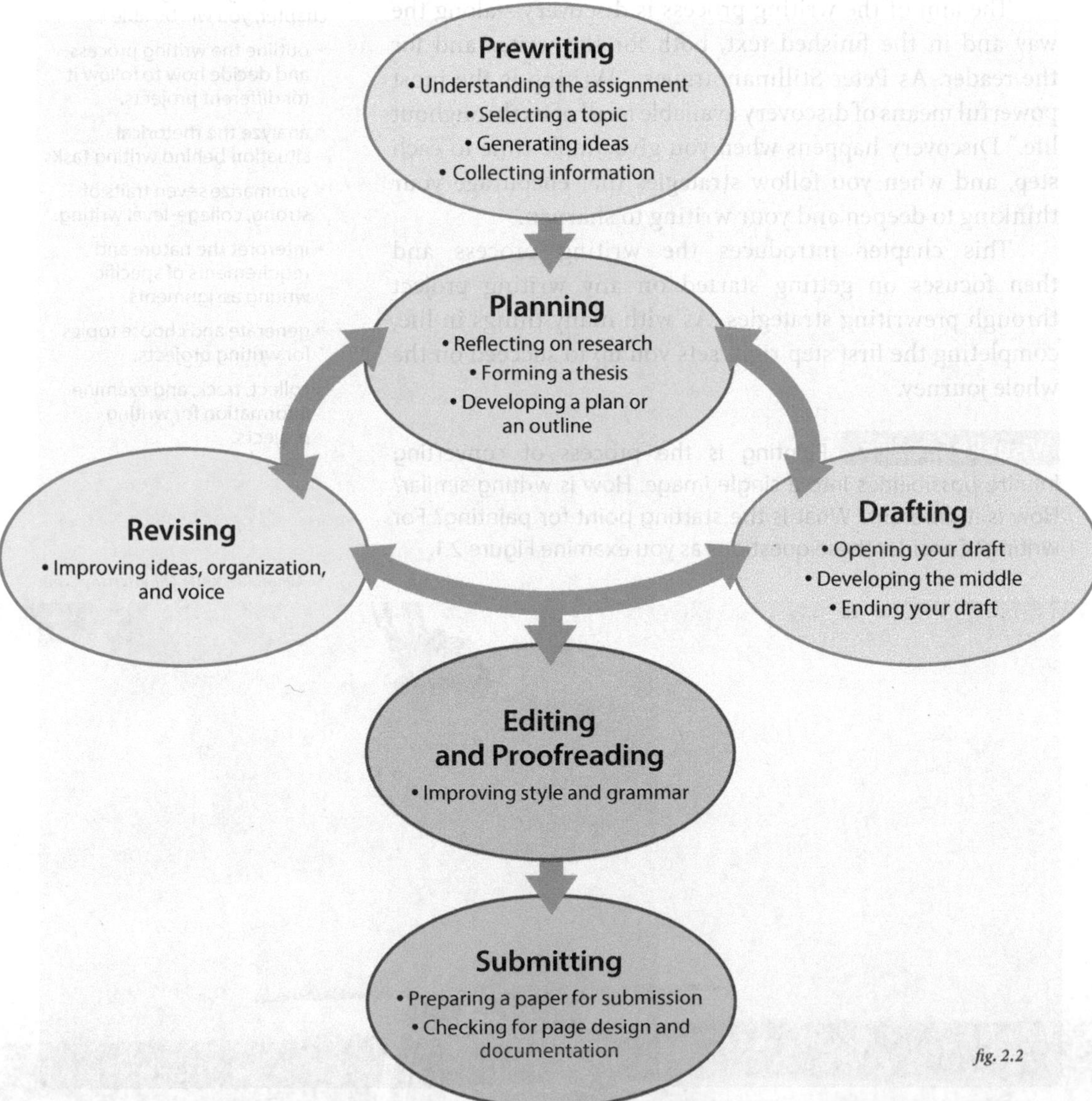

fig. 2.2

Adapt the Process to Your Project

The writing process shown on the previous page is flexible, not rigid. As a writer, you need to adapt the process to your situation and assignment. To do so, consider these essential principles.

- **Writing tends not to follow a straight path.** While writing begins with an assignment or a need and ends with a reader, the journey in between is often indirect. The steps in the flowchart show that when you write, you sometimes move back and forth between steps, meaning that the process is recursive. For example, during the revision phase, you may discover that you need to draft a new paragraph or do more research.
- **Each assignment presents distinct challenges.** A personal essay may develop best through clustering or freewriting; a literary analysis through close reading of a story; a lab report through the experimental method; and a position paper through reading of books and journal articles, as well as through careful and balanced reasoning. Moreover, an assignment may or may not involve extensive research and working with sources.
- **Writing can involve collaboration.** From using your roommate as a sounding board for your topic choice to working with a group to produce a major report, college writing is not solitary writing. In fact, many colleges have a writing center to help you refine your writing assignments. (See pages 89–91 for more.)
- **Each writer works differently.** Some writers do extensive prewriting before drafting, while others do not. You might develop a detailed outline, whereas someone else might draft a brief list of topics. Experiment with the strategies introduced in chapters 2–7, adopting those that help you.
- **Good writing can't be rushed.** Although some students regard pulling an all-nighter as a badge of honor, good writing takes time. A steady, disciplined approach will generally produce the best results. For example, by brainstorming or reading early in a project, you stimulate your subconscious mind to mull over issues, identify problems, and project solutions—even while your conscious mind is working on other things. Similarly, completing a first draft early enough gives you time to revise objectively.
- **Different steps call for attention to different writing issues.** As you use the writing process, at each stage keep your focus where it belongs:
  1. While getting started, planning, and drafting, focus on global issues: ideas, structure, voice, format, and design.
  2. During revising, fix big content problems by cutting, adding, and thoroughly reworking material. (Our experience is that students benefit the most from revising—but spend the least time doing it!)
  3. While editing and proofreading, pay attention to small, local issues—word choice, sentence smoothness, and grammatical correctness. Worrying about these issues early in the writing process interrupts the flow of drafting and wastes time on material that may later be deleted.

Understanding the Rhetorical Situation

Rhetoric is the art of using language effectively. As Aristotle, Quintilian, and others have explained, your language is effective when all aspects of your message fit the rhetorical situation (Figure 2.3). For any writing project, then, prewriting can begin with analyzing the rhetorical situation that lies behind the project. By doing so, you get the project in focus. The diagram and discussion below explain what is involved in such rhetorical analysis.

Rhetorical Situation

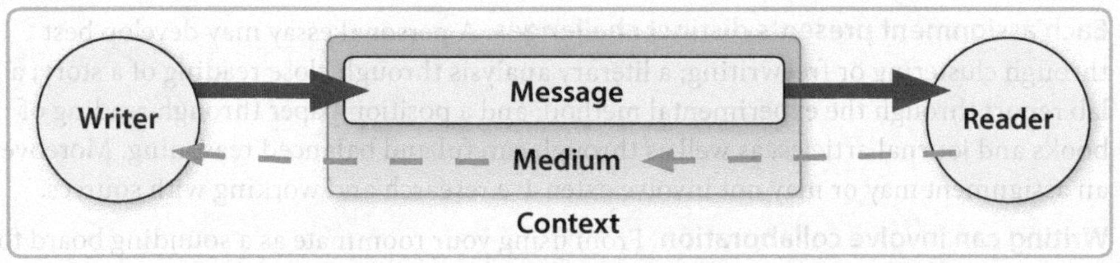

fig. 2.3

Think of Your Role as the Writer

Are you writing as a concerned citizen, a student in a class, a friend relating a story, a reporter providing news, or a blogger giving an opinion? Your role in writing and otherwise communicating affects the level of language you use, the voice you adopt, the types of details you include, the evidence you cite to support a claim, and so on.

Understand Your Subject

To truly understand your subject, you need to gather and assimilate all relevant details about it, including its history, makeup, function, and impact on people and culture. Knowing those details will help you narrow your focus to a specific thesis and develop it well.

Working with Sources As you search for information, think about which types of sources are recommended or expected for the assignment. Which should be avoided?

Understand Your Purpose

Key words in an assignment—such as *analyze, explain, defend,* or *describe*—tell you what the purpose of the writing is supposed to be. Understanding why you are writing helps you choose an organizational strategy, such as classification, definition, or process. (See pages 32–33.)

Working with Sources Think of the sources that will most help you achieve your purpose, whether to entertain, compare, inspire, enlighten, and so on.

Understand Your Audience

For any writing task, you must understand your audience in order to develop writing that meets their needs. To assess your audience, answer questions like these:

- Who are my readers: instructor? classmates? Web users?
- What do they know about my topic, and what do they need to know?
- How well do they understand the terminology involved?
- What are their attitudes toward the topic and toward me?
- How well do they read written English—or visuals such as graphs and charts?
- How will they use my writing (as entertainment or to complete a task)?

Note: Answers to such questions will help you develop meaningful sentences (pages 95–102), choose appropriate words (pages 103–108), and select relevant visuals.

Working with Sources Ask yourself what sources your reader will best understand and most respect. What sources will add to your credibility and authority?

Understand the Medium (Form)

Many communication options are available for every message. Academic forms include essays, analyses, reports, proposals, research papers, reviews, and so on. It is important to understand the form of the assignment. What works well in a narrative about a past experience would not work as well in a lab report. Also, each of these forms can contain multiple media: written elements, graphics, photos, drawings, videos, audios, links, and so on. Understanding the overall medium and the media within it will help you succeed.

Working with Sources Make sure you understand the way that sources are to be cited in the form of communication you are using. (See 465–532 for MLA and APA styles.)

Think About the Context

Think about how this assignment relates to others in the course. Consider these issues:

- **Weight:** Is this an everyday assignment, a weekly or biweekly one, or the big one?
- **Assessment:** Find out how the assignment will be graded. What traits will your instructor look for? Will your writing be assessed with a rubric? (See page 30.)
- **Intent:** Make certain that you understand the goals of the assignment and understand what your instructor wants you to get out of it.

Note: If the writing you are doing is not in response to an assignment, think about the environment in which the message will be read. What is the history of this issue? What is the current climate like? What might the future be?

Working with Sources If you are writing material that will be reviewed and debated by others in your field, think about what sources you would most want your writing to appear in. Make certain you understand the submission guidelines for the source.

Aiming for Writing Excellence

What makes your writing strong enough to engage and enlighten readers? As already suggested on pages 28–29, that depends in part on the rhetorical situation: what your purpose is, who your readers are, and so on. Writing excellence can be measured by the depth of what you learn through writing, as well as by what your reader gains through reading. However, while the world of writing is so diverse that no formula or prescription can state definitively what makes for strong writing, we can point to common traits that describe such writing. Consider the relevance of these traits at the beginning of any writing project.

Common Traits of College Writing

Quality writing shows strengths in the traits below, which range from global issues to local, sentence-level issues.

- **Strong ideas** are what you discover and develop through your writing. They are what make your content substantial and meaningful. These elements include a clear, sharp thesis or theme; strong and balanced reasoning; and accurate, supportive information that is properly credited.
- **Logical organization** creates the structure and flow of your writing. Through organization, reasoning is delivered through a clear chain of ideas, a unified whole. Typically, an engaging opening focuses discussion, the middle effectively develops the main idea, and a closing offers conclusions and points forward—all in paragraphs that are well developed (unified, coherent, and complete).
- **Engaging voice** refers to how your writing "sounds" to readers—the attitude, pacing, and personality that come through. An engaging voice sounds authentic and natural, engaged with the topic. Moreover, the tone—whether serious, playful, or sarcastic—is confident but also sincere and measured, fitting the writing occasion.
- **Clear word choice** carries your meaning. In your writing, the vocabulary should fit the topic, purpose, and audience. Phrasing should be clear throughout—language that readers will understand, precise terminology and plain English whenever possible.
- **Smooth sentences** express complete thoughts in a good blend of sentence lengths (short and punchy, long and thoughtful) and patterns (loose, balanced, and periodic). Such sentences use phrases and clauses in logical and expressive ways—energetically, economically, gracefully.
- **Correct writing** follows the conventions of language (grammar, punctuation, mechanics, usage, and spelling), as well as standards of citation and documentation (e.g., MLA, APA).
- **Professional document design** refers to the appearance of your writing on the page, the screen, and so on. Such design includes the document's format (e.g., essay, lab report, presentation, Web site), its page layout (e.g., margins, headings, bullets, white space), its typography (typefaces, type sizes, and type styles), and its use of tables and visuals.

Common Traits in Action

What do these common traits look like in a typical piece of college writing? Spurred on by a funny experience, student writer Mary Bruins researched the word *gullible* and wrote this essay. Study the paper to explore why it represents strong freshman-level college writing.

Ideas
Clear focus, engaging thesis, and precise content

Organization
Lively opening, well-structured middle, and thoughtful closing

Voice
Informed and engaging tone

Words
Precise, lively, clear phrasing

Sentences
Smooth, varied, and graceful constructions

Correctness
Error-free prose

Design
Attractive format, page layout, and typography

The Gullible Family

The other day, my friend Loris fell for the oldest trick in the book: "Hey, 1
somebody wrote *gullible* on the ceiling!" Shortly after mocking "Gullible Loris" for looking up, I swallowed the news that Walmart sells popcorn that pops into the shapes of cartoon characters. And so, as "Gullible Mary," I decided to explore what our name means, and who else belongs to our Gullible family. What I learned is that the family includes both people and birds, related to each other by our willingness to "swallow."

A gullible person will swallow an idea or argument without questioning its 2
truth. Similarly, the gull (a long-winged, web-footed bird) will swallow just about anything thrown to it. In fact, the word *gullible* comes from *gull*, and this word can be traced back to the Germanic word *gwel* (to swallow). Both *gull* and *gwel* are linked to the modern word *gulp*, which means "to swallow greedily or rapidly in large amounts." It's not surprising, then, that Loris and I, sisters in the Gullible family, both eagerly gulped (like gulls) the false statements thrown to us.

Swallowing things this quickly isn't too bright, and gull (when referring to a 3
bird or person) implies that the swallower is immature and foolish. For example, gull refers to an "unfledged" fowl, which the *Grolier Encyclopedia* describes as either "an immature bird still lacking flight feathers," or something that is "inexperienced, immature, or untried." These words describe someone who is fooled easily, and that's why *gull*, when referring to a human, means "dupe" or "simpleton." In fact, since 1550, *gullet*, which means "throat," has also meant "fooled."

To illustrate this usage, the *Oxford English Dictionary* quotes two authors who 4
use *gull* as a verb meaning to fool. "Nothing is so easy as to gull the public, if you only set up a prodigy," writes Washington Irving. William Dean Howells uses the word similarly when he writes, "You are perfectly safe to go on and gull imbeciles to the end of time, for all I care."

Both of these authors are pretty critical of gullible people, but does *gullible* have 5
only negative connotations? Is there no hope for Gullibles like Loris and me? C. O. Sylvester Marson's comments about *gullible* may give us some comfort. He links *gullible* to "credulous, confiding, and easily deceived." At first, these adjectives also sound negative, but *credulous* does mean "to follow implicitly." And the word *credit* comes from the Latin word *credo* (meaning "I believe"). So what's bad about that? In other words, isn't wanting to believe other people a good thing? Why shouldn't Loris and I be proud of at least that aspect of our gull blood? We want to be positive—and we don't want to be cynics!

Understanding the Assignment

Each college instructor has a way of personalizing a writing assignment, but most assignments will spell out (1) the objective, (2) the task, (3) the formal requirements, and (4) suggested approaches and topics. An important step, therefore, is to read the assignment carefully, noting the options and restrictions that are part of it. The suggestions below will help you do that. (Also see pages 116–118 for one writer's approach.)

Read the Assignment

Certain words in the assignment explain what main action you must perform. Here are some words that signal what you are to do:

Key Words

Analyze: Break down a topic into subparts, showing how those parts relate.
Argue: Defend a claim with logical arguments.
Classify: Divide a large group into well-defined subgroups.
Compare/contrast: Point out similarities and/or differences.
Define: Give a clear, thoughtful definition or meaning of something.
Describe: Show in detail what something is like.
Evaluate: Weigh the truth, quality, or usefulness of something.
Explain: Give reasons, list steps, or discuss the causes of something.
Interpret: Tell in your own words what something means.
Reflect: Share your well-considered thoughts about a subject.
Summarize: Restate someone else's ideas very briefly in your own words.
Synthesize: Connect facts or ideas to create something new.

Options and Restrictions

The assignment often gives you some choice of your topic or approach but may restrict your options to suit the instructor's purpose. Note the options and restrictions in the following short sample assignment:

> Reflect on the way a natural disaster or major historical event has altered your understanding of the past, the present, or the future.
>
> **Options:** (1) You may choose any natural disaster or historical event.
> (2) You may focus on the past, present, or future.
> (3) You may examine any kind of alteration.
>
> **Restrictions:** (1) You must reflect on a change in your understanding.
> (2) The disaster must be natural.
> (3) The historical event must be major.

Relate the Assignment to the Goals of the Course

1. How much value does the instructor give the assignment? (The value is often expressed as a percentage of the course grade.)
2. What benefit does your instructor want you to receive?
    - Strengthen your comprehension?
    - Improve your research skills?
    - Deepen your ability to explain, prove, or persuade?
    - Expand your style?
    - Increase your creativity?
3. How will this assignment contribute to your overall performance in the course? What course goals (often listed in the syllabus) does it address?

Relate the Assignment to Other Assignments

1. Does it build on previous assignments?
2. Does it prepare you for the next assignment?

Relate the Assignment to Your Own Interests

1. Does it connect with a topic that already interests you?
2. Does it connect with work in your other courses?
3. Does it connect with the work you may do in your chosen field?
4. Does it connect with life outside school?

Reflect on the Assignment

1. **First impulses:** How did you feel when you first read the assignment?
2. **Approaches:** What's the usual approach for an assignment like this? What's a better way of tackling it?
3. **Quality of performance:** What would it take to produce an excellent piece of writing?
4. **Benefits:** What are the benefits to your education? To you personally? To the class? To society?
5. **Features:** Reflect further on four key features of any writing assignment.
    - **Purpose:** What is the overall purpose of the assignment—to inform, to explain, to analyze, to entertain? What is the desired outcome?
    - **Readers:** Should you address your instructor? Your classmates? A general reader? How much does the reader already know about the topic? What type of language should you use?
    - **Form:** What are the requirements concerning length, format, and due date?
    - **Assessment:** How will the assignment be evaluated? Which of the traits discussed on pages 30–31 are important to this assignment? How can you be sure that you are completing the assignment correctly?

Developing a Topic

For some assignments, finding a suitable topic may require little thinking on your part. If an instructor asks you to summarize an article in a scholarly journal, you know what you will write about—the article in question. But suppose the instructor asks you to analyze a feature of popular culture in terms of its impact on society. You won't be sure of a specific writing topic until you explore the possibilities. Keep the following points in mind when you conduct a topic search. Your topic must . . .

- meet the requirements of the assignment.
- be limited in scope.
- seem reasonable (that is, be within your means to research).
- genuinely interest you.

Limit the Subject Area

Many of your writing assignments may relate to general subject areas you are currently studying. Your task, then, is to select a specific topic related to the general area of study—a topic limited enough that you can treat it with sufficient depth in the number of pages and preparation time allowed for the assignment. The following examples show the difference between general subjects and limited topics:

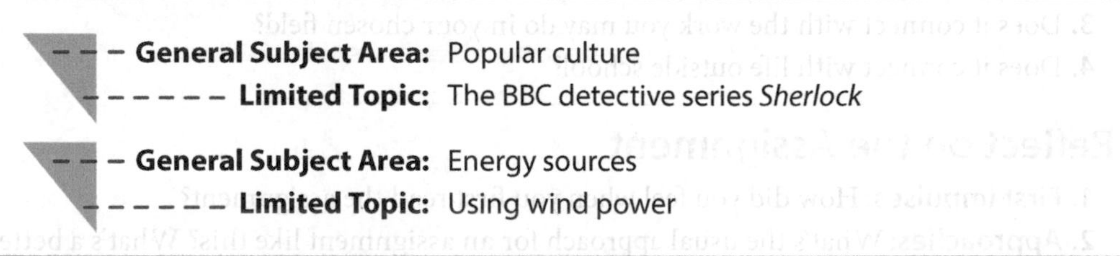

Conduct Your Search

Finding a writing idea that meets the requirements of the assignment should not be difficult, if you know how and where to look. Follow these steps:

1. **Check your class notes and handouts** for ideas related to the assignment.
2. **Search the Internet.** Type in a keyword or phrase (the general subject stated in the assignment) and see what you can find.
3. **Consult indexes, guides, and other library references.** Subscription databases such as EBSCOhost, for example, list current articles published on specific topics and where to find them. (See pages 414–417.)
4. **Discuss the assignment** with your instructor or an information specialist.
5. **Use one or more of the prewriting strategies** described on the following pages to generate possible writing ideas.

Explore Possible Topics

You can generate topic possibilities by using the following strategies. These same strategies can be used when you've chosen a topic and want to develop it further.

Journal Writing

Write in a journal on a regular basis. Reflect on your personal feelings, develop your thoughts, and record the happenings of each day. Periodically go back and underline ideas that you would like to explore in writing assignments. In the following journal-writing sample, the writer came up with an idea for a writing assignment about the societal impacts of popular culture.

> I read a really disturbing news story this morning. I've been thinking about it all day. In California a little girl was killed when she was struck by a car driven by a man distracted by a billboard ad for lingerie featuring a scantily clothed woman. Not only is it a horrifying thing to happen, but it also seems to me all too symbolic of the way that sexually charged images in the media are putting children, and especially girls, in danger. That reminds me of another news story I read this week about preteen girls wanting to wear the kinds of revealing outfits that they see in music videos, TV shows, and magazines aimed at teenagers. Too many of today's media images give young people the impression that sexuality should begin at an early age. This is definitely a dangerous message.

Listing

Freely list ideas as they come to mind, beginning with a key concept related to the assignment. (Brainstorming—listing ideas in conjunction with members of a group—is often an effective way to extend your lists.) The following is an example of a student's list of ideas for possible topics on the subject of news reporting:

Aspect of popular culture: News reporting

- Sensationalism
- Sound bites rather than in-depth analysis
- Focus on the negative
- Shock radio
- Shouting matches pretending to be debates
- Press leaks that damage national security, etc.
- Lack of observation of people's privacy
- Bias
- Contradictory health news confusing to readers
- Little focus on "unappealing" issues like poverty
- Celebration of "celebrity"

Clustering

When you create a cluster, you visualize connections between concepts, things, and events. To begin the clustering process, write a key word or phrase related to the assignment in the center of your paper. Circle it, and then cluster ideas around it. Circle each idea as you record it, and draw a line connecting it to the closest related idea. Keep going until you run out of ideas and connections. Figure 2.4 is a student's cluster on the subject of sports:

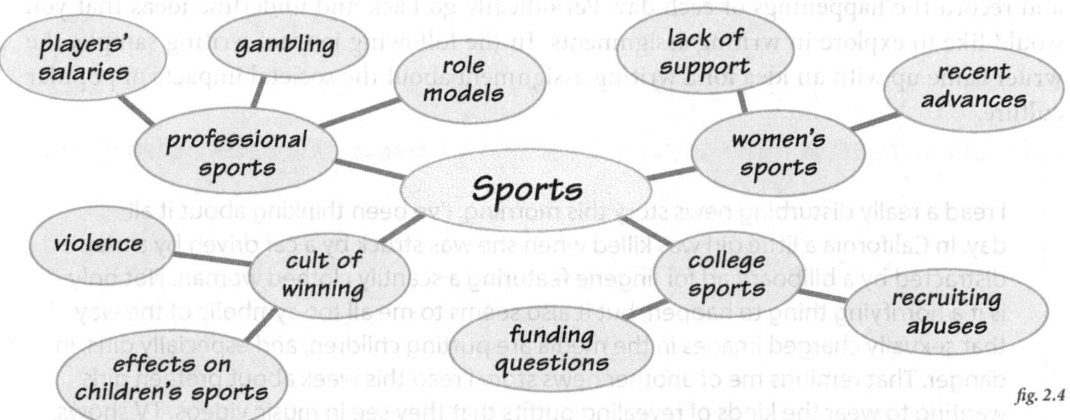

fig. 2.4

fyi After four or five minutes of listing or clustering, scan your work for an idea to explore in a freewriting. A writing idea should begin to emerge during this freewriting session. (See page 37.)

Freewrite to Discover and Develop a Topic

Freewriting is the writing you do without having a specific outcome in mind. You simply write down whatever pops into your head as you explore your topic. Freewriting can serve as a starting point for your writing, or it can be combined with any of the other prewriting strategies to help you select, explore, focus, or organize your writing. If you get stuck at any point during the composing process, you can return to freewriting as a way of generating new ideas.

Reminders

- **Freewriting helps you get your thoughts down on paper.** (Thoughts are constantly passing through your mind.)
- **Freewriting helps you develop and organize these thoughts.**
- **Freewriting helps you make sense out of things that you may be studying or researching.**
- **Freewriting may seem awkward at times, but just stick with it.**

The Process

- **Write nonstop and record whatever comes into your mind.** Follow your thoughts instead of trying to direct them.
- **If you have a particular topic or assignment to complete, use it as a starting point.** Otherwise, begin with anything that comes to mind.
- **Don't stop to judge, edit, or correct your writing;** that will come later.
- **Keep writing even when you think you have exhausted all of your ideas.** Switch to another angle or voice, but keep writing.
- **Watch for a promising writing idea to emerge.** Learn to recognize the beginnings of a good idea, and then expand that idea by recording as many specific details as possible.

The Result

- **Review your writing and underline the ideas you like.** These ideas will often serve as the basis for future writings.
- **Determine exactly what you need to write about.** Once you've figured out what you are required to do, you may then decide to do a second freewriting exercise.
- **Listen to and read the freewriting of others.** Learn from your peers.

Freewriting

Write nonstop for ten minutes or longer to discover possible writing ideas. Use a key concept related to the assignment as a starting point. You'll soon discover potential writing ideas that might otherwise have never entered your mind. Note in the following example that the writer doesn't stop writing even when he can't think of anything to say. Note also that he doesn't stop to correct typos and other mistakes.

> Popular culture. What does that include? Television obviously but that's a pretty boring subject. What else? Movies, pop music, video games. Is there a connection between playing violent video games and acting out violent behavior? Most video players I know would say no but sometimes news reports suggest a connection. Is this something I'd want to write about? Not really. What then? Maybe I could think about this a different way and focus on the positive effects of playing video games. They release tension for one thing and they can really be challenging. Other benefits? They help to kill time, that's for sure, but maybe that's not such a good thing. I would definitely read more if it weren't for video games, TV, etc. Maybe I could write about how all the electronic entertainment that surrounds us today is creating a generation of nonreaders. Or maybe I could focus on whether people aren't getting much physical exercise because of the time they spend with electronic media. Maybe both. At least I have some possibilities to work with.

Researching Your Topic

Writer and instructor Donald Murray said that "writers write with information. If there is no information, there will be no effective writing." How true! Before you can develop a thoughtful piece of writing, you must gain a thorough understanding of your topic; to do so, you must carry out the necessary reading, reflecting, and researching. Writing becomes a satisfying experience once you can speak with authority about your topic. Use the following guidelines when you start collecting information. (Also see "Research and Writing" in this book.)

- Determine what you already know about your topic. (Use the strategies below this bulleted list.)
- Consider listing questions you would like to answer during your research. (See page 39.)
- Identify and explore possible sources of information. (See page 40.)
- Carry out your research following a logical plan. (See pages 49–55.)

Find Out What You Already Know

Use one or more of the following strategies to determine what you already know about a writing topic.

1. **Focused freewriting:** At this point, you can focus your freewriting by (1) exploring your limited topic from different angles or (2) approaching your freewriting as if it were a quick draft of the actual paper. A quick version will tell you how much you know about your topic and what you need to find out.
2. **Clustering:** Try clustering with your topic serving as the nucleus word. Your clustering should focus on what you already know. (See page 36.)
3. **Five W's of writing:** Answer the five W's—Who? What? When? Where? and Why?—to identify basic information on your subject. Add How? to the list for better coverage.
4. **Directed writing:** Write whatever comes to mind about your topic, using one of the modes listed below. (Repeat the process as often as you need to, selecting a different mode each time.)

Describe it: What do you see, hear, feel, smell, and taste?
Compare it: What is it similar to? What is it different from?
Associate it: What connections between this topic and others come to mind?
Analyze it: What parts does it have? How do they work together?
Argue it: What do you like about the topic? What do you not like about it? What are its strengths and weaknesses?
Apply it: What can you do with it? How can you use it?

Ask Questions

To guide your collecting and researching, you may find it helpful to list questions about your topic that you would like to answer. Alternatively, you can use the questions that follow to guide your research.

	Description	Function	History	Value
PROBLEMS	• What is the problem? • What type of problem is it? • What are its parts? • What are the signs of the problem?	• Who or what is affected by it? • What new problems might it cause in the future?	• What is the current status of the problem? • What or who caused it? • What or who contributed to it?	• What is its significance? Why? • Why is it more (or less) important than other problems? • What does it symbolize or illustrate?
POLICIES	• What is the policy? • How broad is it? • What are its parts? • What are its most important features?	• What is the policy designed to do? • What is needed to make it work? • What are or will be its effects?	• What brought about this policy? • What are the alternatives?	• Is the policy workable? • What are its advantages and disadvantages? • Is it practical? • Is it a good policy? Why or why not?
CONCEPTS	• What is the concept? • What are its parts? • What is its main feature? • Whom or what is it related to?	• Who has been influenced by this concept? • Why is it important? • How does it work?	• When did it originate? • How has it changed over the years? • How might it change in the future?	• What practical value does it have? • Why is it superior (or inferior) to similar concepts? • What is its social worth?

ajt / Shutterstock.com

Identify Possible Sources

Finding meaningful sources is one of the most important steps you will take as you prepare to write. (That's why Part 3 of this text is dedicated to research instruction. See especially chapters 19–21.) Listed below are tips that will help you identify good sources:

1. **Give yourself enough time.** Finding good sources of information may be time-consuming. Books and periodicals you need may be checked out, your computer service may be down, and so on.
2. **Be aware of the limits of your resources.** Print material may be out-of-date. Online information may be more current, but it may not always be reliable. (See pages 384–387 for ways to help you evaluate information.)
3. **Use your existing resources to find additional sources of information.** Pay attention to books, articles, and individuals mentioned in reliable sources of information you find as you research.
4. **Ask for help.** The specialists in your school library can help you find information that is reliable and relevant. These people are trained to find information; don't hesitate to ask for their help.
5. **Bookmark useful Web sites.** Include reference works and academic resources related to your major.

Explore Different Sources of Information

Of course, books and Web sites are not the only possible sources of information. Primary sources such as interviews, observations, and surveys may lead you to a more thorough and meaningful understanding of a topic. (See pages 399–430.)

Primary Sources	Secondary Sources
Interviews	Articles
Observations	Reference book entries
Participation	Books
Surveys	Web sites

Carry Out Your Research

As you conduct your research, try to use a variety of reliable sources. It's also a good idea to choose an efficient note-taking method before you start. You will want to take good notes on the information you find and record all the publishing details necessary for citing your sources. (See pages 390–393.)

Reserve a special part of a notebook or file on your computer to question, evaluate, and reflect on your research as it develops. Reflection helps you make sense of new ideas, refocus your thinking, and evaluate your progress.

Track Sources

Follow these strategies for tracking sources and taking notes.

- **Track resources in a working bibliography.** Once you find a useful book, journal article, news story, or Web page, record identifying information for the source. For more help, see pages 388–389.
- **Use a note-taking system that respects sources.** Essentially, your note-taking system should help you keep an accurate record of useful information and ideas from sources while also allowing you to engage those sources with your own thinking. For a discussion of possible systems, see pages 390–393.
- **Distinguish summaries, paraphrases, and quotations.** As you read sources, you will find material that answers your questions and helps you achieve your writing purpose. At that point, decide whether to summarize, paraphrase, or quote the material:
    - **A summary** pulls just the main points out of a passage and puts them in your own words: Summarize source material when it contains relevant ideas and information that you can boil down.
    - **A paraphrase** rewrites a passage point by point in your own words: Paraphrase source material when all the information is important but the actual phrasing isn't especially important or memorable.
    - **A quotation** records a passage from the source word for word: Quote when the source states something crucial and says it well. Note: In your notes, always identify quoted material by putting quotation marks around it.

Summarizing, paraphrasing, and quoting are treated more fully on pages 394–396. Here is a brief example, with the original passage coming from Coral Ann Howells' *Alice Munro*, published in 1998 by Manchester University Press as part of its Contemporary World Writers series.

Original: "To read Munro's stories is to discover the delights of seeing two worlds at once: an ordinary everyday world and the shadowy map of another imaginary or secret world laid over the real one, so that in reading we slip from one world into the other in an unassuming domestic sort of way."

Summary: Munro's fiction moves readers from recognizable reality into a hidden world.

Paraphrase: Reading Munro's fiction gives readers the enjoyment of experiencing a double world: day-to-day reality and on top of that a more mysterious, fantastic world, with the result that readers move smoothly between the worlds in a seamless, ordinary way.

Quotation: Munro's fiction takes us into "the shadowy map of another imaginary or secret world laid over the real one."

Critical Thinking and Writing: Applications

Once you have used the instruction in this chapter to get started on a writing project, there might be more to think about. Through the activities below, apply what you have learned.

1. **Wise Words:** Writer Ralph Fletcher shares, "When I write, I am always struck at how magical and unexpected the process turns out to be." Would you describe the writing process you follow as "magical" and "unexpected"? Explain.
2. **Writing Reset:** Reread one of your recent essays. Does the writing show that you thoroughly understood your subject, met the needs of your readers, and achieved your purpose? How does it measure against the traits of strong writing? What traits in your writing are strong? Which need work?
3. **Living Today:** Getting started techniques help you engage with topics thoughtfully. Many areas of contemporary life—whether in health, the environment, the arts, or work—could benefit from our thoughtful engagement. Select one of these broad subject areas and engage it by doing the following: Using the strategies on pages 34–37, brainstorm possible topics and select one. Then use the strategies on pages 38–39 to explore what you know about that topic and what you need to learn.
4. **Photo Op:** This chapter opens with a photograph on page 25 (Figure 2.1) and a diagram of the writing process on page 26 (Figure 2.2). With these images in mind, find or make a photo, diagram, or other graphic that captures your sense of the writing process as a whole or of getting started in particular.

Learning-Objectives Checklist ✓

Have you achieved this chapter's learning objectives? Check your progress with the items below, revisiting topics in the chapter as needed. I have . . .

____ outlined the writing process, from getting started to submitting (26).

____ adapted the writing process to a specific writing project, taking into account the assignment challenges and my own writing habits (27).

____ analyzed the rhetorical situation for a specific writing project so as to make good decisions about my approach, tone, and content (28–29).

____ differentiated seven traits of strong, college-level writing and assessed my relative strengths and weaknesses with respect to these traits (30–31).

____ identified an assignment's key words, options, and restrictions, and related the assignment to course goals, other assignments, and my own interests (32–33).

____ developed and chosen a strong topic for a writing project by limiting the subject, conducting an exploratory search, and using prewriting techniques (34–37).

____ identified what I already know about the topic, generated questions to research, formulated a list of possible resources, and worked with those sources, while carefully tracking my use of these sources (38–41).

MindTap® Practice skills that you have learned in this chapter and receive automatic feedback. Reflect on your writing process.

Chapter 3

Planning

MindTap®

Understand the goals of the chapter and complete a warm-up activity online.

Some of us are meticulous planners. We organize our lives in advance and formulate strategies for completing every task. Others of us live more in the moment, believing that whatever needs to get done will get done, with or without a plan.

In writing, author and instructor Ken Macrorie calls for a blend of these two approaches: "Good writing," says Macrorie, "is formed partly through plan and partly through accident." In other words, too much early planning can get in the way of the discovery aspect of writing, while not enough planning can harm the focus and coherence of your writing.

Learning Objectives

By working through this chapter, you will be able to

- re-examine the rhetorical situation with an eye to planning your writing.
- generate a focused, thoughtful working thesis.
- determine the pattern of development suggested by your thesis.
- produce a plan or outline for your writing.

Visually Speaking Carefully study Figure 3.1. What does the photograph suggest about the role that planning plays in military life? What might be some of its benefits and drawbacks? Does such planning in any way parallel planning to write? How might planning your writing be different from what you see in the image?

U.S. Air Force photo/Master Sgt. Jack Braden

fig. 3.1

Revisiting the Rhetorical Situation

Use the following planning checklist to help you decide whether to move ahead with your planning or reconsider your topic.

Rhetorical Checklist

Writer

___ Am I interested in this topic?

___ How much do I know about this topic, and how much do I need to learn?

Subject

___ Does the topic fit with the subject requirements of the assignment?

___ Is the topic the right size—not too general or too specific—for the assignment?

___ What sources have I found so far, and how helpful have they been at deepening my understanding of the subject?

Purpose

___ What are the specific goals of the assignment?

___ Am I writing to entertain, inform, explain, analyze, persuade, reflect?

Form

___ What form should I create: essay, proposal, report, review?

Audience

___ Will my readers be interested in this topic? How can I interest them?

___ What do they know and need to know about it? What opinions do they have?

Context

___ What weight does this assignment have in terms of my grade?

___ How will the assignment be assessed?

Working with Sources

For projects that involve research, consider how the rhetorical situation can guide your use of sources:

1. **For your subject**, which sources offer reliable information and analysis that have shaped your thinking and pointed toward a working thesis?
2. **To achieve your purpose** (to entertain, inform, analyze, and/or persuade), which resources/sources should be featured in your writing?
3. **Given your audience,** which resources will help you create credibility with the audience and clarify the topic for them?

Forming Your Thesis Statement

After you have completed enough research and collecting, you may begin to develop a more focused interest in your topic. If all goes well, this narrowed focus will give rise to a thesis for your writing. A thesis statement identifies your central idea. It usually highlights a special condition or feature of the topic, expresses a specific claim about it, or takes a stand.

State your thesis in a sentence that effectively expresses what you want to explore or explain in your essay. Sometimes a thesis statement develops early and easily; at other times, the true focus of your writing emerges only after you've written your first draft.

Find a Focus

A general subject area is typically built into your writing assignments. Your task, then, is to find a limited writing topic and examine it from a particular angle or perspective. (You will use this focus to form your thesis statement.) Figure 3.2 shows this process.

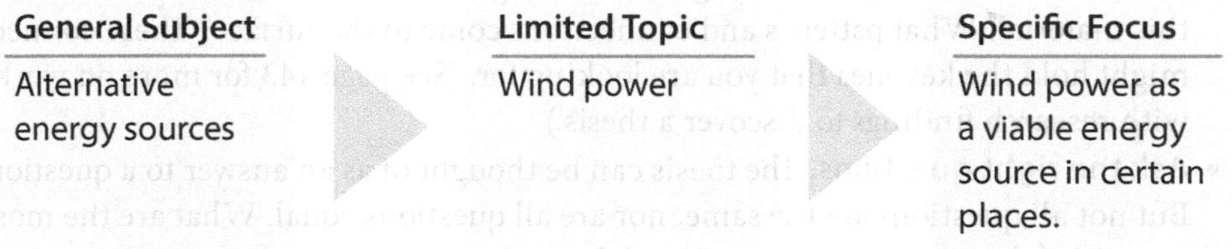

fig. 3.2

State Your Thesis

You can use the formula in Figure 3.3 to write a thesis statement for your essay. A thesis statement sets the tone and direction for your writing. Keep in mind that at this point you're writing a *working thesis statement*—a statement in progress, so to speak. You may change it as your thinking on the topic evolves.

a manageable or limited topic	+	a specific claim	=	an effective thesis statement
wind power		provides a viable energy source in the plains states		Wind power provides a viable energy source in the plains states.

fig. 3.3

Working with Sources Sometimes your writing can take direction specifically from your sources. You may consider making your thesis a response to a specific source. For example, if one source is especially strong or especially contrary to your own thinking, you could shape your thesis as an affirmation of the strong source's authority or as a rebuttal to the contrary source's claims.

Refine Your Thesis

Once you have drafted your working thesis, you can move on to thinking about organizing your essay. However, it may be helpful to pause, consider why the thesis is so important, and find ways to strengthen your working thesis before moving forward. Consider the following:

Why is the thesis so important for your writing? The thesis is the controlling idea of your essay—the main point or assertion about the topic. As such, the thesis is central to your essay. It sets a direction for your writing and represents your contribution to the larger "conversation" on the topic. Without a solid thesis, an essay lacks direction, purpose, and pressure; it too easily falls into traps of diffusion and disorganization. With a good thesis, an essay takes on purpose, becomes naturally organized, and takes the reader on a journey.

How can you discover, develop, and refine your thesis? You can improve your chances of developing a strong thesis by doing the following:

- **Reflect on your findings.** Prewriting strategies and research should generate ideas and information for your writing. Both during and after these activities, reflect on all this material. What patterns and connections come to the surface? These connections might hold the key idea that you are looking for. (See page 443 for more on working with research findings to discover a thesis.)
- **Ask the right questions.** The thesis can be thought of as an answer to a question. But not all questions are the same, nor are all questions equal. What are the most meaningful questions about your topic?
- **Apply concepts from the field.** Some writing calls for a practical, concrete thesis (e.g., the steps that should be followed to create an attractive and informative Web page). However, most essay writing centers on concepts and principles (e.g., the key principles of Web design). What are the central concepts at the heart of your topic? What principles are common in the field of knowledge to which the topic belongs? Can you apply concepts from other fields of knowledge to your topic?

What is the difference between a weak and a strong thesis? A strong thesis is narrowly focused rather than broad, making it manageable for the assignment. It is challenging rather than simplistic—rarely a simple summary, a straightforward statement of fact, or a pure opinion (a taste or preference that cannot really be argued). Here are three examples:

Weak thesis: lacks depth, functions as a cliché, offers a broad or vague generalization

> Writing is an important skill.

Good thesis: demonstrates some higher level thinking, such as analysis and argument

> Reading and writing function symbiotically: strengthening one skill improves the other.

Strong thesis: shows complexity, tension, or even risk (surprise, challenge, paradox)

> In a college or university, writing needs to become much more than an academic exercise: it must function as part of an authentic internal and communal dialogue on consequential issues.

Using a Thesis to Pattern Your Writing

An organizing pattern for your essay may be built into your assignment. For example, you may be asked to develop an argument or to write a process paper. When a pattern is not apparent, one may still evolve naturally during the research and information-collecting steps. If this doesn't happen, take a careful look at your thesis statement.

Let Your Thesis Guide You

An effective thesis will often suggest an organizing pattern. Notice how the thesis statements that follow direct and shape the writing to follow. (Also see page 19.)

Thesis (Focus) for a Personal Narrative

Writers of personal narratives do not always state a thesis directly, but they will generally have in mind an implied theme or main idea that governs the way they develop their writing. In the following thesis, the writer relates that his experience of prison, painful as it was, allows him to share four insights about prison life and the prison system. (See the full essay on pages 156–158.)

> At first I talked about the most painful things: that your children grow up without you, that you never get to hold your lover, kiss your mother, or walk down a quiet street in the rain. But I decided that I didn't like sharing that pain with strangers. I put together four talking points about how prison changes a middle-class, educated white man.

Thesis for an Essay of Definition

An essay of definition explores the denotation, connotation, and history of a term. In the following thesis statement, the writer names the two words he will explore—*deft* and *daft*—and provides an overview of the definition essay. (See the full essay on page 182.)

> Let me see if I can explain the original meaning and also how *daft* and *deft* came to part company.

Thesis for an Essay of Classification

An essay of classification identifies the main parts or categories of a topic and then examines each one. In the following thesis, the writer identifies four ways to discuss literature, and he examines each one in turn. (See the full essay on pages 283–285.)

> There are four main perspectives, or approaches, that readers can use to converse about literature.

Thesis for a Process Essay

Process essays are organized chronologically. As indicated in the following thesis, the writer of this essay will explain how cancer cells multiply and affect the body. (See the full essay on pages 212–213.)

> When a cell begins to function abnormally, it can initiate a process that results in cancer.

Thesis for an Essay of Comparison

The writer of the following thesis aims to make sense of the similarities and differences between traditional and online bullying by building on the distinction between urban and rural bullying. (See the full essay on pages 244–247.)

> In some ways, when it comes to bullying, the Internet has made the world more rural. Before the Internet, bullying ended when you withdrew from whatever environment you were in. But now, the bullying dynamic is harder to contain and harder to ignore.

Thesis for a Cause-and-Effect Essay

A cause-and-effect essay usually begins with one or more causes followed by an explanation of the effects, or with a primary effect followed by an explanation of the causes. In the following thesis, the writer suggests that an increased emphasis on teamwork in the workplace may short-circuit creativity, which often relies on solitude and an introspective character. (See the full essay on pages 259–263.)

> Research strongly suggests that people are more creative when they enjoy privacy and freedom from interruption. And the most spectacularly creative people in many fields are often introverted.

Thesis for a Position Essay

A position paper first introduces a topic and then states a position in its thesis. The following thesis statement defines the writer's position on fatherlessness. (See the full essay on pages 358–362.)

> Fatherlessness is the most harmful demographic trend of this generation. Yet, despite its scale and social consequences, fatherlessness is a problem that is frequently ignored or denied.

Thesis for an Essay Proposing a Solution

In the following thesis, the writer addresses the problem of low self-esteem in girls by arguing that the solution can be found in strengthening mother-daughter ties. (See the full essay on pages 337–341.)

> The fact that mothers have a significant impact on their daughters during the process of identity development is supported by research everywhere. Solid mother-daughter relationships are essential to combating the media's unrealistic and unattainable sense of beauty and in building self-esteem in young girls.

Developing a Plan or an Outline

Prior to drafting, it makes sense to develop a working plan for the structure of your writing. Your approach to planning may differ from one type of writing to another. For a short personal essay, a few brief points may be all you need to get started on a narrative; by contrast, for a major research project, you may want to develop a full, formal outline. Whatever choices you make, planning gives you a map to get started—a helpful tool for preventing writer's block and keeping you on course. To do effective planning, consider the following strategies.

Discovering organization in your thesis. As discussed on the previous pages, a working thesis sets direction for your writing. With this principle in mind, your goal is to shape the essay as a unified whole around the thesis. To find that unity, ask questions like these:

- **What support is implied in the phrasing of my working thesis?** Examine the key terms and phrases for hints of where your writing needs to go. Try turning those elements into questions that need to be answered, and then order those questions logically.
- **Does my thesis naturally suggest a specific method of development?** For example, in terms of your assignment, you may have drafted a working thesis that calls for support in a problem-solution, cause-effect, or compare-contrast pattern. Not only is this concept shown on the previous two pages, but it is also explored more fully in Part II of this text, "Reader: Strategies and Samples."
- **Where should I place my thesis in relation to the overall structure of my writing?** Frequently, the thesis is placed at the end of the introduction, paving the way for elaboration and support. However, in some writing, the thesis might come toward the middle (e.g., problem-solution writing) or the end (e.g., some position papers). In fact, in some narrative writing, the thesis might be implied only, not stated.

Looking to your prewriting. What organizational hints are in your notes? Explore how your notes suggest a way of proceeding. See how points collect under key ideas.

Structuring writing for the development of ideas. A strong essay is much more than a static list of points in support of a thesis, each point standing alone and equal in weight. You may recognize this approach as the five-paragraph high-school hamburger: introduction (top bun), three supporting points (meat), and conclusion (bottom bun). If this is the type of essay that you are used to cooking up, it's time to take your cooking skills to the next level. A more mature essay is about idea development, with each idea building upon or deepening the previous one. To be forward-looking in your planning, ask these questions:

- **What do I need to provide so the reader understands my thinking?** To carry your reader into a deeper understanding of the topic, you need to structure your thinking for your reader, not for yourself. You might, for example, need to begin by explaining the historical or social context of your topic, by supplying definitions of key terms for your analysis, or by reviewing the commonly held positions on the issue. Only then can you proceed.

- **How can I build sections that move from the known to the new?** Consider how you might "scaffold" your essay by building each new point on top of the previous one, now understood by the reader. This strategy is the "known-new" pattern.

Experimenting with mapping methods. You may be comfortable with using one strategy to organize all your essays—traditional outlining, for example. However, trying other methods may unlock creative possibilities that you had not imagined. Below is a list of five mapping strategies, each of which is elaborated on the pages that follow.

- **Quick List:** A brief listing of main points (See Figure 3.4.)
- **Topic Outline:** A more formal plan, including main points and essential details (See page 51.)
- **Sentence Outline:** A formal plan, including main points and essential details, written as complete sentences (See page 52.)
- **Writing Blueprints:** Basic organizational strategies preferred for different forms of writing (See page 53.)
- **Graphic Organizer:** An arrangement of main points and essential details in an appropriate chart or diagram (See pages 54–55.)

Quick Lists

Though listing is the simplest of all the methods of organization, it can help you take stock of your main ideas and get a sense of what further research or planning needs to be done. There is no right or wrong way to go about listing. The key is to come up with a system that works best for you. Figure 3.4 shows two examples that you may consider: **the basic bulleted list,** which briefly lists the main points you will discuss, and a **T Chart,** which lists the main points on one side and a supporting detail on the other side.

Sample Basic List

Topic: Different ways to discuss literature ——— Topic

- Focus on the text itself
- Focus on the text and the reader
- Focus on the author of the text
- Focus on ideas outside of literature

(Main Points)

Sample T Chart

Topic: Different ways to discuss literature ——— Topic

Approach	Emphasis
Text-centered approach	Structure and rules
Audience-centered approach	Relationship between reader and text
Author-centered approach	The writer's life
Idea-centered approach	Interpretation via specific ideology or field of knowledge

fig. 3.4

Topic Outline

If you have a good deal of information to sort and arrange, you may want to use a **topic outline** for your planning. In a topic outline, you state each main point and essential detail as a word or phrase. Before you start constructing your outline, write your working thesis statement at the top of your paper to help keep you focused on the subject. (Do not attempt to outline your opening and closing paragraphs unless you are specifically asked to do so.)

An effective topic outline is parallel in structure, meaning the main points (I, II, III) and essential details (A, B, C) are stated in the same way. Notice how the sample outline in Figure 3.5 uses a parallel structure, making it easy to follow.

Sample Topic Outline

Thesis: There are four main perspectives, or approaches, that readers can use to converse about literature. ← Topic

I. Text-centered approaches ← Main Points
- **a.** Also called formalist criticism
- **b.** Emphasis on structure of text and rules of genre ← Supporting Details
- **c.** Importance placed on key literary elements

II. Audience-centered approaches
- **a.** Also called rhetorical or reader-response criticism
- **b.** Emphasis on interaction between reader and text

III. Author-centered approaches
- **a.** Emphasis on writer's life
- **b.** Importance placed on historical perspective
- **c.** Connections made between texts

IV. Ideological approaches
- **a.** Psychological analysis of text
- **b.** Myth or archetype criticism
- **c.** Moral criticism
- **d.** Ecocriticism
- **e.** Sociological analysis

fig. 3.5

Maxx-Studio / Shutterstock.com

INSIGHT Planning is adaptable. Some writers prefer to generate an outline before they begin writing, while others prefer to make a more detailed outline after having written a draft. In the latter strategy, an outline can serve as a tool for evaluating the logic and completeness of the paper's organization.

Sentence Outline

A **sentence outline**, such as the one in Figure 3.6, uses complete sentences to explain the main points and essential details in the order that they will be covered in the main part of your essay. Such an outline can help you develop your ideas when writing the paper.

Sample Sentence Outline

Thesis: There are four main perspectives, or approaches, that readers can use to converse about literature. — Thesis

I. A text-centered approach focuses on the literary piece itself. — Main Points
  - **a.** This approach is often called formalist criticism.
  - **b.** This method of criticism examines text structure and the rules of the genre. — Supporting Details
  - **c.** A formalist critic determines how key literary elements reinforce meaning.

II. An audience-centered approach focuses on the "transaction" between text and reader.
  - **a.** This approach is often called rhetorical or reader-response criticism.
  - **b.** A rhetorical critic sees the text as an activity that is different for each reader.

III. An author-centered approach focuses on the origin of a text.
  - **a.** An author-centered critic examines the writer's life.
  - **b.** This method of criticism may include a historical look at a text.
  - **c.** Connections may be made between the text and related works.

IV. The ideological approach applies ideas outside of literature.
  - **a.** Some critics apply psychological theories to a literary work.
  - **b.** Myth or archetype criticism applies anthropology and classical studies to a text.
  - **c.** Moral criticism explores the ethical dimensions of literature.
  - **d.** Ecocriticism examines the environmental implications of a text.
  - **e.** Sociological approaches include Marxist, feminist, and minority criticism.

fig. 3.6

Working with Sources

When your writing project involves sources, the planning phase will include a great deal of sorting through material. Outlining can help you organize your primary and secondary sources to best support your thesis. As you organize your research in your outline, ask these questions:

- Where and how should I work with primary sources—interviews, surveys, analyses, observations, experiments, and other data I have collected?
- Where and how should I bring in secondary sources—scholarly books, journal articles, and the like?

Writing Blueprints

The writing blueprints in Figures 3.7–3.10 lay out basic organizational strategies for different forms of writing. The blueprints may help you arrange the details of your essay or even find holes in your research.

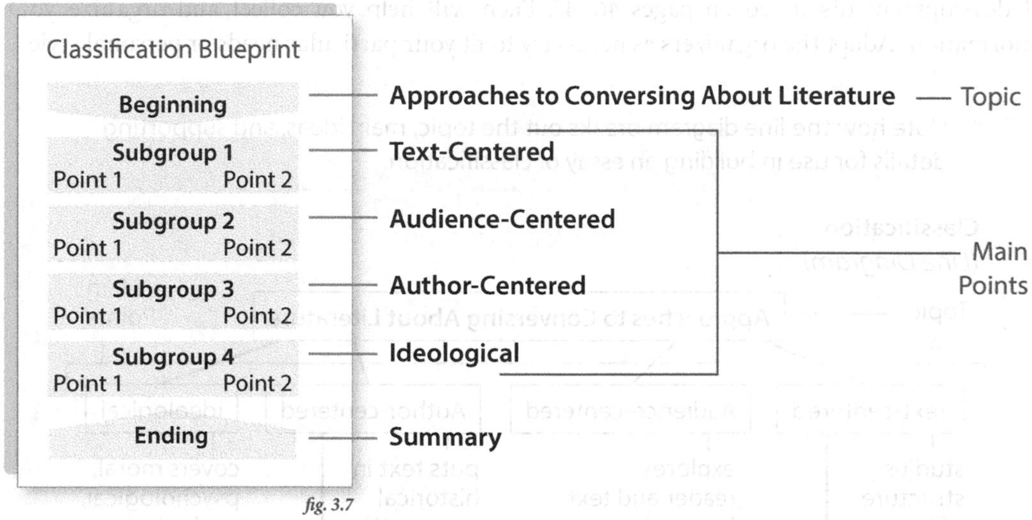

fig. 3.7

Comparison-Contrast Blueprint

Point by Point	*Subject by Subject*	*Similarities-Differences*
Beginning	**Beginning**	**Beginning**
Point A Subject 1 Subject 2	**Subject 1**	**Similarities**
Point B Subject 1 Subject 2	**Subject 2**	**Differences**
Ending	**Ending**	**Ending**

fig. 3.8

Cause-Effect Blueprint

Cause-Focused	*Effect-Focused*
Beginning	**Beginning**
Cause	**Effect**
Cause	**Effect**
Cause	**Effect**
Effect(s)	**Cause(s)**
Ending	**Ending**

fig. 3.9

Problem-Solution Blueprint

Problem(s)

Solution(s)

Objection(s)

Rebuttal(s)

fig. 3.10

Graphic Organizers

If you are a visual person, you might prefer a graphic organizer when it comes to arranging your ideas for an essay or a report. Graphic organizers can help you map out ideas and illustrate relationships among them. The organizers in Figures 3.11–3.17 are related to the methods of development discussed on pages 46–47. Each will help you collect and organize your information. Adapt the organizers as necessary to fit your particular needs or personal style.

Note how the line diagram breaks out the topic, main ideas, and supporting details for use in building an essay of classification.

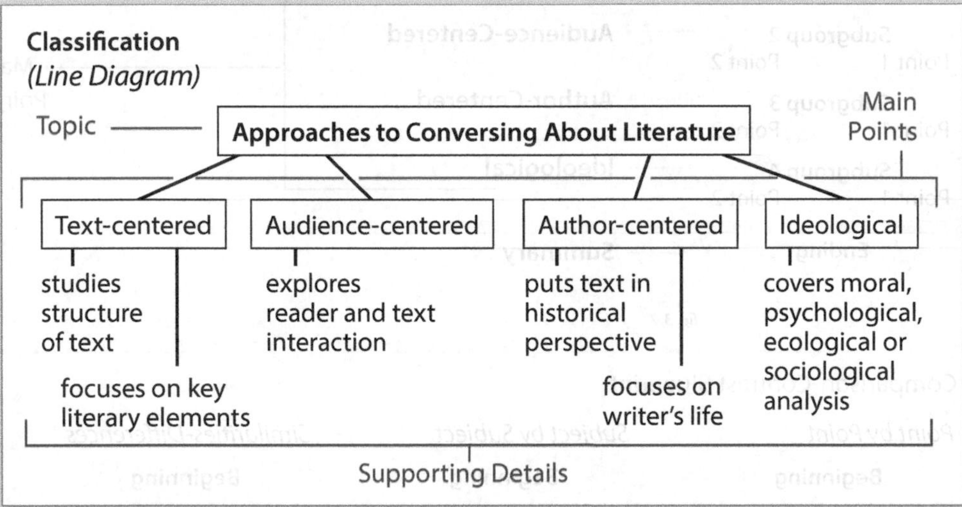

fig. 3.11

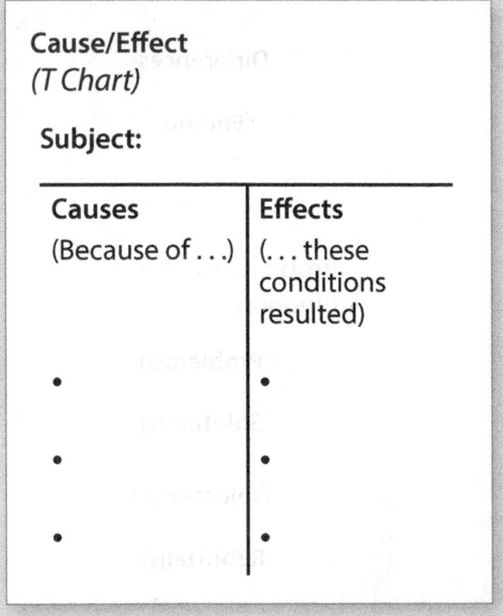

fig. 3.12

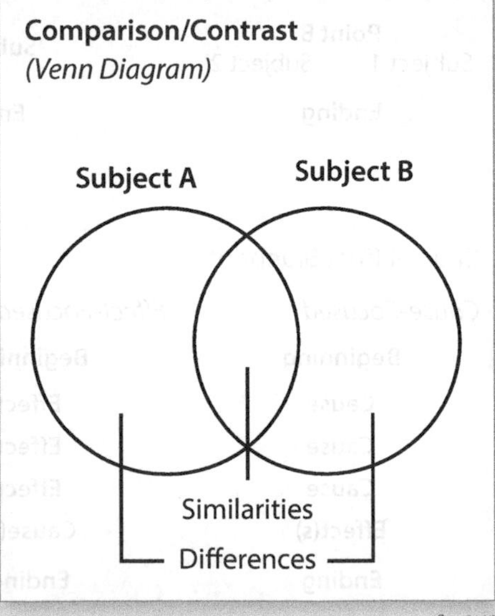

fig. 3.13

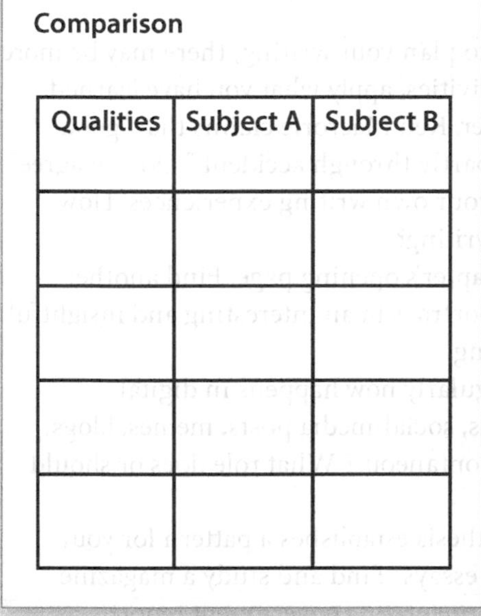

fig. 3.14

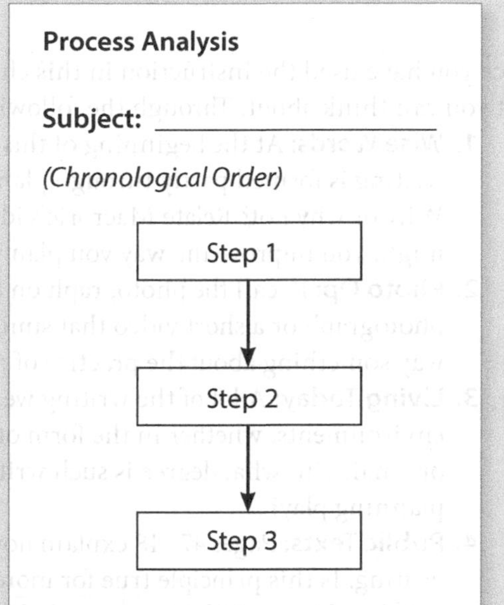

fig. 3.15

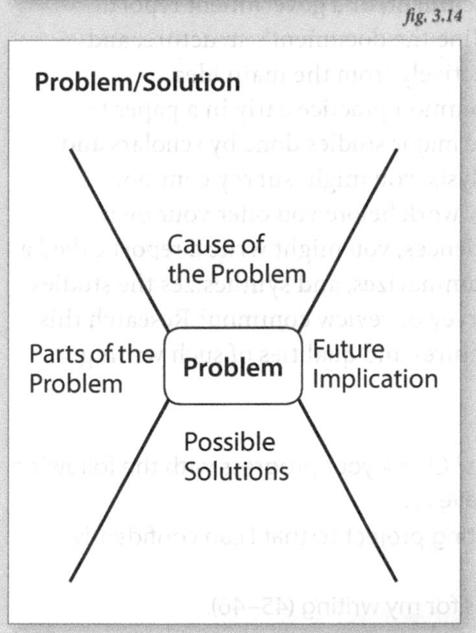

fig. 3.16

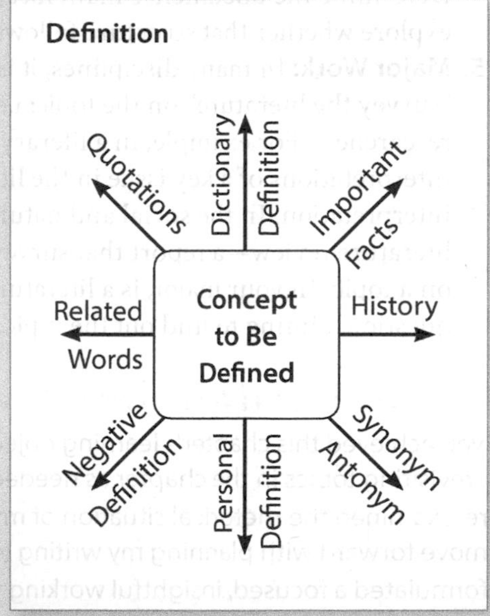

fig. 3.17

blackdaiya / Shutterstock.com

Critical Thinking and Writing: Applications

Once you have used the instruction in this chapter to plan your writing, there may be more that you can think about. Through the following activities, apply what you have learned.

1. **Wise Words:** At the beginning of this chapter, Ken Macrorie claims that "good writing is formed partly through plan and partly through accident." Do you agree? Why or why not? Relate Macrorie's idea to your own writing experiences. How might you improve the way you plan your writing?
2. **Photo Op:** Recall the photograph on the chapter's opening page. Find another photograph or a short video that similarly portrays in an interesting and insightful way something about the practice of planning.
3. **Living Today:** A lot of the writing we do regularly now happens in digital environments, whether in the form of tweets, social-media posts, memes, blogs, or emails. To what degree is such writing spontaneous? What role does or should planning play?
4. **Public Texts:** Pages 47–48 explain how the thesis establishes a pattern for your writing. Is this principle true for more than essays? Find and study a magazine article, a blog, a Web page, a workplace document, or a government report. Determine the document's main idea, outline the document's structure, and explore whether that structure follows effectively from the main idea.
5. **Major Work:** In many disciplines, it is a common practice early in a paper to "survey the literature" on the topic: i.e., the major studies done by scholars and researchers. For example, in a literary analysis, you might survey common interpretations of a key issue in the literary work before you offer your own interpretation. In the social and natural sciences, you might write a report called a literature review—a report that surveys, summarizes, and synthesizes the studies on a topic. In your major, is a literature survey or review common? Research this question, aiming to find out the typical features and qualities of such writing.

Learning-Objectives Checklist ✓

Have you achieved this chapter's learning objectives? Check your progress with the following items, revisiting topics in the chapter as needed. I have . . .

____ re-examined the rhetorical situation of my writing project so that I can confidently move forward with planning my writing (44).

____ formulated a focused, insightful working thesis for my writing (45–46).

____ analyzed my working thesis so as to choose a pattern of organization (47–48).

____ generated a plan for my writing, whether a quick list, a topic outline, a formal sentence outline, a blueprint, or a graphic organizer (49–55).

MindTap® Practice skills that you have learned in this chapter and receive automatic feedback. Reflect on your writing process.

Chapter 4

Drafting

French novelist Anatole France once said that one of his first drafts could have been written by a schoolboy, his next draft by a bright college student, his third draft by a superior graduate, and his final draft "only by Anatole France." Think in those terms as you write your first draft. Your main objective is to get ideas down; you'll have a chance later to improve your writing.

This chapter provides instruction for drafting a college-level essay. You'll find specific advice for creating the three main parts and arranging information—the writing moves that enable you to develop your thinking and impact readers.

Visually Speaking How is drafting like sketching? Note the hand with the pencil in Figure 4.1. What does it suggest about the process of drafting? Then again, are there important differences between sketching and drafting?

MindTap®

Understand the goals of the chapter and complete a warm-up activity online.

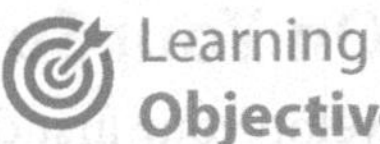

Learning Objectives

By working through this chapter, you will be able to

- re-examine the rhetorical situation as preparation for drafting.
- describe and explain the parts or "major moves" of essays.
- compose an effective opening for your writing.
- generate a substantial middle to follow the opening.
- produce a closing that effectively ends your draft.
- effectively integrate source material into your draft.

Sergey Sarychev / Shutterstock.com

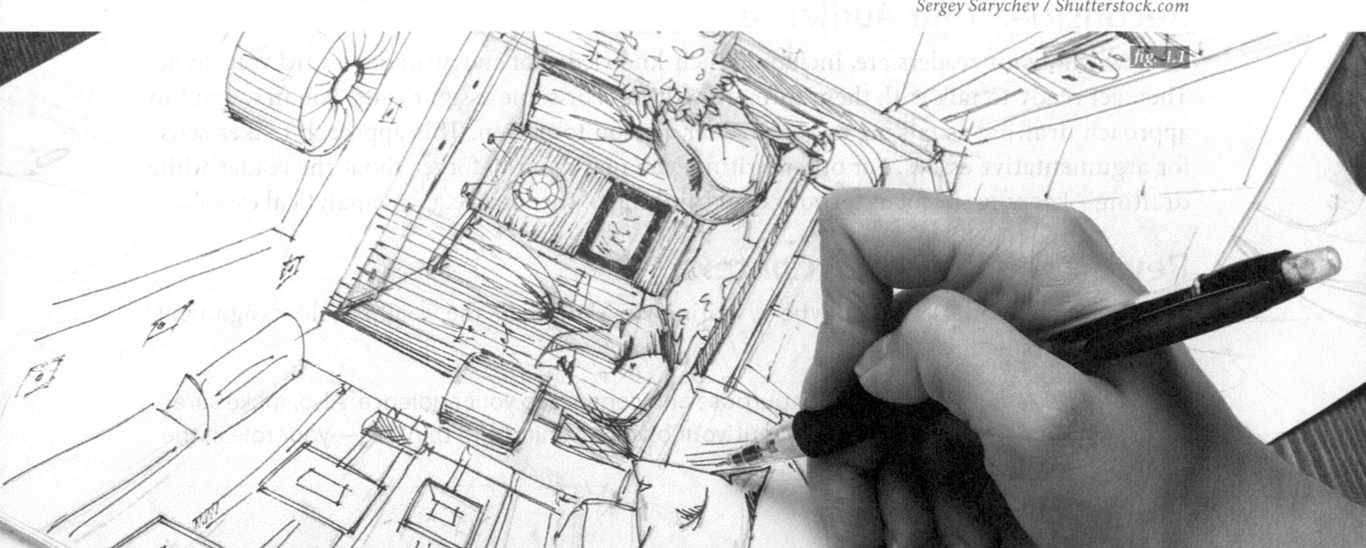
fig. 4.1

Reconsider the Rhetorical Situation

As you prepare to write, think about the parts of the rhetorical situation:

Think About Your Role

Are you writing as a student, a citizen, a friend, a member of a scholarly community or discipline? Use a voice that represents you well.

Focus On Your Subject

As you develop your first draft, these strategies can help you keep your subject in focus.

- **Use your outline, writing plan, or diagram** as a general guide, but don't feel absolutely bound by it. Try to develop your main points, but allow new ideas to emerge naturally.
- **Write freely** without being too concerned about neatness and correctness. Concentrate on developing your ideas, not on producing a final copy.
- **Include as much detail as possible**, continuing until you reach a logical end point.
- **Complete your first draft** in one or two sittings.
- **Use the most natural voice you can** so that the writing will flow smoothly. If your voice is too formal during drafting, you'll be tempted to stop and edit your words.
- **Quote sources accurately** by using your word-processing program's copy-and-paste features or by handwriting or typing quotations carefully.

Reconsider Your Purpose

Briefly review (1) what you want your writing to do (your task), (2) what you want it to say (your thesis), and (3) how you want to say it (list of ideas or outline). If helpful, write that purpose or thesis on a file card and keep it nearby as you draft.

Reconsider Your Audience

Review who your readers are, including their knowledge of and attitude toward your topic. Then get ready to talk with them through writing. For some assignments, you may want to approach drafting as talking to your reader, person to person. This approach makes sense for argumentative essays. For other writing, you may want to forget about the reader while drafting—keeping the focus on your own thinking of the topic (e.g., an analytical essay).

Review the Form and Context

Make sure you understand the type of writing you should do, the weight of the assignment, and any assessment issues.

Working with Sources Use sources that aid your purpose and connect to your audience. Also, make sure your sources do not crowd out your own reasoning and thinking—your role in the assignment.

Basic Essay Structure: Major Moves

The chart in Figure 4.2 lists the main writing moves that occur during the development of a piece of writing. Use it as a general guide that you adapt as needed for all of your drafting. Note that especially the middle moves listed offer strategies to use, not a sequence to follow.

Opening

Engage your reader.
Stimulate and direct the reader's attention.

Establish your direction.
Identify the topic and put it in perspective.

Get to the point.
Narrow your focus and state your thesis.

Middle

Advance your thesis.
Provide background information and cover your main points.

Test your ideas.
Raise questions and consider alternatives.

Support your main points.
Add substance and build interest.

Build a coherent structure.
Start new paragraphs and arrange the support.

Use different levels of detail.
Clarify and complete each main point.

Ending

Reassert the main point.
Remind the reader of the purpose and rephrase the thesis.

Urge the reader.
Gain the reader's acceptance and look ahead.

fig. 4.2

Opening Your Draft

The opening paragraph is one of the most important elements in any composition. It should accomplish at least three essential things: (1) engage the reader; (2) establish your direction, tone, and level of language; and (3) introduce your line of thought.

Advice:
- The conventional way of approaching the first paragraph is to view it as a kind of "funnel" that draws a reader in and narrows to a main point. In some situations, the final sentence explicitly states your thesis.

Cautions:
- Don't feel bound by the conventional pattern, which may sound stale if not handled well.
- Don't let the importance of the first paragraph paralyze you. Relax and write.

The information that follows will help you develop your opening. For additional ideas, you can refer to the sample essays in part II of this text, the Reader. (See page 133.)

Engage Your Reader

Your reader will be preoccupied with other thoughts until you seize, stimulate, and direct his or her attention. Here are some effective ways to "hook" the reader:

- **Mention little-known facts about the topic.**

  > Beads may have been what separated human ancestors from their Neanderthal cousins. Yes, beads.

- **Pose a challenging question.**

  > Why would human ancestors spend days carving something as frivolous as beads while Neanderthals spent days hunting mammoths?

- **Offer a thought-provoking quotation.**

  > "The key thing in human evolution is when people start devoting just ridiculous amounts of time to making these [beads]," says archeologist John Shea of Stony Brook University.

- **Tell a brief, illuminating story.**

  > When I walked into the room, I had only to show my hand to be accepted in the group of strangers there. The Phi Delta Kappa ring on my finger—and on all of our fingers—bound us across space and time as a group. Our ancestors discovered the power of such ornamentation forty thousand years ago.

Establish Your Direction

The direction of your line of thought should become clear in the opening part of your writing. Here are some moves you might make to set the right course:

- **Identify the topic (issue).** Show a problem, a need, or an opportunity.
- **Deepen the issue.** Connect the topic, showing its importance.
- **Acknowledge other views.** Tell what others say or think about the topic.

Get to the Point

You may choose to state your main point up front, or you may wait until later to introduce your thesis. For example, you could work inductively by establishing an issue, a problem, or a question in your opening and then build toward the answer—your thesis—in your conclusion. (See page 18 for more on inductive reasoning.) Sometimes, in fact, your thesis may simply be implied. In any case, the opening should at least hint at the central issue or thesis of your paper. Here are three ways to get to the point:

1. **Narrow your focus.** Point to what interests you about the topic.
2. **Raise a question.** Answer the question in the rest of the essay.
3. **State your thesis.** If appropriate, craft a sentence that boils down your thinking to a central claim. You can use the thesis sentence as a "map" for the organization of the rest of the essay. (See pages 45–48 and 372–373.)

Weak Opening

Although the following opening introduces the topic, the writing lacks interesting details and establishes no clear focus for the essay.

> I would like to tell you about the TV show *The Simpsons*. It's about this weird family of five people who look kind of strange and act even stranger. In fact, the characters aren't even real—they're just cartoons.

Strong Opening

In the following essay opener, the writer uses his first paragraph to get his readers' attention and describe his subject. He uses the second paragraph to raise a question that leads him to a statement of his thesis (underlined).

> *The Simpsons,* stars of the TV show by the same name, are a typical American family, or at least a parody of one. Homer, Marge, Bart, Lisa, and Maggie Simpson live in Springfield, U.S.A. Homer, the father, is a boorish, obese oaf who works in a nuclear power plant. Marge is an overprotective, nagging mother with an outrageous blue hairdo. Ten-year-old Bart is an obnoxious, "spiky-haired demon." Lisa is eight and a prodigy on the tenor saxophone and in class. The infant Maggie never speaks but only sucks on her pacifier.
>
> What is the attraction of this yellow-skinned family that stars on a show in which all of the characters have pronounced overbites and only four fingers on each hand? Viewers see a little bit of themselves in everything the Simpsons do. The world of Springfield is a parody of the viewer's world, and even after more than 500 episodes, Americans can't get enough of it. Viewers experience this parody in the show's explanations of family, education, workplace, and politics.

INSIGHT After stating the thesis, the writer forecasts the method of supporting that thesis.

Developing the Middle

The middle of an essay is the place where you do the "heavy lifting." In this part you develop the main points that support your thesis statement.

Advice:
- As you write, you will likely make choices that were unforeseen when you began. Use "scratch outlines" (temporary jottings) along the way to show where your new ideas may take you.

Cautions:
- Writing that lacks effective detail gives only a vague image of the writer's intent.
- Writing that wanders loses its hold on the essay's purpose.

For both of these reasons, always keep your thesis in mind when you develop the main part of your writing. Refer to the guidelines on the next two pages for help. You can refer to the sample essays in this book for ideas.

Advance Your Thesis

If you stated a thesis in the opening, you can advance it in the middle paragraphs by covering your main points and supporting them in these ways.

Explain: Provide important facts, details, and examples.
Narrate: Share a brief story or re-create an experience to illustrate an idea.
Describe: Tell in detail how someone appears or how something works.
Define: Identify or clarify the meaning of a specific term or idea.
Analyze: Examine the parts of something to better understand the whole.
Compare: Provide examples to show how two things are alike or different.
Argue: Use logic and evidence to prove that something is true.
Reflect: Express your thoughts or feelings about something.
Cite authorities: Add expert analysis or personal commentary.

Test Your Ideas

When you write a first draft, you're testing your initial thinking about your topic. You're determining whether your thesis is valid and whether you have enough compelling information to support it. Here are ways to test your line of thinking as you write:

- **Raise questions.** Try to anticipate your readers' questions.
- **Consider alternatives.** Look at your ideas from different angles; weigh various options; reevaluate your thesis.
- **Answer objections.** Directly or indirectly deal with possible problems that a skeptical reader might point out.

Build a Coherent Structure

Design paragraphs as units of thought that develop and advance your thesis clearly and logically. For example, look at the following brief essay, noting how each body paragraph presents ideas with supporting details that build on and deepen the main idea.

MindTap®
Read, highlight, and take notes online.

Seeing the Light

The writer introduces the topic and states his thesis.

All light bulbs make light, so they're all the same, right? Not quite. You have 1
many choices regarding how to light up your life. Two types of bulbs are the traditional incandescent and the newer, more compact fluorescent. By checking out how they're different, you can better choose which one to buy.

The writer starts with a basic explanation of how the two types of light bulbs function differently.

While either incandescent or compact fluorescent bulbs can help you read or 2
find the bathroom at night, each bulb makes light differently. In an incandescent bulb, electricity heats up a tungsten filament (thin wire) to 450 degrees, causing it to glow with a warm, yellow light. A compact fluorescent is a glass tube filled with mercury vapor and argon gas. Electricity causes the mercury to give off ultraviolet radiation. That radiation then causes phosphors coating the inside of the tube to give off light.

The writer shifts his attention to weaknesses of compact bulbs.

Both types of bulbs come in many shapes, sizes, and brightnesses, but compacts 3
have some restrictions. Because of their odd shape, compacts may not fit in a lamp well. Compacts also may not work well in very cold temperatures, and they can't be used with a dimmer switch.

He next explains the strengths of compacts.

On the other hand, while compact fluorescents are less flexible than 4
incandescents, compacts are four times more efficient. For example, a 15-watt compact produces as many lumens of light as a 60-watt incandescent! Why? Incandescents turn only about 5 percent of electricity into light and give off the other 95 percent as heat.

He acknowledges that compacts cost more, but he justifies the cost.

But are compacts less expensive than incandescents? In the short run, no. 5
Whereas a 60-watt incandescent costs about one dollar, a comparable compact can cost about $5.00. However, because compacts burn less electricity—and last 7 to 10 times longer—in the long run, compacts are less expensive.

The writer rephrases his thesis as a challenge.

Now that you're no longer in the dark about light bulbs, take a look at the lamp 6
you're using to read this essay. Think about the watts (electricity used), lumens (light produced), efficiency, purchase price, and lamplife. Then decide how to light up your life in the future.

Make Writing Moves

Drafting the body of your essay can involve using a range of writing moves. Many of these are addressed in part II of this book, where rhetorical modes such as defining and classifying are presented. What follows, however, are some other common writing moves.

Developing an Analogy or Comparison

An analogy is a comparison that a writer uses to explain a complex or unfamiliar phenomenon. For example, in this paragraph, Rob King compares our immune system to mall security.

> The human body is like a mall, and the immune system is like mall security. Because the mall has hundreds of employees and thousands of customers, security guards must rely on photo IDs, name tags, and uniforms to decide who should be allowed to open cash registers and who should have access to the vault. In the same way, white blood cells and antibodies need to use DNA cues to recognize which cells belong in a body and which do not. Occasionally security guards make mistakes, wrestling Kookie the Klown to the ground while DVD players "walk" out of the service entrance, but these problems amount only to allergic reactions or little infections. If security guards become hypervigilant, detaining every customer and employee, the situation is akin to leukemia, in which white blood cells attack healthy cells. If security guards become corrupt, letting thieves take a "five-finger discount," the situation is akin to AIDS. Both systems—mall security and human immunity—work by correctly differentiating friend from foe.

Developing an Example or Illustration

Providing an example or illustration allows you to flesh out an idea by exploring an instance of it. Well developed examples match up with the idea by illustrating and clarifying its various facets. In the following passage from "The Rise of the New Groupthink" (pages 259–263), Susan Cain illustrates how charisma can blind people to actual sources of creativity.

> Culturally, we're often so dazzled by charisma that we overlook the quiet part of the creative process. Consider Apple. In the wake of Steve Jobs's death, we've seen a profusion of myths about the company's success. Most focus on Mr. Jobs's supernatural magnetism and tend to ignore the other crucial figure in Apple's creation: a kindly, introverted engineering wizard, Steve Wozniak, who toiled alone on a beloved invention, the personal computer.
>
> Rewind to March 1975: Mr. Wozniak believes the world would be a better place if everyone had a user-friendly computer. This seems a distant dream—most computers are still the size of minivans, and many times as pricey. But Mr. Wozniak meets a simpatico band of engineers that call themselves the Homebrew Computer Club. The Homebrewers are excited about a primitive new machine called the Altair 8800. Mr. Wozniak is inspired, and immediately begins work on his own magical version of a computer. Three months later, he unveils his amazing creation for his friend, Steve Jobs. Mr. Wozniak wants to give his invention away free, but Mr. Jobs persuades him to co-found Apple Computer.

Presenting and Interpreting Evidence

You may be familiar with the phrase "marshalling evidence," which suggests that this writing move is something of a military campaign. When you pull together, present, and analyze a range of evidence (e.g., statistics, historical records, and expert testimony), you advance your ideas by building a foundation on which your reasoning can stand. In the following paragraph from "The Emancipation of Abe Lincoln" (pages 226–229), Eric Foner offers evidence of Lincoln's complex efforts to end slavery.

> Lincoln's plan sought to win the cooperation of slave holders in ending slavery. As early as November 1861, he proposed it to political leaders in Delaware, one of the four border states (along with Kentucky, Maryland and Missouri) that remained in the Union. Delaware had only 1,800 slaves; the institution was peripheral to the state's economy. But Lincoln found that even there, slave holders did not wish to surrender their human property. Nonetheless, for most of 1862, he avidly promoted his plan to the border states and any Confederates who might be interested.
>
> Lincoln also took his proposal to black Americans. In August 1862, he met with a group of black leaders from Washington. He seemed to blame the presence of blacks in America for the conflict: "but for your race among us there could not be war." He issued a powerful indictment of slavery—"the greatest wrong inflicted on any people"—but added that, because of racism, blacks would never achieve equality in America. "It is better for us both, therefore, to be separated," he said. But most blacks refused to contemplate emigration from the land of their birth

Applying a Concept

A lot of academic writing involves explaining and applying concepts—the key ideas that make sense of subjects. For example, an environmental science student might analyze corn production using the concept of sustainability, or an English student might explain a character's fate through the concept of hubris. In the following passage from "How the Internet Has Changed Bullying" (pages 244–247), Maria Konnikova applies the concept of rural bullying, which she has just explained as distinct from urban bullying, to the relatively new phenomenon of cyberbullying.

> In some ways, when it comes to bullying, the Internet has made the world more rural. Before the Internet, bullying ended when you withdrew from whatever environment you were in. But now, the bullying dynamic is harder to contain and harder to ignore. If you're harassed on your Facebook page, all of your social circles know about it; as long as you have access to the network, a ceaseless stream of notifications leaves you vulnerable to victimhood. Bullying may not have become more prevalent—in fact, a recent review of international data suggests that its incidence has declined by as much as ten percent around the world. But getting away from it has become more difficult.

Stretching an Idea

When you stretch an idea, you are making a writing move that explores the boundaries and portability of the idea. Can it be stretched to include elements and dimensions not normally associated with it? Might it be transported from one field of knowledge to another? Should you shift the direction of discussion by turning the idea upside down? In the following paragraph from "Fatherless America" (pages 358–362), David Blankenhorn explores the possible ramifications of fatherlessness for all of American society, not just specific families.

> If this trend continues, fatherlessness is likely to change the shape of our society. Consider this prediction. After the year 2000, as people born after 1970 emerge as a large proportion of our working-age adult population, the United States will be a nation divided into two groups, separate and unequal. The two groups will work in the same economy, speak a common language, and remember the same national history. But they will live fundamentally divergent lives. One group will receive basic benefits—psychological, social, economic, educational, and moral—that are denied to the other group.
>
> The primary fault line dividing the two groups will not be race, religion, class, education, or gender. It will be patrimony. One group will consist of those adults who grew up with the daily presence and provision of fathers. The other group will consist of those who did not. By the early years of the next [twenty-first] century, these two groups will be roughly the same size.

Exploring a Tension

This writing move attends to the gaps, disagreements, dualisms, and elements of confusion within your topic. Such tensions are often big and obvious, but they may also be small and subtle. Both kinds are worthy of your attention. Such a move may call out the tension, explore its meaning, and possibly seek to resolve it. In the following paragraph from "Death from Below" (see pages 264–267), Brian Phillips introduces opposing, contradictory themes in how the media cover shark attacks.

> Like almost all shark-related media coverage, the summer-of-shark-attacks dossier is depressing and contradictory. It has to be, because it's designed to serve two opposing agendas. It needs to scare us a little, because the fascination that makes sharks prime box-office draws hinges on sharks being real-life sea monsters and thus categorically terrifying. But it also needs to live up to the statistical and ecological responsibility not to vilify sharks. The result is the distinctive, smug tone of self-correcting sensationalism that we associate with shark-attack pseudo-journalism: DID YOU KNOW that these BEINGS OF PURE EVIL AND MALEVOLENCE who WILL NEVER EVER BOTHER YOU also totally YEARN TO EAT YOUR CHILDREN and are VITAL TO THE HEALTH OF OUR PLANET??

Ending Your Draft

Closing paragraphs can be important for tying up loose ends, clarifying key points, or signing off with the reader. In a sense, the entire essay is a preparation for an effective ending; the ending helps the reader look back over the essay with new understanding and appreciation. Many endings leave the reader with fresh food for thought.

Advice:
- Because the ending can be so important, draft a variety of possible endings. Choose the one that flows best from a sense of the whole.

Cautions:
- If your thesis is weak or unclear, you will have a difficult time writing a satisfactory ending. To strengthen the ending, strengthen the thesis.
- You may have heard this formula for writing an essay: "Say what you're going to say, say it, then say what you've just said." Remember, though, if you need to "say what you've just said," say it in new words.
- You may be tempted to begin your conclusion with "In conclusion." As a general rule, don't. This phrase is clichéd. Aim to be more subtle and inventive in beginning your ending.

The information that follows will help you develop your ending. For ideas, you can refer to the sample essays in part II of this book.

Reassert the Main Point

If an essay is complicated, the reader may need reclarification at the end. Show that you are fully addressing the issues that you forecast earlier in the essay.

- **Remind the reader.** Recall what you first set out to do; check off the key points you've covered; or answer any questions left unanswered.
- **Rephrase the thesis.** Restate your thesis in light of the most important support you've given. Deepen and expand your original thesis.
- **Revisit your opening.** As discussed on page 60, your opening may include an interesting fact, question, quotation, or story. In your ending, you could refer to that element again, offering a final thought about it to bring your writing full circle.

Urge the Reader

Your reader may still be reluctant to accept your ideas or argument. The ending is your last chance to gain the reader's acceptance. Here are some possible strategies:

- **Show the implications.** Follow further possibilities raised by your train of thought; be reasonable and convincing.
- **Look ahead.** Suggest other possible connections.
- **List the benefits.** Show the reader the benefits of accepting or applying the things you've said.

INSIGHT When your writing comes to an effective stopping point, conclude the essay. Don't tack on another idea.

Complete and Unify Your Message

Your final paragraphs are your last opportunity to refocus, unify, and otherwise reinforce your message. Draft the closing carefully, not merely to finish the essay but to further advance your purpose and thesis.

Weak Ending

The following ending does not focus on and show commitment to the essay's main idea. Rather than reinforcing this idea, the writing leads off in a new direction.

> I realize I've got to catch my bus. I've spent too much time talking to this woman whose life is a wreck. I give her some spare change and then head off. She doesn't follow me. It's kind of a relief. Toronto is a great city, but sometimes you have weird experiences there. Once a street vendor gave me a free falafel. I didn't want to eat it because maybe something was wrong with it. What a weird city!

Strong Endings

What follows are final paragraphs from two essays in this book. Listen to their tone, watch how they reconsider the essay's ideas, and note how they offer further food for thought. (The first example is a revision of the weak paragraph.)

> I tell her I need to get going. She should go, too, or she'll be late for the hearing. Before getting up, I reach into my wallet and give her two TTC passes and some spare change. I walk her to the street and point her toward Old City Hall. She never thanks me, only looks at me one last time with immense vulnerability and helplessness. Then she walks away.
>
> I wonder as I hurry towards the station if she'll be okay, if her boyfriend really will get out of jail, and if her grandmother will ever take her back. Either way, I think as I cross Bay Street, what more can I do? I have a bus to catch.
>
> (See the full essay on pages 153–155.)

> Passion and power permeate all of Latin America's music. The four major types of music—indigenous, Iberian and Mestizo folk, Afro-American, and popular urban—are as diverse as the people of Latin America, and each style serves a valued need or function in Latinos' everyday lives. As a result, those listening to Latin American music—whether it is a Peruvian Indian's chant, a Venezuelan farmer's whistled tune, a Cuban mambo drummer's vivacious beat, or the Bogotá rock concert's compelling rhythms—are hearing much more than music. They are hearing the passion and power of the Latin American people.
>
> (See the full essay on pages 196–199.)

Working with Sources Save the best for last. Consider using an especially thought-provoking statement, quotation, or detail in your conclusion. Doing so can help you clinch your point.

Working with Sources

If you are using sources, take care not to overwhelm your draft with source material. Keep the focus on your own ideas:

- Avoid strings of references and chunks of source material with no discussion, explanation, or interpretation on your part in between.
- Don't offer entire paragraphs of material from a source (whether paraphrased or quoted) with a single in-text citation at the end. When you do so, your thinking disappears.
- Be careful not to overload your draft with complex information and dense data lacking explanation.
- Resist the urge to simply copy and paste big chunks from sources. Even if you document the sources, your paper will quickly become a patchwork of source material with a few weak stitches (your contribution) holding it together.
- Note the careful use of source material in the following paragraph.

Sample Paragraph Showing Integration of Source Material

Topic sentence: idea elaborating and supporting thesis

Development of idea through reasoning

Support of idea through reference to source material

Concluding statement of idea

Antibiotics are effective only against infections caused by bacteria and should never be used against infections caused by viruses. Using an antibiotic against a viral infection is like throwing water on a grease fire—water may normally put out fires but will only worsen the situation for a grease fire. In the same way, antibiotics fight infections, but they cause the body harm only when they are used to fight infections caused by viruses. Viruses cause the common cold, the flu, and most sore throats, sinus infections, coughs, and bronchitis. Yet antibiotics are commonly prescribed for these viral infections. *The New England Journal of Medicine* reports that 22.7 million kilograms (25,000 tons) of antibiotics are prescribed each year in the United States alone (Wenzel and Edmond, 1962). Meanwhile, the CDC reports that approximately 50 percent of those prescriptions are completely unnecessary ("Antibiotic Overuse" 25). "Every year, tens of millions of prescriptions for antibiotics are written to treat viral illnesses for which these antibiotics offer no benefits," says the CDC's antimicrobial resistance director David Bell, M.D. (qtd. in Bren 30). Such mis-prescribing is simply bad medical practice that contributes to the problem of growing bacterial infection.

Critical Thinking and Writing: Applications

Once you have used the instruction in this chapter to draft your writing, there may be more that you can think about. Through the following activities, apply what you have learned.

1. **Wise Words:** Patricia T. O'Connor says, "All writing begins life as a first draft, and first drafts are never any good. They're not supposed to be." Is this claim true? Why or why not? What do you hope to accomplish with a first draft? How can you make drafting more effective?
2. **Photo Op:** Recall the photograph on the chapter's opening page. Find another photograph or a short video that portrays something about your practices when drafting, or the challenges you face when you sit down to do so.
3. **Making Moves:** Review the chart on page 59 and the "writing moves" on pages 64–66. Based on your own reading and writing, can you identify, name, and describe an additional writing move? Can you supply an example of that move?
4. **Writing Reset:** Choose one of the sample essays in part II of this text. After analyzing the opening, middle, and closing strategies that the writer uses, imagine alternatives to what you find there. Sketch out these alternatives and explain how they would change the writing.
5. **Major Work:** Find one or two examples of the kinds of writing done in or related to your field of study—scholarly articles, online reports, Web sites, and so on. What writing moves seem to be valued in your field? Why?

Learning-Objectives Checklist ✓

Have you achieved this chapter's learning objectives? Check your progress with the following items, revisiting topics in the chapter as needed. I have . . .

____ re-examined the rhetorical situation of my writing project (my role as writer, my subject, my purpose, the audience, the form, and the context) to be better prepared for drafting (58).

____ identified and explained the parts or "major moves" of an essay, including strategies for openings, middles, and closings (59).

____ composed an opening that effectively engages my readers; establishes my direction, tone, and diction level; and introduces my line of thought through a thesis or a theme (60–61).

____ generated a substantial middle that advances my thesis, tests out my ideas, builds a coherent structure, and provides a fitting level of detail (62–63).

____ produced a closing that reasserts my main point in a fresh way, connects with readers, and unifies my writing (67–68).

____ integrated source material so that it supports my thinking rather than encumbers my ideas (69).

MindTap® Practice skills that you have learned in this chapter and receive automatic feedback. Reflect on your writing process.

Chapter 5

Revising

MindTap®

Understand the goals of the chapter and complete a warm-up activity online.

The word revising means "taking another look," so revising is best done after a brief break. Set aside your writing and return to it later with fresh eyes. Also, enlist the fresh eyes of another reader, whether a roommate, a classmate, or someone at the writing center. Revising is all about getting perspective.

Of course, once you have perspective, you need to figure out how to make improvements. This chapter provides numerous strategies for focusing on the global traits of your writing—ideas, organization, and voice. The changes you make should improve the work significantly, perhaps even reshaping it.

Learning Objectives

By working through this chapter, you will be able to

- assess the overall approach that you have taken in your draft.
- critique and improve the ideas, organization, and voice of your draft.
- test and strengthen your paragraphs for unity, coherence, and completeness.
- give and receive helpful feedback by collaborating with classmates.
- understand the role of the writing center and use it to improve your own writing.

Visually Speaking To effectively revise your draft, you need to first "recharge your writing batteries" (Figure 5.1). Practically speaking, what might this idea mean for your own writing?

Alison Hancock / Shutterstock.com

fig. 5.1

Consider Whole-Paper Issues

When revising, first look at the big picture. Take it all in. Determine whether the content is interesting, informative, and worth sharing. Note any gaps or soft spots in your line of thinking. Ask yourself how you can improve what you have done so far. The information that follows will help you address whole-paper issues such as these.

Revisit the Rhetorical Situation

Just as the rhetorical situation helped you to set your direction in writing, it can help you make course corrections. Think about each part of the rhetorical situation.

- **Consider your role.** How are you coming across in this draft? Do you sound authoritative, engaged, knowledgeable, confident? How do you want to come across?
- **Think about your subject.** Have you stated a clear focus? Have you supported it with a variety of details? Have you explored the subject fully?
- **Remember your purpose.** Are you trying to analyze, describe, explain, propose? Does the writing succeed? Do the ideas promote your purpose? Does your organization support the purpose? Is your writing voice helpful in achieving your purpose?
- **Check the form.** Have you created writing that matches the form that your instructor requested? Have you taken best advantage of the form, including graphics or other media, if appropriate?
- **Consider your readers.** Have you captured their attention and interest? Have you provided them the information they need to understand your writing? Have you considered their values, needs, and opinions, and used them to connect?
- **Think about the context.** Is this piece of writing the correct length and level of seriousness for the assignment? Is it on schedule? How does it match up to what others are doing?

Working with Sources

Make sure that your sources work well for each part of the rhetorical situation. Verify that the sources you have used . . .

- reflect well on you, showing that you understand and care about the topic.
- illuminate the subject with accurate, precise, substantial information.
- help you achieve your purpose, whether to inform, persuade, or reflect.
- work well within the form and can be appropriately credited.
- are seen as authoritative by readers.
- are timely and credible in the context.

Consider Your Overall Approach

Sometimes it's better to start fresh if your writing contains stretches of uninspired ideas. Consider a fresh start if your first draft shows one of these problems:

- **The topic is worn-out.** An essay titled "Lead Poisoning" may not sound very interesting. Unless you can approach it with a new twist ("Get the Lead Out!"), consider cutting your losses and finding a fresh topic.
- **The approach is stale.** If you've been writing primarily to get a good grade, finish the assignment, or sound cool, start again. Try writing to learn something, prompt real thinking in readers, or touch a chord.
- **Your voice is predictable or fake.** Avoid the bland "A good time was had by all" or the phony academic "When one studies this significant problem in considerable depth . . . " Be real. Be honest.
- **The draft sounds boring.** Maybe it's boring because you pay an equal amount of attention to everything and hence stress nothing. Try condensing less important material and expanding what's important.
- **The essay is formulaic.** In other words, it follows the "five-paragraph" format. This handy organizing frame may prevent you from doing justice to your topic and thinking. If your draft is dragged down by rigid adherence to a formula, try a more original approach.

Working with Sources Test the balance of reasoning and sources. Make sure your draft is not thin on source material, but also make sure that the source material does not dominate the conversation. Use these tips for balancing reasoning and sources:

1. Before diving into source material within a paragraph or section of your paper, flesh out your thinking more fully. Offer reasoning that elaborates the claim and effectively leads into the evidence.
2. As you present evidence from source material, build on it by explaining what it means. Evidence doesn't typically speak for itself: through analysis, synthesis, illustration, contrast, and other means, you need to show how or why your sources advance your thesis.
3. After you have presented evidence that elaborates on and supports your idea, extend your thoughts by addressing the reader's "So what?" or "Why does this matter?" skepticism.

Revising Your First Draft

Revising helps you turn your first draft into a more complete, thoughtful piece of writing. The following information will help you do that.

Prepare to Revise

Once you've finished a first draft, set it aside (ideally for a few days) until you can look at the draft objectively and make needed changes. If you drafted on paper, photocopy the draft. If you drafted on a computer, print your paper (double-spaced). Then make changes with a good pencil or colored pen. If you prefer revising on the computer, consider using your software editing program. In all cases, save your first draft for reference.

Think Globally

When revising, focus on the big picture—the overall strength of the ideas, organization, and voice.

Ideas: Check your thesis, focus, or theme. Has your thinking on your topic changed? Also think about your readers' most pressing questions concerning this topic. Have you answered these questions? Finally, consider your reasoning and support. Are both complete and sound?

Organization: Check the overall design of your writing, making sure that ideas move smoothly and logically from one point to the next. Does your essay build effectively? Do you shift directions cleanly? Fix structural problems in one of these ways:

- **Reorder** material to improve the sequence.
- **Cut** information that doesn't support the thesis.
- **Add** details where the draft is thin.
- **Rewrite** parts that seem unclear.
- **Improve** links between points by using transitions.

Voice: Voice is your personal presence on the page, the tone and attitude that others hear when reading your work. In other words, voice is the between-the-lines message your readers get (whether you want them to or not). When revising, make sure that the tone of your message matches your purpose, whether it is serious, playful, or satiric.

INSIGHT Don't pay undue attention to spelling, grammar, and punctuation at this early stage in the process. Otherwise, you may become distracted from the task at hand: improving the content of your writing. Editing and proofreading come later.

Revising for Ideas and Organization

As you review your draft for content, make sure the ideas are fully developed and the organization is clear. From your main claim or thesis to your reasoning and your evidence, strengthen your thinking and sequencing.

Examine Your Ideas

Review the ideas in your writing, making sure that each point is logical, complete, and clear. To test the logic in your writing, see pages 323–326.

Complete Thinking

Have you answered readers' basic questions? Have you supported the thesis? The original passage that follows is too general; the revision is clearly more complete.

Original Passage (Too general)

As soon as you receive a minor cut, the body's healing process begins to work. Blood from tiny vessels fills the wound and begins to clot. In less than 24 hours, a scab forms.

Revised Version (More specific)

As soon as you receive a minor cut, the body's healing process begins to work. In a simple wound, the first and second layers of skin are severed along with tiny blood vessels called capillaries. As these vessels bleed into the wound, minute structures called platelets help stop the bleeding by sticking to the edges of the cut and to one another, forming a plug. The platelets then release chemicals that react with certain proteins in the blood to form a clot. The blood clot, with its fiber network, begins to join the edges of the wound together. As the clot dries out, a scab forms, usually in less than 24 hours.

Clear Thesis

Make sure that your writing centers on one main issue or thesis. Although the following original passage lacks a thesis, the revision has a clear one.

Original Passage (Lacks a thesis)

Teen magazines are popular with young girls. These magazines contain a lot of how-to articles about self-image, fashion, and boy-girl relationships. Girls read them to get advice on how to act and how to look. Girls who don't really know what they want are the most eager readers.

Revised Version (Identifies a specific thesis statement)

Adolescent girls often see teen magazines as handbooks on how to be teenagers. These magazines influence the ways they act and the ways they look. For girls who are unsure of themselves, these publications can exert an enormous amount of influence. Unfortunately, the advice about self-image, fashion, and boys found within their pages may do more harm than good.

Examine Your Organization

Good writing has structure. It leads readers logically and clearly from one point to the next. When revising for organization, consider four areas: the overall plan, the opening, the flow of ideas, and the closing.

Overall Plan

Look closely at the sequence of ideas or events that you share. Does that sequence advance your thesis? Do the points build effectively? Are there gaps in the support or points that stray from your original purpose? If you find such problems, consider the following actions:

- **Refine the focus or emphasis** by rearranging material within the text.
- **Fill in the gaps with new material.** Go back to your planning notes.
- **Delete material that wanders** away from your purpose.
- **Use an additional (or different) method of organization.** For example, if you are comparing two subjects, add depth to your analysis by contrasting them as well. If you are describing a complex subject, show the subject more clearly and fully by distinguishing and classifying its parts. (See pages 64–66 for more on organizational methods.)

INSIGHT What is the best method of organization for your essay? The writing you are doing will usually determine the choice. As you know, a personal narrative is often organized by time. Typically, however, you combine and customize methods to develop a writing idea. For example, within a comparison essay you may do some describing or classifying. See pages 62 and 140–141 for more on the common methods of development.

Opening Ideas

Reread your opening paragraph(s). Is the opening organized effectively? Does it engage readers, establish a direction for your writing, and express your thesis or focus? The original opening that follows doesn't build to a compelling thesis statement, but the revised version engages the reader and leads to the thesis.

Original Opening (Lacks interest and direction)

> The lack of student motivation is a common subject in the news. Educators want to know how to get students to learn. Today's higher standards mean that students will be expected to learn even more. Another problem in urban areas is that large numbers of students are dropping out. How to interest students is a challenge.

Revised Version (Effectively leads readers into the essay)

> How can we motivate students to learn? How can we get them to meet today's rising standards of excellence? How can we, in fact, keep students in school long enough to learn? The answer to these problems is quite simple. Give them money. Pay students to study and learn and stay in school.

Flow of Ideas

Look closely at the beginnings and endings of each paragraph. Have you connected your thoughts clearly? (See page 86 for a list of transition words.) The original opening words of the paragraph sequence below, from an essay of description, offer no links for readers. The revised versions use strong transitions indicating spatial organization (order by location).

Original First Words in the Four Middle Paragraphs

There was a huge, steep hill . . .
Buffalo Creek ran . . .
A dense "jungle" covering . . .
Within walking distance from my house . . .

Revised Versions (Words and phrases connect ideas)

Behind the house, there was a huge, steep hill . . .
Across the road from the house, Buffalo Creek ran . . .
On the far side of the creek bank was a dense "jungle" covering . . .
Up the road, within walking distance from my house . . .

INSIGHT Review "Supporting Your Claims" (pages 316–317) and use those strategies to strengthen weak or unconvincing passages.

Closing Ideas

Reread your closing paragraph(s). Do you offer an effective summary, reassert your main point in a fresh way, and provide readers with food for thought as they leave your writing? Or is your ending abrupt, repetitive, or directionless? The original ending that follows is uninspiring; it adds little to the main part of the writing. The revision summarizes the main points in the essay and then urges the reader to think again about the overall point of writing.

Original Ending (Sketchy and flat)

Native Son deals with a young man's struggle against racism. It shows the effects of prejudice. Everyone should read this book.

Revised Version (Effectively ends the writing)

Native Son deals with a young man's struggle in a racist society, but also with so much more. It shows how prejudice affects people, how it closes in on them, and what some people will do to find a way out. Anyone who wants to better understand racism in the United States should read this book.

Tip: To generate fresh ideas for your closing, freewrite answers to questions like these: Why is the topic important to me? What should my readers have learned? Why should this issue matter to readers? What evidence or appeal (pages 316–317) will help readers remember my message and act on it? How does the topic relate to broader issues in society, history, or life?

Revising for Voice and Style

Generally, readers more fully trust writing that speaks in a clear, informed voice. To develop such a voice, keep the focus on your topic, offering the reader rich information and sound thinking. Also, be committed and unpretentious, with transparent sentences and diction. (For more on sentence style and word choice, see pages 97–108.) To revise for voice, check the issues that follow.

Check the Level of Commitment

Consider how and to what degree your writing shows that you care about the topic and reader. The original passage that follows lacks a personal voice, revealing nothing about the writer's connection to—or interest in—the topic. The revision shows the opposite.

Original Passage (Lacks voice)

Cemeteries can teach us a lot about history. They make history seem more real. There is an old grave of a Revolutionary War veteran in the Union Grove Cemetery. . . .

Revised Version (Personal, sincere voice)

I've always had a special feeling for cemeteries. It's hard to explain any further than that, except to say history never seems quite as real as it does when I walk among many old gravestones. One day I discovered the grave of a Revolutionary War veteran. . . .

Check the Intensity of Your Writing

All writing—including academic writing—is enriched by an appropriate level of intensity, or even passion. In the original passage that follows, the writer's concern for the topic is unclear because the piece sounds neutral. In contrast, the revised version exudes energy.

Original Passage (Lacks feeling and energy)

The Dream Act could make a difference for people. It just takes a long time to get any bill through Congress. This bill probably will never get approved. Instead of passing the Dream Act, the country will probably just deport high school students from other countries.

Revised Passage (Expresses real feelings)

Given such debates, it might be a long time before the bill becomes law, thereby dashing the dreams of nearly 65,000 high school students like Maria who can't wait another year because they may already be in deportation proceedings. We need to step up and educate our representatives and senators about the importance of passing the Dream Act on its own instead of including the bill along with other resolutions. We need to urge them to debate and approve the Dream Act now, thereby making Maria's dreams—and the dreams of thousands of students like her—a reality!

Develop an Academic Style

Most college writing requires an academic style. Such a style isn't stuffy; you're not trying to impress readers with ten-dollar words. Rather, you are using language that facilitates a thoughtful, engaged discussion of the topic. To choose the best words for such a conversation, consider the issues that follow.

Personal Pronouns

In some academic writing, personal pronouns are acceptable. Such is the case in informal writing, such as reading responses; personal essays involving narration, description, and reflection; and opinion-editorial essays written for a broad audience. In addition, *I* is correctly used in academic writing rooted in personal research, sometimes called an I-search paper.

Generally, however, avoid using *I, we,* and *you* in traditional academic writing. The concept, instead, is to focus on the topic itself and let your attitude be revealed indirectly. As E. B. White puts it, "To achieve style, begin by affecting none—that is, begin by placing yourself in the background."

No: I really think that the problem of the homeless in Chicago is serious, given the number of people who are dying, as I know from my experience where I grew up.

Yes: Homelessness in Chicago often leads to death. This fact demands the attention of more than lawmakers and social workers; all citizens must address the problems of their suffering neighbors.

Tip: Use the pronoun *one* carefully in academic prose. When it means "a person," *one* can lead to a stilted style if overused. In addition, the pronoun *their* (a plural pronoun) should not be used with *one* (a singular pronoun).

Technical Terms and Jargon

Technical terms and jargon—"insider" words—can be the specialized vocabulary of a subject, a discipline, a profession, or a social group. As such, jargon can be difficult to read for "outsiders." Follow these guidelines:

- **Use technical terms** to communicate with people within the profession or discipline as a kind of shorthand. However, be careful that such jargon doesn't devolve into meaningless buzzwords and catchphrases.
- **Avoid jargon** when writing for readers outside the profession or discipline. Use simpler terms and define technical terms that must be used.

Technical: Bin's Douser power washer delivers 2200 psi p.r., runs off standard a.c. lines, comes with 100 ft. h.d. synthetic-rubber tubing, and features variable pulsation options through three adjustable s.s. tips.

Simple: Bin's Douser power washer has a pressure rating of 2200 psi (pounds per square inch), runs off a common 200-volt electrical circuit, comes with 100 feet of hose, and includes three nozzles.

Level of Formality

Most academic writing (especially research papers, literary analyses, lab reports, and argumentative essays) should meet the standards of formal English. Formal English is characterized by a serious tone; careful attention to word choice; longer and more complex sentences reflecting complex thinking; strict adherence to traditional conventions of grammar, mechanics, and punctuation; and avoidance of contractions.

You may write other papers (personal essays, commentaries, journals, and reviews) in which informal English is appropriate. Informal English is characterized by a personal tone, the occasional use of popular expressions, shorter sentences with slightly looser syntax, contractions, and personal references (*I, we, you*), but it still adheres to basic conventions.

Formal

Formal English, modeled in this sentence, is worded correctly and carefully so that it can withstand repeated readings without seeming tiresome, sloppy, or cute.

Informal

Informal English sounds like one person talking to another person (in a somewhat relaxed setting). It's the type of language that you're reading now. It sounds comfortable and real, not affected or breezy.

Tip: In academic writing, generally avoid slang—words considered outside standard English because they are faddish, familiar to few people, and sometimes insulting.

Unnecessary Qualifiers

Using qualifiers (such as *mostly, often, likely,* or *tends to*) is an appropriate strategy for developing defendable claims in argumentative writing. (See pages 318–319.) However, when you "overqualify" your ideas or add intensifiers (*really, truly*), the result is insecurity—the impression that you lack confidence in your ideas. The cure? Say what you mean, and mean what you say.

Insecure: I totally and completely agree with the new security measures at sporting events, but that's only my opinion.

Secure: I agree with the new security measures at sporting events.

fyi Each academic discipline has its own vocabulary and its own vocabulary resources. Such resources include dictionaries, glossaries, or handbooks. Check your library for the vocabulary resources in your discipline. Use them regularly to deepen your grasp of that vocabulary.

Know When to Use the Passive Voice

Most verbs can be in either the active or the passive voice. When a verb is active, the sentence's subject performs the action. When the verb is passive, the subject is acted upon.

Active: Given the global economy, when U.S. consumers stopped buying cars, Japanese carmakers shared in the rapid economic downturn.

Passive: Given the global economy, when cars were no longer being bought by U.S. consumers, the rapid economic downturn was shared by Japanese carmakers.

Weaknesses of Passive Voice

The passive voice tends to be wordy and sluggish because the verb's action is directed backward, not ahead. In addition, passive constructions tend to be impersonal, making people disappear.

Passive: As a sign of economic recovery, 350,000 job gains were experienced in March 2016.

Active: As a sign of economic recovery, 350,000 workers gained a job in March 2016.

Strengths of Passive Voice

Using the passive voice isn't wrong. In fact, the passive voice has some important uses: (1) when you need to be tactful (say, in a bad-news letter), (2) if you wish to stress the object or person acted upon, and (3) if the actual actor is understood, unknown, or unimportant.

Active: The U.S. government bailed out both GM and Chrysler, two struggling automakers.

Passive: Both GM and Chrysler, two struggling automakers, were bailed out by the U.S. government.

Active: As part of the study, participants drove hybrids for six months.

Passive: As part of the study, hybrids were driven for six months.

Tip: Avoid using the passive voice unethically to hide responsibility. For example, an instructor who says, "Your assignments could not be graded because of scheduling difficulties," might be trying to evade the truth: "I did not finish grading your assignments because I was watching *Game of Thrones*."

Working with Sources Academic writing must be free of plagiarism. Check that you have clearly indicated which material in your draft is summarized, paraphrased, or quoted from another source. (For more help, see pages 432–437.)

Addressing Paragraph Issues

While drafting, you may have constructed paragraphs that are loosely held together, poorly developed, or unclear. When you revise, take a close look at your paragraphs for focus, unity, and coherence (pages 83–88).

Remember the Basics

A paragraph should be a concise unit of thought. Revise a paragraph until it . . .

- is organized around a controlling idea—often stated in a topic sentence that also links back to the previous paragraph in some way.
- consists of supporting sentences that (a) develop the controlling idea through reasoning or (b) offer evidence related to that reasoning.
- concludes with a sentence that summarizes the main point and prepares readers for the next paragraph or main point.
- serves a specific function in a piece of writing—opening, supporting, developing, illustrating, countering, describing, or closing.

Sample Paragraph

Topic sentence

Supporting sentences

Closing sentence

Tumor cells can hurt the body in a number of ways. First, a tumor can grow so big that it takes up space needed by other organs. Second, some cells may detach from the original tumor and spread throughout the body, creating new tumors elsewhere. This happens with lymphatic cancer—a cancer that's hard to control because it spreads so quickly. A third way that tumor cells can hurt the body is by doing work not called for in their DNA. For example, a gland cell's DNA code may tell the cell to produce a necessary hormone in the endocrine system. However, if cancer damages or distorts that code, sick cells may produce more of the hormone than the body can use—or even tolerate (Braun 4). Cancer cells seem to have minds of their own, and this is why cancer is such a serious disease.

Keep the Purpose in Mind

Use these questions to evaluate the purpose and function of each paragraph:

- What function does the paragraph fulfill? How does it add to your line of reasoning or the development of your thesis?
- Would the paragraph work better if it were divided in two—or combined with another paragraph?
- Does the paragraph flow smoothly from the previous paragraph, and does it lead effectively into the next one?

Check for Unity

A unified paragraph is one in which all the details help to develop a single main topic or achieve a single main effect. Test for unity by following these guidelines.

Topic Sentence

Very often the topic of a paragraph is stated in a single sentence called a "topic sentence." Check whether your paragraph needs a topic sentence. If the paragraph has a topic sentence, determine whether it is clear, specific, and well focused. Figure 5.2 presents a formula for writing good topic sentences:

Formula:	**A Limited Topic**	+	**Specific Feeling or Thought**	=	**Topic Sentence**
Example:	The fear that Americans feel		comes partly from the uncertainty related to this attack		The fear that Americans feel comes partly from the uncertainty related to this attack.

fig. 5.2

Placement of the Topic Sentence

Normally the topic sentence is the first sentence in the paragraph. However, it can appear elsewhere in a paragraph.

Middle Placement: Place a topic sentence in the middle when you want to build up to and then lead away from the key idea.

During the making of *Apocalypse Now,* Eleanor Coppola created a documentary about the filming called *Hearts of Darkness:* A Filmmaker's Apocalypse. In the first film, the insane Colonel Kurtz has disappeared into the Cambodian jungle. As Captain Willard searches for Kurtz, the screen fills with horror. **However, as *Hearts of Darkness* relates, the horror portrayed in the fictional movie was being lived out by the production company.** For example, in the documentary, actor Larry Fishburne shockingly says, "War is fun. . . . Vietnam must have been so much fun." Then toward the end of the filming, actor Martin Sheen suffered a heart attack. When an assistant informed investors, the director exploded, "He's not dead unless I say he's dead."

End Placement: Place a topic sentence at the end when you want to build to a climax, as in a passage of narration or persuasion.

When sportsmen stop to reflect on why they find fishing so enjoyable, most realize that what they love is the feel of a fish on the end of the line, not necessarily the weight of the fillets in their coolers. Fishing has undergone a slow evolution over the last century. While fishing used to be a way of putting food on the table, most of today's fishermen do so only for the relaxation that it provides. The barbed hook was invented to increase the quantity of fish a man could land so that he could better feed his family. **This need no longer exists, so barbed hooks are no longer necessary.**

Supporting Sentences

All the sentences in the body of a paragraph should support the topic sentence by reasoning about that idea or supplying evidence (facts, statistics, examples, etc.) related to that reasoning. The closing sentence, for instance, will often summarize the paragraph's main point or emphasize a key detail. If any sentences shift the focus away from the topic, revise the paragraph in one of the following ways:

- **Delete the material** from the paragraph.
- **Rewrite the material** so that it clearly supports the topic sentence.
- **Create a separate paragraph** using the material that doesn't fit.
- **Revise the topic sentence** so that it relates more closely to the support.

Consistent Focus

Examine the following paragraph about fishing hooks. The original topic sentence focuses on the point that some anglers prefer smooth hooks. However, the writer leaves this initial idea unfinished and turns to the issue of the cost of new hooks. In the revised version, unity is restored: The first paragraph completes the point about anglers who prefer smooth hooks; the second paragraph addresses the issue of replacement costs.

Original Paragraph (Lacks unity)

According to some anglers who do use smooth hooks, their lures perform better than barbed lures as long as they maintain a constant tension on the line. Smooth hooks can bite deeper than barbed hooks, actually providing a stronger hold on the fish. Some people have argued that replacing all of the barbed hooks in their tackle would be a costly operation.

Revised Version (Unified)

According to some anglers who do use smooth hooks, their lures perform better than barbed lures as long as the anglers maintain a constant tension on the line. Smooth hooks can bite deeper than barbed hooks, actually providing a stronger hold on the fish. These anglers testify that switching from barbed hooks has not noticeably reduced the number of fish that they are able to land. In their experience, and in my own, enjoyment of the sport is actually heightened by adding another challenge to playing the fish (maintaining line tension).

Some people have argued that replacing all of the barbed hooks in their tackle would be a costly operation. While this is certainly a concern, barbed hooks do not necessarily require replacement. With a simple set of pliers, the barbs on most conventional hooks can be bent down, providing a cost-free method of modifying one's existing tackle. . . .

Paragraphs that contain unrelated ideas lack unity and are hard to follow. As you review each paragraph for unity, ask yourself these questions: Is the topic of the paragraph clear? Does each sentence relate to the topic? Are the sentences organized in the best possible order?

Check for Coherence

When a paragraph is coherent, the parts stay together. A coherent paragraph flows smoothly because each sentence is connected to others by patterns in the language such as repetition and transitions. To strengthen the coherence in your paragraphs, check for the following issues.

Effective Repetition

To achieve coherence in your paragraphs, consider using repetition—repeating words or synonyms where necessary to remind readers of what you have already said. You can also use parallelism—repeating phrase or sentence structures to show the relationships among ideas. At the same time, you will add a unifying rhythm to your writing.

Ineffective: The floor was littered with discarded soda cans, newspapers that were crumpled, and wrinkled clothes.

Effective: The floor was littered with discarded soda cans, crumpled newspapers, and wrinkled clothes. (Three parallel phrases are used.)

Ineffective: Reading the book was enjoyable; to write the critique was difficult.

Effective: Reading the book was enjoyable; writing the critique was difficult. (Two similar structures are repeated.)

Clear Transitions

Linking words and phrases like "next," "on the other hand," and "in addition" connect ideas by showing the relationship among them. There are transitions that show location and time, compare and contrast things, emphasize a point, conclude or summarize, and add or clarify information. (See page 86 for a list of linking words and phrases.) Note the use of transitions in the following examples:

The transition is used to emphasize a point.

The paradox of Scotland is that violence had long been the norm in this now-peaceful land. In fact, the country was born, bred, and came of age in war.

The transition is used to show time or order.

The production of cement is a complicated process. First, the mixture of lime, silica, alumina, and gypsum is ground into very fine particles.

INSIGHT Another way to achieve coherence in your paragraphs is to use pronouns effectively. A pronoun forms a link to the noun it replaces and ties that noun (idea) to the ideas that follow. As always, don't overuse pronouns or rely too heavily on them in establishing coherence in your paragraphs.

Transitions and Linking Words

The words and phrases in Figure 5.3 can help you tie together words, phrases, sentences, and paragraphs.

Words used to show location:

above	behind	down	on top of
across	below	in back of	onto
against	beneath	in front of	outside
along	beside	inside	over
among	between	into	throughout
around	beyond	near	to the right
away from	by	off	under

Words used to show time:

about	during	next	today
after	finally	next week	tomorrow
afterward	first	second	until
as soon as	immediately	soon	when
at	later	then	yesterday
before	meanwhile	third	

Words used to compare things (show similarities):

also	in the same way	likewise
as	like	similarly

Words used to contrast things (show differences):

although	even though	on the other hand	still
but	however	otherwise	

Words used to emphasize a point:

again	for this reason	particularly	to repeat
even	in fact	to emphasize	truly

Words used to conclude or summarize:

all in all	finally	in summary	therefore
as a result	in conclusion	last	to sum up

Words used to add information:

additionally	and	equally important	in addition
again	another	finally	likewise
along with	as well	for example	next
also	besides	for instance	second

Words used to clarify:

for instance	in other words	put another way	that is

fig. 5.3

Note: Use transitions to link, expand, or intensify an idea, but don't add elements carelessly, creating run-on or rambling sentences.

Check for Completeness

A paragraph's sentences should support and expand on the main point. If a paragraph does not seem complete, add information to deepen the reasoning and add more evidence.

Supporting Details

If some of your paragraphs are incomplete, they may lack details. There are numerous kinds of details, including the following:

facts	paraphrases	explanations	definitions
anecdotes	statistics	comparisons	summaries
analyses	quotations	examples	analogies

Add details based on the type of writing you are engaged in.

Describing: Add details that help readers see, smell, taste, touch, or hear it.
Narrating: Add details that help readers understand the events and actions.
Explaining: Add details that help readers understand what it means, how it works, or what it does.
Persuading: Add details that strengthen the logic of your argument.

Specific Details

The original paragraph that follows fails to answer fully the question posed by the topic sentence. In the revised paragraph, the writer uses an anecdote to answer the question.

Original Paragraph (Lacks completeness)

So what is stress? Actually, the physiological characteristics of stress are some of the body's potentially good self-defense mechanisms. People experience stress when they are in danger. In fact, stress can be healthy.

Revised Version (Full development)

So what is stress? Actually, the physiological characteristics of stress are some of the body's potentially good self-defense mechanisms. Take, for example, a man who is crossing a busy intersection when he spots an oncoming car. Immediately his brain releases a flood of adrenaline into his bloodstream. As a result, his muscles contract, his eyes dilate, his heart pounds faster, his breathing quickens, and his blood clots more readily. Each one of these responses helps the man leap out of the car's path. His muscles contract to give him exceptional strength. His eyes dilate so that he can see more clearly. His heart pumps more blood and his lungs exchange more air—both to increase his metabolism. If the man were injured, his blood would clot faster, ensuring a smaller amount of blood loss. In this situation and many more like it, stress symptoms are good (Curtis 25–26).

INSIGHT If a paragraph is getting long, divide it at a natural stopping point. The topic sentence can then function as the thesis for that part of your essay or paper.

Working with Sources Test your evidence to make certain that it provides the support you need, support that meets the following criteria.

- **Accurate:** The information is all correct.
- **Precise:** The data are concrete and specific, not vague and general.
- **Substantial:** The amount of evidence reaches a critical mass—enough to convey the idea and convince readers of its validity.
- **Authoritative:** The evidence comes from a reliable source. Moreover, the information is as close to the origin as possible; it is not a report conveying third-hand information.
- **Representative:** The information fairly represents the range of data on the issue. Your presentation of evidence is balanced.
- **Fitting:** Given your purpose, the topic, and your reader, the evidence is appropriate and relevant for the question or issue you are discussing.

Example: The following resources come from the references list for Julia Sweigert's paper, "The Silent Sibling: How Current Autism Intervention Affects Typically-Developed Siblings," on pages 522–531. While you would need to go to the sources themselves to test their reliability and Julia's use of them in her essay, you can tell a number of things simply from the source details provided. First, the sources are scholarly—published in respected field-of-study journals, as well as by an academic association and a government agency. The articles come from academic databases, and an online search shows that the authors are recognized and respected experts. Finally, the titles indicate that the sources, though likely coming from a specific point of view, are likely balanced and thoughtful. In other words, these sources promise to provide information that is accurate and precise (possibly primary data and certainly data that is properly credited), that is substantial and authoritative (given length and authorship), and that is representative and fitting (showing the range of perspectives on the specific issue Julia is exploring).

References

American Psychiatric Association. (2013). *Diagnostic and Statistical Manual of Mental Disorders. 5th ed.* Arlington, VA: American Psychiatric Association.

Arnold, C., Heller, T., & Kramer, J. (2012). Support needs of siblings of people with developmental disabilities. *Intellectual and Developmental Disabilities, 50*(5), 373-382.

Burke, M., Taylor, J., Urbano, R., & Hodapp, R. (2012). Predictors of future caregiving by adult siblings of individuals with intellectual and developmental disabilities. *Journal on Intellectual and Developmental Disabilities, 117*(1), 33-47.

Centers for Disease Control and Prevention. (2014). Prevalence of autism spectrum disorder among children aged 8 years. *MMWR Surveillance Summaries Publication, 63*(2), 1-21.

Revising Collaboratively

Every writer can benefit from feedback from an interested audience, especially one that offers constructive and honest advice during a writing project. Members of an existing writing group already know how valuable it is for writers to share their work. Others might want to start a writing group to experience the benefits. Your group might collaborate online or in person. In either case, the information on the next two pages will help you get started.

Know Your Role

Writers and reviewers should know their roles and fulfill their responsibilities during revising sessions. Essentially, the writer should briefly introduce the draft and solicit honest responses. Reviewers should make constructive comments in response to the writing.

Provide Appropriate Feedback

Feedback can take many forms, including the three approaches described here.

- **Basic Description:** In this simple response, the reviewer listens or reads attentively and then simply describes what she or he hears or sees happening in the piece. The reviewer offers no criticism of the writing.

  Ineffective: "That was interesting. The piece was informative."
  Effective: First, the essay introduced the challenge of your birth defect and how you have had to cope with it. Then in the next part you . . ."

- **Summary Evaluation:** Here the reviewer reads or listens to the piece and then provides a specific evaluation of the draft.

  Ineffective: "Gee, I really liked it!" or "It was boring."
  Effective: "Your story at the beginning really pulled me in, and the middle explained the issue strongly, but the ending felt a bit flat."

- **Thorough Critique:** The reviewer assesses the ideas, organization, and voice in the writing. Feedback should be detailed and constructive. Such a critique may also be completed with the aid of a review sheet or checklist. As a reviewer, be prepared to share specific responses, suggestions, and questions. But also be sure to focus your comments on the writing, rather than the writer.

  Ineffective: "You really need to fix that opening! What were you thinking?"
  Effective: "Let's look closely at the opening. Could you rewrite the first sentence so it grabs the reader's attention? Also, I'm somewhat confused about the thesis statement. Could you rephrase it so it states your position more clearly?"

Respond According to a Plan

Using a specific plan or scheme like the following will help you give clear, helpful, and complete feedback.

- **OAQS Method:** Use this simple four-step scheme—**Observe, Appreciate, Question,** and **Suggest**—to respond to your peers' writing.

1. **Observe** means to notice what another person's essay is designed to do, and to say something about its design or purpose. For example, you might say, "Even though you are writing about your boyfriend, it appears that you are trying to get a message across to your parents."
2. **Appreciate** means to praise something in the writing that impresses or pleases you. You can find something to appreciate in any piece of writing. For example, you might say, "In this paragraph, you make a very convincing point about our reliance on fossil fuels" or "With your description here, I can actually see his broken tooth and understand how dramatic it is."
3. **Question** means to ask whatever you want to know after you've read the essay. You might ask for background information, a definition, an interpretation, or an explanation. For example, you might say, "Can you tell us what happened when you got to the emergency room?"
4. **Suggest** means to give helpful advice about possible changes. For example, you might say, "With a little more physical detail—especially more sounds and smells—your third paragraph could be the highlight of the whole essay. "

Asking the Writer Questions

Reviewers should ask the following types of questions while reviewing a piece of writing:

- **To help writers reflect on their purpose and audience . . .**
  Why are you writing this?
  Who will read this, and what do they need to know?
- **To help writers focus their thoughts . . .**
  What message are you trying to get across?
  Do you have more than one main point?
  What are the most important examples?
- **To help writers think about their information . . .**
  What do you know about the subject?
  Does this part say enough?
  Does your writing cover all of the basics? (*Who? What? Where? When? Why?* and *How?*)
- **To help writers with their openings and closings . . .**
  What are you trying to say in the opening?
  How else could you start your writing?
  How do you want your readers to feel at the end?

Using the Writing Center

A college writing center or lab is a place where a trained adviser will help you develop and strengthen a piece of writing. You can expect the writing center adviser to do certain things; other things only you can do. For quick reference, refer to Figure 5.4.

Adviser's Job	Your Job
Make you feel at home	Be respectful
Discuss your needs	Be ready to work
Help you choose a topic	Decide on a topic
Discuss your purpose and audience	Know your purpose and audience
Help you generate ideas	Embrace the best ideas
Help you develop your logic	Consider other points of view; stretch your own perspective
Help you understand how to research your material	Do the research
Read your draft	Share your writing
Identify problems in organization, logic, expression, and format	Recognize and fix problems
Teach ways to correct weaknesses	Learn important principles
Help you with grammar, usage, diction, vocabulary, and mechanics	Correct all errors

fig. 5.4

Tips for getting the most out of the writing center

- Visit the center at least several days before your paper is due.
- Take your assignment sheet with you to each advising session.
- Read your work aloud, slowly.
- Expect to rethink your writing from scratch.
- Do not defend your wording—if it needs defense, it needs revision.
- Ask questions. (No question is "too dumb.")
- Request clarification of anything you don't understand.
- Ask for examples or illustrations of important points.
- Write down all practical suggestions.
- Ask the adviser to summarize his or her remarks.
- Rewrite as soon as possible after—or even during—the advising session.
- Return to the writing center for a response to your revisions.

Critical Thinking and Writing: Applications

Once you have used the instruction in this chapter to revise your writing, there may be more that you can think about. Through the following activities, apply what you have learned.

1. **Wise Words:** Doris Lessing has stated that when it comes to writing, "The more a thing cooks, the better." In what sense is revision a crucial stage in that cooking process? Using Lessing's cooking metaphor as a starting point, explore how revision should function in your own writing. How should you let your writing cook?
2. **Photo Op:** The photograph on the first page of this chapter shows an electric car being charged. What other image would capture the nature of revision? Find such an image and share it with classmates. (You might try to create a meme out of the image, as well.)
3. **Living Today:** On pages 78–81, this chapter introduces concepts of voice and style. How are voice and style a reflection of the speaker or writer? Consider a public figure whose speeches or writings you admire. Study one of his or her oral or written statements. What qualities of voice do you discern, and what creates those qualities?
4. **Public Texts:** This chapter explains that strong paragraphs, especially body paragraphs, are unified, coherent, and complete. But do these requirements apply to more than academic essays? Find a print or digital document from a business, government agency, educational institution, or other organization. What paragraphing principles seem to be at work?

Learning-Objectives Checklist ✓

Have you achieved this chapter's learning objectives? Check your progress with the following items, revisiting topics in the chapter as needed. I have . . .

____ re-examined the rhetorical situation of my writing project to be better prepared to revise my draft (72).

____ assessed my overall approach to see if it is stale, predicable, boring, or formulaic (73).

____ examined my ideas for a clear thesis and complete development (75).

____ evaluated the overall organization of my draft, including whether the opening engages readers and sets a direction, the middle clearly traces a line of reasoning, and the closing effectively ends the draft (76–77).

____ examined and improved the voice in my draft, addressing issues of commitment, intensity, academic style, and active vs. passive voice (78–81).

____ examined each paragraph to ensure that it is an effective unit of thought, unified in its topic or effect, coherent through transitions, and complete in its details (82–88).

____ given and received helpful feedback on a draft by collaborating with classmates through techniques such as the OAQS method (89–90).

____ understood the role of the writing center in improving my writing (91).

MindTap® Practice skills that you have learned in this chapter and receive automatic feedback. Reflect on your writing process.

Chapter 6

Editing and Proofreading

MindTap®

Understand the goals of the chapter and complete a warm-up activity online.

Learning Objectives

By working through this chapter, you will be able to

- assess the overall style of your revised draft.
- combine short, simplistic sentences into more substantial ones.
- expand sparse sentences with meaningful details.
- transform stylistically weak sentences through various techniques.
- replace vague, weak, and biased words.
- identify and correct errors in grammar, punctuation, mechanics, usage, and spelling.

Editing and proofreading allow you to fine-tune your writing, making it ready to hand in. When you edit, look first for words, phrases, and sentences that sound awkward, uninteresting, or unclear. When you proofread, check your writing for spelling, mechanics, usage, and grammar errors. Ask one of your writing peers to help you.

The guidelines and strategies given in this chapter will help you edit your writing for style and clarity and proofread it for errors.

Visually Speaking Piano tuning requires special skills and specialized tools (Figure 6.1). What skills and tools do you need to effectively edit and proofread your writing? How are tuning a piano and polishing your writing similar and different?

PhotoHouse / Shutterstock.com

fig. 6.1

Strategies for Polishing Your Writing

When you have thoroughly revised your writing, you need to edit it so that the style is clear, concise, energetic, and varied. A closely related task is proofreading, which involves polishing your prose for correct grammar, punctuation, mechanics, usage, and spelling. To effectively edit and proofread, start with the following strategies.

Review the Overall Style of Your Writing

How does your writing sound? Test it for the following:

1. **Check that your style fits the rhetorical situation.** Does your writing sound as if you wrote it with a clear **goal** in mind? Will your writing sound mature, thoughtful, and direct to **readers**? Does your writing suit the **subject** and your treatment of it?
2. **Check that your style carries the right authority.** Nineteenth-century British author Matthew Arnold puts it this way: "Have something to say and say it as clearly as you can. That is the only secret of style." Does your writing communicate a clear message with a fitting confidence?
3. **Check your sentence style and word choice.** At its heart, your style is about the sentences you craft and the words crafted into those sentences. For that reason, this chapter focuses to a large degree on strengthening sentences through combining, expanding, and varying structures (pages 95–101), as well as on avoiding wordiness and making effective word choices (pages 102–108).

Use Tools and Methods That Work

Here are three tips that will help you edit and proofread effectively:

1. **Do it at the right time, and give yourself the time.** Leave time between revising and editing your paper (at least 24 hours) to give yourself a fresh view of your writing. In addition, don't rush through editing, as doing it well takes patience and concentration.
2. **Review your draft from multiple points of view.** On-screen editing offers you tremendous power and flexibility. Then again, at some point you need to see your words in print on a page. Consider increasing print size and line spacing to create white space that helps you see your writing and make changes. Finally, consider reading your paper aloud or having a classmate do so: hearing your words will help you sense where your sentences fall flat or your grammar breaks down.
3. **Use software editing tools as an aid.** Without relying on them exclusively, use wisely such tools as spell check, grammar check, find-and-replace functions, track-changes tools, and so on. For example, spell check will not catch usage errors such as *it's* versus *its*. In the end, you need to manage the editing process, including your writing tools.

Combining Sentences

Effective sentences often contain several basic ideas that work together to show relationships and make connections. Here are five basic ideas followed by seven examples of how the ideas can be combined into effective sentences.

1. The longest and largest construction project in history is the Great Wall of China.
2. The project took 1,700 years to complete.
3. The Great Wall of China is 1,400 miles long.
4. It is between 18 and 30 feet high.
5. It is up to 32 feet wide.

Edit Short, Simplistic Sentences

A series of short, simplistic sentences creates a choppy effect called primer style. Combine your short, simplistic sentences into longer, more detailed sentences. Sentence combining is generally carried out in the following ways:

- Use a **series** to combine three or more similar ideas.

  > The Great Wall of China is **1,400 miles long,** between **18 and 30 feet high,** and up to **32 feet wide.**

- Use a **relative pronoun** *(who, whose, that, which)* to introduce subordinate (less important) ideas. (See page 589 for help with restrictive and nonrestrictive clauses.)

  > The Great Wall of China, **which is 1,400 miles long and between 18 and 30 feet high,** took 1,700 years to complete.

- Use an **introductory phrase** or **clause.**

  > **Having taken 1,700 years to complete,** the Great Wall of China is the longest construction project in history.

- Use a **semicolon** (and a conjunctive adverb if appropriate). (See page 565.2.)

  > The Great Wall took 1,700 years to complete**;** it is 1,400 miles long and up to 30 feet high and 32 feet wide.

- Repeat a **key word** or phrase to emphasize an idea.

  > The Great Wall of China is the longest construction **project** in history, a **project** that took 1,700 years to complete.

- Use **correlative conjunctions** *(either, or; not only, but also)* to compare or contrast two ideas in a sentence. (See page 554.3.)

  > The Great Wall of China is **not only** up to 30 feet high and 32 feet wide, **but also** 1,400 miles long.

- Use an **appositive** (a word or phrase that renames) to emphasize an idea. (See page 588.1.)

  > The Great Wall of China—**the largest construction project in history**—is 1,400 miles long, 32 feet wide, and up to 30 feet high.

Expanding Sentences

When you edit, expand sentences so as to connect related ideas and make room for new information. Length has no value in and of itself: The best sentence is still the shortest one that says all it has to say. An expanded sentence, however, is capable of saying more—and saying it more expressively.

Use Cumulative Sentences

Modern writers often use an expressive sentence form called the cumulative sentence. A cumulative sentence is made of a general "base clause" that is expanded by adding modifying words, phrases, or clauses. In such a sentence, details are added before and after the main clause, creating an image-rich thought. Here's an example of a cumulative sentence, with the base clause or main idea in boldface:

> In preparation for her Spanish exam, **Julie was studying at the kitchen table,** completely focused, memorizing a list of vocabulary words.

Discussion: Notice how each new modifier adds to the richness of the final sentence. Also notice that each of these modifying phrases is set off by a comma. Here's another sample sentence:

> With his hands on his face, **Tony was laughing halfheartedly,** looking puzzled and embarrassed.

Discussion: Such a cumulative sentence provides a way to write description that is rich in detail, without rambling. Notice how each modifier changes the flow or rhythm of the sentence.

Expand with Details

Here are seven basic ways to expand a main idea:

1. with **adjectives and adverbs:** *halfheartedly, once again*
2. with **prepositional phrases:** *with his hands on his face*
3. with **absolute phrases:** *his head tilted to one side*
4. with **participial (-ing or -ed) phrases:** *looking puzzled*
5. with **infinitive phrases:** *to hide his embarrassment*
6. with **subordinate clauses:** *while his friend talks*
7. with **relative clauses:** *who isn't laughing at all*

INSIGHT To edit sentences for more expressive style, it is best to (1) know your grammar and punctuation (especially commas); (2) practice tightening, combining, and expanding sentences using the guidelines in this chapter; and (3) read good writing carefully, looking for models of well-constructed sentences.

Checking for Sentence Style

Writer E. B. White advised young writers to "approach sentence style by way of simplicity, plainness, orderliness, and sincerity." That's good advice from a writer steeped in style. It's also important to know what to look for when editing your sentences. The information that follows will help you edit your sentences for style and correctness.

Avoid These Sentence Problems

Always check for and correct the following types of sentence problems. When attempting to fix problems in your sentences, turn to the pages listed below for guidelines and examples.

Short, Choppy Sentences: Combine or expand any short, choppy sentences (called primer style); use the examples and guidelines on page 95.

Flat, Predictable Sentences: Rewrite any predictable and uninteresting sentences by varying their structures and expanding them with modifying words, phrases, and clauses. (See pages 98–100.)

Incorrect Sentences: Look carefully for fragments, run-ons, and comma splices. Correct them as needed. (See pages 574–575.)

Unclear Sentences: Edit any sentences that contain unclear wording, misplaced modifiers, dangling modifiers, or incomplete comparisons.

Unacceptable Sentences: Change sentences that include nonstandard language, double negatives, or unparallel constructions.

Unnatural Sentences: Rewrite sentences that contain jargon, clichés, or flowery language. (See page 104.)

Review Your Writing for Sentence Variety

Use the following strategy to review your writing for variety in terms of sentence beginnings, lengths, and types.

- In one column on a piece of paper, list the opening words in each of your sentences. Then decide if you need to vary some of your sentence beginnings.
- In another column, identify the number of words in each sentence. Then decide if you need to change the lengths of some of your sentences.
- In a third column, list the kinds of sentences used (exclamatory, declarative, interrogative, and so on). Then, based on your analysis, use the instructions on pages 98–101 to edit your sentences as needed.

Working with Sources When you integrate a quotation into a text, make sure that the quotation works with the material around it. Either make the quotation a grammatical part of the sentence, or introduce the quotation with a complete sentence followed by a colon.

Vary Sentence Structures

To energize your sentences, vary their structures using one or more of the methods shown on this page and the next.

1. **Vary sentence openings.** If a series of sentences begin the same way, move modifying words, phrases, or clauses to the front of some sentences.

   Unvaried: The problem is not just about wasteful irrigation, though. The problem is also about resistance to change. The problem is that many people have fought against restrictions.

   Varied: However, the problem is not just about wasteful irrigation. It's about resistance to change. When governments have tried to pass regulations, many people have fought against restrictions.

2. **Vary sentence lengths.** Short sentences (ten words or fewer) are ideal for making points crisply. Medium sentences (ten to twenty words) should carry the bulk of your thinking. When well crafted, occasional long sentences (more than twenty words) can develop and expand your ideas.

   Short: Museum exhibitions have become increasingly commercial.

   Medium: To the extent that "access" adequately measures museum performance, art as entertainment "has proven a resounding triumph."

   Long: Shows featuring motorcycles, automobiles, the treasures of King Tutankhamen, the works of Van Gogh, and other blockbuster favorites not only have proven immensely popular but have also offered the promise of corporate underwriting and ample commercial tie-ins.

3. **Vary sentence kinds.** The most common sentence is declarative—it states a point. For variety, try exclamatory, imperative, interrogative, and conditional statements.

   Declarative: Historical records indicate that the lost colonists of Roanoke may have been harboring a dangerous virus: influenza.

   Conditional: If the influenza virus was not present in the New World, then the lost colonists of Roanoke likely served as vectors for the disease.

   Interrogative: That being said, we must now turn to a different question: What happened to those lost colonists?

   Imperative: Let us take steps to ensure that the Lumbee People do not share the fate of the colonists who disappeared from Roanoke.

   Exclamatory: Just as John White discovered over 400 years ago, something is terribly wrong! (Note: generally avoid exclamatory sentences in academic writing.)

4. **Vary sentence arrangements.** Where do you want to place the main point of your sentence? You make that choice by arranging sentence parts into loose, periodic, balanced, or cumulative patterns. Each pattern creates a specific effect.

Loose Sentence

> **Men are frequently mystified by women,** with their unfamiliar rituals, their emotional vitality, and their biological clocks—issues often addressed in romantic comedies.

Analysis: This pattern is direct. It states the main point immediately (bold), and then tacks on extra information.

Periodic Sentence

> While Western culture celebrates romantic love, seen powerfully in its films and romance novels, **in the end, such attraction between a man and a woman fails to sustain a relationship for a lifetime.**

Analysis: This pattern postpones the main point (bold) until the end. The sentence builds to the point, creating an indirect, dramatic effect.

Balanced Sentence

> **The modern romantic comedy often portrays male characters as resistant to or clueless about love**; however, **in Jane Austen's narratives, men's behavior is further complicated by traditional codes of honor.**

Analysis: This pattern gives equal weight to complementary or contrasting points (bold); the balance is often signaled by a comma and a conjunction *(and, but)* or by a semicolon. Sometimes, a conjunctive adverb *(however, nevertheless)* or a transitional phrase *(in addition, even so)* follows the semicolon to further clarify the relationship.

Cumulative Sentence

> In spite of his initially limiting pride, **Mr. Darcy**, now properly proud, **emerges** finally **as the consummate romantic hero**, the anonymous savior of Elizabeth's family, a true gentleman.

Analysis: This pattern puts the main idea (bold) in the middle of the sentence, surrounding it with modifying words, phrases, and clauses.

5. **Use positive repetition.** Although you should avoid needless repetition, you might use emphatic repetition to repeat a key word to stress a point.

Needlessly Repetitive Sentence

> Each year, more than a million young people who read poorly leave high school unable to read well, functionally illiterate.

Emphatic Sentence

> Each year, more than a million young people leave high school functionally illiterate, so **illiterate** that they can't read newspapers, job ads, or safety instructions.

Use Parallel Structure

Coordinated sentence elements should be parallel—that is, they should be written in the same grammatical forms. Parallel structures save words, clarify relationships, and present the information in the correct sequence. Follow these guidelines.

1. **For words, phrases, or clauses in a series,** keep elements consistent.

   Not parallel: I have tutored students in Biology 101, also Chemistry 102, not to mention my familiarity with Physics 200.
   Parallel: I have tutored students in *Biology 101, Chemistry 102,* and *Physics 200.*

   Not parallel: I have volunteered as a hospital receptionist, have been a hospice volunteer, and as an emergency medical technician.
   Parallel: I have done volunteer work as *a hospital receptionist, a hospice counselor,* and *an emergency medical technician.*

2. **Use both parts of correlative conjunctions** *(either, or; neither, nor; not only, but also; as, so; whether, so; both, and)* so that both segments of the sentence are balanced.

   Not parallel: *Not only* did Blake College turn 20 this year. Its enrollment grew by 16 percent.
   Parallel: *Not only* did Blake College turn 20 this year, *but* its enrollment *also* grew by 16 percent.

3. **Place a modifier correctly** so that it clearly indicates the word or words to which it refers.

   Confusing: MADD promotes *severely* punishing and eliminating drunk driving because this offense leads to a *great number* of deaths and sorrow.
   Parallel: MADD promotes eliminating and *severely* punishing drunk driving because this offense leads to *many* deaths and *untold* sorrow.

4. **Place contrasting details in parallel structures** (words, phrases, or clauses) to stress a contrast.

   Weak contrast: The average child spends 24 hours in front of a screen each week and reads for 36 minutes.
   Strong contrast: Each week, the average child *spends more than 24 hours in front of a screen but spends much less than an hour in a book.*

Working with Sources When using sources, smoothly integrate text references to those sources. (For guidelines, see pages 468–475 for MLA and pages 506–509 for APA.)

Avoid Weak Constructions

Avoid constructions that weaken your writing, including the ones that follow.

Nominal Constructions

The nominal construction is both sluggish and wordy. Avoid it by changing the noun form of a verb *(description or instructions)* to a verb *(describe or instruct)*. At the same time, delete the weak verb that preceded the noun.

Nominal Constructions (noun form underlined)	**Strong Verbs** (italicized)
Engineer Tim Schuster *gave a description* . . .	Lydia Balm *provides an explanation* . . .
Schuster *described* . . .	Balm *explains* . . .

Sluggish: In her study of Austen film adaptations, Lydia Balm *provides an explanation* for the narrative power of dance scenes. Dances *offer a symbolization and visualization* of characters in situations of mutual attraction but *nonverbalization.*

Energetic: In her study of Austen film adaptations, Lydia Balm *explains* the narrative power of dance scenes. Dances *symbolize visually* the attraction characters feel for each other but cannot *verbalize.*

Expletives

Expletives such as "it is" and "there is" are fillers that serve no purpose in most sentences—except to make them wordy and unnatural.

Sluggish: *It is* believed by some people that childhood vaccinations can cause autism *There are* several Web sites that promote this point of view quite forcefully. In fact, *it is* also the case that some celebrities advocate this cause.

Energetic: Some people believe that childhood vaccinations can cause autism. Some celebrities and several Web sites forcefully promote this point of view.

Negative Constructions

Sentences constructed upon the negatives *no, not, neither/nor* can be wordy and difficult to understand. It's simpler to state what *is* the case.

Negative: Hybrid vehicles *are not* completely different from traditional cars, as hybrids *cannot* run without gas and *cannot* rely only on battery power that has *not been created* by the gasoline engine.

Positive: Hybrid vehicles are similar to traditional cars, as hybrids do require gas in order to power an internal-combustion engine that in turn powers batteries.

Eliminate Wordiness

Wordy writing taxes the reader's attention. To tighten your writing so that every word counts, cut the following types of wordiness.

Deadwood

Deadwood is filler material—verbal "lumber" that you can remove without harming the sentence. Look for irrelevant information and obvious statements.

Deadwood: GM *must undergo a thorough retooling process if it is to be competitive in the fast-paced, rapidly changing world of today's* global marketplace.
Concise: GM must change to meet global challenges.

Redundancy

Redundancy refers to unnecessary repetition. Check your sentences for words and phrases that say the same thing, doubling up the meaning. Examples: combine together, new beginner, connect up, green in color, round in shape, plan ahead, descend down.

Redundant: Avoid the construction site, and *be sure to pick a different route* if you want to avoid riding over nails and *risking a flat tire.*
Concise: If you want to avoid a flat tire, don't drive through the construction site.

Unnecessary Modifiers

Adjectives and adverbs typically clarify nouns and verbs; however, excessive modifiers make prose dense. Use precise nouns and verbs to avoid the need for modifiers, and avoid intensifying adverbs (*very, extremely, intensely, awfully, especially*).

Wordy: To ensure *very healthy, properly growing* trees, whether *deciduous* or *coniferous*, hire a *licensed, professional* tree surgeon.
Concise: To ensure healthy trees, hire a professional tree surgeon.

Long Phrases and Clauses

Often, a long phrase or clause can be replaced by a shorter phrase or even a single word. Locate prepositional phrases (*at the beginning of the project*) and relative clauses (*who, which, that* clauses) and replace them when possible with simpler words.

Wordy: Among a variety of different devices that could possibly perform the task of preventing the wastage of water, an interesting one is LEPA, also known by many as low-energy precision application, hence the acronym.
Concise: A second device that prevents water waste is LEPA, or low-energy precision application.

Avoiding Vague, Weak, and Biased Words

As you edit your writing, check your choice of words carefully. The information on the next five pages will help you edit for word choice.

Substitute Specific Words

Replace vague nouns and verbs with words that generate clarity and energy.

Specific Nouns

Make it a habit to use specific nouns for subjects. General nouns *(woman, school)* give the reader a vague, uninteresting picture. More specific nouns *(actress, university)* give the reader a better picture. Finally, very specific nouns *(Meryl Streep, Notre Dame)* are the type that can make your writing clear and colorful.

General to Specific Nouns

Person	Place	Thing	Idea
woman	school	book	theory
actor	university	novel	scientific theory
Meryl Streep	Notre Dame	*Pride and Prejudice*	relativity

Vivid Verbs

Like nouns, verbs can be too general to create a vivid word picture. For example, the verb *looked* does not say the same thing as *stared, glared, glanced,* or *peeked.*

- Whenever possible, use a verb that is strong enough to stand alone without the help of an adverb.

  Verb and adverb: John fell down in the student lounge.
  Vivid verb: John collapsed in the student lounge.

- Avoid overusing the "be" verbs (*is, are, was, were*) and helping verbs. Often a main verb can be made from another word in the same sentence.

  A "be" verb: Cole is someone who follows international news.
  A stronger verb: Cole follows international news.

- Use active rather than passive verbs. (Use passive verbs only if you want to downplay who is performing the action in a sentence. See page 81.)

  Passive verb: Another provocative essay was submitted by Kim.
  Active verb: Kim submitted another provocative essay.

- Use verbs that show rather than tell.

  A verb that tells: Dr. Lewis is very thorough.
  A verb that shows: Dr. Lewis prepares detailed, interactive lectures.

Replace Jargon and Clichés

Replace language that is overly technical or difficult to understand. Also replace overused, worn-out words.

Understandable Language

Jargon is language used in a certain profession or by a particular group of people. It may be acceptable to use if your audience is that group of people, but to most ears jargon will sound technical and unnatural.

Jargon: I'm having conceptual difficulty with these academic queries.
Clear: I don't understand these review questions.

Fresh and Original Writing

Clichés are overused words or phrases. They give the reader no fresh view and no concrete picture. Because clichés spring quickly to mind (for both the writer and the reader), they are easy to write and often fail to convey a precise meaning.

an axe to grind
between a rock and a hard place
easy as pie
piece of cake
stick your neck out
throwing your weight around

While clichés fill your writing with tired expressions, using flowery phrases leads to language that is overblown. Such wording is unnecessarily fancy and often sentimental. This type of writing draws attention to itself, interfering with direct communication.

Flowery: The gorgeous beauty of the Great Barrier Reef is fantastically on display in coral of all the colors of the rainbow and in its wondrous variety of delightful tropical fish that soar like eagles through the azure liquid.
Fresh: The beauty of the Great Barrier Reef is displayed in rainbow-colored coral formations and in a rich variety of tropical fish.

Unpretentious Language

Pretentious language aims to sound intelligent but comes off sounding phony. Such language calls attention to itself rather than its meaning; in fact, pretentious words can be so high-blown that meaning is obscured altogether.

Pretentious: Liquid precipitation in the Iberian Peninsula's nation-state of most prominent size experiences altitudinal descent as a matter of course primarily in the region characterized by minimal topographical variation.
Plain: The rain in Spain falls mainly on the plain.

Strive for Plain English

In many ways, plain English is the product of the principles discussed on the previous pages: avoiding jargon, technical language, clichés, flowery phrasing, and pretentious wording. However, plain English also counters these ethically questionable uses of language:

Obfuscation

When writing includes fuzzy terms such as *throughput* and *downlink* that muddy the issue, the result is obfuscation. These words may make simple ideas sound more profound than they really are, or they may make false ideas sound true.

> Through the fully functional developmental process of a streamlined target-refractory system, the military will successfully reprioritize its data throughputs
>
> (*Objection:* What does this mean?)

Ambiguity

Especially when deliberate, ambiguity makes a statement open to two or more interpretations. While desirable in some forms of writing (like poetry and fiction), ambiguity is usually disruptive in academic writing because it obscures the meaning of the words.

> Many women need to work to support their children through school, but they would be better off at home.
>
> (*Objection:* Does *they* refer to *children* or *women*? What does *better off* mean? These words and phrases are unclear.)

Euphemisms

A euphemism is an indirect expression that avoids stating an uncomfortable truth. In your academic writing, choose neutral, tactful phrasing, but avoid euphemisms.

> This economically challenged neighborhood faces some issues concerning mind-enhancing substances and scuffles between youths.
>
> (*Translation:* This impoverished neighborhood is being destroyed by drugs and gangs.)

Doublespeak

When phrasing deliberately seeks either to hide the truth from readers or at least to understate the situation, the result is often doublespeak. Such slippery language is especially a temptation when the writer wields authority, power, or privilege in a negative situation (e.g., a hospital administrator writing a report, as shown in the sentence below). Avoid such verbal misdirection; be clearly honest by choosing precise, transparent phrasing.

> The doctor executed a nonfacile manipulation of newborn.
>
> (*Translation:* The doctor dropped the baby during delivery.)

Change Biased Words

When depicting individuals or groups according to their differences, use language that implies equal value and respect for all people (see Figures 6.2 and 6.3).

Words Referring to Ethnicity

Acceptable General Terms	Acceptable Specific Terms
American Indians, Native Americans	**Cherokee people, Inuit people,** and so forth
Asian Americans (not Orientals)	**Chinese Americans, Japanese Americans,** and so forth
Latinos, Latinas, Hispanics	**Mexican Americans, Cuban Americans,** and so forth
African Americans, blacks "African American" has come into wide acceptance, though the term "black" is preferred by some individuals.	
Anglo Americans (English ancestry), European Americans Use these terms to avoid the notion that "American," used alone, means "white."	

Not Recommended	Preferred
Eurasian, mulatto	**person of mixed ancestry**
nonwhite	**person of color**
Caucasian	**white**
American (to mean U.S. citizen), when writing to international readers	**U.S. citizen**

fig. 6.2

Words Referring to Age

Age Group	Acceptable Terms
up to age 13 or 14	**boys, girls**
between 13 and 19	**youth, teenagers, young men, young women**
late teens and 20s	**young adults, young women, young men**
30s to age 60	**adults, men, women**
60 and older	**older adults, older people** (not elderly)
65 and older	**seniors** (senior citizens also acceptable)

fig. 6.3

Words Referring to Disabilities or Impairments

In the recent past, some writers were choosing alternatives to the term *disabled,* including *physically challenged, exceptional,* or *special.* However, it is not generally held that these new terms are precise enough to serve those who live with disabilities. Of course, degrading labels such as *crippled, invalid,* and *maimed,* as well as overly negative terminology, must be avoided.

Not Recommended	Preferred
handicapped	**disabled**
mentally retarded	**intellectual disability**
birth defect	**congenital disability**
stutter, stammer, lisp	**speech impairment**
an AIDS victim	**person with AIDS**
suffering from cancer	**person who has cancer**
mechanical foot	**prosthetic foot**

Words Referring to Conditions

People with various disabilities and conditions have sometimes been referred to as though they were their condition (*quadriplegics, depressives, epileptics*) instead of people who happen to have a particular disability. As much as possible, remember to refer to the person first, the disability second.

Not Recommended	Preferred
the disabled	**people with disabilities**
cripples	**people who have difficulty walking**
the retarded	**people with a developmental disability**
dyslexics	**students with dyslexia**
neurotics	**patients with neuroses**
subjects, cases	**participants, patients**
quadriplegics	**people who are quadriplegic**
wheelchair users	**people who use wheelchairs**

Additional Terms

Make sure you understand the following terms that address specific impairments:

hearing impairment = partial hearing loss, hard of hearing (not deaf, which is total loss of hearing)

visual impairment = partially sighted (not blind, which is total loss of vision)

communicative disorder = speech, hearing, and learning disabilities affecting communication

Words Referring to Gender

- Use parallel language for both genders:

  The **men** and the **women** rebuilt the school together.
  Hank and **Marie**
  Mr. Robert Gumble, Mrs. Joy Gumble

  Note: The courtesy titles Mr., Ms., Mrs., and Miss ought to be used according to the person's preference.

- Use nonsexist alternatives to words with masculine connotations:

  humanity (not *mankind*) **synthetic** (not *man-made*)
  artisan (not *craftsman*)

- Do not use masculine-only or feminine-only pronouns *(he, she, his, her)* when you want to refer to a human being in general:

  A politician can kiss privacy good-bye when **he** runs for office.
  (not recommended)

  Instead, use *he or she*, change the sentence to plural, or eliminate the pronoun:

  A politician can kiss privacy good-bye when **he** or **she** runs for office.
  Politicians can kiss privacy good-bye when **they** run for office.
  A politician can kiss privacy good-bye when running for office.

- Do not use gender-specific references in the salutation of a business letter when you don't know the person's name:

  Dear Sir: Dear Gentlemen: (neither is recommended)

  Instead, address a position:

  Dear Personnel Officer:
  Dear Members of the Economic Committee:

Occupational Issues

Not Recommended	Preferred
chairman	**chair, presiding officer, moderator**
salesman	**sales representative, salesperson**
clergyman	**minister, priest, rabbi**
male/female nurse	**nurse**
male/female doctor	**doctor, physician**
mailman	**mail carrier, postal worker, letter carrier**
insurance man	**insurance agent**
fireman	**firefighter**
businessman	**executive, manager, businessperson**
congressman	**member of Congress, representative, senator**
steward, stewardess	**flight attendant**
policeman, policewoman	**police officer**

Proofreading Your Writing

The following guidelines will help you check your revised writing for spelling, mechanics, usage, grammar, and form. For additional help, see the Handbook section of this text (pages 533–679).

Review Punctuation and Mechanics

1. **Check for proper use of commas** before coordinating conjunctions in compound sentences, after introductory clauses and long introductory phrases, between items in a series, and so on.
2. **Look for apostrophes** in contractions, plurals, and possessive nouns.
3. **Examine quotation marks** in quoted information, titles, or dialogue.
4. **Watch for proper use of capital letters** for first words in written conversation and for proper names of people, places, and things.

Look for Usage and Grammar Errors

1. **Look for words that writers commonly misuse:** *there/their/they're; accept/except.*
2. **Check for verb use.** Subjects and verbs should agree in number: Singular subjects go with singular verbs; plural subjects go with plural verbs. Verb tenses should be consistent throughout.
3. **Review for pronoun/antecedent agreement problems.** A pronoun and its antecedent must agree in number.

Check for Spelling Errors

1. **Use a spell checker.** Your spell checker will catch most errors.
2. **Check each spelling you are unsure of.** Especially check those proper names and other special words your spell checker won't know.
3. **Consult a handbook.** Refer to a list of commonly misspelled words, as well as an up-to-date dictionary.

Check the Writing for Form and Presentation

1. **Note the title.** A title should be appropriate and lead into the writing.
2. **Examine any quoted or cited material.** Are all sources of information properly presented and documented? (See pages 465–502 and 503–532.)
3. **Look over the finished copy of your writing.** Does it meet the requirements for a final manuscript?

Critical Thinking and Writing: Applications

After you have used the instruction in this chapter to edit and proofread your essay, apply what you learned to the activities that follow.

1. **Wise Words:** The nineteenth-century British writer Matthew Arnold offers this advice to writers about refining their writing: "Have something to say and say it as clearly as you can. That is the only secret of style." Does your own writing demonstrate such a style? What might you do to strengthen clarity in your writing?
2. **Writing Reset:** Choose a writing assignment that you submitted without doing enough polishing. Edit the sentences in this writing for style and correctness using pages 95–101 as a guide. Then use pages 102–108 to edit the writing for wordiness, as well as vague, weak, and biased words. What difference does it make to have carefully edited and proofread the essay?
3. **Word Play:** Combine some of the following ideas into longer, more mature sentences. Write at least four sentences, using page 95 as a guide.

    Dogs can be difficult to train. The necessary supplies include a leash and treats. Patience is also a necessity. Dogs like to please their owners. Training is not a chore for dogs. A well-trained dog is a pleasure to its owner.
4. **Photo Op:** To suggest the nature of editing and proofreading, the chapter's opening page (93) contains a photograph of piano tuning. Find another image, graphic, or cartoon that represents this part of the writing process for you.

Learning-Objectives Checklist ✓

Have you achieved this chapter's learning objectives? Check your progress with the following items, revisiting topics in the chapter as needed. I have . . .

___ re-examined the overall style of my revised draft, including how well that style fits the rhetorical situation (94).

___ combined short, simplistic sentences through techniques of coordination and subordination (95).

___ expanded sparse sentences by making them cumulative, building them up with meaningful and rich details (96).

___ transformed weak sentences by varying sentence openings, lengths, types, and arrangements (97–99).

___ re-formulated sentences to strengthen parallel structure of coordinating elements (100).

___ re-written sentences weakened by nominalizations, expletives, and negative constructions (101).

___ eliminated wordiness within sentences (102), and replaced vague terms with precise nouns and vivid verbs (103).

___ replaced jargon with understandable language and clichés with fresh phrasing (104).

___ replaced any terms showing bias (106–108).

MindTap® Practice skills that you have learned in this chapter and receive automatic feedback. Reflect on your writing process.

Chapter 7

Submitting Writing and Creating Portfolios

MindTap®

Understand the goals of the chapter and complete a warm-up activity online.

By working through this chapter, you will be able to

- design the format and layout of your writing.
- choose an appropriate submission method.
- integrate your writing into a portfolio.
- improve your writing through reader feedback, including your instructor's.

Submitting your writing might be as simple as handing it in to your instructor or posting it to a class wiki, or it might be as involved as submitting it to a journal in your area of study or assembling it with your other works to publish in a portfolio. Whatever the case, sharing your writing makes all the work you have done worthwhile. As writer Tom Liner states, "You learn ways to improve your writing by seeing its effect on others."

This chapter will help you prepare your writing for submission and sharing. When you make your writing public—in whatever form—you are *publishing* it.

Visually Speaking Packages, packaging, packing—how is Figure 7.1 suggestive of what happens at the end of the writing process?

Dmitry Kalinovsky / Shutterstock.com

fig. 7.1

Formatting Your Writing

A good page design makes your writing clear and easy to follow. Keep that in mind when you produce a final copy of your writing.

Strive for Clarity in Page Design

Examine the following design elements, making sure that each is appropriate and clear in your project and in your writing.

Format and Documentation

- **Keep the design clear and uncluttered.** Aim for a sharp, polished look in all your assigned writing.
- **Use the designated documentation form.** Follow all the requirements outlined in the MLA (pages 487–491) or APA (page 521) style guides.

Typography

- **Use an easy-to-read serif font for the main text.** Serif type, **like this**, has "tails" at the tops and bottoms of the letters. For most writing, use a 10- or 12-point type size.
- **Consider using a sans serif font for the title and headings.** In traditional academic writing, typeface and type size should remain consistent throughout (e.g., 12-point Times New Roman.) For other documents, however, consider sans serif type and different sizes for headings. Sans serif type, **like this**, does not have "tails." Use larger, perhaps 18-point, type for your title and 14-point type for any headings. You may also use boldface for headings if they seem to get lost on the page. (Follow your instructor's formatting guidelines.)

Because most people find a sans serif font easier to read on screen, consider a sans serif font for the body and a serif font for the titles and headings in any writing you publish online.

Spacing

- **Follow all requirements for indents and margins.** This usually means indenting the first line of each paragraph five spaces, maintaining a one-inch margin around each page, and double-spacing throughout the paper.
- **Avoid orphans and widows.** Avoid leaving a heading, a hyphenated word, or a single line of a new paragraph alone at the bottom of a page (an orphan). Also avoid carrying over the last line of a paragraph to the top of a new page (a widow).

Graphic Devices

- **Create bulleted or numbered lists to highlight individual items in a list.** But, be selective, using traditional paragraphs when they help you more effectively communicate your message. Writing should not include too many lists.
- **Include charts or other graphics.** Graphics should be neither so small that they get lost on the page, nor so large that they overpower the page.

Submitting Writing and Creating Portfolios

Once you have formatted and proofread your final draft, you should be ready to share your writing. For college assignments, you will often simply turn in your paper to your instructor. However, you should also think about sharing your writing with other audiences, including those who will want to see your writing portfolio.

Consider Potential Audiences

You could reach readers in addition to your instructor by taking these steps:

- Share your writing with peers or family members.
- Submit your work to a local publication or an online journal.
- Post your writing on an appropriate Web site, including your own.

Select Appropriate Submission Methods

There are two basic methods for submitting your work.

- **Paper submission:** Print an error-free copy on quality paper.
- **Electronic submission:** If allowed, send your writing as an email attachment.

Use a Writing Portfolio

There are two basic types of writing portfolios: (1) *a working portfolio* in which you store documents at various stages of development, and (2) *a showcase portfolio* with which you share appropriate finished work. For example, you could submit a portfolio to complete course requirements or to apply for a scholarship, graduate program, or job. The documents below are commonly included in a showcase portfolio:

- A table of contents listing the pieces included in your portfolio
- An opening essay or letter detailing the story behind your portfolio
- A specified number of—and types of—finished pieces
- A cover sheet attached to each piece of writing, discussing the reason for its selection, the amount of work that went into it, and so on
- Evaluation sheets or checklists charting your progress or experiences

Digest Feedback from Readers

Learning to write well is a process of continuous improvement. Moreover, you want your writing to reach readers—to do good work. For both these reasons, pay attention to and learn from the various forms of feedback you receive from readers. Two forms stand out:

- **Instructor Feedback:** Study your instructor's comments on your work, not just the grade. Guided by the traits of strong writing (pages 30–31), review comments and questions, as well as specific grading symbols, to learn where your content, style, and grammar are strong and where they need improvement.
- **Peer Feedback:** Whether it's through conversations with your classmates or online comments about your work, measure the impact of your writing. What succeeded, and what didn't? Why? What might you change to reach readers better?

Critical Thinking and Writing: Applications

After you have used the instruction in this chapter to format and submit your writing, there may be more to think about. Through the activities below, apply what you have learned.

1. **Wise Words:** Catherine Drinker Bowen has argued the following: "Writing is not apart from living. Writing is a kind of double living." As you think about sharing your own writing and adding it to your writing portfolio, does this claim ring true? Why or why not?
2. **Writing Reset:** Choose one of your recent writing assignments and use the instructions on page 112 to assess the quality of your formatting and page design. Edit and redesign the paper as needed.
3. **Photo Op:** The chapter's opening page contains a photograph of a woman packaging materials—meant to visually symbolize the end of the writing process. Find another image, graphic, or cartoon that represents this ending for you. Another option: find or make an image that captures the entire writing process for you.
4. **Living Today:** Using the Internet (including blogging and social media), virtually everyone can self-publish in the broadest sense, for better or worse. What are practical strategies for creating a positive digital writing footprint? What are pitfalls to avoid? Answer these questions by studying your own online postings or those of a public figure.
5. **Major Work:** In your field of study, what writing might go into a professional portfolio? How could this portfolio contribute to your career planning? Research these questions as needed, and begin to put together your portfolio.

Learning-Objectives Checklist ✓

Have you achieved this chapter's learning objectives? Check your progress with the following items, revisiting topics in the chapter as needed. I have . . .

____ produced a clear, reader-friendly page design by developing an overall format that fits the writing assignment and form, following the requirements of a specific style such as MLA or APA, making typographical choices that enhance readability, creating white space as needed, and effectively designing and integrating graphics (112).

____ chosen a submission method, whether paper or digital, that meets readers' needs and the assignment expectations (113).

____ integrated my writing into a portfolio, whether a working or showcase portfolio, so as to track and demonstrate my growth as a writer (113).

____ carefully reviewed and learned from reader feedback, both that of my instructor and of my peers (113).

Chapter 8

One Writer's Process

Understand the goals of the chapter and complete a warm-up activity online.

Learning Objectives

By working through this chapter, you will be able to

- analyze how one writer worked through the writing process to complete an assignment.
- compare this student's process with your own.
- assess how the writing process might help you complete college assignments.

An essay is an attempt to understand a topic more deeply and clearly. That's one of the reasons this basic form of writing is essential in many college courses. It's a tool for both discovering and communicating.

How do you move from an assignment to a finished, polished essay? The best strategy is to take matters one step at a time, from understanding the assignment to submitting the final draft. Don't try to churn out the essay the night before it's due.

This chapter shows how student writer Angela Franco followed the writing process outlined in chapters 2 through 7.

Visually Speaking A rotary or roundabout (Figure 8.1) effectively controls the flow of traffic. How might writing be thought of as involving a flow of traffic? In what ways does the writing process involve rotaries?

Malota / Shutterstock.com

fig. 8.1

Angela's Assignment and Response

In this chapter, you will follow student Angela Franco as she writes an assigned essay for her Environmental Policies class. Start by carefully reading the assignment and discussion below, noting how she thinks through the rhetorical situation.

Angela Examined the Assignment

Angela carefully read her assignment and responded with the notes below.

> "Explain in a two- to three-page essay how a local environmental issue is relevant to the world community. Using *The College Writer* as your guide, format the paper and document sources in MLA style. You may seek revising help from a classmate or from the writing center."

Role

- I'm writing as a student in Environmental Policies, and as a resident of Ontario.

Subject

- The subject is a local environmental issue.

Purpose

- My purpose is to explain how the issue is relevant to all people. That means I must show how this issue affects my audience—both positively and negatively.

Form

- I need to write a two- to three-page essay—that sounds formal.
- I'll need to include a thesis statement, as well as references to my sources using MLA style.

Audience

- My audience will be people like me—neighbors, classmates, and community members.
- I'll need to keep in mind what they already know and what they need to know.

Context

- I'll use the guidelines and checklists in The College Writer to evaluate and revise my writing.
- I'll get editing feedback from Jeannie and from the writing center.

For each step in the writing process, choose strategies that fit your writing situation. For example, a personal essay in an English class might require significant time getting started, whereas a lab report in a chemistry class might require little or none.

Angela Explored and Narrowed Her Assignment

Angela explored her assignment and narrowed its focus by clustering and freewriting.

Angela's Cluster

When she considered environmental issues, Angela first thought of water pollution as a possible topic for her essay. After writing the phrase in the center of her page, she drew from memories, experiences, and readings to list related ideas and details. Notice how she used three different-colored inks to distinguish the topic (blue) from ideas (red) and details (green) (Figure 8.2).

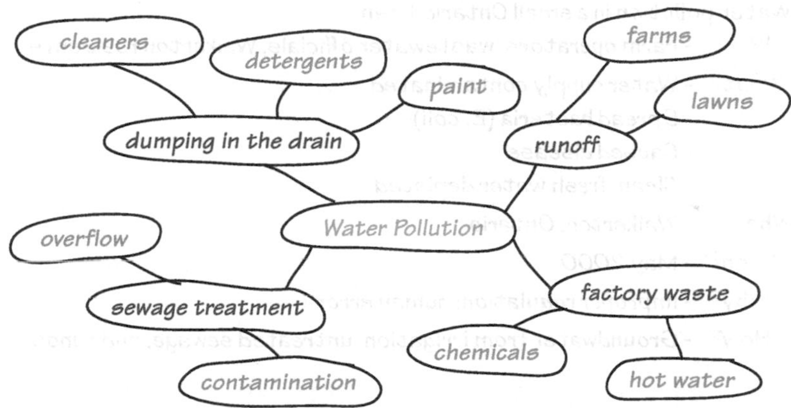

fig. 8.2

Angela's Freewriting

Angela decided to freewrite about the water pollution caused about fifteen years earlier by improper sewage treatment in a small Canadian town.

> I once read an article about the anniversary of a deadly water problem in Walkerton, a small Ontario town. People actually died. The water they drank was contaminated. This is becoming a problem in developed countries like ours. Consider water purification problems on Native reserves, or what happened in Flint, Michigan. I thought this was a problem only in developing countries. So who is responsible for sewage treatment? Who guarantees the safety of our drinking water? How does water get contaminated? Are there solutions for every kind of contamination: mercury, PCBs, sewage?

Angela's Narrowed Assignment

Based on her freewriting, Angela rephrased her assignment to narrow its focus.

> Explain in a two- to three-page essay how a local water pollution problem in a small Ontario town is relevant to the world community.

Angela's Planning

Narrowed Writing Assignment

Explain in a two- to three-page essay how a local water pollution problem in a small Ontario town is relevant to the world community.

Angela reviewed her narrowed assignment and reassessed her topic.

Angela Focused Her Topic

To focus her topic, Angela answered the journalistic questions (five Ws and H).

Topic: Water pollution in a small Ontario town

Who? - Farm operators, wastewater officials, Walkerton residents

What? - Water supply contaminated
- Spread bacteria (E. coli)
- Caused disease
- Clean, fresh water depleted

Where? - Walkerton, Ontario

When? - May 2000

Why? - Improper regulation; human error

How? - Groundwater from irrigation, untreated sewage, and runoff

Angela Researched the Topic

Angela then did some research to check her information and collect more details for her paper. She recorded all the essential data on each source following MLA format and then listed the specific details related to her topic. Here's one source:

"Inside Walkerton: Canada's worst ever E. coli contamination." CBC News, 17 May 2010, cbc.ca/news/canada/inside-walkerton-canada-s-worst-ever-e-coli-contamination-1.887200.

- May 15—water sampled
- May 17—first patients with flu-like symptoms
- May 18—Lab confirms E. coli contamination in water, but Public Utilities Commission (PUC) does not report information.
- May 19—Medical Health Office (MHO) discovers E. coli outbreak, but is assured by the PUC that the water is safe.
- May 20—At least 40 people treated at hospital with bloody diarrhea, but PUC says twice that water is safe.
- May 21—MHO tells people not to drink water, runs their own test.
- May 23—MHO finds E. coli, learns of May 18 memo, and that chlorinator not working for some time.
- May 24—Three adults and a baby die of E. coli.

Angela Decided How to Organize Her Writing

With a focus selected, Angela used the three guidelines below to choose the best organizational pattern for her writing.

Guidelines

1. **Review your assignment** and record your response.

   Assignment:
   Explain in a two- to three-page essay how a recent environmental issue is relevant to the world community.

   Response:
   My assignment clearly states that I need to explain my topic, so I have a general idea of how my paper will be organized.

2. **Decide on your thesis statement** and think about your essay's possible content and organization.

   Thesis Statement:
   The water pollution incident in Walkerton, Ontario, had a devastating effect that every town should learn from.

   Reflection:
   After reading my thesis statement, it's obvious that I'm going to be writing about a problem and its causes.

3. **Choose an overall method** and reflect on its potential effectiveness.

   Reflection:
   Looking at the list of methods, I see that I can use cause/effect or problem/solution. After making two quick lists of my main points using both approaches, I decided to use a problem/solution approach. I will still talk about causes and effects in my essay—they just won't be front and center.

   With problem/solution, I need to first present the problem clearly so that readers can fully understand it and see why it's important. Then I need to explore solutions to the problem—maybe what they did in Walkerton and what we all need to do to make water safe.

fyi Many essays you write will be organized according to one basic method or approach. However, within that basic structure you may want to include other methods. For example, while developing a comparison essay you may do some describing or classifying. In other words, you should choose methods of development that (1) help you understand the topic, and (2) help your reader understand your message.

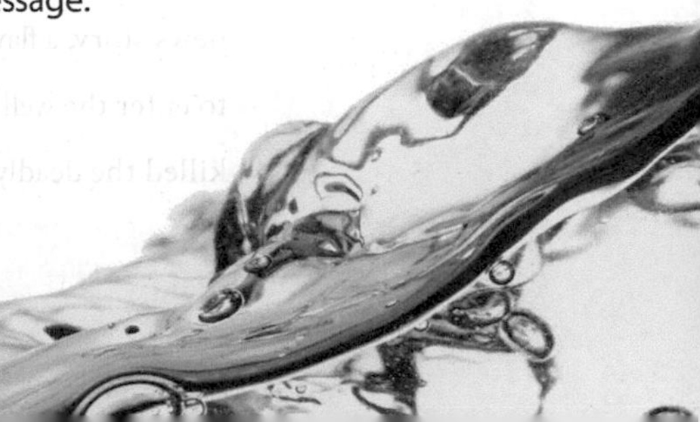

Angela's First Draft

After composing her opening, middle, and closing paragraphs, Angela put together her first draft. She then added a working title.

The writer uses a series of images to get the reader's attention.

The thesis statement (boldfaced) introduces the subject.

The writer describes the cause of the problem.

The writer indicates some of her source material with a citation.

Water Woes

It's a hot day. Several people just finished mowing their lawns. A group of 1
bicyclists—more than 3,000—have been passing through your picturesque town all afternoon. Dozens of Little Leaguers are batting, running, and sweating. What do all these people have in common? They all drinks lots of tap water, especially on hot summer days. They also take for granted that the water is clean and safe. But in reality, the water they drink could be contaminated and pose a serious health risk. **That's just what happened in Walkerton, Ontario, where a water pollution incident had a devastating effect that every town can learn from.**

What happened in Walkerton Ontario? Heavy rains fell on May 12. It wasn't 2
until May 21 that the townspeople were advised to boil their drinking water. The rains washed cattle manure into the town well. The manure contained E coli, a type of bacteria. E coli is harmless to cattle. It can make people sick. Seven days after the heavy rains, people began calling public health officials. The warning came too late. Two people had already died (Wickens).

Once Walkerton's problem was identified, the solutions were known. The 3
government acted quickly to help the community and to clean the water supply. One Canadian newspaper reported that a $100,000 emergency fund was set up to help families with expenses. Bottled water for drinking and containers of bleach for sanitizing and cleaning were donated by local businesses.

So what messed up Walkerton? Basically, people screwed up! According to one 4
news story, a flaw in the water treatment system allowed the bacteria-infested water to enter the well. The manure washed into the well, but the chlorine should have killed the deadly bacteria. In Walkerton, the PUC group fell asleep at the wheel.

The writer covers the solutions that were used to resolve the problem.

At last, the Provincial Clean Water Agency restored the main water and sewage systems by flushing out all of the town's pipes and wells. The ban on drinking Walkerton's water was finally lifted seven months after the water became contaminated. 5

The concluding paragraph stresses the importance of public awareness.

Could any good come from Walkerton's tragedy? Does it have a silver lining? It is possible that more people are aware that water may be contaminated. Today people are beginning to take responsibility for the purity of the water they and their families drink. In the end, more and more people will know about the dangers of contaminated water—without learning it the hard way. 6

Angela Kept a Working Bibliography

As she researched her topic, Angela kept a working bibliography—a list of resources that she thought might offer information helpful to her essay. From the start, she formatted the entries in MLA style. During the writing process, she deleted some resources, added others, and edited the document that became the works-cited list on page 130.

Working Bibliography

Blackwell, Thomas. "Walkerton Doctor Defends Response." *The Edmonton Journal,* 9 Jan. 2001, edmontonjournal.com.

"Inside Walkerton: Canada's Worst Ever E.coli Contamination." *CBC News,* 17 May 2010, cbc.ca/news/canada/inside-walkerton-canada-s-worst-ever-e-coli-contamination-1.887200.

Johnson, Alex. Personal interview. 14 Sept. 2016.

Angela's First Revision

After finishing the first draft, Angela set it aside. When she was ready to revise it, she looked carefully at global issues—ideas, organization, and voice. She wrote notes to herself to help keep her thoughts together.

Angela's comments

I need to give my opening more energy.

Does my thesis still fit the paper?—Yes.

Using time sequence, put this paragraph in better order.

Move this paragraph—it interrupts the discussion of causes.

My voice here is too informal.

Water Woes

It's ~~a~~ [an unusually] hot ~~day~~ [Saturday afternoon]. Several people just finished mowing their lawns. A group of bicyclists ~~—more than 3,000—have been passing through your picturesque town all afternoon~~ [pedal up the street]. Dozens of Little Leaguers are batting, running, and sweating. What do all these people have in common? They all drinks lots of tap water, especially on hot summer days. They also take for granted that the water is clean and safe. But in reality, the water they drink could be contaminated and pose a serious health risk. **That's just what happened in Walkerton, Ontario, where a water pollution incident had a devastating effect that every town can learn from.** 1

What happened in Walkerton Ontario? Heavy rains fell on May 12. It wasn't until May 21 that the townspeople were advised to boil their drinking water. The rains washed cattle manure into the town well. The manure contained E coli, a type of bacteria. E coli is harmless to cattle. It can make people sick. Seven days after the heavy rains, people began calling public health officials. The warning came too late. Two people had already died (Wickens). 2

Once Walkerton's problem was identified, the solutions were known. The government acted quickly to help the community and to clean the water supply. One Canadian newspaper reported that a $100,000 emergency fund was set up to help families with expenses. Bottled water for drinking and containers of bleach for sanitizing and cleaning were donated by local businesses. 3

So what ~~messed up~~ [went wrong in] Walkerton? ~~Basically, people screwed up!~~ [Human error was a critical factor.] [First,] According to one news story, a flaw in the water treatment system allowed the bacteria-infested water to enter the well. [Even after] The manure washed into the well, ~~but~~ the chlorine should have killed the deadly bacteria. In Walkerton, ~~the PUC group fell asleep at the wheel.~~ 4

Explain "fell asleep." Move paragraph three here and combine.

In addition

~~At last,~~ the Provincial Clean Water Agency restored the main water and sewage systems by flushing out all of the town's pipes and wells. The ban on drinking Walkerton's water was finally lifted seven months after the water became contaminated. 5

Cut the clichés.

Could any good come from Walkerton's tragedy? ~~Does it have a silver lining?~~ It is possible that more people are aware that water may be contaminated. Today people are beginning to take responsibility for the purity of the water they and their families drink. In the end, more and more people will know about the dangers of contaminated water—without learning it the hard way. 6

the Public Utilities Commission was responsible for overseeing the testing and treating of the town's water, but they failed to monitor it properly. Apparently, shortcuts were taken when tracking the water's chlorine level, and as a result, some of the water samples were mislabeled. There was also a significant delay between the time that the contamination was identified and the time it was reported.

Angela's Second Revision

Angela revised her draft, taking into account the questions and suggestions she received from a peer. His comments are in the margin, and Angela's changes, including a new opening and closing, are in red.

Reviewer's comments

> Could you make the opening more relevant and urgent?

> Could you clarify your focus on the topic?

> Add the year and other specific details.

> Make sure you document all source material—you have just one citation in your draft.

Angela's Changes

Water Woes

WARNING: City tap water is polluted with animal waste. Using the water for drinking, cooking, or bathing could cause sickness or death. 1

According to the Seirra Club, run-off pollutants from farm cites are steadily seeping into our streams, lakes, reservoirs and wells. Because much of our drinking water comes from these resources, warnings like the one above are already posted in a number of U.S. and Canadian communities, and many more postings will be needed ("Water Sentinels"). As the Seirra Club argues, the pollution and related warnings are serious, and failure to take them seriously could be deadly. For example, about fifteen years ago the citizens of Walkerton Ontario learned that the water that they believed to be clean was actually poisoned. 2

The events ~~What happened~~ in Walkerton, began ~~Ontario? Heavy rains fell~~ on May 12, 2000, when heavy rains ~~. The rains~~ washed cattle manure into the town well. The manure contained E coli, a type of bacteria. E coli is harmless to cattle. It can make people sick. Seven days after the heavy rains, people began calling public health officials to complain of nausea and diarrhea. It wasn't until May 21 that the townspeople were advised to boil their drinking water. The warning came too late. Two people had already died, and more than 2,000 were ill (Wickens). 3

Several factors contributed to the terrible tragedy in Walkerton, including human error. ~~So what went wrong in Walkerton? Human error was acritical factor.~~ First, according to The Edmonton Journal, ~~one news story,~~ a flaw in the water treatment system allowed the bacteria-infested water to enter the well. Even after the manure washed into the well, the chlorine should have killed the deadly bacteria (Blackwell). In Walkerton, the Public Utilities Commission was responsible for overseeing the testing and treating of the town's water, but it failed to monitor it properly. Apparently, shortcuts were taken when tracking the water's chlorine level, and as a result, some of the water samples 4 were mislabeled. There was also a significant delay between the time that the contamination was identified and the time it was reported.

Use active voice.

Once Walkerton's problem was identified, ~~the solutions were known.~~ The government acted quickly to help the community ~~and to clean the water supply.~~ 5

The Edmonton Journal
~~One Canadian newspaper~~ reported a $100,000 emergency fund was set up to help
Local businesses donated
families with expenses. Bottled water for drinking and containers of bleach for basic sanitizing and cleaning ~~were donated by local businesses.~~ In addition, the Provincial Clean Water Agency restored the main water and sewage systems by flushing out all of the town's pipes and wells. The ban on drinking Walkerton's water was finally lifted. Seven months after the water became contaminated.

Consider adding details—maybe an entire paragraph—calling readers to action, and stating your thesis clearly.

6 **As the Sierra Club warned and the citizens of Walkerton learned, water purity is a life-and-death issue. Fortunately, both the United States and Canada have been addressing the problem. For example, since 2001, more states and provinces are tightening their clean-water standards, more communities have begun monitoring their water quality, and more individuals have been using water-filtration systems, bottled water, or boiled tap water. However, a tragedy like that in Walkerton could happen again, as recent problems with water quality in Flint, Michigan, show. To avoid such horror, all of us must get involved by demanding clean tap water in our communities and by promoting the polices and procedures needed to achieve that goal.**

Angela's Edited Draft

When Angela began editing, she read each of her sentences aloud to check for clarity and smoothness. **The first page of Angela's edited copy is shown below.**

The writer revises the title.

Water Woes [in Walkerton]

Warning: City tap water is polluted with animal waste. Using the water for drinking, cooking, or bathing could cause sickness or death. 1

She qualifies her statement, replacing "will" with "might."

She rewrites and combines several choppy sentences.

Angela deletes unnecessary words.

According to the Seirra Club, run-off pollutants from farm cites are steadily 2
seeping into our streams, lakes, reservoirs[,] and wells. Because much of our drinking
water comes from these resources, warnings like the one above are already posted
in a number of U.S. and Canadian communities, and many more postings ~~will~~ [might] be
~~needed~~ [in the future] ("Water Sentinels). As the Seirra Club argues, the pollution and related
warnings are serious, and failure to take them seriously could be deadly. For
example, about fifteen years ago the citizens of Walkerton Ontario learned that the
water that they believed to be clean was ~~actually~~ [tragically] poisoned.

The events in Walkerton began on May 12, 2000, when heavy rains washed 3
cattle manure into the town well. The manure contained ~~E coli.~~ a bacteria [commonly called] E coli.
[While E coli] is harmless to cattle. ~~It~~ [it] can make people sick. Seven days after the heavy rains,
people began calling public health officials to complain of nausea and diarrhea. It
wasn't until May 21 that the townspeople were advised to boil their drinking water.
The warning came too late. Two people had already died, and more than 2,000 were
ill (Wickens).

Several factors contributed to the ~~terrible~~ tragedy in Walkerton, including 4
human error. First, according to *The Edmonton Journal*, a flaw in the water
treatment system allowed the ~~bacteria~~ infested water to enter the well (Blackwell).
Even after the manure washed into the well, the chlorine . . .

Angela's Proofread Draft

Angela reviewed her edited copy for punctuation, agreement issues, and spelling. **The first page of Angela's proofread essay is shown below.**

Water Woes in Walkerton

Warning: City tap water is polluted with animal waste. Using the water for drinking, cooking, or bathing could cause sickness or death. 1

The writer corrects errors that the spell checker did not pick up.

According to the Seirra Club, run-off pollutants from farm cites [s] are steadily 2
seeping into our streams, lakes, reservoirs, and wells. Because much of our drinking water comes from these resources, warnings like the one above are already posted in a number of U.S. and Canadian communities, and many more postings might be needed in the future ("Water Sentinels"). As the Seirra Club argues, the pollution and related warnings are serious, and failure to take them seriously could be deadly. For example, about fifteen years ago the citizens of Walkerton, Ontario, learned that the water that they believed to be clean was tragically poisoned.

She adds a comma between the city and province.

The events in Walkerton began on May 12, 2000, when heavy rains washed 3
cattle manure into the town well. The manure contained bacteria commonly called E. coli. While E. coli is harmless to cattle, it can make people sick. Seven days after the heavy rains, people began calling public health officials to complain of nausea and diarrhea. It wasn't until May 21 that the townspeople were advised to boil their drinking water. The warning came too late. Two people had already died, and more than 2,000 were ill (Wickens).

She adds periods and italicizes "E. coli" to show that it is a scientific term.

Several factors contributed to the tragedy in Walkerton, including human error. 4
First, according to *The Edmonton Journal,* a flaw in the water treatment system allowed the infested water to enter Walkerton's well (Blackwell). Even after the manure washed into Walkerton's well ~~into the well,~~ the chlorine should have . . .

She adds a word for clarity.

Angela's Finished Essay

After proofreading and formatting her essay, Angela added a heading and page numbers. She also added more documentation and a works-cited list at the end.

The writer revises the title.

The warning is emphasized with red print.

An appropriate font and type size are used.

Franco 1

Angela Franco

Professor Kim Van Es

English 101

18 October 2016

Clean Water Is Everyone's Business

Warning: City tap water is polluted with animal waste.
Using the water for drinking, cooking, or bathing
could cause sickness or death.

According to the Sierra Club, run-off pollutants from farm sites are steadily seeping into our streams, lakes, reservoirs, and wells. Because much of our drinking water comes from these resources, warnings like the one above are already posted in a number of U.S. and Canadian communities, and many more postings might be needed in the future ("Water Sentinels"). As the Sierra Club argues, the pollution and related warnings are serious, and failure to take them seriously could be deadly. For example, a about fifteen years ago the citizens of Walkerton, Ontario, learned that the water that they believed to be clean was tragically poisoned.

The events in Walkerton began on May 12, 2000, when heavy rains washed cattle manure into the town well. The manure contained the bacteria commonly called *E. coli*. While *E. coli* is harmless to cattle, it can make people sick. Seven days after the heavy rains, people began calling public health officials to complain of nausea and diarrhea. It wasn't until May 21 that the townspeople were advised to

Author's last name and page number are cited on each page.

Each claim or supporting point is backed up with reasoning and evidence.

The writer continues to give credit throughout the essay.

Franco 2

boil their drinking water. The warning came too late. Two people had already died, and more than 2,000 were ill (Wickens).

Several factors contributed to the tragedy in Walkerton, including human 3
error. First, according to *The Edmonton Journal*, a flaw in the water treatment system allowed the infested water to enter Walkerton's well (Blackwell). Even after the manure washed into Walkerton's well, the chlorine should have killed the deadly bacteria. In Walkerton, the Public Utilities Commission was responsible for overseeing the testing and treating of the town's water, but it failed to monitor the procedure properly ("Walkerton's Water-Safety"). Apparently, shortcuts were taken when tracking the water's chlorine level, and as a result, some of the water samples were mislabeled. There was also a significant delay between the time that the contamination was identified and the time it was reported.

Once Walkerton's problem was identified, the government acted quickly to help 4
the community. In its December 7, 2000, edition, *The Edmonton Journal* reported that a $100,000 emergency fund was set up to help families with expenses. Local businesses donated bottled water for drinking and containers of bleach for basic sanitizing and cleaning. In addition, the Provincial Clean Water Agency restored the main water and sewage systems by flushing out all of the town's pipes and wells. Seven months after the water became contaminated, the ban on drinking Walkerton's water was finally lifted.

As the Sierra Club warns and the citizens of Walkerton learned, water purity 5
is a life-and-death issue. Fortunately, both the United States and Canada have

Franco 3

been addressing the problem. For example, since 2001, more states and provinces have been tightening their clean-water standards, more communities have been monitoring their water quality, and more individuals have been using water-filtration systems, bottled water, or boiled tap water. However, a tragedy like that in Walkerton could happen again, as recent problems with water quality in Flint, Michigan, show. To avoid such horror, all of us must get involved by demanding clean tap water in our communities and by promoting the policies and procedures needed to achieve that goal.

The writer restates her thesis in the last sentence.

Franco 4

Works Cited

Sources used are listed correctly, in alphabetical order.

Each entry follows MLA rules for content, format, and punctuation.

Blackwell, Thomas. "Walkerton Doctor Defends Response." *The Edmonton Journal,* 9 Jan. 2001, edmontonjournal.com.

"Walkerton's Water-Safety Tests Falsified Regularly, Utility Official Admits." *The Edmonton Journal,* 7 Dec. 2000, edmontonjournal.com.

"Water Sentinels: Keeping It Clean around the U.S.A." *Sierra Club,* Jan. 2016, sierraclub.org/water-sentinels.

Wickens, Barbara. "Tragedy in Walkerton." *Maclean's,* 5 June 2000, business.highbeam.com/4341/article-1G1-62959012/tragedy-walkerton-contaminated-water-brings-death-and.

Critical Thinking and Writing: Applications

After you have reviewed Angela's writing process, there may be more to think about. Through the activities below, apply what you have learned.

1. **Wise Words:** Scott Russell Sanders suggests that "essays are experiments in making sense of things." Does Sanders' statement ring true? What makes such experiments flop or succeed? What kinds of "sense" do essays create?
2. **Photo Op:** The chapter's opening page contains an aerial photograph of a roundabout—a bird's-eye view of traffic. What other bird's-eye view image might resemble the writing process for you? What would that image show?
3. **Living Today:** Because she was writing an essay for a college course, Angela took her writing carefully through all the steps of the full writing process. For your formal writing assignments, you want to do the same. But what about the many forms of writing that we do today outside the college classroom? In what situations should you use the full writing process? How might you use an abbreviated or condensed process in other situations?
4. **Writing Reset:** How does Angela's writing process differ from the process you typically follow? Review the work that you did to complete a recent writing assignment. What elements of the process did you complete productively? Where were the weaknesses and gaps? What would you do differently now?
5. **Major Work:** Based on the assignment instructions, Angela documented and formatted her paper following the MLA system. In your field of study, what system are you expected to follow? What are the key features of that system?

Learning-Objectives Checklist ✓

Have you achieved this chapter's learning objectives? Check your progress with the following items, revisiting topics in the chapter as needed. I have . . .

____ analyzed how Angela Franco worked through the writing process:

- examining the assignment (116)
- narrowing the topic (117)
- researching her topic and organizing her thoughts (118–119)
- completing her first draft (120–121)
- revising the draft by herself and then through peer review (122–125)
- and editing and proofreading her essay (126–127).

____ compared Angela's process with the process that I normally follow, considering strengths and weaknesses of my own approach.

____ assessed how I might tailor the writing process shown by Angela and outlined in chapters 2–7 to my own writing habits and my college writing assignments.

MindTap® Practice skills that you have learned in this chapter and receive automatic feedback. Reflect on your writing process.

Traits of College Writing: A Checklist

Early in chapter 2, you learned about the common traits of excellent college writing (pages 30–31). The following checklist is a reminder of those traits. You can use it to check any of your finished writing assignments.

Stimulating Ideas *The writing . . .*

____ presents interesting and important information.
____ maintains a clear focus or purpose—centered on a thesis, theme, concern, or question.
____ develops the focus through a line of thought or reasoning elaborated with sufficient details or evidence.
____ holds the reader's attention (and answers her or his questions).

Logical Organization

____ includes a clear beginning, middle, and ending.
____ contains specific details, arranged in an order that builds understanding with readers.
____ uses transitions to link sentences and paragraphs.

Engaging Voice

____ speaks in a sincere, natural way that fits the writing situation.
____ shows that the writer really cares about the subject.

Appropriate Word Choice

____ contains specific, clear words.
____ uses a level of language appropriate for the type of writing and the audience.

Overall Sentence Fluency

____ flows smoothly from sentence to sentence.
____ displays varied sentence beginnings and lengths.
____ follows a style that fits the situation (e.g., familiar versus academic).

Correct, Accurate Copy

____ adheres to the rules of grammar, spelling, and punctuation.
____ follows established documentation guidelines.

Reader-Friendly Design

____ exhibits a polished, professional design in terms of overall format, page layout, and typographical choices.
____ makes the document attractive and easy to read.
____ is formatted correctly in MLA or APA style.

II. Reader:
Strategies and Samples

Sergey Peterman / Shutterstock.com

Reader: Strategies and Samples

Chapter 9

Forms of College Writing

MindTap®

Understand the goals of the chapter and complete a warm-up activity online.

In college, professors in nearly all fields give writing assignments. Why? Because they know that writing helps you learn course material today and use that knowledge in subsequent college courses and in the workplace. Similarly, college writing develops the thinking skills needed in a field of study and a profession.

This chapter begins by showing the big picture of college writing: the three divisions into which most college curricula are divided, and the academic departments that constitute each division. The chapter then offers instruction in the methods of inquiry and forms of writing typical to each division's disciplines.

Visually Speaking Study Figure 9.1 and consider the possible comparison between modes of transportation and forms of writing. What might the analogy suggest regarding the distinctions between different forms of writing?

Learning Objectives

By working through this chapter, you will be able to

- identify and classify fields of study in the college curriculum.
- differentiate and explain writing in the humanities, the social sciences, and the natural and applied sciences.
- analyze the nature of writing in your own field of study or a major that interests you.
- identify personal, analytical, and argumentative modes of writing.
- transition from one mode to another.

Artens / Shutterstock.com

fig. 9.1

Three Curricular Divisions

Based on each department's field of study, the college curriculum is generally divided into three groups: humanities, social sciences, and natural and applied sciences. These groups are then subdivided into specific departments, such as biology, chemistry, and physics. Below you will find an explanation of each division, along with its common departments.

Humanities

Scholars and students within this division study human culture, both past and present. They examine topics such as the history of civilization, cultural institutions and trends, religious beliefs and practices, languages and their use, and artwork and performance skills. This division includes the following departments:

Archeology	Ethnic Studies	Modern Languages	Theater Arts
Asian Studies	Film Studies	Music	Theology
Dance	Graphic Design	Philosophy	Visual Arts
English	History	Religion	Women's Studies

Social Sciences

Scholars and students in this division study human behavior and societies using research strategies adapted from the natural sciences. For example, a researcher may develop a hypothesis regarding a topic or phenomenon, and then devise an experiment to test that hypothesis. Students study economic systems, correctional programs, and personality disorders. Departments in this division include the following:

Anthropology	Economics	Geophysics	Psychology
Business	Education	Government	Social Work
Communication	Genetics	Health & Phys. Ed.	Sociology
Criminology	Geography	Political Science	Urban Planning

Natural and Applied Sciences

The natural sciences (such as biology, zoology, and chemistry) focus on specific aspects of nature, such as animal life, plant life, and molecular structures. In contrast, the applied sciences (such as mathematics, computer science, and engineering) consider how to use science-based information to understand concepts and develop artifacts. Here are some of the departments in this division:

Agriculture	Biology	Environment	Physics
Agronomy	Botany	Forestry	Physiology
Anatomy	Chemistry	Mathematics	Public Health
Architecture	Computer Science	Nutrition	Space Science
Astronomy	Engineering	Oceanography	Zoology

Writing in the Humanities

In a humanities class (e.g., English, history, and theater arts), your study and writing likely focus on various types of texts, broadly understood: primary texts, such as poems, novels, historical records, and philosophical essays, as well as secondary sources (books and periodical articles). Such study is largely concerned with the world of ideas, whether creative, historical, or theoretical. Your writing will likely have the character described below.

The Purpose of Inquiry

Humanities study aims to understand more deeply some aspect of human experience and humanity's place in the world, whether that aspect of experience relates to the artistic and imaginative, the historical, the spiritual, the linguistic, or the world of ethics. As a result, writing in the humanities tends to be thesis-driven, focused on a central idea that is explored through coherent analysis and argument.

Forms of Humanities Writing

In humanities courses, you will likely write essays and research papers of this sort: interpretive analyses and arguments on a specific topic, theoretical studies of key concepts in the discipline, and book reviews or broader bibliographic surveys. Here are typical forms:

- **Analysis of a Text or Art Work:** Such a study closely examines a specific work in order to understand more fully what it means, how it communicates, and so on.
- **A Review of the Literature on a Topic:** This form of research writing identifies and synthesizes the studies that have been published on a specific issue or question.
- **A Book, Film, Music, or Performance Review:** Applying general criteria for excellence, reviews evaluate the quality, impact, strengths, and weaknesses of a specific text or art work.

Examples: "Latin American Music: A Diverse and Unifying Force" (page 196), "*The Revenant*: A Brutal Masterpiece" (page 298), "'Let Evening Come': An Invitation to the Inevitable" (page 287).

Humanities Research Methods

As the forms of writing above suggest, the humanities involve the careful "reading" of primary texts, artifacts, and events. In addition, humanities projects involve a careful investigation of past scholarship on a topic so that the writer can add his or her voice to the ongoing discussion or dialogue. With their focus on "reading," the humanities value skills of interpretation—sensitivity to the primary text, thoughtful use of evidence from the text, attention to the textual context, awareness of theoretical frameworks for understanding texts, insightful theses about texts, and the rhetorical skills involved in analysis and argument. In such research, the following resources may be especially helpful:

- "Analyzing Texts, Documents, Records, and Artifacts" (pages 404–405)
- MLA Documentation (chapter 23, pages 465–502, and www.mla.org)

Writing in the Social Sciences

In a social sciences class (e.g., psychology, sociology, business, education), your writing will likely explore some dimension of the way that people behave, individually or within groups, whether the group is just two people or an entire society. Your writing will likely have the following character.

The Purpose of Inquiry

Broadly, the social sciences aim to understand, through using an adapted version of the natural-science experimental method, the rules and conventions that govern human behavior and societies. As such, social-sciences thinking tends to be hypothesis-driven, seeking not only to describe behavior but also to predict it. To that end, the social sciences involve observing, measuring, and testing various forms of behavior.

Forms of Social-Science Writing

With their focus on behavior and social laws, social scientists typically write reports, often as teams of researchers. Here are specific types of writing that you might do:

- **A Literature Review:** This form of research writing identifies and synthesizes the studies that have been published on a specific behavioral or social issue.
- **An Experiment Report:** Such a report describes a specific experiment designed to test a hypothesis about behavior, and then share and analyze the results.
- **A Field Report:** Whether based on observations, interviews, or surveys, such a report shares insights gathered through such contact with human subjects.
- **A Case Study:** Such a study describes and examines actual individuals and situations so as to understand them more deeply.

Examples: "Familiar Strangers" (page 254), "The Rise of the New Groupthink" (page 259), "Mother-Daughter Relationships: Harmful or Helpful" (page 337), APA sample research paper (page 522)

Social-Science Research Methods

Like scholars in the natural sciences, social scientists tend to use the experimental method to test out observation-based hypotheses. Some social-science research, however, is more subjective, involving a speculative approach to the mysteries of human consciousness, emotions, and the like. Because much social-science research is observation-based, much of the thinking is rooted in mathematics, particularly statistical analysis. Focused on testing hypotheses, such research pays careful attention to variables, controls, experiment replication, and case studies. Objective analysis of all the data is valued. The following resources may be especially helpful:

- "Conducting Surveys" (pages 402–403), "Conducting Interviews" (pages 406–407), and "Making Observations" (page 408)
- APA Documentation (chapter 24, pages 503–532, and www.apa.org)

Writing in the Natural and Applied Sciences

In a natural- or applied-science class (e.g., botany, chemistry, engineering, and oceanography), your writing will explore some aspect of the physical, natural world. Such writing seeks to explore and explain the nature of the world that we inhabit and are part of, as well as the natural laws that govern that world. If your major is in the natural or applied sciences, your writing will likely have the following character.

The Purpose of Inquiry

Broadly, natural science aims to explain observations in the light of current theories, observations that are typically not now explicable. The goal of the scientist—or more likely team of scientists—is to arrive at an explanation, stimulate discussion, and prompt further research. As such, scientific thinking tends to be hypothesis driven: it begins with a possible explanation rooted in current knowledge, makes an experiment-related prediction, observes and measures results, and then accepts, rejects, or modifies the possible explanation.

Forms of Natural-Science Writing

With their focus on natural phenomena, natural scientists typically write research reports. Here are types of writing that you might do:

- **Lab or Field Reports:** Sometimes called IMRAD reports (introduction, method, results, and discussion), such reports share the results of experiments and measured observations.
- **Literature Reviews:** These reports summarize and synthesize all the current research on a specific topic, perhaps also examining the theories that underlie the topic.
- **Technical Reports:** Applied research might involve writing technical reports aimed at proposing practical solutions to a specific problem or challenge.

Examples: "Wayward Cells" (page 212), "Defining *Mathematics*" (page 178), and "Sample Research Paper: Science IMRAD Report" (page 457)

Natural-Science Research Methods

Natural scientists practice two predominant research methods: laboratory experiments and field work. Both rooted in objective attention to phenomena, laboratory research follows the strict procedures of the experimental method while field work relies on careful, often quantifiable observation. Both forms for research value insightful hypothesizing, carefully collecting and analyzing data (typically in a lab notebook or a field journal), and thoughtfully relating the results to past research and current theories. The following resources might be helpful:

- "Making Observations" (page 408)
- Council of Science Editors (councilscienceeditors.org)

The Rhetorical Modes

The chapters in this part of *The College Writer* are largely organized by the type of writing: personal essay, analytical essay, and argumentative essay. However, this division also features the rhetorical modes—thinking patterns that characterize writing in part or in whole. These thinking patterns are at work in your academic writing, so learning them and practicing them create a foundation for all your assignments.

The Modes as Thinking Framework

Each rhetorical mode involves a thinking move that allows you to deepen your understanding of a topic, to explore it and make claims about it.

Personal-Writing Modes

Personal-writing modes focus on experience, especially the writer's experience—whether of places, people, or events—with the goal of vividly sharing that experience with readers.

- **Narration** tells a story, whether in the form of a brief anecdote, a personal essay, a short story, or a book-length novel. (See pages 144–145.)
- **Description** evokes material reality (e.g., birds outside a window) through appealing to the senses (sight, hearing, touch, taste, and smell). (See pages 145–146.)
- **Reflection** involves rumination—a kind of speculation that extends narration and description toward personal and universal meaning. (See pages 147.)

Analytical Modes

Analytical modes involve mentally "breaking down" a topic in an effort to reveal structures and logical relationships that hold it together.

- **Definition** seeks to clarify the meaning of a term (e.g., human trafficking, mathematics, excellence). (See Chapter 11, pages 173–192.)
- **Classification** organizes into categories large or complex sets of things: weightlifters and their motivations, musical genres popular in Latin America, or positions on climate change. (See Chapter 12, pages 193–208.)
- **Process** analysis explains how a specific phenomenon unfolds in time—stage by stage, step by step. The phenomenon might be natural (the development of cancer), historical (emancipation), or cultural (end-of-life care). (See Chapter 13, pages 209–232.)
- **Comparison-contrast** analysis examines the similarities and/or differences between two or more topics in order to illuminate their distinctiveness and/or their commonalities, whether the topics are cultural characteristics, human and animal suffering, or traditional and cyber bullying. (See Chapter 14, pages 233–250.)
- **Cause-effect** analysis examines the forces that bring about specific results—focusing on the forces at work (causes), the results (effects), or both. As such, cause-effect reasoning explores why and how questions about a wide range of topics, for example, why creativity requires solitude. (See Chapter 15, pages 251–278.)

Argumentative Modes

Argumentative modes are persuasive in nature, aiming to convince readers to accept claims about topics that are typically controversial or at least problematic.

- **Position papers** take a stand on a topic (e.g., incarceration, a controversial statue on campus), either arguing for a specific claim or arguing against a claim with which the writer disagrees. (See page 333.)
- **Call-to-action essays** move beyond taking a position on a controversial topic to pressing readers to take a step in response to that position—a concrete action or a general change in behavior. (See page 334.)
- **Problem-solution** analysis proposes specific changes to address a specific challenge. This mode thus presses readers to care about a problem, embrace the recommended solution, and (sometimes) even implement the solution. (See page 335.)

The Modes at Work

In academic writing, a specific rhetorical mode might dominate a piece of writing, giving the essay structure and direction from start to finish, such as in an essay classifying types of student weightlifters (pages 200–201). However, the rhetorical modes are more often seamlessly combined in your writing, all serving the specific mental work you are doing with your topic. For example, your main purpose might be to explain how a knuckleball works (cause-effect), but in doing so you also walk through a typical pitch delivery (process) and describe the distinctly different ball movement of other pitches such as fast balls and curve balls (contrast). Indeed, it is fair to say that the rhetorical modes build and rely on each other: analytical writing can contain narrative, descriptive, and reflective elements; argumentative writing, in turn, depends upon effective analytical moves to bolster its claims.

Example: In order to explain the nature of prosopagnosia, Audrey Torrest uses *narration* and *description* to describe its *effects*, and she uses *definition* to identify its *cause*.

> Dr. Smith stood beside a fellow neurobiologist on the campus of Washington University in St. Louis. While engrossed in conversation, Smith noticed from the corner of his eye an undergraduate walking in their direction. At first he thought nothing of it, but as she approached, it dawned on him that she was looking directly at him. "Strange," he thought. He tried to ignore her and continue his conversation, but when she was about 20 feet away he heard her laugh. Upon hearing the sound, the unfamiliar undergraduate who had been staring so intently at him morphed into his daughter. Smith had been unable to recognize her.
>
> Dr. Smith suffers from a unique condition known as prosopagnosia or face blindness. Historically, most documented cases have been due to brain damage suffered after maturity from head trauma, stroke, or degenerative diseases. . . . (See page 254.)

Critical Thinking and Writing: Applications

After you have carefully read the chapter, apply what you have learned in the situations that follow.

1. **Curricular Survey:** Using its online or print catalog, review your college's curriculum—its organization into divisions, disciplines, and courses. What does that big picture reveal about knowledge, inquiry, and learning in your school? How might you apply that knowledge and learning in your career?
2. **Writing Analysis:** Using what you have learned in this chapter about inquiry in the humanities, social sciences, and natural sciences, browse through chapters 10–24, identifying essays, research papers, and other forms of writing that relate to the different divisions and disciplines. Read closely two or three samples that interest you, analyzing the thinking and writing strategies that the authors use.
3. **Major Analysis:** Consider the major that you have chosen, or select a program that interests you. Then research the thinking and writing skills practiced in this field:
   a. **In the college catalog, study the programs and courses in the department.** What do these reveal about the structure of knowledge, the major issues, and writing practices in the field?
   b. **Using library and digital resources, find and study scholarly writing in this field.** What does this writing reveal about the thinking strategies valued, as well as the writing forms used?
   c. **How is knowledge from this field presented in writing to the broader culture?** Explore this question by researching an issue in the field as it is discussed in the popular print and digital media.

Learning-Objectives Checklist ✓

Have you achieved this chapter's learning objectives? Check your progress with the following items, revisiting topics in the chapter as needed. I have . . .

____ identified the three traditional curricular divisions—including their area of knowledge and typical disciplines or majors within each (136).

____ differentiated and explained the purpose of inquiry, the forms of writing, and the research methods in the humanities, the social sciences, and the natural and applied sciences (137–139).

____ analyzed how writing works in my field of study or a major that interests me, including in the program itself, in scholarly writing, in popular writing, and in professions to which the major leads.

____ examined the nature and function of these modes: narration, description, and reflection (140); definition (140), classification (140), process (140), comparison-contrast (140), and cause-effect (140); position (141), call-to-action (141), and problem-solution (141).

____ noted how the modes are used individually and together.

Chapter **10**

Narration, Description, and Reflection

Understand the goals of the chapter and complete a warm-up activity online.

Learning Objectives

By working through this chapter, you will be able to

- critique and create the elements of narrative writing.
- analyze and effectively utilize strategies for descriptive writing.
- evaluate and use reflective-writing strategies such as natural observation and meaningful thesis thinking.
- create and integrate enriching anecdotes in personal and academic writing.
- develop a well-organized personal essay that includes narration, description, and/or reflection.

Personal essays often tell stories—not ones that the writers made up, but ones that they lived. Whatever the topics, the stories should help readers see, hear, touch, and taste those details that make the experiences come alive. To do that, writers must carefully describe key aspects of the experience. But they might also reflect on why the experiences are important—exploring their personal and shared meanings.

When reading such personal essays, do so with an open mind—seeking to go where writers guide you, to experience what they carefully describe, and to analyze how they craft their work.

As you prepare to write your own story, get ready to relive it yourself—to reexperience all that you felt, thought, or sensed during the event. In addition, be ready to learn something new about the experience, about others, and even about yourself.

Visually Speaking Carefully study the photograph in Figure 10.1. What story does it suggest? What elements of narration, description, and reflection might the story include?

igor.stevanovic / Shutterstock.com

fig. 10.1

Strategies for Personal Essays

Personal essays typically present and explore some dimension of the writer's experience by blending **narration, description,** and **reflection**. This blending often follows a **fluid organization**. Whether you are reading or writing a personal narrative, start with the **rhetorical situation** and then consider the strategies that follow.

The Rhetorical Situation

To put a personal essay in context, consider the rhetorical situation that gives rise to it:

- **Purpose:** The goal of such writing is to explore topics or issues with which writers have a personal connection. A writer's aim is to deepen his or her own insight while sharing it with readers.
- **Readers:** Most personal essays are written for a general audience, though they may be directed to a specific segment of society. The writer hopes that his or her personal experience will speak universally—that readers will empathize and connect with it.
- **Topic:** Writers address any topic that they find meaningful and worth exploring through the lens of personal experience and reflection—often events, people, and places from their own lives.

Example: In "The Muscle Mystique" (pages 159–161), Barbara Kingsolver focuses on a **topic** meaningful to her own life, her sense of physical weakness and her attempts to "buff up." Her **purpose** is to gain insight into her own situation, comical as it is, but also to explore more fully the cultural significance of bodybuilding and exercise. Her **readership** would rightly be described as a general public, but the essay may also be directed at fellow "weaklings" and at bodybuilding enthusiasts.

Principles of Narration

Personal essays often center on engaging narratives—stories that focus on meaningful events and people. That's the case, for example, with "Story Time: A True Story" (pages 150–152) and "Spare Change" (pages 153–155), where the writers tell stories that stand on their own. The following elements are central to a well-crafted narrative:

Action: This refers to the unfolding sequence of events shaped into a meaningful whole, a force that drives narrative forward. Consider these strategies:

- **Handling chronology:** Narrative is time-sensitive, so a good narrative handles time effectively through clear temporal markers, verb tenses, and time transitions. Moreover, the narrative manages temporal pacing by focusing in on key events and compressing or summarizing less significant action. Finally, the narrative may "escape" strict chronology by beginning in the middle of the action before going back to the beginning, as well as by using flashbacks and foreshadowing.
- **Clarifying action:** Narratives move forward energetically when writers use precise, engaging, and suggestive verbs. Example: "Outside the restaurant, Goodman **leapfrogged** across rocks into the middle of the broad, taupe-colored Panjshir River

to **pose**, **mugging** and **clowning**, for pictures. **Driving** back to the base, she **hooted** with delight whenever we **passed** a scatter of scruffy red hens **pecking** listlessly along the roadside or **huddled** in a dirt yard."

- **Shaping a plot:** A narrative's overall pattern may take many forms, but the traditional structure builds tension and complication toward a climactic moment of decision or discovery, followed by aftermath and resolution.

Character: While events (what happened and why) are often the focus of a narrative, frequently the narrative's focus is character—what the events reveal about people. Characters need to be well-developed and engaging in order to reveal things about life and human nature. Narrative shows people feeling, thinking, acting, and interacting.

Dialogue: Conversations are used in narrative to reveal character, advance the action, and embody the conflict. Typically chosen for significant moments in the action, such dialogue should be natural in word choice, voice, and sentence rhythms (reflecting dialects if needed).

Narrative Perspective: In a personal narrative, the writer is typically the narrator—the voice telling the story. However, the narrative voice might be in the foreground (participating in the action) or the background (observing the action).

Setting: Action happens and people live within specific places and times—the narrative's setting. Settings put events and characters in physical, historical, and cultural context.

Sample Narrative Paragraph

Taken from "Story Time: A True Story" (pages 150–152), the paragraph below narrates moments of calm after a frightening argument.

> I don't know when or how I fell asleep, but it couldn't have been for long according to my clock. It was 3:30 when I had last looked, and now it was 4:00. My sister was sleeping next to me, her face red from hot tears, but otherwise so peaceful that I hardly believed I was awake. I gently disentangled myself from her, slowly took down the blockade from my door, and then silently crept through the house to see if anyone was awake.

Principles of Description

Effective descriptive passages (of places, people, and objects) offer precise, evocative details that help readers thoughtfully experience the essay's topic. Such description may aim for fidelity—objectivity through accurate and complete details, including measurements and so on. Or the description may aim to create a dominant impression, a sense of the person, place, or object that is rooted in carefully selected details that work through imagination, association, and symbolism. For example, "The Muscle Mystique" (pages 159–161) is filled with vivid descriptions of places and people. Such strong description draws attention to different strategies: naming, detailing, ordering, and comparing (see page 146 for more).

Naming: At its base, description identifies things, and the beginning of such identification is naming—among available terms, choosing words that precisely or suggestively clarify the nature of what is being described.

Detailing: Description appeals to the senses through concrete details, details that may be precise but also rich in connotations and associations. Details that appeal to sight create a mental picture for readers; sounds and smells tend to evoke feelings and memories; taste and touch generate a sense of intimacy.

Ordering: While they may involve a single detail, descriptions are often much fuller. In that case, writers may need to (1) establish a vantage point from which readers will see the object, (2) orient the object in space, and (3) lead readers systematically through the description (e.g., left to right, top to bottom, back to front).

Comparing: Descriptions may be clarified and deepened through comparisons. Here are three common options:

- **Simile** is a comparison of two things in which *like* or *as* is used. Example: "My friends have given me an official item of exercise equipment that looks like a glob of blue putty."
- **Metaphor** is a comparison in which one thing is said to be another, establishing an identity. (Neither *like* nor *as* is used.) Example: "I can't deny the place [health club] was a lekking ground."
- **Personification** is a device in which the author speaks of or describes an animal, object, or idea as if it were a person. Example: "The moon is lonesome without you, but I look at it each night as it rises and see you staring back at me."

Sample Descriptive Paragraph

The paragraph below is the opening paragraph in Teresa Zsuffa's "Spare Change" (pages 153–155). Note how in describing the urban setting she appeals to multiple senses, offers precise details, evokes a feeling of unease, and ends with a metaphor ("starry distance").

> This grime is infectious. The smell of old cigarettes and expired perfume is constricting my throat and turning my stomach. But here I am again on the underground subway platform, changing trains at Bloor-Yonge in Toronto, the weight of my backpack thrusting me forward with the Friday morning rush hour crowd. When the subway doors open I hurry inside and look around frantically, as usual. There is an empty seat to my left, but everyone is keeping a safe four-foot distance, as if the seat will suck them in and destroy them if they sit down. Or at least destroy the facade put on with a Ralph Lauren suit, a Coach handbag, or a pair of authentic Gucci sunglasses. Not like the fake five-dollar ones I picked up from a Chinatown vendor just yesterday. The others keep their starry distance; when I sit down, I see why.

Principles of Reflection

In a personal essay, strong reflective passages—from single sentences to entire paragraphs—relay the writer's observations and insights regarding the nature, impact, and value of the experience. In some personal essays, such reflection is minimal (e.g., essays that are primarily narrative in nature, such as "Spare Change"). However, some essays are rich in reflection, particularly when the writer's purpose is to explore psychological and cultural complexity, as in "Finding Ashton" (pages 162–169) and "The Muscle Mystique" (pages 159–161). Consider these reflection strategies:

Natural Observation: Reflection within a personal essay should have an organic feel—arising naturally out of the material presented, out of the narration and description. That reflection can be thematically implied or openly stated, depending on the writer's purpose. Essentially, however, the reflection should be honest, meaningful, and thought-provoking for readers, pressing them to connect with and universalize the experience. For that reason, reflection is often stated using the pronoun I, but a connection to other people is stated or implied, perhaps through comparison-contrast.

Thesis Thinking: The key idea of a personal essay typically grows out of the writer's questions about the meaning of the experience. More than a simple statement of fact or a clichéd opinion, the thesis should follow these guidelines:

- **The thesis expresses some complexity about the experience**—mixed feelings (ambivalence), tensions, or paradox. The thesis is rarely a blunt, simplistic "This is the moral of the story" statement, as it doesn't do justice to the fullness of the experience or the complications of the narrative. Example: Many marriages demonstrate the notion that opposites attract—with painful consequences for everyone involved.
- **The thesis may be stated openly or simply implied.** If stated, it can be positioned in a variety of places in the essay, though toward the middle or end seems best: action and description build inductively toward insight.

Sample Reflective Paragraph

In the paragraph below, from "Finding Ashton" (pages 162–169), Melissa Pritchard reflects on why she had tried to escape from the life that she was living, and what she had found outside her security zone.

> Sometimes we run away to be reclaimed, to be reassured that if we are not wholly understood, at least we are loved. When I came home, my daughters let it be known how worried they had been, shocked and even hurt that their mother would go somewhere, anywhere, without asking or even telling them. I had left home like an impetuous child, wanting to be found. Instead I had found Ashton and was opened to love beyond my familiar, given circle.

Principles of Organization

If a personal essay centers on a narrative, the organization will largely be determined by chronology, arranged according to the logic of the plot. (See, for example, "Spare Change," pages 153–155.) Generally, the structure of a personal essay tends to be fluid—flowing more freely than a traditional academic essay. Consider these strategies:

Opening: The opening seeks to get readers' attention, usher them into the world of the essay, and orient them to the topic through techniques like these: a memory, an image, an idea, a conflict, a puzzle, a moment from the middle or near the end of the story. Remember that personal essays don't always need to open at the beginning of the story; they can start from the middle or end of the action.

Middle: The body of the essay may weave together elements of narration, description, and reflection to deepen interest, and possibly to build toward a climax—a moment of discovery or decision. This process may involve

- bringing together "strands" of the past and the present
- introducing tensions, complications, and conflicts
- focusing on key moments, episodes, and encounters (including dialogue)
- foreshadowing what is to come or creating a puzzle to be solved
- comparing events, settings, or characters
- moving from a broad view to a narrow focus or vice versa

Closing: Traditional narratives follow the climax with the fallout and resolution (revealing the results of conflict, the outcome). Other narratives, however, aim to be more open-ended. The ending might also focus on authentic reflection (without trite moralism) that leaves readers with food for thought. Finally, it might supply a surprise, a dramatic turn of events, or it might return to the opening in some way.

Reading Personal Writing

On the following pages, you will find personal essays written by both students and professional authors. As you read, consider these questions:

1. Does the essay center on narrative? How is that narrative developed through action, character, dialogue, narrative perspective, and setting? Do you find the narrative engaging?
2. What roles does description play in the essay, and what descriptive techniques are used? Are there descriptions that grab your attention? Why?
3. What ideas or themes evolve from the story? Is reflection stated or implied? Can you locate a thesis, or is it implied? Can you put it in your own words? Why does the writer care about this topic, and how do you feel about it in the end? What have you learned?
4. How does the essay unfold? How are narrative, description, and reflection blended?

Brief Narratives: Anecdotes

A common narrative is the anecdote—a brief story that enlivens your writing while introducing a topic or illustrating an idea. Read the anecdotes below, along with the essays from which they are taken. Then assess the anecdotes' effectiveness.

Anecdote Introducing a Topic

The other day, my wife, watching our son-in-law with his large hands gracefully tie the shoelaces of his little daughter, remarked, "You really are deft." Ever the cynic, I remarked, "He's not only deft, he's daft." I talk that sort of nonsense frequently, but as I said this, I began to wonder. What if *deft* and *daft* come from the same root and once meant the same thing? A quick trip to the dictionary showed that, indeed, they did once mean the same thing (though my wife thought me daft when I first suggested it).

From "Deft or Daft," page 182

Anecdote Illustrating a Process

Imagine a room containing a large group of people all working hard toward the same goal. Each person knows his or her job, does it carefully, and cooperates with other group members. Together, they function smoothly—like a well-oiled machine.

Then something goes wrong. One guy suddenly drops his task, steps into another person's workstation, grabs the material that she's working with, and begins something very different—he uses the material to make little reproductions of himself, thousands of them. These look-alikes imitate him—grabbing material and making reproductions of themselves. Soon the bunch gets so big that they spill into other people's workstations, getting in their way, and interrupting their work. As the number of look-alikes grows, the work group's activity slows, stutters, and finally stops.

A human body is like this room, and the body's cells are like these workers. . . .

From "Wayward Cells," page 212

Anecdote Illustrating a Trait

Dr. Smith stood beside a fellow neurobiologist on the campus of Washington University in St. Louis. While engrossed in conversation, Dr. Smith noticed from the corner of his eye an undergraduate walking in their direction. At first he thought nothing of it but as she approached, it dawned on him that she was looking directly at him. "Strange," he thought. . . .

Dr. Smith suffers from a unique condition known as prosopagnosia . . .

From "Familiar Strangers," page 254

Sample Personal Essays

Personal essays can focus on a wide range of topics as writers narrate, describe, and reflect upon their experiences. The essays that follow suggest that range as they explore family life, subway encounters, incarceration, health club antics, and a soldier's desire to live.

MindTap®
Read, highlight, and take notes online.

Exploring a Tense Situation

In the opening two paragraphs of this essay, student writer Brandalynn S. Buchanan begins a story about a young girl (the narrator) and her little sister, barricaded in an upstairs bedroom. In the third paragraph, in italics, Buchanan begins a second story—a dramatic tale about a little princess, a fearsome dragon, brave knights, and a king. She then develops both plots side-by-side until the closing, when she reveals how the two stories are related.

Story Time: A True Story

When the walls would shake with curses, we lay together in my room. We should 1
not have been listening to our father's tirade; it was against the rules to hear what he said. If he came upstairs and thought we had been listening, it would be our own fault for whatever happened. So we told ourselves a story.

She was a young child, crying in my arms and soaking the sleeve of the 2
uncomfortable shirt I had not been allowed to change out of. To watch her live this life was like watching a small flower try to grow. A gentle rain it could endure, but having gallon after fermented gallon dropped on it threatened to bend, break, and eventually drown this gentle plant. She would wince when he said our names, and I would cover her ears so she could pretend that she hadn't been listening. Think of something else. Anything else. We're not really here.

A long time ago, Baby, in a land of magic and heroes . . . 3

"I don't give a shit!" The bed shook. "Disrespectful brats wouldn't listen to me . . ." 4

. . . there was a brave little princess who lived in a tall tower. Below the brave princess 5
lived a fearsome dragon with thick scales over thin bones. The princess was afraid of the dragon, and she wanted nothing more than to be saved from his grasp.

Something broke downstairs—I spent a moment hoping it wasn't my computer 6
because I had homework on it, then immediately felt guilty. There were more precious things downstairs to worry about. We had been trapped up here for two hours now, and we knew that we had to rest if we did not want everyone to see how tired we were in the morning. Sleep was necessary, obedient, and absolutely impossible.

The queen was trapped in the dungeon, and she knew that she could do nothing 7
to help the princess. She could scream at the dragon, and sometimes that worked. If

he were busy in the dungeon, then the princess was safe in her tower.

"Please, Jeff, the neighbors . . ." I heard my mother plead down below, and I wanted to go to her, but who would stay with the girl? 8

There were other castles around her own, but somehow the dragon had used magic to make himself invisible to the residents who lived there. Every now and then they might hear him roar, but they mistook it for the thundering sky. If they were asked, they'd tell tales of the sweet princess next door. 9

We heard a loud cracking but did not know what it was. In the morning, when I would quickly scan the downstairs rooms before running to school, I would see the hole in the kitchen wall. 10

"I want them to hear! I want this whole damn town to hear me, I'll burn it to the ground—I swear to God!" 11

Even though she was hidden by the magic of the dragon, the princess's story began to spread, and brave knights bearing crosses came to the castle. They'd storm the moat with swords and shields, but when they approached the gates, the dragon changed his form into that of a handsome king. The king would bring the knights in, show them the beautiful castle, and then introduce them to the princess. She knew that if he chose to do so, he could instantly turn back into a dragon and kill the knights, so she told them that she was not in danger. They rode away from the castle, and the princess went back to her tower to hide and to watch them disappear over the horizon. 12

"People coming in here telling me how to raise my damn kids!" I leaned forward and checked the blockade that I had put in front of my door. When he spoke about us, he usually remembered that other people were in the house too, and that was the worst thing that could happen. 13

I heard his footsteps approaching up the stair . . . they stopped . . . and he went back to yelling at our mother. I sighed in relief, and the little girl started breathing again. I hadn't realized she had been holding her breath. 14

The dragon sent the princess outside sometimes because he knew that people would be suspicious if he didn't. During those precious minutes of freedom, she walked with other girls her age and laughed and smiled, but told no one of the terror she faced. She didn't want anyone to know that a fierce dragon was in her home. 15

But the princess was smart, good, and brave. The dragon knew this, and that was why, to break her faith in herself, he roared and told her that she was weak, cowardly, and stupid. 16

However, he never could break her self-confidence. No matter how lonely she got in her tower, or how singed her beautiful brown hair was from the fire shooting up the staircase, the princess wouldn't give up hope. Because his words came from hate, they meant nothing and slid over her like sand on glass—leaving their scratches but never destroying her. She knew that she was strong, that she was good, and that one day— 17

I don't know when or how I fell asleep, but it couldn't have been for long according to my clock. It was 3:30 when I had last looked, and now it was 4:00. My sister was sleeping next to me, her face red from hot tears, but otherwise so peaceful that I hardly believed I was awake. I gently disentangled myself from her, slowly took down the blockade from my door, and then silently crept through the house to see if anyone was awake. But I could hear and see nothing, except the darkness that hung in the air, warning of danger nearby. 18

I went back to my room and picked up my princess, carrying her to her room and tucking her in bed. Then I returned to my room and lay alone on my bed, my mind too busy to sleep. No matter how hard I searched, I could not think of an ending for the story. Hours later I fell into a fitful knight's rest. 19

Reading for Better Writing

1. *Connections:* In this essay, the narrator protects her little sister by creating a fantasy world into which the two girls can periodically escape their raging father downstairs. What role have fantasy worlds played in your life? Are they related in some way to fears, or to something else?
2. *Comprehension:* Re-read the real-life story (in regular print) by itself, and then read the imaginary story (in italics) by itself. How do specific characters and events in one narrative mirror or reflect specific characters or events in the other narrative. Taken together, how do the parallel stories help you understand the family's situation?
3. *Writing Strategies:* A good narrative requires a clear chronology and a vivid sense of place. Cite strategies that Brandalynn uses to show time unfolding, to signal her transitions from one story to the other, and to create a sense of the real world and the fantasy world.

Your Project: As you search for a topic for your own narrative, think about events in your life in which one person earnestly tried to help someone in need or in danger. Consider why those efforts succeeded or failed, and why such stories may be worth writing.

Narrating an Encounter

"Spare Change" is the first part of student writer Teresa Zsuffa's "A Diary of Chance Encounters," an essay that explores her experiences of living in Toronto. The piece below recounts a challenging encounter with the face of poverty.

"Spare Change"

This grime is infectious. The smell of old cigarettes and expired perfume 1
is constricting my throat and turning my stomach. But here I am again on the
underground subway platform, changing trains at Bloor-Yonge in Toronto, the weight
of my backpack thrusting me forward with the Friday morning rush hour crowd.
When the subway doors open I hurry inside and look around frantically, as usual.
There is an empty seat to my left, but everyone is keeping a safe four-foot distance, as
if the seat will suck them in and destroy them if they sit down. Or at least destroy the
facade put on with a Ralph Lauren suit, a Coach handbag, or a pair of authentic Gucci
sunglasses. Not like the fake five-dollar ones I picked up from a Chinatown vendor just
yesterday. The others keep their starry distance; when I sit down, I see why.

She must be about twenty-nine. Her orange track-pants are worn and faded, her 2
T-shirt is far too big, and her powder blue sweatshirt is tied around her waist. Her
face and teeth are stained, hair greasy and unkempt. A part of me feels sorry for her.
Another part follows the crowd and is careful not to make eye contact.

"Excuse me," she says, perching on the edge of her seat, leaning forward and 3
clasping the metal pole with two hands. No one turns. "Excuse me, which stop do I
take to the Old City Hall?" One man shrugs and shakes his head while pretending to
check his phone. I feel guilt, but it's easily subdued. After all, she wasn't asking me.

I am deeply engrossed in my Nicholas Sparks novel by the time the driver 4
announces "Dundas Station." As I stuff the book back into my purse and make my way
towards the doorway, I'm irritated to see that she also stands up—one stop early for
Old City Hall. Doesn't she know she should stay on until Queen? Oh well, she'll figure
it out, I reason. The Toronto Transit Commission officers can help her.

I let her off the subway before me. Finally I'm free. 5

But then she stops on the platform and turns her head, like a puppy making sure 6
her owner is following close behind. No eye contact, I remind myself, and try to walk
past but she falls into step with me.

"Can I help you carry your bag?" 7

I may look like a tourist, but I'm smarter. "No, thanks," I reply. 8

"Well it just looks pretty heavy." We reach the escalator and the staircase and 9
I take the left side, where I can climb the steps and go up twice as fast as those just
standing there on the right and enjoying the ride. But it doesn't work; the woman is
still at my heels.

"Are you going somewhere?" she asks. 10

"Yeah, I have to get to the Greyhound station, I'm going out of town." 11

"Oh." Now we are standing in front of the underground entrance to the Eaton 12
Center. The Atrium on Bay is to my right, on the other side of which is the bus station and my ticket out of this alien city that is now my home. The woman stands frozen and looks around trying to get her bearings. I start to walk away but hesitate. Looking back, I see her blinking and flinching as people shove past her. She reminds me of a small child lost at a summer carnival.

I check my watch—quarter past eight. I just missed an express shuttle, and the 13
next bus to Niagara Falls, where my father lives, won't be leaving for another forty-five minutes. Something pulls me back to the woman, and against all sworn Torontonian rules, I ask if she needs help.

Her dull brown eyes light up. "I need to find the Old City Hall." 14

"Okay," I nod. "I'll take you." I lead her through the glass doors into the city's 15
busiest mall. It's the fastest way from Dundas to Queen Street, and from there she will need to walk only a few blocks west. As we're walking, I'm aware of the stares I'm getting from people I'll never see again.

"So where are you from?" I ask. 16

"Sudbury." And I'm instantly speechless. What is this woman doing so far from 17
home? How did she get here? I ask why she's in the city.

"My boyfriend. He's in jail, and they're letting him go today. I came to take him 18
back home with me after his hearing."

While we walk past Mexx, Aritzia, and Abercrombie, I learn that she had taken a 19
bus from Sudbury the day before and spent the night on a park bench. Her boyfriend is forty-two years old and has been in jail for the past ten months. I don't ask why. She proudly tells me she was a crack addict and that she's been clean for three months.

"I just got out of rehab," she says. "Now maybe my grandma will take me back in." 20

"Back in?" 21

"Yeah, she kicked me out. She told me I wasn't allowed to be a hooker anymore, 22
but I got caught bringing someone home once."

I have no idea how to talk to a prostitute, never mind one who is so open about 23
everything she's done, but this woman seems to like me and trust me. The next thing I know, I'm offering to buy her breakfast before she meets up with her boyfriend.

There's a McDonald's at the southernmost side of the Eaton Centre, overlooking 24
the Queen Street entrance. I tell her she can have anything she wants. An Egg McMuffin? Fruit and yogurt? But all she wants is Coke and a hash-brown. I order her two.

We sit down at a freshly wiped table by the window. Beside us, two men in grey 25
suits sip coffee over an array of files and spreadsheets. They pause in their conversation to stare at us—the student traveler and the bedraggled prostitute. I tell the woman a little about my life, and ask more about hers and her grandmother. She says that they used to go to church together, when she was little, but she hasn't been since. She takes another bite of her hash-brown and tells me she's now twenty-one. Only twenty-one, and her boyfriend is forty-two. She talks about the drugs and the providence of God.

"I know that he helped me stop," she says. "I've been clean for three months, can you believe that? That's a miracle! It has to be a miracle." 26

At this point all I can do is smile. 27

"I wish I could get my boyfriend to quit," she says, staring off. Then she suddenly leans forward and asks, "Do you know how hard it is? Have you ever done crack?" 28

"No." 29

"Pot, at least?" 30

"No. Sorry." I'm not sure why I'm apologizing for never having tried drugs, but the way her face drops and she shifts her eyes makes me feel guilty. As though I can never fully understand her because I've never experienced the things she has. 31

"Well you should try it," she urges. "It's really good." 32

"Maybe one day." I glance at my watch. It's now quarter-to, and I still need to stand in line to buy my ticket and get to the right platform. I wonder why I'm not panicking yet. 33

I tell her I need to get going. She should go, too, or she'll be late for the hearing. Before getting up, I reach into my wallet and give her two TTC passes and some spare change. I walk her to the street and point her toward Old City Hall. She never thanks me, only looks at me one last time with immense vulnerability and helplessness. Then she walks away. 34

I wonder as I hurry towards the station if she'll be okay, if her boyfriend really will get out of jail, and if her grandmother will ever take her back. Either way, I think as I cross Bay Street, what more can I do? I have a bus to catch. 35

Reading for Better Writing

1. *Connections:* Teresa Zsuffa writes about her sometimes unsettling encounter with someone whose experiences and values are different from her own. Have you had a similar experience? Where and when did it happen, and what was the outcome?
2. *Comprehension:* In your own words, summarize the plot, especially the opening and closing scenes. Then explain what Teresa and the other young woman may have learned about themselves and each other through their encounter.
3. *Writing Strategies:* The central character in the essay is presented primarily through description, comparisons, and dialogue. Identify such passages, exploring what they communicate about the woman and how effectively they work.

Your Project: Think about the experience (or encounter) that you cited in your answer to question one above. What did you learn—or not learn—from the experience? Why do you care—or not care—about this person today? Why does thinking about the experience make you amused, embarrassed, jealous, or something else? Might the experience be a good topic for your own essay?

Examining a Failed Institution

James Kilgore is a lecturer and research scholar at the University of Illinois at Urbana-Champaign, as well as a convicted felon who spent six and a half years in prison. In this essay, published in 2015, he describes prison life and his effort to deal with the stigma of having been incarcerated. As you read the essay, note how he reflects on his experiences and uses them to support his critique of current incarceration policies. In addition to this essay, Kilgore has written a number of books, including *Understanding Mass Incarceration: A People's Guide to the Key Civil Rights Struggle of Our Time.*

What I Learned in Prison

I was paroled to Champaign, Illinois in 2009, after serving six and a half years in federal and state prisons in California. When I arrived in Illinois, I ducked questions about my years behind bars. People would ask me where I had been before. "California," I'd say. "What were you doing there?" I'd look away and mumble something about being a writer (I did write a lot in prison) or just say "a lot of things." 1

Since I'm an older white guy, with no tattoos or bulging biceps and all my teeth, no one assumes I'm a thug or a meth cook. Class and race stereotypes help steer people away from specifics. 2

Then one day I met a man at a birthday party who started in on the "where were you before you came to Champaign?" routine. I didn't feel like playing the game anymore. "I was in prison," I told him. He went bug-eyed. All he could do was repeat the word "prison." 3

I, on the other hand, felt great. I realized the power of truth, even if it does come with stigma and judgment. Since we have nearly 20 million people in the United States with felony convictions and an estimated 65 million with some kind of criminal record, people need to get used to dealing with "background" as part of people's biographies. Of course, those millions are not spread evenly. Many black folks either have a family member with a felony or have one themselves. Ditto if you are Native American or transgender. It's not much different in Latino communities, especially if we acknowledge that immigration detention is the same as imprisonment. 4

After that fateful birthday party, people began asking me: "What was prison like?" At first I talked about the most painful things: that your children grow up without you, that you never get to hold your lover, kiss your mother, or walk down a quiet street in the rain. But I decided that I didn't like sharing that pain with strangers. I put together four talking points about how prison changes a middle-class, educated white man. 5

First, the abnormal becomes normal. This occurs in ways that you might expect: You get called "inmate" or referred to by your prison number, not your name. You get handcuffed and put in waist chains and leg shackles when you have to leave the prison to see a doctor (and at other times when the guards see fit). 6

But the most abnormal thing that becomes normal is the endless stream of black, brown, and poor white bodies flowing through those gates. And those bodies will spend 10, 20, 30 years in prison. Some will do life or double life or life without parole. I had one friend who was doing 555 years. Most of those prisoners have not committed 7 crimes that any rational society would punish so severely.

When I was in the federal prison at Lompoc, I was a GED teacher. One of my best students was Weldon Angelos, whose case exposes the madness of mass incarceration. He is serving 55 years for selling marijuana while possessing a gun—with no prior record, a family, and a job. Even his judge says he should never have gotten such a long sentence. I met too many Weldons behind those walls. 8

Second, there isn't much violence in prison. That always shocks people because they think that men in prison spend their days stabbing and raping each other. But instead, people find ways to live together: to share tight spaces and meager resources in a way that puts getting along at the center of their lives. I have a lot of respect for that. 9

The minute you arrive at a new prison yard, someone will approach you, find out where you are from, connect you to one of your "homies," and make sure you have the basics needed to survive: soap, deodorant, a couple of Top Ramens, a pair of shower shoes. The assumption is that we all have to live together in this hellhole, so let's find a way to do that; let's make sure no one starves, no one stinks, no one has to walk around in bare feet. 10

Every prison has a well-developed service economy, all run by prisoners. I have paid for the following from my comrades-in-arms: a massage, getting my shirts ironed, a haircut, a delicious burrito, oatmeal cookies stolen from the kitchen, color portraits of my entire family, a picture frame made from old potato-chip wrappers, and, of course, white lightning and the prison wine known as pruno. People find ways to make money, to barter, to improve their lives through systems of production and cooperation. 11

You can cram 150 "convicts" into a converted gym and make them sleep on triple bunks, and they will develop a way to get along without violence. They will make rules, carve out territory, and respect boundaries. Anyone who breaks the rules may be forced to do a few burpees or even get "checked" (punched), but the rules are clear. If you put 150 CEOs or MacArthur geniuses in the same space, they wouldn't do half as well. 12

My next point contradicts Point No. 2: Prisons are steeped in hate and violence. Guards generally loathe prisoners. Since so many prisons are located in rural areas with mostly white populations, whereas those locked up are overwhelmingly poor people of color from big cities, prison hatred has a powerful racial tinge. Most guards have learned how to avoid using the N-word, but institutional racism lurks just below the surface. 13

Then there is white supremacy. In prison I acquired the social skill of making polite conversation with someone with a swastika tattoo on his forehead or a nicely inked "thank God I'm white" across the back of his neck. Prisons are hotbeds of white supremacy, a special form of hatred that keeps prison populations divided and makes it difficult to mount resistance to the myriad ways in which the institutions violate the rights of their charges. Unfortunately, the ideology spills out into the streets. 14

While I hate white supremacy, I don't hate all white supremacists. Most are victims of circumstances—but still dangerous. 15

Finally, in prison you always know someone is benefiting from locking you up. 16

People make money designing those crepe-paper suits they put on you when you move to another prison. Companies like Bob Barker ("America's Leading Detention Supplier") profit from a range of disgusting products, like one-inch razors and canvas shoes with black and white stripes on the side. Other companies make millions designing and building prisons and supplying them with everything from food to toilet paper.

Guards are the most obvious profiteers. They're constantly cooking up overtime schemes. Thousands of guards in California make more than $100,000, and last year more than 100 had paychecks surpassing $180,000. That's a criminal misuse of taxpayers' money. 17

Prison changed me. I'm a little less fun now, less prone to look for the lighter side of things. I do try. But most days, prison is all I can talk about. I've become an obsessed campaigner against incarceration, against the madness of solving social problems with concrete and steel cages. My obsession may not make me an ideal party guest, but I can't think of a better way to spend my time. 18

Reading for Better Writing

1. *Connections:* In his essay, James Kilgore asserts that the incarceration system in the U.S. is exploitative, abusive, and de-humanizing. What have you learned through reading about or experiencing the system? Does your knowledge and/or experience support or contradict Kilgore's claims? Explain.
2. *Comprehension:*
   a. Prisons and penitentiaries are sometimes called "correctional institutions," implying that they strengthen society by "correcting" deviant behavior. Would Kilgore agree with this claim? Why? Cite details in his essay to support your answer.
   b. In paragraph 9, Kilgore says, "Second, there isn't much violence in prison." But in paragraph 13, he says, "My next point contradicts Point No. 2: Prisons are steeped in hate and violence." What does he suggest by these (apparently) contradictory statements?
3. *Writing Strategies:* Kilgore develops his personal essay through researched data, personal anecdotes, and reflection. Find an example of each and explain how he uses it to advance his thesis.

Your Project: Kilgore's essay critiques what he believes to be an institution that fails to accomplish what it is intended to do. What other institutions are important to you? Consider researching and writing about an institution that you believe either succeeds or fails to achieve its mission.

Reflecting on a Cultural Trend

The following essay by Barbara Kingsolver is taken from her book, *High Tide in Tucson.* In the essay, she describes her brief experience as a bodybuilding wannabe, and she reflects on how she "outgrew" her need to buff up.

The Muscle Mystique

The baby-sitter surely thought I was having an affair. Years ago, for a period of three whole months, I would dash in to pick up my daughter after "work" with my cheeks flushed, my heart pounding, my hair damp from a quick shower. I'm loath to admit where I'd really been for that last hour of the afternoon. But it's time to come clean. 1

I joined a health club. 2

I went downtown and sweated with the masses. I rode a bike that goes nowhere at the rate of five hundred calories per hour. I even pumped a little iron. I can't deny the place was a lekking ground: guys stalking around the weight room like prairie chickens, nervously eying each other's pectorals. Over by the abdominal machines I heard some of the frankest pickup lines since eighth grade ("You've got real defined deltoids for a girl"). A truck perpetually parked out front had vanity plates the read: LFT WTS. Another one, PRSS 250, I didn't recognize as a vanity plate until I understood the prestige of bench pressing 250 pounds. 3

I personally couldn't bench press a fully loaded steam iron. I didn't join the health club to lose weight, or to meet the young Adonis who admired my (dubiously defined) deltoids. I am content with my lot in life, save for one irksome affliction: I am what's known in comic-book jargon as the ninety-eight-pound weakling. I finally tipped the scales into three digits my last year of high school, but "weakling" I've remained, pretty much since birth. In polite terminology I'm cerebral; the muscles between my ears are what I get by on. The last great body in my family was my Grandfather Henry. He wore muscle shirts in the days when they were known as BVDs, under his cotton work shirt, and his bronze tan stopped midbiceps. He got those biceps by hauling floor joists and hammering up roof beams every day of his life, including his last. How he would have guffawed to see a roomful of nearly naked bankers and attorneys, pale as plucked geese, heads down, eyes fixed on a horizon beyond the water cooler, pedaling like bats out of hell on bolted-down bicycles. I expect he'd offer us all a job. If we'd pay our thirty dollars a month to *him*, we could come out to the construction site and run up and down ladders bringing him nails. That's why I'm embarrassed about all this. I'm afraid I share his opinion of unproductive sweat. 4

Actually, he'd be more amazed than scornful. His idea of fun was watching Ed Sullivan or snoozing in a recliner, or ideally, both at once. Why work like a maniac on your day off? To keep your heart and lungs in shape. Of course. But I haven't noticed any vanity plates that say GD LNGS. The operative word here is vanity. 5

Standards of beauty in every era are things that advertise, usually falsely: "I'm rich and I don't have to work." How could you be a useful farmhand, or even an efficient clerk-typist, if you have long, painted fingernails? Four-inch high heels, like the bound feet of Chinese aristocrats, suggest you don't have to do *anything* efficiently, except maybe put up your tootsies on an ottoman and eat bonbons. (And I'll point out here that aristocratic *men* wore the first high heels.) In my grandmother's day, women of all classes lived in dread of getting a tan, since that betrayed a field worker's station in life. But now that the field hand's station is occupied by the office worker, a tan, I suppose, advertises that Florida and Maui are within your reach. Fat is another peculiar cultural flip-flop: in places where food is scarce, beauty is three inches of subcutaneous fat deep. But here and now, jobs are sedentary and calories are relatively cheap, while the luxury of time to work them off is very dear. It still gives me pause to see an ad for a weight-loss program that boldly enlists: "First ten pounds come off free!" But that is about the size of it, in the strange food-drenched land of ours. After those first ten, it gets expensive. 6

As a writer I could probably do my job fine with no deltoids at all, or biceps or triceps, so long as you left me those vermicelli-sized muscles that lift the fingers to the keyboard. (My vermicellis are *very* well defined.) So when I've writ my piece, off I should merrily go to build a body that says I don't really have a financial obligation to sit here in video-terminal bondage. 7

Well, yes. But to tell the truth, the leisure body and even the GD LNGS are not really what I was after when I signed up at Pecs-R-Us. What I craved, and long for still, is to be *strong*. I've never been strong. In childhood, team sports were my most reliable source of humiliation. I've been knocked breathless to the ground by softballs, basketballs, volleyballs, and once, during a wildly out-of-hand game of Red Rover, a sneaker. In every case I knew my teammates were counting on me for a volley or a double play or anyhow something more than clutching my stomach and rolling upon the grass. By the time I reached junior high I wasn't even the last one picked anymore. I'd slunk away long before they got to the bottom of the barrel. 8

Even now, the great mortification of my life is that visitors to my home sometimes screw the mustard and pickle jar lids back on so tightly *I can't get them open!* (The visitors probably think they are just closing them enough to keep the bugs out.) Sure, I can use a pipe wrench, but it's embarrassing. Once, my front gate stuck, and for several days I could only leave home by clambering furtively through the bougainvilleas and over the garden wall. When a young man knocked on my door to deliver flowers one sunny morning, I threw my arms around him. He thought that was pretty emotional, for florists' mums. He had no idea he'd just casually pushed open the Berlin Wall. 9

My inspiration down at the health club was a woman fire-fighter who could have knocked down my garden gate with a karate chop. I still dream about her triceps. But I've mostly gotten over my brief fit of muscle envy. Oh, I still make my ongoing, 10

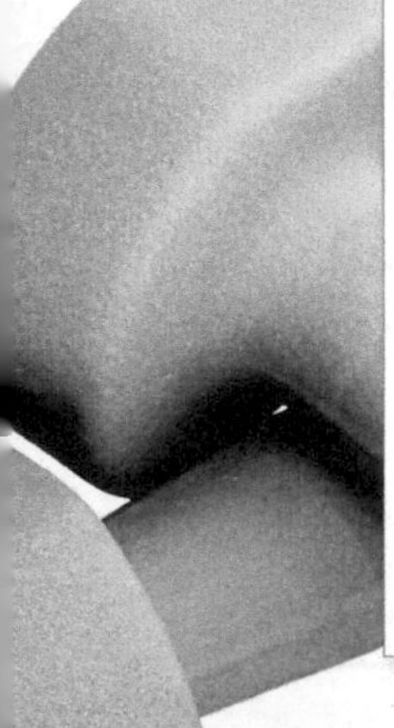

Brittny / Shutterstock.com

creative stabs at bodybuilding: I do "girl pushups," and some of the low-impact things from Jane Fonda's pregnant-lady workout book, even if I'm not. I love to run, because it always seems like there's a chance you might actually get somewhere, so I'll sometimes cover a familiar mile or so of our county road after I see my daughter onto the school bus. (The driver confessed that for weeks he thought I was chasing him; he never stopped.) And finally, my friends have given me an official item of exercise equipment that looks like a glob of blue putty, which you're supposed to squeeze a million times daily to improve your grip. That's my current program. The so-called noncompetitive atmosphere of the health club whipped me, hands down. Realistically, I've always known I was born to be a "before" picture. So I won't be seen driving around with plates that boast: PRSS 250.

Maybe: OPN JRS. 11

Reading for Better Writing

1. *Connections:* Review the opening few paragraphs and explain how the writer introduces her subject and sets the tone for the essay. Cite words and phrases that you find interesting, engaging, or funny. How do your own experiences with exercise and health relate to Kingsolver's?
2. *Comprehension:*
   a. Kingsolver entitles her essay, "The Muscle Mystique." What does "mystique" mean and in what sense are muscles or bodybuilding a "mystique"?
   b. In the third paragraph, Kingsolver describes the health club as a "lekking ground." What does "lekking" mean, and what does it suggest about the "muscle mystique"?
3. *Writing Strategies:*
   a. Define "self-deprecating humor" and cite examples in paragraphs 1–7. How does Kingsolver use such humor? Would these passages be as funny if Kingsolver were describing others' foibles rather than her own?
   b. Find two or three passages that you consider reflective writing and explain how they enrich the text.

Your Project: In paragraph 6, Kingsolver describes how the "standards of beauty" in her grandmother's generation are very different from the "standards of beauty" in Kingsolver's generation. Are there other standards that your parents or grandparents claim have substantively changed from their generations to yours? Consider exploring in your own essay how, why, and to what effect this change has occurred.

Seeking and Finding

Melissa Pritchard teaches creative writing at Arizona State University and is the author of eight books, including *Disappearing Ingenue, Late Bloomer,* and *The Odditorium.* In this essay, which is included in her book, *A Solemn Pleasure: To Imagine, Witness, and Write,* she tells a story about life, death, and love, all of which she experienced while "finding" her friend, Ashton.

Finding Ashton

When I was 9, I ran away. I was soon discovered a few blocks from home by a 1
supercilious, sneering neighbor boy nobody much liked named Eddie. He marched me back to my mother but not before the shock of that short freedom, the vastness of the world, and the mixed mercies of people caring about me had all made a deep impression.

Now I was running again, this time from my own life. On the fifth anniversary of 2
my father's death, my mother had suffered a stroke that left her paralyzed; she died ten months later, in April 2008. I flew to Hawaii that autumn and scattered handful after handful of my parents' mingled dust into the Pacific Ocean they had loved.

Death, I discovered, uncorks sentimentality. I made myself throw out the pair 3
of shoes my dad had been wearing the day he died (what was I going to do? bronze them? wear them?) though I kept a lock of my mother's dyed, champagne-colored hair. I had locks of my children's hair, too—two daughters now with homes of their own, lives of their own. I was a professor at a large university, a published novelist, a successful, self-sufficient woman. But waking up every morning to a large, empty house was a new, unexpected shriving. I felt as if my skeleton were gone, as if I had been filleted, deboned. I was standing, but barely. Wearing an exoskeleton of books, accomplishments, and titles, I fled to a children's poetry project in the brothels of Calcutta, then to an all-women's medical mission in Ecuador. After that, who knew? I was drawn to places of suffering that surpassed my own.

I didn't think about any of this rationally. This was not self-awareness. I was 4
simply an old, old child orphaned by death, a mother with unneeded mothering skills, an ex-wife with decades of memories, not all of them bad. A woman bereft, floundering, ashamed of her weakness, fearful for her future, beginning with the next five minutes.

It was January 2009, and I had managed to keep my next destination and 5
assignment, as an embedded journalist interviewing female soldiers, a secret from my daughters. With body armor purchased online, military-issue winter underwear,

notebooks, tape recorder, vitamins, stale PowerBars, and a nagging conscience, I arrived at Bagram Airfield, 47 kilometers north of Kabul, and sent a quick email from the media operations office, letting my children know I was now in Afghanistan, under the protection of the U.S. Air Force. I would, I promised, be safely home in two weeks.

Under leaden winter skies, nine air force and army soldiers, bulky with gear and weapons, waited on rain-darkened gravel near tan, mud-splashed Humvees to begin the drive north to their small forward operating base (FOB) in Panjshir Province. The youngest, Air Force Sr. Airman Ashton Goodman, 21, stood beside me in camouflage uniform with pistol, carbine, knife, heavy boots, and helmet, explaining that as a vehicles "op" (short for vehicle operator dispatcher), she maintained and drove Humvees, Land Cruisers, "whatever has wheels." She added that she couldn't wait to drive one of the newer Mine-Resistant Ambush-Protected all-terrain vehicles, a paleolithic-looking monster built to survive roadside bombs, improvised explosive devices (IEDs), and ambushes. A former supply truck driver on mine-infested roads in Iraq, Goodman was about two months into her new deployment in this relatively peaceful, "model" province. 6

Established in 2005 by combined American military, civilian, and NATO forces, the Panjshir Provincial Reconstruction Team (PRT), working closely with the Afghan people, was responsible for diverse humanitarian efforts, from medical clinics and vaccination programs to schools and engineering and agricultural projects. Although at the time its 70-member team was the smallest of the 26 PRT sites throughout Afghanistan, FOB Lion was considered a showcase. I was going there to write about the five female soldiers on that team. 7

My initial impression of the diminutive, blue-eyed, athletic Sr. Airman Goodman that bleak afternoon at Bagram was of a wholesome G.I. Jane action figure come to life. She'd missed her dream of becoming a fighter pilot, she later told me, by being one inch under the air force height requirement. 8

Vaulting lightly into the driver's seat of an armored Humvee, Goodman, as she liked to be called, secured her helmet and eye shield, adjusted her radio, and gave a wisecrack rallying cry, "All right, let's kick anus!" as we pulled out of Bagram, a three-vehicle convoy heading to FOB Lion, about 120 kilometers north, in the Hindu Kush mountains. Goodman's acronym-laced patter over the radio, her belting out of lines from Bon Jovi's "Never Say Die" ("I love that song," she says. "It pretty much defines my view of life: Never quit, death is just a part of life, and brotherhood and camaraderie are paramount") distracted me from morbid musings on the odds of our being blown up by an IED, a stark possibility made plain in an earlier briefing. When 9

I wasn't trying to see out of the grimy porthole window, I was admiring Goodman's expert handling of her armored Humvee. IEDs, buried beneath roads, and vehicle-borne IEDs, often suicide bombs, were the main cause of military casualties in Afghanistan, but Goodman's courage and calm skill gave an illusion of safety. My survival was in her young hands.

It seemed unlikely this soldier and I would find any personal connection. Mine 10
was a comfortable, private life of travel, writing, and teaching, hers a life of service in a war zone, little privacy or comfort, a stringent, daily regimen of monotony and risk. We were generations apart. Yet in the five days I spent with Goodman, I found that beneath her veneer of military protocol and discipline, beneath her bravado, kill-talk, and cussing, she was surprisingly vulnerable, coltish. She was also ravenous for adventure. As we drove from one PRT mission to the next in this harsh, mountainous province, visiting medical clinics, a fledgling radio station, a girls' school, an international aid drop, I learned she was earning a degree in biology, planned to be a veterinarian, was an amateur photographer and an aspiring author, writing "little stories," she said, to relieve stress. She had just started Rosetta Stone Spanish lessons and confessed to missing bubble baths. She had a tattoo on her left forearm, *Studium Nunquam Intereo*—"spirit never dies."

Wondering how much of Goodman's tough-girl act was a coping mechanism, I 11
asked about the difficulties of being a young woman and a wartime soldier. "Balancing my femininity within a male-dominated military has actually posed a problem," she told me. "I always feel that I have to prove myself. It's like I have two personas: my butch military side and my dorky, girlie side—it's a constant struggle."

I had no doubt Goodman would prove fearless in battle, and it was humbling to 12
know she would give her life to protect mine, a stranger's. Yet civilian life presented its own battles; it was from these, as well as her own self-doubt, that I wanted to protect her.

On my second day in Panjshir, headed back to FOB Lion after visiting a remote 13
medical clinic in the district of Shutol, our two-vehicle convoy of military women and mujahideen guards was caught in a sudden blizzard. Navigating the dirt road, a slick, hairpin descent, with heavy snow falling and sticking faster than the windshield wipers could clear the glass, Goodman, jaw clenched, half-humming, half-singing a children's song, managed to keep the Land Cruiser from sliding off the road and plunging into a rocky ravine. Concerned about the less-experienced driver behind her ("He's got a wife and new baby at home"), she signaled that she was stopping, braked, then jumped out to help three elderly Afghan men standing beside a rust-

eaten sedan, its grille nosed tight into an ochre cleft of the mountainside. Within minutes, Goodman freed the car. Politely thanking her, the men got back into their ancient vehicle and proceeded down the sinuous road, with Goodman, still humming, following behind.

On another day, we stopped for lunch at the only restaurant in Panjshir, a pale green, threadbare café on the riverside, serving typical Afghan fare—kebabs, pilau, and a kind of nan I had never seen—the pieces huge and snowshoe shaped. Goodman grinned as she tore into hers—"I love this stuff," she said. At the end of our meal, the rest of us handed over all of our extra nan, which she happily wrapped in her hijab, the traditional Muslim headscarf the five U.S. military women wore as a sign of cultural respect whenever they left the base. Each of the women had a collection of colorful scarves bought in local markets; during my visit, I was given a fringed, amber-colored hijab, which I still have. 14

Outside the restaurant, Goodman leapfrogged across rocks into the middle of the broad, taupe-colored Panjshir River to pose, mugging and clowning, for pictures. Driving back to the base, she hooted with delight whenever we passed a scatter of scruffy red hens pecking listlessly along the roadside or huddled in a dirt yard. Crazy about birds, especially chickens, she also lavished an almost impish affection on shunned creatures like slugs, frogs, and mice. She unabashedly mothered dogs, birds, babies of all kinds, anything innocent and sweetly alive, and it wasn't hard to imagine what a wonderful mother she would be. When I asked about her boyfriend, she said his name was David, David Flint, and that he was in the army, fighting in Afghanistan. Like her, he was from Indianapolis, and she couldn't wait to get back home to "raise a whole bunch of chickens," since David liked them, too. She didn't want to say much more, reluctant, perhaps, to jinx her future happiness. 15

On the fourth day, after hiking down a snowy mountain trail to another tiny medical clinic, we sat, five military women, a translator, and I, on floor cushions in an unheated mud-and-straw room, drinking tea with two doctors and a midwife in a black burka, discussing how many babies had been born since the PRT's last visit. Afterward, as we trudged single-file back up to our vehicles, Goodman launched into a snowball fight. Everyone joined in, sniping snowballs at one another, until Goodman, cheeks burning pink, fell backward laughing, scissoring her arms and legs, making an angel, uneven and solitary against the flat expanse of snow. 16

Even when serious and quiet, Goodman blazed with uncommon energy. On the day before I left Panjshir to return to Bagram, she met me in the base's chilly community room, the last of the interviews for my magazine story. Minus weapons, 17

with her golden brown hair pulled back into a shiny, clubbed ponytail, she looked startlingly young, precociously mature, self-effacing yet eager for the novelty of being interviewed. As she answered questions about her decision to join the military and admitted her hope of being a published writer one day, I watched her surface toughness drop away, saw that she was no different from my own daughters, from the young women who were my university students. Like them, she was eager to create a life that mattered. In that paneled room with its faux-leather black furniture, with an artificial Christmas tree, shorn of ornaments, keeping shadowy watch in one corner, a shy, sudden affection bloomed between us.

Later that night, after dinner, she sat close beside me in the chow hall, examining photographs on my digital camera, images from recent trips to India, Scotland, Italy, France, and England. As she asked about the people and places in the pictures, she confessed her desire to travel the world, to see it all—and the frank hunger and hope on her thoughtful, unmarked face moved me. 18

"Ashton, you're so young. You have lots of time." 19

Handing the camera back to me, she said, "I want to go to Africa." 20

After I returned home, we kept in touch. When I asked to read some of her work, she emailed two of her "humble writings," signing off with an embarrassed "Eek, Ashton." Emotional honesty was the hardest thing to teach writing students; her stories were bold, unflinchingly truthful. "You have an absolute gift," I wrote back. "I'm excited to read your books," she answered. 21

It was April now, springtime, and Ashton emailed photographs—an Afghan mother holding her newborn daughter, a puppy the soldiers had adopted, a pale, downy cluster of baby chicks, and panoramic views of the richly green, lush Panjshir Valley. In our interview, she had talked about her time in Iraq as a driver for line haul convoys, routing supplies on IED-infested roads. "One of our guys was killed by a mine, and I was the first to know," she told me. "I wasn't supposed to tell anyone, so I was just walking around with this knowledge. After people were informed, I became one of the comforters. Afterward, it was really bad. We'd have to drive every day on the same road where it had happened, see the bomb hole, the trail of his blood. I went through a period of being really shaken up, stressed-out, shaking, scared. Then I knew it was about fate, God, coincidence. When it was my time, it was my time. After that I wasn't scared." The most surprising thing about the mission in Panjshir, she went on, was how peaceful it was. She didn't have to be as guarded or as afraid of the people: "It's unlikely any of them has a bomb strapped to his chest." 22

Assigned by her PRT commander to serve on women's affairs, Ashton had begun 23 attending weekly meetings, or *shuras*, with local Afghan women. She told me that she was impressed by their intelligence and tenacity. “It infuriates me that women here are treated as second-class citizens. I’d like to see a woman with her own shop, a woman doctor. It will take generations, though. They need infrastructure, schools, clean water, and clean places to slaughter animals rather than by the side of the road. I’d really like to come back here in 20 years and show my kids how we helped.”

Early in May, she invited me to be a friend on Facebook, a form of communication 24
I was new to, ambivalent about, but willing to try. She added me to her personal email list along with her parents, her little brother, Levi, and her boyfriend, David. We all got to read and congratulate her on her first publication, “Panjshir PRT Medics Improve Medical Sanitation,” an article on the U.S. Air Force Web site.

In a private email, she described a brief trip home. “I did go on leave in March. It 25
was a relief to get away, even though I love it here. The tension and stress were starting to get to me, and I was cranky and irritable. When I got back, I was my normal self again. The hardest part about being home was getting used to the complete freedom. I could wear what I wanted, shower without flip-flops, wear my hair down. I cried a lot, too. Home is a place for me to heal. It felt good to get it all out and have my mom hold me while I did. I’m still a momma’s girl and always will be. Love, Ashton.”

It was May 29, and I had worked all day on my article. I’d spent most of the 26
afternoon revising, trying to capture Ashton’s seemingly contradictory passion for Disney movies (her favorites were *The Little Mermaid* and *The Lion King*) and her tastes in music—techno, heavy metal, JPop (Japanese pop), and especially European power metal. “The lyrics are awesome because they always talk about being proud warriors like they’re freaking ancient Celts fighting for the motherlands . . .”

Tired but still thinking about Ashton—had I gotten her right?—I went into 27
my kitchen, began to scroll idly through Facebook, skimming the bright chatter of friends, before stopping cold at what had to be a callous joke, a notice posted by the Flanner and Buchanan Funeral Centers: *Sr. Airman Ashton Lynn Marie Goodman, 21, of Indpls., died May 26, 2009, while serving in Afghanistan. She was born June 14, 1987 at Beale Air Force Base, CA. Ashton was in the U.S. Air Force 43rd Airlift Wing serving as a driver for Panjshir (Afghanistan) Provincial Reconstruction Team. She was a . . .* Abruptly, the notice stopped. Beside it was an official air force photograph, stamp-sized, of a barely recognizable Ashton, in dark blue dress uniform and peaked cap, looking like some nostalgic 1940s, studio-lit version of herself. Numb with shock, I clicked over to her page to prove it was a joke, a mistake, but found only grieving messages from family, friends, her boyfriend, David. Crying now, frantically clicking

Steve Collender / Shutterstock.com

for details, facts, calling a military friend in Afghanistan, calling local friends, still fastened to the Internet, I located the Department of Defense casualty list and found the official air force announcement saying that she had died near Bagram Airfield of wounds sustained from an improvised explosive device.

I returned to her Facebook page, staring blindly at accumulating condolences. There were details of the funeral. The burial. Donations could be made to the World Wildlife Fund. Her father wrote that he had flown to Dover Air Force Base and "brought his pumpkin home." I responded with a short, stumbling sympathy note. I read every anguished message from David, fighting somewhere in Afghanistan, unable to attend Ashton's ceremony at Bagram Airfield, where her body was formally loaded onto a transport plane home. 28

The moon is lonesome without you, but I look at it each night as it rises and see you staring back at me. I hope you are at peace. I miss you baby. Always fighting strong for your dreams, my little hummingbird. —David 29

My mother had always loved birds, especially hummingbirds. She had promised to send me a sign, once she had passed, that her spirit was still alive; hours after her death, a hummingbird hovered at my window, looking in at me for an unmistakably long time. I called to my sister to come see this tiny, iridescent creature shimmering in midair, gazing at us through the glass, its wings beating up to 80 times per second, backward and forward, in the symbol for infinity. The hummingbird returned the next day and again on the third morning as I sat in the garden praying to my mother for help, for comfort—it came, jeweled messenger, shaking the air inches from my face before darting away. I never saw it again. 30

Ashton was killed less than three weeks before her 22nd birthday. The birthday package David sent to Panjshir was returned, unopened. One of the first things he will do once he returns home to Indiana is find the tall pine tree Ashton lies buried beneath and share with his little hummingbird the gift he had chosen to delight her. 31

Sometimes we run away to be reclaimed, to be reassured that if we are not wholly understood, at least we are loved. When I came home, my daughters let it be known how worried they had been, shocked and even hurt that their mother would go somewhere, anywhere, without asking or even telling them. I had left home like an impetuous child, wanting to be found. Instead I had found Ashton and was opened to love beyond my familiar, given circle. 32

There are three photographs of Ashton I keep returning to. The first, taken days before her death, shows her sitting in a circle with Afghan women, wearing her favorite blue hijab, rain-like sparkles along the hem, her face turned to the camera, smiling serenely, as if telling the world she is glad to be fighting for justice with words now, not 33 weapons. She looks like she does in most of her pictures—a bit indifferent to, or unsure of, her own prettiness. And it may have been the lighting, but in this photo, one of her last, she looks calm, radiant, ethereal.

Hardest to look at is the newswire image I had come across online: Ashton's remains in a flag-draped transfer case being lowered from a transport plane at Dover Air Force Base. 34

Finally, there is the photograph she chose for her Facebook home page: Ashton, balanced lightly on the edge of a cliff overlooking Panjshir Valley, arms raised high, lifted in a triumphant "Yes!" to life. Beneath the photo, this caption: 35

Don't forget to send me some love!!!! My address is Sr. Airman Ashton Goodman PRT Panjshir, APO AE 09354 I love getting cards and stuff in the mail. :):):):):) 36

Reading for **Better Writing**

1. *Connections:* In her opening paragraph, Melissa Pritchard describes how she ran away as a child, and then as an adult. Consider a time when you (or someone close to you) ran away. How does that experience compare with Pritchard's experiences in terms of motivation to run, cost of running, and lessons learned?
2. *Comprehension:*
   a. In paragraph 3, while describing how she coped with her parents' deaths, Pritchard writes, "Death, I discovered, uncorks sentimentality." What does she mean by the statement, and how does it relate to her subsequent sentences that describe how she disposes of her parents' possessions?
   b. Compare and contrast Pritchard and Ashton, including their ages, personalities, goals, concerns, and careers. How are the characters similar and different? What do you understand about each woman at the end of the essay?
   c. Explain what Pritchard means in paragraph 32 where she writes, "I had left home like an impetuous child, wanting to be found. Instead I had found Ashton and was opened to love beyond my familiar, given circle."
3. *Writing Strategies:* Review paragraphs 9 and 13, noting the details used to describe Ashton. How do these details help you understand her? What other techniques does Pritchard use to describe Ashton? Find two additional passages using these techniques and explain their effect.

Your Project: This narrative is about two different people who inadvertently meet, share a challenging trek, and through the process, learn much about each other, themselves, and life itself. For your own writing, consider treks, pilgrimages, and travels that you or someone close to you has experienced.

Writing Guidelines

Planning

1. **Select a topic.** The most promising topics are experiences that gave you insights into yourself, and possibly into others as well. To identify such topics, consider the categories below and then list whatever experiences come to mind:
   - Times when you felt *secure, hopeful, distraught, appreciated, confident, frightened, exploited,* or *misunderstood.*
   - Times when you made a decision about *lifestyles, careers, education,* or *religion.*
   - Events that tested your *will, patience, self-concept,* or *goals.*
   - Events that changed or confirmed your assessment of *a person, a group,* or *an institution.*

   Tip: List topics in response to the following statement: *Reflect on times when you first discovered that the world was strange, wonderful, complex, frightening, small, full, or empty.* How did these experiences affect you?

2. **Get the big picture.** Once you have chosen a topic, gather your thoughts by brainstorming or freewriting in response to questions like these:
   - Where did the experience take place and what specific sights, sounds, and smells distinguish the place?
   - Who else was involved, and what did they look like, act like, do, and say?
   - What were the key or pivotal points in your experiences and why?
   - What led to these key moments and what resulted from them?
   - How did your or others' comments or actions affect what happened?
   - What did others learn from this experience—and what did you learn?
   - Did the experience end as you had hoped? Why or why not?
   - What themes, conflicts, and insights arose from the experience?
   - How do your feelings now differ from your feelings then? Why?

   Tip: To find out more details about the event or people involved, sort through photo albums and home videos to trigger memories; talk to someone who shared your experiences; consult your journal, old letters, and saved digital communications, such as email.

3. **Probe the topic and reveal what you find.** The mind-searching aspect of writing this essay happens while asking so-why questions: *So why does this picture still make me smile?* or *Why does his comment still hurt?* or *Why did I do that when I knew better*—or *Did I know better?* Your readers need to experience what you experienced, so don't hide what's embarrassing, or painful, or still unclear.

4. **Get organized.** Review your brainstorming or freewriting, and highlight key details, quotations, or episodes. Then list the main events in chronological order, or use a cluster to help you gather details related to your experiences.

Drafting

5. **Write the first draft.** Rough out the first draft. Then test your narration and description by asking whether the quotations, details, and events are accurate and clear. Test your reflection by asking whether it explains how the experience affected you.

Revising

6. **Review the draft.** After taking a break, read your essay for truthfulness and completeness. Does it include needed details and questions?
7. **Get feedback.** Ask a classmate to read your paper and respond to it.
8. **Improve the ideas, organization, and voice.** Use your own review and peer review to address these issues:

____ **Ideas:** The essay offers readers an engaging, informative look into your life, personality, and perspective.

____ **Organization:** The essay includes (1) an inviting opening that pictures the setting, introduces the characters, and forecasts the themes; (2) a rich middle that develops a clear series of events, nuanced characters, and descriptions; and (3) a satisfying closing that completes the experience and unifies the essay's ideas.

____ **Voice:** The tone is fair, and it fits the experience. The voice is genuine and inviting.

Editing

9. **Edit and proofread your essay.** Polish your writing by addressing these items:

____ **Words:** The words in descriptive and narrative passages *show* instead of *tell about;* they are precise and rich, helping readers imagine the setting, envision the characters, and vicariously experience the action. The words in reflective passages are insightful and measured.

____ **Sentences:** The sentences in descriptive and reflective passages are clear, varied in structure, and smooth. The sentences in dialogue accurately reflect the characters' personalities, regional diction, and current idioms.

____ **Correctness:** The copy includes no errors in spelling, mechanics, punctuation, or grammar.

____ **Page Design:** The design is attractive and follows assigned guidelines.

Publishing

10. **Publish your writing** by sharing your essay with friends and family, posting it on a Web site, or submitting it to a journal or newspaper.

MindTap® Request help and feedback from a tutor. If required, participate in peer review, submit your paper for a grade, and view instructor comments online.

Critical Thinking and Writing: Applications

Once you have finished your narrative essay, there may be more to think about. Consider how to apply what you have learned in the situations below.

1. **Living Today:** Anecdotes, as explained on page 149, are brief stories used in academic writing to enliven the prose while introducing a topic or illustrating a point. But anecdotes are also commonly used in workplace writing, such as sales letters (to verify a product's quality), campaign brochures (to illustrate a politician's character), or proposals (to support the value of what is proposed). Study a document with an anecdote and analyze how it does (or does not) advance the document's goal.
2. **Public Texts:** Public and private organizations use narratives to tell their "stories" or enhance their reputations. For example, a hospital may advertise its obstetrics ward by broadcasting on TV mothers and fathers, who are holding their newly born babies, tell how the birthing process and care of the babies was enhanced by the hospital's exemplary doctors, nurses, and facilities. Critique one or more of these mini-dramas by assessing whether the settings seem "staged," the dialogue sounds authentic, and the characters are believable.
3. **Major Work:** Consider your major and your future career. What is the focus of this field of study and this profession? Where and how do people in this profession use anecdotes or longer narratives? Why will doing it well matter? Research these questions to get the answers you need.

Learning-Objectives Checklist ✓

Have you achieved this chapter's learning objectives? Check your progress with the items below, revisiting topics in the chapter as needed. I have . . .

____ successfully identified, critiqued, and created these elements of narrative writing: setting, character, plot, dialogue, and theme (144–145).

____ developed engaging, vivid, and well-organized descriptive writing that includes precise words and sensory appeals (145–146).

____ integrated into my personal writing appropriate analytical strategies such as interesting comparisons and contrasts (146).

____ written reflective passages that include honest, relevant, and fitting observations (147).

____ successfully analyzed my writing situation in order to determine when, why, and how to use anecdotes (149).

____ blended techniques of narration, description, and reflection to craft a personal essay that enables readers to share my experience and to understand its broad significance (170–171).

____ developed a well-organized personal essay with an engaging opening, a rich and substantive middle, and a complementary closing (170–171).

MindTap® Practice skills that you have learned in this chapter and receive automatic feedback. Reflect on your writing process.

Chapter 11

Definition

MindTap®

Understand the goals of the chapter and complete a warm-up activity online.

By working through this chapter, you will be able to

- investigate how writers' situations inform their definition writing.
- critically examine and critique both brief and extended definitions.
- research all elements of a word's meaning.
- compose well-researched and well-reasoned brief and extended definitions.
- produce enriching anecdotes, quotations, comparisons, and contrasts, along with smooth transitions.

Most forms of academic and workplace writing—from essays and reports to proposals and literature reviews—include brief (one- or two-sentence) definitions of terms, sometimes called formal definitions. Although this chapter will help you read and write those, its main purpose is to help you understand and write longer, essay-length pieces sometimes called extended definitions.

Such definitions clarify and deepen readers' understanding of a term—whether it refers to something concrete or abstract. When reading such essays, consider how the writers "extend" your understanding of their topics, often using examples, illustrations, comparisons, and anecdotes to do so.

Visually Speaking Figure 11.1 pictures a woman studying a tableau of figures. Can you read the message that the figures convey? Try to define one or more figures. What does the image suggest about how people use language?

kravka / Shutterstock.com

fig. 11.1

Strategies for Definition Essays

Definition clarifies meaning through an equation: **term x = explanation y.** The writer must show that explanation *y* on the right amounts to the same thing as the term (or referent) *x* on the left. Depending on a writer's situation (purpose, readers, and topic), she or he might develop a succinct one-sentence formal definition or a six-page extended definition.

The Rhetorical Situation

To put definition writing in context, consider the situation that gives rise to it:

- **Purpose:** Writers compose definitions for many reasons—to define a misunderstood term, to plumb the meaning of a complex concept, or to entertain readers. Their writing purpose—and readers—affect what form the writing takes. For example, a writer explaining to high school students the classical concept of *catharsis* might begin by offering a one-sentence, formal definition of the term, *tragic hero*.
- **Readers:** People who read definitions also do so for different reasons, which affect the type of definitions they seek. For example, one reader may find a term unclear but want only a brief definition. Another reader may find a term very confusing and want a lengthy analysis of it, including its etymology. A third reader may understand what the term means but want to learn how a writer might expand its meaning.
- **Topic:** For any definition, the topic is a term. But what terms do writers typically focus on, and how does the term itself affect the form and style of the definition? That again depends on the writer's purpose and readers. For example, David Schelhaas writes extended definitions for a radio audience. He chooses words that will interest his listeners, and he defines the terms in a playful, narrative style (page 182). In contrast, Shon Bogar writes a lengthy academic essay analyzing the economic roots of a number of serious social abuses. To help readers understand his argument, he first defines one of those abuses, human trafficking (pages 176–177).

Principles of Definition Writing

Definition writing depends on the principles explained on this page and the next.

Examining a term's denotative (or literal) meaning, connotative (or suggested) meaning, and etymology (or historical meaning). By studying one or more of these, writers gain a foundational understanding of their topics and commonly find poignant details that lead to fresh insights. For an example, see Schelhaas's essay on page 182.

Writing precise definitions. As Chase Viss demonstrates in his essay, "Defining *Mathematics*" (pages 178–181), a definition that is sufficiently precise for high school students may be imprecise or incorrect for college students.

Seeking accurate, authoritative sources. For information on how to evaluate the credibility of a source, see pages 384–387.

Using anecdotes, examples, illustrations and comparisons. Writers use strategies such as these to engage readers and help them imagine a situation, visualize details, and discern subtle connotations. For example, in her essay "On *Excellence*" (187–189), Cynthia Ozick defines *excellence* in part by sharing numerous, entertaining anecdotes that illustrate how her mother is similar to or different from other members of their family.

Inserting transitions that lead into and out of definitions. When composing a definition within a longer piece of writing, writers typically insert a transition that introduces the definition and explains why it is relevant or needed. After the definition, writers then insert another transition that leads readers back into the discussion that follows. For example, look at how Bogar's opening sentence in the sample paragraph introduces the term that he is defining and explains why the definition is needed.

Avoiding logical fallacies. Definitions are weakened by logical fallacies such as oversimplification (323), half-truths (325), ambiguity (326), and slanted language (326). Writers need to edit their definitions to correct any poor reasoning.

Sample Definition Paragraph

In his essay analyzing the economic roots of various social and sexual abuses, Shon Bogar writes a two-paragraph definition of the term, *human trafficking* (pages 176–177). In his first paragraph that follows, he states why the definition is needed, and he then defines the term by comparing and contrasting it with two related terms.

Human trafficking, in particular, is a term that is difficult to define properly, but it must first be clarified if the problem itself is to be addressed. To begin, migration, human smuggling, and human trafficking are distinct but related phenomena, and incorrect definitions would put different groups of people in the wrong category, with potentially dire consequences. For example, the Trafficking Victims Prevention Act (TVPA), which came into law in 2000, requires the U.S. government to ensure that victims of trafficking are not jailed or "otherwise penalized solely for unlawful acts as a direct result of being trafficked" (U.S. Department of State, 2004), whereas illegal immigrants are still subject to deportation and criminal proceedings. The U.S. State Department recognizes the potentially "confusing" difference between smuggling and human trafficking, so it defines human smuggling as "the procurement or transport for profit of a person for illegal entry in a country" (2004). However, even if the smuggling involves "dangerous or degrading conditions," the act is still considered smuggling, not human trafficking, and so smuggling is considered an immigration matter, not necessarily a human rights issue (2004).

Reading Definition Writing

As you read definition essays, consider these questions:

1. What claims are made about the term's denotative and connotative meanings?
2. Is the definition current, relevant, complete, and clear?
3. Does the definition accurately explain the term's past and current usage?
4. Do clear transitions link the definition to the writing that precedes and follows it?

Sample Definition Essays

This chapter includes four sample extended definitions. As you read each piece, consider how the writer's purpose, readers, and topic might have affected how she or he shaped the essay's content, voice, organization, and style.

MindTap®
Read, highlight, and take notes online.

Defining Key Terms Within an Essay

This excerpt comes from a research paper by student writer Shon Bogar. The paper focuses on the problems of human trafficking and slavery as phenomena associated with current trends in globalization. After reviewing global economic trends since the end of the Cold War, Bogar defines the key terms that readers must understand if they are to comprehend the problem. The ellipses at the beginning and ending of this excerpt indicate that the original essay extends beyond what is shown here.

Economic Disparities Fuel Human Trafficking

. . . . These great economic disparities, from extreme poverty to fabulous wealth, have helped fuel the international trade in human cargo, as those people with nothing seek a better life serving those with excess. 1

The buying, selling, and forced exploitation of people—slavery—is not a new phenomenon. Most nations and most cultures have, at one time or another, enslaved others and been themselves enslaved in turn. The pattern continues today; in fact, slavery exists far beyond the developing world and reaches into the comfortable First World of the United States, Europe, Japan, and Australia. However, examining current trends in the trade of human cargo shows that trafficking and slavery are extremely difficult to define and understand, and that they coexist with and are codependent upon each other. These problems, moreover, have a variety of complex causes and too few solutions that offer a realistic possibility of ending this global abomination. 2

Human trafficking, in particular, is a term that is difficult to define properly, but it must first be clarified if the problem itself is to be addressed. To begin, migration, human smuggling, and human trafficking are distinct but related phenomena, and incorrect definitions would put different groups of people in the wrong category, with potentially dire consequences. For example, the Trafficking Victims Prevention Act (TVPA), which came into law in 2000, requires the U.S. government to ensure that victims of trafficking are not jailed or "otherwise penalized solely for unlawful acts as a direct result of being trafficked" (U.S. Department of State, 2004), whereas illegal immigrants are still subject to deportation and criminal proceedings. The U.S. State Department recognizes the potentially "confusing" difference between smuggling and human trafficking, so it defines human smuggling as "the procurement or transport for profit of a person for illegal entry in a country" (2004). However, even if the smuggling involves "dangerous or degrading conditions," the act is still considered smuggling, not human trafficking, and so smuggling is considered an immigration 3 matter, not necessarily a human rights issue (2004).

What distinguishes trafficking from smuggling is the element of exploitation, 4
including but not limited to "fraud, force, or coercion" (U.S. Department of State, 2004). With this distinction in mind, the United Nations Convention Against Transnational Organized Crime has developed this standard definition of human trafficking: "the recruitment, transportation, transfer, harbouring or receipt of persons, by means of the threat or use of force or other forms of coercion, of abduction, of fraud, of deception, of the abuse of power, or of a position of vulnerability or of the giving or receiving of payments or benefits to achieve the consent of a person having control over another person, for the purpose of exploitation" (U.N. Resolution 25, 2001). To unravel the U.N. legalese, human trafficking involves any use of force, coercion, fraud, or deception by those with power so as to exploit people, primarily by moving them into some form of slavery. Under this definition, smuggling can become trafficking if the smugglers have used any means of deception. Unfortunately, the requirement that the smuggler/trafficker be aware of the "victim's final circumstances" makes distinguishing between smuggling and trafficking an inexact science (U.S. Department of State, 2004), and it creates a new set of problems in combating trafficking apart from smuggling. Nevertheless, this definition of human trafficking is a helpful starting point from which the United Nations and governments around the globe can start to fight the trafficking and eventual enslavement of people.

All difficulties of definition aside, human trafficking and slavery are real problems— 5
historical problems that have taken new shapes due to globalization. In fact, today human trafficking is linked to millions of people experiencing multiple forms of slavery, from traditional "chattel slavery" to sexual slavery to debt bondage. . . .

Reading for Better Writing

1. *Connections:* Bogar asserts that human trafficking is a cruel and common practice. Have you been affected by this practice in some way—in your experiences, in your family's history, or in your reading or viewing?
2. *Comprehension:*
   a. Without looking back at Bogar's definition, define "human trafficking" in a sentence or two.
   b. What is his thesis, and how do each of the three main paragraphs advance that claim?
3. *Writing Strategies:* Note the sources that he uses to develop his definitions. Why are these sources appropriate for the terms? What other sources might be useful?

Your Project: Review several papers that you have written and select one with an undefined (or poorly defined) term. Then write a definition that precisely defines the term, and insert smooth transitions leading into and out of it.

Defining an Academic Discipline

In his essay, "The Philosophy of Mathematics," student writer Chase Viss wrote the following definition of *mathematics*. Note how he organizes the passage by first analyzing a common definition that he finds inadequate and then developing his own, more scholarly definition.

Defining *Mathematics*

Throughout elementary, middle, and high school, most students experience mathematics solely through classes that involve the manipulation of numbers, variables that represent numbers, figures that can be represented by numbers, and functions, which act on numbers to produce more numbers. Given this experience, these students might define *mathematics* as the study of numbers and their applications—a definition that would suit their needs. However, students enrolled in college-level mathematics courses soon learn that mathematics has a much more general foundation. For example, classes like Discrete Structures and Abstract Algebra address systems such as Sentential Logic, Set Theory, and Group Theory—systems that often intersect the world of numbers. However, numbers are by no means necessary for their study. Set Theory, for instance, involves sets of numbers such as the Rationals and the Reals, but the foundation of Set Theory is a set of axioms and definitions about objects, sets, and operations that do not emphasize numbers at all. Should this deviation exclude basic Set Theory from mathematics? Similarly, the study of Group Theory often involves numbers, but its axioms certainly do not require that members of a group actually be numbers. Clearly, if these abstract systems are to be included in the study of mathematics, then the prerequisite of numbers must be removed from its definition. 1

So, if not numbers, then what do all mathematical systems have in common? After studying various mathematical topics, students will begin to see that every area of mathematics has its own foundation of axioms—general assumptions used to derive necessary conclusions using accepted rules of logic and calculation. Sometimes, these axioms and rules are clearly laid out like those in Euclid's Elements, in which each assumed definition, common notion, and postulate is stated and then used in logical proofs to determine more complex, necessary propositions. In other systems, starting axioms, definitions, and deduction rules are less obvious. For 2 example, the Ancient Mesopotamians did not explicitly write out the foundational assumptions of their mathematical system, but does this imply that none were present? The Babylonians must have shared a set of assumptions such as the definition of numbers and operations, accepted algorithms for arithmetic, and rules for solving equations and calculating the area/volume of figures. These general principles can be inferred from the particular examples given in their scrolls. Without these universal assumptions, the practice of Babylonian mathematics would have varied from scribe to scribe. The consistency of their system required that while teaching mathematics, the instructor must have shared with the student, whether explicitly or implicitly, the basic assumptions/axioms and rules for calculation from which their entire system was derived. In this same way, all mathematical systems must have a starting set of axioms and accepted methods for deducing new propositions.

"[A]ll mathematical systems must have a starting set of axioms and accepted methods for deducing new propositions."

If this is true, should mathematics be defined as the practice of deduction from a set of axioms using accepted forms of logic? While this is a characteristic of any mathematical system, the study and practice of mathematics generally requires more than just deducing propositions. In order for students to deduce anything, they must first have an idea about the concept they are trying to prove. But how can they already have knowledge about a proposition if they have not yet derived it through deduction? Additionally, the starting axioms of any mathematical system are, by nature, assumed and therefore impossible to achieve through deduction. Where do they come from and why are they chosen? Typically, foundational axioms, along with all necessary definitions, are chosen through mathematical intuition, the theorizing of general principles based on the observation of particular instances. For example, after combining two sets of objects, one might observe that if an object belonged to either of the first two sets, then it will belong to the resulting combined set. Based on this physical phenomenon, the definition of set union, one of the foundational operations of set theory, is formed. This example may seem incredibly obvious, but it demonstrates that axioms and definitions are chosen because they seem "true" in real life. Discovering mathematical propositions that are not starting axioms is usually more difficult. Archimedes discovered many of his propositions through "The Method," or by investigating mathematical relationships mechanically before attempting to formally deduce them. Nevertheless, it is clear that before deduction can be done in any mathematical system, intuition must provide the starting points for the system and propositions for which it is designed to prove.

Finally, if mathematics is the study of certain deductive systems, something in its definition must differentiate mathematics from other axiomatically presented sciences such as physics. The distinguishing characteristic of mathematics is that it emphasizes the properties, relationships, and interactions of abstract concepts, such as quantity, magnitude, functions, sets, or geometric figures. Some of these concepts, like quantity, seem like fairly concrete ideas, but the study of mathematics does not involve physical instances of quantities as much as it explores the concept of quantity abstracted away from any physical representation. Similarly, the study of shapes in geometry does not usually involve actual, concrete figures but rather the idealized shapes abstracted away from these figures. Of course, just because mathematics involves primarily the abstract does not mean it cannot be applied to physical situations. Because its concepts are derived from physical phenomena and their properties/relationships are formed by intuition, mathematics can be used to make accurate predictions about the natural world and, therefore, can be applied in countless practical situations. 4

"The distinguishing characteristic of mathematics is that it emphasizes the properties, relationships, and interactions of abstract concepts, . . ."

When studying and describing these mathematical concepts, teachers and students generally represent them and their relationships using symbols or words. However, notation is only a secondary characteristic of any mathematical system as symbolism for certain concepts can vary from culture to culture. Mathematics, therefore, is not a study of symbols, but the abstract concepts the symbols represent. 5

Once students have explored areas of mathematics outside the traditional, calculus-based curriculum of middle and high school, they will be prepared to give mathematics a much more appropriate definition than just the study of numbers. One reasonable definition would be the study of any formal deductive system, formed and guided by intuition, involving the properties, relationships, and interactions of abstract concepts. This definition includes all areas of advanced mathematics instead of just restricting it to numerical studies. Also, this definition allows for a greater appreciation of mathematics. Reducing mathematics to numbers can easily cause students to value it exclusively due to its practical applications. However, with a broader definition in mind, students at all levels will see that another significant reason to study mathematics is that it expands and sharpens both their deductive and their intuitive capabilities—tools that will prove valuable in every possible field of study. 6

Reading for Better Writing

1. *Connections:* Chase Viss wrote this definition in order to more clearly understand the nature and function of mathematics, his academic major. How might writing an extended definition of your major help you more clearly grasp what you are studying?
2. *Comprehension:* In his opening paragraph, Chase presents a common definition of *mathematics* and then points out this definition's weaknesses. Explain why he finds it weak, and how his own definition corrects these weaknesses.
3. *Writing Strategies:*
   a. How does analyzing the weak definition help Chase articulate a stronger definition? Cite details that support your answer.
   b. Describe how Chase uses questions in paragraphs 2 and 3 to develop his definition.
   c. Explain how the opening sentence in paragraph 4 functions as a transition and as a topic sentence.

Your Project: Reflect on your answer to question 1, and consider writing a detailed extended definition of your major. You could begin by listing questions that you or others have asked about it. You could also look in your college's—and in other colleges'—catalogues and Web sites to see how they define and illustrate the major. Then assess how these sources help answer your questions, or raise additional questions.

Distinguishing Related Terms

Professor David Schelhaas delivered the following definition on his weekly radio program, *What's the Good Word?*

Deft or Daft

The other day, my wife, watching our son-in-law with his large hands gracefully tie the shoelaces of his little daughter, remarked, "You really are deft." Ever the cynic, I remarked, "He's not only deft, he's daft." I talk that sort of nonsense frequently, but as I said this, I began to wonder. What if *deft* and *daft* come from the same root and once meant the same thing? A quick trip to the dictionary showed that, indeed, they did once mean the same thing (though my wife thought me daft when I first suggested it). 1

Let me see if I can explain the original meaning and also how *daft* and *deft* came to part company. *Daft* originally meant mild or gentle. The Middle English *dafte* comes from the Old English *gadaefte*, which has as its underlying sense fit or suitable. Quite likely, mild or gentle people were seen as behaving in a way that was fit and suitable. 2

Gradually, however, the mild, gentle meaning descended in connotation to mean crazy or foolish. First, animals were described as daft—that is, without reason—and eventually people also. The word *silly*, which once meant happy or blessed, slid down the same slope. So that explains where *daft* got its present meaning. 3

But how does *deft*, meaning skillful or dexterous, fit into the picture? Again, if we start with the Old English meaning of *fit* or *suitable*, we can see a connection to *skillful*. In fact, the root of *gadaefte*, which is *dhabh*, to fit, carries with it the sense of a joiner or an artisan, someone who skillfully made the ends or corners of a cupboard or piece of furniture fit neatly together. From *fit* to *skillful* to *dexterous*. Thus we see how one root word meaning *fit* or *suitable* went in two different directions—one meaning crazy, the other meaning skillful. 4

These days it is usually considered much better to be deft than to be daft. But don't be too sure. It is good to remind ourselves that one person's deftness might very well appear as daftness to another. 5

This is David Schelhaas asking, "What's the Good Word?" 6

Reading for Better Writing

1. *Connections:* What similar terms (like *deft* or *daft*) have you—or someone you know—misused? Who was present, and how did they respond?
2. *Comprehension:* In your own words, describe the evolution of *deft* and *daft*.
3. *Writing Strategies:*
   - **a.** Review Schelhaas's opening and closing. Are they effective?
   - **b.** Describe his tone. Is it effective for a radio show and an informal essay? Explain.

Illustrating a Term

Amy Tan is an award-winning writer whose many books include *The Joy Luck Club, The Kitchen God's Wife, The Bonesetter's Daughter,* and *The Valley of Amazement*. When asked to respond to the writing prompt "confession," she relayed the following personal experience that concludes with an urgent confession.

Confession

1 *"My mother had a very difficult childhood, having seen her own mother kill herself. So she didn't always know how to be the nurturing mother that we all expect we should have."* —Amy Tan

2 My mother has Alzheimer's disease. Often her thoughts reach back like the winter tide, exposing the wreckage of a former shore. Often she's mired in 1968, the year my older brother and father died. This was also the year that she took me and my younger brother across an ocean to Switzerland, a place so preposterously different that she knew she had to give up grieving simply to survive. That year, she remembers, she was very, very sad. I too remember. I was sixteen then, and I recall a late-night hour when my mother and I were arguing in a chalet, that tinder box of emotions where we lived.

3 She had pushed me into the small bedroom we shared, and as she slapped me about the head, I backed into a corner, to a room that looked out upon the lake, the Alps, the beautiful outside world. My mother was furious because I had a boyfriend. She said he was a drug addict, a bad man who would use me for sex and throw me away like leftover garbage. "Stop seeing him!" she ordered. I shook my head. The more she beat me, the more implacable I became, and this in turn fueled her outrage. "You didn't love your daddy or Peter! When they die you not even sad." I kept my face to the window, unmoved. What does she know about sad? She sobbed and beat her chest. "I'd rather kill myself first than see you destroy your life!" Suicide. How many times had she threatened that before? "I wish you the one die! Not Peter, not Daddy." She had just confirmed what I had always suspected. Now she flew at me with her fists. "I rather kill you! I rather see you die!" And then perhaps horrified by what she had just said, she fled the room.

4 Thank God that was over. Suddenly she was back. She slammed shut the door, latched it, then locked it with a key. I saw the flash of a meat cleaver just before she pushed me to the wall and brought the blade's edge to within an inch from my throat. Her eyes were like a wild animal's, shiny, fixated on the kill. In an excited voice she said she was going to kill me first, then my younger brother, then herself, the whole

family destroyed. She smiled, her chest heaving, as she asked me, "Why don't you cry?" She pressed the blade closer and I could feel her breath gusting on my face as she ranted, hoarse and incoherent. Was she bluffing? I wasn't afraid. If she did kill me, so what? Who would care? While she rambled, a voice within me was whimpering. "This is sad, this so sad."

5 For ten minutes, fifteen, who knows how long, I perched between these two thoughts—that it didn't matter if I died, that it would be eternally sad if I did—until all at once I felt a snap, then a rush of hope into a vacuum, and I was crying, and then I confessed, "I want to live. Please let me live."

6 Since that day I've wondered if my mother really meant to kill me. I needed to know, yet I couldn't ask. Not until now. Now she remembers me differently. Now she recalls that I was a good girl, so good she never had to spank me, not once that she can recall.

Reading for Better Writing

1. *Connections:* Consider the word *confession*. What experiences come to mind? Choose one and think about who confessed, what was said, why, and how those who were present responded. As you reflect on the confession now, do you think it was warranted? Why?
2. *Comprehension:*
   a. Re-read Amy Tan's three opening sentences. What does each one tell you about Amy and her mother? Why might Amy have chosen to open with these details?
   b. Summarize what happens in paragraphs 2, 3, and 4. Then explain how these events drive Amy to make the confession, "I want to live. Please let me live."
   c. Why might Amy call this a confession rather than a plea? Precisely what is she confessing, and to what effect?
3. *Writing Strategies:* Amy writes this extended definition as a narrative with a setting, plot, and characters. What does this strategy enable her to communicate about a confession that she could not communicate in a dictionary-style definition?

Your Project: Review your answer to question 1, and then, without pausing, freewrite for twenty minutes on the experience that you cited. If what you produced looks promising, draft and refine your own essay that illustrates the term, *confession*.

Defining a Stage of Life

In response to the writing prompt, "Beginnings," Susan Sontag wrote the following essay in which she first explains why she finds the term—when applied to her career—uninteresting. However, she then explains why she finds the term—when applied to her writing process—both intimidating and elating. (This essay is from *Three Minutes or Less: Life Lessons from America's Greatest Writers.*)

Beginnings

I could tell you about my bereft childhood with parents as remote as fairy-tale royalty living as far away as one could imagine. My father dying in China. My mother after her return to America—I was then six—continuing to be more absent than not. I could tell you about my precocious ardent relation to the written word, which had me reading books by the age of four—writers begin as bewitched readers—and beginning to write at age seven. At eight, one of my mother's suitors, in an unsuccessful attempt to win my vote, gave me a typewriter, and by nine I began to self-publish. I discovered in a magazine an account of a printing process called hectographing, so primitive even I could master it. My paper, which came out weekly or bi-weekly in some two dozen copies and ran to at least four purple-inked pages, consisted exclusively of my stories, poems, playlets, and bloodthirsty tirades against Hitler, Mussolini, and Tojo. 1

I note that I began as a rather prolific writer and have been steadily devolving from the blessed state ever since. The childhood of a misfit, in large measure a voluntary misfit, in which other children seemed terrifying, school boring and depressive as well as terrifying, and being at home in bed with a book was not just the safest but the freest place to be. I had that familiar writer's childhood with all its bliss-ridden pathos. There was everything except the elementary schoolteacher or interesting older relative who befriended me, gave me books to read, encouraged my dreams of becoming a writer. I had no such mentor and I take pride in being a pioneer of my own self. 2

To speak thus, to evoke one's beginnings, implies of course that one has begun in obscurity, in provincial isolation, in anguish, in a delirious dream of emulation, that it is begun and one goes on. It is to be someone for whom beginnings are long past, to be recollected with rue, with complacency, with pride, with the distinctive fondness that one reserves for oneself. But I would rather speak of the fact that to be a writer, for me, is to be always at the beginning. I have never had what, it seems to me, most writers have—a sense of mastery. For unlike, say, the art of the surgeon, that of the writer 3 does not, through years of practicing it, become less difficult. It doesn't get easier. Surprisingly, it gets harder. There are no uplands of accomplishment. The permission given to the self to be expressive steadily, unremittingly as a vocation, feels as if it could be withdrawn at any time. Each time feels like a new beginning, one that has to triumph over a lengthening set of obstacles and inhibiting forms of self-awareness and ambition.

I could hardly be more American. American not only in that I understand myself 4
as self-created, American in that I respect nothing as much as self-transformation and that I feel myself perennially capable of a radical new beginning. Thus, my beginnings in the usual sense didn't interest me very much. What interests me is the beginning that I make quite unarmed, filled with anxiety and elation each day that I'm able to write, as if I were writing for the first time or, more precisely, as if I were at last writing something with which I am not too dissatisfied so that I can go on from this piece of writing to the next, to the real beginning.

Reading for Better Writing

1. *Connections:* What were your *beginnings* as a reader, writer, athlete, singer, student, best friend, or whatever? Were you just born good at your quest, or did you stumble at first, occasionally tumbling into knee-bruising, arm-breaking falls? Describe your beginnings at this feat.
2. *Comprehension:*
   a. Sontag describes what the word *beginnings* means to her, first as a writer learning her trade, and second as a writer starting a new piece of writing. Why does she find the first phenomenon uninteresting and the second one fascinating?
   b. Explain what Sontag means in her last sentence where she refers to her beginning a new piece of writing as "the real beginning."
3. *Writing Strategies:* Review Sontag's first paragraph, noting the grim details of her early childhood. How does she use these details to clarify what she labels in her last sentence as "the real beginning"?

Your Project: Review your answer to question 1, and then consider writing an extended definition about that beginning in your life. Include in your essay passages in which you reflect on why the experience is one that you remember, possibly value, and may find formative.

Defining a Personal Trait

Cynthia Ozick is an American writer known for her fiction, poetry, and essays on Jewish American life. In 2005, she was nominated for the Man Booker International Prize for lifetime achievement in literature.

On *Excellence*

In my Depression childhood, whenever I had a new dress, my cousin Sarah would get suspicious. The nicer the dress was, and especially the more expensive it looked, the more suspicious she would get. Finally she would lift the hem and check the seams. This was to see if the dress had been bought or if my mother had sewed it. Sarah could always tell. My mother's sewing had elegant outsides, but there was something catch-as-catch-can about the insides. Sarah's sewing, by contrast, was as impeccably finished inside as out; not one stray thread dangled. 1

My uncle Jake built meticulous grandfather clocks out of rosewood; he was a perfectionist and sent to England for the clockworks. My mother built serviceable radiator covers and a serviceable cabinet, with hinged doors, for the pantry. She built a pair of bookcases for the living room. Once, after I was grown and in a house of my own, she fixed the sewer pipe. She painted ceilings, and also landscapes; she reupholstered chairs. One summer she planted a whole yard of tall corn. She thought herself capable of doing anything, and did everything she imagined. But nothing was perfect. There was always some clear flaw, never visible head-on. You had to look underneath where the seams were. The corn thrived, though not in rows. The stalks elbowed one another like gossips in a dense little village. 2

"Miss Brrrroooobaker," my mother used to mock, rolling her Russian r's, whenever I crossed a *t* she had left uncrossed, or corrected a word she had misspelled, or became impatient with a *v* that had tangled itself up in a *w* in her speech. ("Vvventriloquist," I would say. "Vventriloquist," she would obediently repeat. And the next time it would come out "wiolinist.") Miss Brubaker was my high school English teacher, and my mother invoked her name as an emblem of raging finical obsession. "Miss Brrrroooobaker," my mother's voice hoots at me down the years, as I go on casting and recasting sentences in a tiny handwriting on monomaniacally uniform paper. The loops of my mother's handwriting—it was the Palmer Method—were as big as hoops, spilling generous splashy ebullience. She could pull off, at five minutes' notice, a satisfying dinner for ten concocted out of nothing more than originality and panache. But the napkin would be folded a little off-center, and the spoon might be on the wrong side of the knife. She was an optimist who ignored trifles; for her, God was not in the details but in the intent. And all these culinary and agricultural efflorescences were extracurricular, accomplished in the crevices and niches of a fourteen-hour business day. When she scribbled out her family memoirs, 3 in heaps of dog-eared notebooks or on the backs of old bills or on the margins of last year's calendar, I would resist typing them; in the speed of the chase she often omitted words like "the," "and," "will." The same flashing and bountiful hand fashioned and fired ceramic pots, and painted brilliant autumn views and vases of imaginary flowers and ferns, and decorated ordinary Woolworth platters with lavish enameled gardens. But bits of the painted petals would chip away.

Lavish: my mother was as lavish as nature. She woke early and saturated the 4
hours with work and inventiveness, and read late into the night. She was all profusion, abundance, fabrication. Angry at her children, she would run after us whirling the cord of the electric iron, like a lasso or a whip; but she never caught us. When, in the seventh grade, I was afraid of failing the Music Appreciation final exam because I could not tell the difference between "To a Wild Rose" and "Barcarolle," she got the idea of sending me to school with a gauze sling rigged up on my writing arm, and an explanatory note that was purest fiction. But the sling kept slipping off. My mother gave advice like mad—she boiled over with so much passion for the predicaments of strangers that they turned into permanent cronies. She told intimate stories about people I had never heard of.

Despite the gargantuan Palmer loops (or possibly because of them), I have always 5
known that my mother's was a life of—intricately abashing word!—excellence: insofar as excellence means ripe generosity. She burgeoned, she proliferated; she was endlessly leafy and flowering. She wore red hats and called herself a gypsy. In her girlhood she marched with the suffragettes and for Margaret Sanger and called herself a Red. She made me laugh, she was so varied: like a tree on which lemons, pomegranates, and prickly pears absurdly all hang together. She had the comedy of prodigality.

My own way is a thousand times more confined. I am a pinched perfectionist, 6
the ultimate fruition of Miss Brubaker; I attend to crabbed minutiae and am self-trammeled through taking pains. I am a kind of human snail, locked in and condemned by my own nature. The ancients believed that the moist track left by the snail as it crept was the snail's own essence, depleting its body little by little; the farther the snail toiled, the smaller it became, until it finally rubbed itself out. That is how perfectionists are. Say to us "Excellence," and we will show you how we use up our substance and wear ourselves away, while making scarcely any progress at all. The fact that I am an exacting perfectionist in a narrow strait only, and nowhere else, is hardly to the point, since nothing matters to me so much as a comely and muscular sentence. It is my narrow strait, this snail's road: the track of the sentence I am writing now; and when I have eked out the wet substance, ink or blood, that is its mark, I will begin the next sentence. Only in reading out sentences am I perfectionist; but then there is nothing else I know how to do, or take much interest in. I miter every pair of abutting sentences as scrupulously as Uncle Jake fitted one strip of rosewood against

another. My mother's worldly and bountiful hand has escaped me. The sentence I am writing is my cabin and my shell, compact, self-sufficient. It is the burnished horizon—a merciless planet where flawlessness is the single standard, where even the inmost seams, however hidden from a laxer eye, must meet perfection. Here "excellence" is not strewn casually from a tipped cornucopia, here disorder does not account for charm, here trifles rule like tyrants.

I measure my life in sentences, and my sentences are superior to my mother's, 7
pressed out, line by line, like the lustrous ooze on the underside of the snail, the snail's secret open seam, its wound, leaking attar. My mother was too mettlesome to feel the force of a comma. She scorned minutiae. She measured her life according to what poured from the horn of plenty, which was her ample, cascading, elastic, susceptible, inexact heart. My narrower heart rides between the tiny horns of the snail, dwindling as it goes.

And out of this thinnest thread, this ink-wet line of words, must rise a visionary 8
fog, a mist, a smoke, forging cities, histories, sorrows, quagmires, entanglements, lives of sinners, even the life of my furnace-hearted mother: so much wilderness, waywardness, plenitude on the head of the precise and impeccable snail, between the horns.

Reading for Better Writing

1. *Connections:* Choose a person (possibly yourself) who interests you. What one word captures her or his core identity? What five additional words list key related traits?
2. *Comprehension:* Ozick asserts that both she and her mother display excellence, depending on how the term is defined. Cite ways in which each woman achieves excellence.
3. *Writing Strategies:*
   a. What words and phrases does Ozick use to define *excellence*, and how does contrasting her mother's life with her own enable Cynthia to further define the term?
   b. To develop her definition, Ozick lists words with meanings similar to *excellence*. What other techniques does she use, or could she use?
   c. Find instances where Ozick lists one term or idea after another to refine her definition. How would her meaning change if she had used only one word?

Your Project: To discover a word similar to *excellence* for your own writing, select a place that you find frightening, mysterious, inspiring, incredibly dull, or otherwise unique. What word captures the core quality of this place? Consider using one or more of Ozick's writing strategies to draft an extended definition of the word.

Writing Guidelines

Planning

1. **Select a topic.** Beneath headings like these, list words that you'd like to explore:
    - Words related to an art or sport:
    - Words that are (or should be) in the news:
    - Words that are overused, unused, or abused:
    - Words that make you laugh or worry:
    - Words that do (or don't) describe you:

    Tip: The best topics are abstract nouns *(truth, individualism)*, complex terms *(code blue, dementia)*, or words connected to a personal experience *(excellence, deft, daft)*.

2. **Identify what you know.** To discern what you already know about the topic, write freely about the word, letting your writing go where it chooses. Explore both your personal and your academic connections with the word.

3. **Gather information.** To find information about the word's history, usage, and grammatical form, use strategies such as these:
    - **Consult a general dictionary**, preferably an unabridged dictionary; list both denotative (literal) and connotative (associated) meanings for the word.
    - **Consult specialized dictionaries** that define words from specific disciplines or occupations: music, literature, law, medicine, and so on.
    - If helpful, **interview experts** on your topic.
    - **Check reference books** such as *Bartlett's Familiar Quotations* to see how famous speakers and writers have used the word.
    - **Research the word's etymology and usage** by consulting appropriate Web sources such as dictionary.com and merriam-webster.com.
    - **Do a general search on the Web** to see where the word pops up in titles of songs, books, or films; company names, products, and ads; nonprofit organizations' names, campaigns, and programs; and topics in the news.
    - **List synonyms** (words meaning the same—or nearly the same) and antonyms (words meaning the opposite).

4. **Compress what you know.** Based on your freewriting and research, try writing a formal, one-sentence definition that satisfies the following equation:

    Equation: Term = larger class + distinguishing characteristics

    Examples: Swedish pimple = fishing lure + silver surface, tubular body, three hooks
    melodrama = stage play + flat characters, contrived plot, moralistic theme
    Alzheimer's = dementia + increasing loss of memory, hygiene, social skills

5. **Get organized.** To organize the information that you have, and to identify details that you may want to add, fill out a graphic organizer like the one on page 55.

Drafting

6. Draft the essay. Review your outline as needed to write the first draft.

- **Get the reader's attention and introduce the term.** If you are organizing the essay from general to specific, consider using an anecdote, an illustration, or a quotation to set the context. If you are organizing the essay from specific to general, consider including an interesting detail from the word's history or usage. When using a dictionary definition, avoid the dusty phrase "According to *Webster* . . . "
- **Show your readers precisely what the word means.** Build the definition in paragraphs that address distinct aspects of the word: common definitions, etymology, usage by professional writers, and so on. Link paragraphs so that the essay unfolds the word's meaning layer by layer.
- **Review your main point and close your essay.** (You might, for example, conclude by encouraging readers to use—or not use—the word.)

Revising

7. Improve the ideas, organization, and voice. Ask a classmate or someone from the college's writing center to read your essay for the following:

___ **Ideas:** Is each facet of the definition **clear**, showing precisely what the word does and does not mean? Is the definition **complete**, telling the reader all that she or he needs to know in order to understand and use the word?

___ **Organization:** Does the **opening** identify the word and set the context for what follows? Are the **middle** paragraphs cohesive, each offering a unit of information? Does the **closing** wrap up the message and refocus on the word's core meaning?

___ **Voice:** Is the voice informed, engaging, instructive, and courteous?

Editing

8. Edit the essay by addressing these issues:

___ **Words:** The words are precise and clear to the essay's readers.

___ **Sentences:** The sentences are complete, varied in structure, and readable.

___ **Correctness:** The copy includes no errors in spelling, usage, punctuation, grammar, or mechanics.

___ **Design:** The page design is correctly formatted and attractive.

Publishing

9. Publish the essay. Share your writing with interested readers, including friends, family, and classmates. Submit the essay to your instructor.

MindTap® Request help and feedback from a tutor. If required, participate in peer review, submit your paper for a grade, and view instructor comments online.

Critical Thinking and Writing: Applications

After you have finished your definition essay, consider how to apply what you have learned in the following situations.

1. **Technical Writing:** In the passage excerpted from "Economic Disparities Fuel Human Trafficking" (pages 176–177), Shon Bogar defines terms that readers must grasp in order to understand the rest of his essay. This strategy is commonly used by writers in academia, especially in the natural or applied sciences. Choose a scientific document (your own or someone else's) that includes a word or concept needing clarification. Define the topic and insert the definition into the text, along with transitions that smoothly lead the reader into and out of the definition.
2. **Living Today:** New devices often spawn new terms (e.g., reality TV, eBooks, digital natives, smart phones) that re-define more traditional terms. Choose such a term and explore what the traditional term meant, what the new term means, how it evolved, and how the new device has affected current practices.
3. **Writing Reset:** In her essay "On Excellence," Cynthia Ozick defines *excellence* by comparing and contrasting herself and her mother. Using one of your unique experiences or acquaintances, draft your own paragraph on *excellence.*
4. **Public Texts:** Good writing uses words, sentences, and organization that the intended readers can readily understand. To test this principle, select a term used in your discipline (e.g., *fraction, sonnet, filibuster, quorum, carpet bagger, photosynthesis, osmoses, muscle spasm).* Then using the Internet, textbooks, or library resources, find two definitions of the term: the first for high school students and the second for college students. Compare and contrast the definitions.

Learning-Objectives Checklist ✓

Have you achieved this chapter's learning objectives? Check your progress with the following items, revisiting topics in the chapter as needed. I have . . .

___ carefully examined the qualities of effective brief and extended definitions (174–175).

___ investigated how writers' consideration of their situations helps them focus and refine their definitions (174–175).

___ researched and analyzed a word's roots, prefix, suffix, denotations, connotations, etymology, and usage (190–191).

___ developed well-reasoned, research-based, brief and extended definitions (190–191).

___ critiqued others' writing and my own for logical fallacies such as oversimplification, half-truths, ambiguity, and slanted language (323–326).

___ utilized enriching anecdotes, quotations, comparisons, and contrasts, along with smooth transitions leading into and out of these passages (190–191).

___ evaluated the quality of my ideas, organization, and voice, revising and editing where needed (190–191).

MindTap® Practice skills that you have learned in this chapter and receive automatic feedback. Reflect on your writing process.

Chapter 12

Classification

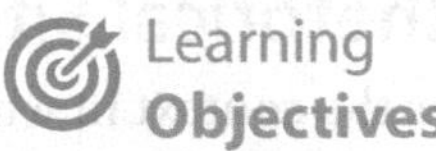

Understand the goals of the chapter and complete a warm-up activity online.

Classification is an organizational strategy that helps writers make sense of large or complex sets of things. A writer using this strategy breaks the topic into individual items or members that can be sorted into clearly distinguishable groups or categories. For example, if writing about the types of residents who live in assisted-care facilities, a nursing student might classify them according to various physical and/or mental limitations.

By sorting residents in this way, the writer can discuss them as individuals, as representatives of a group, or as members of the body as a whole. By using an additional strategy such as comparison-contrast, she or he can show both similarities and differences between individuals within a group, or between one group and another.

Visually Speaking To learn more about reading and writing classification essays, look at Figure 12.1 and consider what it suggests about the challenges and benefits of classifying things. How might using classification in writing be similar to warehousing products?

Learning Objectives

By working through this chapter, you will be able to

- interpret and critique writers' use of classification reasoning.
- devise a classification plan that aligns with your writing situation.
- create a logical grouping scheme that includes clear criteria for sorting.
- utilize a classification grid to identify your topic's components and to sort them into groups.
- compose an analytical essay using primarily classification reasoning (with other analytical strategies, as needed).

Baloncici / Shutterstock.com

fig. 12.1

Strategies for Classification Essays

In writing rooted in classification, you create logical categories into which people, places, things, or concepts can be grouped. Categorization makes sense of a body of information by showing how members of the group are both related and differentiated. Classification, then, can reveal something about the overarching structure of the whole, the nature of a particular category, or the distinctive features of one member of the group.

The Rhetorical Situation

Consider the context in which writers use classification reasoning:

- **Purpose:** Writers classify a body of information to explain its order, to clarify relationships, and to "locate" specific items within a larger structure. For example, in her essay, "Latin American Music . . ." (pages 196–199), Kathleen Marsh's purpose is to explain how the many types of Latin American music reflect Latinos' cultural identity and impact social change.
- **Readers:** While readership can vary greatly, writers using classification are seeking to illuminate the deeper order of a topic, either to enhance readers' understanding or to support an argument. For example, Marsh's criteria for classifying types of Latin American music help her readers (college students) understand the history and cultural impact of Latinos' diverse forms of music.
- **Topic:** Writers typically use classification with topics that include a complex body of individual items. For example, Marsh's topic is the nature and function of Latin American music—thousands of songs. To address the topic, she sorts the songs into four categories that clarify music's diverse roles in Latino culture.

Principles of Classification Writing

Classification writing depends on the principles that follow.

Establishing clear criteria for grouping. Given his or her purpose for classifying, the writer finds a basis or standard for categorizing items. This standard becomes the "common denominator" for the ordering scheme. For example, trees could be grouped as follows:

- **Size:** types of trees grouped by height categories
- **Geography:** trees common to different areas, zones, or elevations
- **Structure or composition:** division by leaf type (deciduous vs. coniferous)
- **Purpose:** windbreak trees, shade trees, flowering trees, fruit trees, etc.

Creating a logical and orderly classification scheme. These guidelines apply:

- As they sort items into groups, writers seek . . .
    - **consistency**—applying the same sorting criterion in the same way.
    - **exclusivity**—creating groups that are distinct and do not overlap.
    - **completeness**—fitting all elements from a larger group into the subgroups with no elements left over.

- To keep the classification structure manageable, writers usually limit the number of main categories to six.
- Subcategories distinguish the elements that comprise a category. To further distinguish elements within the whole, subcategories can be broken into smaller groups. See Figure 12.2.
- When explaining the classification scheme, writers present the categories and subcategories in a logical order, selecting a sequence that will help readers digest the overall scheme and see connections and differences between categories.
- Sometimes, writers complement their discussion with graphics (tables, charts, diagrams) that help readers understand the overall scheme and individual categories.

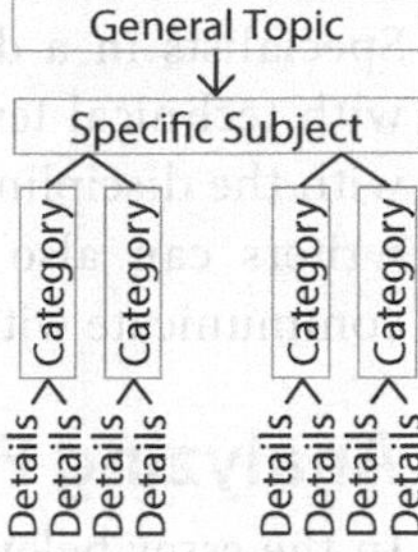

fig. 12.2

- When classifying ideas or theoretical practices, writers might illustrate each. For example, in his classification essay on pages 283–285, John Van Rys identifies four approaches to literary criticism. He then illustrates each one by describing how a critic using it might critique the poem, "My Last Duchess."

Sample Classification Paragraph

The following paragraph is from the essay cited above. Note how Van Rys first describes the fourth approach to literary criticism, and then gives an example of each subgroup in it.

> The fourth approach to criticism applies ideas outside of literature to literary works. Because literature mirrors life, argue these critics, disciplines that explore human life can help us understand literature. Some critics, for example, apply psychological theories to literary works by exploring dreams, symbolic meanings, and motivation. Myth or archetype criticism uses insights from psychology, cultural anthropology, and classical studies to explore a text's universal appeal. Moral criticism, rooted in religious studies and ethics, explores the moral dilemmas literary works raise. Marxist, feminist, and minority criticism are, broadly speaking, sociological approaches to interpretation. While the Marxist examines the themes of class struggle, economic power, and social justice in texts, the feminist critic explores the just and unjust treatment of women as well as the effect of gender on language, reading, and the literary canon. The critic interested in race and ethnic identity explores similar issues, with the focus shifted to a specific cultural group.

Reading Classification Writing

As you read the essays on the following pages, consider these questions:

1. Does the writer explain the classification scheme, and is this reasoning logical, given his or her topic and purpose? Explain.
2. Are the number of categories sufficient, given the size and diversity of the topic?
3. Are the categories consistent, exclusive, and complete? Explain.
4. Are the categories presented in a clear, logical order?

Sample Classification Essays

Specialists in a discipline will commonly use classification—along with technical terminology—to analyze a topic for readers familiar with the discipline. However, as shown in the essays in this chapter, writers can also use classification and nontechnical language to communicate with readers.

MindTap® Read, highlight, and take notes online.

Analyzing Forms of Music

In the essay below, student writer Kathleen Marsh uses classification strategies to describe the nature of Latin American music and to explain how the music both reflects and affects Latin American culture.

Latin American Music: A Diverse and Unifying Force

On September 20, 2009, Latin pop, rock, and salsa rhythms danced through the air in Havana's Plaza de la Revolución as more than one million people gathered to witness Paz Sin Fronteras II (Peace Without Borders II). These benefit concerts brought together performers from Cuba, Puerto Rico, Ecuador, and Venezuela. Juanes, a popular Colombian singer who headlined the concerts, explained the event's passion and power like this: "Music becomes an excuse to send a message that we're all here together building peace, that we are here as citizens and this is what we want, and we have to be heard" (Hispanic 17). His statement demonstrates Latinos' belief that their music has the power to unify Latin American people, synthesize their cultural activities, and address their diverse needs. To understand how the music (which is as diverse as Latin America's people) can do this, it is helpful to sort the many forms of music into four major types and consider what each type contributes to Latin American society. *1*

One type is indigenous music, a group of musical forms that connect the human and the spiritual. Archeological evidence indicates that indigenous musical cultures of the Americas began over 30,000 years ago. Over time the first instruments, which were stone and clay sound-producing objects, evolved into wind instruments such as flutes and windpipes. An example of indigenous music connecting the human and spiritual is found among Aymara-speaking musicians in the Lake Titicaca Region of *2*

Peru. The people of this region use music to mesh pre-Columbian agricultural rites with current Catholic practices. For instance, during feasts such as the annual Fiesta de la Candelaria (Candlemas Feast), celebrants use Sicus (panpipes), pincullos (vertical duct flutes), cajas (drums), chants, dances, and costumes—in combination with Catholic symbolism—to celebrate the gift of staple crops such as corn and potatoes (Indigenous 328, 330).

A second type, Iberian and Mestizo (mixed) folk music, enrich Latinos' everyday lives in a variety of forms, including liturgical music, working songs, and mariachi tunes. For example, whereas the traditional Catholic mass featured organ music, more recent Catholic services such as the Nicaraguan Peasant Mass use the acoustic guitar along with the colorful sounds of the marimba, maracas, and melodies from popular festivals. As a result, worshipers find the music inviting and the passionate lyrics (which can cite issues of economic or political injustice) socially relevant. 3

> "Iberian and Mestizo (mixed) folk music, enrich Latinos' everyday lives in a variety of forms, including liturgical music, working songs, and mariachi tunes."

Another form of folk music known as tonadas (or tunes) are used as serenades and working songs. For example, in Venezuela, workers might whistle or sing tonadas while milking, plowing, or fishing (Tonadas). These vocal duets, which also can be accompanied by guitar, have pleasant harmonies, two main melodies, and faster tempos ("Iberian and mestizo folk music" 338, 341). 4

The mariachi band, a final form of folk music, adds festivity to Mexicans' many celebrations. With its six to eight violins, two trumpets, and a guitar, the band creates a vibrant, engaging sound. During birthdays or feast days, these bands commonly set up on streets and below windows where they awaken the residents above to the sounds of "Las Mañ Anitas," the traditional song for such days. Mariachis are also hired for baptisms, weddings, quinceañeras (the fifteenth birthday for a Mexican girl), patriotic holidays, and funerals (History of the Mariachi). 5

Afro-American music, the third type of Latin American music, infuses passion 6 and power in its percussion-driven dances and complex rhythm structures. These songs and dances, performed throughout the Caribbean, function as an entertaining, unifying force among Latin people ("Afro-American" 345-6). The energy of Afro-American music is clear in genres such as the mambo and the rumba dances. The rumba, an Afro-Caribbean dance, is highly improvisational and exciting. The quinto (a high-pitched drum) establishes a dialogue with a solo voice and challenges the male dancer, while the tumbadora and palitos (sticks on woodblock) provide a contrast with regular, unchanging rhythm patterns.

The mambo, an Afro-Cuban dance, became popular in Havana, Cuba. In the 7
1940s, nightclubs throughout Latin America caught the energy of this fast tempo song and dance. Arsenio Rodríguez' "Bruca Managuá" exemplifies this form. Because of the song's sound and lyrics, many black Cubans consider the piece to be an anthem of Afro-Cuban pride and resistance:

I am Calabrí, black by birth/nation, 8
Without freedom, I can't live, 9
Too much abuse, the body is going to die. 10
(Oxford Encyclopedia for Latinos and Latinas in the United States. 218) 11

Urban popular music, the fourth type of Latin American music, combines 12
a dynamic sound with poignant appeals for social change, appeals that resonate with many listeners. The styles of this type of music include rock, heavy metal, punk, hip-hop, jazz, reggae, and R&B. During the September 20, 2009 Paz Sin Fronteras II concerts described earlier, urban popular music was common fare. As U.S. representative Jim McGovern observed, the message of the concerts was to "circumvent politics . . . using the medium of music to speak directly to young people, to change their way of thinking, and leave behind the old politics, hatred, prejudices, and national enmities that have locked too many people in patterns of conflict, violence, poverty, and despair. It is an attempt to break down barriers and ask people to join in common purpose" (Paz Sin Fronteras II). Popular urban musicians such as Juanes utilize music not only to entertain but also to unite Latinos in a universal cause.

Passion and power permeate all of Latin America's music. The four major types of 13
music—indigenous, Iberian and Mestizo folk, Afro-American, and popular urban—

are as diverse as the people of Latin America, and each style serves a valued need or function in Latinos' everyday lives. As a result, those listening to Latin American music—whether it is a Peruvian Indian's chant, a Venezuelan farmer's whistled tune, a Cuban mambo drummer's vivacious beat, or the Bogotá rock concert's compelling rhythms—are hearing much more than music. They are hearing the passion and power of the Latin American people.

Note: The Works Cited page is not shown. For an example, see pages 500–501.

Reading for Better Writing

1. *Connections:* In her essay, Kathleen Marsh identifies four broad categories of Latin music, examining specific genres and songs within each group. How does Kathleen's essay speak to your own musical tastes? If you were to categorize what you listen to and/or why, what would be revealed?
2. *Comprehension:* Review the opening in which Marsh introduces her topic, thesis, and choice to sort the music into four categories. What is the main point of her classification scheme for Latin American music? Describe her categories and what is distinctive about each.
3. *Writing Strategies:*
   a. What strategies does Marsh use to distinguish the four types of music and the various forms within those groups? Are the strategies effective? Why?
   b. Identify words with which she describes the tone and tenor of the music. Is the word choice helpful? Why?
   c. Review the instructions at the bottom of page 194 regarding the three guidelines for creating a logical classification scheme: consistency, exclusivity, and completeness. Then analyze Marsh's classification scheme and explain why it does or does not exemplify the three guidelines.
   d. In the last sentence, she re-states and re-phrases her thesis. Is this sentence an effective closing?

Your Project: For your own writing, consider areas of culture similar to Latin American music. For example, you could categorize varieties of American music, or you could examine TV programs, video games, films, or fiction.

Analyzing Weight Lifters

In the following essay, student writer Hillary Gammons seeks to identify the diverse bunch of college students working out in the weight room. To clarify who they are and why they lift weights, she sorts them into four groups: health enthusiasts, toners, athletes, and body builders. As you read the essay, assess whether Hillary's classification plan helps her analyze her topic, address her college readers, and achieve her writing purpose.

Why We Lift

I had heard rumors about it before I ever left for college, and once I moved into the dorm, I realized it was not just a rumor. I needed a way to combat the "freshman fifteen," that dreaded poundage resulting from a combination of late-night pizzas, care-package cookies, and cafeteria cheesecakes. So, my roommate and I headed to the university gym, where the weight-training rooms are filled with student "chain gangs" sweating and clanging their way through a series of mechanical monsters. As I looked around, it became obvious that people work out for quite different reasons. Health enthusiasts, toning devotees, athletes, and bodybuilders seem to be the main categories of those lifting weights. 1

Some students lift weights as part of an exercise program aimed at maintaining or improving health. They have heard how strong abdominals reduce lower-back problems. They have learned that improved flexibility can help to reduce tension buildup and prevent headaches and other problems related to prolonged periods of sitting or studying. They know that combining weights with aerobic exercise is an efficient way to lose weight. A person who exercises can lose weight while continuing to eat well because increased muscle mass burns more calories. Typical weight-lifting routines for health enthusiasts are around 20 minutes, three times a week. 2

The toners' routine is different because they want smoothly defined muscles. Not surprisingly, this group includes many young women. Lifting weights can target problem spots and help shape up the body. To develop solid arms, these people use dumbbells and a bench press. Other equipment focuses on achieving toned legs, abdominals, and buttocks. Toning workouts must be done more often than three times a week. I talked to a few young women who lift weights (after aerobic activity of some kind) for about 30 minutes, five times a week. 3

Athletes also lift weights. Volleyball, rowing, basketball, football—all these sports require weight training. It may seem obvious that a football player needs to be muscular and strong, but how do other athletes benefit from weight lifting? Muscles are a lot like brains: the more they are used, the more they can do. Strong muscles can increase a person's speed, flexibility, endurance, and coordination. Consider the competition required in various sports—different muscle groups matter more 4 to different athletes. For example, while runners, especially sprinters, need bulging thighs for quick starts and speed, basketball players need powerful arms and shoulders for endless shots and passes. And while gymnasts want overall muscle strength for balance and coordination, football players develop large muscles for strength, speed, and agility. For all members of this group, however, weight lifting is a vital part of their training.

5 One last group that cannot be ignored are the people who lift weights to become as big and strong as possible. I worked out with a guy who is about 6 feet 2 inches and weighs more than 200 pounds. He bench-presses more than I weigh. In a room devoted to dumbbells and barbells (also known as free weights), bodybuilders roar, bulk-boosting battle cries as they struggle to lift super heavy bars. After you spend only a short time in this grunt room, it is clear that the goal for bodybuilders is not simply to be healthy, toned, or strong. These lifters want muscles for both strength and show—muscles that lift and bulge. For this reason, many participants spend little time on aerobic activity and most of their time lifting very heavy weights that build bulk and strength. My partner works out for an hour or more, five days a week.

6 Not everyone fits neatly into these four categories. I work out to be healthy and toned, and find that I can benefit from lifting only three times a week. Weight lifting has become more and more popular among college students who appreciate exercise as a great stress reliever. And for me, the gym proves to be the best place to combat the dreaded "freshman fifteen."

Reading for Better Writing

1. *Connections:* Describe your own experience of weight rooms and weightlifting. How does Hillary Gammon's explanation of why people lift weights help you understand something of your own relationship to weight training?
2. *Comprehension:* Gammons classifies weight lifters according to their reasons for lifting. What are the four categories, and what distinguishes each from others? What is the main point of her classification?
3. *Writing Strategies:*
   a. Gammons opens and closes her essay by describing her own interest in weight lifting. What are the strengths and weaknesses of this approach?
   b. Gammons sorts weight lifters into four groups; however, in the first sentence in paragraph 6, she notes, "Not everyone fits neatly into these four categories." Explain why this admission does or does not weaken her argument.

Your Project: Gammons classifies a group of people with whom she is familiar. For your own writing, consider groups of people whom you know or belong to, such as gamers, social activists, movie buffs, members of a religious institution, and so on.

"Why We Lift" by Hillary Gammons

Analyzing Rhetorical Positions on Climate Change

Stewart Brand, author of *Whole Earth Discipline: An Ecopragmatist Manifesto,* published this essay in December 2009. In the piece, he argues that the climate-change debate is better understood as advocating four main perspectives—not two.

Four Sides to Every Story

1 Climate talks have been going on in Copenhagen for a week now, and it appears to be a two-sided debate between alarmists and skeptics. But there are actually four different views of global warming. A taxonomy of the four:

2 **DENIALISTS** They are loud, sure and political. Their view is that climatologists and their fellow travelers are engaged in a vast conspiracy to panic the public into following an agenda that is political and pernicious. Senator James Inhofe of Oklahoma and the columnist George Will wave the banner for the hoax-callers.

3 "The claim that global warming is caused by man-made emissions is simply untrue and not based on sound science," Mr. Inhofe declared in a 2003 speech to the Senate about the Kyoto accord that remains emblematic of his position. "CO2 does not cause catastrophic disasters—actually it would be beneficial to our environment and our economy. . . . The motives for Kyoto are economic, not environmental—that is, proponents favor handicapping the American economy through carbon taxes and more regulations."

4 **SKEPTICS** This group is most interested in the limitations of climate science so far: they like to examine in detail the contradictions and shortcomings in climate data and models, and they are wary about any "consensus" in science. To the skeptics' discomfort, their arguments are frequently quoted by the denialists.

5 In this mode, Roger Pielke, a climate scientist at the University of Colorado, argues that the scenarios presented by the United Nations Intergovernmental Panel on Climate Change are overstated and underpredictive. Another prominent skeptic is the physicist Freeman Dyson, who wrote in 2007: "I am opposing the holy brotherhood of climate model experts and the crowd of deluded citizens who believe the numbers predicted by the computer models. . . . I have studied the climate models and I know what they can do. The models solve the equations of fluid dynamics, and they do a very good job of describing the fluid motions of the atmosphere and the oceans. They do a very poor job of describing the clouds, the dust, the chemistry and the biology of fields and farms and forests."

6 **WARNERS** These are the climatologists who see the trends in climate headed toward planetary disaster, and they blame human production of greenhouse gases as the primary culprit. Leaders in this category are the scientists James Hansen, Stephen Schneider and James Lovelock. (This is the group that most persuades me and whose views I promote.)

7 "If humanity wishes to preserve a planet similar to that on which civilization developed and to which life on earth is adapted," Mr. Hansen wrote as the lead author of an influential 2008 paper, then the concentration of carbon dioxide in the atmosphere would have to be reduced from 395 parts per million to "at most 350 p.p.m."

CALAMATISTS There are many environmentalists who believe that industrial 8
civilization has committed crimes against nature, and retribution is coming. They quote the warners in apocalyptic terms, and they view denialists as deeply evil. The technology critic Jeremy Rifkin speaks in this manner, and the writer-turned-activist Bill McKibben is a (fairly gentle) leader in this category.

In his 2006 introduction for *The End of Nature*, his famed 1989 book, Mr. 9
McKibben wrote of climate change in religious terms: "We are no longer able to think of ourselves as a species tossed about by larger forces—now we are those larger forces. Hurricanes and thunderstorms and tornadoes become not acts of God but acts of man. That was what I meant by the 'end of nature.'"

The calamatists and denialists are primarily political figures, with firm ideological 10
loyalties, whereas the warners and skeptics are primarily scientists, guided by ever-changing evidence. That distinction between ideology and science not only helps clarify the strengths and weaknesses of the four stances, it can also be used to predict how they might respond to future climate developments.

If climate change were to suddenly reverse itself (because of some yet 11
undiscovered mechanism of balance in our climate system), my guess is that the denialists would be triumphant, the skeptics would be skeptical this time of the apparent good news, the warners would be relieved, and the calamatists would seek out some other doom to proclaim.

If climate change keeps getting worse, then I would expect denialists to grasp 12
at stranger straws, many skeptics to become warners, the warners to start pushing geoengineering schemes like sulfur dust in the stratosphere, and the calamatists to push liberal political agendas—just as the denialists said they would.

Reading for Better Writing

1. *Connections:* Based upon Steward Brand's categories, how would you characterize your own thinking about climate change? Brand published this essay in 2009. Has the climate-change debate altered since then? How and why?
2. *Comprehension:* Identify Brand's thesis and describe each of the four categories that he outlines. How does his classification thinking help him develop the thesis?
3. *Writing Strategies:*
   a. Brand sorts the debaters into four groups. What strategies does he use to distinguish their viewpoints? Are these strategies effective? Why?
   b. Examine Brand's opening paragraph and closing paragraphs (11 and 12). How do these frame his classification of climate-change positions?

Your Project: Brand uses classification to expand the positions on a controversial issue. For your own writing, think of other difficult issues often reduced to two choices or positions (e.g., illegal immigration, unions, health insurance, free college tuition). Use classification to expand the possible positions.

Analyzing How Readers Read

Jessica Seigel is an award-winning journalist. In the essay below, she explains how readers should respond to nuanced literary devices such as symbols, themes, and allegories.

The Lion, the Witch and the Metaphor

THOUGH it's fashionable nowadays to come out of the closet, lately folks are piling in—into the wardrobe, that is, to battle over who owns Narnia: secular or Christian lovers of C. S. Lewis's stories. 1

Children, of course, have been slipping through the magic cupboard into the mythical land for 50 years without assistance from pundits or preachers (though fauns and talking badgers have been helpful). But now that the chronicles' first book, *The Lion, the Witch and the Wardrobe,* has been made into a Disney movie, adults are fighting to claim the action. And that means analyzing it. Or not. 2

The 7-year-old who sat next to me during a recent showing said, "This is really scary." It was scary when the White Witch kills the lion Aslan, who dies to save the loathsome Edmund before rising to help him and his siblings vanquish evil. But adults reducing the story to one note—their own—are even scarier. One side dismisses the hidden Jesus figure as silly or trivial, while the other insists the lion is Jesus in a story meant to proselytize. They're both wrong. 3

As a child, I never knew that Aslan was "Jesus." And that's a good thing. My mother recently remarked that if she'd known the stories were Christian, she wouldn't have given me the books—which are among my dearest childhood memories. 4

But parents today will not be innocent of the religious subtext, considering the drumbeat of news coverage and Disney's huge campaign to remind churchgoing audiences of the film's religious themes. The marketing is so intense that the religious Web site HollywoodJesus.com even worried that ham-fisted promotion might ruin it for non-Christians. 5

But a brief foray into Criticism 101 shows that the wardrobe is big enough for everyone. Symbolism, for example, is when one thing stands for another but is not the thing itself. Psychoanalysts, for instance, have interpreted "The Wonderful Wizard of Oz" as Dorothy's quest for a penis—that is, retrieving the witch's broomstick. Does that symbolism—if you buy it—make Dorothy a pervert? No, because it's hidden. That's the point. Overt and covert meaning can exist independently. 6

Those with a fiduciary, rather than phallic bent, might prefer the theory that L. Frank Baum's Oz stories are a Populist manifesto, with the yellow brick road as the gold standard, the Tin Man as alienated labor, Scarecrow as oppressed farmers, and so on. (And surely some Jungian theory about the collective unconscious explains why both Oz and Narnia are populated by four heroic characters fighting an evil witch.) 7

Yes, it's allegory land, a place that strings symbols together to create levels of meaning, which a determined scholar has actually quantified as ranging from two to seven layers. (No word on why not eight.) Allegory, the oldest narrative technique, often involves talking animals, from Aesop's fox with the grapes to Dr. Seuss's Yertle 8 the Turtle, supposedly a Hitler figure.

Does that twist the Seuss tale into a political treatise on fascism? No, it adds another level for adults, it teaches morals (even the meekest can unseat the powerful, etc.), and it's fun—when plain little Mack burps, he shakes the bad king Yertle from his throne built on turtles. 9

But which layer is more important—the surface or beneath? Deep thinkers specialize in hidden meanings (building demand, of course, for their interpretive expertise). An Oxford English professor, Lewis himself explored the depths in his scholarly books. But he also defended the literal, lamenting in his essay "On Stories" how modern criticism denigrates the pleasures of a good yarn—and that was 50 years ago. 10

While critics today call it "fallacy" to interpret a work by citing the author's intentions, Lewis left a road map for us marked with special instructions for not annoying children. In his essay "Sometimes Fairy Stories May Say Best What's to Be Said," he denounced as "moonshine" the idea that he wrote the Narnia chronicles to proselytize the young. The lion Aslan, he wrote, bounded into his imagination from his experience as a Christian, coming to him naturally as should all good writing. 11

"Let the pictures tell you their own moral," he advised in "On Three Ways of Writing for Children." "If they don't show you a moral, don't put one in." 12

In keeping with that advice, the Narnia chronicles don't beat you on the head—nor does the faithful movie adaptation. If everyone stays on his own level—the surface for adventurers, and the depths for believers—we can all enjoy, so long as the advertisers stay out of the way. 13

Reading for Better Writing

1. *Connections:* Have you read one of C.S. Lewis's *Narnia* chronicles, or a similar allegory? How old were you at the time? Did you understand that the story was an allegory, and how did that understanding (or lack of understanding) affect your reading experience?
2. *Comprehension:*
   a. Describe the two conflicting groups (or viewpoints) in this article.
   b. Summarize Seigel's argument and explain why you do or do not agree.
3. *Writing Strategies:* In the final paragraph, Seigel differentiates the two categories as "adventurers" and "believers." Are her subgroups consistent, exclusive, and complete? For example, could a reader be both an adventurer and a believer? How might a third (or fourth) category affect Seigel's argument?

Your Project: Would Seigel's categories of "adventurers" and "believers" apply to other narratives? For your own writing, consider classifying readers for books with which you are familiar, such as the Harry Potter series or *The Hunger Games*.

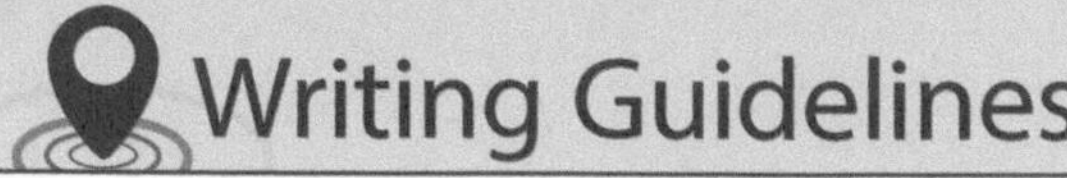

Writing Guidelines

Planning

1. **Select a topic.** Begin by reviewing the project options listed at the end of each sample essay. For more topic ideas, write a few general headings like the academic headings in Figure 12.3; then list two or three related topics under each heading. Finally, pick a topic that is characterized by a larger set of items or members that can best be explained by ordering them into categories.

Engineering	Biology	Social Work	Education
Machines	Whales	Child welfare	Learning styles
Bridges	Fruits	Organizations	Testing Methods

fig. 12.3

2. **Look at the big picture.** Do preliminary research to get an overview of your topic. Review your purpose (to explain, persuade, inform, and so on), and consider which classification criteria will help you divide the subject's content into distinct, understandable categories.
3. **Choose and test your criterion.** Choose a criterion for creating categories. Make sure it produces groups that are *consistent* (the same criterion are used throughout the sorting process), *exclusive* (groups are distinct—no member fits into more than one group), and *complete* (each member fits into a subgroup with no member left over).
4. **Gather and organize information.** Gather information from reliable sources. To organize your information, take notes, possibly using a classification grid like the one shown in Figure 12.4. Set up the grid by listing the classification criteria down the left column and listing the groups in the top row of the columns. Then fill in the grid with appropriate details. (The grid in Figure 12.4 lists the classification criterion and groups discussed in "Latin American Music . . . ," pages 196–199.)

Classification Criteria	Group #1	Group #2	Group #3	Group #4
	Indigenous music	Iberian and Mestizo	Afro-American music	Urban popular music
Historical qualities/functions	• Trait #1 • Trait #2 • Trait #3	• Trait #1 • Trait #2 • Trait #3	• Trait #1 • Trait #2 • Trait #3	• Trait #1 • Trait #2 • Trait #3

fig. 12.4

Note: If you do not use a grid, consider using an outline to organize your thoughts.

5. **Draft a thesis.** Draft a working thesis that states your topic and identifies your classification scheme. Include language introducing your criteria for classifying groups.

Drafting

6. Draft the essay. Write your first draft, using organization planned in step 4.

- **Opening:** Get the readers' attention, introduce the subject and thesis, and give your criteria for dividing the subject into categories.
- **Middle:** Develop the thesis by discussing each category, explaining its traits, and showing how it is distinct from the other groups. For example, in the middle section of "Four Ways to Talk About Literature," the writer first shows the unique focus of each of the four approaches to literary criticism, and then illustrates each approach by applying it to the same poem, "My Last Duchess" (see pages 283–285).
- **Closing:** Reflect on and tie together the classification scheme. While the opening and middle of the essay separate the subject into distinct categories, the closing may bring the groups back together. For example, Van Rys closes by identifying characteristics that the four subgroups have in common (see pages 284–285).

Revising

7. Improve the ideas, organization, and voice. Ask a classmate or someone from the writing center to read your essay, looking for the following:

___ **Ideas:** Are the classification criteria logical and clear, resulting in categories that are consistent, exclusive, and complete? Does the discussion include appropriate examples that clarify the nature and function of each group?

___ **Organization:** Does the essay include (1) an engaging opening that introduces the subject, thesis, and classification criteria, (2) a well-organized middle that distinguishes groups, shows why each group is unique, and supports these claims with evidence, and (3) a unifying closing that restates the main idea and its relevance?

___ **Voice:** Is the tone informed, courteous, and rational?

Editing

8. Edit the essay. Polish your writing by addressing these issues:

___ **Words:** The words distinguishing classifications are used uniformly.

___ **Sentences:** The sentences and paragraphs are complete, varied, and clear.

___ **Correctness:** No usage, grammatical, or mechanical errors are present.

___ **Page Design:** The design follows MLA, APA, CMS, or CSE formatting rules.

Publishing

9. Publish the essay by sharing it with your instructor and classmates, publishing it on a Web site, or submitting it to a print or online journal.

MindTap® Request help and feedback from a tutor. If required, participate in peer review, submit your paper for a grade, and view instructor comments online.

Critical Thinking and Writing: Applications

After you have finished your classification essay, consider how to apply what you have learned in the following situations.

1. **Living Today:** Unscrupulous news sites and blogs published on the Web often include articles based on an erroneous claim that a complex topic is "simply" a two-option issue. This type of claim, called either-or thinking, is a logical fallacy (see page 323). Choose a complex topic and research the Web to find such an either-or argument. Then find a piece that categorizes positions in a more nuanced way.
2. **Sports Talk:** Fully understanding a sport or game requires knowing how it is played, including the rules. Choose a sport or game that you enjoy, and create a classification scheme for different types of plays or moves. How does your scheme help you understand that sport or game?
3. **Social Situation:** Frequently, social sciences categorize people into generations. Here, for example, is a common scheme: (a) Generation Z/Boomlets, born after 2001; (b) Generation Y/Millennial, born between 1981 and 2000 (c) Generation X, born between 1965 and 1980, (d) Baby Boomers, born between 1946 and 1964, and (e) Mature/Silents, born between 1927 and 1945. Given your own experience, describe what characterizes each generation, consider what generation you belong to, and reflect on the strengths and limits of the generation concept.

Learning-Objectives Checklist ✓

Have you achieved this chapter's learning objectives? Check your progress with the following items, revisiting topics in the chapter as needed. I have . . .

____ critically read others' classification essays, assessing their organizational schemes for consistency, exclusivity, and completeness (194–195).

____ examined how these writers craft their analyses in accordance with their purposes, topics, and readers (194–195).

____ evaluated my own writing situation and developed a classification framework that helped me analyze my topic as required in my writing assignment (206–207).

____ devised a logical classification scheme that includes clear grouping criteria (206–207).

____ created and used a classification grid (1) to logically break down the topic into groups of components, (2) to explain why the groups are unified, complete, and distinct, and (3) to show how the groups together comprise one entity (206–207).

____ used additional analytical strategies such as definition and compare-contrast to clarify similarities and differences between groups (174–175 and 234–235).

____ drafted, revised, and edited an essay that effectively uses classification reasoning to analyze a topic and to present the analysis in clear, logical writing (206–207).

MindTap® Practice skills that you have learned in this chapter and receive automatic feedback. Reflect on your writing process.

Chapter 13

Process

MindTap®

Understand the goals of the chapter and complete a warm-up activity online.

Process writing helps us understand our world and ourselves by answering interesting questions like these: How does cancer spread? How do believers in Islam prepare a body for burial? How did Abraham Lincoln come to advocate the "Emancipation Proclamation"?

Writing that answers questions like these analyzes a process by breaking it down into steps, often grouping the steps into stages or phases. In addition to explaining the process, sometimes the writing also examines related causes and effects. Such papers are developed and formatted as essays, and the information in this chapter will help you read and write them.

However, writing that explains how readers can complete a process typically takes the form of technical instructions.

Visually Speaking Figure 13.1 captures a moment in a process. What is the process, and what writing strategies would you use to explain how to do the process?

Learning Objectives

By working through this chapter, you will be able to

- examine and assess writers' use of process reasoning.
- investigate a process so as to outline its nature and its workings.
- analyze the process, identifying its steps and related causes and effects.
- sequence the process chronologically, using transitions to link phases or steps.
- compose an analytical essay using primarily process thinking (with other analytical strategies, as needed).

Tyler Olson / Shutterstock.com

fig. 13.1

Strategies for Process Writing

Analyzing a process is an effort to explain how something happens, works, is made, or is done. The process may be natural (a phenomenon that occurs in nature, including human nature), performative (mechanical, something people do), or historical/cultural (events in time and/or within communities or groups).

The Rhetorical Situation

To put process writing in context, consider the situation that gives rise to it:

- **Purpose:** Writers write process essays in order to analyze and explain how an event or other phenomenon transpires. To that end, they first offer an overview of the process and then explain how each step leads logically to the next, and how all the steps together complete the process. (If the writer wants to help readers work through a process themselves, he or she writes instructions.)
- **Readers:** In all process writing, the text should meet the needs of all its readers, including those who know the least about the topic. To do this, writers should (1) include all the information that readers need, (2) use language that they understand, and (3) define unfamiliar or technical terms.
- **Topic:** In academic process writing, the topics are usually course-related phenomena that interest the writer and offer readers insight into the field of study. Topics addressed in professional publications should interest and educate their readers.

Example: In her essay "Wayward Cells" (pages 212–213), Kerry Mertz analyzes her **topic**: the process through which cancer cells overtake and destroy healthy cells. Her **purpose** is to help her **readers** (non-experts—college students and others without detailed technical knowledge) understand how and why the process occurs.

Principles of Process Writing

Analytical process writing should follow these principles:

Being clear and complete. Shape the analysis based on (1) how readers will use it, and (2) what they already know about it. Aim to deepen their current knowledge about how the process unfolds and what principles are at work.

Offering an overview. In order to understand individual parts of or moments in the process, readers generally need the big picture. Start, then, by explaining the process's essential principle, its goal, or its main product and/or result. That overview statement can often serve as the thesis statement. ***Example:*** *When a cell begins to function abnormally, it can initiate a process that results in cancer.*

Making the process manageable. A process essay unfolds effectively and clearly when the process is presented in manageable segments. First identify the process's major phases or stages (perhaps limiting these to three or four). Then break each stage into discrete steps or events, grouping actions in clear, logical ways.

Making the process familiar. To help readers understand the writing, use precise terms, well-chosen adjectives, and clear action verbs. Consider, as well, using comparisons for unfamiliar parts of the process, likening, for example, the growth of hair to the growth of grass. Finally, design graphics such as flowcharts, time lines, or sequential drawings that display the process. (See the sample flowchart in Figure 13.2.)

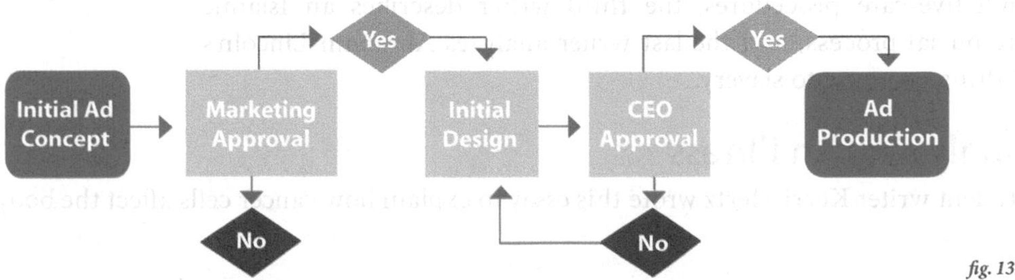

fig. 13.2

Signaling temporal relationships. Because process analysis is time related, readers need clear references to the order of events. Consider using terms such as *step, phase, stage;* transition words such as *first, second, next, finally;* or actual numbering systems (1, 2, 3).

Sample Process Paragraph

In his essay "The Emancipation of Abe Lincoln" (pages 226–229), Eric Foner identifies stages in the development of Lincoln's support for the "Emancipation Proclamation." In the following paragraph, Foner describes a series of events included in one of these stages:

> In the summer of 1862, a combination of events propelled Lincoln in a new direction. Slavery was disintegrating in parts of the South as thousands of slaves ran away to Union lines. With the war a stalemate, more Northerners found themselves agreeing with the abolitionists, who had insisted from the outset that slavery must become a target. Enthusiasm for enlistment was waning in the North. The Army had long refused to accept black volunteers, but the reservoir of black manpower could no longer be ignored. In response, Congress moved ahead of Lincoln, abolishing slavery in the District of Columbia, authorizing the president to enroll blacks in the Army and freeing the slaves of pro-Confederate owners in areas under military control. Lincoln signed all these measures that summer.

Reading Process Writing

As you read process essays, consider these questions:

1. Does the essay identify the process, outline its stages, explain individual steps, and (if appropriate) discuss causes and effects?
2. Does the writer effectively state and support his or her claims?
3. Does the writer use precise language and define unfamiliar terms?
4. Are steps organized chronologically and clearly linked with transitions?

Sample Process Essays

This chapter includes four essays illustrating how writers analyze processes to illuminate the central nature of the phenomena. The first writer explains how cancer develops, the second writer critiques palliative-care procedures, the third writer describes an Islamic pre-burial process, and the last writer analyzes Abraham Lincoln's shifting response to slavery.

MindTap®
Read, highlight, and take notes online.

Analyzing an Illness

Student writer Kerri Mertz wrote this essay to explain how cancer cells affect the body.

Wayward Cells

Imagine a room containing a large group of people all working hard toward the same goal. Each person knows his or her job, does it carefully, and cooperates with other group members. Together, they function smoothly—like a well-oiled machine. 1

Then something goes wrong. One guy suddenly drops his task, steps into another person's workstation, grabs the material that she's working with, and begins something very different—he uses the material to make little reproductions of himself, thousands of them. These look-alikes imitate him—grabbing material and making reproductions of themselves. Soon the bunch gets so big that they spill into other people's workstations, getting in their way, and interrupting their work. As the number of look-alikes grows, the work group's activity slows, stutters, and finally stops. 2

A human body is like this room, and the body's cells are like these workers. If the body is healthy, each cell has a necessary job and does it correctly. For example, right now red blood cells are running throughout your body carrying oxygen to each body part. Other cells are digesting that steak sandwich that you had for lunch, and others are patching up that cut on your left hand. Each cell knows what to do because its genetic code—or DNA—tells it what to do. When a cell begins to function abnormally, it can initiate a process that results in cancer. 3

The problem starts when one cell "forgets" what it should do. Scientists call this "undifferentiating"—meaning that the cell loses its identity within the body (Pierce 75). Just like the guy in the group who decided to do his own thing, the cell forgets its job. Why this happens is somewhat unclear. 4

The problem could be caused by a defect in the cell's DNA code or by something in the environment, such as cigarette smoke or asbestos (German 21). Causes from inside the body are called genetic, whereas causes from outside the body are called carcinogens, meaning "any substance that causes cancer" (Neufeldt and Sparks 90). In either case, an undifferentiated cell can disrupt the function of healthy cells in two ways: by not doing its job as specified in its DNA and by not reproducing at the rate noted in its DNA. 5

Most healthy cells reproduce rather quickly, but their reproduction rate is controlled. For example, your blood cells completely die off and replace themselves 6 within a matter of weeks, but existing cells make only as many new cells as the body needs. The DNA codes in healthy cells tell them how many new cells to produce. However, cancer cells don't have this control, so they reproduce quickly with no stopping point, a characteristic called "autonomy" (Braun 3). What's more, all their "offspring" have the same qualities as their messed-up parent, and the resulting overpopulation produces growths called tumors.

Tumor cells can hurt the body in a number of ways. First, a tumor can grow so big that it takes up space needed by other organs. Second, some cells may detach from the original tumor and spread throughout the body, creating new tumors elsewhere. This happens with lymphatic cancer—a cancer that's hard to control because it spreads so quickly. A third way that tumor cells can hurt the body is by doing work not called for in their DNA. For example, a gland cell's DNA code may tell the cell to produce a necessary hormone in the endocrine system. However, if cancer damages or distorts that code, sick cells may produce more of the hormone than the body can use—or even tolerate (Braun 4). Cancer cells seem to have minds of their own, and this is why cancer is such a serious disease. 7

Fortunately, there is hope. Scientific research is already helping doctors do amazing things for people suffering with cancer. One treatment that has been used for some time is chemotherapy, or the use of chemicals to kill off all fast-growing cells, including cancer cells. (Unfortunately, chemotherapy can't distinguish between healthy and unhealthy cells, so it may cause negative side effects such as damaging fast-growing hair follicles, resulting in hair loss.) Another common treatment is radiation, or the use of light rays to kill cancer cells. One of the newest and most promising treatments is gene therapy—an effort to identify and treat chromosomes that carry a "wrong code" in their DNA. A treatment like gene therapy is promising because it treats the cause of cancer, not just the effect. Year by year, research is helping doctors better understand what cancer is and how to treat it. 8

Much of life involves dealing with problems like wayward workers, broken machines, or dysfunctional organizations. Dealing with wayward cells is just another problem. While the problem is painful and deadly, there is hope. Medical specialists and other scientists are making progress, and some day they will help us win our battle against wayward cells. 9

Reading for Better Writing

1. *Connections:* Reflect on your experiences with cancer in your family or beyond. Then re-read Mertz's last two sentences. Do you share her optimism?
2. *Comprehension:* Explain how the essay both describes and analyzes the process.
3. *Writing Strategies:*
   a. What does the analogy in the opening and closing accomplish?
   b. How does the writer use transitions between steps?

Your Project: Consider researching and analyzing a health-related process that interests you.

Analyzing Medical Procedures

"No Risky Chances" is an essay excerpted from the book, *Being Mortal: Medicine and What Matters in the End.* In both texts, author and physician Dr. Atul Gawande critiques traditional procedures used by physicians to care for patients during their last stages of life. "Lacking a coherent view of how people might live successfully all the way to the very end," he says, "we have allowed our fates to be controlled by medicine, technology, and strangers."

No Risky Chances:
The Conversation That Matters Most

1 I learned about a lot of things in medical school, but mortality wasn't one of them. Although I was given a dry, leathery corpse to dissect in anatomy class in my first term, our textbooks contained almost nothing about aging or frailty or dying. The purpose of medical schooling was to teach how to save lives, not how to tend to their demise.

2 I had never seen anyone die before I became a doctor, and when I did, it came as a shock. I'd seen multiple family members—my wife, my parents, and my children—go through serious, life-threatening illnesses, but medicine had always pulled them through. I knew theoretically that my patients could die, of course, but every actual instance seemed like a violation, as if the rules I thought we were playing by were broken.

3 Dying and death confront every new doctor and nurse. The first times, some cry. Some shut down. Some hardly notice. When I saw my first deaths, I was too guarded to weep. But I had recurring nightmares in which I'd find my patients' corpses in my house—even in my bed.

4 I felt as if I'd failed. But death, of course, is not a failure. Death is normal. Death may be the enemy, but it is also the natural order of things. I knew these truths abstractly, but I didn't know them concretely—that they could be truths not just for everyone but also for this person right in front of me, for this person I was responsible for.

5 You don't have to spend much time with the elderly or those with terminal illness to see how often medicine fails the people it is supposed to help. The waning days of our lives are given over to treatments that addle our brains and sap our bodies for a sliver's chance of benefit. These days are spent in institutions—nursing homes and intensive-care units—where regimented, anonymous routines cut us off from all the things that matter to us in life.

6 As recently as 1945, most deaths occurred in the home. By the 1980s, just 17 percent did. Lacking a coherent view of how people might live successfully all the way

to the very end, we have allowed our fates to be controlled by medicine, technology, and strangers.

But not all of us have. That takes, however, at least two kinds of courage. The first is the courage to confront the reality of mortality—the courage to seek out the truth of what is to be feared and what is to be hoped when one is seriously ill. Such courage is difficult enough, but even more daunting is the second kind of courage—the courage to act on the truth we find. 7

A few years ago, I got a late night page: Jewel Douglass, a 72-year-old patient of mine receiving chemotherapy for metastatic ovarian cancer, was back in the hospital, unable to hold food down. For a week, her symptoms had mounted: They started with bloating, became waves of crampy abdominal pain, then nausea and vomiting. 8

Her oncologist sent her to the hospital. A scan showed that, despite treatment, her ovarian cancer had multiplied, grown, and partly obstructed her intestine. Her abdomen had also filled with fluid. The deposits of tumor had stuffed up her lymphatic system, which serves as a kind of storm drain for the lubricating fluids that the body's internal linings secrete. When the system is blocked, the fluid has nowhere to go. The belly fills up like a rubber ball until you feel as if you will burst. 9

But walking into Douglass' hospital room, I'd never have known she was so sick if I hadn't seen the scan. "Well, look who's here!" she said, as if I'd just arrived at a cocktail party. "How are you, doctor?" 10

"I think I'm supposed to ask you that," I said. 11

She smiled brightly and pointed around the room. "This is my husband, Arthur, whom you know, and my son, Brett." She got me grinning. Here it was, 11 at night, she couldn't hold down an ounce of water, and she still had her lipstick on, her silver hair was brushed straight, and she was insisting on making introductions. 12

Her oncologist and I had a menu of options. A range of alternative chemotherapy regimens could be tried to shrink the tumor burden, and I had a few surgical options too. I wouldn't be able to remove the intestinal blockage, but I might be able to bypass it, I told her. Or I could give her an ileostomy, disconnecting the bowel above the blockage and bringing it through the skin to empty into a bag. I would also put in a couple of drainage catheters—permanent spigots that could be opened to release the fluids from her blocked-up drainage ducts or intestines when necessary. Surgery risked serious complications—wound breakdown, leakage of bowel into her abdomen, infections—but it was the only way she might regain her ability to eat. 13

I also told her that we did not have to do either chemo or surgery. We could provide medications to control her pain and nausea and arrange for hospice care at home. 14

This is the moment when I would normally have reviewed the pros and cons. But 15 we are only gradually learning in the medical profession that this is not what we need to do. The options overwhelmed her. They all sounded terrifying. So I stepped back and asked her a few questions I learned from hospice and palliative care physicians, hoping to better help both of us know what to do: What were her biggest fears and concerns? What goals were most important to her? What trade-offs was she willing to make?

Not all can answer such questions, but she did. She said she wanted to be without pain, nausea, or vomiting. She wanted to eat. Most of all, she wanted to get back on her feet. Her biggest fear was that she wouldn't be able to return home and be with the people she loved. 16

I asked what sacrifices she was willing to endure now for the possibility of more time later. "Not a lot," she said. Uppermost in her mind was a wedding that weekend that she was desperate not to miss. "Arthur's brother is marrying my best friend," she said. She'd set them up on their first date. The wedding was just two days away. She was supposed to be a bridesmaid. She was willing to do anything to make it, she said. 17

Suddenly, with just a few simple questions, I had some guidance about her priorities. So we made a plan to see if we could meet them. With a long needle, we tapped a liter of tea-colored fluid from her abdomen, which made her feel at least temporarily better. We gave her medication to control her nausea. We discharged her with instructions to drink nothing thicker than apple juice and to return to see me after the wedding. 18

She didn't make it. She came back to the hospital that same night. Just the car ride, with its swaying and bumps, made her vomit, and things only got worse at home. 19

We agreed that surgery was the best course now and scheduled it for the next day. I would focus on restoring her ability to eat and putting drainage tubes in. Afterward, she could decide if she wanted more chemotherapy or to go on hospice.

She was as clear as I've seen anyone be about her goals, but she was still in doubt. The following morning, she cancelled the operation. "I'm afraid," she said. She'd tossed all night, imagining the pain, the tubes, the horrors of possible complications. "I don't want to take risky chances," she said. 20

Her difficulty wasn't lack of courage to act in the face of risks; it was sorting out how to think about them. Her greatest fear was of suffering, she said. Couldn't the operation make it worse rather than better? 21

It could, I said. Surgery offered her the possibility of being able to eat again and a very good likelihood of controlling her nausea, but it carried substantial risk of giving her only pain without improvement or adding new miseries. She had, I estimated, a 75 percent chance that surgery would make her future better, at least for a little while, and a 25 percent chance it'd make it worse. 22

The brain gives us two ways to evaluate experiences like suffering—how we 23
apprehend such experiences in the moment and how we look at them afterward. People seem to have two different selves—an *experiencing self* who endures every moment equally and a *remembering self* who, as the Nobel Prize–winning researcher Daniel Kahneman has shown, gives almost all the weight of judgment afterward to just two points in time: the worst moment of an ordeal and the last moment of it. The remembering self and the experiencing self can come to radically different opinions about the same experience—so which one should we listen to?

This, at bottom, was Jewel Douglass' torment. Should she heed her remembering 24
self—or, in this case, anticipating self—which was focused on the worst things she might endure? Or should she listen to her experiencing self, which would likely endure a lower average amount of suffering in the days to come if she underwent surgery rather than just going home—and might even get to eat again for a while?

I left feeling that, at least this once, we had done it right. 25

In the end, a person doesn't view his life as merely the average of its moments— 26
which, after all, is mostly nothing much, plus some sleep. Life is meaningful because it is a story, and a story's arc is determined by the moments when something happens. Unlike your experiencing self, which is absorbed in the moment, your remembering self is attempting to recognize not only the peaks of joy and valleys of misery but also how the story works out as a whole. That is profoundly affected by how things ultimately turn out. Football fans will let a few flubbed minutes at the end of a game ruin three hours of bliss—because a football game is a story, and in stories, endings matter.

Jewel Douglass didn't know if she was willing to face the suffering that surgery 27
might inflict and feared being left worse off. "I don't want to take risky chances," she said. She didn't want to take a high-stakes gamble on how her story would end. Suddenly I realized, she was telling me everything I needed to know.

We should go to surgery, I told her, but with the directions she'd just spelled out— 28
to do what I could to enable her to return home to her family while not taking "risky chances." I'd put in a small laparoscope. I'd look around. And I'd attempt to unblock her intestine only if I saw that I could do it fairly easily. If it looked risky, I'd just put in tubes to drain her backed-up pipes. I'd aim for what might sound like a contradiction in terms: a palliative operation—an operation whose overriding priority was to do only what was likely to make her feel immediately better.

She remained quiet, thinking. 29

Her daughter took her hand. "We should do this, Mom," she said. 30

"OK," Douglass said. "But no risky chances." 31

When she was under anesthesia, I made a half-inch incision above her belly 32 button. I slipped my gloved finger inside to feel for space to insert the fiberoptic scope. But a hard loop of tumor-caked bowel blocked entry. I wasn't even going to be able to put in a camera.

I had the resident take the knife and extend the incision upward until it was large 33
enough to see in directly and get a hand inside. There were too many tumors to do anything to help her eat again, and now we were risking creating holes we'd never be able to repair. Leakage inside the abdomen would be a calamity. So we stopped.

No risky chances. We shifted focus and put in two long, plastic drainage tubes. 34
One we inserted directly into her stomach to empty the contents backed up there; the other we laid in the open abdominal cavity to empty the fluid outside her gut. Then we closed up, and we were done.

I told her family we hadn't been able to help her eat again, and when Douglass 35
woke up, I told her too. Her daughter wept. Her husband thanked us for trying. Douglass tried to put a brave face on it. "I was never obsessed with food anyway," she said.

The tubes relieved her nausea and abdominal pain greatly—"90 percent," she said. 36
The nurses taught her how to open the gastric tube into a bag when she felt sick and the abdominal tube when her belly felt too tight. We told her she could drink whatever she wanted and even eat soft food for the taste. Three days after surgery, she went home with hospice care to look after her.

Before she left, her oncologist and oncology nurse practitioner saw her. Douglass 37
asked them how long they thought she had. "They both filled up with tears," she told me. "It was kind of my answer."

A few days later, she and her family allowed me to stop by her home after work. 38
She answered the door, wearing a robe because of the tubes, for which she apologized. We sat in her living room, and I asked how she was doing.

OK, she said. "I think I have a measure that I'm slip, slip, slipping," but she had 39
been seeing old friends and relatives all day, and she loved it. She was taking just Tylenol for pain. Narcotics made her drowsy and weak, and that interfered with seeing people.

She said she didn't like all the contraptions sticking out of her. But the first time 40
she found that just opening a tube could take away her nausea, she said, "I looked at the tube and said, 'Thank you for being there.' "

Mostly, we talked about good memories. She was at peace with God, she said. I left 41
feeling that, at least this once, we had done it right. Douglass' story was not ending the way she ever envisioned, but it was nonetheless ending with her being able to make the choices that meant the most to her.

Two weeks later, her daughter Susan sent me a note. "Mom died on Friday 42
morning. She drifted quietly to sleep and took her last breath. It was very peaceful. My

dad was alone by her side with the rest of us in the living room. This was such a perfect ending and in keeping with the relationship they shared."

I am leery of suggesting that endings are controllable. No one ever really has control; physics and biology and accident ultimately have their way in our lives. But as Jewel Douglass taught me, we are not helpless either—and courage is the strength to recognize *both* of those realities. We have room to act and shape our stories—although as we get older, we do so within narrower and narrower confines. 43

Reading for Better Writing

1. *Connections:* In paragraphs 3 and 4, Gawande writes, "When I saw my first deaths . . . I felt as if I'd failed. But death, of course, is not a failure. Death is normal. Death may be the enemy, but it is also the natural order of things." What losses have you experienced among family and friends? Is it your experience that death is normal, the natural order?
2. *Comprehension:*
   a. In paragraph 6, he writes, "Lacking a coherent view of how people might live successfully all the way to the very end, we have allowed our fates to be controlled by medicine, technology, and strangers." What does he mean? How does Jewel Douglass' story that follows this statement relate to it?
   b. In paragraph 15, Gawande asks his patient three questions. Re-read the questions and explain how they helped him prescribe effective treatment.
   c. Gawande explores two processes in his essay: the process of dying and procedures for treating the dying. What does he illuminate about each?
3. *Writing Strategies:*
   a. Much of Gawande's essay explores a single case. What techniques does he use to present the process of treating Jewel Douglass during her last weeks and days? Consider his organizing events into stages or phases, his use of transitions, and other strategies.
   b. Paragraph 34 begins with this sentence, "*No risky chances.*" To what effect?
   c. What does the essay's closing do to bring the analysis of death and dying treatments to a close?

Your Project: For your own writing, consider exploring processes similar to those Gawande analyzes. For example, consider other phases of human growth, development, and aging (e.g., the development of the fetus in the womb, infancy, childhood, adolescence). Or consider a medical process that treats a condition or disease that interests you or connects to your life.

Describing a Pre-Burial Procedure

In this essay, Reshma Memon Yaqub, an accomplished writer and editor, describes the solemn Islamic practice of washing and shrouding a body to prepare it for burial. As you read the essay, note how, as the process proceeds, Yaqub's respect for the practice grows, leading to her closing profession: "To God we belong, and to God we return." (The essay was published in the 2011 edition of *Best American Essays*.)

The Washing

I hadn't planned to wash the corpse. 1

But sometimes you just get caught up in the moment. 2

Through a series of slight miscalculations, I am the first of the deceased woman's relatives to arrive at the March Funeral Home in west Baltimore on this Monday morning. The body of the woman whom everyone in the family refers to simply as Dadee, which means "grandmother" in Urdu, is scheduled to arrive at 10 a.m., after being released from Howard County General Hospital in Columbia. I get to the funeral home at 10 a.m. and make somber chitchat with the five women from the local mosque who have volunteered to help with funeral preparations, which includes washing the deceased's body. 3

According to Islamic practices, family members of the same gender as the deceased are expected to bathe and shroud the body for burial. But because it's such a detailed ritual, and because so many second-generation American Muslim families have yet to bury a loved one here, mosques have volunteers to assist grieving families. These women have come from the Islamic Society of Baltimore, where Dadee's funeral prayer service will be held this afternoon. 4

When the body arrives at 11:30 a.m., I am still the only family member here, and the body-washers naturally usher me in to join them for the ritual cleansing. It feels too late to tell them that technically I'm not a relative. When I first met the women an hour ago and spoke to them in my halting Urdu, it seemed unnecessary to explain that I was only about to become Dadee's relative. That she was the visiting grandmother of the woman engaged to marry my younger brother. That she had flown in from South Africa just ten days earlier to attend the upcoming wedding. That the only time I'd ever seen Dadee was last night at the hospital, a few hours after she died of sudden cardiac arrest, and then I hadn't even seen her face. When I had arrived at the hospital after getting the call from my brother, a white sheet was already drawn up over Dadee's face and tucked around her slight, eight-decade-old frame. 5

But the body-washers are understandably in a bit of a hurry. They've been kept waiting. And these genuinely kind women, five middle-aged homemakers, have their own responsibilities to get back to. I call my brother's finance to tell her that the women want to start the hour-long washing, and she gives the go-ahead because she and her parents are still at the hospital. I tell the washers they can start, and they look at me expectantly. "Let's go," they say in Urdu. "Uh, okay," I reply. It's not that I don't want to wash the body. It's actually something I've wanted to experience for a while. Earlier in the year, I told the funeral coordinator at my mosque to keep me in mind if the need ever arose when I'm available. A few years ago, I attended a daylong workshop on how to perform the ritual. It's just, I didn't think today was going to be the day. I didn't think this was going to be my first body. I had come here, on this fall day in 2008, only to offer emotional support to my future sister-in-law and her mother. 6

I mutely follow the women through a heavy door marked "Staff Only," then down a flight of concrete stairs into the recesses of the funeral home. I'm starting to feel as though I'm trapped in one of those old *I Love Lucy* episodes, where Lucille Ball finds herself stomping grapes or smuggling cheese and has no idea how to stop this runaway train. We reach a large open room, where I see some gurneys and a simple coffin—upholstered in blue fabric with a white interior. Another doorway leads into a smaller private room that has been set up for ritual washings such as these, one of the volunteers tells me. From the doorway, I see Dadee's form in her hospital-issue white body bag, zipped all the way up. She is lying on a metal gurney, which, with its slightly raised edges, looks like a giant jellyroll pan. It has a quarter-sized hole at the bottom near Dadee's feet, and the silver tray is tilted slightly so the water we will use drains into a utility sink. 7

I am not afraid of dead bodies. I have seen one up close three times in my thirty-six years: in high school at the funeral of a friend's father; as a police reporter when I took a tour of the local morgue; and more recently when a friend's ill baby died. But this is the first time I will touch a corpse, and that I am a little nervous about. But I'm also grateful for the opportunity. In Islam, it is a tremendous honor to give a body its final cleansing. The reward is immense—the erasure of forty major sins from your lifetime's record. Few people I know have ever washed a body. Because my parents and their peers moved here from Pakistan as young adults, most of them missed the natural opportunity to wash their own parents' or grandparents' bodies when they passed away overseas. And because few of my Muslim peers have lost their parents, we are two generations that don't know what to do when the time comes. 8

I feel blessed not to be experiencing my first washing with one of my own loved ones, when I would be numb from loss. I would have had little time to prepare myself because Muslims are buried immediately after death—the same day when possible. There is no embalming, no makeup, no Sunday finery for the deceased. There is no wake, no long speech, no cherry-wood coffin, with brass handles. There is simply the ritual washing, the shrouding in plain white cloth, a funeral prayer that lasts five minutes, and then the burial—preferably the body straight into the dirt, but, when required by law, placed in a basic coffin. 9

Body-washers put on sterile scrubs to protect us from whatever illness may have stricken the deceased. First I tie on a large paper apron. Then come rubber gloves. I see one of the women pull on a second pair of gloves over the first, and I follow. Next are puffy paper sleeves that attach from elbow to wrist and are tucked into the gloves. Then big paper booties. And finally a face mask with a large transparent plastic eye shield. By the end, I look like a cross between an overzealous nail technician and a Transformer. 10

I watch the women unzip Dadee from her body bag. As it opens, I see her face for the first time. Muslims believe that at the moment of death, when a soul that's headed to heaven emerges from its body, it slips out as easily as a drop of water spilling from a jug. But a soul that's headed to less heavenly places emerges with great difficulty, like a thorny branch being ripped through a pile of wet wool. I'm relieved that Dadee's face is peaceful, the way you hope somebody's grandmother's face would appear. 11

I stand by Dadee's feet, on her right side, and watch the women gently lift and rock Dadee to free her from the body bag. She's still dressed in her blue-and-white hospital gown. One of the women slowly lifts the gown, while another drapes Dadee with one of the same long aprons that we are all wearing. Not for one moment are any private areas of the body exposed. In the ritual Islamic bathing, the body is to be given the utmost respect. Not only is it to stay covered at all times, but the washers are to remain forever silent about anything negative or unusual they may witness—for example, if there is an unexpected scar, or deformity, or tattoo. In this, a human's most vulnerable of moments, she is guaranteed protection by her family and community. 12

It is time to begin the washing. A thin rubber hose is attached to the faucet in the utility sink, and one of the women turns on the water, adjusting it until it is comfortably warm, as prescribed by Islamic tradition. Because I'm the only "relative" in the room, I'm expected to perform the lion's share of the washing, but the women see that I have no idea what I'm doing, so they resume control, leaving me in charge 13 of the feet. The first time I touch Dadee's feet, I am surprised. I expect the corpse to be cold, but it feels warm. Then again, she left this shell less than a day earlier. Perhaps these things take time.

A Muslim's body is generally washed three times from head to toe with soap and 14 clean water. The right side is washed first, then the left. During the final washing, a softly fragranced oil is rubbed onto the body. The body has to be repeatedly tilted from one side to the other, and it is harder than I expected to maneuver the dead weight of a human form. Dadee's feet keep getting in the way of the hole at the bottom of the table, and every few minutes, the water pools up there and I have to lift her leg.

Fifteen minutes into the washing, my brother's fiancée and her mother knock at 15 the door. The granddaughter is too distraught to join in and watches tearfully from the doorway. But Dadee's daughter-in-law dons the gear and steps into her family role. She is understandably traumatized, having been the one to find Dadee collapsed at their home in Columbia last night and having performed CPR to try to revive her. This is her first time washing a body too. I can't tell if she wants me to stay and keep washing, or leave, because we've met just a handful of times in the three months since my brother proposed to her daughter. But she doesn't say anything, so I stay.

Washing a body in this way, it's 16 impossible not to flash forward to your own ending. I have lain on a table like this before, draped strategically with white cloth, comforting hands laid on me. But that was just for a massage at the Red Door Spa. When I imagine my own washing, I see myself being handled by loved ones: my two oldest friends, Farin and Sajeela; my brothers' wives; my mother and mother-in-law. I've also asked two women at my mosque whom I adore to participate. Maybe I'll live long enough to have a daughter-in-law in the room with me. Should I be so lucky, even a granddaughter. The more I see, the more I appreciate the way a Muslim's body is handled after death. There is so much gentleness, so much privacy. The body isn't left unattended in the short span between death and burial. It unnerves me when, walking through the funeral home's hallway, I look into a room and see a dead man lying on a gurney, unattended. I wonder how long he has been there, how he has been handled, who has had access to him. Whether the water that ran over his body was warmed.

"Washing a body in this way, it's impossible not to flash forward to your own ending."

The body-washers pass the rubber hose back and forth to each other and to me 17 and my soon-to-be relative, who strokes her mother-in-law's hair and washes it. At the end, we dry Dadee with clean white towels and slide several towels underneath her, with their edges hanging over the sides of the gurney. We then roll her gurney into the adjacent room where the coffin awaits for her transport to the mosque. We station her gurney next to a second one, where one of the women has already laid out Dadee's funeral shroud, called a kafan, made of five white cloths of different sizes. We use the towels underneath Dadee as handles to lift her to the second gurney. Pieces of the white fabric are folded around Dadee's body and secured with ropelike strands of the same cloth. One of the volunteers, Rabia Marfani, assembles these fabric kits at home, using cotton/polyester bed sheets that she buys at Wal-Mart.

When the cloth that wraps the hair back is tied on Dadee, she seems strangely transported. She looks so small and fragile, like a little girl with a bonnet tied around her hair. Finally, a large cloth is folded around the entire body, completely enclosing her. It's tied shut with the ropelike strands, and the body looks almost like a wrapped gift. Together we lift Dadee into the coffin. One of the women shows me and Dadee's daughter-in-law how to open the fabric around Dadee's face, should any of her family members ask to see her one last time at the Janazah prayer service at the mosque. 18

Afterward, I hug each of the body-washers and thank them deeply for their help. Although Dadee is not exactly my relative, I feel as though these women have done me a huge personal favor, expecting nothing in return. When I ask Marfani why she has participated in this custom more than thirty times in her fifty years, she replies: "It's our obligation. And there is so much reward from God . . . One day I will also be lying there, and somebody will do this to me." She started as a teenager in Pakistan, assisting when her grandmother and aunt passed away. She encourages younger women to volunteer or just watch, because this knowledge needs to be passed on. 19

We all then raise our hands and pray, asking God to forgive Dadee's sins, to give her the best in the next life. I inwardly alternate between speaking to God and speaking to Dadee. I ask God to welcome her; I wish Dadee good luck on this ultimate pilgrimage. Islam teaches us that after the soul is removed from the body, it briefly faces God to learn its fate, then is returned to the body while on its way to the grave. There it awaits its full reckoning on the Day of Judgment. Though Dadee is no longer of this world, she can continue to earn blessings based on what she has left behind—through righteous offspring who pray for her forgiveness, through knowledge that she has spread to others, or through charitable work whose effects outlast her. 20

I pray for Dadee, and I also apologize to her for a mistake she doesn't know I 21 nearly made. In today's mail, after the funeral, Dadee's family will receive my hand-addressed invitation to her for a wedding reception hosted by my parents. Earlier this week, I had argued with my brother over the unnecessary expense of mailing separate invitations to multiple family members at the same address. I had considered just sending a joint one. In the end, how grateful I am that I did it his way. Of course you deserve your own invitation, Dadee, after flying across the world to witness your granddaughter's wedding.

I ask God one last time to have mercy on her soul. As I pick up my purse and turn 22
to leave the room, I address my final words to both of them: "Innaa lillaahi wa-innaa ilaihi raje' oon." To God we belong, and to God we return.

Reading for Better Writing

1. *Connections:* What serious religious or cultural ceremony have you experienced or witnessed? What was the setting and process? Who participated, and what did you or others do? What did you learn about the ceremony and about yourself?
2. *Comprehension:*
   a. Describe the setting, participants, purpose of the ceremony, and steps in the process.
   b. Who is the narrator, and how does she get involved in the process? What does she know about the ceremony when the essay opens, and what does she learn by participating in it?
3. *Writing Strategies:*
   a. Review the opening five paragraphs, note details, and explain how they set a tone of mystery and intrigue.
   b. Examine one of the longer paragraphs. How is the paragraph structured to explain part of the process?
   c. Review the last sentence. How does it work to bring the presentation of the pre-burial process to a close?

Your Project: What rituals, ceremonies, and practices, whether in religion or other areas of life, interest you? How are these processes to be understood in terms of how they developed and how they make sense of human experience? Consider one such practice for your own writing.

Analyzing a Policy

Eric Foner is a professor of history at Columbia University and the author of numerous publications, including *The Fiery Trial: Abraham Lincoln and American Slavery* and the essay that follows. He published the essay on December 31, 2012, one day before the 150th anniversary of Lincoln's signing the "Emancipation Proclamation."

The Emancipation of Abe Lincoln

ONE hundred and fifty years ago, on January 1, 1863, Abraham Lincoln presided over the annual White House New Year's reception. Late that afternoon, he retired to his study to sign the "Emancipation Proclamation." When he took up his pen, his hand was shaking from exhaustion. Briefly, he paused—"I do not want it to appear as if I hesitated," he remarked. Then Lincoln affixed a firm signature to the document. 1

Like all great historical transformations, emancipation was a process, not a single event. It arose from many causes and was the work of many individuals. It began at the outset of the Civil War, when slaves sought refuge behind Union lines. It did not end until December 1865, with the ratification of the 13th Amendment, which irrevocably abolished slavery throughout the nation. 2

But the Emancipation Proclamation was the crucial turning point in this story. In a sense, it embodied a double emancipation: for the slaves, since it ensured that if the Union emerged victorious, slavery would perish, and for Lincoln himself, for whom it marked the abandonment of his previous assumptions about how to abolish slavery and the role blacks would play in post-emancipation American life. 3

There is no reason to doubt the sincerity of Lincoln's statement in 1864 that he had always believed slavery to be wrong. During the first two years of the Civil War, despite insisting that the conflict's aim was preservation of the Union, he devoted considerable energy to a plan for ending slavery inherited from prewar years. Emancipation would be undertaken by state governments, with national financing. It would be gradual, owners would receive monetary compensation and emancipated slaves would be encouraged to find a homeland outside the United States—this last idea known as "colonization." 4

Lincoln's plan sought to win the cooperation of slave holders in ending slavery. As early as November 1861, he proposed it to political leaders in Delaware, one of the four border states (along with Kentucky, Maryland and Missouri) that remained in the Union. Delaware had only 1,800 slaves; the institution was peripheral to the state's economy. But Lincoln found that even there, slave holders did not wish to surrender their human property. Nonetheless, for most of 1862, he avidly promoted his plan to the border states and any Confederates who might be interested. 5

Lincoln also took his proposal to black Americans. In August 1862, he met with a group of black leaders from Washington. He seemed to blame the presence of blacks in America for the conflict: "but for your race among us there could not be war." 6

He issued a powerful indictment of slavery—"the greatest wrong inflicted on any people"—but added that, because of racism, blacks would never achieve equality in America. "It is better for us both, therefore, to be separated," he said. But most blacks refused to contemplate emigration from the land of their birth.

In the summer of 1862, a combination of events propelled Lincoln in a new 7
direction. Slavery was disintegrating in parts of the South as thousands of slaves ran away to Union lines. With the war a stalemate, more Northerners found themselves agreeing with the abolitionists, who had insisted from the outset that slavery must become a target. Enthusiasm for enlistment was waning in the North. The Army had long refused to accept black volunteers, but the reservoir of black manpower could no longer be ignored. In response, Congress moved ahead of Lincoln, abolishing slavery in the District of Columbia, authorizing the president to enroll blacks in the Army and freeing the slaves of pro-Confederate owners in areas under military control. Lincoln signed all these measures that summer.

The hallmark of Lincoln's greatness was his combination of bedrock principle 8
with open-mindedness and capacity for growth. That summer, with his preferred approach going nowhere, he moved in the direction of immediate emancipation. He first proposed this to his cabinet on July 22, but Secretary of State William H. Seward persuaded him to wait for a military victory, lest it seem an act of desperation.

Soon after the Union victory at Antietam in September, Lincoln issued the 9
Preliminary Emancipation Proclamation, a warning to the Confederacy that if it did not lay down its arms by January 1, he would declare the slaves "forever free."

Lincoln did not immediately abandon his earlier plan. His annual message to 10
Congress, released on Dec. 1, 1862, devoted a long passage to gradual, compensated abolition and colonization. But in the same document, without mentioning the impending proclamation, he indicated that a new approach was imperative: "The dogmas of the quiet past, are inadequate to the stormy present," he wrote. "We must disenthrall our selves, and then we shall save our country." Lincoln included himself in that "we." On Jan. 1, he proclaimed the freedom of the vast majority of the nation's slaves.

The Emancipation Proclamation is perhaps the most misunderstood of the 11
documents that have shaped American history. Contrary to legend, Lincoln did not free the nearly four million slaves with a stroke of his pen. It had no bearing on slaves in the four border states, since they were not in rebellion. It also exempted certain parts of the Confederacy occupied by the Union. All told, it left perhaps 750,000 slaves in bondage. But the remaining 3.1 million, it declared, "are, and henceforward shall be free."

The proclamation did not end slavery in the United States on the day it was issued. 12
Indeed, it could not even be enforced in most of the areas where it applied, which were under Confederate control. But it ensured the eventual death of slavery—assuming the

Union won the war. Were the Confederacy to emerge victorious, slavery, in one form or another, would undoubtedly have lasted a long time.

A military order, whose constitutional legitimacy rested on the president's war powers, the proclamation often disappoints those who read it. It is dull and legalistic; it contains no soaring language enunciating the rights of man. Only at the last minute, at the urging of Treasury Secretary Salmon P. Chase, an abolitionist, did Lincoln add a conclusion declaring the proclamation an "act of justice." 13

Nonetheless, the proclamation marked a dramatic transformation in the nature of the Civil War and in Lincoln's own approach to the problem of slavery. No longer did he seek the consent of slave holders. The proclamation was immediate, not gradual, contained no mention of compensation for owners, and made no reference to colonization. 14

In it, Lincoln addressed blacks directly, not as property subject to the will of others but as men and women whose loyalty the Union must earn. For the first time, he welcomed black soldiers into the Union Army; over the next two years some 200,000 black men would serve in the Army and Navy, playing a critical role in achieving Union victory. And Lincoln urged freed slaves to go to work for "reasonable wages"—in the United States. He never again mentioned colonization in public. 15

Having made the decision, Lincoln did not look back. In 1864, with casualties mounting, there was talk of a compromise peace. Some urged Lincoln to rescind the proclamation, in which case, they believed, the South could be persuaded to return to the Union. Lincoln refused. Were he to do so, he told one visitor, "I should be damned in time and eternity." 16

Wartime emancipation may have settled the fate of slavery, but it opened another vexing question: the role of former slaves in American life. Colonization had allowed its proponents to talk about abolition without having to confront this issue; after all, the black population would be gone. After January 1, 1863, Lincoln for the first time began to think seriously of the United States as a biracial society. 17

While not burdened with the visceral racism of many of his white contemporaries, Lincoln shared some of their prejudices. He had long seen blacks as an alien people who had been unjustly uprooted from their homeland and were entitled to freedom, but were not an intrinsic part of American society. During his Senate campaign in Illinois, in 1858, he had insisted that blacks should enjoy the same natural rights as whites (life, liberty and the pursuit of happiness), but he opposed granting them legal equality or the right to vote. 18

By the end of his life, Lincoln's outlook had changed dramatically. In his last public address, delivered in April 1865, he said that in reconstructing Louisiana, and by implication other Southern states, he would "prefer" that limited black suffrage be implemented. He singled out the "very intelligent" (educated free blacks) and "those who serve our cause as soldiers" as most worthy. Though hardly an unambiguous 19 embrace of equality, this was the first time an American president had endorsed any political rights for blacks.

And then there was his magnificent second inaugural address of March 4, 1865, 20
in which Lincoln ruminated on the deep meaning of the war. He now identified the institution of slavery—not the presence of blacks, as in 1862—as its fundamental cause. The war, he said, might well be a divine punishment for the evil of slavery. And God might will it to continue until all the wealth the slaves had created had been destroyed, and "until every drop of blood drawn with the lash, shall be paid by another drawn by the sword." Lincoln was reminding Americans that violence did not begin with the firing on Fort Sumter, S.C., in April 1861. What he called "this terrible war" had been preceded by 250 years of the terrible violence of slavery.

In essence, Lincoln asked the nation to confront unblinkingly the legacy of 21
slavery. What were the requirements of justice in the face of this reality? What would be necessary to enable former slaves and their descendants to enjoy fully the pursuit of happiness? Lincoln did not live to provide an answer. A century and a half later, we have yet to do so.

Reading for Better Writing

1. *Connections:* Reflect on someone who positively impacted your life. Then think about the people and events in her or his life that shaped the qualities that positively affected you. If you were to tell this person's story, what details would you include? Why?
2. *Comprehension:*
   - **a.** Review Eric Foner's claim (in paragraph two) that emancipation was a process, not a single event. What does he mean, and how does he support this claim?
   - **b.** Identify a passage in which Foner analyzes how specific events caused a shift in Lincoln's thinking. How does this passage advance his thesis?
3. *Writing Strategies:*
   - **a.** Describe how Foner introduces his topic and thesis.
   - **b.** Cite examples showing how he builds transitions that (a) link stages in the process and (b) link specific events within a stage.

Your Project: For your own writing, choose another historical character (e.g., Cesar Chavez, Malcolm X, Henry Standing Bear, Shirley Chisholm, or Eleanor Roosevelt) who sought to bring about significant social change. Then research the person's life and career so as to analyze the process by which she or he became an important social activist.

Writing Guidelines

Planning

1. **Select a topic.** Begin by reviewing the project options listed at the end of each sample essay. To generate more topic ideas, review the following prompts.
   - A course-related process
   - A process in nature
   - A process in the news
   - A process that helps you get a job
2. **Review the process.** Use your knowledge of the topic to fill out an organizer like the one in Figure 13.3. List the subject at the top, each of the steps in chronological order, and the outcome at the bottom. For a complex process, break it down into stages or phases first; then outline the steps or events within each phase.

   Process Analysis
   Subject:
   - **Step #1**
   - **Step #2**
   - **Step #3**

   Outcome:

   fig. 13.3

3. **Research the process.** Find all the information that you need to fully understand the process yourself and to clearly explain it to your readers. To guide your research, you might list headings and related questions like these:
   - **Context:** When, where, how, and why does the process transpire? How is the context related to the nature of the process?
   - **Content:** What individual steps—or groups of steps—make up the process?
   - **Order:** In what order do the steps take place? Is the order important? Why?
   - **Connections:** What links steps to steps or links stages to stages and how?
   - **Causes:** What causes each individual step or event—or what causes the process as a whole? How can I distinguish between false causes (page 325) and actual causes?
   - **Effects:** What is the outcome of each step or event—and what is the outcome of the whole process? What side effects are associated with the outcome?
   - **Materials:** What materials are used in the process and how do they affect it?
   - **History:** When did this process begin? How has it changed over time and why?
   - **Personnel:** Who is involved in the process? Why? How do they affect the process, and how does it affect them?
   - **Cost:** What is the financial cost? The emotional cost? The environmental cost?
   - **Impact:** How does the process affect my community, my friends, or me?
4. **Organize information.** Revise the organizer as needed. Then develop an outline, including steps listed in the organizer, as well as supporting details from your research.

Drafting

5. **Write the first draft.** Write the document using the following guidelines.
   - **Opening:** Introduce the topic and give an overview of the process, possibly forecasting its main stages. Explain why the process is important.

- **Middle:** Clearly describe each step in the process, and link steps with transitions such as *first, second, next, finally,* and *while.* Explain the importance of each step, and how it is linked to other steps in the process. If the process is complex and has many steps, consider grouping them into 3-5 phases or stages. Describe the outcomes of steps and phases, as well as the overall outcome and relevance of the process. Depending on your purpose for writing, you might also analyze the causes and effects related to specific steps, or to the entire process.
- **Closing:** Summarize the process and restate key points as needed, such as why understanding the process has value. If appropriate, explain follow-up activity, such as how readers might learn more about the topic.

Revising

6. Improve the ideas, organization, and voice. Evaluate the following:

___ **Ideas:** Is the process presented as a unified phenomenon that includes a logical series of stages and steps? Are all claims clear, rational, and supported with reliable evidence? Are assertions regarding causes and effects relevant and explained fully? Does the writing include logical fallacies such as false cause (page 325), broad generalization (page 325), and false analogy (page 326)?

___ **Organization:** Does the essay include an opening that introduces the process, offers an overview, and states the thesis; a middle that describes stages and steps clearly and correctly; and a closing that unifies the essay?

___ **Voice:** Is the tone informed, concerned, and objective? Are sensitive issues well researched, addressed respectfully, and shown to be relevant?

Editing

7. Edit the essay. Polish your writing by addressing the following:

___ **Words:** The words are precise, clear, and correct. Technical terms are correct, used uniformly, and defined.

___ **Sentences:** The sentences are smooth, varied in structure, and engaging.

___ **Correctness:** The usage, grammar, punctuation, and spelling are correct.

___ **Page Design:** The page design is attractive and features steps in the process. Essays are correctly formatted in MLA or APA style.

Publishing

8. Publish the essay by offering it to instructors, students, and nonprofit agencies working with the process.

MindTap® Request help and feedback from a tutor. If required, participate in peer review, submit your paper for a grade, and view instructor comments online.

Critical Thinking and Writing: Applications

Once you have finished your process essay, there may be more to think about. Consider how to apply what you have learned in the following situations.

1. **Living Today:** Think about a time or phase in your life during which your understanding of—or position on—an issue, event, or other topic changed. What was the process you went through? Was it smooth or rough, the outcome positive or negative? How would you divide the process into stages?
2. **Major Issue:** In what ways is your field of study focused on processes? Through reading and discussion, develop a list of such processes and consider why understanding these processes is central to mastering that field of knowledge.
3. **Public Texts:** Every day, we encounter process writing in the form of instructions—recipes, Google Map directions, assembly guidelines, game rules, and so on. Find and examine one such set of instructions. What strategies make instructions useful? What weaknesses make them frustrating for readers?
4. **Photo Op:** As shown with Figure 13.1 on page 209 and Figure 13.2 on page 211, visuals can be effective aids to explaining a process. Considering your own process essay, what photographs, charts, or other visuals would you include to clarify the process? Where and how would you position these in your writing?

Learning-Objectives Checklist ✓

Have you achieved this chapter's learning objectives? Check your progress with the following items, revisiting topics in the chapter as needed. I have . . .

____ examined what process essays are, why they are written, and how they are used to analyze and explain phenomena (210–211).

____ analyzed the content and evaluated the quality of process essays (210–211).

____ researched a process, analyzed it, identified steps in the process, and found reliable evidence that distinguishes related causes and effects (230–231).

____ presented this information in a well-crafted essay that introduces the topic, offers an overview of the process, describes the steps clearly in chronological order, links the steps effectively, and explains the overall outcome or impact of the process (230–231).

____ revised the essay for weaknesses in organization and voice, and corrected errors in logic such as false cause, broad generalization, and false analogy (230–231).

____ edited the essay for errors in grammar, punctuation, spelling, and mechanics (230–231).

MindTap® Practice skills that you have learned in this chapter and receive automatic feedback. Reflect on your writing process.

Chapter 14

Comparison and Contrast

In his plays, William Shakespeare creates characters, families, and even plot lines that mirror each other. As a result, we see Hamlet in relation to Laertes and the Montagues in relation to the Capulets. In the process, we do precisely what the writer wants us to do—we compare and contrast the subjects. The result is clarity and insight: by thinking about both subjects in relation to each other, we understand each one more clearly.

But writers in college and in the workplace also use comparison-contrast as an analytical strategy. To help you read and write such documents, the following pages include instructions and four model essays.

Visually Speaking Look closely at Figure 14.1. What do you see? What does the photo suggest about how comparing and contrasting help one analyze and understand a topic?

MindTap®

Understand the goals of the chapter and complete a warm-up activity online.

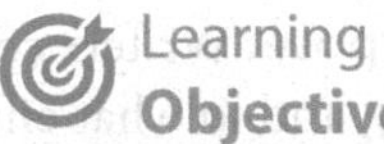

Learning Objectives

By working through this chapter, you will be able to

- examine and assess writers' use of comparison-contrast reasoning.
- differentiate between subject-by-subject and trait-by-trait strategies for comparison-contrast.
- use transitional words and supporting details to clarify compare-contrast claims.
- establish a clear basis for comparison between two or more topics.
- choose clear elements or features for comparison
- compose an analytical essay using primarily compare-contrast reasoning (with other analytical strategies).

Mazzzur / Shutterstock.com

fig. 14.1

Strategies for Comparison-Contrast Essays

Comparison-contrast writing holds two or more things, phenomena, or concepts side by side—with comparison focusing on similarities, and contrast focusing on differences. By looking at subjects side-by-side, we more clearly see their unique and shared traits.

The Rhetorical Situation

Consider the context in which writers use comparison-contrast reasoning:

- **Purpose.** Writers commonly compare and contrast subjects in order to explain how, why, and to what effect their distinguishing features make the subjects similar or different. Depending on their purpose, writers may focus on the similarities between seemingly dissimilar things, or on the differences between things that seem similar.
- **Readers.** A writer using comparison-contrast reasoning may have virtually any reader in mind—the instructor for a student essay or potential clients for a marketing document. Whatever the situation, the writer believes that his or her comparative analysis of the topic will enrich readers' understanding of that topic.
- **Topic.** Writers address a wide range of topics through comparison-contrast: people, events, phenomena, technologies, problems, products, stories, and so on.

Example: In "Beyond the Polite Smile" (pages 236–237), the writer's **topics** are the two communities of which she is a part: her Cantonese-speaking Chinese community in which her name is Pang Jing-Ling, and her English-speaking community in which her name is Janice Pang. Her **purpose** is to help **readers** (classmates and professor) understand how she is shaped by—and responds to—each group's customs, expectations, and opportunities. To that end, she compares and contrasts the traits of two communities.

Principles of Comparison-Contrast Writing

Comparison-contrast writing should be guided by the principles that follow:

Establishing a solid basis for comparison. Comparable items are types of the same thing (e.g. two rivers, two bodies of water, the atmosphere and oceans). Moreover, the subjects are of the same order—one cannot simply be an example of the other: e.g., all lakes and Lake Michigan. Whereas such a discussion would work as an example or illustration, the topics are not truly comparable.

Developing criteria (standards, features, etc.) on which to base the comparison. For example, a comparison of two characters in a play might focus on their backgrounds, their actions, their psychology, their fate, and so on. Once writers choose the criteria, those criteria must be applied consistently. For help comparing and contrasting subjects, use a Venn Diagram (Figure 14.2), listing the subjects' differences on the left or right, and their similarities in the center.

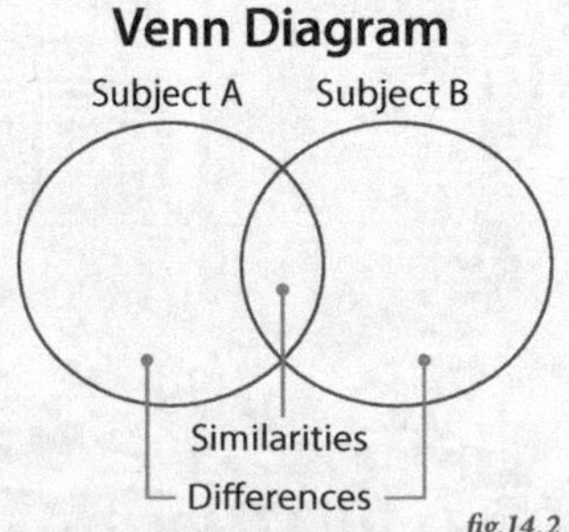

fig.14.2

Considering comparison-contrast. For example, comparison-contrast may be:

- the framework for the entire essay, offering a compare-contrast thesis and structuring the discussion around appropriate points of comparison, or
- a strategy used in a paragraph or a section of an essay, comparing and contrasting details to illuminate an idea.

Phrasing a compare-contrast thesis to clarify relationships. Consider these templates:

- **Emphasizing similarities:** Whereas [subjects A and B] appear quite different in terms of their __________, they show important similarities in that __________.
- **Emphasizing differences:** Whereas [subjects A and B] appear quite similar in terms of their __________, they are essentially different in that __________.

Sample thesis: While *Zero Dark Thirty* and *Argo* both dramatize historical events, *Zero's* portrayal of events is more historically accurate than *Argo*'s.

Organizing your comparison to clarify similarities and differences for readers. Writers have two choices for organizing comparisons so as to illuminate the topics.

- **Whole vs. whole** discusses items separately, giving a strong overview of each. This pattern works well with short, simple comparisons.
- **Point by point** discusses items together, criterion by criterion. This pattern stresses fine distinctions, making sense for long, complex comparisons.

Sample Comparison-Contrast Paragraph

In her essay "How the Internet Has Changed Bullying" (page 244), Maria Konnikova uses comparison-contrast terms such as *more, before, but, harder,* and *as much as.*

> In some ways, when it comes to bullying, the Internet has made the world *more rural. Before* the Internet, bullying ended when you withdrew from whatever environment you were in. *But now,* the bullying dynamic is *harder to contain* and *harder to ignore.* If you're harassed on your Facebook page, all of your social circles know about it; as long as you have access to the network, a ceaseless stream of notifications leaves you vulnerable to victimhood. Bullying may not have become *more prevalent*—in fact, a recent review of international data suggests that its incidence has declined by *as much as* ten per cent around the world. *But getting away* from it has become *more difficult.*

Reading Comparison-Contrast Writing

As you read the essays on the following pages, consider these questions:

1. Does the writer compare these topics to stress similarities, differences, or both?
2. What features or traits of the topics are compared? Why?
3. How does the writer present the topics and the criteria for comparison?
4. What conclusion does the writer develop through compare-contrast analysis?

Sample Comparison-Contrast Essays

Writers compare and contrast in order to help readers more fully understand topics through what is distinct about each and what they share. For example, in the essays that follow, the writers compare and contrast American vs. Asian cultures, treatment of humans vs. treatment of whales, and in-person bullying vs. Internet bullying.

MindTap®
Read, highlight, and take notes online.

Analyzing Two Cultures

Janice Pang, a student at the University of California at Davis, wrote the following essay, entered it in the school's annual writing contest, and was honored by having the paper published in *Prized Writing, 2014–2015*. In that text, she introduces her essay by saying, "My writing distills my views about language and identity into a narrative about culture, family, and personal growth." As you read Pang's essay, note how she uses comparison-contrast to clarify those views.

Beyond the Polite Smile

"You were an easy baby." 1

Over tea, my mother tells me that I came out smiling. I had held my contented expression for three minutes until the doctor firmly patted my bottom, eliciting a shriek and an avalanche of tears. This, the doctor ensured my parents, meant I was normal. 2

Over the ruckus of the restaurant—chopsticks clinking against porcelain, high-pitched howls of Cantonese—my mother coolly explains the origin of my Chinese name: Pang Jing-Ling. A quiet spirit; a series of syllables lodged in my throat. 3

Bringing the cup to my mouth, I blow on the tea and wonder whether I embody my name or my name embodies me. Brown rice swirls in a pool of dark leaves. I gulp, swallowing my thoughts. 4

When my parents introduce me to friends and relatives—Pang Jing-Ling, the quiet spirit—I don my polite smile; the one I use with Cantonese-speaking elders whose sentiments I cannot fully understand, but to whom I must demonstrate extreme agreeability. A polite smile does not reveal any teeth but ever-so-slightly crinkles the eyes and curls the lips. A polite smile is practiced, perfected over 21 years. 5

"She's very good," adults observe. They do not speak to me, but about me. Over me, "*Hoh guay.*" 6

I do not question the validity of their statements—that I'm quiet, that I'm shy. Rather, I accept them. Internalize them. Smile. 7

My parents speak Cantonese to scold me and to gossip with their friends, mouths shifting to accommodate native tongues. I know to listen. 8

In this language, I have never learned to respond or to speak for myself. I have, 9 however, become competent in obeying, in declining and thanking. Unable to translate more complex thoughts, I reduce Cantonese to a language of submission.

English, on the other hand, is a language I command. My public education taught 10
me to stick with five-paragraph formats; to use semicolons sparingly; to write in complete sentences. After years of practicing these rules, I learned to break them.

With thoughts and the agency to voice them, I have the privilege of playing with 11
syntax. I complicate sentences within dashes; I dismantle every subject, object, and verb.

In the spaces where I communicate in English—at work, in class, with friends—I 12
wrangle hellish clients, I challenge problematic texts, I correct everyone's grammar. Anything but quiet, my voice refuses to be passive.

Understanding that I grew up with a repression of language, and a language of 13
repression, I now have a greater appreciation for language that affirms. I use English to make sense of Cantonese, dissecting the language I have such trouble speaking beyond single syllables. I explore each character's meaning—its intricate shape and sound. Familiarizing my tongue with this language, I feel the corners of my polite smile relax.

Reading for Better Writing

1. *Connections:* What practices (e.g., spoken languages, clothing styles, social etiquette, figures of speech, popular sports, forms of art) distinguish the culture of your community? Which of these do you appreciate, dislike, or identify with?
2. *Comprehension:*
   a. Pang titles her essay, "Beyond the Polite Smile." What does she mean by "beyond" and "polite"? What does the smile communicate to those whom she smiles at? What does it hide?
   b. Compare and contrast (a) her demeanor (and smile) when using the Cantonese language with (b) her demeanor (and smile) when using the English language.
   c. Explain what she means by, "I grew up with a repression of language, and a language of repression"?
3. *Writing Strategies:*
   a. Pang uses precise terms to distinguish her two cultures. Cite examples and explain why her word choice is or is not effective.
   b. Pang organizes her essay by first describing her Cantonese character and then contrasting it with her English character. What is the effect of using this subject-by-subject approach rather than the trait-by-trait structure?

Your Project: Consider comparing and contrasting the community in which you grew up and your current college community. How does being in each community affect your attitude, behavior, or self-concept?

Analyzing Human Compassion

Marina Keegan (1989-2012) was an award-winning writer whose work was read on NPR and published in *The New York Times* and NewYorker.com. She accomplished all this and more before, just weeks after graduating from Yale University, a tragic car accident took her life. In this essay, by comparing and contrasting two distinct situations, Keegan analyzes what inspires human compassion.

Why We Care About Whales

1 When the moon gets bored, it kills whales. Blue whales and fin whales and humpback, sperm, and orca whales: centrifugal forces don't discriminate.

2 With a hushed retreat, the moon pulls waters out from under fins and flippers, oscillating them backward and forward before they slip outward. At nighttime, the moon watches its work. Silver light traces the strips of lingering water, the jittery crabs, the lumps of tangled seaweed.

3 Slowly, awkwardly, the whales find their footing. They try to fight the waves, but they can't fight the moon. They can't fight the world's rotation or the bathymetry of oceans or the inevitability that sometimes things just don't work out.

4 More than two thousand cetaceans die from beaching every year. Occasionally they trap themselves in solitude, but whales are often beached in groups, huddled together in clusters and rows. Whales feel cohesion, a sense of community, of loyalty. The distress call of a lone whale is enough to prompt its entire pod to rush to its side—a gesture that lands them nose to nose in the same sand. It's a fatal symphony of echolocation, a siren call to the sympathetic.

5 The death is slow. As mammals of the Cetacea order, whales are conscious breathers. Inhalation is a choice, an occasional rise to the ocean's surface. Although their ancestors lived on land, constant oxygen exposure overwhelms today's creatures.

6 Beached whales become frantic, captives to their hyperventilation. Most die from dehydration. The salty air shrinks their oily pores, capturing their moisture. Deprived of the buoyancy water provides, whales can literally crush themselves to death. Some collapse before they dry out—their lungs suffocating under their massive bodies—or drown when high tides cover their blowholes, filling them slowly while they're too weak to move. The average whale can't last more than twenty-four hours on land.

7 In their final moments, they begin belching and erupting in violent thrashing. Finally, their jaws open slightly—not all the way, but just enough that the characteristic illusion of a perpetual smile disappears. This means it's over. I know this because I watched as twenty-three whale mouths unhinged. As twenty-three pairs of whale eyes glazed over.

I had woken up that morning to a triage center outside my window. Fifty or so 8
pilot whales were lying along the stretch of beach in front of my house on Cape Cod, surrounded by frenzied neighbors and animal activists. The Coast Guard had arrived while I was still sleeping, and guardsmen were already using boats with giant nets in an attempt to pull the massive bodies back into the water. Volunteers hurried about in groups, digging trenches around the whales' heads to cool them off, placing wet towels on their skin, and forming assembly lines to pour buckets of water on them. The energy was nervous, confused, and palpably urgent.

Pilot whales are among the most populous of the marine mammals in the 9
cetacean order. Fully grown males can measure up to twenty feet and weigh three tons, while females usually reach sixteen feet and 1.5 tons.

Their enormity was their problem. Unlike the three dolphins that had managed to 10
strand themselves near our house the previous summer, fifty pilot whales were nearly impossible to maneuver. If unfavorable tidal currents and topography unite, the larger species may be trapped. Sandbars sneak up on them, and tides tie them back.

People are strange about animals. Especially large ones. Daily, on the docks of 11
Wellfleet Harbor, thousands of fish are scaled, gutted, and seasoned with thyme and lemon. No one strokes their sides with water. No one cries when their jaws slip open.

Pilot whales are not an endangered species, yet people spend tens of thousands of 12
dollars in rescue efforts, trucking the wounded to aquariums and in some places even airlifting them off beaches. Perhaps the whales' sheer immensity fosters sympathy. Perhaps the stories of Jonah or Moby Dick do the same. Or maybe it's that article we read last week about that whale in Australia understanding hand signals. Intelligence matters, doesn't it? Brain size is important, right? Those whales knew they were dying. They have some sort of language, some sort of emotion. They give birth, for God's sake! There aren't any pregnant fish in the Wellfleet nets. No communal understanding of their imminent fatality.

I worry sometimes that humans are afraid of helping humans. There's less risk 13
associated with animals, less fear of failure, fear of getting too involved. In war movies, a thousand soldiers can die gruesomely, but when the horse is shot, the audience is heartbroken. It's the *My Dog Skip* effect. The *Homeward Bound* syndrome.

When we hear that the lady on the next street over has cancer, we don't see the 14
entire town flock to her house. We push and shove wet whales all day, then walk home through town past homeless men curled up on benches—washed up like whales on the curbsides. Pulled outside by the moon and struggling for air among the sewers. They're suffocating too, but there's no town assembly line of food. No palpable urgency, no airlifting plane.

15 Fifty stranded whales are a tangible crisis with a visible solution. There's camaraderie in the process, a *Free Willy* fantasy, an image of Flipper in everyone's mind. There's nothing romantic about waking up a man on a park bench and making him walk to a shelter. Little self-righteous fulfillment comes from sending a check to Oxfam International.

16 Would there be such a commotion if a man washed up on the beach? Yes. But stranded humans don't roll in with the tide—they hide in the corners and the concrete houses and the plains of exotic countries we've never heard of, dying of diseases we can't pronounce.

17 In theory I can say that our resources should be concentrated on saving human lives, that our SAVE THE WHALES T-shirts should read SAVE THE STARVING ETHIOPIANS. Logically, it's an easy argument to make. Why do we spend so much time caring about animals? Yes, their welfare is important, but surely that of humans is more so.

18 Last year a nonprofit spent $10,000 transporting a whale to an aquarium in Florida, where it died only three days after arriving. That same $10,000 could have purchased hundreds of thousands of food rations. In theory, this is easy to say.

19 But when I was looking in the eye of a dying pilot whale at four in the morning, my thoughts were not so philosophical. Four hours until high tide. Keep his skin moist. Just three hours now. There wasn't time for logic. My rationality had slipped away with the ebbing dance of the waves.

20 I had helped all day. We had managed to save twenty-seven of the fifty whales, but twenty-three others were deemed too far up shore, too old, or already too close to death. That night, after most of the volunteers had gone home, I went back outside my bedroom to check on the whales.

21 It was mid-tide, and the up-shore seaward still crunched under my bare feet. The water was rising. The moonlight drifted down on the salt-caked battlefield, reflected in the tiny pools of water and half-shell oysters.

22 It was easy to spot the living whales. Their bodies, still moist, shone in the moonlight. I weaved between carcasses, kneeling down beside an old whale that was breathing deeply and far too rapidly for a healthy pilot.

23 I put my hands on his nose and placed my face in front of his visible eye. I knew he was going to die, and he knew he was going to die, and we both understood that there was nothing either of use could do about it.

24 Beached whales die on their sides, one eye pressed into the sand, the other facing up and forced to look at the moon, at the orb that pulled the water out from under its fins.

25 There's no echolocation on land. I imagine dying slowly next to my mother or a

lover, helplessly unable to relay my parting message. I remember trying to convince myself that everything would be fine. But he wouldn't be fine. Just like the homeless man and the Ethiopian aren't fine.

Perhaps I should have been comforting one of them, placing my hands on their shoulders. Spending my time and my money and my life saving those who walked on two legs and spoke without echoes. 26

The moon pulled the waters forward and backward, then inward and around my ankles. Before I could find an answer, the whale's jaw unclenched, opening lightly around the edges. 27

Reading for Better Writing

1. *Connections:* Have you witnessed a sick or injured animal struggle to live? Where did the event happen, when, and why? How did you respond at the time, and how does recalling the event now make you feel—especially in light of reading Keegan's essay?
2. *Comprehension:*
   a. Summarize Keegan's essay. What is her topic, how does she introduce it, and how does she entice us to care about it? What passages do you find most engaging?
   b. What is her thesis, and what does she compare and contrast in order to develop the thesis?
   c. Describe her attitude toward her topic and cite passages that convey this attitude.
3. *Writing Strategies:*
   a. In the opening sentences, Keegan uses personification to describe the moon. What is the effect of beginning this way?
   b. For the first half of the essay (paragraphs 1-12), Keegan explores the human response to the beaching of whales. What techniques does she use to help readers understand this situation?
   c. At paragraph 13, Keegan turns from stranded whales to stranded people. What techniques does she use to compare and contrast the two situations?
   d. How do the opening and closing paragraphs frame Keegan's essay?

Your Project: Review your answer to question 1. Then consider writing an essay in which you compare and/or contrast your experience with Keegan's. Another option would be to consider other connections and distinctions between humans and animals.

Analyzing a Journey

In the following untitled essay, Barbara Kingsolver, a well-traveled novelist, poet, journalist and more, playfully compares and contrasts traits of Japanese culture with corresponding traits of American culture.

1 My Great-Aunt Zelda went to Japan and took an abacus, a bathysphere, a conundrum. That was a game we used to play. All you had to do was remember everything.

2 Then I grew up and went to Japan myself. It was 1992. I was warned to expect a modern place. People said, "Take appliances, battery packs, cellular technology," but I arrived in Kyoto an utter foreigner, unprepared. Yes, there are electric streetcars. Also golden pagodas and more invisible guidelines for politeness than I could fathom. When I stepped on a streetcar, a full head taller than everyone, I became an awkward giant. I took up too much space. I bumped into people. I crossed my arms when I listened, which it turns out is brazen. I didn't know how to eat noodle soup with chopsticks and I did it wrong. I never expected in the sweltering heat that a woman should wear stockings, but every woman in Kyoto wore nylon stockings. Coeds in shorts on the tennis courts wore stockings. I wore skirts and sandals; people averted their eyes.

3 When I went to Japan I took my attitude, my bare naked legs, my callous foreign ways. I was mortified. The Japanese language accommodates no insults, only infinite degrees of apology. I memorized the direst one. "*Sumimasen*" It means, "I wish I were dead!" In the public bath I couldn't get the hang of showering with a hand-held nozzle while sitting fourteen inches from a stranger. I sprayed my elderly neighbor with cold water. In the face. "*Sumimasen*!" She just stared, dismayed by the foreign menace.

> "The Japanese language accommodates no insults, only infinite degrees of apology."

4 I visited a Japanese friend, and in her small, perfect house I spewed my misery. "Everything I do is wrong!" I wailed like a child. "I'm a blight on your country."

5 "Oh no," she said calmly. "To forgive, for us, is the highest satisfaction. To forgive a foreigner, ah! Even better. You have probably made many people happy."

6 When I went to Japan I took my abject good will, my baleful excuses, my

cringing remorse. I couldn't remember everything so I gave myself away, evidently a kind of public service. I prepared to return feeling empty-handed.

7 On the runway in Osaka Airport we sat in a typhoon, waiting to leave for Los Angeles. Suddenly our flight was canceled. Air-traffic control had been struck by lightning. No flight possible until the following day. "We are so sorry," the pilot said. "You will be taken to a hotel, fed, brought back tomorrow." Disembarking, we found an airline official posted in the exit port for the sole purpose of saying to each and every passenger, "Terrible, Terrible. *Sumimasen*" Other travelers nodded with indifference, but not me. I took the startled gentleman by the hands and practically kissed him. "You have no idea," I said, "how thoroughly I forgive you."

Reading for Better Writing

1. *Connections:* Consider Barbara Kingsolver's embarrassment in this essay. Have you ever had difficulty understanding what someone said, or getting another person to understand you? Where did this take place, when, why, and what was the outcome? How did you feel?
2. *Comprehension:*
   a. In response to the prompt, "journeys," Kingsolver wrote this brief essay about her trip to Japan. What experiences does she describe, and what details does she offer about each?
   b. What does she learn about Japanese culture, American culture, cultural miscommunication, and about herself?
3. *Writing Strategies:*
   a. Kingsolver writes with self-deprecating humor. Identify examples and explain why they are funny. How does she use comparison and contrast to help readers picture an event and appreciate its humor?
   b. Find two descriptive passages that you enjoy, and explain how her word choice enlivens the prose.

Your Project: Consider writing an essay about two people or two groups who had significantly different assessments or interpretations of the same person, issue, or event. In your essay, use comparison and contrast as needed to analyze the situation.

Analyzing Internet Bullying

As a contributor to *The New Yorker,* Maria Konnikova writes regularly about psychology and science. In the essay that follows, she uses comparison-contrast to analyze how and why bullying has changed during the last few decades. Konnikova's books include *Mastermind: How to Think Like Sherlock Holmes* and *The Confidence Game*. (Her essay is from the October 21, 2015 edition of *The New Yorker.*)

How the Internet Has Changed Bullying

This summer, *American Psychologist*, the official journal of the American Psychological Association, released a special issue on the topic of bullying and victimization. Bullying is, presumably, as old as humanity, but research into it is relatively young: in 1997, when Susan Swearer, one of the issue's two editors, first started studying the problem, she was one of the first researchers in the United States to do so. Back then, only four states had official statutes against bullying behavior, and the only existing longitudinal work had come out of Scandinavia, in the seventies. After Columbine, however, the landscape changed. The popular narrative at the time held that the shooters, Eric Harris and Dylan Klebold, had been bullied, and that idea—which has since been challenged—prompted a nationwide conversation about bullying, which researchers around the country began studying in earnest. This special issue marks one of the first attempts to systematically review what we've learned in the last two decades—and, especially, to explore whether and how the Internet has changed the bullying landscape. 1

In some ways, bullying research has affirmed what we already know. Bullying is the result of an unequal power dynamic—the strong attacking the weak. It can happen in different ways: through physical violence, verbal abuse (in person or online), or the management of relationships (spreading rumors, humiliation, and exclusion). It is usually prolonged (most bullies are repeat offenders) and widespread (a bully targets multiple victims). Longitudinal work shows that bullies and victims can switch places: there is an entire category of bully-victims—people who are victims in one set of circumstances and perpetrators in another. Finally, emerging research demonstrates that bullying follows us throughout life. Workplace and professional bullying is just as common as childhood bullying; often, it's just less obvious. (At work—one hopes—people don't steal your bicycle or give you a wedgie.) 2

To date, no one has systematically studied how different bullying settings affect 3 bullying behavior—whether bullying in the Northeast differs from bullying in the Midwest, or whether bullying in certain cultures, neighborhoods, or professions comes with its own characteristics. What Swearer has noticed, however, in her nearly two decades of bullying research is a persistent—and seemingly fundamental—environmental distinction between urban and rural bullying. In urban and even mid-sized city environments, anonymity is possible. Even if you're bullied in school, you can have a supportive friend group at your local pickup basketball game. And there are multiple schools and multiple neighborhoods, which means you can float from one to the other, leaving bullying behind you in the process.

By contrast, in rural settings, "There aren't options," Swearer said, when we 4
spoke earlier this month. "It's impossible to get away." The next school may be a hundred miles distant, so you are stuck where you are. What's more, everyone knows everyone. The problems of reporting a bully—or, if you are a bully, of becoming less of one—become much more intractable, because your reputation surrounds you, and behavioral patterns are harder to escape. "Your world becomes an isolated and small place," Swearer says. Isolation itself, she points out, can lead to a sense of helplessness and lack of control—feelings that are associated with some of the worst, most persistent psychological problems in any population, including bullying.

In some ways, when it comes to bullying, the Internet has made the world 5
more rural. Before the Internet, bullying ended when you withdrew from whatever environment you were in. But now, the bullying dynamic is harder to contain and harder to ignore. If you're harassed on your Facebook page, all of your social circles know about it; as long as you have access to the network, a ceaseless stream of notifications leaves you vulnerable to victimhood. Bullying may not have become more prevalent—in fact, a recent review of international data suggests that its incidence has declined by as much as ten percent around the world. But getting away from it has become more difficult.

The inescapability of "cyberbullying" has huge consequences not just for children 6
but also for adults. While workplace bullying is still a new field of study, adults seem to experience bullying just as much as kids do. A 2012 study from the University of Nottingham and the University of Sheffield, in the U.K., found that eight out of ten of the three hundred and twenty adults surveyed across three different universities had been victims of cyberbullying in the last six months; about a quarter reported feeling

humiliated or ignored, or being the subject of online gossip, at least once a week. The effects of adult bullying can be just as severe, if not more so, than those of childhood bullying. While students can go to their teachers if they're being bullied, if you report your boss, you could be out of a job. And adult victims of cyberbullying tend to suffer higher levels of mental strain and lower job satisfaction than those subjected to more traditional forms of bullying. An undermining colleague can be put out of mind at the end of the day. But someone who persecutes you over email, social networks, or anonymous comments is far more difficult to avoid and dismiss.

Many forms of adult bullying are uncomfortably close to the sorts of shaming behaviors outlined by Jon Ronson in his recent book, *"So You've Been Publicly Shamed."* Ronson documents the rise of cyberbrigades, which unite in virtual outrage, on Twitter, Reddit, or elsewhere online, to disparage someone's words or behavior. Participants often feel that their abusive actions flow from justified outrage—but all bullies think that their behavior is justified. "We know from moral disengagement work that all bullies feel morally justified in their actions," Swearer pointed out. Ask people why they bully, and they rarely say, "Because I can." They say, "Because I need to." Bullies believe they are teaching someone a lesson; they claim that their victims are, through their own actions or faults, asking for it, and that they need to be called out and corrected. "They say it's retaliatory. 'I just retaliated,' " Swearer said. "They build narratives of their behaviors." Many of the bullies Swearer has dealt with don't seem to have realized that what they did was bullying: they demonstrate "a lack of insight and self-awareness." Instead, they see themselves as righteous crusaders. 7

In children, it's possible to instill self-awareness about bullying through schoolwide interventions. Catherine Bradshaw, a psychologist and associate dean at the University of Virginia who studies bullying prevention, has found that the most effective approaches are multilayered and include training, behavior-modification guidelines, and systems for detailed data collection. (More, in other words, than a stray assembly or distributed book.) Unfortunately, the equivalent for adults can be hard to find. Many adult bullies hide behind the idea that bullying happens only among children. They conceive of themselves as adults who know better and are offering their hard-earned wisdom to others. The Internet makes that sort of certainty easier to attain: looking at their screens, adult bullies rarely see the impact of their 8 words and actions. Instead, they comfortably bask in self-righteous glory. The U.K. study from 2012 found that online bystanders, too, are disengaged. Observing the actions of cyberbullies, they were less concerned than when they watched in-person bullying.

In short, the picture that's emerged suggests that the Internet has made bullying 9
both harder to escape and harder to identify. It has also, perhaps, made bullies out of some of us who would otherwise not be. We are immersed in an online world in which consequences often go unseen—and that has made it easier to deceive ourselves about what we are doing. The first step to preventing bullying among adults, therefore, might be simple: introspection.

Reading for Better Writing

1. *Connections:* Do you know anyone who has been a perpetrator or victim of cyberbullying? How did it start, how was it done, and what was the outcome?
2. *Comprehension:*
   - **a.** Summarize paragraph 2 in which Konnikova describes bullying and offers examples.
   - **b.** In paragraphs 3 and 4, she compares and contrasts urban bullying with rural bullying. How are they similar and different?
   - **c.** In paragraph 5 Konnikova says, "In some ways, when it comes to bullying, the Internet has made the world more rural." What does she mean, and what does this claim suggest about the danger of cyberbullying?
   - **d.** How is adult bullying similar to or different from adolescent or teen bullying?
3. *Writing Strategies:*
   - **a.** Konnikova compares in-person bullying to cyberbullying, urban bullying to rural bullying, and adolescent and teen bullying to adult bullying. How does she develop each of these comparisons? How does each advance her argument?
   - **b.** She supports her claims by quoting authorities and citing research. Find two examples and explain how each one strengthens her argument.
   - **c.** Review the last paragraph. How does it bring the essay to a close?

Your Project: Bullying is just one behavior that has been impacted by the digital revolution. Consider comparing-contrasting another behavior similarly impacted (e.g., reading, dating, researching, shopping, traveling).

Writing Guidelines

Planning

1. **Select a topic.** Begin by reviewing the project options listed at the end of each sample essay. To generate more topic ideas, list subjects that are similar and/or different in ways that you find interesting, perplexing, disgusting, infuriating, charming, or informing. Then choose two subjects whose comparison and/or contrast gives the reader some insight into who or what they are. ***Note:*** Make sure that the items have a solid *basis* for comparison. Comparable items are types of the same thing (e.g., two rivers, two characters, two films, two mental illnesses, two theories).
2. **Get the big picture.** Using a computer or a paper and pen, create three columns as shown in Figure 14.3. Brainstorm a list of traits under each heading.

Features Peculiar to Subject #1	Shared Features	Features Peculiar to Subject #2

fig. 14.3

3. **Gather information.** Review your list of features, highlighting those that could provide insight into one or both subjects. Research the subjects, using hands-on analysis when possible. Consider writing your research notes in the three-column format shown in Figure 14.3.
4. **Draft a working thesis.** Write a sentence stating the core of what you learned about the subjects: what essential insight have you reached about the similarities and/or differences between the topics? If you're stuck, try completing the following sentence. (Switch around the terms "similar" and "different" if you wish to stress similarities.)

   Whereas ____________ and ____________ seem similar, they are different in several ways, and the differences are important because ____________.

5. **Get organized.** Decide how to organize your essay. Generally, *subject by subject* works better for short, simple comparisons. *Trait by trait* works better for longer, more complex comparisons, in that you hold up the topics side by side, trait by trait (see Figure 14.4). Consider, as well, the order in which you will discuss the topics and arrange the traits, choices that depend on what you want to feature and how you want to build and deepen the comparison.

Subject by Subject:	**Trait by Trait:**
Introduction	Introduction
Subject #1	Trait A
• Trait A	• Subject #1
• Trait B	• Subject #2
Subject #2	Trait B
• Trait A	• Subject #1
• Trait B	• Subject #2

fig. 14.4

Drafting

6. **Write your first draft.** Review your outline and draft the paper.

Subject-by-subject pattern:

- **Opening:** get readers' attention, introduce the subjects, and offer a thesis.
- **Middle:** discuss the first subject, then analyze the second subject, discussing traits parallel to those you addressed with the first subject.
- **Conclusion:** summarize similarities, differences, and implications.

Trait-by-trait pattern:

- **Opening:** get readers' attention, introduce the subjects, and offer a thesis.
- **Middle:** compare and/or contrast the two subjects trait by trait; include transitions that help readers look back and forth between the two subjects.
- **Conclusion:** summarize the key relationships and note their significance.

Revising

7. **Get feedback.** Ask someone to read your paper, looking for a clear thesis, an engaging introduction, a middle that compares and/or contrasts parallel traits in a logical order, and a unifying closing.

8. **Rework your draft.** Based on feedback, revise for the following issues:

___ **Ideas:** The points made and conclusions drawn from comparing and contrasting provide insight into both subjects.

___ **Organization:** The structure, whether subject by subject or trait by trait, helps readers grasp the similarities and differences between the subjects.

___ **Voice:** The tone is informed, involved, and genuine.

Editing and Proofreading

9. **Carefully edit your essay.** Look for the following issues:

___ **Words** are precise, clear, and defined as needed.

___ **Sentences** are clear, well reasoned, varied in structure, and smooth.

___ **Correctness:** The writing is clean and properly formatted.

___ **Page design** is attractive and follows MLA or APA guidelines.

Publishing

10. **Publish your essay.** Share your writing by submitting it to your instructor, posting it on a Web site, sharing it with friends and family who might be interested in the topic, crafting a presentation or demonstration, or reshaping your comparison as a blog.

MindTap® Request help and feedback from a tutor. If required, participate in peer review, submit your paper for a grade, and view instructor comments online.

Critical Thinking and Writing: Applications

After you have finished your comparison-contrast essay, consider how to apply what you have learned in the following situations.

1. **Living Today:** In the workplace, people commonly use comparison-contrast reasoning to complete tasks such as selecting employees, choosing materials and equipment, and designing marketing plans. Think about your current or future job and list ways in which sound comparison-contrast reasoning will help you succeed.
2. **Career Plan:** Choose two or three occupations that interest you. Researching them as needed, compare and contrast their required training, social benefits, financial rewards, availability, required experience, and personal appeal. Consider using this information to write or update your career plan.
3. **Writing Reset:** Select a piece of your writing that could be improved. Then compare your writing with similar papers written by classmates or available on the Internet. Identify strategies for improving your ideas, organization, and voice.
4. **Cultural Insight:** Research two ethnic groups that interest you. Then use comparison and contrast to analyze their systems of government, religious practices, penal institutions, educational systems, or healthcare programs.
5. **Sports Talk:** Compare and contrast two coaches in the same sport, examining issues such as their philosophies of the game, personalities, experiences as players, win-loss records, coaching strategies, teams coached, awards, and titles.

Learning-Objectives Checklist ✓

Have you achieved this chapter's learning objectives? Check your progress with the following items, revisiting topics in the chapter as needed. I have . . .

____ interpreted comparison-contrast essays, ascertaining how the writers' purposes, readers, and topics may have shaped their patterns of reasoning (234–235).

____ examined subject-by-subject and trait-by-trait organizational patterns, identifying their similarities, differences, strengths, and weaknesses (234–235).

____ established a logical basis for a comparison claim by analyzing topics of the same order or type (248–249).

____ developed a reasonable comparison by assessing each subject using the same criteria in the same manner (248–249).

____ supported my comparison-contrast reasoning with precise details, as well as with transitional words that clarify similarities and differences (86).

____ strengthened my compare-contrast writing by using effective revising and editing strategies (248–249).

____ used additional analytical strategies (such as definition) to illustrate a point or develop a claim (174–175).

____ planned, drafted, revised, and polished a logical comparison-contrast essay (248–249).

MindTap® Practice skills that you have learned in this chapter and receive automatic feedback. Reflect on your writing process.

Chapter 15

Cause and Effect

Now, why did that happen? We ask this question every day at home, in college, and on the job in order to understand and cope with things that happen in our lives. For example, knowing why a computer crashed will help us avoid that problem, and knowing the causes and effects of a disease such as diabetes can help us control the condition. In other words, cause and effect reasoning helps us deal with everyday issues, whether large or small.

In a cause and effect essay, the writer develops the thesis through cause and effect reasoning. That is, she or he analyzes and explains the causes, the effects, or both the causes and the effects of a phenomenon. In addition, the writer may use other analytical strategies (such as definition or classification) to clarify a concept or further develop a claim. This chapter includes instructions and samples that will help you read and write cause-effect analyses.

Visually Speaking Carefully study Figure 15.1. What cause-effect relationships are shown? What writing strategies could you use to analyze the phenomenon pictured?

MindTap®

Understand the goals of the chapter and complete a warm-up activity online.

Learning **Objectives**

By working through this chapter, you will be able to

- understand, interpret, and critique writing that utilizes cause-effect reasoning.
- analyze a phenomenon by identifying and explaining its causes and effects.
- identify and correct related logical fallacies.
- support cause-effect reasoning with detailed, reliable evidence.
- clarify cause-effect relationships by inserting transitional words.
- draft, revise, and edit an essay that uses cause-effect reasoning in conjunction with other relevant analytical modes.

Strahil Dimitrov / Shutterstock.com

fig. 15.1

Strategies for Cause-Effect Essays

Cause-effect thinking can move in two directions. First, it can explore the effects of a particular event, action, or phenomenon—the logical results, actual or anticipated. Second, it can trace backward from a particular result to those forces that created the results—the causes. As writers think through causes and effects, their job is to establish and explain solid cause-effect links, as discussed in the strategies below.

The Rhetorical Situation

To put cause-effect writing in context, consider the situation that gives rise to it:

- **Purpose.** Writers use cause-effect analysis to deepen understanding regarding how specific forces work to bring about particular results. In academia and the workplace, cause-effect logic operates in many forms of writing—from persuasive essays and lab reports to project proposals and market analyses. In each situation, writers use cause-effect thinking to explain a phenomenon or to prove a point.
- **Readers.** The readers of cause-effect writing typically understand the topic at a basic level but want or need a deeper understanding of the forces operating within it so as to make decisions about or take positions on it.
- **Topic.** Cause-effect topics are phenomena—events, occurrences, developments, processes, problems, conditions, and so on—that need to be more fully explained in terms of their operating forces.

Example: In "Familiar Strangers" (pages 254–258), Audrey Torrest's **topic** is a condition known as *congenital prosopagnosia* or face blindness. Her **purpose** is to help **readers** (classmates and professor) understand the causes and effects of the disorder.

Principles of Cause-Effect Writing

Cause-effect writing depends upon the logical principles explained below.

Exploring cause-effect links. Such writing tests all possible explanations for a given phenomenon's causes and effects. Consider these options:

- **Causes:** What forces can be designated primary or root causes? What forces are secondary or contributing causes? Which causes are immediate (near), and which are remote (distant)? What cause-effect "evidence" is simply coincidental? What evidence—measurements, testimony, and so on—supports or disproves the causal links? Can the links be tested?
- **Effects:** What are the primary, secondary, and ripple effects? Which are main effects and which are side effects, which immediate and which long-term? What is the seriousness or strength of each effect? What aspects of the cause led to the various effects? Do the effects themselves become causes of a different set of effects in a kind of "chain reaction"?

Establishing a cause-effect thesis. The thesis is an insight growing out of careful study of the topic, often following one of these templates:

- **Focus on causes:** Based on a close examination of the forces at work, we can conclude that A and B are the fundamental causes of C.
- **Focus on effects:** Based on a close examination of the forces at work, we can conclude that the most important results of A have been X, Y, and Z.

Example: When people around the globe watch Hollywood blockbuster films, they absorb a distorted vision of U.S. culture that fuels misunderstanding and, in fact, undermines the government's "war on terror."

Supplying reliable cause-effect evidence. Cause-effect analysis is based on a logical interpretation of the evidence, analysis that avoids these problems: (1) relying extensively on circumstantial evidence, (2) drawing firm conclusions without adequate support, and (3) mistaking sequence for a cause-effect link (see the *false-cause fallacy*, page 325).

Organizing cause-effect analysis to feature the chain of reasoning. The phrasing of the thesis implies a certain method of developing and supporting the thesis—a way of proceeding with and handling the cause-effect evidence. Generally, writers structure their essays according to the direction of analysis (from effect to causes or from cause to effects). It is often necessary to begin by exploring background in order to situate the cause-effect analysis.

Sample Cause-Effect Paragraph:

By no means purporting to tell the whole story, the HTM [History That Matters approach to historical study] reduces the past to its pith or essence. Like the Ten Commandments, it identifies specific shalts and shalt nots. Like the Sermon on the Mount, it prescribes a code of behavior. In doing so, the HTM makes the past usable. Endlessly reiterated in political speech and reinforced by popular culture, the "lessons" of this usable past prescribe what the United States—the indispensable nation—is called upon to do and what it must refrain from doing.

Reading Cause-Effect Writing

As you read the essays on the following pages, consider these questions:

1. Is the writer's rationale for writing informed, reasonable, and convincing?
2. Who is the intended audience, and does the essay present all the necessary information?
3. Is the topic clearly identified and explored as a phenomenon?
4. Is the thesis clear, and is the argument free of logical fallacies?
5. Are the writer's claims sufficiently limited, focused, and logical?

Sample Cause-Effect Essays

Cause-effect essays can address a wide range of topics—from phenomena in nature to events in the news. In the following essays, writers address topics as varied as a face-recognition disorder, groupthink, shark attacks, the impacts of new technologies on human intelligence, and strategies for historical analysis.

MindTap®
Read, highlight, and take notes online.

Analyzing a Cognitive Disorder

Audrey Torrest is a student at the University of California at Davis where she took the class, "Writing in the Health Professions." For one of her assignments, she chose the topic *prosopagnosia*, researched related texts, interviewed a scholar who has the disorder, and wrote the following essay. She subsequently entered her essay in the university's annual writing contest where it was awarded publication in the book *Prized Writing, 2014–2015*.

Familiar Strangers

Dr. Smith stood beside a fellow neurobiologist on the campus of Washington University in St. Louis. While engrossed in conversation, Smith noticed from the corner of his eye an undergraduate walking in their direction. At first he thought nothing of it, but as she approached, it dawned on him that she was looking directly at him. "Strange," he thought. He tried to ignore her and continue his conversation, but when she was about 20 feet away he heard her laugh. Upon hearing the sound, the unfamiliar undergraduate who had been staring so intently at him morphed into his daughter. Smith had been unable to recognize her. 1

Dr. Smith suffers from a unique condition known as prosopagnosia, or face blindness. Historically, most documented cases have been due to brain damage suffered after maturity from head trauma, stroke, or degenerative diseases. Recently, however, studies have demonstrated that many more people suffer from prosopagnosia without experiencing neurological damage (Avidan, Hasson, Malach, & Behrmann, 2005). Smith suffers from this form of face blindness, known as congenital prosopagnosia. Although he spent the vast majority of his life unaware of his condition, Dr. Smith, now 54 years old, acknowledges that it all makes sense in retrospect. 2

As a kid, Smith moved around a lot because his father worked for General Electric 3 and was transferred every couple of years. Dr. Smith always felt like a newcomer and never realized that it was unusual to have difficulties recognizing people after a year or two of being in the same place. At family reunions, his relatives eventually figured out that he couldn't recognize them and began to greet him with announcements of their identities: "You probably don't remember me . . . I am so-and-so." Since these people were all in the context of the family reunion, it was obvious to the young Dr. Smith that they were relatives, but none of them looked familiar. At one point he moved back into a school district where he had lived five years prior and was disconcerted to find that he couldn't recognize any of his former friends. He justified this by concluding that everybody had changed and grown up and the only reason they could recognize him was because he was the "new guy."

In college, when Smith and his roommate were in a group, he grew tired of Smith's asking him to identify people. Consequently, when someone approached the pair, the roommate habitually greeted the person by name, thereby identifying the individual for Smith and averting his embarrassment. At the time, Smith believed that he had difficulty recalling names, not realizing that his real problem was recognizing faces. 4

Then, at the University of Rochester Medical School, Dr. Smith learned about prosopagnosia. Medical students often perceive in themselves symptoms of diseases that they are studying. Upon learning about prosopagnosia, Smith thought that perhaps he was somewhere along the spectrum, on the lesser end of it even. Unlike the cliché of medical students who misdiagnose themselves with illnesses they are studying, Smith's self-diagnosis was accurate, though his perception of its severity was not. In reality, Smith is significantly impaired. 5

Imagine standing in a sea of unfamiliar faces every morning when you go to class. In medical school, Smith struggled to recognize his classmates despite being in small classes every day with the same people. At the beginning of the school year before classes began, he acquired a little book with everyone's picture in it. Thinking that he had trouble remembering names, Smith tried to memorize the people 6

"Imagine standing in a sea of unfamiliar faces every morning when you go to class."

in the book by matching the names with the pictures. This turned out to be of no help. Although he eventually reached a point where he could identify the pictures, when the time came to apply what he had memorized to real people, Smith was unsuccessful. The pictures were static, located in particular places on the page, with people wearing particular clothes. But in the classroom, without the clothing and position clues, identifying the actual people was impossible.

Later, while living in Boston, Dr. Smith had a daughter. When she was about six months old, Smith and his wife began taking her to daycare. Often, he or his wife dropped her off, and the other would pick her up. Whenever his wife dropped her off, he wouldn't know what his daughter was wearing that day. Picking up his daughter would then prove to be an immense challenge because he lacked the clues he needed to recognize her. As Dr. Smith said, "You can't walk into a daycare and ask people which child is yours." In order to avoid this awkward situation, Smith usually arrived when the daycare was about to close, ensuring that his daughter would be one of the few kids left. 7

After 40 or so years of unusual experiences and inexplicable challenges, the mystery was finally solved when Dr. Smith was giving a talk in Pittsburgh and prefaced it by mentioning that he was not great with names and faces and that people shouldn't feel insulted if he didn't recognize them. Marlene Behrmann, a researcher who studies prosopagnosia, happened to be in the audience and asked if he would be willing to do some testing. Smith was reluctant initially, stating that he believed he was within the spectrum of normalcy, but she persisted and he eventually gave in. Following a series of tests, Behrmann diagnosed Smith with congenital prosopagnosia. Since congenital prosopagnosia frequently runs in families, Smith's children were both tested but were found to be unaffected. Smith believes that his father may also have prosopagnosia, but he refuses to get tested. 8

When I met Dr. Smith, I asked him to describe what he experiences when he first sees someone's face. He described this by comparing the differences between human and bird vision. Since humans have three types of cones with different photopsins—red, green, and blue—we are said to have trichromatic vision. Birds, on the other hand, have four cones, or tetrachromatic vision (Goldsmith, 1991). This means that there is a whole spectrum of colors that humans are missing but birds can see. In this sense, 9 all humans are colorblind. So what does prosopagnosia feel like to Dr. Smith? Well, it feels like nothing at all. Individuals with prosopagnosia do not sense that they are missing anything, any more than you or I feel that we are missing any aspects of our color vision. Nevertheless, prosopagnosia can result in tremendous difficulties with human interactions since face recognition plays such a pivotal role in cognition and socialization.

> "Individuals with prosopagnosia do not sense that they are missing anything, any more than you or I feel that we are missing any aspects of our color vision."

10 The human face provides a number of important cues for recognition of individuals. Although people with prosopagnosia exhibit difficulty with conscious recognition—the identification of specific facial features—they demonstrate a relatively normal ability to recognize faces unconsciously through emotional responses and other subtle social cues. Smith sometimes "hitchhikes on other people's facial recognition systems." Essentially, he looks at others for signs of recognition and uses their responses to conclude whether he knows them or not. Dr. Smith relies on a variety of other cues but perhaps depends most heavily on context to aid him in the identification process. When he goes to the park, for example, he recognizes his friends by their dogs. Interestingly, Smith is unsure about whether his facial recognition deficit also applies to animals. This is in part because it is difficult to objectively evaluate one's own facial recognition abilities and also because, in the case of dogs, it is not generally their faces that one recognizes but rather their breed. Although context can be an incredibly useful tool, sometimes it simply doesn't work. "One thing that I occasionally do is that I'll meet someone in two different contexts and I'll think they are two different people, or I'll meet two people around the same time and I'll think they're the same person," Smith stated. He can usually identify a person spatially, but when the person begins to move around, Smith loses his contextual anchors and can no longer recognize him or her.

11 Although individuals with prosopagnosia rely heavily on context and emotional responses to compensate for the difficulties they have with facial recognition, they continue to encounter broad challenges. Currently, no formal treatment is available.

The most important thing prospagnosiacs can do is inform people about their condition so that others will not be offended when they are not recognized. When I asked Dr. Smith at the end of the discussion if there was anything else he would like to mention, he replied, "Don't be insulted if I run into you tomorrow or a month from now and have absolutely no idea that I've met you before."

Note: The References page is not shown. For an example, see pages 530–531.

Reading for Better Writing

1. *Connections:* Recall a time when you met someone who looked familiar, but you could not remember her or his name. Or recall a time when you met another person, addressed the individual by name, but he or she did not recognize you. In either case, what did you and your acquaintance do next? How did you feel? Why? How does recalling the event help you understand this essay?
2. *Comprehension:*
   a. Summarize Audrey Torrest's essay, including details about the nature of prosopagnosia, how Dr. Smith learned that he had the condition, and how he compensated for it as a child and as an adult.
   b. Describe a few occasions when other people recognized Smith's disability. In each case, how did the individuals respond, and how do you think their responses made him feel?
3. *Writing Strategies:*
   a. Torrest uses multiple anecdotes. Identify three, summarize each story, describe how it is used, and explain why it does or does not help you understand the causes and effects of prosopagnosia.
   b. In paragraphs two and eight, Torrest supports her claims by citing three academic experts. Do the citations support her assertions? Explain.

Your Project: Other conditions that may impede one's ability to communicate with others might be poor eyesight, poor hearing, brain trauma, brain stroke, brain cancer, or cognitive disorders such as dementia, depression, or Alzheimer's. Choose one, research it, and consider writing about how the condition may affect one's communication skills.

Analyzing a Trend

Susan Cain is a Harvard-trained attorney, a businessperson, a negotiations consultant, and the author of a number of books and articles, including *Quiet: The Power of Introverts in a World That Can't Stop Talking.* In the following essay, she defines *New Groupthink* and analyzes its causes and effects. (The essay was published in the January 13, 2012 edition of *The New York Times.*)

The Rise of the New Groupthink

Solitude is out of fashion. Our companies, our schools and our culture are in thrall to an idea I call the New Groupthink, which holds that creativity and achievement come from an oddly gregarious place. Most of us now work in teams, in offices without walls, for managers who prize people skills above all. Lone geniuses are out. Collaboration is in. 1

But there's a problem with this view. Research strongly suggests that people are more creative when they enjoy privacy and freedom from interruption. And the most spectacularly creative people in many fields are often introverted, according to studies by the psychologists Mihaly Csikszentmihalyi and Gregory Feist. They're extroverted enough to exchange and advance ideas, but see themselves as independent and individualistic. They're not joiners by nature. 2

One explanation for these findings is that introverts are comfortable working alone—and solitude is a catalyst to innovation. As the influential psychologist Hans Eysenck observed, introversion fosters creativity by "concentrating the mind on the tasks in hand, and preventing the dissipation of energy on social and sexual matters unrelated to work." In other words, a person sitting quietly under a tree in the backyard, while everyone else is clinking glasses on the patio, is more likely to have an apple land on his head. (Newton was one of the world's great introverts: William Wordsworth described him as "A mind for ever/ Voyaging through strange seas of Thought, alone.") 3

Solitude has long been associated with creativity and transcendence. "Without great solitude, no serious work is possible," Picasso said. A central narrative of many religions is the seeker—Moses, Jesus, Buddha—who goes off by himself and brings profound insights back to the community. 4

Culturally, we're often so dazzled by charisma that we overlook the quiet part of the creative process. Consider Apple. In the wake of Steve Jobs's death, we've seen a profusion of myths about the company's success. Most focus on Mr. Jobs's supernatural magnetism and tend to ignore the other crucial figure in Apple's creation: a kindly, introverted engineering wizard, Steve Wozniak, who toiled alone on a beloved invention, the personal computer. 5

Rewind to March 1975: Mr. Wozniak believes the world would be a better place if everyone had a user-friendly computer. This seems a distant dream—most computers are still the size of minivans, and many times as pricey. But Mr. Wozniak meets a simpatico band of engineers that call themselves the Homebrew Computer Club. The Homebrewers are excited about a primitive new machine called the Altair 8800. Mr. Wozniak is inspired, and immediately begins work on his own magical version of a computer. Three months later, he unveils his amazing creation for his friend, Steve Jobs. Mr. Wozniak wants to give his invention away free, but Mr. Jobs persuades him to cofound Apple Computer. 6

The story of Apple's origin speaks to the power of collaboration. Mr. Wozniak wouldn't have been catalyzed by the Altair but for the kindred spirits of Homebrew. And he'd never have started Apple without Mr. Jobs. 7

But it's also a story of solo spirit. If you look at how Mr. Wozniak got the work done—the sheer hard work of creating something from nothing—he did it alone. Late at night, all by himself. 8

Intentionally so. In his memoir, Mr. Wozniak offers this guidance to aspiring inventors: "Most inventors and engineers I've met are like me . . . they live in their heads. They're almost like artists. In fact, the very best of them are artists. And artists work best alone . . . I'm going to give you some advice that might be hard to take. That advice is: Work alone. . . . Not on a committee. Not on a team." 9

And yet. The New Groupthink has overtaken our workplaces, our schools and our religious institutions. Anyone who has ever needed noise-cancelling headphones in her own office or marked an online calendar with a fake meeting in order to escape yet another real one knows what I'm talking about. Virtually all American workers now spend time on teams and some 70 percent inhabit open-plan offices, in which no one has "a room of one's own." During the last decades, the average amount of space allotted to each employee shrank 300 square feet, from 500 square feet in the 1970s to 200 square feet in 2010. 10

Our schools have also been transformed by the New Groupthink. Today, elementary school classrooms are commonly arranged in pods of desks, the better to foster group learning. Even subjects like math and creative writing are often taught as committee projects. In one fourth-grade classroom I visited in New York City, students engaged in group work were forbidden to ask a question unless every member of the group had the very same question. 11

The New Groupthink also shapes some of our most influential religious institutions. Many mega-churches feature extracurricular groups organized around every conceivable activity, from parenting to skateboarding to real estate, and expect 12 worshipers to join in. They also emphasize a theatrical style of worship—loving Jesus out loud, for all the congregation to see. "Often the role of a pastor seems closer to that of church cruise director than to the traditional roles of spiritual friend and counselor," said Adam McHugh, an evangelical pastor and author of *Introverts in the Church*.

Some teamwork is fine and offers a fun, stimulating, useful way to exchange ideas, 13
manage information and build trust.

But it's one thing to associate with a group in which each member works 14
autonomously on his piece of the puzzle; it's another to be corralled into endless meetings or conference calls conducted in offices that afford no respite from the noise and gaze of co-workers. Studies show that open-plan offices make workers hostile, insecure and distracted. They're also more likely to suffer from high blood pressure, stress, the flu and exhaustion. And people whose work is interrupted make 50 percent more mistakes and take twice as long to finish it.

Many introverts seem to know this instinctively, and resist being herded together. 15
Backbone Entertainment, a video game development company in Emeryville, Calif., initially used an open-plan office, but found that its game developers, many of whom were introverts, were unhappy. "It was one big warehouse space, with just tables, no walls, and everyone could see each other," recalled Mike Mika, the former creative director. "We switched over to cubicles and were worried about it—you'd think in a creative environment that people would hate that. But it turns out they prefer having nooks and crannies they can hide away in and just be away from everybody."

Privacy also makes us productive. In a fascinating study known as the Coding 16
War Games, consultants Tom DeMarco and Timothy Lister compared the work of more than 600 computer programmers at 92 companies. They found that people from the same companies performed at roughly the same level—but that there was an enormous performance gap between organizations. What distinguished programmers at the top-performing companies wasn't greater experience or better pay. It was how much privacy, personal workspace and freedom from interruption they enjoyed. Sixty-two percent of the best performers said their workspace was sufficiently private compared with only 19 percent of the worst performers. Seventy-six percent of the worst programmers but only 38 percent of the best said that they were often interrupted needlessly.

Solitude can even help us learn. According to research on expert performance by 17
the psychologist Anders Ericsson, the best way to master a field is to work on the task that's most demanding for you personally. And often the best way to do this is alone. Only then, Mr. Ericsson told me, can you "go directly to the part that's challenging to

you. If you want to improve, you have to be the one who generates the move. Imagine a group class—you're the one generating the move only a small percentage of the time."

Conversely, brainstorming sessions are one of the worst possible ways to stimulate creativity. The brainchild of a charismatic advertising executive named Alex Osborn who believed that groups produced better ideas than individuals, workplace-brainstorming sessions came into vogue in the 1950s. "The quantitative results of group brainstorming are beyond question," Mr. Osborn wrote. "One group produced 45 suggestions for a home-appliance promotion, 56 ideas for a money-raising campaign, 124 ideas on how to sell more blankets." 18

But decades of research show that individuals almost always perform better than groups in both quality and quantity, and group performance gets worse as group size increases. The "evidence from science suggests that business people must be insane to use brainstorming groups," wrote the organizational psychologist Adrian Furnham. "If you have talented and motivated people, they should be encouraged to work alone when creativity or efficiency is the highest priority." 19

The reasons brainstorming fails are instructive for other forms of group work, too. People in groups tend to sit back and let others do the work; they instinctively mimic others' opinions and lose sight of their own; and, often succumb to peer pressure. The Emory University neuroscientist Gregory Berns found that when we take a stance different from the group's, we activate the amygdala, a small organ in the brain associated with the fear of rejection. Professor Berns calls this "the pain of independence." 20

The one important exception to this dismal record is electronic brainstorming, where large groups outperform individuals; and the larger the group the better. The protection of the screen mitigates many problems of group work. This is why the Internet has yielded such wondrous collective creations. Marcel Proust called reading a "miracle of communication in the midst of solitude," and that's what the Internet is, too. It's a place where we can be alone together—and this is precisely what gives it power. 21

My point is not that man is an island. Life is meaningless without love, trust and friendship. 22

And I'm not suggesting that we abolish teamwork. Indeed, recent studies suggest that influential academic work is increasingly conducted by teams rather than by individuals. (Although teams whose members collaborate remotely, from separate universities, appear to be the most influential of all.) The problems we face in science, economics and many other fields are more complex than ever before, and we'll need to stand on one another's shoulders if we can possibly hope to solve them. 23

But even if the problems are different, human nature remains the same. And most 24 humans have two contradictory impulses: we love and need one another, yet we crave privacy and autonomy.

To harness the energy that fuels both these drives, we need to move beyond the 25
New Groupthink and embrace a more nuanced approach to creativity and learning. Our offices should encourage casual, cafe-style interactions, but allow people to disappear into personalized, private spaces when they want to be alone. Our schools should teach children to work with others, but also to work on their own for sustained periods of time. And we must recognize that introverts like Steve Wozniak need extra quiet and privacy to do their best work.

Before Mr. Wozniak started Apple, he designed calculators at Hewlett-Packard, a 26
job he loved partly because HP made it easy to chat with his colleagues. Every day at 10 a.m. and 2 p.m., management wheeled in doughnuts and coffee, and people could socialize and swap ideas. What distinguished these interactions was how low-key they were. For Mr. Wozniak, collaboration meant the ability to share a doughnut and a brainwave with his laid-back, poorly dressed colleagues—who minded not a whit when he disappeared into his cubicle to get the real work done.

Reading for Better Writing

1. *Connections:* Was group work stressed in your grade school and high school? Were you seated in pods to encourage interaction with classmates? Is group work stressed in your college classes, and does it help or hinder your learning? Explain.
2. *Comprehension:*
   - **a.** In your own words, state Susan Cain's thesis, paraphrase her definition of *New Groupthink*, and summarize her primary argument.
   - **b.** List four claims she makes about the causes and effects of New Groupthink.
   - **c.** What does she say in paragraphs 11 and 12 regarding the effects of New Groupthink in schools and churches?
3. *Writing Strategies:*
   - **a.** Describe how Cain uses the Steve Wozniak anecdote. Is it effective? Why?
   - **b.** When and how does she use researched evidence? How does that research support cause-effect reasoning?

Your Project: Choose an exceptionally successful teaching strategy used by one of your high school teachers: e.g. group discussion, oral or written report, project proposal, peer editing, research project, blogging, or debate. Then consider writing an essay in which you use cause-effect reasoning to analyze what and why it did (or did not) help you learn.

Analyzing Fear of Sharks

Brian Phillips currently writes for *MTV News* and previously wrote for *Grantland*. He has published his work in a number of venues including *Slate, The New York Times Magazine, The New Republic, The Hudson Review,* and *Poetry*. In this essay, published in 2015 at the Web site *Grantland*, he analyzes what causes the general public's fascination with—and fear of—shark attacks.

Death From Below: Our Summer of Shark Attacks

This summer marks the 40-year anniversary of *Jaws*, and this Friday marks the five-day anniversary of champion surfer Mick Fanning being attacked by a great white shark during a competition on live television. On Wednesday another surfer had "a good chunk" of his arm ripped off by a shark near the French island of Réunion, in the Indian Ocean, where in April an 8-foot bull shark killed a 13-year-old surfer named Elio Canestri, tearing off his arms and legs, according to tabloid reports, before hauling his body out to sea. In the waters off North Carolina, an area that normally sees one or two shark incidents per year, at least eight swimmers have been attacked since the start of June, including two teenagers, bitten 90 minutes apart near Oak Island, who survived only after each having an arm amputated. In May, a man was bitten to death by a bull shark while snorkeling off the coast of New Caledonia, in the South Pacific, just two weeks after a 65-year-old woman was found floating facedown near Maui, with lacerations on her chest indicating that she had been killed by a shark of uncertain species. 1

It has been, in other words, a summer of shark attacks. Some summers are. The cultural grammar of these summers is so familiar by now that you can probably fill in the signifiers. Local TV reporters say "just when you thought it was safe to go back in the water." Click-driven, news-adjacent content producers roll out "How to Survive a Shark Attack" listicles. Their colleagues in the news-of-the-weird department trawl the shallows for stories about, say, people building their own personal shark cages to take swimming. Shark experts, who probably mutter "a better chance of dying from a bee sting" in their sleep at this point, go on NPR, where they say "a better chance of dying from a bee sting." 2

Like almost all shark-related media coverage, the summer-of-shark-attacks dossier is depressing and contradictory. It has to be, because it's designed to serve two opposing agendas. It needs to scare us a little, because the fascination that makes sharks prime box-office draws hinges on sharks being real-life sea monsters and thus categorically terrifying. But it also needs to live up to the statistical and ecological responsibility not to vilify sharks. The result is the distinctive, smug tone of self- 3 correcting sensationalism that we associate with shark-attack pseudo-journalism: DID YOU KNOW that these BEINGS OF PURE EVIL AND MALEVOLENCE who WILL NEVER EVER BOTHER YOU also totally YEARN TO EAT YOUR CHILDREN and are VITAL TO THE HEALTH OF OUR PLANET?

There being no alternative to human nature, you can understand the need for this; forget to remind people that sharks, in some phenomenally theoretical way, are our friends, and the next thing you know humanity is nuking the oceans. Still, this kind of coverage always seems to exist in denial of some basic truth. We all know that we have a one in 11.5 million chance of being attacked by a shark, that we are more likely to be killed by a toaster oven than by a great white, and so on. Yet we also know, whenever we are more than a few feet deep in the ocean, that there is a shark somewhere near us. We know this deeply, and we also know that it is about to come for us. The sun is sparking on the surface of the water. The waves are shushing the laughter we hear from the shore. Our little naked legs are kicking in the murk beneath us, and somewhere under them . . . 4

I read about divers swimming up through angelic columns of hammerheads. I read about fins seen from far off. As a child I remember being so convinced I was about to be seized by a shark that I had to nerve myself to stay in the water; I lived in Oklahoma, and was in a public swimming pool. Unless we are talking about an actual death, we have largely relegated sharks, in the post-post-*Jaws* universe, to a category of fun—sharks are kitsch, sharks are stuffed animals, sharks are light entertainment. Sharks are a kind of shadow puppet that we throw upon the wall to frighten landlocked children. The certainty that we have conquered nature is implicit in our feeling of responsibility toward it. Look at the shadow, though, and you see a plausible emblem of an old universe, one in which children have a reason to be frightened. That is what I keep thinking about. 5

I keep thinking about the direction of horrible death. Horrible death normally comes at you from above or from one side, so there is something especially terrorizing about the death that comes from below. Even the words sound like an H.P. Lovecraft novella. *The Death from Below*—you picture Ebenezer Pratt, Miskatonic University's most intrepid philologist, struggling on the surface of a mauve ocean while rainbow-colored tentacles swirl up from the nothing beneath him. 6

My point is that a shark attack cannot be compared to, say, being hit by a runaway train, vaporized by a bomb, tackled by a lion, strangled by a psychopath, or, to venture out from the real world into the zone of the fantastic to which shark attacks also belong, being incinerated by a dragon or crushed in the talons of a giant bird. I 7 imagine that these are unpleasant ways to die. But evolution has at least programmed you with a minimal ability to understand them. When you see the disaster coming down on you, instinct tells you to run, flinch, curl up, cover your head—all inadequate responses, but at least they are responses. When the shark materializes in the gloom below you, instinct goes hideously blank, because simply with respect to the position of the threat vis-à-vis your own body, your brain does not grasp what is happening. You are a tourist in the physics of fluids. You do not speak the language, and the cab driver is demanding to be paid.

Falling, perhaps, has something in common with a shark attack; I mean falling 8
from a great height. This is another case in which fate seems to rush up to you from below. One difference is that when you are falling from a great height, you are very likely to know you are doing it, whereas you are not likely to know the shark is gaping toward you until the moment when it strikes. Another difference is that when you are falling, your only enemy is the ground, and while the ground presents a troublingly ironic problem to the falling person, at least the ground is not a dead-eyed monster that pulls you into the depths trailing a cloud of blood like the plume of smoke from a train.

The deep ocean is always both thrilling 9
and appalling, because it represents a boundary in our experience of nature. Up to this point, survival; beyond this point, the void. To compare the deep sea to space is actually misleading: Mars and Venus have been mapped in far more detail than the ocean floor. Human eyes have seen less than 5 percent of the sea. I am thinking here of the monsters that mapmakers used to draw in around the edges of the known world. What if some of the monsters were real? The sharks that attack humans are not really deep-sea creatures (although there are deep-sea sharks), but great whites have been tracked into the bathypelagic zone, at nearly 4,000 feet. This is the realm of colossal squid and bioluminescence and things that look like fronds and move like the hammers of a piano.

"The deep ocean is always both thrilling and appalling, because it represents a boundary in our experience of nature. Up to this point, survival; beyond this point, the void."

If they notice us at all, the creatures that live at this depth are mostly indifferent 10
to us. The shark that attacked Mick Fanning, experts say, might not have been trying to hurt him at all, might only have been vaguely curious about what he was. But indifference in this context is as frightening as the hostility that sometimes follows it, because it is the indifference of another world.

11 At Réunion, the island off whose western coast 13-year-old Elio Canestri was killed, the number of shark attacks—18 in four years, seven of them fatal—has led to a ban on surfing. In several of these cases, the victims knowingly broke the ban. What I am trying to say is that the terror shark attacks inspire may be as apt a perspective on our position in the universe as the scientific calm that seeks to moderate it. The calm depends on the conviction that we are a threat to nature and that nature is not a threat to us. But that is a comforting delusion. We are capable of killing all the sharks, of killing everything that swims, flies, or walks. We are also vulnerable bodies that can be torn to pieces by wind, water, animals, and accidents. To regard these things with horror may be irresponsible. It at least allows for a kind of involved wonder at the scope of this planet, which we have the power to destroy but not to defend ourselves from.

Reading for Better Writing

1. *Connections:* Has an animal ever attacked you? When, where, and how did the attack take place? Describe the creature and exactly what happened. Did you experience physical or emotional injuries, or fear? Explain.
2. *Comprehension:*
   a. Summarize Brian Phillip's analysis of shark attacks, including the types of sharks that attack, and when, where, and how they attack.
   b. What does he claim causes sharks to attack? Explain.
   c. What does he claim regarding the physical and emotional effects—especially the fear of a surprise attack from below?
   d. How does the media contribute to (and profit from) this fear?
3. *Writing Strategies:*
   a. Phillips uses anecdotes to open his essay. Why and to what effect?
   b. Cite words and sentences that illustrate Phillips' informal writing style. Why might the style be effective for Grantland's (his publisher's) readers?
   c. Explain how Phillips' last sentence both re-states and expands his thesis.

Your Project: As noted in the introduction, Phillips writes about the public's fascination with—and fear of—sharks. What other subjects inspire both fascination and fear? For your own essay, consider exploring the causes and effects at work in one such subject.

Analyzing the Effects of Technology

Steven Pinker is a Harvard College Professor and the Johnstone Family Professor of Psychology at Harvard University. He writes frequently for magazines such as *The New York Times*, *Time*, and *The New Republic*, and he has written numerous books including *The Stuff of Thought*, *The Blank Slate*, *Words and Rules*, *How the Mind Works*, and *The Language Instinct*. In the essay below, published in *The New York Times*, Pinker analyzes how our current use of electronic technologies affects our ability to think deeply and process information.

Mind Over Mass Media

New forms of media have always caused moral panics: the printing press, newspapers, paperbacks and television were all once denounced as threats to their consumers' brainpower and moral fiber. 1

So too with electronic technologies. PowerPoint, we're told, is reducing discourse to bullet points. Search engines lower our intelligence, encouraging us to skim on the surface of knowledge rather than dive to its depths. Twitter is shrinking our attention spans. 2

But such panics often fail basic reality checks. When comic books were accused of turning juveniles into delinquents in the 1950s, crime was falling to record lows, just as the denunciations of video games in the 1990s coincided with the great American crime decline. The decades of television, transistor radios and rock videos were also decades in which I.Q. scores rose continuously. 3

For a reality check today, take the state of science, which demands high levels of brainwork and is measured by clear benchmarks of discovery. These days scientists are never far from their email, rarely touch paper and cannot lecture without PowerPoint. If electronic media were hazardous to intelligence, the quality of science would be plummeting. Yet discoveries are multiplying like fruit flies, and progress is dizzying. Other activities in the life of the mind, like philosophy, history and cultural criticism, are likewise flourishing, as anyone who has lost a morning of work to the Web site *Arts & Letters Daily* can attest. 4

Critics of new media sometimes use science itself to press their case, citing research that shows how "experience can change the brain." But cognitive neuroscientists roll their eyes at such talk. Yes, every time we learn a fact or skill the wiring of the brain changes; it's not as if the information is stored in the pancreas. But the existence of neural plasticity does not mean the brain is a blob of clay pounded into shape by experience. 5

Experience does not revamp the basic information-processing capacities of the brain. Speed-reading programs have long claimed to do just that, but the verdict was rendered by Woody Allen after he read *War and Peace* in one sitting: "It was about Russia." Genuine multitasking, too, has been exposed as a myth, not just by laboratory studies but by the familiar sight of an S.U.V. undulating between lanes as the driver cuts deals on his cellphone. 6

Moreover, as the psychologists Christopher Chabris and Daniel Simons show in their new book *The Invisible Gorilla: And Other Ways Our Intuitions Deceive Us,* the effects of experience are highly specific to the experiences themselves. If you train people to do one thing (recognize shapes, solve math puzzles, find hidden words), they get better at doing that thing, but almost nothing else. Music doesn't make you better at math, conjugating Latin doesn't make you more logical, brain-training games don't make you smarter. Accomplished people don't bulk up their brains with intellectual calisthenics; they immerse themselves in their fields. Novelists read lots of novels, scientists read lots of science. 7

The effects of consuming electronic media are also likely to be far more limited than the panic implies. Media critics write as if the brain takes on the qualities of whatever it consumes, the informational equivalent of "you are what you eat." As with primitive peoples who believe that eating fierce animals will make them fierce, they assume that watching quick cuts in rock videos turns your mental life into quick cuts or that reading bullet points and Twitter postings turns your thoughts into bullet points and Twitter postings. 8

Yes, the constant arrival of information packets can be distracting or addictive, especially to people with attention deficit disorder. But distraction is not a new phenomenon. The solution is not to bemoan technology but to develop strategies of self-control, as we do with every other temptation in life. Turn off email or Twitter when you work, put away your Blackberry at dinner time, ask your spouse to call you to bed at a designated hour. 9

And to encourage intellectual depth, don't rail at PowerPoint or Google. It's not as if habits of deep reflection, thorough research and rigorous reasoning ever came naturally to people. They must be acquired in special institutions, which we call universities, and maintained with constant upkeep, which we call analysis, criticism and debate. They are not granted by propping a heavy encyclopedia on your lap, nor are they taken away by efficient access to information on the Internet. 10

The new media have caught on for a reason. Knowledge is increasing exponentially; human brainpower and waking hours are not. Fortunately, the Internet and information technologies are helping us manage, search and retrieve our collective intellectual output at different scales, from Twitter and previews to e-books and online encyclopedias. Far from making us stupid, these technologies are the only things that will keep us smart. 11

Reading for Better Writing

1. *Connections:* Estimate the average number of hours that you spend each day using devices such as computers, notepads, cellphones, TVs, electronic games, and traditional phones. Has that number changed during the last ten years, and has the change affected your habits, personality, or skills? How?
2. *Comprehension:*
   a. Review Pinker's opening paragraph in which he introduces his topic by suggesting that current allegations regarding the negative impact of electronic technologies are similar to past allegations of other media. Paraphrase his claim.
   b. The essay is organized as a series of critics' arguments asserting the negative impact of new media, followed by Pinker's counterarguments. Summarize the core exchanges and explain how the point-counterpoint format clarifies both sides of the argument.
3. *Writing Strategies:*
   a. Pinker is a scholar aiming to analyze an academic topic with thoughtful, well-researched arguments in an informed, academic tone. Cite passages that illustrate this voice.
   b. However, Pinker is also a writer aiming to engage and inform readers who have likely not studied the topic themselves. Identify passages in which his examples and word choice illustrate his effort to connect with these readers.
   c. Do the opening and closing paragraphs effectively frame the argument? Explain.

Your Project: Aside from the electronic technologies that Pinker discusses, what technologies have radically changed life in the last 100 years? What causes and/or effects are at work in one of these technologies? How might you use Pinker's point-counterpoint strategy to distinguish your claims regarding cause-effect relationships from opposing claims regarding those relationships.

Analyzing an Analytical Strategy

Dr. Andrew J. Bacevich is professor emeritus of history and international relations at Boston University and author of *America's War for the Greater Middle East*. In the essay below, he argues that the History That Matters (HTM) approach to the study of history is academically dishonest, diminishing the integrity and value of history. (The essay was published in the November 1, 2015 edition of *The Chronicle for Higher Education*.)

History That Makes Us Stupid

"History is now and England," T.S. Eliot wrote in 1942. Not anymore. Today, as far as most Americans are concerned, the History That Matters centers on the recent past—the period from 1914 to 1989, to be exact—and on the United States. That's a big problem—one for which today's academic historians bear no small responsibility. 1

In Donald Rumsfeld's famous taxonomy of known knowns, known unknowns, and unknown unknowns, the History That Matters (HTM) occupies its own special niche. That niche consists of mythic knowns. 2

All history is selective and interpretive. In the HTM, mythic knowns determine the process of selection and interpretation. Chief among the mythic knowns to which most Americans (academic historians excepted) subscribe are these: 3

- that history itself has an identifiable shape, direction, and destination;
- that history is purposeful, tending toward the universal embrace of values indistinguishable from American values;
- that in the interests of propagating those values, history confers on the United States unique responsibilities and prerogatives.

By no means purporting to tell the whole story, the HTM reduces the past to its pith or essence. Like the Ten Commandments, it identifies specific shalts and shalt nots. Like the Sermon on the Mount, it prescribes a code of behavior. In doing so, the HTM makes the past usable. Endlessly reiterated in political speech and reinforced by popular culture, the "lessons" of this usable past prescribe what the United States—the indispensable nation—is called upon to do and what it must refrain from doing. 4

This usable past finds expression in a straightforward narrative depicting the 20th century as the first American Century, shaped throughout by the actions (or inaction) of the United States. Although incorporating setbacks and disappointments, the narrative culminates in reassuring triumph. On balance, things are headed in the right direction. 5

The drama unfolded in three acts, each centered on a large-scale military undertaking. 6

The first, World War I, occurred between 1914 and 1918. When this conflict began, Americans were having none of it. Yet after considerable hesitation, urged on by a president who believed it incumbent upon the New World to save the Old, they took the plunge. The United States went off to fight. Woodrow Wilson declared, "for the ultimate peace of the world and for the liberation of its peoples," a stirring vision considerably at odds with the actual war aims of the belligerents on both sides. 7

Alas, before permanent peace was fully achieved and the liberation of peoples well and truly won, Americans began having second thoughts and reneged on Wilson's vow. World War I thereby set the stage for another even more horrific conflict just two decades later, widely attributed to the refusal of Americans to fulfill the duties to which destiny had summoned them. 8

In the interim, historians had mounted an energetic challenge to this interpretation of World War I. In effect, revisionists such as Harry Elmer Barnes, eventually joined by Charles A. Beard, launched a pre-emptive attack on the HTM, arguing that U.S. entry into the Great War had been a huge blunder. Ever so briefly, scholarship reflected and reinforced the mood of the moment. When the moment passed, however, revisionism fell out of fashion and the HTM's onward march resumed. 9

As an episode in the History That Matters, therefore, World War I is presented as a missed opportunity, a warning of the consequences that result when the United States fails to lead. 10

Act II began in 1939 or 1938 or 1936 or 1933—the date dependent on the "lesson" to which you're calling attention—but ended definitively in 1945. World War II offered Americans a second chance to get it right. The war pitted good against evil, freedom against slavery, civilization against barbarism, and democracy against dictatorship. 11

Not merely in myth but also in fact, World War II was all of these things. But it was much more as well. It was a winner-take-all contest between rival claimants to Pacific dominion, between competing conceptions of how to govern peoples deemed inferior, and between two decidedly different brands of totalitarianism, one of them aligned with the United States. 12

One thing World War II was emphatically not: a war to avert genocide. The fate of European Jews facing extermination at the hands of Nazi Germany was an afterthought. 13

Per Rumsfeld, we might categorize these realities as discomfiting knowns. Crediting Europe's liberation to the Anglo-American alliance—forged by Franklin and Winston singing "Onward Christian Soldiers" onboard HMS *Prince of Wales*—makes 14 for a suitably uplifting story. Acknowledging the Red Army's far larger contribution to defeating the Nazi menace—with Eastern Europeans paying a steep price for their "liberation" at Soviet hands—only serves to complicate things. The HTM has a decided aversion to complications.

Lasting considerably longer than the first two acts combined, Act III ran from 15
roughly 1947 to 1989 and consisted of many scenes, some of which resisted easy incorporation into the HTM: nuclear arsenals containing thousands of weapons, partnerships with unsavory despots, coups and assassination plots by the bushel, not to mention Korea, the Bay of Pigs, the Missile Crisis, and Vietnam, all capped off with the Leader of the Free World exchanging pleasantries in Beijing with Red China's murderous Great Helmsman. All of this made it difficult to cast Act III as a virtuous sequel to Act II.

Historians took note. A new generation of revisionists, the disciples of William 16
Appleman Williams prominent among them, challenged the official line depicting the Cold War as another round of good pitted against evil. At least briefly, the past seemed up for grabs. For a time—the last time—a debate among American historians engaged broad public attention.

The end of the Cold War deflected this challenge, and the HTM emerged in 17
mature form. To wide applause, a political scientist announced that history itself had ended. That ending validated the mythic knowns underpinning the HTM from the outset. History's trajectory and purpose now appeared self-evident, as did America's extraordinary singularity.

In 1992, an unproven presidential candidate reduced the History That Matters to 18
a homely parable. "I am literally a child of the Cold War," Bill Clinton began.

> My parents' generation wanted little more than to return from a world war and resume the blessedly ordinary joys of home and family and work. Yet . . . history would not let them rest. Overnight, an expansionist Soviet Union summoned them into a new struggle. Fortunately, America had farsighted and courageous leaders . . . who roused our battle-weary nation to the challenge. Under their leadership, we helped Europe and Japan rebuild their economies, organized a great military coalition of free nations, and defended our democratic principles against yet another totalitarian threat.

In declaring his fealty to the HTM, Clinton hoped to establish his credibility as 19
a would-be statesman. Yet implicit in his succinct and sanitized account was a handy template for dealing with challenges to come.

But of course history had not ended, and when new challenges appeared, policy 20
makers reflexively reverted to that very same template. "We have seen their kind before," George W. Bush reassured his badly shaken countrymen after 9/11.

> They're the heirs of all the murderous ideologies of the 20th century. By 21
> sacrificing human life to serve their radical visions, by abandoning every value except the will to power, they follow in the path of fascism, Nazism, and totalitarianism. And they will follow that path all the way to where it ends in history's unmarked grave of discarded lies.

For President Bush, the need for a large-scale military enterprise comparable to 22
those that had made the 20th century an American Century was self-evident. The Global War on Terrorism, in effect, constituted an addendum to the HTM—a fourth act in history's onward march. To emphasize the continuities, some observers styled the U.S. response to 9/11 as World War IV, with the Cold War retroactively designated World War III.

Alas, by whatever name, World War IV has proved a bust. Fifteen years after it 23
began, victory is nowhere in sight.

Meanwhile, the ostensibly usable past has 24
become a straitjacket. Finding solace in its familiarity, Americans remain firmly moored to the HTM, although Acts I and III have taken a backseat to Act II. Hence the innumerable comparisons of Iran to Nazi Germany and Barack Obama to Neville Chamberlain, along with predictions of Israelis marching compliantly off to death camps, inspired by the Iran nuclear deal.

"The task for historians this time around is to reframe the entire 20th century . . ."

The prevailing version of the usable past is worse than unusable. In the United 25
States, it obstructs serious debate over the use and misuse of power. No less than was the case in the 1920s-30s and 1960s-70s, the times call for revisionism. The task for historians this time around is to reframe the entire 20th century, seeing it for the unmitigated disaster that it was and recognizing its profound moral ambiguity without, however, succumbing to moral equivalence.

To cling to the History That Matters is to make real learning impossible. 26
Yet for academics to critically engage the HTM in a way that might affect public understanding of the past requires a revival of fields that have become decidedly unhip. The HTM is essentially a war and politics narrative, and the present-day historical profession does not emphasize political, diplomatic, and military themes.

Today it's race, class, gender, and sexuality that claim pride of place. The effect, whether intended or not, is that comforting fantasies go unchallenged and lodge themselves ever more deeply in the public consciousness. So the "Good War" remains ever good, with the "Greatest Generation" ever great.

Not without reason, members of the historical profession tend to view the HTM as a caricature or cartoon. Yet their very disdain provides one explanation for why it persists. In effect, the myths sustaining this fatuous narrative go unchallenged. For ordinary citizens, "history" becomes what they see on TV—the History Channel!—or what they hear from agenda-peddling politicians. 27

So among Americans at least, count on the HTM to endure—history that lets us feel good, even as it makes us stupid. 28

Reading for Better Writing

1. *Connections:* In his essay, Bacevich claims that the HTM approach to historical analysis produces false accounts of historical events—accounts that make the students who read them, stupid. What news story have you read (or seen on TV) that you believe presented a simplistic or false story on the topic? Explain.
2. *Comprehension:*
   a. In the opening paragraph, Bacevich identifies what he calls "a big problem." In your own words, explain what the problem is, who caused it, and how.
   b. In paragraph 3, he identifies three "mythic knowns." Why does he (cynically) call them *knowns*? What does he mean by *mythic*? And how might the three beliefs make students of history stupid?
   c. In paragraphs 7–14, he analyses events in World Wars I and II. Summarize his analysis and explain how he uses these claims to support his thesis.
3. *Writing Strategies:*
   a. In paragraph 6, Bacevich says that HTM's historical narrative is a "drama unfolded in three acts." How does he use that metaphor in paragraphs 10-15 to explain and critique HTM? Is the strategy effective?
   b. He concludes the essay with a one-sentence paragraph. Explain why this sentence is or is not a strong closing.

Your Project: In his essay, Bacevich explores how a limited or false idea of history affects society. In other areas of knowledge or life, what simplistic or wrong ideas are at work, with what effects? Consider one such myth for your own writing.

Writing Guidelines

Planning

1. **Select a topic.** Begin by reviewing the project ideas at the end of each sample essay. Then think about categories such as those listed below and brainstorm phenomena related to each category. From the list, choose a topic and analyze its causes, its effects, or both.
   - **Society:** nurse, doctor, and engineer shortages; home-grown terrorists; elder and spouse abuse; shifting ethnic ratios; college student debt; super bugs; bitcoin use
   - **Environment:** decreasing bees, shale-oil pollution, noise pollution, lead-poisoned water, decreasing mines, increasing nuclear power plants, forest fires, earthquakes
2. **Narrow and research the topic.** State your topic and below it, list related causes and effects in two columns (see Figure 15.2). Next, do preliminary research to expand the list and distinguish primary causes and effects from secondary ones. Revise your topic as needed to address only primary causes and/or effects that research links to a specific phenomenon.

Cause-effect Topic: ____________

Causes (Because of)	Effects (this results)
1. ________	1. ________
2. ________	2. ________
3. ________	3. ________

fig. 15.2

3. **Draft and test your thesis.** Based on your preliminary research, draft a working thesis (you may revise it later) that introduces the topic, along with the causes and/or effects you intend to discuss. Limit your argument to only those points you can prove.
4. **Gather and analyze information.** Research your topic, looking for clear evidence that links specific causes to specific effects. As you study the phenomenon, distinguish between primary and secondary causes (main and contributing), direct and indirect results, short-term and long-term effects, and so on. At the same time, test your analysis to avoid mistaking a coincidence for a cause-effect relationship. Use the list of logical fallacies (see pages 323–326) to weed out common errors in logic. For example, finding chemical pollutants in a stream running beside a chemical plant does not "prove" that the plant caused the pollutants.
5. **Get organized.** Develop an outline that lays out your thesis and argument in a clear pattern. Under each main point asserting a cause-effect connection, list details from your research that support the connection. (See Figure 15.3.)

Thesis: ____________

Point #1	Point #2	Point #3
• Supporting details	• Supporting details	• Supporting details
• Supporting details	• Supporting details	• Supporting details

fig. 15.3

Drafting

6. **Use your outline to draft the essay.** Try to draft the essay's overall argument before you attempt to revise it. As you write, show how each specific cause led to each specific effect, citing examples as needed. To show those cause-effect relationships, use transitional words like the following:

• accordingly	• for this purpose	• since	• therefore
• as a result	• for this reason	• so	• thus
• because	• hence	• such as	• to illustrate
• consequently	• just as	• thereby	• whereas

Revising

7. **Get feedback.** Ask a peer reviewer to read your essay for an engaging opening, a thoughtful cause-effect thesis, clear and convincing reasoning that links specific causes to specific effects, and a closing that deepens and extends the cause-effect analysis.
8. **Revise the essay.** Whether your essay presents causes, effects, or both, use the checklist below to trace and refine your argument.

    ___ **Ideas:** The essay explains the causes and/or effects of the topic in a clear, well-reasoned analysis. The analysis is supported by credible information and free of logical fallacies.

    ___ **Organization:** The structure helps clarify the cause-effect relationships through a well traced line of thinking, and the links between the main points, supporting points, and evidence are clear.

    ___ **Voice:** The tone is informed, polite, logical, and measured.

Editing and Proofreading

9. **Edit the essay for clarity and correctness.** Check for the following:

    ___ **Words:** The diction is precise and clear, and technical or scientific terms are defined. Causes are linked to effects with transitional words and phrases.

    ___ **Sentences:** Structures are clear, varied, and smooth.

    ___ **Correctness:** The grammar, punctuation, mechanics, usage, and spelling are correct.

    ___ **Design:** The format, layout, and typography fit the situation; any visuals used enhance the written analysis and clarify the paper's cause-effect reasoning.

Publishing

10. **Publish your essay.** Share your writing by submitting it to your instructor, posting it on the class's or department's Web site, or turning it into a presentation.

MindTap® Request help and feedback from a tutor. If required, participate in peer review, submit your paper for a grade, and view instructor comments online.

Critical Thinking and Writing: Applications

Apply what you have learned about critical thinking through reading, viewing, and writing by completing these activities.

1. **Career Plans:** How is cause-effect reasoning used in your discipline? Cite common applications and for each, explain who uses it, why, how, and to what end. If writing is involved, describe the document types, topics, likely writers, and readers. Finally, assess your ability to use cause-effect reasoning, and how you might hone those skills through course work, internships, or workplace experiences.
2. **Living Today:** In her essay, Susan Cain analyzes how the "New Groupthink" can limit the creative efforts of group members. Reflect on your own experiences working with groups. Did you ever witness the New Groupthink? If you did, describe its causes and effects, including how your role in the group supported or challenged the phenomenon.
3. **Media Watch:** In "Death From Below: Our Summer of Shark Attacks," Brian Phillips suggests that the media produce—and benefit from—exaggerated shark-attack stories that generate the public's fear of sharks. In this situation, how might the media benefit from fear mongering? In what other situations do organizations or individuals inspire (or cause) fear for their own gain? Explain.
4. **Side Effects:** In "Familiar Strangers," Audrey Torrest describes how Dr. Smith learned that his inability to recognize faces was caused by congenital prosopagnosia. Do you or someone you know have a puzzling condition or disability? Does the individual know and accept its causes and effects? Explain.

Learning-Objectives Checklist ✓

Have you achieved this chapter's learning objectives? Check your progress with the following items, revisiting topics in the chapter as needed. I have . . .

____ examined, interpreted, and critiqued arguments that utilize cause-effect reasoning (252–253).

____ analyzed a phenomenon by identifying and explaining its primary and secondary causes and effects (252–253).

____ developed a credible cause-effect thesis based on my study of the topic (276–277).

____ explained how and why a given cause is linked to one or more related effects (276).

____ identified and corrected logical fallacies related to cause-effect thinking (323–326).

____ supported my cause-effect reasoning with current, reliable, and detailed evidence (276–277).

____ clarified cause-effect relationships through the effective use of transitional words and phrases (277).

____ used cause-effect reasoning along with other analytical strategies to effectively plan, draft, revise, and polish a cogent, logical essay (276–277).

MindTap® Practice skills that you have learned in this chapter and receive automatic feedback. Reflect on your writing process.

Chapter 16

Reading Literature: A Case Study in Analysis

Understand the goals of the chapter and complete a warm-up activity online.

In college, analyzing a literary text is a critical, interpretive process. For that reason, the process must begin with a deep reading of a poem, short story, play, or other literary work. When you research and write the essay, you assume that your readers have also read the text, and your aim is to illuminate some not-fully-understood dimension of the work: the motivations of a particular character, the image patterns of a lyric, the historical context of a Renaissance play, and so on.

In this way, literary analysis is a special form of the analytical writing explained in chapters 11–15. In this application of analysis, your primary research is reading, rereading, and thinking through the literary text itself in order to develop a sound, insightful interpretation; secondary research supplements your primary reading by providing a range of support, from historical background to scholarly criticism.

Learning Objectives

By working through this chapter, you will be able to

- examine and assess writers' analyses of literature and the arts.
- investigate how writers' situations inform their analyses.
- use literary terms and concepts to evaluate others' analyses and enrich your own.
- conduct primary and secondary research to analyze a literary text or other artwork.
- develop an analysis with an insightful thesis, clear reasoning, and sound evidence.

Visually Speaking What might Figure 16.1 suggest about the relationship between art and life? Explain.

Lee Snider Photo Images / Shutterstock.com

fig. 16.1

Strategies for Analyzing Literature and the Arts

Analyzing the arts is something that most people do (at least informally) every day, whether they're reading reviews of concerts or albums, responding to paintings or photographs in public places, or assessing the value of a film or TV drama. However, this chapter explains a more formal, research-based analysis that is carefully articulated in well-crafted writing. To understand how and why writers produce such analyses, it's helpful to examine the rhetorical situations that give rise to them.

The Rhetorical Situation

Consider the context in which writers analyze literature and the arts:

- **Purpose:** Most writers aim to describe the work's features, to explain how it impacts an audience, and to understand its essential qualities. However, writers reviewing (rather than only analyzing) an artwork focus more on its strengths and weaknesses.
- **Readers:** In college, the primary readers for writing about the arts are students and instructors; outside of the classroom, art news stories and reviews are written for any community members interested in art events, art-related issues, or books.
- **Topic:** The topic might be one artwork (e.g., a sculpture, novel, or film), multiple works created by the same artist (e.g., a series of poems or paintings), a group performance (e.g., a play, an opera, or a symphony), an individual performance (e.g., a pianist, an actor, or a dancer), or critical approaches to an art.

Example: In "'Let Evening Come' An Invitation to the Inevitable" (pages 287–288), Sherry Van Egdom's primary readers are her professor and classmates. Her topic is the poem, "Let Evening Come" (page 286), and her purpose is to explain what and how the poem communicates to her.

Principles of Literary-Analysis Writing

Literary-analysis writing depends on the principles that follow.

Understanding approaches to literary analysis. Literary texts can be interpreted through different critical approaches or schools. Each school, with its specific foci and questions, offers a way of "conversing" about a text. The four basic approaches are as follows:

1. **Formalist criticism** focuses on the literary text itself, especially its structure and genre.
2. **Rhetorical criticism** is audience-centered, focused on the "transaction" between text and reader.
3. **Historical criticism** focuses on the historical context of the literary text, including its author.
4. **Ideological criticism** applies ideas outside of literature (e.g., psychology, mythology, feminism, postcolonialism, environmentalism) to literary texts.

To learn how writers from each school approach literary criticism, read John Van Rys's essay "Four Ways to Talk About Literature" (pages 283–285).

Understanding literary terms that help you read and write about the arts. The terms used to address specific art forms, such as the three examples below, help writers read literature carefully and discuss their topics precisely. To refine your reading skills, learn how the literary elements that these terms identify shape or enrich a literary work. Then when reading a piece of literature, think about how these elements impact what you feel, see, and think. (For definitions of common literary terms, see pages 302–305.)

- **Poetry:** Writers might describe word sounds with terms such as *assonance, consonance,* and *alliteration*; rhythmic effects with words such as *iambic* or *trochaic meter*; and figurative language with words such as *metaphor* and *simile.*
- **Fiction:** Writers might describe diction with terms such as *archaic, colloquial,* or *slang*; narrative method with phrases such as *first person* and *third person*; or genre with terms such as *satire* or *melodrama.*
- **Plays and Films:** To describe characters, writers use terms such as *antagonist, protagonist,* or *tragic hero*; to discuss plots, they use words such as *exposition, rising action,* and *denouement*; or to describe a setting, they might use *stage picture, proscenium arch,* or *thrust stage.*

Understanding primary and secondary research. Writers' reading of a literary text—primary research—is usually the focus of their analyses. However, secondary research can serve many purposes, such as these:

- **Biographical research:** Learning about the author's life may enrich a writer's analysis by helping the person to explore sources of inspiration, personal and literary influences, and modes of thought. Such insights might be gained through learning about the author's childhood, cultural and ethnic background, education, writing apprenticeship, and relationships. Caution: Writers must be careful not to make simplistic connections between biographical details and literary texts (e.g., that the speaker of a poem or the narrator of a story is the author in a direct sense; that because the novelist grew up in the 1960s, the female characters are radical feminists; or that the author's intention must direct an interpretation of the text).
- **Research into historical and cultural context:** Such research illuminates the text by clarifying important contextual issues and historical details. These issues might be the historical realities surrounding the text's writing, its content, and its reception (past and present). Or the issues might be cultural concepts relevant to the text: class, economics, technology, religious institutions and practices, and so on.
- **Research into literary concepts:** This type of secondary research deepens the writer's understanding of literary issues and techniques. For example, he or she might read about methods and theories of irony, or might study the nature of tragedy with the aim of enriching the analysis of the text.
- **Research into theory:** Such research strengthens the writer's understanding of the philosophical and ideological underpinnings of a particular literary school or theorist. Theoretical research—whether into reader-response theory, deconstruction, feminism, or the ideas of a particular theorist such as Mikhail Bakhtin—informs and directs the writer's analysis of the literary text.

- **Research into scholarly interpretations:** In such research, writers join the critical conversation about the text, a conversation that might have been going on for a few years, a few decades, or a few centuries. Many scholarly articles and books will likely offer interpretations of the text—ways of reading, analyzing, and understanding some aspect of the work, typically from a particular point of view. Reading these sources can strengthen a writer's own interpretation in the following ways:
  - She can locate her own reading within the critical conversation, placing her interpretation in context.
  - She can refine her own reading through critical engagement, exploring why different readers interpret the text as they do (comparing their perspectives and values with her own).
  - She can create a critical survey early in her paper, one that reviews the interpretive schools on the issues addressed and makes space for her own reading.
  - Within her essay, she might use the critical comment of a scholar to (a) add expert support to her interpretive argument, (b) create a starting point for further reflection and analysis, or (c) present a claim with which she disagrees.

Focusing on Research Essentials: In a literary analysis project, a writer should use secondary sources carefully and avoid these problems:

- **Substituting his own interpretation** of the text with the readings offered by secondary sources. If he finds himself continually talking about other people's interpretations or simply parroting their interpretations, he needs to get back to his own interpretation in his own voice.
- **Limiting his secondary research** to opinions that he gathers off the free Web (including sites such as Spark Notes and Cliff Notes). Instead, he should rely on substantial sources in academic journals and scholarly books.

Reading Literary-Analysis Writing

As you read the essays on the following pages, consider these questions:

1. Does the writer understand the elements of the art form, what distinguishes a quality artwork, and how to assess those qualities?
2. Does the essay explore nuances such as ironies, motifs, symbols, and allusions?
3. Does the essay have a clear thesis and logical claims, all supported by relevant evidence?
4. Is the tone informed, respectful, and honest?
5. Does the writing sound informed regarding the foci and approaches of schools of literary criticism?
6. Does the writing use literary terms correctly and effectively? (See the list of literary terms on pages 302–305.)
7. Does the writing correctly document both primary and secondary sources?

Approaches to Literary Criticism

In the following essay, Professor John Van Rys describes four schools of (or approaches to) literary criticism. He then illustrates each approach by describing how a critic using it might analyze Robert Browning's poem, "My Last Duchess." The complete text of this poem is available on pages 289–290, along with follow-up ideas for discussing and analyzing it.

MindTap®

Read, highlight, and take notes online.

Four Ways to Talk About Literature

Have you ever been in a conversation in which you suddenly felt lost—out of the loop? Perhaps you feel that way in your literature class. You may think a poem or short story means one thing, and then your instructor suddenly pulls out the "hidden meaning." Joining the conversation about literature—in class or in an essay—may indeed seem daunting, but you can do it if you know what to look for and what to talk about. There are four main perspectives, or approaches, that you can use to converse about literature. 1

Text-centered approaches focus on the literary piece itself. Often called *formalist criticism*, such approaches claim that the structure of a work and the rules of its genre are crucial to its meaning. The formalist critic determines how various elements (plot, character, language, and so on) reinforce the meaning and unify the work. For example, the formalist may ask the following questions concerning Robert Browning's poem "My Last Duchess": How do the main elements in the poem—irony, symbolism, and verse form—help develop the main theme (deception)? How does Browning use the dramatic monologue genre in this poem? 2

Audience-centered approaches focus on the "transaction" between text and reader—the dynamic way the reader interacts with the text. Often called *rhetorical* or *reader-response criticism*, these approaches see the text not as an object to be analyzed, but as an activity that is different for each reader. A reader-response critic might ask these questions of "My Last Duchess": How does the reader become aware of the duke's true nature if it's never actually stated? Do men and women read the poem differently? Who were Browning's original readers? 3

Author-centered approaches focus on the origins of a text (the writer and the historical background). For example, an author-centered study examines the writer's life—showing connections, contrasts, and conflicts between his or her life and the 4 writing. Broader historical studies explore social and intellectual currents, showing links between an author's work and the ideas, events, and institutions of that period. Finally, the literary historian may make connections between the text in question and earlier and later literary works. The author-centered critic might ask these questions of "My Last Duchess": What were Browning's views of marriage, men and women, art, class, and wealth? As an institution, what was marriage like in Victorian England (Browning's era) or Renaissance Italy (the duke's era)? Who was the historical Duke of Ferrara?

The fourth approach to criticism applies ideas outside of literature to literary works. Because literature mirrors life, argue these critics, disciplines that explore human life can help us understand literature. Some critics, for example, apply psychological theories to literary works by exploring dreams, symbolic meanings, and motivation. Myth or archetype criticism uses insights from psychology, cultural anthropology, and classical studies to explore a text's universal appeal. Moral criticism, rooted in religious studies and ethics, explores the moral dilemmas literary works raise. Connecting literature and environmental studies, ecocriticism examines the nature-culture relationship expressed by literary texts, the importance of the natural world to them. Marxist, feminist, minority, and postcolonial criticism are, broadly speaking, sociological approaches to interpretation. While the Marxist examines the themes of class struggle, economic power, and social justice in texts, the feminist critic explores the just and unjust treatment of women as well as the effect of gender on language, reading, and the literary canon. The critic interested in race and ethnic identity explores similar issues, with the focus shifted to a specific cultural group, while the postcolonial critic examines the dynamics of colonialism found in literature of formerly colonized people. 5

Such ideological criticism might ask a wide variety of questions about "My Last Duchess": What does the poem reveal about the duke's psychological state and his personality? How does the reference to Neptune deepen the poem? What does the poem suggest about the nature of evil and injustice? In what ways are the duke's motives class-based and economic? How does the poem present the duke's power and the duchess's weakness? What is the status of women in this society? 6

If you look at the variety of questions critics might ask about "My Last Duchess," you see both the diversity of critical approaches and the common ground between them. In fact, interpretive methods actually share important characteristics: (1) a close 7 attention to literary elements such as character, plot, symbolism, and metaphor; (2) a desire not to distort the work; and (3) a sincere concern for increasing interest in and understanding of a text. In actual practice, critics may develop a hybrid approach to criticism, one that matches their individual questions and concerns about a text. Now that you're familiar with some of the questions defining literary criticism, exercise your own curiosity (and join the ongoing literary dialogue) by discussing a text that genuinely interests you.

Reading for Better Writing

1. *Connections:* How would you describe yourself as a reader? What types of writing do you enjoy, and how do you typically go about reading those works? How do your reading practices relate to the types of "conversation" described in this essay? Does this essay encourage you to change or broaden your reading habits in particular ways?
2. *Comprehension:* Briefly outline the four approaches to interpretation described in this essay—their focus, goals, and methods.
3. *Writing Strategies:*
   - **a.** In the opening paragraph, Van Rys creates a focus; he also establishes a tone and an approach to the topic. How would you characterize that tone and approach? What strategies does the writer use to engage readers?
   - **b.** In introducing the four approaches to reading, Van Rys follows the same pattern with each. Describe that pattern and explain how it works to clarify each category.
   - **c.** The writer uses a poem to illustrate the four critical approaches. How does the illustration clarify the discussion? Does the illustration work even if the reader hasn't read the poem?
   - **d.** Examine the order in which the writer examines the four categories. What is the effect of following this specific order? Is there a particular logic or progression? How is the presentation of the fourth category different from the previous three?
   - **e.** How does the closing paragraph enrich or complicate the discussion of the approaches? In what way do the introduction and conclusion frame the essay?

Your Project: Consider testing a critical approach more fully by analyzing some dimension of "My Last Duchess" on pages 289–290.

Analyzing a Poem

In the essay on the following two pages, student writer Sherry Van Egdom analyzes the form and meaning of the poem below, "Let Evening Come," by American poet Jane Kenyon. Born in 1947 and raised on a farm near Ann Arbor, Michigan, Kenyon settled in New Hampshire at Eagle Pond Farm after she married fellow poet Donald Hall. During her life, Kenyon struggled with her faith, with depression, and with cancer. At the time of her death in 1995 from leukemia, she was the poet laureate of New Hampshire.

Before you read the student writer's analysis, read the poem aloud to enjoy its sounds, rhythm, images, diction, and comparisons. Then read the piece again to grasp more fully how the poem is structured, what it expresses, and how its ideas might relate to your life. Finally, read Van Egdom's analysis and answer the questions that follow it.

Let Evening Come

Let the light of late afternoon
shine through chinks in the barn, moving
up the bales as the sun moves down.

Let the crickets take up chafing
as a woman takes up her needles
and her yarn. Let evening come.

Let dew collect on the hoe abandoned
in long grass. Let the stars appear
and the moon disclose her silver horn.

Let the fox go back to its sandy den.
Let the wind die down. Let the shed
go black inside. Let evening come.

To the bottle in the ditch, to the scoop
in the oats, to air in the lung
let evening come.

Let it come, as it will, and don't
be afraid. God does not leave us
comfortless, so let evening come.

Analysis of Kenyon's Poem

In the essay below, student writer Sherry Van Egdom Doyle analyzes "Let Evening Come." Watch how she develops the essay by introducing the poem, describing how it unfolds, and then examining its structure, ideas, poetic devices, and theme.

"Let Evening Come": An Invitation to the Inevitable

The work of American poet Jane Kenyon is influenced primarily by the circumstances and experiences of her own life. She writes carefully crafted, deceptively simple poems that connect both to her own life and to the lives of her readers. Growing out of her rural roots and her struggles with illness, Kenyon's poetry speaks in a still voice of the ordinary things in life in order to wrestle with issues of faith and mortality (Timmerman 163). One of these poems is "Let Evening Come." In this poem, the poet takes the reader on a journey into the night, but she points to hope in the face of that darkness. 1

That movement toward darkness is captured in the stanza form and in the progression of stanzas. Each three-line stanza offers a self-contained moment in the progress of transition from day to night. The first stanza positions the reader in a simple farm setting. Late afternoon fades into evening without the rumble of highways or the gleam of city lights to distract one's senses from nature, the peace emphasized by the alliteration of "l" in "Let the light of late afternoon." As the sun sinks lower on the horizon, light seeps through cracks in the barn wall, moving up the bales of hay. In the second stanza, the crickets get busy with their nighttime noises. Next, a forgotten farm hoe becomes covered with dew drops, and the silvery stars and moon appear in the sky. In the fourth stanza, complete blackness arrives as a fox returns to its empty den and the silent wind rests at close of day. The alliteration of "d" in "den" and "die down" gives a sinking, settling feeling (Timmerman 176). In the fifth stanza, a bottle and scoop keep still, untouched in their respective places, while sleep comes upon the human body. In the final stanza, Kenyon encourages readers to meet this emerging world of darkness without fear. 2

Within this stanza progression, the journey into the night is intensified by strong images, figures of speech, and symbols. The natural rhythm of work and rest on the farm is symbolized by the light that rises and falls in the first stanza (Timmerman 175). The simile comparing the crickets taking up their song to a woman picking up her knitting suggests a homespun energy and conviction. The moon revealing her "silver horn" implies that the moon does not instantly appear with brightness and beauty but rather reveals her majesty slowly as the night comes on. The den, the wind, and the shed in stanza four stress a kind of internal, hidden darkness. Then stanza five focuses on connected objects: the thoughtlessly discarded bottle resting in the ditch, oats and the scoop for feeding, human lungs and the air that fills them. Kenyon mentions the air in the lung after the bottle, ditch, scoop, and oats in order to picture humanity taking its position among the established natural rhythm of the farm (Harris 31). 3

The refrain, "let evening come," is a powerful part of the poem's journey toward darkness, though critics interpret the line differently. Judith Harris suggests that it symbolizes an acceptance of the inevitable: Darkness will envelop the world, and night will surely come, just as mortality will certainly take its toll in time. This acceptance, in turn, acts as a release from the confinement of one's pain and trials in life. Rather than wrestle with something that cannot be beaten or worry about things that must be left undone, Kenyon advises herself and her readers to let go (31). Night intrudes upon the work and events of the day, perhaps leaving them undone just as death might cut a life short and leave it seemingly unfinished. 4

By contrast, John Timmerman argues that "let" is used twelve times in a supplicatory, prayer-like manner (176). The final two lines, in turn, act as a benediction upon the supplications. The comfort of God is as inevitable as the evening, so cling to faith and hope and let evening come. Although the Comforter is mentioned only in the last two lines, that statement of faith encourages readers to find a spiritual comfort in spite of the coming of the night. 5

When asked how she came to write "Let Evening Come," Jane Kenyon replied that it was a redemptive poem given to her by the Holy Ghost. When there could be nothing—a great darkness and despair, there is a great mystery of love, kindness, and beauty (Moyers 238). In the poem's calm journey into the night, Kenyon confronts darkness and suffering with a certain enduring beauty and hope (Timmerman 161). Death will come, but there remains divine comfort. "Let Evening Come" encourages readers to release their grip on the temporary and pay attention to the Comforter who reveals Himself both day and night. 6

Note: The Works Cited page is not shown. For an example, see pages 500–501.

Reading for Better Writing

1. *Connections:* When you think of the evening, what images and associations come to mind? Can you recall a particularly memorable evening? What made it memorable, and how does it compare with the evening scene Kenyon describes?
2. *Comprehension:* What essential reading of Kenyon's poem does Van Egdom offer? What are the main elements of her reading?
3. *Writing Strategies:*
   a. Review the opening and closing paragraphs. How do they create a framework for the writer's analysis of the poem?
   b. In her essay, Van Egdom refers to the poet's life and to ideas from secondary sources. What do these references add to her analysis of the poem?

Your Project: Has "Let Evening Come" inspired you to read more of Kenyon's poetry? Find another Kenyon poem and develop your own reading of it.

A Poem to Analyze

Now that you have read Jane Kenyon's "Let Evening Come" and Sherry Van Egdom's analysis of the poem, extend your poetry reading and interpretation skills by analyzing "My Last Duchess," the poem shown below and referenced throughout "Four Ways to Talk About Literature" on pages 283–285.

Robert Browning, a British Victorian poet, first published "My Last Duchess" in 1842. The poem is a dramatic monologue, meaning that the speaker (Duke of Ferrara) is imagined as speaking to a silent listener (an agent for a count with whom the duke is attempting to negotiate another marriage after the death of his first wife). The duke speaking in the poem is believed to be the historical Alfonso Il d'Este (1533–1598), who at the age of 25 married 14-year-old Lucrezia di Cosimo de Medici, the figure in the portrait being described by the duke. It is suspected that when Lucrezia died at the age of 17, she had been poisoned by her husband, the duke.

With this background in mind, engage "My Last Duchess" by doing the following, either on your own or with classmates:

1. **Read the poem aloud** (more than once, if helpful), paying attention to the rhythms and sounds at work.
2. **Work through the poem slowly,** line by line, to sort out what the duke is saying to the agent and why he would be saying it.
3. **Through freewriting, explore your response to the poem**—the story that it tells, the voice and personality of the duke, the ethical puzzle that it presents, or anything else that strikes you about this dramatic monologue.
4. **Use the following resources** to develop a fuller interpretation of the poem:
   - The discussion of primary and secondary research for literary analysis on pages 281–282.
   - "Four Ways to Talk About Literature" on pages 283–285.
   - The literary terms and poetry terms on pages 302–305.

My Last Duchess

That's my last Duchess painted on the wall,
Looking as if she were alive. I call
That piece a wonder, now: Frà Pandolf's hands
Worked busily a day, and there she stands.
Will't please you sit and look at her? I said
"Frà Pandolf" by design, for never read
Strangers like you that pictured countenance,
The depth and passion of its earnest glance,
But to myself they turned (since none puts by
The curtain I have drawn for you, but I)
And seemed as they would ask me, if they durst,

How such a glance came there; so, not the first
Are you to turn and ask thus. Sir, 'twas not
Her husband's presence only, called that spot
Of joy into the Duchess' cheek: perhaps
Frà Pandolf chanced to say "Her mantle laps
Over my Lady's wrist too much," or "Paint
Must never hope to reproduce the faint
Half-flush that dies along her throat": such stuff
Was courtesy, she thought, and cause enough
For calling up that spot of joy. She had
A heart—how shall I say?—too soon made glad,
Too easily impressed; she liked whate'er
She looked on, and her looks went everywhere.
Sir, 'twas all one! My favour at her breast,
The dropping of the daylight in the West,
The bough of cherries some officious fool
Broke in the orchard for her, the white mule
She rode with round the terrace—all and each
Would draw from her alike the approving speech,
Or blush, at least. She thanked men,—good! but thanked
Somehow—I know not how—as if she ranked
My gift of a nine-hundred-years-old name
With anybody's gift. Who'd stoop to blame
This sort of trifling? Even had you skill
In speech—(which I have not)—to make your will
Quite clear to such an one, and say, "Just this
Or that in you disgusts me; here you miss,
Or there exceed the mark"—and if she let
Herself be lessoned so, nor plainly set
Her wits to yours, forsooth, and made excuse,
—E'en then would be some stooping, and I choose
Never to stoop. Oh sir, she smiled, no doubt,
Whene'er I passed her; but who passed without
Much the same smile? This grew; I gave commands;
Then all smiles stopped together. There she stands
As if alive. Will't please you rise? We'll meet
The company below, then. I repeat,
The Count your master's known munificence
Is ample warrant that no just pretence
Of mine for dowry will be disallowed;
Though his fair daughter's self, as I avowed
At starting, is my object. Nay, we'll go
Together down, sir. Notice Neptune, though,
Taming a sea-horse, thought a rarity,
Which Claus of Innsbruck cast in bronze for me!

"My Last Duchess," by Robert Browning. Used under the public domain.

Analyzing a Short Story

As with analyzing poetry, interpreting fiction—whether short stories or novels—requires careful attention to the text. In the case of fiction, that reading involves considering elements of story: plot, setting, character, theme, symbolism, and so on. It also involves reading the story in light of your questions about the narrative, the issues and puzzles you wish to understand more deeply.

On pages 295–297, student writer Julia Jansen offers her interpretation of a well-known story by Ernest Hemingway, "A Clean, Well-Lighted Place." Read the story carefully, paying attention to the situation presented, the characters, and the dialogue. What do you understand regarding this story? Then read Jansen's interpretation, comparing her reading with yours.

A Clean, Well-Lighted Place

1 It was very late and everyone had left the cafe except an old man who sat in the shadow the leaves of the tree made against the electric light. In the day time the street was dusty, but at night the dew settled the dust and the old man liked to sit late because he was deaf and now at night it was quiet and he felt the difference. The two waiters inside the cafe knew that the old man was a little drunk, and while he was a good client they knew that if he became too drunk he would leave without paying, so they kept watch on him.

2 "Last week he tried to commit suicide," one waiter said.

3 "Why?"

4 "He was in despair."

5 "What about?"

6 "Nothing."

7 "How do you know it was nothing?"

8 "He has plenty of money."

9 They sat together at a table that was close against the wall near the door of the cafe and looked at the terrace where the tables were all empty except where the old man sat in the shadow of the leaves of the tree that moved slightly in the wind. A girl and a soldier went by in the street. The street light shone on the brass number on his collar. The girl wore no head covering and hurried beside him.

10 "The guard will pick him up," one waiter said.

11 "What does it matter if he gets what he's after?"

12 "He had better get off the street now. The guard will get him. They went by five minutes ago."

13 The old man sitting in the shadow rapped on his saucer with his glass. The younger waiter went over to him.

"What do you want?" 14

The old man looked at him. "Another brandy," he said. 15

"You'll be drunk," the waiter said. The old man looked at him. The waiter went 16
away.

"He'll stay all night," he said to his colleague. "I'm sleepy now. I never get into bed 17
before three o'clock. He should have killed himself last week."

The waiter took the brandy bottle and another saucer from the counter inside the 18
cafe and marched out to the old man's table. He put down the saucer and poured the glass full of brandy.

"You should have killed yourself last week," he said to the deaf man. 19

The old man motioned with his finger. "A little more," he said. The waiter poured 20
on into the glass so that the brandy slopped over and ran down the stem into the top saucer of the pile.

"Thank you," the old man said. 21

The waiter took the bottle back inside the cafe. He sat down at the table with his 22
colleague again. "He's drunk now," he said.

"He's drunk every night." 23

"What did he want to kill himself for?" 24

"How should I know." 25

"How did he do it?" 26

"He hung himself with a rope." 27

"Who cut him down?" 28

"His niece." 29

"Why did they do it?" 30

"Fear for his soul." 31

"How much money has he got?" 32

"He's got plenty." 33

"He must be eighty years old." 34

"Anyway I should say he was eighty." 35

"I wish he would go home. I never get to bed before three o'clock. What kind of 36
hour is that to go to bed?"

"He stays up because he likes it." 37

"He's lonely. I'm not lonely. I have a wife waiting in bed for me." 38

"He had a wife once too." 39

"A wife would be no good to him now." 40

"You can't tell. He might be better with a wife." 41

"His niece looks after him. You said she cut him down." 42

"I know." 43

"I wouldn't want to be that old. An old man is a nasty thing." 44

“Not always. This old man is clean. He drinks without spilling. Even now, drunk. 45
Look at him.”

“I don’t want to look at him. I wish he would go home. He has no regard for those 46
who must work.”

The old man looked from his glass across the square, then over at the waiters. 47

“Another brandy,” he said, pointing to his glass. The waiter who was in a hurry 48
came over.

“Finished,” he said, speaking with that omission of syntax stupid people employ 49
when talking to drunken people or foreigners. “No more tonight. Close now.”

“Another,” said the old man. 50

“No. Finished.” The waiter wiped the edge of the table with a towel and shook his 51
head.

The old man stood up, slowly counted the saucers, took a leather coin purse from 52
his pocket and paid for the drinks, leaving half a peseta tip.

The waiter watched him go down the street, a very old man walking unsteadily 53
but with dignity.

“Why didn’t you let him stay and drink?” the unhurried waiter asked. They were 54
putting up the shutters. “It is not half-past two.”

“I want to go home to bed.” 55

“What is an hour?” 56

“More to me than to him.” 57

“An hour is the same.” 58

“You talk like an old man yourself. He can buy a bottle and drink at home.” 59

“It’s not the same.” 60

“No, it is not,” agreed the waiter with a wife. He did not wish to be unjust. He was 61
only in a hurry.

“And you? You have no fear of going home before your usual hour?” 62

“Are you trying to insult me?” 63

“No, hombre, only to make a joke.” 64

“No,” the waiter who was in a hurry said, rising from pulling down the metal 65
shutters. “I have confidence. I am all confidence.”

“You have youth, confidence, and a job,” the older waiter said. “You have 66
everything.”

“And what do you lack?” 67

“Everything but work.” 68

“You have everything I have.” 69

“No. I have never had confidence and I am not young.” 70

“Come on. Stop talking nonsense and lock up.” 71

“I am of those who like to stay late at the cafe,” the older waiter said. “With all 72 those who do not want to go to bed. With all those who need a light for the night."

"I want to go home and into bed." 73

"We are of two different kinds," the older waiter said. He was now dressed to go 74
home. "It is not only a question of youth and confidence although those things are very beautiful. Each night I am reluctant to close up because there may be some one who needs the cafe."

"Hombre, there are bodegas open all night long." 75

"You do not understand. This is a clean and pleasant cafe. It is well lighted. The 76
light is very good and also, now, there are shadows of the leaves."

"Good night," said the younger waiter. 77

"Good night," the other said. Turning off the electric light he continued the 78
conversation with himself. It was the light of course but it is necessary that the place be clean and pleasant. You do not want music. Certainly you do not want music. Nor can you stand before a bar with dignity although that is all that is provided for these hours. What did he fear? It was not a fear or dread. It was a nothing that he knew too well. It was all a nothing and a man was a nothing too. It was only that and light was all it needed and a certain cleanness and order. Some lived in it and never felt it but he knew it all was nada y pues nada y nada y pues nada. Our nada who art in nada, nada be thy name thy kingdom nada thy will be nada in nada as it is in nada. Give us this nada our daily nada and nada us our nada as we nada our nadas and nada us not into nada but deliver us from nada; pues nada. Hail nothing full of nothing, nothing is with thee. He smiled and stood before a bar with a shining steam pressure coffee machine.

"What's yours?" asked the barman. 79

"Nada." 80

"Otro loco mas," said the barman and turned away. 81

"A little cup," said the waiter. 82

The barman poured it for him. 83

"The light is very bright and pleasant but the bar is unpolished," the waiter said. 84

The barman looked at him but did not answer. It was too late at night for 85
conversation.

"You want another copita?" the barman asked. 86

"No, thank you," said the waiter and went out. He disliked bars and bodegas. 87
A clean, well-lighted cafe was a very different thing. Now, without thinking further, he would go home to his room. He would lie in the bed and finally, with daylight, he would go to sleep. After all, he said to himself, it's probably only insomnia. Many must have it.

Analysis of a Short Story

In the essay below, student writer Julia Jansen interprets Hemingway's "A Clean, Well-Lighted Place." Note how she introduces the story, states her thesis, and then develops that idea through careful attention to the setting, the characters, and the dialogue.

"A Clean, Well-Lighted Place": Emotional Darkness

Known for his dark perspective, Ernest Hemingway portrayed life as depressing in many of his literary works. One such story is "A Clean, Well-Lighted Place," set in a tidy, well-lit café where two waiters serve drinks to an elderly patron. Here, Hemingway symbolizes the loneliness and emptiness that reside within many ordinary people, particularly the elderly. The concept of nada and the contrast between dark and light demonstrate the emotional darkness that shrouds especially the story's two older characters. In this story, rich with terse dialogue and sharp detail, Hemingway relays his vision of a dark and depressing world that is softened only by patience, compassion, and dignity. This vision can be sensed in the symbolic use of light and dark, the debate between the younger and older waiters, and the inner conflicts of the two older characters. 1

Though quite short, "A Clean, Well-Lighted Place" uses light and dark imagery extensively to convey symbolically the characters' situation, especially the elderly patron's. When first mentioned, the elderly man is said to be sitting "in the shadow the leaves of the tree made against the electric light" (Hemingway 288). Though simple, this description reveals at least two details that are crucial to understanding the elderly man's loneliness; these details center on shade and electric light. Because there is electric light, one can assume the place is well-lit, which is also later revealed in the reflections of the older waiter, who says "it is well lighted" (290). Well-lighted, pleasant cafés are places where people can go to feel like they are part of a community even if they are alone (King). The pleasant, clean atmosphere creates a sense of order and happiness that the elderly man apparently values. Because he chooses to frequent a pleasant place of light, one might assume that he too is happy. However, this is not the case, as is evidenced by the second detail of the phrase describing the elderly man's sitting position: he is "in the shadow the leaves of the tree made against the electric light" (288). While there is light all over the café, the elderly man chooses to sit in the only spot offering darkness. These images suggest that there is a darkness in his life, which is evident through the information one waiter reveals regarding the man: "Last week he tried to commit suicide" (288). The shade in which he sits reflects the dark emotional state in which he resides. The shade is a place where he can sit surrounded by light yet remain unseen by others, still in emotional and physical darkness (King). The light of the café may ward off the physical and emotional darkness of the early morning, but the electric light offers only a temporary release (Bassett). 2

Beyond the light and dark symbolism, Hemingway uses the dialogue between 3
the younger and older waiters to deepen this vision of life. The younger waiter, increasingly frustrated that the old patron doesn't pay up and leave, wants to go home to his wife who waits for him in bed. In fact, at one point the young waiter says to the deaf old man "You should have killed yourself last week" (288). However, the older waiter recognizes the elderly patron's yearning for relief and sympathizes with the now-drunk man. For this reason, the older waiter defends the elderly patron's loitering against the younger waiter's wish to go home. The younger waiter believes the old man should "buy a bottle and drink at home," to which the older waiter responds, "Each night I am reluctant to close up because there may be some one who needs the café . . . You do not understand" (Hemingway 290). The contrast between the younger waiter's impatience with the old customer and the older waiter's empathy softens the story's dark vision by introducing compassion. After the young waiter goes home, the older waiter continues the conversation by himself, justifying why the elderly man should not have to drink alone at home or in a bar: "[One cannot] stand before a bar with dignity although that is all that is provided for these hours" (290). In contrast to the well-lighted café, bars and other places of the night are darker, louder, and more likely to draw in groups of people (King). In nearly every sense, the café is a preferred place for people who seek to ward off their loneliness and despair, to find some dignity in the darkness.

Hemingway's vision of human dignity in the face of life's darkness is deepened 4
by the story's presentation of the struggles experienced by the elderly characters—the source of their suffering. With respect to the elderly patron, one waiter reflects that the unhappiness that drove the old man to attempt suicide was not caused by lack of financial means; he says the old man "has plenty of money" (288). Although he is cared for by a niece, the elderly patron has lost his wife. In his old age, this man seems to sense that hope and happiness are out of reach, and the only option is to retain his self-respect by drinking without spilling, responding to the young waiter's demeaning comments with politeness, and walking home "unsteadily but with dignity" (289). For his part, the older waiter is more explicit about the sources of his unhappiness. He says to the younger, "You have youth, confidence, and a job . . . you have everything" (290). By contrast, the older waiter has only a job. When both the elderly patron and the younger waiter are gone, the older waiter has no clean, well-lighted place to stay, so he turns to the last resort: a bar. He relates his desire for a more cheerful place when he says to the bartender, "The light is very bright and pleasant but the bar is unpolished" (291). His comment is not met with a reply, suggesting that even when he is with others, the older waiter is profoundly lonely. The older waiter demonstrates his sense of life's meaninglessness when referencing what he calls the nada, or the nothing.

The narrator reflects, "What did he fear? It was not fear or dread. It was a nothing that he knew too well. It was all a nothing and a man was nothing too" (291). This sad outlook offers little sign of hope or redemption, which is made more obvious through the older waiter's version of the Lord's Prayer. The waiter replaces most of the words of the prayer with nada, saying, "Our nada who art in nada . . ." (291). This simple yet sad revelation reveals the waiter's hopelessness on a deeper level than before and shows that he views religion as a poor antidote to his loneliness (King). Some people turn to God in times of loneliness and desperation, but the older waiter and the elderly man seemingly cannot, finding temporary comfort only in the well-lighted café.

By portraying these struggles, Hemingway encourages readers to empathize with 5
the two elderly characters. The inner conflicts that they experience are effectively revealed through the light and dark symbolism and through the contrasting perspectives of the young and old waiters. Though it may offer a depressing view of life, "A Clean, Well-Lighted Place" softens that vision with an emphasis on patience, compassion, and human dignity. While Hemingway portrays life as sad, he also suggests that a few clean, well-lighted places remain.

Note: The Works Cited page is not shown. For an example, see pages 500–501.

Reading for Better Writing

1. *Connections:* According to Julia Jansen, Hemingway's story focuses on the need for a clean, well-lighted place within the world's darkness. What darkness do you see, feel, and experience in this world? Do you have your own clean, well-lighted place of refuge? Or is more of life "well-lit," in your opinion, than Hemingway's story suggests?
2. *Comprehension:* What essential interpretation of "A Clean, Well-Lighted Place" does Jansen's essay offer? What points does she offer in support of that interpretation?
3. *Writing Strategies:*
   - **a.** In part, Jansen's analysis focuses on the story's setting. How does she discuss the setting? What does she make of it?
   - **b.** Jansen's analysis focuses primarily on the three central characters of the story: the old patron in the café, the younger waiter, and the older waiter. How does her analysis make sense of each character?

Your Project: For your own writing, choose a short story that you find engaging as a narrative but also rich in its presentation of character, a story that also challenges your vision and understanding of life.

Analyzing a Film

During the last century, film has clearly become a dominant form of storytelling, entertainment, and art. As with analyzing poetry and fiction, interpreting film involves close attention to the medium and its various conventions and components—the camera work, acting, character development, cinematography, scene development, and more that constitute film's particular way of presenting images and narratives.

One form of film analysis is the film review. In the review below, Dr. James C. Schaap (who has written more than two dozen books, including nine novels and three collections of short stories) reviews *The Revenant*, especially director Iñárritu's treatment of the Hugh Glass tale, which Schaap compares to Frederick Manfred's approach to the same story in his novel *Lord Grizzly*. He begins the essay by calling attention to the image in Figure 16.2.

The Revenant: A Brutal Masterpiece

fig. 16.2

H0nzaM/Shutterstock.com

1 I hope you'll agree that there is some beauty in this image, an elegance to what Emerson called "the frolic architecture" of snow, something dazzling in its loveliness. That having been said, no one would really want to be here. It's twenty below. Even a buffalo would move south.

2 *The Revenant* is a film-making masterpiece that's both beautiful and just plain awful to watch. Its sheer violence is matched only by the frightful deprivation Hugh Glass endures when he drags his bloody, broken self out of pure wilderness, a place, by the way, where the word *Disney* has absolutely no meaning. Alejandro G. Iñárritu's *The Revenant* is not for the faint of heart. Brace yourself. Its magnificence is as compelling as it is repellent.

3 Like Shakespeare, Iñárritu is working with materials long ago established, in this

case among the great sagas of the American West, the story of Hugh Glass, a dying trapper left on his own by companions who understand their own lives are in jeopardy if they wait to watch, mercifully, for their companion to die. They leave.

This story is pure rags-to-riches Americana in a way, because Hugh Glass is not 4
dead, nor will he die. It's revenge that he breathes, revenge that gives him life. The story goes that Hugh Glass pulled himself up and away from death itself even though he had no bootstraps. Slowly, with pain that's just as unendurable to imagine as it is to witness, he returns to the fort in search of Fitzgerald, the man who left him behind.

In origin, the myth belongs to South Dakota. Glass was mauled by a she-bear 5
somewhere near Lemmon, but eventually fought the elements, hand over hand, all the way back to Fort Kiowa, near Chamberlain, a 200-mile trek. Iñárritu chooses to set the story in the Canadian Rockies, which only makes the suffering more profound—and without a doubt more profoundly beautiful.

That's the material Iñárritu is bending and shaping in *The Revenant*, the myth 6
many have repeated, retold, rewritten. Mostly, he's following Robert Punke's *The Revenant: A Novel of Revenge*.

The power of the original story—of the myth itself—is that at its climax it refuses 7
to deliver what it promises all along. Call it what you will—retribution, spite, anger, hate—what gives Hugh Glass life is not simply a refusal to die but a gorging thirst for revenge that never happens. When he finds Fitzgerald, Glass doesn't kill him. That unforgettable end is what keeps the story alive.

If Hugh Glass had murdered the man who left him for dead, storytellers of the 8
American West would not have retold the story that created the myth. Had Hugh Glass simply put a gun to Fitzgerald's temple, no one would have been surprised and the story wouldn't have been mythologized. That he doesn't is the shock that lifts the story into the level of what's unimaginable.

Frederick Manfred (1912-1994), a Western novelist of significant power, took a 9
shot at the Hugh Glass story when he wrote *Lord Grizzly*, his rendition of the tale, published in 1954 and nominated for a National Book Award. *Lord Grizzly* has probably outsold all of the other Manfred novels combined. It's one of five he called his "Buckskin Man Tales," stories of the Northern Plains where he lived, a region he loved.

Fred Manfred's real name was Feike Feikema. He was born somewhere around 10
Doon, Iowa. He loved his father but worshiped his mother, Alice Van Engen, a deeply religious woman born and reared in the Christian Reformed Church, who made sure her precocious oldest son got his education in Christian schools.

It is fair to say that his people, his tribe, the Dutch Reformed, "received him not," a rejection that sometimes pained him. Once upon a time, Manfred told me that he couldn't understand why it was that the men and women he grew up with had such faint toleration for his work, when the most famous novel he'd ever written was really all about forgiveness, the central thrust of orthodox Christianity. Manfred's problems with the community of his youth and childhood are a fascinating topic, but what's interesting about that statement in the shadow of *The Revenant* is his assessment of the Hugh Glass story: "it's all about forgiveness." 11

Iñárritu thinks so too, but he changes motivations, even hypes the revenge by giving Glass a son, Hawk, by way of a Native wife, a son who is with him because Glass's dearly beloved wife was murdered in a massacre. Iñárritu plays with the myth the way Shakespeare played with the story of *Hamlet, Prince of Denmark*. 12

Before the trek that made Glass famous, Fitzgerald murders Hawk in this new telling, which makes Glass's motivation in *The Revenant* something greater than revenge. His son's death reshapes the cause into a desire for justice in the American frontier, where there are no courts of law. If the score that needs to be settled is a matter of justice, then forgiveness is really of little importance, which makes Manfred's assessment of the shape of the Hugh Glass story irrelevant. 13

That's a shame. Whether or not Manfred is right is not the point. We're all free to alter the shape of the Hugh Glass story because it belongs to American mythology. But I think it's fair to point out that the reshaping which Iñárritu has given us in this simply incredible film does make the story more Hollywood and, if Manfred was right, less, well, divine. 14

There are distractions in this film, a film that will create untold dissertations in film schools, I'm sure. Iñárritu risks melodrama now and then, as if he can't stop himself. The horror and deprivation are so painfully acute that Iñárritu appears to think he has no limits to what he can show. At some moments near the end, the story gets a little heavy-handed, even preposterous. The horror of the story doesn't need this embellishment. 15

Another distraction is the amazement an audience can't help but feel about how on earth the movie was shot. Iñárritu was committed to natural light; therefore, frequently the crew could shoot only when the light was there—and *there*, in this case, is wilderness areas so remote you wonder if any other human beings have ever been even close. Reportedly, crew members quit in droves when they were forced to live in 16 those conditions. When you watch this film, you have to stop once in a while and just shake your head at how it was done.

And then there is the myth itself. One of the reasons Shakespeare's audience found his *Hamlet* so interesting, or so say the scholars, is that his audience already knew the story; what interested them was how the playwright would tell it. I really loved watching this telling of the Hugh Glass story unfold, loved watching it play the myth itself. 17

The Revenant is not for everyone. The film spares nothing, soft-pedals nothing, refuses to restrain itself. It is a magnificent film that will, I'm sure, take home a number of major awards. 18

But *The Revenant* is not easy to watch. It's brutal and unceasing; it revels in beauty that's difficult to see. It's an amazing rendition of a grueling, bloody story we've already enjoyed for more than a century. 19

Reading for Better Writing

1. *Connections:* If you have seen *The Revenant,* did it impact you as powerfully as Schaap describes its impact on him? If you haven't seen this film, can you point to another film that has impacted you in potent ways? Can you explain why?
2. *Comprehension:* What is Schaap's essential assessment of *The Revenant*? What are the main points that he uses in support of this assessment, and what does the essay teach about the larger context of the film's story?
3. *Writing Strategies:*
   a. Schaap begins his review with a winter-scene photograph. What sense does this opening make? How does he connect the image and the film?
   b. Examine passages in which Schaap describes the film. What kind of language does he use? What do his descriptions add to the review?
   c. Schaap puts the film in context by referring to Shakespeare's *Hamlet* and Frederick Manfred's *Lord Grizzly.* What do such discussions add to Schaap's analysis of the film?
   d. How would you describe the tone of Schaap's review? Are there particular ways that he achieves balance in his assessment?

Your Project: For your own writing, find a film that is similarly based on a legend or a written text such as a novel that you have read. Like Schaap, review the film in light of its debt to the legend or a written narrative.

Literary Terms

Your analysis of novels, poems, plays, and films will be deeper and more sophisticated if you understand the most common literary terms.

Allusion is a reference to a person, a place, or an event in history or literature.

Analogy is a comparison of two or more similar objects, suggesting that if they are alike in certain respects, they will probably be alike in other ways, too.

Anecdote is a short summary of an interesting or humorous, often biographical event.

Antagonist is the person or thing actively working against the protagonist, or hero.

Climax is the turning point, an intense moment characterized by a key event.

Conflict is the problem or struggle in a story that triggers the action. There are five basic types of conflict:

- **Person versus person:** One character in a story is in conflict with one or more of the other characters.
- **Person versus society:** A character is in conflict with some element of society: the school, the law, the accepted way of doing things, and so on.
- **Person versus self:** A character faces conflicting inner choices.
- **Person versus nature:** A character is in conflict with some natural happening: a snowstorm, an avalanche, the bitter cold, or any other element of nature.
- **Person versus fate:** A character must battle what seems to be an uncontrollable problem. Whenever the conflict is a strange or unbelievable coincidence, the conflict can be attributed to fate.

Denouement is the outcome of a play or story. See ***Resolution***.

Diction is an author's choice of words based on their correctness or effectiveness.

- **Archaic** words are old-fashioned and no longer sound natural when used, such as "I believe thee not" for "I don't believe you."
- **Colloquialism** is an expression that is usually accepted in informal situations and certain locations, as in "He really grinds my beans."
- **Heightened language** uses vocabulary and sentence constructions unlike that of standard speech or writing, as in much poetry and poetic prose.
- **Profanity** is language that shows disrespect for someone or something regarded as holy or sacred.
- **Slang** is the everyday language used by group members among themselves.
- **Trite** expressions lack depth or originality, or are overworked or not worth mentioning in the first place.
- **Vulgarity** is language that is generally considered common, crude, gross, and, at times, offensive. It is sometimes used in fiction, plays, and films to add realism.

Exposition is the introductory section of a story or play. Typically, the setting, main characters, and themes are introduced, and the action is initiated.

Falling action is the action of a play or story that follows the climax and shows the characters dealing with the climactic event or decision.

Figure of speech is a literary device used to create a special effect or to describe something in a fresh way. The most common types are *antithesis, hyperbole, metaphor, metonymy, personification, simile,* and *understatement.*

- **Antithesis** is an opposition, or contrast, of ideas.

  > "It was the best of times, it was the worst of times, it was the age of wisdom, it was the age of foolishness . . ." — Charles Dickens, *A Tale of Two Cities*

- **Hyperbole** (hi-pur′ ba-lee) is an extreme exaggeration or overstatement.

  > "I have seen this river so wide it had only one bank."
  > —Mark Twain, *Life on the Mississippi*

- **Metaphor** is a comparison of two unlike things in which no word of comparison (*as* or *like*) is used: "Life is a banquet."
- **Metonymy** (ma-ton′a-mee) is the substituting of one term for another that is closely related to it, but not a literal restatement.

  > "Friends, Romans, countrymen, lend me your ears." (The request is for the attention of those assembled, not literally their ears.)

- **Personification** is a device in which the author speaks of or describes an animal, object, or idea as if it were a person: "The rock stubbornly refused to move."
- **Simile** is a comparison of two unlike things in which *like* or *as* is used.

  > "She stood in front of the altar, shaking like a freshly caught trout."
  > —Maya Angelou, *I Know Why the Caged Bird Sings*

- **Understatement** is stating an idea with restraint, often for humorous effect. Mark Twain described Aunt Polly as being "prejudiced against snakes." (Because she hated snakes, this way of saying so is *understatement.*)

Genre refers to a category or type of literature based on its style, form, and content. The mystery novel is a literary genre.

Imagery refers to words or phrases that a writer uses to appeal to the reader's senses.

> "The sky was dark and gloomy, the air was damp and raw . . ."
> —Charles Dickens, *The Pickwick Papers*

Irony is a deliberate discrepancy in meaning. There are three kinds of irony:

- **Dramatic irony,** in which the reader or the audience sees a character's mistakes or misunderstandings, but the character does not.
- **Verbal irony,** in which the writer says one thing and means another ("The best substitute for experience is being sixteen").
- **Irony of situation,** in which there is a great difference between the purpose of a particular action and the result.

Mood is the feeling that a piece of literature arouses in the reader: *happiness, sadness, peacefulness, anxiety,* and so forth.

Paradox is a statement that seems contrary to common sense yet may, in fact, be true: "The coach considered this a good loss."

Plot is the action or sequence of events in a story. It is usually a series of related incidents that build upon one another as the story develops. There are five basic elements in a plot line: *exposition, rising action, climax, falling action,* and *resolution.*

Point of view is the vantage point from which the story unfolds.

- In the **first-person** point of view, the story is told by one of the characters: "I stepped into the darkened room and felt myself go cold."
- In the **third-person** point of view, the story is told by someone outside the story: "He stepped into the darkened room and felt himself go cold."
- **Third-person narrations** can be *omniscient*, meaning that the narrator has access to the thoughts of all the characters, or *limited*, meaning that the narrator focuses on the inner life of one central character.

Protagonist is the main character or hero of the story.

Resolution (or denouement) is the portion of the play or story in which the problem is solved. The resolution comes after the climax and falling action and is intended to bring the story to a satisfactory end.

Rising action is the series of conflicts or struggles that build a story or play toward a fulfilling climax.

Satire is a literary tone used to ridicule or make fun of human vice or weakness, often with the intent of correcting, or changing, the subject of the satiric attack.

Setting is the time and place in which the action of a literary work occurs.

Structure is the form or organization a writer uses for her or his literary work. A great number of possible forms are used regularly in literature: parable, fable, romance, satire, farce, slapstick, and so on.

Style refers to how the author uses words, phrases, and sentences to form his or her ideas. Style is also thought of as the qualities and characteristics that distinguish one writer's work from the work of others.

Symbol is a person, a place, a thing, or an event used to represent something else. For example, the dove is a symbol of peace.

Theme is the statement about life that a particular work shares with readers. In stories written for children, the theme is often spelled out clearly at the end. In more complex literature, the theme will often be more complex and will be implied, not stated.

Tone is the overall feeling, or effect, created by a writer's use of words. This feeling may be serious, mock-serious, humorous, satiric, and so on.

Poetry Terms

Alliteration is the repetition of initial consonant sounds in words.

> "Our gang paces the pier like an old myth . . ."
> —Anne-Marie Oomen, "Runaway Warning"

Assonance is the repetition of vowel sounds without the repetition of consonants.

> "My words like silent rain drops fell . . ." —Paul Simon, "Sounds of Silence"

Blank verse is an unrhymed form of poetry. Each line normally consists of ten syllables in which every other syllable, beginning with the second, is stressed. As blank verse is often used in very long poems, it may depart from the strict pattern from time to time.

Consonance is the repetition of consonant sounds. Although it is very similar to alliteration, consonance is not limited to the first letters of words:

> ". . . and high school girls with clear-skin smiles . . ." —Janis Ian, "At Seventeen"

Foot is the smallest repeated pattern of stressed and unstressed syllables in a verse (see below).

- **Iambic:** an unstressed followed by a stressed syllable (re-peat′)
- **Anapestic:** two unstressed followed by a stressed syllable (in-ter-rupt′)
- **Trochaic:** a stressed followed by an unstressed syllable (old′-er)
- **Dactylic:** a stressed followed by two unstressed syllables (o′-pen-ly)
- **Spondaic:** two stressed syllables (heart′-break′)
- **Pyrrhic:** two unstressed syllables (Pyrrhic seldom appears by itself.)

Onomatopoeia is the use of a word whose sound suggests its meaning, as in *clang or buzz.*

Refrain is the repetition of a line or phrase of a poem at regular intervals, especially at the end of each stanza. A song's refrain may be called the *chorus.*

Rhythm is the ordered or free occurrences of sound in poetry. Ordered or regular rhythm is called meter. Free occurrence of sound is called *free verse.*

Stanza is a division of poetry named for the number of lines it contains:

- **Couplet:** two-line stanza
- **Triplet:** three-line stanza
- **Quatrain:** four-line stanza
- **Quintet:** five-line stanza
- **Sestet:** six-line stanza
- **Septet:** seven-line stanza
- **Octave:** eight-line stanza

Verse is a metric line of poetry. It is named according to the kind and number of feet composing it: *iambic pentameter, anapestic tetrameter,* and so on. (See ***Foot.***)

- **Monometer:** one foot
- **Dimeter:** two feet
- **Trimeter:** three feet
- **Tetrameter:** four feet
- **Pentameter:** five feet
- **Hexameter:** six feet
- **Heptameter:** seven feet
- **Octometer:** eight feet

Writing Guidelines

Planning

1. **Select a topic.** Choose a work of literature or another artwork with which you are familiar or about which you are willing to learn.
2. **Understand the work.** Read or experience it thoughtfully (two or three times, if possible), looking carefully at its content, form, and overall effect.
   - **For plays and films,** examine the plot, props, setting, characters, dialogue, lighting, costumes, sound effects, music, acting, and directing.
   - **For novels and short stories,** focus on point of view, plot, setting, characters, style, diction, symbols, and theme. (See pages 302–304.)
   - **For poems,** examine diction, tone, sound patterns, figures of speech (e.g., metaphors), symbolism, irony, structure, genre, and theme. (See page 305.)
   - **For music,** focus on harmonic and rhythmic qualities, lyrics, and interpretation.
3. **Develop a focus and approach.** Take notes on what you experience, using the list above to guide you. Seek to understand the whole work before you analyze the parts. Select a dimension of the work as a focus, considering what approach to analyzing that element might work. (See "Four Ways to Talk About Literature" on pages 283–285.)
4. **Organize your thoughts.** Review the notes that you took as you analyzed the work. What key insights has your analysis led you to see? Make a key insight your thesis, and then organize supporting points logically in an outline.

Drafting

5. **Write the first draft.**

   Opening: Use ideas like the following to gain your readers' attention, identify your topic, narrow the focus, and state your thesis:
   - Summarize your subject briefly. Include the title, the author or artist, and the literary form or performance.

     Example: Michael Ondaatje's poem "The Time Around Scars," a poem written in quasi-free verse, deals with scars, the stories they tell, and the people who can and cannot share these stories.
   - Start with a quotation from the work and then comment on its importance.
   - Open with a general statement about the artist's style or aesthetic process.

     Example: Flannery O'Connor's stories are filled with characters who are bizarre, freakish, devious, and sometimes even murderous.
   - Begin with a general statement about the plot or performance.

     Example: In Stephen Spielberg's movie *War of the Worlds*, Ray Ferrier and his two children flee from their New Jersey home in a stolen minivan.

- Assert your thesis. State the key insight about the work that your analysis has revealed—the insight your essay will seek to support.

Middle: Develop or support your focus by following this pattern:

- State the main points, relating them clearly to the focus of your essay.
- Support each main point with specific details or direct quotations.
- Explain how these details prove your point.

Conclusion: Tie key points together and assert your thesis or evaluation in a fresh way, leaving readers with a sense of the larger significance of your analysis.

Revising

6. Improve the ideas, organization, and voice. Review your draft for its overall content and tone. Ask a classmate or writing-center tutor for help, if appropriate.

___ **Ideas:** Does the essay show clear and deep insight into specific elements of the text, artwork, or performance? Is that insight effectively developed with specific references to the work itself?

___ **Organization:** Does the opening effectively engage the reader, introduce the text or artwork, and focus attention on an element or issue? Does the middle carefully work through a "reading" of the work? Does the conclusion reaffirm the insight into the work and expand the reader's understanding?

___ **Voice:** Does the tone convey a controlled, measured interest in the text or artwork? Is the analytical attitude confident but reasonable?

Editing

7. Edit and proofread the essay by checking issues like these:

___ **Words:** Language, especially terminology, is precise and clear.

___ **Sentences:** Constructions flow smoothly and are varied in length and structure; quotations are effectively integrated into sentence syntax.

___ **Correctness:** The copy includes no errors in spelling, usage, punctuation, grammar, or mechanics.

___ **Design:** The page design is correctly formatted and attractive; references are properly documented according to the required system (e.g., MLA).

Publishing

8. Publish your essay. Submit your essay to your instructor, but consider other ways of sharing your insights about this work or artist—blogging, submitting a review to a periodical, or leading classmates in a discussion.

MindTap® Request help and feedback from a tutor. If required, participate in peer review, submit your paper for a grade, and view instructor comments online.

Critical Thinking and Writing: Applications

Once you have written your own analysis of a poem, story, or film, there may be more to think about. Consider how to apply what you have learned in the situations below.

1. **Living Today:** While traditional poetry and fiction continue to find audiences, the rise of different media has created new and different spaces for poetic language and for stories. Consider where and how you encounter poetry and story in your daily life. How do the analytical skills from this chapter help you engage these elements?
2. **Major Work:** As discussed in "Four Ways to Talk About Literature" (pages 283–285), ideological criticism borrows concepts from other disciplines such as psychology, cultural studies, and environmental studies. In your discipline (if it isn't English), might various forms of literature enrich your study of the subject matter? How are close attention to language and an understanding of story relevant to your field of study?
3. **Art Crawl:** While this chapter focuses on poems and stories (with some attention to film), you might extend your literary analysis skills into other art forms. Explore the possibilities by completing one of these activities:
   a. Attend a concert with classmates. Afterward, discuss the style of the music, the performance of the singer or group, and the content of the lyrics. Note the age of the audience and discuss how and why it responded as it did. Finally, discuss whether you found the concert worthwhile.
   b. Visit an art gallery and examine an exhibit that engages you. Describe what you find appealing or intriguing and explain why. Also explain what value this exhibit might have for your community.

Learning-Objectives Checklist ✓

Have you achieved this chapter's learning objectives? Check your progress with the following items, revisiting topics in the chapter as needed. I have . . .

____ critically examined and assessed analyses of literature and the arts for clarity, reasoning, insight, and the writer's critical perspective (280–282).

____ assessed how each analyst's critique of an artwork might be informed by her or his purpose, readers, and topic (280–282).

____ effectively used arts-related terminology and concepts to accurately critique others' analyses and to informatively craft my own (302–305).

____ analyzed and evaluated an artwork by addressing relevant issues, including its content, form, style, special features, and impact on audiences and scholarly critics (306–307).

____ written an analysis that has an insightful thesis, clear reasoning, and relevant supporting evidence from and about the work (306–307).

____ examined (and revised where needed) my ideas, organization, and voice for weaknesses such as inadequate supporting evidence or misused literary terms (306–307).

MindTap® Practice skills that you have learned in this chapter and receive automatic feedback. Reflect on your writing process.

Chapter 17

Strategies for Argumentation and Persuasion

"I wasn't convinced." "I just didn't buy it." Maybe you've said something similar while watching a political debate, viewing a TV ad, or discussing an issue in class or at work. You simply didn't find the argument logical or convincing.

College is a place where big issues get argued out—in class and out. To participate in that dialogue, you must be able to read and listen to others' arguments, analyze them, and build your own.

This chapter will help you do that. It explains what argumentation is and the different forms it can take. It shows you how to identify weak arguments, and how to construct strong ones. The next chapter then applies these concepts to your writing of an argument that takes a position, calls for action, and/or solves a problem.

Visually Speaking Carefully study Figure 17.1. What do you see in the foreground, the middle distance, and the background? What story do you imagine the photo is telling? In what ways is that story an argument?

Understand the goals of the chapter and complete a warm-up activity online.

Learning Objectives

By working through this chapter, you will be able to

- structure arguments according to common patterns.
- effectively engage opposing perspectives and alternatives.
- make appeals to *ethos, pathos,* and *logos*.
- support claims with convincing reasoning and fitting evidence.
- distinguish and develop three types of claims.
- reason with and support claims through various types of evidence.
- identify and correct logical fallacies.

fig. 17.1

Understanding Arguments

What is an argument? Formally, an *argument* is a series of statements arranged in a logical sequence, supported with sound evidence, and expressed powerfully so as to sway your reader or listener. Arguments appear in a variety of places:

- A research paper about online surveillance by government agencies such as the NSA.
- An analysis of Ernest Hemingway's "A Clean, Well-Lighted Place" (a short story).
- A debate about the ethics of watching pirated films on the Internet.

Sample Essay of Argumentation

Perhaps the best way to understand written arguments—why and how they are made—is to read one. The following argument was written by Malcolm Gladwell, author of *The Tipping Point, Blink, Outliers, What the Dog Saw,* and *David and Goliath*. Gladwell, who writes regularly for *The New Yorker* magazine, was born in England and grew up in Canada. In "No Mercy," a 2006 commentary, he takes a stand on the punishment of students. As you read his argument, consider how it is constructed and how it works. Look for appeals to logic, credibility, and emotion. Then as you learn about argumentative strategies in the rest of this chapter, come back to this essay to explore those strategies at work.

MindTap®
Read, highlight, and take notes online.

No Mercy

In 1925, a young American physicist was doing graduate work at Cambridge University, in England. He was depressed. He was fighting with his mother and had just broken up with his girlfriend. His strength was in theoretical physics, but he was being forced to sit in a laboratory making thin films of beryllium. In the fall of that year, he dosed an apple with noxious chemicals from the lab and put it on the desk of his tutor, Patrick Blackett. Blackett, luckily, didn't eat the apple. But school officials found out what happened, and arrived at a punishment: the student was to be put on probation and ordered to go to London for regular sessions with a psychiatrist. 1

Probation? These days, we routinely suspend or expel high-school students for doing infinitely less harmful things, like fighting or drinking or taking drugs—that is, for doing the kinds of things that teenagers do. This past summer, Rhett Bomar, the starting quarterback for the University of Oklahoma Sooners, was cut from the team when he was found to have been "overpaid" (receiving wages for more hours than he worked, with the apparent complicity of his boss) at his job at a car dealership. Even in Oklahoma, people seemed to think that kicking someone off a football team for having cut a few corners on his job made perfect sense. This is the age of zero tolerance. Rules are rules. Students have to be held accountable for their actions. Institutions must 2 signal their expectations firmly and unambiguously: every school principal and every college president, these days, reads from exactly the same script. What, then, of a student who gives his teacher a poisoned apple? Surely he ought to be expelled from school and sent before a judge.

Suppose you cared about the student, though, and had some idea of his situation 3
and his potential. Would you feel the same way? You might. Trying to poison your tutor is no small infraction. Then again, you might decide, as the dons at Cambridge clearly did, that what had happened called for a measure of leniency. They knew that the student had never done anything like this before, and that he wasn't well. And they knew that to file charges would almost certainly ruin his career. Cambridge wasn't sure that the benefits of enforcing the law, in this case, were greater than the benefits of allowing the offender an unimpeded future.

Schools, historically, have been home to this kind of discretionary justice. You 4
let the principal or the teacher decide what to do about cheating because you know that every case of cheating is different—and, more to the point, that every cheater is different. Jimmy is incorrigible, and needs the shock of expulsion. But Bobby just needs a talking to, because he's a decent kid, and Mary and Jane cheated because the teacher foolishly stepped out of the classroom in the middle of the test, and the temptation was simply too much. A Tennessee study found that after zero-tolerance programs were adopted by the state's public schools the frequency of targeted offenses soared: the firm and unambiguous punishments weren't deterring bad behavior at all. Is that really a surprise? If you're a teenager, the announcement that an act will be sternly punished doesn't always sink in, and it isn't always obvious when you're doing the thing you aren't supposed to be doing. Why? Because you're a teenager.

Somewhere along the way—perhaps in response to Columbine—we forgot 5
the value of discretion in disciplining the young. "Ultimately, they have to make right decisions," the Oklahoma football coach, Bob Stoops, said of his players, after jettisoning his quarterback. "When they do not, the consequences are serious." Open and shut: he sounded as if he were talking about a senior executive of Enron, rather than a college sophomore whose primary obligation at Oklahoma was to throw a football in the direction of young men in helmets. You might think that if the University of Oklahoma was so touchy about its quarterback being "overpaid" it ought to have kept closer track of his work habits with an on-campus job. But making a fetish of personal accountability conveniently removes the need for institutional accountability. (We court-martial the grunts who abuse prisoners, not the commanding officers who let the abuse happen.) To acknowledge that the causes of our actions are complex and muddy seems permissive, and permissiveness is the hallmark

of an ideology now firmly in disgrace. That conservative patron saint Whittaker Chambers once defined liberalism as Christ without the Crucifixion. But punishment without the possibility of redemption is worse: it is the Crucifixion without Christ.

As for the student whose career Cambridge saved? He left at the end of the academic year and went to study at the University of Göttingen, where he made important contributions to quantum theory. Later, after a brilliant academic career, he was entrusted with leading one of the most critical and morally charged projects in the history of science. His name was Robert Oppenheimer. 6

Reading for Better Writing

1. *Connections:* What school punishments have you experienced or witnessed? What was the story behind those punishments? What do you think about those punishments now, particularly in relation to Gladwell's discussion?
2. *Comprehension:*
   - **a.** According to Gladwell, what is the issue with school punishments? What essential points does he make about them?
   - **b.** Gladwell references Robert Oppenheimer (paragraphs 1, 3, and 6), Rhett Bomar (paragraphs 2 and 5), Columbine (paragraph 5), Enron (paragraph 5), and Christ (paragraph 5). What is the point of each of these illustrations or references? If necessary, briefly research them.
3. *Writing Strategies:*
   - **a.** Gladwell weaves into his argument a contrast of two cases, Robert Oppenheimer and Rhett Bomar. What are the differences, and how does this analysis support Gladwell's argument? How is his commentary structured around this contrast?
   - **b.** How does Gladwell acknowledge and address opposing points of view about school punishment? What strategies does he use to encourage readers to trust his judgment?
   - **c.** At the beginning of paragraph 3, Gladwell uses the pronoun "you" as part of a "what if" appeal to readers. Here and elsewhere in the essay, what is the impact of Gladwell speaking directly to readers?
   - **d.** Gladwell's argument offers a logical critique of "zero tolerance" policies. What logical errors seem to be at the heart of zero tolerance?

Your Project: Like Gladwell, consider policies, practices, or behaviors with which you disagree. Conversely, look at an issue that you support but is critiqued by others. Consider writing your own commentary as a reply to a position on that policy, practice, or behavior.

Structuring Arguments

The shape of an argument often emerges organically as you think about and research an issue. While you have a lot of freedom about how to shape arguments, two patterns have become popular methods of doing so: Toulmin and Rogerian. In what follows, you will find a brief introduction to each method. Use these introductions to guide your choices for specific arguments.

Understand Toulmin Argumentation

Made popular by British philosopher Stephen Toulmin in his book *The Uses of Argument* (1958), this method lends structure to the way people naturally make arguments. Not exactly formal logic, this pattern offers a practical approach that allows writers and their readers to wrestle over debatable issues through sound thinking. Toulmin's elements do not map out a strict sequence of elements, but writers may draw upon the elements to unfold their thinking within a paragraph or for an entire essay. Many of these elements are addressed more fully later in this chapter (pages 315–322), but here is an overview:

- **Claims** The debatable statement the writer aims to prove or support.

  > Planting trees is a practical step to fight climate change.

- **Qualifiers** Any limits the writer puts on claims in order to make those claims more reasonable, precise, and honest.

  > *Although it is a small step*, planting trees is *one* practical way that *many* people can fight climate change.

- **Support** The reasoning that the writer offers to explain and defend the claim; the evidence that the writer offers to back up the reasoning and thereby ground the claim (various forms of data, information, experience, narratives, authority, and so on).

  > According to the UN, "Deforestation causes 12-18 percent of the world's carbon emission, almost equal to all the CO2 emissions from the global transport sector."

- **Warrants** The logical glue that holds together claims, reasons, and evidence; the assumptions, principles, and values (sometimes unstated), that lie behind the writer's reasoning.

  > Stopping climate change is more important than the economic benefits of deforestation.

- **Backing** When warrants aren't shared or understood by readers, the special reasoning and evidence writers offer to convince readers to accept those principles.

  > Recent research has determined that the 32 million acres of forest lost each year make a significant contribution to global warming.

- **Conditions of Rebuttal** The writer's anticipation of and response to possible objections; his or her sense of other perspectives and positions.

  > Economies dependent on deforestation can take a number of steps toward sustainable practices.

Understand Rogerian Argumentation

While the Toulmin approach emphasizes proving a claim through reasoning and evidence (swaying the reader to the writer's side), the Rogerian method aims at consensus building, connection, respect for differences, and collaboration. Borrowed from the therapeutic work of psychologist Carl Rogers, the pattern begins with the idea that disputes and differences cannot be resolved unless each disputant can fully, fairly, and sympathetically state the other's situation and position. The Rogerian approach, in other words, aims to offer an antidote to angry confrontation, divisiveness, and polarized thinking.

Making its way into rhetoric and composition, Rogers's psychological method has resulted in argumentative patterns that are sometimes called "invitational" in that they are grounded in careful listening with the aim of getting people to work together, disagreeing respectfully when agreement cannot be reached. This philosophy has led rhetoric scholars to develop a four-part Rogerian structure:

1. **Introduction:** As completely, richly, and fairly as possible, the writer describes the issue, disagreement, conflict, or problem—showing that he or she fully respects and understands the range of positions or alternatives available.
2. **Contexts:** Grounding the issue in a broader context or background, the writer explores situations in which different positions are valid and sensible.
3. **Writer's Position:** The writer then offers his or her perspective, stating a position but also explaining the conditions or circumstances under which this position is valid.
4. **Benefits to Opponent:** The writer explains to readers, who may hold a different position, how they would gain from agreeing with the writer's position, the writer thus arguing that the position is mutually beneficial.

Choose an Approach

While the Rogerian method is less common than the Toulmin method, both are good choices under the right circumstances. In fact, you should aim to learn how to use both approaches. To choose an approach or to perhaps develop your own hybrid structure for a particular project, consider these rhetorical issues:

- **Your Goal** Are you aiming to sway readers to your position, putting yourself out there as taking a strong stand? Or are you hoping to build bridges, arrive at consensus, or bring about reconciliation in a hurting situation?
- **Your Readers** Whom are you trying to reach with your argument? Are you seeking their respect for your position, even their adoption of it? Or are you aiming to build a collaborative relationship with specific readers, to enter a dialogue with them?
- **The Topic** Does the issue lend itself to one approach over the other? How charged is the topic, and what is at stake in the argument?
- **Your Beliefs and Style** What approach to argumentation feels natural to your own character and consistent with your values?

Engaging the Opposition

A key element of any argument is engaging alternatives and opposing points of view. Whether you use the Toulmin or Rogerian approach, you should think of an argument as an intelligent, lively dialogue with readers. Anticipate their questions, concerns, objections, and counterarguments. Then follow these guidelines.

Make Concessions

By offering concessions—recognizing points made by the other side—you acknowledge your argument's limits and the truth of other positions. Paradoxically, such concessions strengthen your overall argument by making it seem more credible. Concede your points graciously, using words such as the following:

Admittedly	Granted	I agree that	I cannot argue with
It is true that	You're right	I accept	No doubt
Of course	I concede that	Perhaps	Certainly it's the case

> While it is true that foot-and-mouth disease is not dangerous to humans, other animal diseases are.

Develop Rebuttals

Even when you concede a point, you can often answer that objection by rebutting it. A good rebuttal is a small, tactful argument aimed at a weak spot in the opposing argument. Try these strategies:

1. **Point out the counterargument's limits** by putting the opposing point in a larger context. Show that the counterargument omits something important.
2. **Tell the other side of the story.** Offer an opposing interpretation of the evidence, or counter with stronger, more reliable, more convincing evidence.
3. **Address logical fallacies in the counterargument.** Check for faulty reasoning or emotional manipulation. (See the fallacies on pages 323–326.) For example, if the counterargument presents a half-truth, present "the rest of the story."

> It is true that Chernobyl occurred more than 30 years ago, so safety measures for nuclear reactors have been greatly improved. However, that single accident is still affecting millions of people exposed to the radiation.

Consolidate Your Claim

After making concessions and rebutting objections, you may need to regroup. Restate your claim so carefully that the weight of your whole argument can rest on it.

> Although it is not ideal, burning fossil fuels is still a better option than nuclear power until renewable energy sources become more available.

Arguing Through Appeals

For your argument to be persuasive, it must not only be logical, but also "feel right." It must treat readers as real people by appealing to their common sense, hopes, pride, and notion of right and wrong. How do you appeal to all these concerns? Do the following: (1) build credibility, (2) appeal to *pathos* by focusing on readers' values and needs, and (3) appeal to *logos* through sound reasoning.

Appeal to *Ethos*

Sound arguments are rooted in *ethos*—a sense of the writer's character and credibility. As the connection between the words *ethos* and *ethics* suggests, a persuasive argument is so trustworthy that readers can change their minds painlessly. To build credibility, observe these rules:

- **Be thoroughly honest.** Demonstrate integrity toward the topic—don't falsify data, spin evidence, or ignore facts. Document your sources and cite them wherever appropriate. Moreover, use reputable, reliable sources; by doing so, you "borrow" the credibility of authorities.
- **Make realistic claims, projections, and promises.** Avoid emotionally charged statements, pie-in-the-sky forecasts, and undeliverable deals.
- **Develop and maintain trust.** From your first word to your last, develop trust—in your attitude toward the topic, your treatment of readers, and your respect for opposing viewpoints.

Appeal to *Pathos*

When your argument seeks to connect with people emotionally, it appeals to *pathos*. When combined with appeals to *ethos* and *logos*, appeals to *pathos* can powerfully motivate readers to accept, believe, change, and/or act. But you want to avoid playing on readers' emotions. Instead, connect your argument with readers' needs and values. Follow these guidelines:

- **Know your real readers.** Who are they—peers, professors, or fellow citizens? What are their allegiances, their worries, their dreams?
- **Picture readers as resistant.** Accept that your readers, including those inclined to agree with you, need convincing. Think of them as alert, cautious, and demanding—but also interested.
- **Use appeals that match needs and values.** Your argument may support or challenge readers' needs and values. To understand those needs, study the table below, which is based loosely on the thinking of psychologist Abraham Maslow. Maslow's hierarchy ranks people's needs on a scale from the most basic to the most complex. The table begins at the bottom with *having necessities* (a basic need) and ends at the top with *helping others* (a more complex need). For example, if you're writing to argue for more affordable housing for the elderly, you'd argue differently to legislators (whose focus is on *helping others*) than to the elderly who need the housing (whose focus is on *having necessities*). Follow the guidelines in Figure 17.2.

- Use appeals that match the foremost needs and values of your readers.
- If appropriate, constructively challenge those needs and values.
- Whenever possible, phrase your appeals in positive terms.
- After analyzing your readers' needs, choose a persuasive theme for your argument—a positive benefit, advantage, or outcome that readers can expect if they accept your claim. Use this theme to help readers to care about your claims.

Reader needs . . .	Use persuasive appeals to . . .
To make the world better by helping others	values and social obligations
To achieve by being good at something, getting recognition	self-fulfillment, status, appreciation
To belong by being part of a group	group identity, acceptance
To survive by avoiding threats, having necessities	safety, security, physical needs

fig. 17.2

Appeal to *Logos*

Arguments stand or fall on their logical strength; for that reason, the rest of this chapter offers instruction in making sound claims, reasoning with and supporting those claims, and avoiding logical fallacies. However, your readers' acceptance of your logic is often affected more by the emotional appeal of your ideas and evidence. To avoid overly emotional appeals, follow these guidelines:

- **Engage readers positively.** Appeal to their better natures—to their sense of honor, justice, social commitment, altruism, and enlightened self-interest. Avoid appeals geared toward ignorance, prejudice, selfishness, or fear.
- **Use a fitting tone.** Use a tone that is appropriate for the topic, purpose, situation, and audience.
- **Aim to motivate, not manipulate, readers.** While you do want them to accept your viewpoint, it's not a win-at-all-costs situation. Avoid bullying, guilt-tripping, name calling, and exaggerated tugs on heartstrings.
- **Don't trash-talk the opposition.** Show tact, respect, and understanding. Focus on issues, not personalities.
- **Use arguments and evidence that readers can understand and appreciate.** If readers find your thinking too complex, too simple, or too strange, you've lost them.

INSIGHT Remember the adage: The best argument is so clear and convincing that it sounds like an explanation.

Making and Qualifying Claims

An argument that appeals effectively to *ethos, pathos,* and *logos* centers on a claim—a debatable statement. That claim is the thesis, or key point you wish to explain and defend so well that readers agree with it. A strong claim has the following traits:

- **It's clearly arguable**—it can be vigorously debated.
- **It's defendable**—it can be supported with sufficient arguments and evidence.
- **It's responsible**—it takes an ethically sound position.
- **It's understandable**—it uses clear terms and defines key words.
- **It's interesting**—it is challenging and worth discussing, not bland and easily accepted.

Distinguish Claims From Facts and Opinions

A claim is a conclusion drawn from logical thought and reliable evidence. A fact, in contrast, is a statement that can be checked for accuracy. An opinion is a personally held taste or attitude. A claim can be debated, but a fact or an opinion cannot.

Fact: During the last three years, no major accident has occurred in a nuclear power plant in the U.S.

Opinion: I think nuclear power plants are safe.

Claim: Nuclear power and fossil fuels are two major methods of energy production, and nuclear power could be seen as the "greener" option. However, the risks of nuclear power far outweigh its benefits, making fossil fuels the safer and more environmentally friendly option.

Note: While the fact's accuracy can easily be checked, the opinion statement simply offers a personal feeling. Conversely, the claim states an idea that can be supported with reasoning and evidence.

Distinguish Three Types of Claims

Truth, value, and policy—these types of claims are made in an argument. The differences among them are important because each type has a distinct goal.

- **Claims of truth** state that something is or is not the case. As a writer, you want readers to accept your claim as trustworthy.

> The Arctic ice cap will melt completely during the summer as early as 2080.
>
> The cholesterol in eggs is not as dangerous as previously feared.
>
> **Comment:** Avoid statements that are (1) obviously true or (2) impossible to prove. Also, truth claims must be argued carefully because accepting them (or not) can have serious consequences.
>
> *Sample Essay:* "The Prison Problem," pages 346–348

- **Claims of value** state that something does or does not have worth. As a writer, you want readers to accept your judgment.

> Volunteer reading tutors provide a valuable service.
>
> Many music videos fail to present positive images of women.
>
> **Comment:** Claims of value must be supported by referring to a known standard or by establishing an agreed-upon standard. To avoid a bias, base your judgments on the known standard, not on your feelings.
>
> *Sample Essay:* "The Gravest Threat to Colleges Comes from Within," pages 355–357

- **Claims of policy** state that something ought or ought not to be done. As a writer, you want readers to approve your course of action.

> Special taxes should be placed on gas-guzzling SUVs.
>
> The developer should not be allowed to fill in the pond where the endangered tiger salamander lives.
>
> **Comment:** Policy claims focus on action. To arrive at them, you must often first establish certain truths and values; thus an argument over policy may include both truth and value claims.
>
> *Sample Essay:* "Remedying an E-Waste Economy," pages 342–345

Develop a Supportable Claim

An effective claim balances confidence with common sense. Follow these tips:

- **Avoid all-or-nothing, extreme claims.** Propositions using words that are overly positive or negative—such as *all, best, never,* and *worst*—may be difficult to support. Statements that leave no room for exceptions are easy to attack.

> **Extreme:** All people charged for a DUI should never be allowed to drive again.

- **Make a truly meaningful claim.** Avoid claims that are obvious, trivial, or unsupportable. None is worth the energy needed to argue the point.

> **Obvious:** Some people are against oil pipelines.
>
> **Trivial:** Oil pipelines are good at moving oil.
>
> **Unsupportable:** Building oil pipelines is immoral.

- **Use qualifiers to temper your claims.** Qualifiers are words or phrases that make claims more reasonable. Notice the difference between these two claims:

> **Unqualified:** Star athletes take far too many academic shortcuts.
>
> **Qualified:** Some star athletes take improper academic shortcuts.

Note: The "qualified" claim is easier to defend because it narrows the focus and leaves room for exceptions. Use qualifier words or phrases like these:

almost	if done correctly	maybe	tends to
before 2016	in one case	might	typically
frequently	likely	probably some	usually

Supporting Your Claims

A claim stands or falls on its support. It's not the popular strength of your claim that matters, but rather the strength of your reasoning and evidence. To develop strong support, consider how to select and use evidence.

Gather Evidence

Several types of evidence can support claims. To make good choices, review each type, as well as its strengths and weaknesses.

- **Observations and anecdotes** share what people (including you) have seen, heard, smelled, touched, tasted, and experienced. Such evidence offers an "eyewitness" perspective shaped by the observer's viewpoint, which can be powerful but may also prove narrow and subjective.

  > A generation ago, an American child could reasonably expect to grow up with his or her father. Today, an American child can reasonably expect not to.

- **Statistics** offer concrete numbers about a topic. Numbers don't "speak for themselves," however. They need to be interpreted and compared properly—not slanted or taken out of context. They also need to be up-to-date, relevant, and accurate.

  > Pennsylvania spends $30 million annually in deer-related costs.
  >
  > Wisconsin has an estimated annual loss of $37 million for crop damage alone.

- **Tests and experiments** provide hard data developed through the scientific method, data that must nevertheless be carefully studied and properly interpreted.

  > According to the two scientists, the rats with unlimited access to the functional running wheel ran each day and gradually increased the amount of running; in addition, they started to eat less.

- **Graphics** provide information in visual form—from simple tables to more complex charts, maps, drawings, and photographs. When poorly done, however, graphics can distort the truth.
- **Analogies** compare two things, creating clarity by drawing parallels. However, every analogy breaks down if pushed too far.

  > It is obvious today that America has defaulted on this promissory note insofar as her citizens of color are concerned. Instead of honoring this sacred obligation, America has given the Negro people a bad check; a check which has come back marked "insufficient funds." But we refuse to believe that the bank of justice is bankrupt.
  >
  > —Martin Luther King, Jr.

- **Expert testimony** offers insights from an authority on the topic. Such testimony always has limits: Experts don't know it all, and they work from distinct perspectives, which means that they can disagree.

> One specialist opposed to drilling is David Klein, a professor at the Institute of Arctic Biology at the University of Alaska–Fairbanks. Klein argues that if the oil industry opens up the ANWR for drilling, the number of caribou will likely decrease because the calving locations will change.

- **Illustrations, examples, and demonstrations** support general claims with specific instances, making such statements seem concrete and observable. Of course, an example may not be your best support if it isn't familiar.

> Think about how differently one can frame Rosa Parks' historic action. In prevailing myth, Parks—a holy innocent—acts almost on whim. . . . The real story is more empowering: It suggests that change is the product of deliberate, incremental action.

- **Analyses** examine parts of a topic through thought patterns—cause/effect, compare/contrast, classification, process, or definition. Such analysis helps make sense of a topic's complexity, but muddles the topic when poorly done.

> If colorism lives underground, its effects are very real. Darker-skinned African-American defendants are more than twice as likely to receive the death penalty as lighter-skinned African-American defendants for crimes of equivalent seriousness. . . .

- **Predictions** offer insights into possible outcomes or consequences by forecasting what might happen under certain conditions. Like weather forecasting, predicting can be tricky. To be plausible, a prediction must be rooted in a logical analysis of present facts.

> Fortunately, there is hope. Scientific research is already helping doctors do amazing things for people suffering with cancer. One treatment that has been used for some time is chemotherapy, or the use of chemicals to kill off all fast-growing cells, including cancer cells. . . . One of the newest and most promising treatments is gene therapy. . . ."

Use Evidence

Finding evidence is one thing; using it well is another. You want to reason with the evidence effectively, to use that evidence to advance and deepen your argument—to "thicken" it, so to speak. To marshal evidence in support of your claim, follow three guidelines:

1. **Go for quality and variety, not just quantity.** More evidence is not necessarily better. Instead, aim for sound evidence in different forms. Quality evidence is . . .
    - **accurate:** correct and verifiable in each detail.
    - **complete:** filled with pertinent facts.
    - **concrete:** filled with specifics.
    - **relevant:** clearly related to the claim.
    - **current:** reliably up-to-date.
    - **authoritative:** backed by expertise, training, and knowledge.
    - **appealing:** able to influence readers.

2. **Use inductive and deductive patterns of logic.** Depending on your purpose, use inductive or deductive reasoning. (See page 18.)

   Induction: Inductive reasoning works from the particular toward general conclusions. In a persuasive essay using induction, look at facts first, find a pattern in them, and then lead the reader to your conclusion.

   > For example, in "No Mercy" (pages 310–312), Malcolm Gladwell first narrates and reflects on two case studies of student misbehavior, Robert Oppenheimer and Rhett Bomar. He then draws the conclusion that a sharp shift has happened in school discipline from discretionary justice to zero tolerance, and that this shift is a bad thing.

   Deduction: Deductive reasoning—the opposite of inductive reasoning—starts from accepted truths and applies them to a new situation so as to reach a conclusion about it. For deduction to be sound, be sure the starting principles or facts are true, the new situation is accurately described, and the application is logical.

   > For example, in "The Gravest Threat to Colleges Comes from Within" (pages 355–357), Scott Bass and Mary Clark first establish the principle of academic freedom and its value. They then apply that principle to a trend in higher education toward student criticism of materials taught, complaints about speakers brought to campus, and requests for accommodations and "trigger warnings."

3. **Reason using valid warrants.** To make sense, claims and their supporting reasons must have a logical connection. That connection is called the *warrant*—the often unspoken thinking used to relate the reasoning to the claim. If warrants are good, arguments hold water; if warrants are faulty, then arguments break down. In other words, beware of faulty assumptions.

   Check the short argument outlined below. Which of the warrants seem reasonable and strong, and which seem weak? Where does the argument fail?

   > **Reasoning:** If current trends in water usage continue, the reservoir will be empty in two years.
   >
   > **Claim:** Therefore, Emeryville should immediately shut down its public swimming pools.

   Unstated Warrants or Assumptions:

   > It is not good for the reservoir to be empty.
   > The swimming pools draw significant amounts of water from the reservoir.
   > Emptying the pools would help raise the level of the reservoir.
   > No other action would better prevent the reservoir from emptying.
   > It is worse to have an empty reservoir than an empty swimming pool.

INSIGHT Because an argument is no stronger than its warrants, you must make sure that your reasoning clearly and logically supports your claims.

Identifying Logical Fallacies

Fallacies are false arguments—that is, bits of fuzzy, dishonest, or incomplete thinking. They may crop up in your own thinking, in your opposition's thinking, or in such public "arguments" as ads, political appeals, and talk shows. Because fallacies may sway an unsuspecting audience, they are dangerously persuasive. By learning to recognize fallacies, however, you may identify them in opposing arguments and eliminate them from your own writing. In this section, logical fallacies are grouped according to how they falsify an argument. Afterward, the relevance of these fallacies is shown in an essay, "Executive Deception: Four Fallacies about Divestment, and One Big Mistake" (pages 327–329).

Distorting the Issue

The following fallacies falsify an argument by twisting the logical framework.

- **Bare Assertion** The most basic way to distort an issue is to deny that it exists. This fallacy claims, "That's just how it is."

  > The private ownership of handguns is a constitutional right. (*Objection:* The claim shuts off discussion of the U.S. Constitution, the legal process of amending the Constitution, or the reasons for regulation.)

- **Begging the Question** Also known as circular reasoning, this fallacy arises from assuming in the basis of your argument the very point you need to prove.

  > We don't need a useless film series when students have computers and other devices. (*Objection:* There may be uses for a public film series that private video viewing can't provide. The word "useless" begs the question.)

- **Oversimplification** This fallacy reduces complexity to simplicity. Beware of phrases like "It's a simple question of." Serious issues are rarely simple.

  > Capital punishment is a simple question of protecting society.

- **Either/Or Thinking** Also known as black-and-white thinking, this fallacy reduces all options to two extremes. Frequently, it derives from a clear bias.

  > Either this community develops light-rail transportation or the community will not grow in the future. (*Objection:* The claim ignores the possibility that growth may occur through other means.)

- **Complex Question** Sometimes by phrasing a question a certain way, a person ignores or covers up a more basic question.

  > Why can't we bring down the prices that corrupt gas stations are charging? (*Objection:* This question ignores a more basic question—"Are gas stations really corrupt?")

- **Straw Man** In this fallacy, the writer argues against a claim that is easily refuted. Typically, such a claim exaggerates or misrepresents the opponents' position.

  > Those who oppose euthanasia must believe that individuals who are terminally ill deserve to suffer.

Sabotaging the Argument

These fallacies falsify the argument by twisting it. They destroy reason and replace it with something hollow or misleading.

- **Red Herring** This strange term comes from the practice of dragging a stinky fish across a trail to throw tracking dogs off the scent. When a person puts forth a volatile idea that pulls readers away from the real issue, readers become distracted. Suppose the argument addresses drilling for oil in the Arctic National Wildlife Refuge (ANWR) of Alaska, and the writer begins with this statement:

> In 1989, the infamous oil spill of the *Exxon Valdez* led to massive animal deaths and enormous environmental degradation of the coastline. (*Objection:* Introducing this notorious oil spill distracts from the real issue—how oil drilling will affect the ANWR.)

- **Misuse of Humor** Jokes, satire, and irony can lighten the mood and highlight a truth; when humor distracts or mocks, however, it undercuts the argument. What effect would the mocking tone of this statement have in an argument about tanning beds in health clubs?

> People who use tanning beds will just turn into wrinkled old prunes or leathery sun-dried tomatoes!

- **Appeal to Pity** This fallacy engages in a misleading tug on the heartstrings. Instead of using a measured emotional appeal, an appeal to pity seeks to manipulate the audience into agreement.

> Affirmative action policies ruined this young man's life. Because of them, he was denied admission to Centerville College.

- **Use of Threats** A simple but unethical way of sabotaging an argument is to threaten opponents. More often than not, a threat is merely implied: "If you don't accept my argument, you'll regret it."

> If we don't immediately start drilling for oil in the ANWR, you will soon face hour-long lines at gas stations from New York to California.

- **Bandwagon Mentality** Someone implies that a claim cannot be true because a majority of people are opposed to it, or it must be true because a majority support it. (History shows that people in the minority have often had the better argument.) At its worst, such an appeal manipulates people's desire to belong or be accepted.

> It's obvious to intelligent people that cockroaches live only in the apartments of dirty people. (*Objection:* Based on popular opinion, the claim appeals to a kind of prejudice and ignores scientific evidence about cockroaches.)

- **Appeal to Popular Sentiment** This fallacy consists of associating your position with something popularly loved: the American flag, baseball, apple pie. Appeals to popular sentiment sidestep thought to play on feelings.

> Anyone who has seen *Bambi* could never condone hunting deer.

Drawing Faulty Conclusions from the Evidence

This group of fallacies falsifies the argument by short-circuiting proper logic in favor of assumptions or faulty thinking.

- **Appeal to Ignorance** This fallacy suggests that because no one has proven a particular claim, it must be false; or, because no one has disproven a claim, it must be true. Appeals to ignorance unfairly shift the burden of proof onto someone else.

  > Flying saucers are real. No scientific explanation has ruled them out.

- **Hasty or Broad Generalization** Such a claim is based on too little evidence or allows no exceptions. In jumping to a conclusion, the writer may use intensifiers such as *all, every,* or *never.*

  > Today's voters spend too little time reading and too much time being taken in by 30-second sound bites. (*Objection:* Quite a few voters may, in fact, spend too little time reading about the issues, but it is unfair to suggest that this is true of everyone.)

- **False Cause** This well-known fallacy confuses sequence with causation: If *A* comes before *B*, *A* must have caused *B*. However, *A* may be one of several causes, or *A* and *B* may be only loosely related, or the connection between *A* and *B* may be entirely coincidental.

  > Since that new school opened, drug use among young people has skyrocketed. Better that the school had never been built.

- **Slippery Slope** This fallacy argues that a single step will start an unstoppable chain of events. While such a slide may occur, the prediction lacks evidence.

  > If we legalize marijuana, it's only a matter of time before hard drugs follow and America becomes a nation of junkies and addicts.

Misusing Evidence

These fallacies falsify the argument by abusing or distorting the evidence.

- **Impressing with Numbers** In this case, the writer drowns readers in statistics and numbers that overwhelm them into agreement. In addition, the numbers haven't been properly interpreted.

  > At 35 ppm, CO levels factory-wide are only 10 ppm above the OSHA recommendation, which is 25 ppm. Clearly, that 10 ppm is insignificant in the big picture, and the occasional readings in some areas of between 40 and 80 ppm are aberrations that can safely be ignored. (*Objection:* The 10 ppm may be significant, and higher readings may indicate real danger.)

- **Half-Truths** A half-truth contains part of but not the whole truth. Because it leaves out "the rest of the story," it is both true and false simultaneously.

  > The new welfare bill is good because it will get people off the public dole. (*Objection:* This may be true, but the bill may also cause undue suffering for some truly needy individuals.)

- **Unreliable Testimonial** An appeal to authority has force only if the authority is qualified in the proper field. If he or she is not, the testimony is irrelevant. Note that fame is not the same thing as authority.

  > On her talk show, Alberta Magnus recently claimed that most pork sold in the United States is tainted. (*Objection:* Although Magnus may be an articulate talk show host, she is not an expert on food safety.)

- **Attack Against the Person** This fallacy, also called an "*ad hominem* attack," directs attention to a person's character, lifestyle, or beliefs rather than to the issue.

  > Would you accept the opinion of a candidate who experimented with drugs in college?

- **Hypothesis Contrary to Fact** This fallacy relies on "if only" thinking. It bases the claim on an assumption of what would have happened if something else had, or had not, happened. Being pure speculation, such a claim cannot be tested.

  > If only multiculturalists hadn't pushed through affirmative action, the United States would be a united nation.

- **False Analogy** Sometimes a person will argue that X is good (or bad) because it is like Y. Such an analogy may be valid, but it weakens the argument if the grounds for the comparison are vague or unrelated.

  > Don't bother voting in this election; it's a stinking quagmire. (*Objection:* Comparing the election to a "stinking quagmire" is unclear and exaggerated.)

Misusing Language

Essentially, all logical fallacies misuse language. However, three fallacies falsify the argument particularly by the misleading use of words.

- **Obfuscation** This fallacy involves using fuzzy terms like *throughput* and *downlink* to muddy the issue. These words may make simple ideas sound more profound than they really are, or they may make false ideas sound true.

  > Through the fully functional developmental process of a streamlined target-refractory system, the U.S. military will successfully reprioritize its data throughputs. (*Objection:* What does this sentence mean?)

- **Ambiguity** Ambiguous statements can be interpreted in two or more opposite ways. Although ambiguity can result from unintentional careless thinking, writers sometimes use ambiguity to obscure a position.

  > Many women need to work to support their children through school, but they would be better off at home. (*Objection:* Does *they* refer to *children* or *women*? What does *better off* mean? These words and phrases can be interpreted in opposite ways.)

- **Slanted Language** By choosing words with strong positive or negative connotations, a writer can draw readers away from the true logic of the argument. Here is an example of three synonyms for the word stubborn that the philosopher Bertrand Russell once used to illustrate the bias in slanted language:

  > I am firm. You are obstinate. He is pigheaded.

Identifying Fallacies in Others' Arguments

While it is important to identify and avoid fallacies in your own arguments, it is also valuable (though not necessarily appreciated) to point out logical errors in others' arguments. This is one strategy for engaging opposition within your own writing. In the following essay, Kathleen Dean Moore structures her whole essay around four logical fallacies in the arguments of university administrators who defend not divesting their university's finances of investments in fossil fuels. Moore is a distinguished professor emerita of philosophy at Oregon State University. She is the author or coeditor of several books, including the recently published *Great Tide Rising: Toward Clarity and Moral Courage in a Time of Planetary Change*. As you read her essay, examine how she explains and illustrates each fallacy, and note how each of her claims advances her thesis.

Executive Deception: Four Fallacies About Divestment, and One Big Mistake

It pains this old logic professor to read university officials' arguments against divesting their institutions of investments in fossil fuels, not because their refusal to divest is wrong-headed, although I believe it is, but because their logic is so awful. 1

A sample of Ivy League universities' antidivestment statements offers a primer in the fallacies that students are warned against in Logic 101. Here are four: 2

The ad hominem argument: "I find a troubling inconsistency in the notion that, as an investor, we should boycott [the oil-and-gas industry, while we] are extensively relying on those companies' products and services," writes Drew Faust, president of Harvard University. 3

The assumption is that those who rely on fossil fuels do not have the moral authority to take a stand against them. This is an ad hominem (to the man) attack, which turns the focus from the argument itself to the person or institution making the argument. The attack might be fair if the university had freely chosen fossil fuels from an array of options. It did not. Over generations, fossil fuels have been built into the structure of our lives, our buildings, our cities. Big Oil works hard to perpetuate that dependency and to radically constrict choices, as it lobbies against renewable energies, influences the election of officials who will vote against alternative transportation, hires hacks to confuse the public about the scientific consensus on climate change, making sure that colleges (and all the rest of us) are forced to use fossil fuels. It's the ultimate triumph of the industry that even as it is externalizing its environmental costs, it is also externalizing its shame. And university officials making this argument haplessly cooperate to disempower their own moral voices and those of their students. 4

The straw argument: "Brown's holdings are much too small for divestiture to 5
reduce corporate profits," writes Christina Paxson, president of Brown University.

Of course Brown's divestment, or anyone else's, will not cripple the fossil-fuel 6
industry. The author and divestment leader Bill McKibben publicly affirms that it will not. Divestment isn't designed to destroy. It is designed to save, and what is imperiled here is the integrity of the university. A university has an overriding responsibility to advance the well-being of its students, which means that it is flat wrong to profit from industries that will devastate their future.

The Ivy League response is a classic straw argument, a cynical or careless 7
misconstruing of the divestment argument. Instead of addressing the real issue of moral integrity, the president substitutes a scarecrow so flimsy that it might be made of straw. Easy enough to knock down the bogus argument, but the serious one remains.

The false dichotomy: "Yale will have its greatest impact in meeting the climate 8
challenges through its core mission: research, scholarship, and education," claims the Yale Corporation Committee on Investor Responsibility.

Maybe so. But that doesn't mean that Yale should not study, educate, and at 9
the same time divest from fossil fuels. Divest or educate? This is not a forced choice between alternatives. In fact, divestment may be a university's greatest opportunity for moral education, for instruction in the foundational moral imperative to let your values guide your decisions.

"Climate change is a grave threat to human welfare," the committee goes on 10
to say. If so, then Yale should throw everything it's got at the threat. Research? Yes. Scholarship? Yes. Education? Beyond a doubt. Divestment? Absolutely, and anything else it can pull out of the hat. Addressing climate change is going to require the greatest exercise of the moral and technological imagination the world has ever seen. The future is no place for slackers.

The hasty generalization. "Logic and experience indicate that barring 11
investments in [fossil fuels] would—especially for a large endowment reliant on sophisticated investment techniques, pooled funds, and broad diversification—come at a substantial economic cost." Harvard again.

It's sometimes logical to make predictions about the future on the basis of past 12
experience, but only if you can assume that the future will resemble the past. When the future threatens to be staggeringly different from the past, reliance on experience is a hasty, often expensive mistake in reasoning.

Never before has life on the planet been so deeply threatened by a single 13 energy technology—burning fossil fuels. And never before have there been so many alternative ways to generate energy. Never have the costs of alternatives fallen so rapidly.

It's a new world. Whether because of new technologies, new regulations, a global 14
crisis of conscience, a global economy utterly devastated by climate change, or who knows what, the world will divest itself of the fossil-fuel economy, and probably sooner rather than later. The investors who quickly respond to a changing world have the best chance to prosper; the laggards will be left holding the bag.

And so we come to the big mistake: "The [university] endowment is a resource, 15
not an instrument to impel social or political change." Harvard.

Oh, yes it is. By profiting from Big Oil, the university endowment casts a very 16
public vote for short-term, short-sighted profit and against the victims of that business plan—future generations, plants and animals, the world's poor and displaced—and the university's own students. Shame.

Reading for Better Writing

1. *Connections:* Where and how do you use fossil fuels in your own life? How would you characterize your dependence on them? Have you taken steps to lessen that dependence? On a different scale, does your college or university have a policy on divestment in fossil fuels? What rationale, if any, does your school offer for or against divestment?
2. *Comprehension:* For each of the four fallacies Moore discusses, restate the logical error and summarize how college administrators make the error.
3. *Writing Strategies:*
   a. Moore both starts and ends her essay with some sharp statements. What is the effect of doing so? How do these statements frame her discussion, putting it in a larger context.
   b. For each fallacy, Moore quotes directly from administrators and then explains the fallacious reasoning in the quotation. What is the effect of this method and pattern?

Your Project: Fossil-fuel divestment is just one issue on which people are susceptible to thinking fallaciously. With what other contentious, difficult issues would people make logical errors? Consider choosing such a topic, researching what people think about it, and writing an exposé of the common fallacies people make.

Critical Thinking and Writing: Applications

Once you have finished learning and practicing strategies for argumentation, there may be more to think about. Consider how to apply what you have learned in the following situations.

1. **Photo Op:** The chapter's opening page contains a photograph of crosses in front of a nuclear power plant—an image of an argument. Consider another controversial issue, and find or create an image that similarly makes a claim about that issue.
2. **Living Today:** What role does argument play in our daily lives and decisions? Reflect on an area of your life where you rely on arguments—consumer purchases, politics, sports, and so on. Examine the arguments that you make in that area of life, as well as the arguments that you listen to: do they follow sound argumentation strategies?
3. **Public Texts:** Editorials in periodicals are often brief arguments. Find, read, and analyze an editorial on an issue that interests you:
   - **a.** What approach does the editorial take—Toulmin, Rogerian, something else?
   - **b.** How does the editorial present and address opposing points of view?
   - **c.** In what ways does the editorial appeal to *ethos*? How does it build credibility?
   - **d.** In its appeals to *pathos*, does the editorial connect with needs and values?
   - **e.** What is the editorial's main claim? Is it a claim of truth, value, or policy?
   - **f.** What arguments does the editorial offer to support that claim? Is the reasoning logical? Are the warrants behind the reasoning sound?
   - **g.** What types of evidence does the writer provide to support his or her reasoning? Is the evidence valid, sufficient, current, and accurate?
   - **h.** How would you characterize the overall success or failure of this argument?

Learning-Objectives Checklist ✓

Have you achieved this chapter's learning objectives? Check your progress with the following items, revisiting topics in the chapter as needed. I have . . .

____ identified different approaches to argumentation (313–314).
____ practiced addressing alternatives and opposing perspectives (315).
____ analyzed and practiced appeals to *ethos, pathos,* and *logos* (316–317).
____ analyzed the nature and effects of truth, value, and policy claims (318–319).
____ revised arguments, correcting these weaknesses: all-or-nothing claims, obvious claims, trivial assertions, and claims lacking needed qualifiers (319).
____ analyzed the strengths and weaknesses of nine types of evidence (320–321).
____ linked claims and their supporting reasons with valid warrants (322).
____ identified and corrected logical fallacies in others' arguments and in my own (323–326).
____ drafted, revised, and edited a brief argument that critiques a policy or practice or that reveals logical fallacies in a position.

MindTap® Practice skills that you have learned in this chapter and receive automatic feedback. Reflect on your writing process.

Arguing for Positions, Actions, and Solutions

Written arguments aim to move people by changing their minds, behaviors, and actions. Doing so isn't easy, as readers may be indifferent, resistant, or opposed to your thinking. To move them, your writing needs to overcome this inertia.

Perhaps you want your readers to take action on e-waste, to adopt your position on sex-selective abortions, or to leave a controversial statue where it is. Whatever the debatable issue your writing addresses, it must construct a sound argument that speaks logically to readers' reason, convinces them to trust you, and appeals to their values and better natures.

Such arguments typically follow a pattern, singly or blended: taking a position, calling for action, or solving a problem. This chapter introduces these patterns, while also helping you apply the principles outlined in chapter 17.

Visually Speaking Look closely at Figure 18.1. Is it a moving, compelling photograph? What point does it seem to make? In particular, what does it suggest about making arguments?

MindTap®

Understand the goals of the chapter and complete a warm-up activity online.

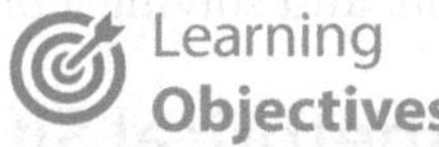

Learning Objectives

By working through this chapter, you will be able to

- examine written arguments sympathetically and critically.
- identify logical fallacies that are especially damaging in persuasive writing.
- develop measured, reasonable claims—position statements, calls to action, or solutions to problems.
- support claims with convincing reasoning and fitting evidence.
- write a compelling argumentative essay that effectively appeals to credibility, values, and reason.

spirit of america / Shutterstock.com

fig. 18.1

Strategies for Argumentative Writing

Argumentative writing takes many forms: essays, editorials, position papers, proposals, to name a few. Whatever the form, argumentative writing goes out on a limb by examining a controversy, a debatable issue, or a problem. Such writing goes beyond careful analysis of the issue by asking questions like these: Why should we care? What should we believe? What can we do? To learn how to go out on a limb without breaking it, writers need to understand the rhetorical situation behind their writing and follow the principles for taking a stand, calling for action, and solving a problem.

The Rhetorical Situation

To construct an argument, writers start by thinking about the purpose, the readers, and the specific topic of their writing.

- **Purpose:** Writers produce argumentative papers to inform readers about the nature and relevance of a topic, to convince them to take a stand on it, and possibly to move them to take action. If the topic can be defined as a problem, the writer's goal is to persuade readers of a solution. More limited goals might be to convince readers to care about the topic and to at least respect the writer's argument.
- **Readers:** A writer may address a variety of readers: people opposed to the argument, uncertain what to think about the issue, or unaware that an issue exists. The audience may even be those who agree with the writer's point of view but are looking for sensible reasons. Good writers shape the content, organization, and tone of their arguments to effectively address such intended readers.
- **Topic:** The topics addressed in argumentative writing are debatable issues about which informed people can reasonably disagree. Therefore, as a reader, you will learn more about a paper's topic by focusing not only on the writer's position, call to action, or solution, but also on the reasoning that he or she uses to develop the argument, including attention to alternatives.

Example: In "Fatherless America" (pages 358–362), David Blankenhorn's ***purpose*** is to convince readers that the absence of fathers from families is a serious, damaging trend, one with many long-term, harmful consequences for American society. The ***topic*** of fatherlessness is debatable, in the sense that some might argue that fatherhood can be restricted to a biological function, leaving mothers to more ably raise children, while others would claim that the traditional nuclear family is the only accepted pattern. Published in a book of the same title, this excerpt shows Blankenhorn, the founder of the Institute for American Values, speaking to ***readers*** who are well-educated—possibly legislators and other decision-makers, feminists, social workers, and ultimately fathers and mothers, current and soon-to-be.

Principles: Taking a Stand

Writing that takes a position examines a controversial or debatable issue, and it then articulates and defends a specific stance on that issue. Effectively taking a position depends on the principles that follow.

Researching, exploring, and respecting all available positions. Before settling on a particular position, writers need to openly and thoroughly examine all the options—getting inside different stances, objectively examining the reasoning and evidence, and weighing the pluses and minuses. Doing so helps writers better determine where to stand and prepares them to speak to all the alternatives.

Making a stance reasonable and measured. A solid position must go beyond a pure opinion that is shouted shrilly. (Whereas an opinion may be uninformed and inherited, writers *think* their way into a position.) Writers are certainly free to advance their position forcefully, but they also need to do so thoughtfully and respectfully: conceding points, addressing objections, and softening the stance (if necessary) with qualifiers. Essentially, writers need to determine whether to advance their positions firmly or to seek a fair and reasonable compromise, working their way out of embattled and entrenched thinking. Such position statements can be phrased as affirmations or as arguments against a claim:

- **Position statement:** *Barbed fishing hooks should be banned in favor of smooth hooks in order to protect fish stocks.*
- **Argument against a claim:** *Contrary to Breton's contention, violent video games do not make boys more violent in adulthood.*

Rooting the position in sound analysis and reliable evidence. Writers need to show how the evidence weighs in favor of their position—not verbal aggression, bluster, or the fervor of their feelings. The evidence needs to be sound, soundly reasoned with, and complete: writers should not hide, ignore, or lightly dismiss evidence that does not support their position. In addition, the reasoning needs to be solid in these ways:

- **Built on an analytical foundation:** For a position to hold up, writers may need to carefully *define* key terms in the debate or even the issue itself. Similarly, they may need to position the issue historically (*process* analysis), exploring how and why the issue arose. Finally, effective *comparison-contrast* makes sense of the range of possible positions on the issue.
- **Sensitive to logical fallacies:** Writers need to be aware of specific thinking errors within the debate, address them in opposing positions, and avoid them in their own stance. Particularly problematic is either-or thinking (page 323), a kind of dualistic logic that reduces an issue to two polar opposite possibilities. Similarly, writers need to avoid broad generalizations (page 325) and oversimplification (page 323).

Principles: Calling for Action

Change is tough, so calling others to action in writing can be especially challenging. In this sense, call-to-action writing not only takes a position on an issue (encouraging readers to adopt or at least respect that position, as discussed above) but also presses readers to take the next logical step—translating that stance into concrete action or behavioral change. Persuading readers to act relies on writing principles like these:

Rooting the writing in sound reasoning. Asking readers to act must be built on a foundation of trustworthy evidence and sound reasoning. Because action is involved, writers need to get it right. Especially important is cause-effect analysis—reasoning that can sort out the forces at work in an issue and predict the consequences of action. Similarly, call-to-action writing needs to avoid logical fallacies such as half-truths, unreliable testimonials, and false analogies (pages 323–329).

Building credibility through an encouraging but measured voice. A writer's aim is to motivate, not manipulate. To that end, the tone in most call-to-action writing should communicate an objective urgency, though in some situations humor works well to deflate some tension and open a new perspective on the issue. Above all, the writing should never sound threatening or engage in guilt-tripping in order to prompt action. Not only is such an approach ethically questionable, but it also tends to have an effect opposite to the one desired.

Convincing readers to care about the issue. Motivating readers to act begins with encouraging them to embrace the issue as their own. Writers do so by sharing compelling anecdotes and illustrations that put a human face on the issue, by correcting misunderstandings or commonly held views about the issue (often through the voices of respected experts), and by making sound appeals to shared needs and values (page 316). Through such strategies, writers change readers' view of the issue.

Motivating readers to undertake a doable action. First of all, writers must imagine points of resistance for readers—those thoughts and feelings that make them reluctant to act. With these realities in mind, writers need to then determine what is a doable action, a concrete step or general change that is within reach for readers. Can a writer expect readers to re-examine their spending habits, to stop using a word thoughtlessly, to contribute to organizations that fight poverty? That doable action then becomes the theme and thesis of the writing, what it builds towards. Here are some examples of calls to doable action:

- *It's time for all consumers to learn more about where their food comes from and how it gets to their table.*
- *Sign the online petition and boycott Company X until it changes its unethical sourcing practices.*
- *Whatever your race, connect with the Black Lives Matter movement on your campus or in your community. Add your voice to the chorus calling for real racial reconciliation.*

Principles: Proposing a Solution

Sometimes, the issue on which writers take a position can be described as a *problem*, and the action they call for a *solution*. Explaining a problem flows naturally into arguing for a solution. For the problem-solution writer, the task is to convince the reader that the solution matches the problem. Doing so requires practicing a range of strategies.

Rooting the argument in quality research. A proposal stands or falls on the quality of both the reasoning and its support. Writers convince the reader of their credibility by going to reliable sources for quality evidence ranging from the statistical to the historical, and by doing their homework concerning debates about the problem, its broader context, and past attempts at solutions.

Thinking creatively. While problem-solution thinking needs to be sound, it must also be creative. Writers do so by thinking beyond what has already been done, by considering alternative perspectives on both the problem and possible solutions, and by bringing to bear on the problem ideas from other fields of knowledge. Proposal writing requires a willingness to challenge the status quo and a mind that is open to creative possibilities—a willingness to ask, "What's really wrong here, and how can we fix it?"

Considering ethical issues. Inherently, problem-solution writing involves an ethical dimension. It involves realizing that whereas some people may be harmed by the problem, other people may benefit from its existence. Such writing can require seeking common ground on some of life's most enduring challenges. And it attempts to motivate readers to embrace a specific solution, a change that the writer stands behind and that might fail partly or wholly. Smart writers are aware of and speak to these ethical dimensions.

Presenting Problems. The first part of a proposal typically lays out the problem. The aim here is not only to convince readers that the problem exists but to persuade them to care about it enough to seek a solution. Laying out the problem involves strategies like these:

- **A measured approach:** Writers determine how deeply to treat and explain the problem based on what their audience needs and the level of seriousness inherent to the problem. The more unfamiliar the problem, the more serious it is, the more resistant the readers, the more extensive the damage caused by the problem, the longer its history—the deeper the writer must go into presenting the problem in all its complexity, the more serious his or her tone.
- **Sound analysis:** Problems make sense when they are precisely defined (What is it?), vividly described (What does it look like?), explored as a narrative (What's the story?), explained as a process (When and how did it develop?), and/or probed for causes and effects (What brought about the problem? What are its consequences?).

Arguing for Solutions. When writers turn from problems to solutions, they approach the heart of their writing—their thesis about what will end the problem or at least mitigate its harmful consequences. (The thesis thus often comes part-way through the essay, not at the beginning.) Arguing for a solution involves strategies like the ones that follow:

- **Criteria for a successful solution:** Writers establish a measurement for what a solution must accomplish, what it must look like.
- **Comparison of all options:** Using these criteria, writers boldly explore all possible solutions, weighing and balancing them against each other in terms of how they attack root causes and bring about real benefits. In addition, writers consider past attempts at solutions, to what degree these succeeded, and how they still fell short.
- **Support for the best solution (or a series of related solutions):** The best solution is not superficial, one that temporarily treats surface harms. Nor is it a vague suggestion that something must be done. Instead, writers need to present a solution in precise and exact terms, addressing possible objections and explaining the positive outcomes that will result and the negative consequences that will be avoided.
- **Feasibility:** Writers need to show that their solution is workable, not just an empty wish. They do so by considering the resources required, mapping out how the solution should be implemented, and addressing any roadblocks to success.

Sample Argumentative Paragraph

In any essay, a writer might make an argumentative point not necessarily central to the essay's purpose but worthy of consideration. For example, in "The Rise of the New Groupthink" Susan Cain spends most of her essay exploring the dynamics at work in solitary and group work; however, toward the end she turns to the following argument:

> To harness the energy that fuels both these drives [our need for both others and privacy], we need to move beyond the New Groupthink and embrace a more nuanced approach to creativity and learning. Our offices should encourage casual, cafe-style interactions, but allow people to disappear into personalized, private spaces when they want to be alone. Our schools should teach children to work with others, but also to work on their own for sustained periods of time. And we must recognize that introverts like Steve Wozniak need extra quiet and privacy to do their best work.

Reading Persuasive Writing

As you read each essay on the following pages, consider these questions (noting how many of them connect with the elements of argumentation you learned in Chapter 17):

1. In what sense is the topic debatable? Is it stated fairly and fully?
2. What stance does the writer take among the available positions on the topic?
3. Does the writer also call for action, or does he or she present a solution to a problem? If yes, is the writer convincing?
4. Is the writer's argument well reasoned and effectively supported with reliable evidence? Is it free of logical fallacies?
5. Is the tone measured and free of manipulative language?
6. What topics, ideas, and strategies does the essay inspire for your own writing?

Sample Argumentative Essays

The essays on the following pages address a wide range of issues—from e-waste to AIDS in Africa. Of particular interest, a number of the essays consider campus debates, continuing the theme begun in Chapter 17 with Malcolm Gladwell's "No Mercy" on pages 310–312 and Kathleen Dean Moore's "Executive Deception" on pages 327–329. As you read, engage the arguments, study the strategies used, and consider how the essays might inspire your own writing.

MindTap®

Read, highlight, and take notes online.

Taking a Stand on Female Self-Esteem

As a psychology student, Sara Wiebenga wrote the following essay to explore the influence of mothers on their daughters' self-esteem, given the large influence of media in girls' lives. As you read, look for places where the author takes a stand.

Mother-Daughter Relationships: Harmful or Helpful?

"Look like this and you will find love." "Eat this and you will be skinny." "Wear these clothes and you will be popular." These are just a few of the messages the media portray in commercials, on the Internet, and on billboards. These messages are everywhere, complete with thin women wearing next to nothing and men snuggled in closely. In fact, "[y]oung girls are bombarded by millions of images of digitally manipulated, airbrushed beauty every day, and research tells us this onslaught can often be responsible for feelings of low self-esteem" (Shields, 2007). Models spend hours having their hair and makeup done to enhance their overall look and to cover up any blemishes. After the photo shoot, editors retouch the photos in order to create the "perfect" image. But with all of this makeup, hair product, and digital editing, "the definition of beauty [has] become limiting and unattainable" (Dove, 2012). Research by Dove's "Campaign for Real Beauty" shows that "only 4% of women worldwide consider themselves beautiful" (Dove, 2011). What message is this sending to young girls? The fact that mothers have a significant impact on their daughters during the process of identity development is supported by research everywhere. Solid mother-daughter relationships are essential to combat the media's unrealistic standards of beauty and to build girls' healthy self-esteem. 1

Unrealistic advertisements are destroying girls' self-esteem and body image. The media portrays beauty that is not attainable by anyone—models have flawless, spot- 2 free skin and long, wavy hair; pout their perfectly plump lips to match their big eyes with clump-free lashes; and are too thin for their own wellbeing. The media not only applauds these superficial traits but also uncritically promotes them (Spettigue, 2004). Dove has started a campaign that encourages women to embrace their real and inner beauty, regardless of what culture says. Its "Evolution" video shows the transformation of an average-looking woman with no makeup into a billboard model. She has her hair curled perfectly, her makeup done flawlessly, and the photos are taken with just the right angle of lighting. Afterwards, a computer screen is shown with a mouse rapidly clicking various areas of the woman's face—elongating her neck, defining her jawline, enlarging her eyes, and more. The video shows that even photos of supposedly perfect models are significantly retouched before the photos are publicized. The advertisements are not realistic at all; makeup alone could not replicate the model's image. It is for this reason that a Lancôme advertisement featuring Julia Roberts was banned in the United Kingdom (Swinson, 2011). Roberts, who is naturally stunning, does not need any digital editing in order to look beautiful. But the photo had been "manipulated to the extent that L'Oreal, which owns Lancôme, could not prove the makeup's ability to replicate such flawlessness" (Swinson, 2011).

3 Unfortunately, women who are unaware of these photo-shoot practices may feel inferior when comparing themselves to the photo images, and these feelings can damage their self-esteem. As Shields (2007) points out, the link between the number of cases of low self-esteem among girls and the images of female perfection portrayed on billboards and in magazines is undeniable. In fact, the Dove research team found that in a recent survey, 77% of women felt fat, ugly, and depressed when faced with pictures of beautiful models or celebrities. Furthermore, Dohnt (2006) found that girls who watched television shows with an emphasis on appearance (such as *Friends*) were less satisfied with their overall appearance than those who didn't watch TV. Dohnt (2006) adds that soap operas and televised music clips that "present women as thin and attractive . . . have also been correlated with body dissatisfaction and disordered eating in adolescents." Extensive research shows a correlation between the overload of advertisements with which young girls are bombarded and a decrease in self-esteem. Furthermore, the average girl has seen more than 77,000 advertisements by the age of 12 (Shields, 2007).

4 As part of a study done by Dove during its "Campaign for Real Beauty," girls were asked to keep journals of the beauty images they were exposed to over a three-day period, and then record their reactions in the journal. One of the girls who

participated in the study said this: "The images I see in magazines make me feel sad because I know I could never be that beautiful" (Shields, 2007). She felt as if she could never achieve the image that the media portrayed as true beauty. Furthermore, Shields (2007) notes that over 90% of girls regularly feel stressed and anxious about their appearance. In another study, Dove asked girls how they felt about themselves. Most of the girls discussed appearance and their desire to be accepted by their peers. One of the girls answered "I want to be skinny" while another one said that "no one really looks for your personality" (A Girl's Self-Esteem, n.d.). Sadly, the media is polluting girls' minds to the point that the girls feel inferior and inhibited. In fact, six out of ten girls avoid doing the things they love or going to events because they lack body confidence (Dove, 2013).

Although research clearly links the media's advertisements and the decrease in girls' self-esteem, some writers disagree. They argue that the media does not significantly diminish self-esteem and that adolescents should not accept advertisements as personal criticism. These writers claim that advertisements are inescapable, so girls and women should accept seeing other people more beautiful than themselves. However, girls cannot insulate themselves from the media's demeaning message. Dohnt (2006) notes that regular reading of women's magazines does diminish girls' self-esteem. In addition, Swinson (2011) observes that whereas girls know that models go through hair, makeup, and wardrobe changes, "the pressure to conform to such narrow ideals is overwhelming." 5

So what might help girls deal with this pressure? Dove created a video called "Onslaught" that opens with a shot of a smiling seven-year-old girl, afterwards cutting abruptly to a barrage of beauty-industry images: "Scantily clad models bear down from billboards; make-up adverts promote products promising to make viewers 'younger, lighter, thinner, firmer'; and gruesome footage shows women altering their bodies through surgery" (Shields, 2007). At the end of the clip, a black screen with white letters cautions parents: "Talk to your daughter, before the beauty industry does" (Beauty Pressure, n.d.). Dove's campaign highlights the importance of strong mother-daughter relationships in fighting against the pressure the media imposes on girls of all ages. 6

In another video, Dove argues that "things won't change until we change them" (A Girl's Self-Esteem, n.d.) and that there is a link between a mother's influence and her daughter's ideas about body image and self-confidence (Dove, 2013). If mothers become more aware of their own attitudes and have a positive outlook towards their 7 own bodies, their daughters will notice. This awareness will in turn help girls stand up to cultural influences that undermine their own sense of beauty and self worth (Dove, 2013). Because parents play a central role in establishing their children's beliefs and values, mothers and fathers need to emphasize the important aspects of the true definition of beauty. Beauty does not come merely from outward appearance, but also from respectable character. In a recent survey, girls were asked which traits they like most about themselves and in what ways they were unique. Most of the answers referred to various personality traits rather than looks. For example, one girl said that she is not scared to be weird, another said she can see the best in people, and still another said that she "[doesn't] try to be something like in the magazines" (What Makes You Beautiful, n.d.). Mothers should aim to boost self-esteem in their daughters by highlighting character traits rather than appearance (Dohnt, 2006). Moms need to "intervene at critical times" (Dove, 2013) and discuss how to address confidence issues. Dove tells mothers to stay curious and help their daughters identify and appreciate their beauty, both inside and out. In fact, Dove (2011) notes that "the best role model is a woman who knows who she has been and who she wants to become, while being proud of who she is today."

Some critics argue that parents do not play a major role in their children's lives because children do not listen to their parents anyway. Statistics show, however, that girls listen to their mothers more than to anyone else. "Recent research has focused on parents, particularly mothers, as influential role models for younger girls 5-8 years of age" (Dohnt, 2006). Young girls are often seen shadowing their mothers, imitating the way they talk and act in hopes one day of becoming like them. Therefore, mothers who are insecure about their own image will have a negative effect on their daughters' self-esteem. In fact, McFadden's (2011) research shows that young women spend 30-40% of the day thinking about body image, with 46% of these women focusing on it because their mothers did. Talking about diets, weight loss, or ugliness, along with judging other women based on their appearance, shows a young girl that her mother has succumbed to the media's ridiculous standards of beauty. These standards will further undermine a daughter's confidence—interpersonally, academically, professionally, and sexually—into adulthood (McFadden, 2011). In addition, girls will not talk to their parents about body image if their mothers do not find themselves beautiful because the girls believe their moms will not be able to support them: "A mother's inability to appreciate the female body and authentic female sexuality causes daughters to lose 8 faith in their mother's ability to be confident role models of health and happiness" (McFadden, 2011). Clearly, mothers must be self-assured in order to help their daughters develop positive body image.

The relationship between a mother and her daughter significantly affects a girl's self-confidence and self-perception. Whereas the media constantly pressures girls to conform to its unrealistic standards of beauty, wise mothers help their daughters set and achieve their own healthy standards of beauty and success. For example, one mother recently listed ten things on her blog that she wants her daughter to know about working out and looking beautiful, commenting on the notion that exercise should not be a means to fit into "*that* dress," but rather a way to see the world and feel good about yourself. Beauty comes from within, and it is evident that when someone is confident in who she is as a person, she is more beautiful to those around her. Number eight on this mother's blog is this: "If you feel beautiful, you look beautiful" (Harrington, 2013). To counter the destructive influence of the media, all females need to share this message, and it starts with mothers. 9

Note: The References section is not shown. For an example, see pages 530–531.

Reading for Better Writing

1. *Connections:* Whether you are male or female, how would you characterize the influence of your mother in your life? How does Sara Wiebenga's essay speak to your relationships and experience? Have various media interfered with that relationship?
2. *Comprehension:* In your own words, what is the position that Wiebenga takes? What are the main ideas that lead her to take that position? What is the most memorable evidence that she uses?
3. *Writing Strategies:* Throughout the essay, Wiebenga references Dove's "Campaign for Real Beauty." Examine those references, asking why and how she uses them, as well as how effectively they support her argument about mother-daughter relationships.

Your Project: As you search for a topic for your own argumentative essay, consider this question: Today, how do modern media enhance life? How do they harm life? Is there a particular medium (e.g., film or TV show genre, Web site such as Twitter) that you wish to defend or critique?

Solving the Problem of E-Waste

Student writer Rachel DeBruyn wrote the following essay out of a concern for the environment and for developing-world work conditions. As you read, consider how she presents both the problem of e-waste and her solution for it.

Remedying an E-Waste Economy

Desktops, laptops, monitors, keyboards, iPhones, iPads . . . we buy them, use them, and wear them out. And then we recycle them. But are our electronics being recycled the way we think they are? We assume that a team of trained individuals meticulously disassembles our used electronics—referred to as e-waste—in a large recycling plant full of conveyer belts and safety equipment. Most often, however, this is not the case. Despite international legislation and state pressures, many Western firms ship the electronic waste produced by our homes and businesses to countries such as India, China, and Ghana. It is in the developing world that the globe's most vulnerable population contends with some of the globe's most hazardous waste. 1

Electronic refuse is not like other household waste. It contains toxic metals such as lead, mercury, cadmium, barium, beryllium, chromium (Boudier), phosphor, arsenic plastics, flame retardants, and more (Zhou). In fact, almost every element on the periodic table can be found in most electronics (Townsend). When e-waste is not properly dealt with through recycling, incineration, or safe landfill storage (Townsend), its toxic components can seep into soil, leak into water, and enter into the air (Oteng-Ababio). Once these hazardous elements enter the environment, they severely interfere with ecological functions (Akinseye). In addition, humans who are exposed to these toxins face consequences to their health: lead causes brain and nerve damage (as well as death) through chronic exposure; mercury hinders brain and kidney performance as well as fetus development through bio-accumulation in the food chain; arsenic causes cancer and death through contact with its dust particles; and cadmium causes kidney damage (and eventually death) through water and air contact. Unfortunately, these are only a few of the hazardous materials that make their way into the environment and thus into contact with the people who live in that environment (Akinseye). 2

Since many components of e-waste interfere with environmental functions and harm human health, proper disposal of electronics is crucial for the world's wellbeing. Nevertheless, despite the high ecological costs of improper e-waste disposal, the economic costs of proper recycling are also high. Rather than paying for the labor-intensive process and real estate costs associated with e-waste recycling, Western firms prefer shipping waste out of their countries (Boudier). By shipping out electronic refuse, the developed world pays neither the ecological nor the economic costs of its disposal. However, the only ones who can afford these costs are developed countries. 3

The electronic waste being shipped out of the West travels to countries with fragile, emerging economies. Neither adequate infrastructure nor knowledge exists in the developing world to properly handle or recycle these imports. Training and equipment are expensive, so developing countries send illegally imported e-waste to impoverished communities where unskilled workers, especially children, make a living by breaking down and selling its valuable components ("E-Waste from Antwerp to Ghana"). An observational study done in India found that with no knowledge of the most efficient ways to disassemble electronics, laborers beat, burn, and melt their materials using rudimentary tools and their bare hands. They expose themselves to a wide range of toxins through skin contact and by inhaling the smoke from burning (Zhou). Without an understanding of the toxicity of their materials, uninformed laborers also pollute their environment. Workers dump the used acid from acid baths (a popular metal extraction method), filled with residual toxins, into the sewage system that flows into nearby waterways (Boudier). Anything that is not sellable after the metal is extracted is sent to landfills. Landfills in countries like India are not suitable for hazardous material, so the toxic elements leach into the soil (Zhou). Disadvantaged workers across the world protect neither themselves nor the air, water, and soil of their environment from the hazardous contents of e-waste (Oteng-Ababio). Without proper technology and knowledge, those who handle electronic refuse in developing countries cannot prevent the harm associated with e-waste disassembly. 4

International efforts have been made to halt the movement of electronic waste across state borders and into vulnerable countries. The most notable international regulatory system is the Basel Convention, which bans all cross-border movements of inoperative electronics. But due to inconsistency between individual state regulations, international control such as Basel is hard to maintain (Zhou). Developed countries easily circumvent any bans by claiming that the e-waste being shipped overseas is for second-hand use ("E-Waste Hell"). As a result of a severe lack of regulation in global ports, inspectors can prevent only a small fraction of waste from being shipped. In the Port of Antwerp, for example, four inspectors are responsible for monitoring the eight million containers that pass through the port each year ("E-waste from Antwerp to Ghana"). The quantity of electronic refuse being generated and transported is staggering. Computers—which represent only a portion of all e-waste—become obsolete globally at a growing rate of 100 million per year (Sawyer). Greenpeace estimates that each year roughly 12 million tons of electronics are illegally shipped to Asia alone (Boudier). For developing countries receiving the vast quantities of e-waste, it is impossible to stop the flow. 5

How can we free the developing world from its role as "the industrial world's trash can" (Boudier)? The most obvious solution is to stop all shipments of electronic refuse to the developing world, thereby keeping hazardous waste out of communities 6 that do not have the knowledge to process it. The flow of waste out of the industrial world could be slowed with improved regulations and increased policy maintenance. Yet the real solution to handling e-waste is not to keep it in the West. The issue is not that simple. Stopping the movement of waste to the developing world would mean cutting off a major source of its income. Entire communities have come to depend on earning a living by extracting and selling metals from electronics. A hierarchy of income generation has emerged around e-waste, beginning with shop-owners who find functioning electronics among the waste to sell, down to the children who pick over the shattered remains and trade what precious materials they can find ("E-Waste Hell"). If the West successfully strengthened its regulation against electronic waste exports, countless numbers of people would lose their means of livelihood.

If the West did, however, reduce its shipments of e-waste, it could be argued that those who depend on selling the components of electronics could find new forms of employment. Yet other sources of livelihood are not as profitable, and the surge of people seeking income would throw the entire labor force into stronger competition. Salvaging and selling the rare and valuable metals found in electronic waste is lucrative (Boudier). The industrial world needs rare metals (which are not found in abundance in nature) to continue producing electronics. Those who can salvage and recycle rare metals can sell them for an excellent price. For example, it is estimated that a forty-foot container of television sets can fetch up to 7,000 pounds in the markets of Ghana, and this is only the first level of the e-waste economic hierarchy ("Britain's E-waste Illegally Leaking"). Although laborers could find new forms of income if e-waste shipments ceased, there is a better solution. 7

Instead of ceasing e-waste exports and cutting off a major source of income in the world's poorest countries, the trade of e-waste must be fully legalized. Additionally, developing countries must be empowered to properly handle the waste they receive. The main problem for the developing world is that this otherwise profitable trade is causing health issues in its laborers and their communities. Ignorance of safety and a lack of proper protection prevent laborers from fully benefitting from their work. To encourage a safe, legal framework of e-waste disposal, training and technology must be provided as a part of pre-existing (or new) international aid efforts. If a system of proper hazardous material handling could be established and regulated, many people in the developing world would have jobs as sustainable as the influx of electronics. If health threats are the major hindrance in the e-waste economy that has emerged, training and technology to prevent such harm make it possible for the West's trash to become the developing world's raw materials ("Mountains of E-Waste"). 8

Continuing to send waste to the world's poorest countries is not an excuse to continue producing (or to produce more) waste. E-waste is an inevitable by-product of the Industrial Age, but we must keep in mind that the level of waste should be 9 controlled. Our electronics should have the longest life possible before being properly and sustainably disassembled. Currently, our electronic trash is contributing to sickness and death in the developing world. The West unloads its hazardous waste on other countries to avoid the costs and consequences of dealing with it itself. To remedy the harm we are causing, we must empower workers to earn a living in a manner that does not harm their health.

10 The consequences of our actions, regardless of our ignorance towards them, are wreaking destruction in parts of the globe we may never see. Yet we are equally as responsible for our neighbors abroad as we are for our neighbors next door. In finding a solution to the problems we have caused, we must always seek the solution that best benefits those we have wronged. The developing world is suffering health consequences due to our e-waste, but they have also built an economy dependent on it. Instead of rushing to fix the problem the way we assume is best, we must consider carefully what the developing world needs most: a safe way to ensure financial security. In achieving this, we would not only remedy the suffering we have caused, but we would empower our neighbors to flourish.

Note: The Works Cited page is not shown. For an example, see pages 500–501.

Reading for Better Writing

1. *Connections:* What role do various electronics play in your life? Can you list e-waste that you and your family have created over the years, and can you recall how you disposed of it? How has Rachel DeBruyn's essay raised your awareness of e-waste?
2. *Comprehension:* Starting with the opening paragraph, sketch or outline what DeBruyn's essay presents about the e-waste problem and its solution.
3. *Writing Strategies:*
   a. In the first section of her paper (paragraphs 1-5), DeBruyn identifies and explains the problem: what does she do to encourage readers to both understand and own the problem?
   b. In the second section of her paper (paragraphs 6-10), DeBruyn explores possible solutions, identifies the solution she believes will work, and then supports that solution: what strategies does she use to support her solution?
   c. Look again at DeBruyn's opening and closing paragraphs: what does she do to start and finish her argument?

Your Project: For your own writing, consider other forms of waste: of time; of food by homes, restaurants, and grocery stores; of talent; of water; of landscape; of life. What waste would you care to solve in your writing?

Taking a Considered Position on Prison

In the following editorial, published in the September 29, 2015 edition of *The New York Times*, David Brooks argues that many current prison-sentencing practices are unfair, unnecessary, and destructive. As you read the piece, note how he develops his position on the topic by describing the problem, identifying possible causes, examining potential solutions, and finally, presenting his own solution.

The Prison Problem

Pretty much everybody from Barack Obama to Carly Fiorina seems to agree that far too many Americans are stuck behind bars. And pretty much everybody seems to have the same explanation for how this destructive era of mass incarceration came about. 1

First, the war on drugs got out of control, meaning that many nonviolent people wound up in prison. Second, mandatory-minimum sentencing laws led to a throw-away-the-key culture, with long, cruel and pointlessly destructive prison terms. 2

It's true that mass incarceration is a horrific problem. Back in the 1970s the increase in incarceration did help reduce the crime rate, maybe accounting for a third of the drop. But today's incarceration levels do little to deter crime while they do much to rip up families, increase racial disparities and destroy lives. 3

The popular explanation for how we got here, however, seems to be largely wrong, and most of the policy responses flowing from it may therefore be inappropriate. 4

The drug war is not even close to being the primary driver behind the sharp rise in incarceration. About 90 percent of America's prisoners are held in state institutions. Only 17 percent of these inmates are in for a drug-related offense, or fewer than one in five. 5

Moreover, the share of people imprisoned for drug offenses is dropping sharply, down by 22 percent between 2006 and 2011. Writing in *Slate*, Leon Neyfakh emphasized that if you released every drug offender from state prison today, you'd reduce the population only to 1.2 million from 1.5 million. 6

The war on drugs does not explain the rocketing rates of incarceration, and ending that war, wise or not, will not solve this problem. 7

The mandatory-minimum theory is also problematic. Experts differ on this, but some of the most sophisticated work with the best data sets has been done by John Pfaff of Fordham Law School. When I spoke with Pfaff on Monday I found him to be wonderfully objective, nonideological and data-driven. 8

His research suggests that while it's true that lawmakers passed many measures 9
calling for long prison sentences, if you look at how much time inmates actually served, not much has changed over the past few decades. Roughly half of all prisoners have prison terms in the range of two to three years, and only 10 percent serve more than seven years. The laws look punitive, but the time served hasn't increased, and so harsh laws are not the main driver behind mass incarceration, either.

So what does explain it? Pfaff's theory is that it's the prosecutors. District 10
attorneys and their assistants have gotten a lot more aggressive in bringing felony charges. Twenty years ago they brought felony charges against about one in three arrestees. Now it's something like two in three. That produces many more plea bargains and many more prison terms.

I asked Pfaff why prosecutors are more 11
aggressive. He's heard theories. Maybe they are more political and they want to show toughness to raise their profile to impress voters if they run for future office. Maybe the police are bringing stronger cases. Additionally, prosecutors are usually paid by the county but prisons by the state, so prosecutors tend not to have to worry about the financial costs of what they do.

"In reality, reducing mass incarceration means releasing many once-violent offenders. That may be the right thing to do in individual cases, but it's a knotty problem."

Pfaff says there's little evidence so far to prove any of these theories, since the 12
prosecutorial world is largely a black box. He also points out that we have a radically decentralized array of prosecutors, with some elected and some appointed. Changing their behavior cannot be done with one quick fix.

Some politicians and activists suggest that solving this problem will be easy— 13
just release the pot smokers and the low-level dealers. In reality, reducing mass incarceration means releasing many once-violent offenders. That may be the right thing to do in individual cases, but it's a knotty problem.

Two final points. Everybody is railing against the political establishment and 14
experts and experienced politicians. But social problems are invariably more complex than they look. The obvious explanation for most problems is often wrong. It takes experience and craftsmanship to design policies that grapple with the true complexity of reality.

Finally, recategorizing a problem doesn't solve it. In the 1970s, we let many people 15
out of mental institutions. Over the next decades we put many people into prisons. But the share of people kept out of circulation has been strangely continuous. In the real world, crime, lack of education, mental health issues, family breakdown and economic hopelessness are all intertwined.

Changing prosecutor behavior might be a start. Lifting the spirits of inmates, as 16
described in the outstanding *Atlantic* online video "Angola for Life," can also help. But the fundamental situation won't be altered without a comprehensive surge, unless we flood the zone with economic, familial, psychological and social repair.

Reading for Better Writing

1. *Connections:* What role has prison played in your life—a near one, a distant one? Have you ever been imprisoned, know someone now in prison, visited or ministered to someone in prison? Or is prison for you simply an institution referenced in police dramas and on news sites? Consider how David Brooks's thinking relates to your experiences.
2. *Comprehension:* Brooks presents misconceptions about the prison problem and then tries to clear those up. What are those essential misconceptions? What seems to be true about high rates of incarceration?
3. *Writing Strategies:*
   a. At the start of his essay, Brooks presents the common explanations for high incarceration rates and then argues against these: how does he do so, using what reasoning and evidence?
   b. Part way through the essay, Brooks turns to an expert, John Pfaff: how does Brooks introduce Pfaff and then use Pfaff's expertise to develop a position about imprisonment?
   c. Brooks concludes with "Two final points": are these simply add-ons, or are they central to his argument?

Your Project: As you consider topics for your own argumentative essay, reflect on other dimensions of crime and punishment: victim impacts, torture and human rights, war crimes, the legalization of marijuana, and so on. Are you intrigued by one of these issues?

Taking a Position on a Campus Statue

In 2015, a controversy erupted over a statue of Jefferson Davis on the campus of the University of Texas at Austin. In response to the administration's decision to move the statue to a less prominent location on campus, two professors at the university, Al Martinich (philosophy) and Tom Palaima (classics) wrote the following opinion piece. As you read, ask yourself how they support the position boldly stated already in their title.

Why Removing the Jefferson Davis Statue Is a Big Mistake

The removal of Jefferson Davis's statue from its prominent location on the campus 1
of the University of Texas at Austin this week may appear to end the university's difficult struggle to shake off its historical embrace of racist values and practices. It does not.

Removing the statue is a serious moral and ethical mistake. Remembering 2
our lamentable behavior in the past is an important part of helping to ensure that a similar behavior does not recur, especially if that remembering does what colleges, particularly public colleges, were created to do: produce educated citizens who can make sound ethical decisions.

"Remember the reason the statue of Jefferson Davis was erected in the first place 3
and what it symbolized for over eight decades" is not as pithy as "Remember the Alamo." But it is just as important. Remembering the long and inglorious success of racism in our institution and our society is as important as remembering a glorious defeat in battle.

The controversy about this and other Confederate statues on campus is nothing 4
new. People of conscience who understood what they symbolized created enough of a stir that the university's two immediate past presidents appointed committees to study what to do with the statues. The presidents decided to do nothing.

Recent troubling events in our country gave UT-Austin and its current president, 5
Gregory L. Fenves, a third chance to do the right thing. He came up with a solution that is arguably worse than the original problem.

The statue controversy should not be viewed as a provincial squabble. It is an 6
instance of the general failure of many public institutions of higher education to own up to their own histories. Remembering those histories offers moral and political lessons for our society as a whole.

For more than 80 years, Jefferson Davis and three other Confederate heroes were 7
honored conspicuously on the campus's main mall. Fenves justified removing the Davis statue alone among them because, he said, Davis has no connection with the university. But the presence of his statue is the connection. The more than symbolic

embrace of Davis's values explains why African-Americans were not admitted to UT-Austin, which was founded in 1881, until the 1950s, and why the university vigorously resisted integration during the civil-rights era.

Instead of finally speaking out against Confederate values, the three other statues 8
of Confederate heroes—Gen. Robert E. Lee; Gen. Albert Sidney Johnston, who was Lee's commanding officer before the war in charge of suppressing American Indians; and John H. Reagan, postmaster general of the Confederacy and first chairman of the Railroad Commission of Texas—will remain in place.

Fenves's reasoning contains many statements that have little force. For example, 9
the argument that Davis has no connection with the University of Texas is true insofar as he was never a student, professor, regent, or donor there. Yet that is irrelevant, since the same is true of Lee, who was in Texas for a few years as an Army officer keeping American Indian populations in check.

Lee's more significant association is his toleration of slavery. He spent time away 10
from Texas to settle the estate of his father-in-law, who owned hundreds of slaves. He first hired an overseer who would "make them [the slaves] do their duty." His desire to be "considerate and kind to the negroes" did not stop him from exploiting them as animate tools, whipping, jailing and selling to slave traders those who insisted on their freedom. He did not hesitate to break up families of slaves who had been together for generations.

The only connection that General Johnston and John H. Reagan have to the 11
University of Texas is that their statues, too, stand for the values of the Old South.

Saving the face of Jefferson Davis by removing his statue comes at an additional 12
cost. In addition to the tens of thousands of dollars to be spent on its new housing, the statue of Woodrow Wilson that long stood opposite Davis's was also removed, because leaving it in place would have created an asymmetry that would have invited questions: "Why is nothing here?" "If something used to be here, why is it gone?"

The university's leaders do not want these questions asked. But a university should 13
be a safe place for free and open thought, discussion, and exploration. It should invite these very questions. It also should answer them.

UT-Austin should unequivocally acknowledge its history and assert its 14
commitment to do better. We should have retained all the statues. As it is now, we should put plaques on the remaining statues and on Davis's when it gets to its final, high-dollar place of honor. The plaques should have texts such as this: "The University of Texas at Austin regrets its long association with people who supported the system of segregation that denied equality to African-Americans and other oppressed minorities as if it were an acceptable part of civilized life."

The university's decision in the case of the Confederate statues runs counter to the 15 core values it has long promoted. Carved in large letters prominently across the façade of the south entrance of the UT Tower are the liberating words of John 8:32: "Ye shall know the truth and the truth shall make you free." The motto on the official seal of the university reads *Disciplina Praesidium Civitatis:* "A cultivated mind is the guardian genius of democracy." The recent decision is not faithful to those values, nor is it in keeping with our university motto: "What starts here changes the world."

All human lives matter, including historical lives. For over a century, people of 16 color in Texas were treated as unworthy of the full rights and privileges of American citizens. We should not segregate any part of our past in a moral skeleton closet. Keeping, contextualizing, and explaining the Confederate statues and their history would convert those artworks into tools of historical witness to wrongs done and too long tolerated. And they would serve as conspicuous examples of how to change moral direction within our society.

Reading for Better Writing

1. *Connections:* How would you describe your own connection to and experience of the South? What about your knowledge of racial history in that region? What about statues? Are the statues on your campus (if there are some) particularly meaningful? What do they represent?
2. *Comprehension:* Early in their piece, Martinich and Palaima claim that "[r]emoving the statue is a serious moral and ethical mistake." Outline the reasons that they give after this statement.
3. *Writing Strategies:*
   a. The authors are direct in stating their position right away: what is the effect of doing so?
   b. In paragraphs 4–7, Martinich and Palaima put the statue debate in context: what does context add?
   c. In paragraph 9, the authors criticize the university president's reasoning: what weaknesses do they point out, and how effective is their critique?
   d. In the final three paragraphs, how do Martinich and Palaima drive home their position? Are their strategies an effective way to close their argument?

Your Project: To find a topic for your own argumentative essay, consider other public objects and activities that are similarly controversial: art works or installations, development projects, buildings, parks, pipelines, memorials, and so on. Does one of these debates interest you?

Addressing AIDS in Africa

Kofi A. Annan, a past Secretary General of the United Nations, wrote the following essay in order to urge readers worldwide to help address the suffering caused by AIDS and famine in Africa.

In Africa, AIDS Has a Woman's Face

A combination of famine and AIDS is threatening the backbone of Africa—the women who keep African societies going and whose work makes up the economic foundation of rural communities. For decades, we have known that the best way for Africa to thrive is to ensure that its women have the freedom, power, and knowledge to make decisions affecting their own lives and those of their families and communities. At the United Nations, we have always understood that our work for development depends on building a successful partnership with the African farmer and her husband. 1

Study after study has shown that there is no effective development strategy in which women do not play a central role. When women are fully involved, the benefits can be seen immediately: families are healthier; they are better fed; their income, savings and reinvestment go up. And, what is true of families is true of communities and, eventually, of whole countries. 2

But today, millions of African women are threatened by two simultaneous catastrophes: famine and AIDS. More than 30 million people are now at risk of starvation in southern Africa and the Horn of Africa. All of these predominantly agricultural societies are also battling serious AIDS epidemics. This is no coincidence: AIDS and famine are directly linked. 3

Because of AIDS, farming skills are being lost, agricultural development efforts are declining, rural livelihoods are disintegrating, productive capacity to work the land is dropping, and household earnings are shrinking—all while the cost of caring for the ill is rising exponentially. At the same time, H.I.V. infection and AIDS are spreading dramatically and disproportionately among women. A United Nations report released last month shows that women now make up 50 percent of those infected with H.I.V. worldwide—and in Africa that figure is now 59 percent. Today, AIDS has a woman's face. 4

AIDS has already caused immense suffering by killing almost 2.5 million Africans this year alone. It has left 11 million African children orphaned since the 5 epidemic began. Now it is attacking the capacity of these countries to resist famine by eroding those mechanisms that enable populations to fight back—the coping abilities provided by women.

In famines before the AIDS crisis, women proved more resilient than men. Their survival rate was higher, and their coping skills were stronger. Women were the ones who found alternative foods that could sustain their children in time of drought. Because droughts happened once a decade or so, women who had experienced previous droughts were able to pass on survival techniques to younger women. Women are the ones who nurture social networks that can help spread the burden in times of famine. 6

". . . AIDS is eroding the health of Africa's women, it is eroding the skills, experience and networks that keep their families and communities going."

But today, as AIDS is eroding the health of Africa's women, it is eroding the skills, experience and networks that keep their families and communities going. Even before falling ill, a woman will often have to care for a sick husband, thereby reducing the time she can devote to planting, harvesting and marketing crops. When her husband dies, she is often deprived of credit, distribution networks or land rights. When she dies, the household will risk collapsing completely, leaving children to fend for themselves. The older ones, especially girls, will be taken out of school to work in the home or the farm. These girls, deprived of education and opportunities, will be even less able to protect themselves against AIDS. 7

Because this crisis is different from past famines, we must look beyond relief measures of the past. Merely shipping in food is not enough. Our effort will have to combine food assistance and new approaches to farming with treatment and prevention of H.I.V. and AIDS. It will require creating early-warning and analysis systems that monitor both H.I.V. infection rates and famine indicators. It will require new agricultural techniques, appropriate to a depleted work force. It will require a renewed effort to wipe out H.I.V.-related stigma and silence. 8

It will require innovative, large-scale ways to care for orphans, with specific measures that enable children in AIDS-affected communities to stay in school. Education and prevention are still the most powerful weapons against the spread of H.I.V. Above all, this new international effort must put women at the center of our strategy to fight AIDS. 9

Experience suggests that there is reason to hope. A recent United Nations report shows that H.I.V. infection rates in Uganda continue to decline. In South Africa, infection rates for women under 20 have started to decrease. In Zambia, H.I.V. rates show signs of dropping among women in urban areas and younger women in rural areas. In Ethiopia, infection levels have fallen among young women in the center of Addis Ababa. 10

We can and must build on those successes and replicate them elsewhere. For that, we need leadership, partnership, and imagination from the international community and African governments. If we want to save Africa from two catastrophes, we would do well to focus on saving Africa's women. 11

Reading for Better Writing

1. *Connections:* What is your experience of the suffering that happens in some parts of Africa? Do you or your family contribute to relief efforts or sponsor a child? Are you African by citizenship or heritage? How does Annan's piece impact your thinking about the continent and its challenges?
2. *Comprehension:* Annan's essay is about famine, AIDS, and Africa's women. What does he communicate about the connections between these topics?
3. *Writing Strategies:* Annan's essential call to action is for individuals, organizations, and nations to support Africa's women as a solution to entrenched problems. What reasons lead Annan to this conclusion? What evidence does he use to support this conclusion?

Your Project: As you search for a topic for your own argumentative essay, consider other entrenched and difficult problems, whether near or far: strife in the Middle East, home-grown terrorism, underemployment, the gap between rich and poor. Are you interested in getting at real solutions to such vexing problems?

Taking Action on Academic Freedom

Scott A. Bass is provost and Mary L. Clark is dean of academic affairs at American University. This essay, addressed primarily to other academics, was published in October 2015 in response to trends on campuses involving student criticism of materials taught, including requirements for accommodations such as "trigger warnings." As you read this argument, consider how professors' concerns for academic freedom relate to your concerns as a student.

The Gravest Threat to Colleges Comes from Within

We are experiencing one of the greatest threats to the university as we know it. It 1
is not about enrollments, revenues, regulation, rankings, or leadership. It is about the ability to engage in unfettered debate at American colleges. It is about the assurance of intellectual freedom, about what can and cannot be discussed.

Colleges face criticism from students and others uncomfortable with the points 2
of view expressed in the classroom and by individual faculty members. Provocative art, revealing films, graphic literary portrayals, and controversial speech are understandably uncomfortable for those who find such work contrary to their beliefs. Yet it is this type of work—controversial at times—that has enlightened the world.

Throughout history, colleges have been sites for the creation of knowledge and 3
its dissemination to new generations. The creative spirit of the scholars in higher education, along with the protection afforded by academic freedom, has ensured innovation. Basic research that appears to have little practical application has helped cure disease, led to breakthroughs in science, and fostered understanding of the world. Presentation of counterculture perspectives, art, and literature has contributed to the next generation of leaders' understanding of social and political movements. Disclosures of business and government practices have increased transparency and improved quality of products and services.

Many of the things we take for granted were once controversial, even heretical. 4
Political dissent in the 1950s, which created a climate of fear for professors, serves as a not-too-distant example. Yet a key tenet of college has been the freedom to pursue novel questions. In the mid-12th century, the University of Bologna originated the concept of academic freedom such that scholars could pursue inquiry without risk of persecution. With 900 years of tradition, academic freedom is something to cherish and protect.

Our newest and greatest threat, however, comes not from external pressures, but 5
from inside the university itself. Around the country, students have been rebelling against certain assignments, topics, or speakers. Some students object to material

presented and readings assigned, asserting that assignments are upsetting, triggering anxieties or violating personal beliefs. After all, some argue, they are paying for the experience and should have a say in what they are exposed to and taught.

Colleges have taken pride in building more-diverse communities as a way for students to learn from one another in a safe space. Yet rather than being a place where divergent points of view are discussed and debated, the campus is increasingly becoming a site of tension and acrimony, resulting in a restricted exchange of perspectives. With nuanced public discourse on the wane and increased volume and vitriolic exchanges in the public space writ large, students increasingly come to college with little appreciation for civilized, engaged, and thoughtfully probing discourse. 6

College administrators now face questions: Should students vote on the selection of speakers? Are permitted points of view determined by majorities or even the most vocal minorities? Should the library develop a rating system not unlike that of the motion-picture industry, in which we would label our holdings as to level of controversy? Should certain courses be labelled with disclaimers or warnings? 7

Higher education must be prepared to uphold academic freedom. If we deny one speaker, restrict one book, or limit one faculty member, we have abandoned the very purpose of our institutions. College was never intended to be another entertainment industry or a customized consumer product. The campus is among the few places remaining where ideas—even those that are abhorrent to all or most audiences—may be freely expressed. In the spirit of academic freedom, students have every right to protest uncomfortable points of view. They do not, however, have a right to deny the communication of ideas, expression, inquiry, or creative works in an academic setting. 8

In this climate, the American University's Faculty Senate has unanimously approved a Resolution on Freedom of Academic Expression. It states in part: 9

> American University is committed to protecting and championing the right to freely communicate ideas—without censorship—and to study material as it is written, produced, or stated, even material that some members of our community may find disturbing or that provokes uncomfortable feelings. This freedom is an integral part of the learning experience and an obligation from which we cannot shrink. . . . 10
>
> Faculty may advise students before exposing them to controversial readings and other materials that are part of their curricula. However, the Faculty Senate does not endorse offering "trigger warnings" or otherwise labelling controversial 11

material in such a way that students construe it as an option to "opt out" of engaging with texts or concepts, or otherwise not participating in intellectual inquiries.

Faculty should direct students who experience personal difficulties from exposure to controversial issues to resources available at American University's support-services offices. 12

In issuing this statement, the Faculty Senate affirms that shielding students from controversial material will deter them from becoming critical thinkers and responsible citizens. Helping them learn to process and evaluate such material fulfills one of the most important responsibilities of higher education. 13

Freedom of academic expression is what makes college a remarkable place for personal growth and learning. It also facilitates college's role as an incubator for the creation of knowledge. We hope all college communities will stand in support of this core value. 14

Reading for Better Writing

1. *Connections:* Have you been in a course where "trigger warnings" were given or controversial materials labeled? Have certain topics, events, and discussions on campus made you uncomfortable? From your perspective as a student, what does academic freedom look like and mean?
2. *Comprehension:* The title and first sentence of this essay use the word "threat." What exactly is that threat, where does it come from, and why does it matter, according to Bass and Clark?
3. *Writing Strategies:*
   a. To a large degree, this argument depends on defining academic freedom and defending its importance. What strategies do Bass and Clark use to do so?
   b. In paragraphs 2 and 5-8, the writers characterize the problem on campuses today. How do they describe the problem? Is it a fair presentation of the student perspective?
   c. Toward the end, Bass and Clark include a long quotation. What is the effect of that quotation? Does it work well here?

Your Project: As you search for a topic for your own argumentative essay, consider other forms of freedom and the restrictions sometimes placed on them. Or consider specific controversies on your campus—the place and value of sports, political events such as Israeli Anti-Apartheid demonstrations, fraternity hazing, and so on.

Taking a Position on Fatherhood

David Blankenhorn, the founder and president of the Institute for American Values, is a Harvard graduate and the author of numerous publications, including *The Future of Marriage*. In the essay below, taken from his book, *Fatherless America*, Blankenhorn argues that America is losing its understanding of and appreciation for fatherhood.

Fatherless America

The United States is becoming an increasingly fatherless society. A generation ago, an American child could reasonably expect to grow up with his or her father. Today, an American child can reasonably expect not to. Fatherlessness is now approaching a rough parity with fatherhood as a defining feature of American childhood. 1

This astonishing fact is reflected in many statistics, but here are the two most important. Tonight, about 40 percent of American children will go to sleep in homes in which their fathers do not live. Before they reach the age of eighteen, more than half of our nation's children are likely to spend at least a significant portion of their childhoods living apart from their fathers. Never before in this country have so many children been voluntarily abandoned by their fathers. Never before have so many children grown up without knowing what it means to have a father. 2

Fatherlessness is the most harmful demographic trend of this generation. It is the leading cause of declining child well-being in our society. It is also the engine driving our most urgent social problems, from crime to adolescent pregnancy to child abuse to domestic violence against women. Yet, despite its scale and social consequences, fatherlessness is a problem that is frequently ignored or denied. Especially within our elite discourse, it remains largely a problem with no name. 3

If this trend continues, fatherlessness is likely to change the shape of our society. Consider this prediction. After the year 2000, as people born after 1970 emerge as a large proportion of our working-age adult population, the United States will be a nation divided into two groups, separate and unequal. The two groups will work in the same economy, speak a common language, and remember the same national history. But they will live fundamentally divergent lives. One group will receive basic benefits—psychological, social, economic, educational, and moral—that are denied to the other group. 4

The primary fault line dividing the two groups will not be race, religion, class, education, or gender. It will be patrimony. One group will consist of those adults who grew up with the daily presence and provision of fathers. The other group will consist of those who did not. During the early years of this [twenty-first] century, these two 5 groups already are roughly the same size.

Surely a crisis of this scale merits a response. At a minimum, it requires a serious debate. Why is fatherhood declining? What can be done about it? Can our society find ways to invigorate effective fatherhood as a norm of male behavior? Yet, to date, the public discussion on this topic has been remarkably weak and defeatist. There is a prevailing belief that not much can—or even should—be done to reverse the trend. 6

When the crime rate jumps, politicians promise to do something about it. When the unemployment rate rises, task forces assemble to address the problem. As random shootings increase, public health officials worry about the preponderance of guns. But when it comes to the mass defection of men from family life, not much happens. 7

There is debate, even alarm, about specific social problems. Divorce. Out-of-wedlock childbearing. Children growing up in poverty. Youth violence. Unsafe neighborhoods. Domestic violence. The weakening of parental authority. But in these discussions, we seldom acknowledge the underlying phenomenon that binds together these otherwise disparate issues: the flight of males from their children's lives. In fact, we seem to go out of our way to avoid the connection between our most pressing social problems and the trend of fatherlessness. 8

We avoid this connection because, as a society, we are changing our minds about the role of men in family life. As a cultural idea, our inherited understanding of fatherhood is under siege. Men in general, and fathers in particular, are increasingly viewed as superfluous to family life: either as expendable or as part of the problem. Masculinity itself, understood as anything other than a rejection of what it has traditionally meant to be male, is typically treated with suspicion and even hostility in our cultural discourse. Consequently, our society is now manifestly unable to sustain, or even find reason to believe in, fatherhood as a distinctive domain of male activity. 9

The core question is simple: Does every child need a father? Increasingly, our society's answer is "no" or at least "not necessarily." Few idea shifts in this century are as consequential as this one. At stake is nothing less than what it means to be a man, who our children will be, and what kind of society we will become. 10

This [essay] is a criticism not simply of fatherlessness but of a culture of fatherlessness. For, in addition to losing fathers, we are losing something larger: our idea of fatherhood. Unlike earlier periods of father absence in our history, we now face more than a physical loss affecting some homes. We face a cultural loss affecting every home. For this reason, the most important absence our society must confront is not the absence of fathers but the absence of our belief in fathers. 11

In a larger sense, this [essay] is a cultural criticism because fatherhood, much 12 more than motherhood, is a cultural invention. Its meaning for the individual man is shaped less by biology than by cultural script or story—a societal code that guides, and at times pressures, him into certain ways of acting and of understanding himself as a man.

Like motherhood, fatherhood is made up of both a biological and a social dimension. Yet in societies across the world, mothers are far more successful than fathers at fusing these two dimensions into a coherent parental identity. Is the nursing mother playing a biological or social role? Is she feeding or bonding? We can hardly separate the two, so seamlessly are they woven together. 13

But fatherhood is a different matter. A father makes his sole biological contribution at the moment of conception—nine months before the infant enters the world. Because social paternity is only indirectly linked to biological paternity, the connection between the two cannot be assumed. The phrase "to father a child" usually refers only to the act of insemination, not to the responsibility for raising a child. What fathers contribute to their offspring after conception is largely a matter of cultural devising. 14

Moreover, despite their other virtues, men are not ideally suited to responsible fatherhood. Although they certainly have the capacity for fathering, men are inclined to sexual promiscuity and paternal waywardness. Anthropologically, human fatherhood constitutes what might be termed a necessary problem. It is necessary because, in all societies, child well-being and societal success hinge largely upon a high level of paternal investment: the willingness of adult males to devote energy and resources to the care of their offspring. It is a problem because adult males are frequently—indeed, increasingly—unwilling or unable to make that vital investment. 15

Because fatherhood is universally problematic in human societies, cultures must mobilize to devise and enforce the father role for men, coaxing and guiding them into fatherhood through a set of legal and extralegal pressures that require them to maintain a close alliance with their children's mother and to invest in their children. Because men do not volunteer for fatherhood as much as they are conscripted into it by the surrounding culture, only an authoritative cultural story of fatherhood can fuse biological and social paternity into a coherent male identity. 16

For exactly this reason, Margaret Mead and others have observed that the supreme test of any civilization is whether it can socialize men by teaching them to be fathers—creating a culture in which men acknowledge their paternity and willingly nurture their offspring. Indeed, if we can equate the essence of the antisocial male with violence, we can equate the essence of the socialized male with being a good father. 17

Thus, at the center of our most important cultural imperative, we find the fatherhood script: the story that describes what it ought to mean for a man to have a child.

Just as the fatherhood script advances the social goal of harnessing male behavior to collective needs, it also reflects an individual purpose. That purpose, in a word, is happiness. Anthropologists have long understood that the genius of an effective culture is its capacity to reconcile individual happiness with collective well-being. By situating individual lives within a social narrative, culture endows private behavior with larger meaning. By linking the self to moral purposes larger than the self, an effective culture tells us a story in which individual fulfillment transcends selfishness, and personal satisfaction transcends narcissism. 18

In this respect, our cultural script is not simply a set of imported moralisms, exterior to the individual and designed only to compel self-sacrifice. It is also a pathway—indeed, our only pathway—to what the founders of the American experiment called the pursuit of happiness. 19

The stakes on this issue could hardly be higher. Our society's conspicuous failure to sustain or create compelling norms of fatherhood amounts to a social and personal disaster. Today's story of fatherhood features one-dimensional characters, an unbelievable plot, and an unhappy ending. It reveals in our society both a failure of collective memory and a collapse of moral imagination. It undermines families, neglects children, causes or aggravates our worst social problems, and makes individual adult happiness—both male and female—harder to achieve. 20

Ultimately, this failure reflects nothing less than a culture gone awry: a culture increasingly unable to establish the boundaries, erect the sign-posts, and fashion the stories that can harmonize individual happiness with collective well-being. In short, it reflects a culture that increasingly fails to "enculture" individual men and women, mothers and fathers. 21

In personal terms, the end result of this process, the final residue from what David Gutmann calls the "deculturation" of paternity, is narcissism: a me-first egotism that is hostile not only to any societal goal or larger moral purpose but also to any save the most puerile understanding of personal happiness. In social terms, the primary results of decultured paternity are a decline in children's well-being and a rise in male violence, especially against women. In a larger sense, the most significant result is our society's steady fragmentation into atomized individuals, isolated from one another and estranged from the aspirations and realities of common membership in a family, a community, a nation, bound by mutual commitment and shared memory. 22

[A good father] is a cultural model, or what Max Weber calls an ideal social type—an anthropomorphized composite of cultural ideas about the meaning of paternity. I call him the Good Family Man. As described by one of the fathers [I] interviewed . . . , a good family man "puts his family first." 23

A good society celebrates the ideal of the man who puts his family first. Because our society is now lurching in the opposite direction, I see the Good Family Man as the principal casualty of today's weakening fatherhood script. And because I cannot imagine a good society without him, I offer him as the protagonist in the stronger script that I believe is both necessary and possible. 24

Reading for Better Writing

1. *Connections:* How do you relate to fatherhood? How would you characterize your own relationship with your father? Your step-father? If you are male, are you yourself a father? Is your family traditional or untraditional? Consider how Blankenhorn's discussion of fatherhood resonates with you.
2. *Comprehension:* Choose one of these statements and unpack its meaning:
   a. Paragraph 9: "Masculinity itself, understood as anything other than a rejection of what it has traditionally meant to be male, is typically treated with suspicion and even hostility in our cultural discourse."
   b. Paragraph 17: "Margaret Mead and others have observed that the supreme test of any civilization is whether it can socialize men by teaching them to be fathers—creating a culture in which men acknowledge their paternity and willingly nurture their offspring."
   c. Paragraph 22: "In personal terms, the end result of this process, the final residue from what David Gutmann calls the 'deculturation' of paternity, is narcissism."
3. *Writing Strategies:*
   a. In paragraphs 1–9, Blankenhorn argues that fatherlessness is an important problem: how does he do so?
   b. In paragraphs 10–12, he explains what he is doing in his writing. Why? What is the effect of these statements?
   c. The rest of the essay is, in a sense, an explanation of what he calls the "fatherhood script" and a defense of its importance. What strategies does Blankenhorn use here? How do these drive the essay toward its conclusion?

Your Project: Consider other scripts people follow, other roles they play: business executive, politician, caregiver, teacher, advocate, and so on. Could you argue for the importance of one of these roles, for the repair of its current damaged state?

Writing Guidelines

Start your project by reviewing what you learned in chapter 17 about effective strategies for constructing arguments: following Toulmin and Rogerian approaches; engaging opposition; and appealing to *ethos, pathos,* and *logos*. Then follow the steps outlined below.

Planning

1. **Select a debatable topic.** Begin by reviewing the project options listed at the end of each sample essay. For more topic ideas, list issues about which you feel passionately, that impact your life, and/or that divide people. Think about problems that people face in different areas of life: at home or work, in society, in nature. Consider community problems, international issues, disaster-relief efforts, educational outreach programs, environmental clean-up efforts, social movements, or political campaigns. Then choose a topic that is debatable, significant, current, and manageable. Finally, test it: is the issue real and serious?

2. **Identify and analyze your audience.** You could have a range of readers, from those opposed to your argument to those indifferent to it. Consider these questions:
   - What do readers know about the issue? What are their questions and concerns?
   - Why might they accept change or resist it? What position, action, or solution would they prefer?
   - What reasoning and evidence would convince them?
   - Which of their needs and values are clearly related to the issue?

3. **Narrow your focus and determine your purpose.** Should you focus on one aspect of the issue or all of it? Will your goal be to take a stance on the issue, persuade your readers to change, or to solve a problem? Let that goal guide your research and writing.

4. **Get inside the issue.** Start by taking stock of what you already know and believe about the topic. Where do your knowledge and attitudes come from? How does your thinking need to be tested, to grow? Then study the issue fully and carefully:
   - Research the issue or problem—its various causes and effects, its larger context and history, forecasts of where it's going, and so on. Immerse yourself in the topic.
   - Investigate all possible angles on the issue: different positions, possible actions, solutions. Think creatively about what's best and what's possible.
   - Set up "opposing viewpoints" columns in which you list arguments of those who advocate for different positions, solutions, and so on. Consider how attractive each might be to your readers.

5. **Develop a working thesis—your position, the action, or the solution.** By now, you may have sharpened or even radically changed your initial thinking on the topic.

Before you organize and draft your essay, reflect on those changes. Depending on your approach, try one of these patterns:

- **Position Statement:** I believe this to be true about [topic]: [main claim].
- **Action Statement:** On the issue of [focused topic], I believe [main claim]. Therefore, we must change by [recommended action].
- **Solution to Problem:** Given that the problem is [its essential nature or cause], the best solution is to [specific fix].

6. **Organize your argument and support.** Review the patterns on pages 313–314, but consider as well a structure or flow that will be most convincing to your readers. Where might you begin? What background might they need? What sequence of claims would build an effective chain of reasoning? Where should you address alternatives, options, and opposition? How can you finish strong? Consider these options:
   - **Traditional Pattern:** Introduce the issue, state your main claim, support it, address and refute opposition, and restate your main claim.
   - **Blatant Confession:** Place your main claim in the very first sentence, and then run with it.
   - **Delayed Gratification:** Describe various positions on the topic, compare and contrast them, and then make your main claim and defend it.
   - **Changed Mind:** If research changed your mind, describe where you started and then explain how and why this change happened.
   - **Winning Over:** If readers will oppose your main claim, address their concerns by anticipating each objection and answering each question.

Drafting

7. **Write your first draft.** Rough out your argument, working on the parts that follow, though not necessarily in this order:
   - **Opening:** Seize the reader's attention, possibly with a bold title—or raise concern for the issue with a dramatic story, a pointed example, a vivid picture, a thought-provoking question, or a personal confession. Supply background information that readers need to understand the issue or problem.
   - **Development:** Deepen, clarify, and support your main claim, using solid logic and reliable support. Address opposing views fairly as part of a clear, well-reasoned argument that helps readers understand and accept your position. Throughout, be mindful of readers' needs and values, as well as your own credibility and the credibility of your sources.

- **Closing:** End on a lively, thoughtful note that stresses your commitment to your position, emphasizes the importance of the action called for, or encourages adoption of your solution.

Revising

8. Improve the ideas, organization, and voice. Ask a classmate or someone from the college's writing center to read your position paper for the following:

___ **Ideas:** Is the main claim clearly stated and effectively qualified and refined? Do the reasoning and support help the reader understand and appreciate the main claim?

___ **Organization:** Does the opening effectively raise the issue? Does the middle offer a carefully sequenced development and defense of the claim? Does the closing successfully drive home the position, call to action, or solution?

___ **Voice:** Is the voice thoughtful, measured, committed, and convincing?

Editing

9. Edit and proofread the essay by addressing these issues:

___ **Words:** Language is precise, concrete, and lively—no jargon, clichés, or insults.

___ **Sentences:** Constructions vary in length and flow smoothly. Syntax clearly and carefully conveys reasoning about the evidence.

___ **Correctness:** The copy includes no errors in spelling, usage, punctuation, grammar, or mechanics.

___ **Design:** The page design is correctly formatted and attractive, a compelling part of the argument; research is accurately documented according to the required system (e.g., MLA, APA).

Publishing

10. Publish your essay. Submit your argumentative essay according to your instructor's requirements. In addition, seek a forum for stating your position, calling people to act, or presenting a solution—with peers in a discussion group or debate, with relatives, online in a blog or forum.

MindTap® Request help and feedback from a tutor. If required, participate in peer review, submit your paper for a grade, and view instructor comments online.

Critical Thinking and Writing: Applications

Once you have finished your argumentative essay, there may be more to think about. Consider how to apply what you have learned in the situations that follow.

1. **Wise Words:** One of Aesop's fables goes like this: "Passion is often more effectual than force." Is argumentative writing a form of passion? How is such passion different from force, perhaps even opposed to force?
2. **Photo Op:** Recall the photograph on this chapter's opening page. Find another photograph or a short video that similarly portrays the nature of argumentation in an interesting and insightful way. As an alternative, find a photograph or other graphic that could be incorporated into your own argumentative essay.
3. **Living Today:** Contemporary America is filled with issues that seem to have opposing poles but no middle ground: gun control, immigration, abortion, and the war on terror, to name just a few. Choose an issue like this, and then research news commentaries, editorials, blogs, and comment threads that characterize the opposing positions. Given what you have learned about argumentation, can you explain what is going on in these entrenched oppositions?
4. **Public Texts:** Written arguments can be found throughout the digital landscape: at sites sponsored by news organizations, political groups, businesses, and not-for-profits. Choose an organization that interests you, relates to your life, or perhaps even aggravates you. Then go to its Web site, and search for a page containing an argument: a position, a call to action, or a solution to a problem. Assess how well the argument works.
5. **Major Work:** Consider your major and your future career. What is the focus of this field of study and this profession? Where and how will argument be part of what you do? Why will doing it well matter? Research these questions to get the answers you need.

Learning-Objectives Checklist ✓

Have you achieved this chapter's learning objectives? Check your progress with the following items, revisiting topics in the chapter as needed. I have . . .

___ critically examined argumentative essays for well-crafted claims, reliable evidence, and valid warrants (313–322).

___ identified logical fallacies in others' writing and corrected them in my own writing, especially oversimplification, either/or thinking, appeals to pity, personal attacks, false cause, and slanted language (323–326).

___ developed measured, reasonable claims, whether position statements, calls to action, or solutions to problems (333–335).

___ researched and written a convincing argumentative essay that communicates in a measured but confident voice and appeals to readers' needs and values (363–365).

MindTap® Practice skills that you have learned in this chapter and receive automatic feedback. Reflect on your writing process.

III. Research and Writing

Furtseff / Shutterstock.com

Chapter 19

Getting Started: From Planning Research to Evaluating Sources

At first glance, research looks like a dry-as-dust business carried out by obsessed scholars in dim libraries and mad scientists in cluttered laboratories. Research couldn't be further from the reality of your life.

But is it? Consider car tires. Before these were mounted, scientists researched which materials would resist wear and which adhesives would keep treads on steel belts. Sloppy research could cause blowouts; good research builds safe tires.

For you, the rewards of research projects can be great—new insights into a subject that really interests you, a deepened understanding of your major or profession, reliable knowledge to share with others, and sharpened thinking skills. This chapter will help you get started on such a project.

Visually Speaking Figure 19.1 shows one form of research in action. Study the details. What does this image suggest about research? What other images would capture other dimensions of research today?

MindTap®

Understand the goals of the chapter and complete a warm-up activity online.

Learning Objectives

By working through this chapter, you will be able to

- interpret the rhetorical situation for research.
- identify the phases of the research process.
- focus a research assignment into a manageable project.
- identify primary, secondary, and tertiary sources.
- generate a research plan.
- choose different information resources and sites.
- perform keyword searches.
- examine and evaluate print and digital resources.
- produce a working bibliography.
- choose a note-taking system.
- summarize, paraphrase, and quote source material.

kurhan / Shutterstock.com

fig. 19.1

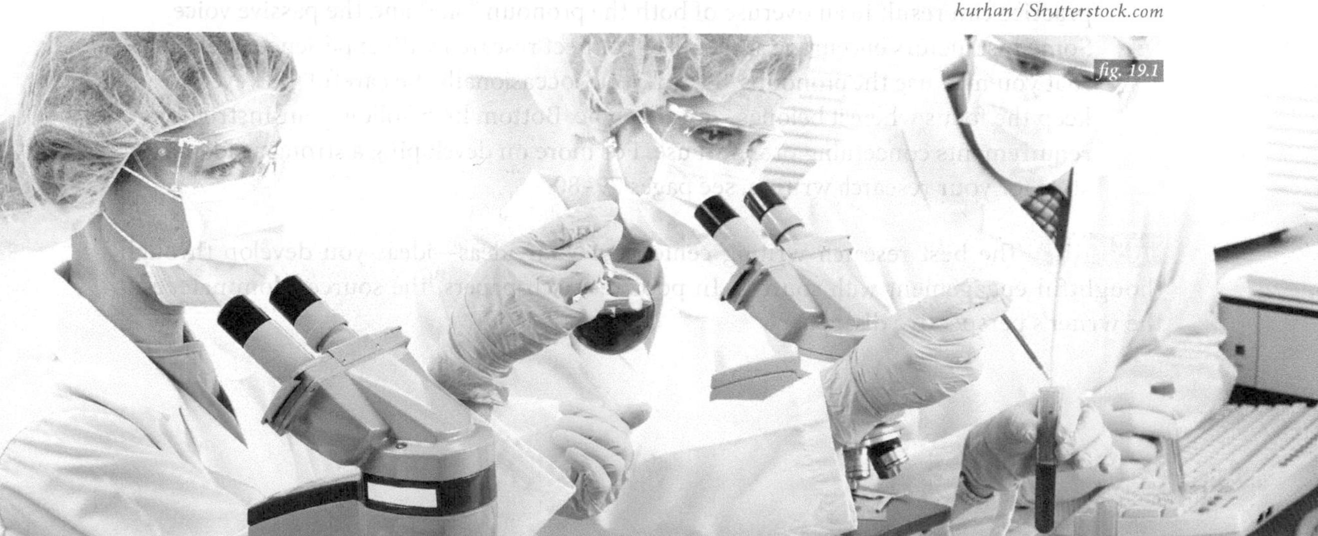

Papers with Documented Research: Quick Guide

When you work on a research project, you ask important questions, look systematically for answers, and share your conclusions with readers. The rhetorical situation for such a project centers on the writer's purpose of inquiring into a topic so as to advance understanding for him- or herself and the reader. In other words, it's all about curiosity, discovery, and dialogue.

- **Starting Point:** The assignment usually relates to a course concept, so consider what your instructor wants you to learn and how your project will be evaluated. Then take ownership of the project by looking for an angle that makes the writing relevant for you.
- **Purpose:** The project requires you to conduct research and share results. Your main goal is to discover the complex truth about a topic and clarify that discovery for others.
- **Form:** The traditional research paper is a fairly long essay (5 to 15 pages) complete with thesis, supporting paragraphs, integrated sources, and careful documentation. However, you may be asked to shape your research into a field report, a Web site, or a multimedia presentation.
- **Audience:** Traditionally, research writing addresses "the academic community," a group made up mainly of instructors and students. However, your actual audience may be more specific: addicted smokers, all Floridians, fellow immigrants, and so on.
- **Voice:** The tone is usually formal or semiformal, but check your instructor's expectations. In any research writing, maintain a thoughtful, confidently measured tone. After all, your research has made you somewhat of an authority on the topic.
- **Point of View:** Generally, research writers avoid the pronouns "I" and "you" in an effort to remain properly objective and academic sounding. Unfortunately, this practice can result in an overuse of both the pronoun "one" and the passive voice. Some instructors encourage students to connect research with experience, meaning that you may use the pronouns "I" and "you" occasionally. Be careful, however, to keep the focus where it belongs—on the topic. Bottom line: Follow your instructor's requirements concerning pronoun use. For more on developing a strong academic style for your research writing, see pages 79–80.

INSIGHT The best research writing centers on your ideas—ideas you develop through thoughtful engagement with sources. In poor research papers, the sources dominate, and the writer's perspective disappears.

The Research Process: A Flowchart

The research process involves getting started, planning, conducting the research, and organizing the results. This process is flexible enough to be adapted to diverse research projects. In fact, real research is typically dynamic: You might think during the planning phase that you've nailed down your topic, only to discover a surprising topical detour while conducting research. Generally, however, the research process maps out as shown in Figure 19.2. When you get your assignment—whether to write a five-page paper on pasteurization or to develop a Web site on Middle Eastern political conflicts—review the process and tailor it to the task.

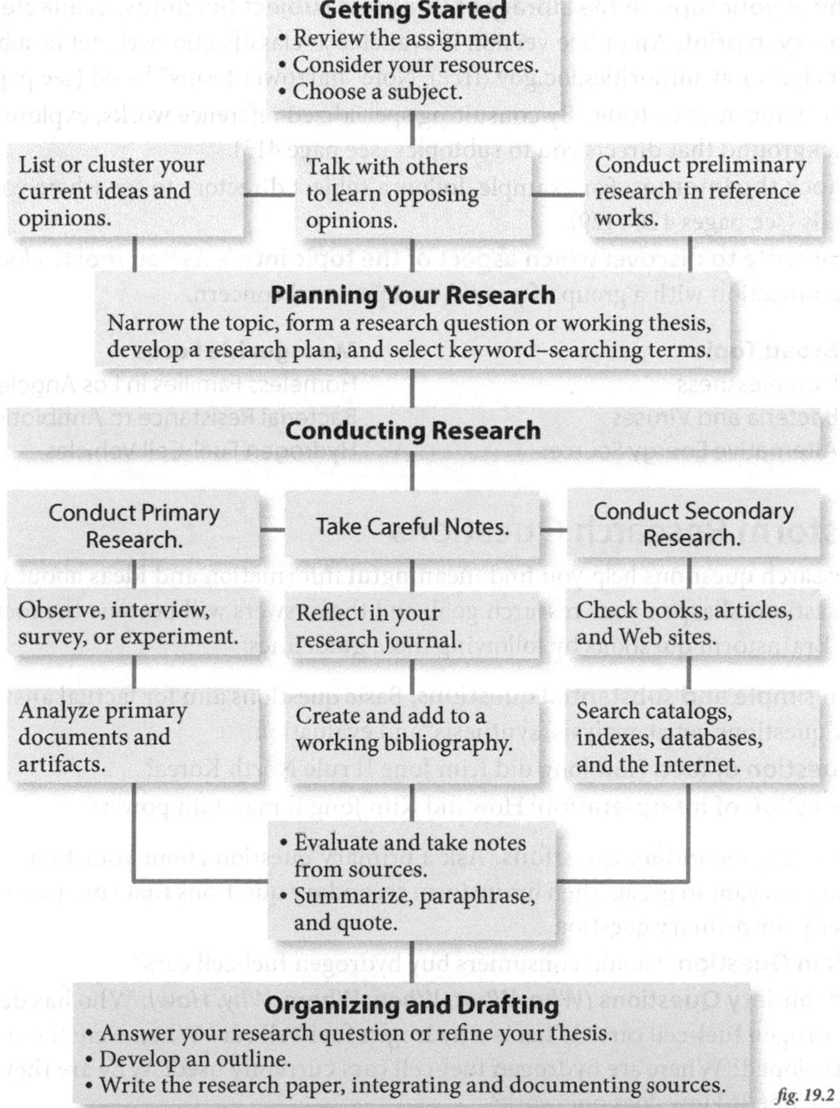

fig. 19.2

Getting Focused

Early in your project, get focused by narrowing your topic, brainstorming research questions, and developing a working thesis. For help understanding assignments and selecting topics, as well as other prewriting strategies, see pages 32–35.

Establish a Narrow, Manageable Topic

To do good research, you need an engaging, manageable topic. Once you have a broad topic, narrow your focus to a specific feature or angle that allows for in-depth research. Try these strategies:

- **Check your topic in the Library of Congress subject headings, available in your library in print.** An online version is available at classificationweb.net (a subscription service) or at authorities.loc.gov (free). Note "narrower terms" listed (see page 382).
- **Read about your topic.** By consulting specialized reference works, explore background that directs you to subtopics (see page 413).
- **Check the Internet.** For example, follow a subject directory to see where your topic leads (see pages 420–429).
- **Freewrite to discover which aspect of the topic interests you most:** a local angle, a connection with a group of people, or a personal concern.

Broad Topic	Manageable Focus
Homelessness	Homeless Families in Los Angeles
Bacteria and Viruses	Bacterial Resistance to Antibiotics
Alternative Energy Sources	Hydrogen Fuel-Cell Vehicles

Brainstorm Research Questions

Good research questions help you find meaningful information and ideas about your topic. These questions sharpen your research goal, and the answers will become the focus of your writing. Brainstorm questions by following these guidelines:

List both simple and substantial questions. Basic questions aim for factual answers. More complex questions get at analysis, synthesis, and evaluation.

- **Question of fact:** How long did Kim Jong Il rule North Korea?
- **Question of interpretation:** How did Kim Jong Il maintain power?

List main and secondary questions. Ask a primary question about your topic—the main issue that you want to get at. Then brainstorm secondary questions that you need to research to answer your primary question.

- **Main Question:** Should consumers buy hydrogen fuel-cell cars?
- **Secondary Questions *(Who, What, When, Where, Why, How)*:** Who has developed hydrogen fuel-cell cars? What is a hydrogen fuel-cell car? When were these cars developed? Where are hydrogen fuel-cell cars currently used? Why are they being developed? How does one work?

Testing Your Main Research Question

____ Is the question so broad that I can't answer it in the project's time and page limits?

____ Is the question so narrow that I won't be able to find sources?

____ Is the question so simple that it will be too easy to answer?

____ Will the question lead to significant sources and an intellectual challenge?

____ Am I committed to answering this question? Does it interest me?

____ Will the question and answers interest my readers?

Develop a Working Thesis

A working thesis offers a preliminary answer to your main research question. As your initial perspective on the topic, a good working thesis keeps you focused during research, helping you decide whether to carefully read a particular book or just skim it, fully explore a Web site or quickly browse through it. Make your working thesis a statement that demands "Prove it!" Don't settle for a simple statement of fact about your topic; instead, choose a working thesis that seems debatable or that requires some explanation. Try this formula:

Formula:

Working Thesis = limited topic + tentative claim, statement, or hypothesis

Examples:

Digital communication technologies are rewiring our brains.

Downtown revitalization will have distinct economic, environmental, and social benefits.

Internet dating is weakening long-term relationships.

Working Thesis Checklist

____ Does my working thesis focus on a single, limited topic?

____ Is my working thesis stated in a clear, direct sentence?

____ Does my working thesis convey my initial perspective about the topic?

____ Do I have access to enough good information to support this working thesis?

____ Does my working thesis direct me to write a paper that meets all assignment requirements?

INSIGHT Your working thesis is written in sand, not stone. It may change as you research the topic because sources may push you in new directions. In fact, such change shows that you are engaging your sources and growing in your thinking.

Understanding Primary, Secondary, and Tertiary Sources

Information sources for your project can be primary, secondary, or tertiary, depending on their nearness to your topic. With your college assignments, you will likely be expected to rely upon primary and secondary sources, not tertiary sources. As part of project planning, then, you need to understand the distinction between primary, secondary, and tertiary sources.

Primary Sources

A primary source is an original source, one that gives firsthand information on a topic: the source is close to the issue or question. This source (such as a log, a person, a document, or an event) informs you directly about the topic, not through another person's explanation or interpretation. Common primary sources are observations, interviews, surveys, experiments, documents, and artifacts. Frequently, you generate the primary source yourself; sometimes, that primary information is available in published form.

> ***Example:*** For a project on Jane Austen's *Pride and Prejudice* in fiction and film, these sources would be primary: the text of the novel itself, the 2005 film adaptation of the novel, Jane Austen's letters, and an interview with a screen writer who adapts novels into films.
>
> **Strengths of Primary Research:** Primary sources produce information precisely tailored to your research needs, giving you direct, hands-on access to your topic. If, for example, you were researching the impact of tornados on communities, interviews with survivors would provide information directly tailored to your project.
>
> **Downsides of Primary Research:** Primary research can take a lot of time and many resources, as well as specialized skills (e.g., designing surveys and analyzing statistics).

Secondary Sources

Secondary sources present information one step removed from the origin: information has been collected, compiled, summarized, analyzed, synthesized, interpreted, and evaluated by someone studying primary sources and other secondary sources. Scholarly studies, journal articles, and documentaries are typical examples of such resources. Typically, you track down secondary resources in your library, through library databases, and on the free Web (see pages 409–429).

> ***Example:*** For a project on Jane Austen's *Pride and Prejudice* in fiction and film, these sources would be secondary: books and articles by scholars on Austen and on film, literary biographies about Austen's life, and film reviews.

Strengths of Secondary Research: Good secondary sources—especially scholarly ones that have gone through a peer review process—offer quality information in the form of expert perspectives on and analysis of your topic. As such, secondary sources can save you plenty of research labor while providing you with extensive data. In addition, secondary sources can help you see your topic from multiple angles through multiple perspectives; they can tell you the story of research done on your topic.

Downside of Secondary Research: Because secondary research isn't written solely with you and your project in mind, you may need to do some digging to find relevant data. Moreover, the information that you do find may be filtered through the researcher's bias. In fact, the original research related through the secondary source may be faulty, a point suggesting that the quality of secondary sources can vary greatly (especially on the free Web). Finally, because knowledge about your topic can grow or radically change over time, secondary sources can become dated.

Tertiary Sources

Some resources are tertiary—essentially reports of reports of research. That is, writers of tertiary sources are not reporting on the primary research they themselves have done but are compiling information based on their reading of secondary sources. Examples of tertiary sources would include some articles in popular magazines and entries in Wikipedia (see page 424).

Example: For a project on Jane Austen's *Pride and Prejudice* in fiction and film, these sources would be tertiary: an online discussion group exchanging thoughts on a recent Austen biography, and a Wikipedia entry on Austen.

Upside of Tertiary Research: Tertiary sources are typically easy to find, easy to access, and easy to read. Note, for example, that a free-Web search of a specific topic frequently lists a Wikipedia entry in the first ten items. Used cautiously, such tertiary sources can serve as one starting point for your research—to find basic facts that you'll likely have to verify elsewhere, some ideas for narrowing your topic, or some leads and links for further research.

Downside of Tertiary Research: The main weakness of tertiary sources is their distance from the original research and information. Because the information and ideas have been passed along in this way, the possibility of error, distortion, gaps, and over-simplification of complex issues is greater than with primary and secondary sources. Generally, tertiary sources lack the reliability and depth necessary for college-level research projects.

fyi Whether a source is primary, secondary, or tertiary often depends on what your focused topic is. For example, if you were studying why power brown-outs happen during heat waves, a newspaper editorial on the topic would be secondary. But if you were focusing on public attitudes towards and responses to brown-outs, the editorial might prove primary. In other words, a given source is not always primary or always secondary: proximity depends on the research context.

Developing a Research Plan

It pays to plan your research, including decisions about primary, secondary, and tertiary sources. In fact, minutes spent planning research can save hours doing research. With your limited topic, main research question, and working thesis in front of you, plan your project more fully using the research tips on the next two pages.

Choose Research Methods

Consider these questions: What do you already know about the topic? What do you need to know? Which resources will help you answer your research question? Which resources does the assignment require? Based on your answers, map out a research plan that draws resources from fitting categories.

Background research: To find information about your topic's context, central concepts, and key terms, take these steps:

- Use the Library of Congress subject headings to find keywords for searching the library catalog, periodical databases, and the Internet (see page 382).
- Conduct a preliminary search of the library catalog, journal databases, and the Internet to confirm that good resources on your topic exist.
- Use specialized reference works to find background information, definitions, facts, and statistics (see page 413).

Field or primary research: If appropriate for your project, conduct field research:

- Use interviews (pages 406–407) or surveys (pages 402–403) to get key information from experts or others.
- Conduct observations or experiments (page 408) to obtain hard data.
- Analyze key documents or artifacts (pages 404–405).

Library research: Select important library resources:

- Use scholarly books to get in-depth, reliable material (pages 409–413).
- Use periodical articles (print or electronic) to get current, reliable information (pages 380–381). Select from news sources, popular magazines, scholarly journals, and trade journals.
- Consider other library resources, such as a documentary, recorded interview, pamphlet, marketing study, or government publication.

Free-Web research: Plan effective free-Web searches using the following:

- Search engines and subject guides: Choose tools that will lead you to quality resources (pages 420–423).
- Expert guidance: Select reputable Web sites that librarians or other experts recommend (page 426).
- Evaluation: Test all Web resources for reliability (pages 426–429).
- Limitations: How many Web resources are you allowed to use, if any?

Get Organized to Do Research

An organized approach to doing your research will save you time, help you work efficiently, and prevent frustration. Get organized by addressing these issues:

Establishing Priorities for Resources, Time, and Effort

- How much research material do you need?
- What range of resources will give you quality, reliable information?
- Which types of research does the assignment specify? Are you limited, for example, in the number of Internet sources you can use?
- What are the project's priorities: What must you do? Which tasks are secondary in nature?
- What weight does the project carry in the course? How should you match your time and effort with that weight?

INSIGHT Gather more information than you could ever use in your paper. That richness gives you choices and allows you to sift for crucial information.

Selecting Research Methods and Systems

- **Given the resources and technologies available, select methods that help you do research efficiently:** signing out hard-copy library holdings or using interlibrary loan; photocopying book sections and journal articles; printing, saving, downloading, bookmarking, or emailing digital materials.
- **Develop a note-taking system.** Choose from the note-card, double-entry notebook, copy-and-annotate, and research-log methods (pages 390–393). In addition, set up a working bibliography (pages 388–389).
- **Choose and review a documentation system.** It's likely that your instructor will designate a system such as MLA (pages 465–502) or APA (pages 503–532). If he or she doesn't do so, then use a method that suits the subject matter and discipline. Review the system's basic rules and strategies.

Establishing a Schedule

The time frame for completing a research project obviously varies from one assignment to the next. What you have to work with is the time frame between getting the assignment and turning in the project at the deadline, whether that time frame is two weeks or two months, along with any intermediate deadlines set by your instructor for specific phases of the project (e.g., topic selection, project proposal, working bibliography, first draft). Generally, however, you should spend about half your time on research and half on writing. To stay on track, sketch out a preliminary schedule with tentative deadlines for completing each phase of your work.

Writing a Research Proposal

For some research projects, you may need to submit a proposal early in the process. The proposal seeks to explain what you plan to research, why, and how. Such a proposal has several aims: (1) to show that the research is valid (makes good scholarly sense), (2) to argue that the research is valuable (will lead to significant knowledge), (3) to communicate your enthusiasm for the project, and (4) to demonstrate that your plan is workable within the constraints of the assignment—all in order to gain your instructor's feedback and approval. Note the parts modeled in the sample proposal.

Understand the Parts of a Research Proposal

1. **Introduction:** In a brief paragraph, state your research idea, explaining why the topic is important and worth researching. Provide any background information that the instructor may need.
2. **Description:** Discuss your proposed research topic by identifying the central issue or concern about the topic, indicating the main question that you want to answer through research, listing secondary questions that relate to the main question, stating a working thesis or hypothesis in response to the main question, and explaining the research outcomes that you expect from the study.
3. **Plan (methods and procedures):** Explain how you plan to answer your questions, how you plan to research your topic. Include an explanation of your primary research (the "firsthand" investigation), a description of research tools you plan to use (e.g., catalogs, reference works, lab equipment, survey software), and a working bibliography indicating your initial survey of resources.
4. **Schedule:** List deadlines that are part of the assignment and deadlines that you've set for yourself.
5. **Approval Request:** Ask for feedback and approval from your instructor.

Sample Research Proposal

The research proposal below offers a student's plan for analyzing Jane Austen's *Pride and Prejudice,* both the novel and the film adaptation.

Film Studies 201 Proposal:
Jane Austen's *Pride and Prejudice* as Fiction and Film

Gwendolyn Mackenzie

Nearly 200 years after her death, Jane Austen's novels still captivate readers, filmmakers, and filmgoers—including me. For my research paper, I will explore one aspect of this phenomenon within *Pride and Prejudice* and the 2005 film adaptation directed by Joe Wright.

Description: Specifically, I want to see how the novel and film explore gender prejudice. My main research question is, "What sense do these texts make of prejudice as it relates to relationships between men and women?" My working thesis is that the 2005 film portrayal of gender inequality in *Pride and Prejudice* highlights and intensifies the issue of gender inequality introduced in the novel.

This study of gender prejudice will allow me (1) to appreciate the treatment of this theme in fiction and in film, (2) to understand film adaptations more fully, and (3) to explain in a small way the Jane Austen phenomenon. As part of the project, I will write a 6-8 page paper.

Plan: My primary research will involve rereading the novel and reviewing the 2005 film adaptation. In terms of secondary research, I have done an initial search of our library's catalog and of EBSCOhost for books and articles. This is my working bibliography:

Primary Sources

Austen, Jane. *Pride and Prejudice: An Authoritative Text, Background and Sources, Criticism.* Edited by Donald J. Gray. Norton, 2001.

Wright, Joe, director. *Pride and Prejudice.* Universal Pictures, 2005.

Secondary Sources

Cartmell, Deborah, and Imelda Whelehan. *Adaptations: From Text to Screen, Screen to Text.* Routledge, 2004.

Crusie, Jennifer. *Flirting with* Pride and Prejudice*: Fresh Perspectives on the Original Chick-Lit Masterpiece.* BenBella, 2005.

Grandi, Roberta. "The Passion Translated: Literary and Cinematic Rhetoric in *Pride and Prejudice* (2005)." *Literature Film Quarterly*, vol. 36, no. 1, 2008, pp. 45-51.

McFarlane, Brian. "Something Old, Something New: 'Pride and Prejudice' on Screen." *Screen Education*, 2005, pp. 6-14.

Stovel, Nora Foster. "From Page to Screen: Dancing to the Altar in Recent Film Adaptations of Jane Austen's Novels." *Persuasions: The Jane Austen Journal*, 2006, pp. 185-198.

Sutherland, Kathryn. *Jane Austen's Textual Lives: From Aeschylus to Bollywood.* Oxford UP, 2007.

Todd, Janet M. *The Cambridge Introduction to Jane Austen*, 2nd ed. Cambridge UP, 2015.

Schedule: Here is my schedule for completing this project:

1. Finish rereading the novel and reviewing the film: November 14.
2. Complete secondary research: November 20.
3. Develop outline for paper: November 23.
4. Finish first draft of paper: November 30.
5. Revise, edit, and proofread paper: December 4.
6. Submit paper: December 6.

Approval Request: Dr. Rajan, I would appreciate your feedback on my proposed project, as well as your approval of my plan.

Exploring Information Resources and Sites

To conduct thorough, creative, but efficient research, you need a sense of which types of resources are available for your project and where to find them. Check Figures 19.3 and 19.4.

Consider Different Information Resources

Examine the range of resources available: Which will give you the best information for your project? While one project (for example, a sociological report on airport behaviors) might require personal, direct sources, another project (for example, the effects of the September 11, 2001, terrorist attacks on the air transportation industry) might depend on government reports, business publications, and journal articles. Generally, a well-rounded research paper relies on a range of quality resources; in particular, it avoids relying on insubstantial Web information.

fig. 19.3

Type of Resource	Examples
Personal, direct resources	Memories, diaries, journals, logs, experiments, tests, observations, interviews, surveys
Reference works (print and electronic)	Dictionaries, thesauruses, encyclopedias, almanacs, yearbooks, atlases, directories, guides, handbooks, indexes, abstracts, catalogs, bibliographies
Books (print and electronic)	Nonfiction, how-to, biographies, fiction, trade books, scholarly and scientific studies
Periodicals and news sources	Print newspapers, magazines, and journals; broadcast news and news magazines; online magazines, news sources, and discussion groups
Audiovisual, digital, and multimedia resources	Graphics (tables, graphs, charts, maps, drawings, photos), audiotapes, CDs, videos, DVDs, Web pages, online databases
Government publications	Guides, programs, forms, legislation, regulations, reports, records, statistics
Business and nonprofit publications	Correspondence, reports, newsletters, pamphlets, brochures, ads, catalogs, instructions, handbooks, manuals, policies and procedures, seminar and training materials

Consider Different Information Sites

Where do you go to find the resources that you need? Consider the information "sites" listed in Figure 19.4, remembering that many resources may be available in different forms in different locations. For example, a journal article may be available in library holdings or in an electronic database.

fig. 19.4

Information Location	Specific "Sites"
People	Experts (knowledge area, skill, occupation) Population segments or individuals (with representative or unusual experiences)
Libraries	General: public, college, online Specialized: legal, medical, government, business
Computer resources	Computers: software, disks Networks: Internet and other online services (email, limited-access databases, discussion, groups, Web sites, blogs, social networks, YouTube, image banks, wikis); intranets
Mass media	Radio (AM and FM) Television (network, public, cable, satellite, Internet) Print (newspapers, magazines, journals)
Testing, training, meeting, and observation sites	Plants, facilities, field sites, laboratories Research centers, universities, think tanks Conventions, conferences, seminars Museums, galleries, historical sites
Municipal, state, and federal government offices	Elected officials, representatives Offices and agencies, Government Printing Office Web sites (GPO, www.gpoaccess.gov)
Business and nonprofit publications	Computer databases, company files Desktop reference materials Bulletin boards (physical and electronic) Company and department Web sites Departments and offices Associations, professional organizations Consulting, training, and business information services

Conducting Effective Keyword Searches

Keyword searching can help you find information in electronic library catalogs, online databases that index periodical articles (for example, EBSCOhost), print indexes to periodical publications (for example, *Business Periodicals Index*), Internet resources, print books, and e-books. Learn to choose keywords and use specific search strategies.

Choose Keywords Carefully

Keywords give you "compass points" for navigating through a sea of information. That's why choosing the best keywords is crucial. Consider these tips:

1. **Brainstorm a list of possible keywords**—topics, titles, and names—based on your current knowledge and/or background reading.
2. **Consult the Library of Congress subject headings.** These headings, available in print or online at classificationweb.net (subscription) or at authorities.loc.gov (free), contain the keywords librarians use when classifying materials. For example, if you looked up *immigrants*, you would find the entry in Figure 19.5, indicating keywords to use and tips to follow (including that the topic may subdivide geographically), along with narrower, related, and broader terms. When conducting subject searches of catalogs and databases, these are the terms that will get you the best results.

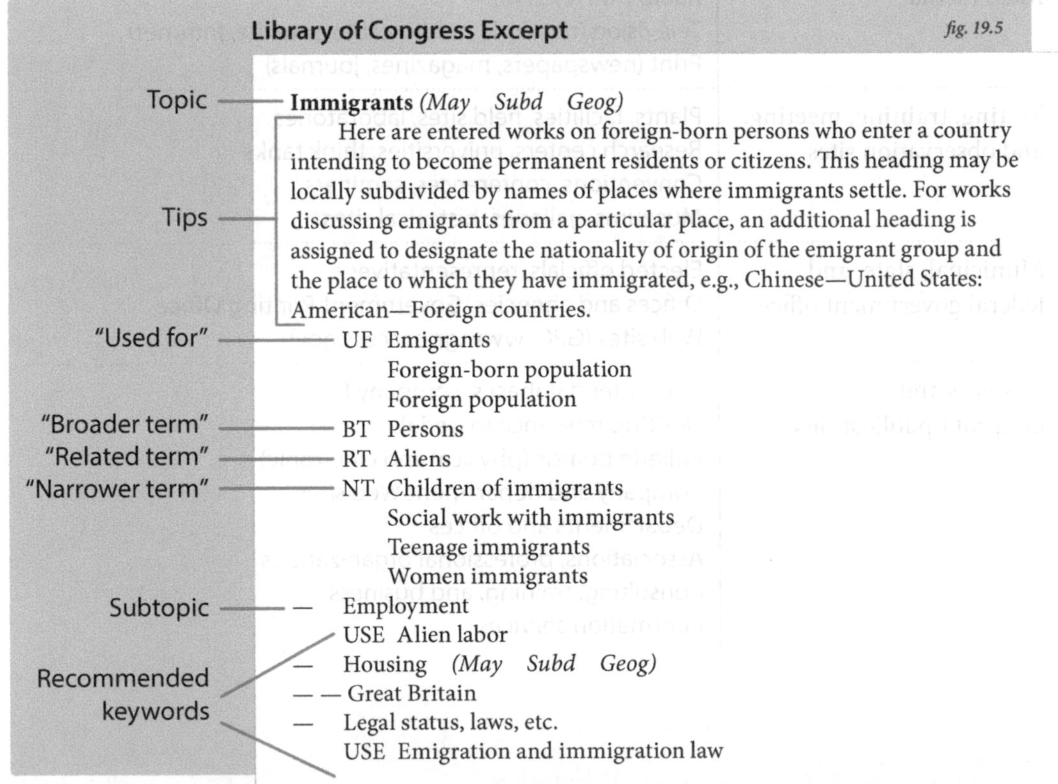

Use Keyword Strategies

The goal of a keyword search is to find quality research sources. To ensure that you identify the best resources available, follow these strategies:

1. **Get to know the database.** Look for answers to these questions:
   - What material does the database contain? What time frames?
   - What are you searching—authors, titles, subjects, full text?
   - What are the search rules? How can you narrow the search?
2. **Use a shotgun approach.** Start with the most likely keyword. If you have no "hits," choose a related term. Once you get some hits, check the citations for clues regarding which words to use as you continue searching.
3. **Use Boolean operators to refine your search.** When you combine keywords with Boolean operators—such as those in Figure 19.6—you will obtain better results.

Boolean Operators

fig. 19.6

Narrowing a Search **And, +, not, -** Use when one term gives you too many hits, especially irrelevant ones.	buffalo and bison *or* buffalo + bison buffalo not water +buffalo –water	Searches for citations containing both keywords Searches for "buffalo" but not "water," so that you eliminate material on water buffalo
Expanding a Search **Or** Combine a term providing few hits with a related word	buffalo or bison	Searches for citations containing either term
Specifying a Phrase **Quotation marks** Indicate that you wish to search for the exact phrase enclosed	"reclamation project"	Searches for the exact phrase "reclamation project"
Sequencing Operations **Parentheses** Indicate that the operation should be performed before other operations in the search string	(buffalo or bison) and ranching	Searches first for citations containing either "buffalo" or "bison" before checking the resulting citations for "ranching"
Finding Variations **Wild card symbols** Depending on the database, symbols such as $, ?, or # can find variations of a word.	ethic# ethic$	Searches for terms like *ethics* and *ethical*

Engaging and Evaluating Sources

Using reliable benchmarks, you should test all sources before you rely on them in your writing. After all, credible sources help your own credibility; sources that aren't credible destroy it. The benchmarks on the next four pages will help you test your sources' usefulness and reliability.

Engage Your Sources

Engaged reading is the opposite of passive reading—treating all sources equally, swallowing whole what's in the material, or looking only for information that supports your opinion. Full engagement involves these practices:

Test each source to see if it's worth reading. When reviewing source citations and generating a working bibliography, study titles, descriptions, lengths, and publication dates, asking these questions:

- How closely related to my topic is this source?
- Is this source too basic, overly complex, or just right?
- What could this source add to my overall balance of sources?

If you were writing about the International Space Station, for example, you might find a ten-page article in *Scientific American* more valuable and insightful than a brief news article on a specific event onboard or a *Star Trek* fan's blog on the topic.

INSIGHT Don't reject a source simply because it disagrees with your perspective. Good research engages rather than ignores opposing points of view.

Skim sources before reading in-depth. Consider marking key pages or passages with sticky notes, tabs, or a digital bookmark.

- Review the author's biography, the preface, and/or the introduction to discover the perspective, approach, scope, and research methods.
- Using your keywords, review any outline, abstract, table of contents, index, or home page to get a sense of coverage.

Read with an open but not an empty mind. Carry on a dialogue with the source, asking questions like "Why?" and "So what?"

- Note the purpose and audience. Was the piece written to inform or persuade? Is it aimed at the public, specialists, supporters, or opponents?
- Read to understand the source: What's clear and what's confusing?
- Relate the source to your research question: How does the source affirm or challenge your ideas? Synthesize what you read with what you know.
- Record your reactions to it—what it makes you think, feel, believe.
- Consider how you might use this source in your writing—key facts, important ideas, opposing perspectives, or examples.
- Check footnotes, references, appendices, and links for leads on other sources.

Rate Source Reliability and Depth

You should judge each source on its own merit. Generally, however, types of sources can be rated for depth and reliability, as shown in Figure 19.7, based on their authorship, length, topic treatment, documentation, publication method, review process, distance from primary sources, allegiances, stability, and so on. Use the information in Figure 19.7 to

1. target sources that fit your project's goals,
2. assess the approximate quality of the sources you're gathering, and
3. build a strong bibliography that readers will respect.

fig. 19.7

Deep, Reliable, Credible Sources

Scholarly Books and Scholarly Articles: largely based on careful research; written by experts for experts; address topics in depth; involve peer review and careful editing; offer stable discussion of topic

Trade Books and Articles in Quality, Specialized Magazines: largely based on careful research; written by experts for educated general audience. ***Sample periodicals:*** *The Atlantic, Scientific American, Nature, Orion*

Government Resources: books, reports, Web pages, guides, statistics developed by experts at government agencies; provided as service to citizens; relatively objective. ***Sample source:*** EPA "Climate Change" Web site

Reviewed Official Online Documents: Internet resources posted by legitimate institutions—colleges and universities, research institutes, service organizations; although offering a particular perspective, sources tend to be balanced.

Reference Works and Textbooks: provide general and specialized information; carefully researched, reviewed, and edited; lack depth for focused research (e.g., general encyclopedia entry).

News and Topical Stories from Quality Sources: provide current affairs coverage (print and online), introduction-level articles of interest to general public; may lack depth and length. ***Sample sources:*** *the Washington Post, the New York Times; Time, Psychology Today;* NPR's *All Things Considered*

Popular Magazine Stories: short, introductory articles often distant from primary sources and without documentation; heavy advertising. ***Sample sources:*** *Glamour, Seventeen, Reader's Digest*

Business and Nonprofit Publications: pamphlets, reports, news releases, brochures, manuals; range from informative to sales-focused.

List Server Discussions, Blog Posts, Social Media Posts Talk Radio Discussions: highly open, fluid, undocumented, untested exchanges and publications; unstable resource.

Unregulated Web Material: personal sites, joke sites, chat rooms, special-interest sites, advertising and junk email (spam); no review process, little accountability, biased presentation.

Tabloid Articles (print and Web): contain exaggerated and untrue stories written to titillate and exploit. ***Sample source:*** *National Enquirer*

Shallow, Unreliable, Not Credible Sources

Evaluate Print and Online Sources

As you work with a source, you need to test its reliability. The benchmarks that follow apply to both print and online sources; note, however, the additional tests offered for Web sources. For more on evaluating material on the Web, see pages 426–428.

Credible author An expert is an authority—someone who has mastered a subject area. Is the author an expert on this topic? What are her or his credentials, and can you confirm them? For example, an automotive engineer could be an expert on hydrogen fuel-cell technology, whereas a celebrity in a commercial would not.

> ***Web test:*** Is an author indicated? If so, are the author's credentials noted and contact information offered (for example, an email address)?

Reliable publication Has the source been published by a scholarly press, a peer-reviewed professional journal, a quality trade-book publisher, or a trusted news source? Did you find this resource through a reliable search tool (for example, a library catalog or database)?

> ***Web test:*** Which individual or group posted this page? Is the site rated by a subject directory or library organization? How stable is the site—has it been around for a while and does material remain available, or is the site "fly-by-night"? Check the site's home page, and read "About Us" pages and mission statements, looking for evidence of the organization's perspective, history, and trustworthiness.

Unbiased discussion While all sources come from a specific perspective and represent specific commitments, a biased source may be pushing an agenda in an unfair, unbalanced, incomplete manner. Watch for bias toward a certain region, country, political party, industry, gender, race, ethnic group, or religion. Be alert to connections among authors, financial backers, and the points of view shared. For example, if an author has functioned as a consultant to or a lobbyist for a particular industry or group (oil, animal rights), his or her allegiances may lead to a biased presentation of an issue.

> ***Web test:*** Is the online document one-sided? Is the site nonprofit (.org), government (.gov), commercial (.com), educational (.edu), business (.biz), informational (.info), network-related (.net), or military (.mil)? Is the site U.S. or international? Is this organization pushing a cause, product, service, or belief? How do advertising or special interests affect the site? You might suspect, for example, the scientific claims of a site sponsored by a pro-smoking organization.

Web Link: Beware especially of masquerade sites—those that appear to be legitimate but are joke sites or, worse, propaganda lures. Check, for example, www.dhmo.org.

Current information A five-year-old book on computers may be outdated, but a forty-year-old book on Abraham Lincoln could still be the best source. Given what you need, is this source's discussion up-to-date?

> ***Web test:*** When was the material originally posted and last updated? Are links live or dead?

Accurate information Bad research design, poor reporting, and sloppy documentation can lead to inaccurate information. Check the source for factual errors, statistical flaws, and conclusions that don't add up.

> ***Web test:*** Is the site information-rich or -poor? More specifically, is it filled with helpful, factual materials or fluffy with thin, unsubstantiated opinions? Can you trace and confirm sources by following links or conducting your own search?

Full, logical support Is the discussion of the topic reasonable, balanced, and complete? Are claims backed up with quality evidence? Does the source avoid faulty assumptions, twisted statistical analysis, logical fallacies, and unfair persuasion tactics? (See pages 323–326, for help.)

> ***Web test:*** Does the Web page offer well-supported claims and helpful links to additional information?

Quality writing and design Is the source well written? Is it free of sarcasm, derogatory terms, clichés, catch phrases, mindless slogans, grammar slips, and spelling errors? Generally, poor writing correlates with sloppy thinking.

> ***Web test:*** Are words neutral ("conservative perspective") or emotionally charged ("fascist agenda")? Are pages well designed—with clear rather than flashy, distracting multimedia elements? Is the site easy to navigate?

Positive relationship with other sources Does the source disagree with other sources? If yes, is the disagreement about the facts themselves or about how to interpret the facts? Which source seems more credible?

> ***Web test:*** Is the site's information logically consistent with print sources? Do other reputable sites offer links to this site?

INSIGHT Engage and evaluate visual resources as thoroughly as verbal materials. For example, ask yourself what tables, graphs, and photos really "say":

- Is the graphic informative or merely decorative?
- Does the graphic create a valid or manipulative central idea? For example, does the image seek to bypass logic by appealing to sexual impulses or to crude stereotypes?
- What does the graphic include and exclude in terms of information?
- Is the graphic well designed and easy to understand, or is it cluttered and distorted?
- Is a reliable source provided?

Creating a Working Bibliography

A working bibliography lists sources you have used and intend to use. It helps you track your research, develop your final bibliography, and avoid plagiarism. Here's what to do:

Select an Efficient Approach for Your Project

Choose an orderly method, such as one of the following:

- **Paper note cards:** Use 3 x 5-inch cards, and record one source per card.
- **Paper notebook:** Use a small, spiral-bound book to record sources.
- **Computer program:** Record source information electronically, either by capturing citation details from online searches or by recording bibliographic information using word-processing software or research software such as TakeNote, EndNote Plus, or Bookends Pro.

Including Identifying Information for Sources

Start by giving each source its own code number or letter: Doing so will help you when drafting and documenting your paper. Then include specific details for each kind of source listed below, shown on the facing page.

A. **Books:** author, title and subtitle, publication details (place, publisher, date)

B. **Periodicals:** author, article title, journal name, publication information (volume, number, date), page numbers

C. **Online sources:** author (if available), document title, site sponsor, database name, publication or posting date, access date, other publication information, URL

D. **Primary or field research:** date conducted, name and/or descriptive title of person interviewed, place observed, survey conducted, document analyzed

Adding Locating Information

Because you may need to retrace your research footsteps, include details about your research path:

A. **Books:** Include the Library of Congress or Dewey call number.

B. **Articles:** Note where and how you accessed them (stacks, current periodicals, microfilm, database).

C. **Web pages:** Record the complete URL (uniform resource locator) or the DOI (digital object identifier), not just the broader site address.

D. **Field research:** Include contact information such as a telephone number or an email address, as well as locating information such as an address or GPS coordinates.

INSIGHT Consider recording bibliographic details in the format of the documentation system you are using—MLA (pages 465–502) or APA (pages 503–532), for example. Doing so now will save time later. In addition, some research software allows you to record bibliographic information and then format it according to a specific system.

Annotate the Source

Add a note about the source's content, focus, reliability, and usefulness, as shown in Figure 19.8.

Sample Working Bibliography Entries

fig. 19.8

A. Book Source Note:

#2

Howells, Coral Ann. *Alice Munro.*

Contemporary World Writers. Manchester UP, 1998.

PS 8576.U57 Z7 1998

Book provides good introduction to Alice Munro's fiction, chapters arranged by Munro's works; contains intro, conclusion, and bibliography; 1998 date means author doesn't cover Munro's recent fiction.

B. Periodical Source Note

#5

Valdes, Marcela. "Some Stories Have to Be Told by Me: A Literary History of Alice Munro." *Virginia Quarterly Review* , vol. 82, no. 3, Summer 2006, pp. 82-90.

EBSCOhost permalink libproxy.redeemer.ca:2048/login?url=http://search.ebscohost.com/login.aspx?direct=true&db=aph&AN=21373060&site=eds-live

Article offers good introduction to Munro's life, her roots in Ontario, her writing career, and the key features of her stories

C. Internet Source Note:

#3

"Alice Munro." Athabasca University Centre for Language and Literature: Canadian Writers. Updated 11 Oct. 2012. Accessed 17 April 2017.

http://www.athabascau.ca/writers/munro.html site offers good introduction to Munro's writing, along with links to bibliography and other resources.

D. Interview Source Note:

#4

Thacker, Robert. Email interview. 7 March 2017.

rthacker@mdu.edu

Author of critical biography on Munro, *Alice Munro: Writing Her Lives,* offered really helpful insights into her creative process, especially useful for story "Carried Away."

Developing a Note-Taking System

Accurate, thoughtful notes create a foundation for your research writing. The trick is to practice some sensible strategies and choose an efficient method.

Develop Note-Taking Strategies

What are you trying to do when you take notes on sources? What you are not doing is (a) collecting quotations to plunk in your project, (b) piling isolated grains of data into a large stack of disconnected facts, or (c) intensively reading and taking notes on every source you find. Instead, use these strategies:

Be selective. Guided by your research questions and working thesis, focus on sources that are central to your project. From these sources, record information clearly related to your limited topic, but also take notes on what surprises or puzzles you. Be selective, avoiding notes that are either too meager or too extensive. Suppose, for example, that you were writing a paper on the engineering challenges associated with building the International Space Station. If you were reading an article on the history and the future of this facility, you might take careful notes on material describing the station's technical details, but not on astronauts' biographies.

Develop accurate, complete records. Your notes should . . .

- Accurately summarize, paraphrase, and quote sources (pages 394–396).
- Clearly show where you got your information.
- Cover all the research you've done—primary research (e.g., interviews, observations), books and periodical articles, and online sources.

Engage your sources. Evaluate what you are reading and develop your own responses. (See pages 384–387.) For example, with an article about the International Space Station, you might test the author's biases, credentials, and logic; and you might respond with knowledge you have gained about other space endeavors.

Take good notes on graphics in sources—tables, line graphs, photographs, maps, and so on. Such graphics are typically packed with information and powerfully convey ideas. (See "Critical Thinking Through Viewing," pages 10–15.)

INSIGHT Different disciplines use different note-taking practices. In your major, learn these practices through courses that introduce you to the subject matter. Here are two examples:

- In literature studies, students conduct literary analyses by annotating print texts. Students may also take notes through keyword searches of e-books (for example, a play by Shakespeare) and reviews of literary criticism.
- In environmental studies, students conduct research by (a) taking notes on published research to develop literature reviews, and (b) using a standard field notebook to collect data, make drawings, and reflect on results.

Employ Note-Taking Systems

A good note-taking system should help you do the following:

- Avoid unintentional plagiarism by developing accurate records, distinguishing among sources, and separating source material from your own ideas.
- Work efficiently at gathering what you need for the project.
- Work flexibly with a wide range of resources—primary and secondary, print and digital, verbal and visual.
- Engage sources through creative and critical reflection.
- Record summaries, paraphrases, and quotations correctly.
- Be accurate and complete so that you need not reread sources.
- Efficiently develop your paper's outline and first draft.

Four note-taking systems are outlined on the pages that follow. Choose the system that works best for your project, or combine elements to develop your own.

System 1: Paper or digital note cards. Using paper note cards is the traditional method of note taking; however, note-taking software is now available with most word-processing programs and special programs like TakeNote, EndNote Plus, and Bookends Pro. Here's how a note-card system works:

1. Establish one set of cards for your bibliography.
2. On a second set of cards, take notes on sources (see Figure 19.9):
   - Record one point from one source per card.
   - Clarify the source: List the author's last name, a shortened title, or a code from the matching bibliography card. Include a page number.
   - Provide a topic or heading: Called a slug, the topic helps you categorize and order information.
   - Label the note as a summary, paraphrase, or quotation of the original.
   - Distinguish between the source's information and your own thoughts.

fig. 19.9

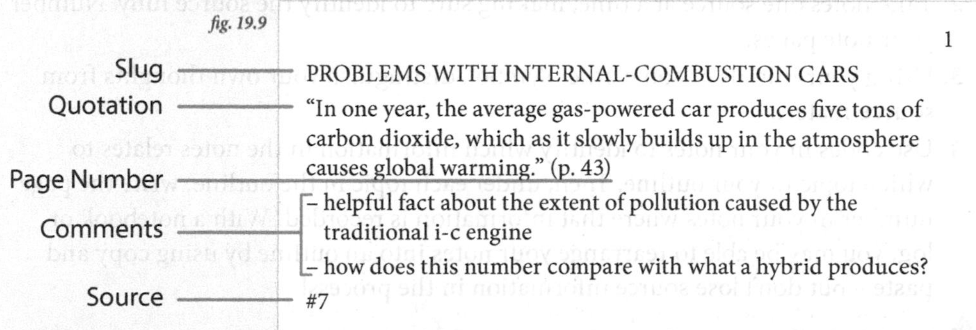

Upside: Note cards are highly systematic, helping you categorize material and organize it for an outline and a first draft.

Downside: The method can be initially tedious and time-consuming.

System 2: Copy (or save) and annotate. The copy-and-annotate method involves working with photocopies, print versions, or digital texts of sources:

1. Selectively photocopy, print, and/or save important sources. Copy carefully, making sure you have full pages, including the page numbers.
2. As needed, add identifying information on the copy—author, publication details, and date. Each page should be easy to identify and trace. When working with books, simply copy the title and copyright pages and keep them with the rest of your notes.
3. As you read, mark up the copy and highlight key statements. In the margins or digital file, record your ideas:
   - Ask questions. Insert a "?" in the margin, or write out the question.
   - Make connections. Draw arrows to link ideas, or make notes like "see page 36."
   - Add asides. Record what you think and feel while reading.
   - Define terms. Note important words that you need to understand.
   - Create a marginal index. Write keywords to identify themes and main parts.

Upside: Copying, printing, and/or saving helps you record sources accurately; annotating encourages careful reading and thinking.

Downside: Organizing material for drafting is inconvenient; when done poorly, annotating and highlighting involve skimming, not critical thinking.

System 3: The computer notebook or research log. The computer notebook or research log method involves taking notes on a computer or on sheets of paper. Here's how it works:

1. Establish a central location for your notes—a notebook, a file folder, a binder, or a digital folder.
2. Take notes one source at a time, making sure to identify the source fully. Number your note pages.
3. Using your initials or some other symbol, distinguish your own thoughts from source material.
4. Use codes in your notes to identify which information in the notes relates to which topic in your outline. Then, under each topic in the outline, write the page number in your notes where that information is recorded. With a notebook or log, you may be able to rearrange your notes into an outline by using copy and paste—but don't lose source information in the process!

Upside: Taking notes feels natural without being overly systematic.

Downside: Outlining and drafting may require time-consuming paper shuffling.

System 4: The double-entry notebook. The double-entry notebook involves parallel note taking—notes from sources beside your own brainstorming, reaction, and reflection. Using a notebook or the columns feature of your word-processing program, do the following:

1. Divide pages in half vertically.
2. In the left column, record bibliographic information and take notes on sources.
3. In the right column, write your responses. Think about what the source is saying, why the point is important, whether you agree with it, and how the point relates to other ideas and other sources. See Figure 19.10 for an example.

Upside: This method creates accurate source records while encouraging thoughtful responses; also, it can be done on a computer.

Downside: Organizing material for drafting may be a challenge.

fig. 19.10

Cudworth, Erika. Environment and Society. Routledge Introductions to Environment Series. Routledge, 2003.	
Ch. 6 "Society, 'Culture' and 'Nature'—Human Relations with Animals"	
chapter looks at how social scientists have understood historically the relationship between people and animals (158)	I've actually had a fair bit of personal experience with animals—the horses, ducks, chickens, dogs, and cats on our hobby farm. Will this chapter make trouble for my thinking?
the word animal is itself a problem when we remember that people too are animals but the distinction is often sharply made by people themselves (159)	Yes, what really are the connections and differences between people and animals? Is it a different level of intelligence? Is there something more basic or fundamental? Are we afraid to see ourselves as animals, as creatures?
"In everyday life, people interact with animals continually." (159)-author gives many common examples	Many examples—pets, food, TV programs, zoos—apply to me. Hadn't thought about how much my life is integrated with animal life! What does that integration look like? What does it mean for me, for the animals?

Summarizing, Paraphrasing, and Quoting Source Material

As you work with sources, you must decide what to put in your notes and how to record it—as a summary, a paraphrase, or a quotation. Use these guidelines:

- How relevant is the passage to your research question or working thesis?
- How strong and important is the information offered?
- How unique or memorable is the thinking or phrasing?

The more relevant, the stronger, and the more memorable the material is, the more likely you should note it. The passage below comes from an article on GM's development of fuel-cell technology. Review the passage; study how the researcher summarizes, paraphrases, and quotes from the source; and then practice these same strategies as you take notes on sources.

From Burns, L. D., McCormick, J. B., and Borroni-Bird, C. E. "Vehicle of Change." *Scientific American 287*(4), 64-73.

When Karl Benz rolled his Patent Motorcar out of the barn in 1886, he literally set the wheels of change in motion. The advent of the automobile led to dramatic alterations in people's way of life as well as the global economy—transformations that no one expected at the time. The ever-increasing availability of economical personal transportation remade the world into a more accessible place while spawning a complex industrial infrastructure that shaped modern society.

Now another revolution could be sparked by automotive technology: one fueled by hydrogen rather than petroleum. Fuel cells—which cleave hydrogen atoms into protons and electrons that drive electric motors while emitting nothing worse than water vapor—could make the automobile much more environmentally friendly. Not only could cars become cleaner, they could also become safer, more comfortable, more personalized—and even perhaps less expensive. Further, these fuel-cell vehicles could be instrumental in motivating a shift toward a "greener" energy economy based on hydrogen. As that occurs, energy use and production could change significantly. Thus, hydrogen fuel-cell cars and trucks could help ensure a future in which personal mobility—the freedom to travel independently—could be sustained indefinitely, without compromising the environment or depleting the earth's natural resources.

A confluence of factors makes the big change seem increasingly likely. For one, the petroleum-fueled internal-combustion engine (ICE), as highly refined, reliable and economical as it is, is finally reaching its limits. Despite steady improvements, today's ICE vehicles are only 20 to 25 percent efficient in converting the energy content of fuels into drive-wheel power. And although the U.S. auto industry has cut exhaust emissions substantially since the unregulated 1960s—hydrocarbons dropped by 99 percent, carbon monoxide by 96 percent and nitrogen oxides by 95 percent—the continued production of carbon dioxide causes concern because of its potential to change the planet's climate.

Summarize Useful Passages

Summarizing condenses in your own words the main points in a passage. Summarize when the source provides relevant ideas and information on your topic.

1. **Reread the passage,** jotting down a few key words.
2. **State the main point in your own words.** Add key supporting points, leaving out examples, details, and long explanations. Be objective: Don't include your reactions.
3. **Check your summary against the original,** making sure that you use quotation marks around any exact phrases you borrow.

Sample Summary:

> While the introduction of the car in the late nineteenth century has led to dramatic changes in society and world economics, another dramatic change is now taking place in the shift from gas engines to hydrogen technologies. Fuel cells may make the car "greener," and perhaps even safer, cheaper, and more comfortable. These automotive changes will affect the energy industry by making it more environmentally friendly; as a result, people will continue to enjoy mobility while transportation moves to renewable energy. One factor leading to this technological shift is that the internal-combustion engine has reached the limits of its efficiency, potential, and development—while remaining problematic with respect to emissions, climate change, and health.

Paraphrase Key Passages

Paraphrasing involves putting a passage from the source into your own words—keeping the content but phrasing it in your own voice and style, so to speak. Typically, you would paraphrase a passage that contains important points, explanations, or arguments but that is not phrased memorably or clearly. The passage might be primarily factual, making direct quotation unnecessary, or the passage might be technical, dense, and complex, requiring that you put it in plainer terms. To paraphrase effectively, follow these steps:

1. **Review the passage** to make sure that you have the gist of the whole.
2. **Go through the passage carefully,** sentence by sentence, doing the following:
   - State the ideas in your own words, substituting terms and defining words as needed.
   - Rework the sentence patterns, as needed—changing syntax, combining clauses, and so on—so that the passage takes on your voice.
   - If you do borrow phrases directly, put them in quotation marks.
3. **Check your paraphrase against the original:** Is the meaning accurate and complete? Have you fairly "translated" the source into your own wording and voice?

Sample Paraphrase of the Second Paragraph in the Passage:

Automobile technology may lead to another radical economic and social change through the shift from gasoline to hydrogen fuel. By breaking hydrogen into protons and electrons so that the electrons run an electric motor with only the by-product of water vapor, fuel cells could make the car a "green" machine. But this technology could also increase the automobile's safety, comfort, personal tailoring, and affordability. Moreover, this shift to fuel-cell engines in automobiles could lead to drastic, environmentally friendly changes in the broader energy industry, one that will be now tied to hydrogen rather than fossil fuels. The result from this shift will be radical changes in the way we use and produce energy. In other words, the shift to hydrogen-powered vehicles could promise to maintain society's valued mobility, while the clean technology would preserve the environment and its natural resources.

Quote Crucial Phrases, Sentences, and Passages

Quoting records statements or phrases in the original source word for word. Quote nuggets only—statements that are well phrased or authoritative:

1. **Note the quotation's context**—how it fits in the author's discussion.
2. **Copy the passage word for word,** enclosing it in quotation marks and checking its accuracy.
3. **If you omit words, note that omission with an ellipsis.** If you change any word for grammatical reasons, put changes in brackets. (See page 451).

Sample Quotation:

"[H]ydrogen fuel-cell cars and trucks could help ensure a future in which personal mobility . . . could be sustained indefinitely, without compromising the environment or depleting the earth's natural resources."

Note: This sentence captures the authors' main claim about the benefits and future of fuel-cell technology.

INSIGHT Whether you are summarizing, paraphrasing, or quoting, aim to be true to the source by respecting the context and spirit of the original. Avoid shifting the focus or ripping material out of its context and forcing it into your own. For example, in the sample passage the authors discuss the limits of the internal-combustion engine. If you were to claim that these authors are arguing that the internal-combustion engine was an enormous engineering and environmental mistake, you would be twisting their comments to serve your own writing agenda.

fyi For instruction on effectively integrating quotations, paraphrases, and summaries into your writing, see pages 448–451.

Avoiding Unintentional Plagiarism

Careful note taking helps prevent unintentional plagiarism. Plagiarism—using source material without giving credit—is treated more fully in chapter 21; essentially, however, unintentional plagiarism happens when you accidentally use a source's ideas, phrases, or information without documenting that material. At the planning stage of your project, you can prevent this problem from happening by adhering to principles of ethical research and following some practical guidelines.

Practice the Principles of Ethical Research

Because of the nature of information and the many challenges of working with it, conducting ethical research can be very complex and involved. To start with, however, commit to these principles of ethical research:

- Do the research and write the paper yourself.
- Adhere to the research practices approved in your discipline.
- Follow school- and discipline-related guidelines for working with people, resources, and technology.
- Avoid one-sided research that ignores or conceals opposition.
- Present real, accurate data and results—not "fudged" or twisted facts.
- Treat source material fairly in your writing.

Practices That Prevent Unintentional Plagiarism

The principles of ethical research above find expression when you prevent unintentional plagiarism. Do so by following these practices:

- Maintain an accurate working bibliography (pages 388–389).
- When taking notes, distinguish source material from your own thinking by using quotation marks, codes, and/or separate columns or note cards.
- When you draft your paper, transfer source material carefully by coding material that you integrate into your discussion, using quotation marks, double-checking your typing, or using copy and paste to ensure accuracy.
- Take time to do the project right—both research and writing. Avoid pulling an all-nighter during which you can't properly work with sources.

Practices That Prevent Internet Plagiarism

An especially thorny area related to unintentional plagiarism centers on the Internet. As with traditional print sources, Internet sources must be properly credited; in other words, Web material cannot simply be transferred to your paper without acknowledgement. So treat Web sources like print sources. And if you copy and paste digital material while taking notes and drafting, always track its origins with codes, abbreviations, or separate columns.

Critical Thinking and Writing: Applications

Once you have studied the instruction in this chapter, you need to apply it to your own research project. The following activities will help you do so.

1. **Research Map:** Using all that you have learned in this chapter, develop a research proposal that identifies a topic of interest to you, clarifies the value of the research, maps out research methods (including a working bibliography of five to ten sources), and establishes a workable schedule.
2. **Source Work:** If you have not already done so, get the resources that you listed in your research proposal's working bibliography. Then do the following:
   a. Identify each source as primary, secondary, or tertiary. Consider the relative value of these sources for your project.
   b. Test the reliability of your sources. Refer to the scale on page 385 and the questions on pages 386–387. Are the sources credible enough for your project?
   c. From your bibliography, choose a short article or a passage from a longer source. Read that material carefully and do the following: (a) write a summary of the material, (b) choose a paragraph and paraphrase it, and (c) choose a key statement to quote directly, indicating why it is worthy of quotation.

Learning-Objectives Checklist ✓

Have you achieved this chapter's learning objectives? Check your progress with the items below, revisiting topics in the chapter as needed. I have . . .

____ analyzed the rhetorical situation of my research project (370).
____ identified the phases of the research process (371).
____ focused my research project by establishing a manageable topic, brainstorming questions, and developing a working thesis (372–373).
____ differentiated the nature and uses of primary, secondary, and tertiary sources (374–375).
____ generated a research plan by choosing research methods and getting organized to do research, as well as composing a research proposal, if required (376–379).
____ chosen fitting information sources from promising information sites (380–381).
____ performed effective keyword searches by choosing productive keywords and implementing search strategies (382–383).
____ critically engaged print and digital sources, evaluating them for depth, reliability, credibility, lack of bias, currency, and accuracy (384–387).
____ produced and maintained an orderly, accurate working bibliography (388–389).
____ chosen a note-taking system that allows me to keep accurate, complete records and engage my sources (390–393).
____ accurately summarized, paraphrased, and quoted material from sources in my notes (394–396).
____ identified principles of ethical research and implemented them in my own project (397).

MindTap® Practice skills that you have learned in this chapter and receive automatic feedback. Reflect on your writing process.

Chapter 20

Conducting Research: Primary, Library, Web

Today, conducting research is both easy and difficult. It's easy because research technology is powerful and many research methods are available. It's difficult because that technology and those methods provide access to so much information—the good, the bad, and the ugly.

How do you meet this challenge and conduct quality research? First, consider whether your project would benefit from primary research—gathering information firsthand by observing sites, interviewing people, and analyzing documents, for example. Second, learn how to use an expert resource—your college library. The library is your gateway to quality print and electronic materials. Third, learn to access reliable resources on the free Web.

Visually Speaking "Libraries are research centers." Think about this statement in light of Figure 20.1, and relate this idea to your own experience of research, inside and outside of libraries.

MindTap®

Understand the goals of the chapter and complete a warm-up activity online.

Learning **Objectives**

By working through this chapter, you will be able to

- choose, design, and conduct primary research for your project.
- identify, locate, retrieve, and work with library resources.
- implement free-Web research tools to locate and evaluate free-Web resources.

Jens Goepfert / Shutterstock.com

fig. 20.1

Planning Primary Research

As discussed on pages 374–375, resources can be primary, secondary, or tertiary. Doing primary research is particularly hands-on and requires careful planning. To do truly useful primary research, you need to choose methods that will gather information directly related to your main research question and learn the proper methods of doing such research. To start your planning, consider these factors:

- **The assignment:** Does the assignment dictate a particular form of primary research?
- **The field of study:** Does the course's subject matter point you towards particularly valued methods of primary research?
- **The topic:** How might your understanding of the topic deepen with information gathered through a particular method?
- **The timing:** How much time do you have for doing primary research?
- **The audience:** What forms of primary research will your readers expect, respect, or value?

Methods of Primary Research

After considering the factors above, review the methods below and choose those that make sense for your project. You can find instruction for each method at the page numbers indicated.

- **Surveys and Questionnaires** (pages 402–403) gather information from representative groups of people as responses you can review, tabulate, and analyze, most often statistically. Whether gathering simple facts or personal opinions, such research can give you strong insights into how the group thinks about your issue; however, it may be difficult to gather complex responses.
- **Analyses of Texts, Documents, Records, and Artifacts** (pages 404–405) involve studying original correspondence, reports, legislation, images, literary works, historical records, and so on. Such research provides a direct experience of your topic and insights into its immediate nature, products, or remnants, but the quality of research depends on how fully and effectively you analyze the "text" in question.
- **Interviews** (pages 406–407) involve consulting people through a question-and-answer dialogue. Interviewees can be either experts on your topic or people who have had a particular experience with the topic, either witnessing it or involved in some way. Interviewing experts can add authoritative input, though experts sometimes disagree. Interviewing someone with experience of your topic can give an inside perspective into its causes and effects, as well as its personal dimensions.
- **Observations** (page 408) involve systematically examining and analyzing places, spaces, scenes, equipment, work, events, and other sites or phenomena. Whether you rely simply on your five senses or use scientific techniques, observation provides a range of information—from personal impressions to precise data (e.g., measurements).

- **Experiments** (see IMRAD report, pages 457–463) test hypotheses—predictions about why things are as they are or happen as they do—so as to arrive at conclusions that can be tentatively accepted, related to other knowledge, and acted upon. Such testing often explains cause-effect relationships for varied natural, social, or psychological phenomena, offering a degree of scientific certainty about the forces at work in your topic.

Principles for Doing Primary Research

Whatever primary research you choose to do, you should conduct that research in a systematic, careful manner in order to generate valid, reliable primary information and ideas. Here are some principles common to doing any method of primary research:

1. **Locate a reliable source.** Make sure, in other words, that the person, place, group, document, or image is the real thing—an authoritative, representative, respected source of information. Whether you find your source in a print publication (e.g., a version of a Shakespeare play published by a scholarly press), on the Internet (e.g., a piece of legislation), in an archive or museum (e.g., a sculpture), through personal contact (e.g., a home visit), or through exploration (e.g., a ravine in your city)—make sure that the source matches your research need and has the right "weight" for your project.
2. **Aim for objectivity.** You should approach most primary research with an objective frame of mind: remain open to the evidence that arises by keeping your wishes in check; otherwise, your research will be slanted and your readers will recognize the biases in your thinking.
3. **Get ready through background research.** That is, don't go cold into your primary research. Do your homework first—learning the key concepts and perspectives on your topic, the theories debated, and the knowledge that has already been built by others. That way, your primary research will grow out of some foundational thinking and be driven by a specific purpose and specific questions.
4. **Use the right tools.** Each method of primary research requires tools—physical tools (e.g., field notebook, instruments), software (e.g., survey software, spreadsheet software), or analytical tools (e.g., the ability to sort out causes and effects). Make sure that you have reliable tools and are using them effectively.
5. **Gather and work with data carefully.** Primary information is only as good as the care with which it is gathered, interpreted, and presented. Keep accurate, complete records of your research; in some projects, you may even have to include such records and "raw data" in an appendix. Above all, work ethically with your data by avoiding errors, gaps, and omissions, and by not fudging your data or doctoring graphics.

If your research involves working with people, typically called "human subjects," strive to (1) do no harm, whether psychological, social, or financial, and (2) respect individual autonomy—participants' rights, dignity, and privacy, for example. Check if your school has a research-ethics committee that reviews, approves, and oversees such research by students.

Conducting Surveys

One source of primary information that you can use for research projects is a survey or questionnaire. Surveys can collect facts and opinions from a wide range of people about virtually any topic. To get valid information, follow these guidelines:

1. **Find a focus.**
   - Limit the purpose of your survey.
   - Target a specific audience.
2. **Ask clear questions.**
   - Phrase questions so they can be easily understood.
   - Use words that are objective (not biased or slanted).
3. **Match your questions to your purpose.**
   - Closed questions give respondents easy-answer options, and the answers are easy to tabulate. Closed questions can provide two choices (*yes* or *no*, *true* or *false*), multiple choices, a rating scale (*poor 1 2 3 excellent*), or a blank to fill.
   - Open-ended questions bring in a wide variety of responses and more complex information, but they take time to complete, and the answers can be difficult to summarize.
4. **Organize your survey so that it's easy to complete.**
   - In the introduction, state who you are and why you need the information. Explain how to complete the survey and when, where, and how to return it.
   - Guide readers by providing numbers, instructions, and headings.
   - Begin with basic questions and end with any complex, open-ended questions that are necessary. Move in a logical order from one topic to the next.
5. **Test your survey before using it.**
   - Ask a friend or classmate to read your survey and help you revise it, if necessary, before printing or posting it.
   - Try out your survey with a small test group. If the test group seems to misunderstand or misinterpret a question, then revise it.
6. **Conduct your survey.**
   - Distribute the survey to a clearly defined group that won't prejudice the sampling (random or cross section).
   - Get responses from a sample of your target group (10 percent at minimum).
   - Tabulate responses carefully and objectively.

Note: To develop statistically valid results, you may need expert help. Check with your instructor. In addition, consider online survey tools such as SurveyMonkey.com and LimeSurvey.org.

Sample Survey

Confidential Survey

The introduction includes the essential information about the survey.

My name is Cho Lang, and I'm conducting research about the use of training supplements. I'd like to hear from you, Alfred University's athletes. Please answer the questions below by circling or writing out your responses. Return your survey to me, care of the Dept. of Psychology, through campus mail by Friday, April 5. Your responses will remain confidential.

The survey begins with clear, basic questions.

1. What is your gender?

2. Circle your year.
   Freshman **Sophomore** **Junior** **Senior**

3. List the sports that you play.

4. Are you presently using a training supplement?
   Yes **No**

   Note: If you circled "no," you may turn in your survey at this point.

The survey asks an open-ended question.

5. Describe your supplement use (type, amount, and frequency).

6. Who supervises your use of this training supplement?
   Coach **Trainer** **Self** **Others**

7. How long have you used it?
   Less than 1 month **1–12 months** **12+ months**

The survey covers the topic thoroughly.

8. How many pounds have you gained while using this supplement?

9. How much has your athletic performance improved?
   None **1** **2** **3** **4** **5** **Greatly**

10. Circle any side effects you've experienced.
    Dehydration **Nausea** **Diarrhea**

Analyzing Texts, Documents, Records, and Artifacts

An original document or record is one that relates directly to the event, issue, object, or phenomenon you are researching. Examining original documents and artifacts can involve studying letters, email exchanges, Tweets, case notes, literary texts, blog posts, sales records, legislation, and material objects such as tools, sculptures, buildings, and tombs. As you analyze such documents and records, you examine evidence in an effort to understand a topic, arrive at a coherent conclusion about it, and support that judgment. How do you work with such diverse documents, records, and artifacts? Here are some guidelines:

Choose Evidence Close to Your Topic

Which texts, documents, records, and artifacts originated from or grew out of the topic you are researching? The closer to the topic, the more primary the source. Select materials that are directly related to your research questions and/or working thesis.

Example: If you were studying English labor riots of the 1830s, you could investigate these primary sources:

- To identify the rioters, names from police reports or union membership lists
- To understand what rioters were demanding, copies of speeches given at demonstrations
- To learn the political response to the riots, political speeches or legislation
- To get at the attitudes of people from that time, newspaper reports, works of art, or novels from the period
- To find people's personal stories and private opinions related to the riots, personal letters, diaries, family albums, gravestones, and funeral eulogies

Put the Document or Artifact in Context

So that the material takes on meaning, clarify its external and internal natures. First, consider its external context—the five W's and H: What exactly is it? Who made it, when, where, why, and how? Second, consider its internal nature—what the document means, based on what it can and cannot show you: What does the language mean or refer to? What is the document's structure? What are the artifact's composition and style?

Example: If you were examining Mary Wollstonecraft's *A Vindication of the Rights of Woman* in a history or women's studies course, you would consider the following:

- **External Context:** who Mary Wollstonecraft was; when and why she wrote *A Vindication* and under what conditions; for whom she wrote it and their response; the type of document it is
- **Internal Context:** Wollstonecraft's essential argument and evidence; the nature of her views, their relationship to her times, and their relevance today

Frame Your Examination with Questions

To make sense of the text, document, record, or artifact, understand what you are looking for and why. List the secondary questions that you want to answer in relation to the main question behind your research project.

> ***Example:*** To study the legislative background behind the development of cleaner cars, such as the hybrid-fuel vehicle, you could access various documents on the Clean Air Act of 1990 (for example, *The Plain English Guide to the Clean Air Act*, an EPA publication). As you study this legislation, you could frame your reading with these additional questions:
> - What are the requirements of the Clean Air Act?
> - What legislation followed the Clean Air Act?
> - Specifically, how do those requirements affect automotive technology?
> - Which research projects will likely influence these requirements?
> - Are schedules for change or deadlines written into the Clean Air Act?

Draw Coherent Conclusions About Meaning

Make sense of the source in relation to your research questions. What connections does it reveal? What important developments? What cause/effect relationships? What themes?

> ***Example:*** A study of the Clean Air Act might lead you to conclusions regarding how environmental legislation relates to the development of hybrid technology—for example, that the United States must produce cleaner cars if it hopes to gain improved air quality.

INSIGHT Studying primary documents and artifacts is central to many disciplines—history, literature, theology, philosophy, political studies, and archaeology, for example. Good analysis depends on asking research questions appropriate for the discipline. With the English labor riots of the 1830s again as an example, here's what three disciplines might ask:

- **Political science:** What role did political theories, structures, and processes play in the riots—both in causing and in responding to them?
- **Art:** How were the concerns of the rioters embodied in the new "realist" style of the mid-1800s? Did artists sympathize with and address an alienated working-class audience? How did art comment on the social structures of the time?
- **Sociology:** What type and quality of education did most workers have in the 1830s? How did that education affect their economic status and employment opportunities? Did issues related to the riots prompt changes in the English educational system? What changes and why?

With these examples in mind, consider your own major: What questions would this discipline ask of the English labor riots, of Mary Wollstonecraft's *A Vindication of the Rights of Woman*, or of the Clean Air Act of 1990 and its related legislation?

Conducting Interviews

The purpose of an interview is simple: To get information, you talk with someone who has significant experience or someone who is an expert on your topic. Use the guidelines below whenever you conduct an interview.

1. **Before the interview,** research the topic and the person you are planning to interview.
   - Arrange the interview in a thoughtful way. Explain to the interviewee your purpose and the topics to be covered.
   - Think about the specific ideas you want to cover in the interview and write questions for each. Addressing the 5 W's and H (*Who? What? Where? When? Why?* and *How?*) is important for good coverage.
   - Organize your questions in a logical order so the interview moves smoothly from one subject to the next.
   - Write the questions on the left side of a page. Leave room for quotations, information, and impressions on the right side.
2. **During the interview,** try to relax so that your conversation is natural and sincere.
   - Provide some background information about yourself, your project, and your plans for using the interview information.
   - Use recording equipment only with the interviewee's permission.
   - Jot down key facts and quotations.
   - Listen actively. Show that you're listening through your body language—eye contact, nods, smiles. Pay attention not only to what the person says, but also to how he or she says it.
   - Be flexible. If the person looks puzzled by a question, rephrase it. If the discussion gets off track, redirect it. Based on the interviewee's responses, ask follow-up questions, and don't limit yourself to your planned questions only.
   - End positively. Conclude by asking if the person wants to add, clarify, or emphasize anything. (Note: important points may come up late in the interview.) Thank the person, gather your notes and equipment, and part with a handshake.
3. **After the interview,** do the appropriate follow-up work.
   - As soon as possible, review your notes. Fill in responses you remember but couldn't record at the time.
   - Analyze the results. Study the information, insights, and quotations you gathered. What do they reveal about the topic? How does the interview confirm, complement, or contradict other sources on the topic? What has the interview added to your understanding?
   - Thank the interviewee with a note, an email, or a phone call.
   - If necessary, ask the interviewee to check whether your information and quotations are accurate.
   - Offer to send the interviewee a copy of your writing.

Sample Interview Note-Taking Sheet

Below, note how the researcher sets up questions for an interview with an automotive engineer regarding hybrid technology. The interviewer begins with identifying information for future reference, and then moves from a basic "connecting" question into the technology's principles, strengths, challenges, and future. On the right, he leaves room (approximately half the sheet) for taking notes.

Interview with Jessica Madison,
automotive engineer for Future Fuel Corporation
(email jmadison@futurefuel.com; phone 555-555-5555)
January 22, 2017: 2:30 p.m.

Notes, quotations, observations:

Preliminaries: thanks/appreciation; introduction of myself; background, purpose, hoped-for outcome of research (report on hybrids' environmental potential)

Initial Question

1. Please tell me about your research into hybrid technology. When and how did you become interested? What discoveries have you made?

Hybrid Technology: Principles

2. How does hybrid technology actually work? What's the principle behind the hybrid vehicle?
3. How is the hybrid engine different from the traditional internal-combustion engine?

Strengths and Challenges

4. What are the strengths of hybrid vehicles?
5. What are some of the challenges of hybrids? Some of the weaknesses?

The Future/Viability

6. Where is hybrid technology going? What's the next generation of clean-car technology?
7. What are the benefits or drawbacks of society investing in hybrids? Why should the average person care about hybrid technologies?
8. Would you like to add or clarify anything about hybrid technologies?

Closing: thank for taking time, offering insights

Making Observations

Observation places you at a site directly related to your topic. Whether you are examining people's behavior, natural phenomena, or a location's features, observation can gather subjective impressions, sensory data, various recordings, or concrete measurements.

Prepare to Observe

1. **Know your goal.** Do you need to understand a place or a process? Solve a problem? Answer a question? What kind of information do you want to gather?
2. **Consider possible perspectives and vantage points.** Should you observe the site passively or interact with it? Should you simply record data or also include impressions? Should you observe from one position or several?
3. **Plan your observation.** Preparation involves both academic and practical issues: doing sufficient background research; listing questions to answer; seeking permission to observe, if needed; taking safety precautions; considering timing issues; and gathering observation tools.

Conduct Your Observations

1. **Be flexible but focused.** Follow your plan, but be open to surprises. Pay attention to the big picture (the context, time frame, and surroundings), but focus on your observational goal by filtering out unnecessary details.
2. **Identify your position.** Where are you in the site? What is your angle? More broadly, what is your personal and/or cultural stance here?
3. **Take notes on specific details and impressions.** While being careful not to miss too much, jot down data for later review—conditions, appearances, actions, events, and so on. If appropriate, focus on your five senses: sight, sound, smell, touch, and taste.
4. **Gather other forms of evidence.** Take measurements, record images and sound, gather samples, interview people, study event programs, get brochures.

Make Sense of Your Observations

1. **Complete and review your notes and evidence.** As soon as possible, flesh out your notes a bit more fully—while your memory is still good. Then examine closely everything that you have written, recorded, and collected, looking for patterns and themes.
2. **List your conclusions.** Describe what has been clarified about your topic through the observation.
3. **Relate your observations to your other research.** Explore how your observations confirm, contradict, complement, or build on other sources of information.

Becoming Familiar with the Library

The library door is your gateway to information. Inside, the college library holds a wide range of research resources, from books to periodicals, from reference librarians to digital databases.

To improve your ability to succeed at all your research assignments, become familiar with your college library system. Take advantage of tours and orientation sessions to learn its physical layout, resources, and services. Check your library's Web site for policies, tutorials, and research tools. The college library offers a variety of resources for your research projects.

Librarians and media specialists: These library specialists are information experts:
- They manage the library's materials and guide you to resources.
- They help you perform online searches.

Collections: The library collects, houses, and provides access to a variety of materials:
- **Books and digital materials**—print books, ebooks, CDs, DVDs, and more.
- **Periodicals**—journals, magazines, and newspapers (print, microform, pdf, and html)
- **Reference materials**—directories, indexes, handbooks, encyclopedias, and almanacs (print and digital)
- **Special collections**—government publications, historical documents, archival materials, and original artifacts

Research tools: The library contains many tools that direct you to materials:
- The online catalog allows you to search everything in the library.
- Subscription databases (Lexis-Nexis, EBSCOhost, ProQuest Direct) point you to abstracts and full-text articles.
- Internet access connects you with other library catalogs and online references.

Special services: Special services may also help you to complete research:
- Interlibrary loan allows you to obtain books and articles not available in your library or online.
- "Hold" allows you to request a book that is currently signed out.
- "Reserve" materials give you access to materials recommended by your instructors or heavily in demand.
- The reference desk can help you find information quickly, point you to the right resources, and help you with a search.
- Photocopiers, scanners, and presentation software help you perform and share your research.

Cross-Curricular Connection: As you advance in your field of study, become especially familiar with the reference holdings, journals, book stacks, and Web resources related to your major.

Searching the Catalog

Library materials are catalogued so they are easy to find. In most college libraries, books, videos, and other holdings are catalogued in an electronic database (see Figure 20.2). To find material, use book titles, author names, and related keyword searching.

Sample Electronic Catalog

fig. 20.2

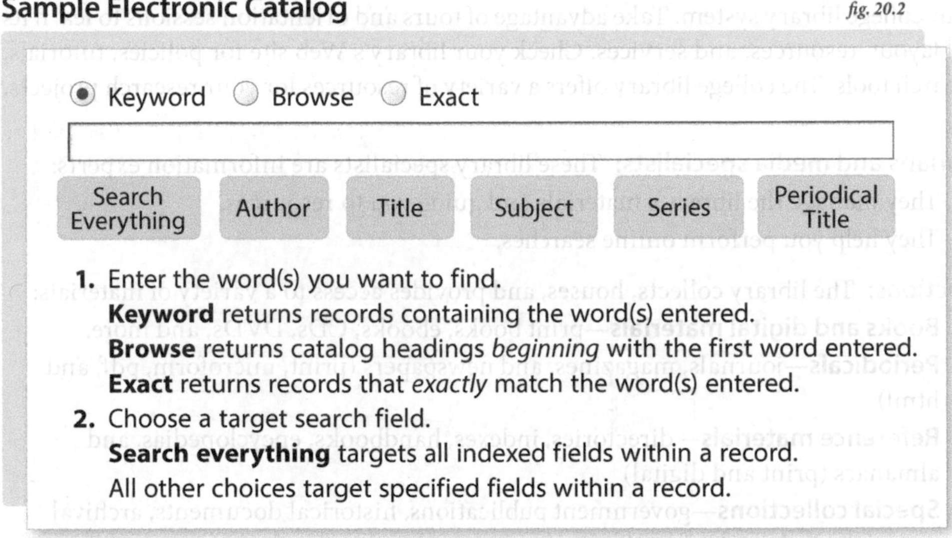

When you find a citation for a book or other resource, the result will provide some or all of the information in Figure 20.3. Use that information to determine whether the resource is worth exploring further and to figure out other avenues of research. Note that a number of items appearing in blue, underlined type provide links to related books and other resources in the catalog.

fig. 20.3

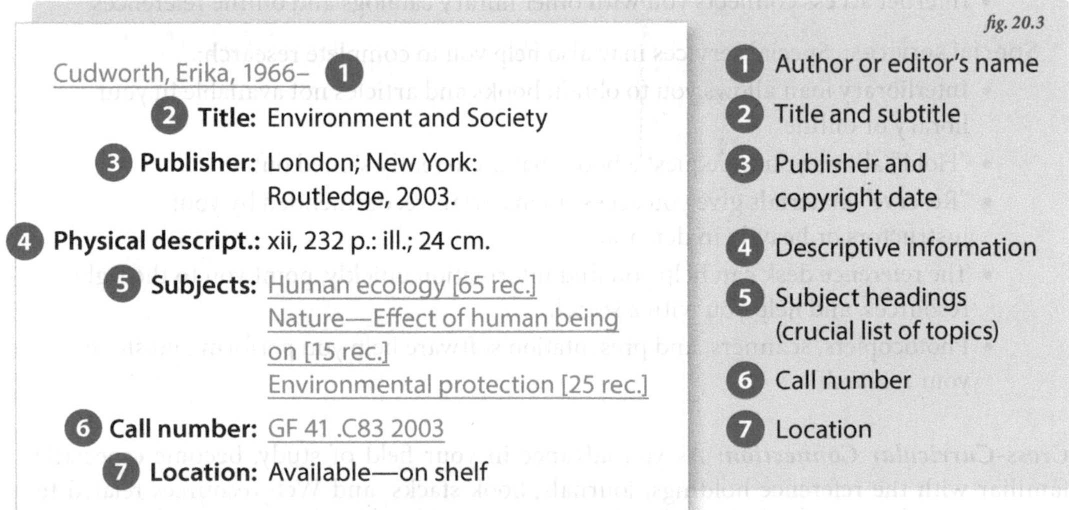

Locating Resources by Call Numbers

Library of Congress (LC) call numbers combine letters and numbers to specify a resource's broad subject area, topic, and authorship or title. Finding a book, DVD, or other item involves combining both the alphabetical and the numerical order. Here is a sample call number for *Arctic Refuge: A Vanishing Wilderness?*:

VIDEO QH84.1.A72 1990

subject area (**QH**) topic number (**84**) subtopic number (**1**) cutter number (**A72**)

To find this resource in the library, first note the tab VIDEO. Although not part of the call number, this locator may send you to a specific area of the library. Once there, follow the parts of the call number one at a time:

1. Find the library section on natural history containing videos with the "QH" designation.
2. Follow the numbers until you reach "84."
3. Within the "84" items, find those with the subtopic "1."
4. Use the cutter "A72" to locate the resource alphabetically with "A," and numerically with "72."

Note: In the LC system, pay careful attention to the arrangement of subject area letters, topic numbers, and subtopic numbers: Q98 comes before QH84; QH84 before QH8245; QH84.A72 before QH84.1.A72.

Classification Systems

The LC classification system combines letters and numbers. The Dewey decimal system, which is used in some libraries, uses numbers only. Figure 20.4 shows a list of the subject classes for both the LC and Dewey systems.

The Library of Congress and Dewey Decimal Systems

fig. 20.4

LC Category		Dewey Decimal	LC Category		Dewey Decimal
A	General Works	000–999	K	Law	340–349
B	Philosophy	100–199	L	Education	370–379
	Psychology	150–159	M	Music	780–789
	Religion	200–299	N	Fine Arts	700–799
C	History: Auxiliary Sciences	910–929	P	Language	800–899
				Literature	400–499
D	History: General and Old World	930–999	Q	Science	500–599
			R	Medicine	610–619
E–F	History of the Americas	970–979	S	Agriculture	630–639
G	Geography	910–919	T	Technology	600–699
	Anthropology	571–573	U	Military Science	355–359, 623
	Recreation	700–799	V	Naval Science	359, 623
H	Social Sciences	300–399	Z	Bibliography and Library Science	010–019
J	Political Science	320–329			020–029

Using Books in Research

Your college library contains a whole range of books for you to use. Unfortunately, for many research projects you simply don't have time to read an entire book, and rarely do the entire contents relate to your topic. Instead, use the strategies outlined below.

Approach the Book Systematically

1. **Identify the book type.** Trade books are typically written for a broad public and published by for-profit presses. Often written by experts, such books can be filled with reliable, useful information for a lay audience, though quality, depth, and reliability can vary. Example: *Flirting with* Pride & Prejudice: *Fresh Perspectives on the Original Chick-Lit Masterpiece*. By comparison, scholarly books are typically written for a specialized audience and college-level students. Published by university presses and other respected scholarly presses, such studies typically provide advanced research findings. Example: *Jane Austen on Screen* (Cambridge University Press).
2. **Check out front and back information.** The title and copyright pages give the book's full title and subtitle; the author's name; and publication information, including publication date and Library of Congress subject headings. The back may contain a note on the author's credentials and other publications.
3. **Scan the table of contents.** Examine the contents page to see what the book covers and how it is organized. Ask yourself which chapters are relevant to your project.
4. **Using key words, search the index.** Check the index for coverage and page locations of the topics most closely related to your project. Are there plenty of pages, or just a few? A scattered mention of key words likely represents more superficial coverage than concentrated, in-depth coverage.
5. **Skim the preface, foreword, or introduction.** The opening materials will often indicate the book's perspective, explain its origin, and preview its contents.
6. **Check appendices, glossaries, or bibliographies.** These special sections may be a good source of tables, graphics, definitions, statistics, and clues for further research.
7. **Carefully read appropriate chapters and sections.** Think through the material you've read and take good notes. (See pages 390–393.) Follow references to authors and other works to do further research on the topic. Study footnotes and endnotes for insights and leads to additional resources.

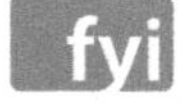

Consider these options for working productively with books:

- When you find a helpful book, browse nearby shelves for more books.
- To confirm a book's quality, check the Internet or a periodical database for a review.
- If your library subscribes to an e-book service such as NetLibrary, you have access to thousands of books in digital form. You can conduct electronic searches, browse or check out promising books, and read them online.

Using Reference Resources

Reference works, whether print or digital, are information-rich resources that can give you an overview of your topic, supply basic facts, share common knowledge about your topic, and offer ideas for focusing and furthering your research. While some reference resources are available on the free Web (see, for example, the discussion of Wikipedia on pages 424–425), your library offers you excellent access to reference resources in both print and digital formats. Consider options like those below.

Check Reference Works That Supply Information

- **Encyclopedias** supply facts and overviews for topics arranged alphabetically. General encyclopedias cover many fields of knowledge: *Encyclopedia Britannica* (online version). Specialized encyclopedias focus on a single topic: *Encyclopedia of American Film Comedy.*
- **Almanacs, yearbooks, and statistical resources,** normally published annually or posted regularly, contain diverse facts. For example, the www.census.gov Web site provides data on population, geography, politics, employment, business, science, industry, and more.
- **Vocabulary resources** supply information on languages. General dictionaries, such as *The American Heritage College Dictionary,* supply definitions and histories for a whole range of words. Specialized dictionaries define words common to a field, topic, or group: *The New Harvard Dictionary of Music.* Bilingual dictionaries translate words from one language to another.
- **Biographical resources** supply information about people. General biographies cover a broad range of people. Other biographies focus on people from a specific group. ***Examples:*** *Who's Who in America, World Artists 1980–1990.*
- **Directories** supply contact information for people, groups, and organizations. ***Examples:*** *USPS ZIP Code Lookup and Address Information* (online).

Check Reference Works That Are Research Tools

- **Guides and handbooks** help readers explore specific topics: *The Handbook of North American Indians, A Guide to Prairie Fauna.*
- **Indexes** point you to useful resources. Whether general or specialized, such indexes are available online in databases your library subscribes to. (See pages 414–417.)
- **Bibliographies** list resources on a specific topic. A good, current bibliography can be used as an example when you compile your own bibliography on a topic.
- **Abstracts,** like indexes, direct you to articles on a particular topic. But abstracts also summarize those materials so you learn whether a resource is relevant before you invest time in locating and reading it. Such abstracts are typically incorporated into many online subscription databases.

Finding Articles Via Databases

Periodicals are publications or broadcasts produced at regular intervals (daily, weekly, monthly, quarterly). Although some periodicals are broad in their subject matter and audience, as a rule they focus on a narrow range of topics geared toward a particular audience.

- **Daily newspapers and newscasts** provide up-to-date information on current events, opinions, and trends—from politics to natural disasters *(Wall Street Journal, USA Today, The NewsHour).*
- **Weekly and monthly magazines** generally provide more in-depth information on a wide range of topics *(Time, Newsweek, 60 Minutes).*
- **Journals**, generally published quarterly, provide specialized scholarly information for a narrowly focused audience *(English Journal).*

With thousands of periodicals available, how do you find helpful articles? Learn (a) which search tools your library offers, (b) which periodicals it has available in which forms, and (c) how to gain access to those periodicals.

Search Online Databases

If your library subscribes to EBSCOhost, Lexis-Nexis, or another database service, use keyword searching (see pages 382–383) to find citations on your topic. You might start with the general version of such databases, such as EBSCOhost's Academic Search Premier, which provides access to more than 4,100 scholarly publications covering all disciplines.

- **Basic Search:** Figure 20.5 shows an EBSCOhost search screen for a search on hybrid electric cars. Notice how limiters, expanders, and other advanced features help you find the highest-quality materials.

fig. 20.5

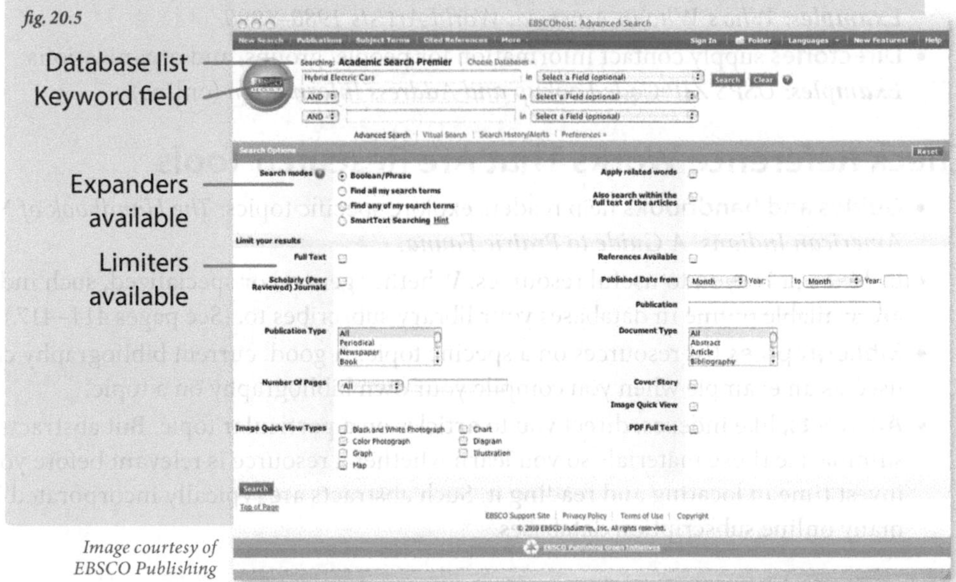

Image courtesy of EBSCO Publishing

- **Advanced Search:** A more focused research strategy would involve turning to specialized databases, which are available for virtually every discipline and are often an option within search services such as EBSCOhost (for example, Business Source Elite, PsycINFO, ERIC) and Lexis-Nexis (for example, Legal, Medical, and Business databases). If a basic search turns up little, turn to specialized databases, seeking help from a librarian if necessary. For a list of specialized databases, see page 417.

Particularly if you need articles published before 1985, you may need to go to the *Readers' Guide to Periodical Literature* or another print index. While databases are converting pre-1985 articles to digital form (for example, the JSTOR database), many excellent periodical articles are available only in print. To use the *Reader's Guide,* consult a librarian.

Generate Citation Lists of Promising Articles

Your database search should generate lists of citations, brief descriptions of articles that were flagged through keywords in titles, subject terms, abstracts, and so on. For example, a search focused on hybrid electric cars leads to the results shown in Figure 20.6. At this point, study the results and do the following:

- Refine the search by narrowing or expanding it.
- Mark specific citations for "capture" or further study.
- Re-sort the results.
- Follow links in a specific citation to further information.

fig. 20.6

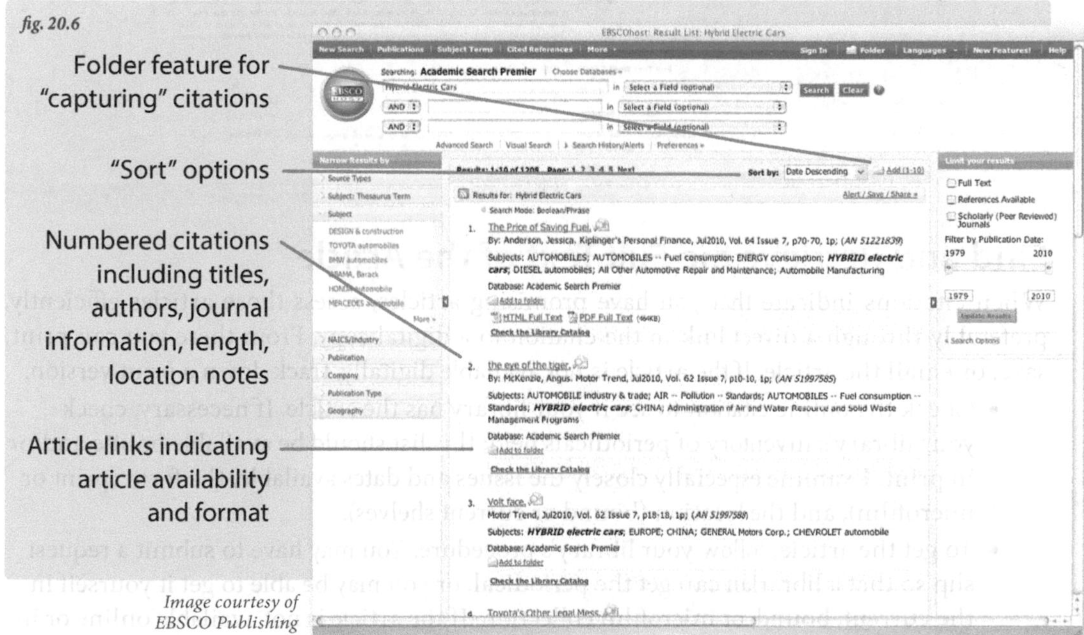

Image courtesy of EBSCO Publishing

Study Citations and Capture Identifying Information

By studying citations (especially abstracts), you can determine three things:

- Is this article relevant to your research?
- Is an electronic, full-text version available?
- If not, does the library have this periodical?

To develop your working bibliography (see pages 388–389), you should also "capture" the article's identifying details by using the save, print, or email function, or by recording the periodical's title, the issue and date, and the article's title and page numbers. These functions are shown in the EBSCOhost citation in Figure 20.7.

fig. 20.7

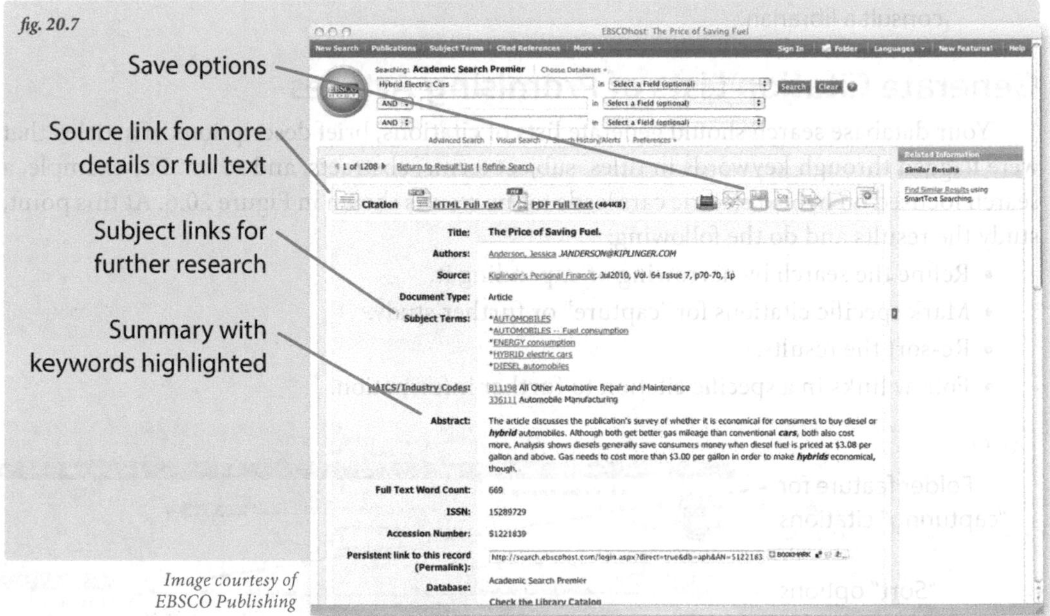

Image courtesy of EBSCO Publishing

Find and Retrieve the Full Text of the Article

When citations indicate that you have promising articles, access those articles efficiently, preferably through a direct link in the citation to a digital copy. From there you can print, save, or email the article. If the article is not available digitally, track down a print version:

- Check the online citation to see if your library has the article. If necessary, check your library's inventory of periodicals held; this list should be available online and/or in print. Examine especially closely the issues and dates available, the form (print or microfilm), and the location (bound or current shelves).
- To get the article, follow your library's procedure. You may have to submit a request slip so that a librarian can get the periodical, or you may be able to get it yourself in the current, bound, or microfilm collection. If the article is not available online or in your library, use interlibrary loan.

Databases for Disciplines

Most libraries offer access to databases from a wide range of disciplines. Check your library's Web site for access to databases like these:

- **Agricola** offers citations from the National Agricultural Library group—with materials focused on issues from animal science to food and nutrition.
- **ARTbibliographies Modern** abstracts articles, books, catalogs, and other resources on modern and contemporary art.
- **CAIRSS for Music** offers bibliographic citations for articles on music-related topics, from music education to music therapy.
- **Communication & Mass Media Complete** offers access to resources on topics like public speaking and TV broadcasting.
- **Engineering E-journal Search Engine** offers free, full-text access to more than 150 online engineering journals.
- **ERIC** offers citations, abstracts, and digests for more than 980 journals in the education field.
- **First Search**, a fee-based information service, offers access to more than 30 scholarly databases in a range of disciplines.
- **GPO**, the Government Printing Office, offers access to records for U.S. government documents (e.g., reports, hearings, judicial rules, addresses, and so on).
- **Health Source** offers access to abstracts, indexing, and full-text material on health-related topics, from nutrition to sports medicine.
- **Ingenta** offers citations for more than 25,000 journals, mostly in the sciences.
- **JSTOR** offers full-text access to scholarly articles in a full range of disciplines, articles once available only in print.
- **Math Database** offers article citations for international mathematics research.
- **Medline** offers access to journals in medicine and medicine-related disciplines through references, citations, and abstracts.
- **MLA Bibliography** provides bibliographic citations for articles addressing a range of modern-language and literature-related topics.
- **National Environmental Publications Internet Site (NEPIS)** offers access to more than 6,000 EPA documents (full text, online).
- **PsycINFO** offers access to materials in psychology and psychology-related fields (for example, social work, criminology, organizational behavior).
- **Scirus** indexes science resources, citing article titles and authors, source publication information, and lines of text indicating the article's content.
- **Vocation and Career Collection** offers full-text access to more than 400 trade- and industry-related periodicals.
- **Worldwide Political Science Abstracts** offers bibliographic citations in politics-related fields, from public policy to international law.

Understanding Internet Basics

Did you know that the World Wide Web and the Internet are not the same? Do you know what the *deep Web* is? Can you identify the parts of a Web page? These two pages provide basic definitions and explanations of the digital world.

- The **Internet** is a vast array of interconnected computers and computer networks. It began in 1969 with the ARPANET, a connection of U.S. government computers. Since then, the Internet has expanded into a worldwide system. Email, cell phones, and satellites all access and use the Internet, as do people on the World Wide Web.
- The **World Wide Web** is a huge collection of Web sites and pages on the Internet, accessible through the hypertext transfer protocol (HTTP). Put simply, this protocol is a set of rules that allow computers to trade information. The World Wide Web was begun in 1989 by a British engineer named Tim Berners-Lee.
- A **uniform resource locator (URL)** is the Web address for each page available on the World Wide Web. Just as every home has a specific street address, every Web site has a specific Web address that allows other computers to find and access it. (See Figure 20.8.)

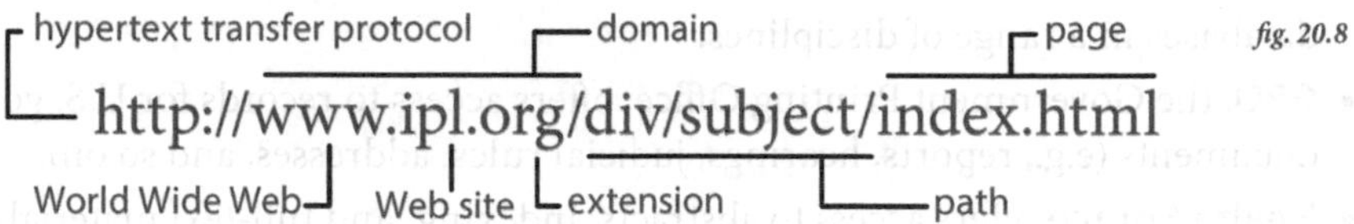

fig. 20.8

- A **domain name** is the Web site address, often beginning with www and ending with an extension that indicates what type of site it is. Here is a list of common domain types:

  .com a commercial or business site
  .gov a government site, for federal, state, or local government
  .edu an educational site
  .org a site for a nonprofit organization
  .net a site for an organization that belongs to the Internet's infrastructure
  .mil a military site
  .biz a business site
  .info an information site

  Such domain names apply particularly to U.S. Web sites. If a Web site originates in another country, the domain typically is a two-letter nation abbreviation. Examples: .ca for Canada; .uk for United Kingdom. Keep this in mind as you access Web sites for your research.

- A **Web browser** is a program on your computer that provides access to the Web. Common browsers include Chrome, Internet Explorer, Firefox, and Safari.

- A **Web page** is a specific grouping of information on the Web (Figure 20.9). Web pages often include text, graphics, photographs, videos, and hyperlinks—which are words or graphics that can be clicked to take the user to different Web pages.
- A **search engine** is a specialized Web page that allows you to find specific terms on sites throughout the Web. Here are some popular search engines:

Google	http://www.google.com
Bing	http://www.bing.com
Yahoo	http://www.yahoo.com

- A **metasearch engine** is a Web page that searches several other search engines at once, compiling the information. Here are some popular metasearch engines:

Ask	http://www.ask.com
Dog Pile	http://www.dogpile.com
Ixquick	http://www.ixquick.com

- A **deep-Web** tool is an Internet search engine or database that can access materials not available to basic search engines, materials found on what is called the *deep Web.*

Deeper Web	http://www.deeperweb.com

Common Web page Elements

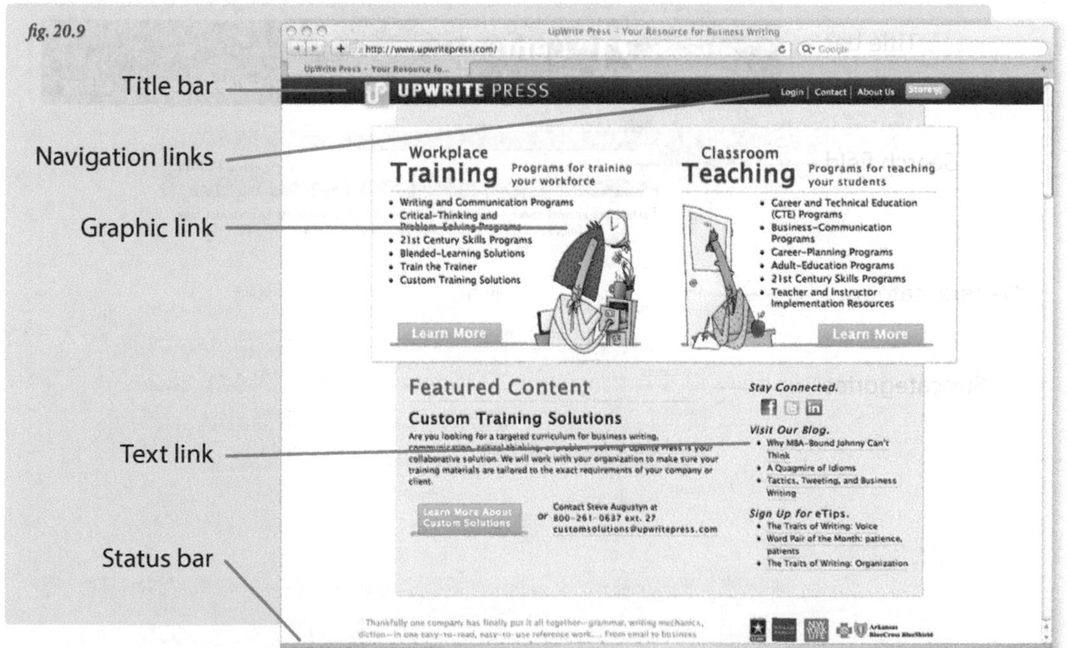

Image courtesy of Thoughtful Learning

Using a Subject Guide/Directory

A subject tree, sometimes called a *subject guide* or *directory*, lists Web sites that have been organized into categories by experts who have reviewed those sites. As such, a subject tree includes sites selected for reliability and quality. For this reason, directories may prove a useful tool for your project, even though they are declining in number and amount of traffic, given the dominance of search engines.

1. **Search out the subject trees available to you.** Check whether your library subscribes to a database in which subject experts have cataloged Internet resources by topic. Here are some common subject directories:

   WWW Virtual Library vlib.org/Overview.html
   DMOZ www.dmoz.org/docs/en/about.html

2. **Follow categories from broad to specific.** A subject tree is arranged from general to specific, so you will need to begin by clicking on a broad category to see a more selective list. Clicking on subcategories will take you to progressively more focused lists. Read the name of a site, review the information beneath the name, check out the domain and extension, and decide if the site is worth exploring. If so, click on it. If not, go back and continue your search. Figure 20.10 illustrates common subject guide elements.

Common Subject Guide Elements

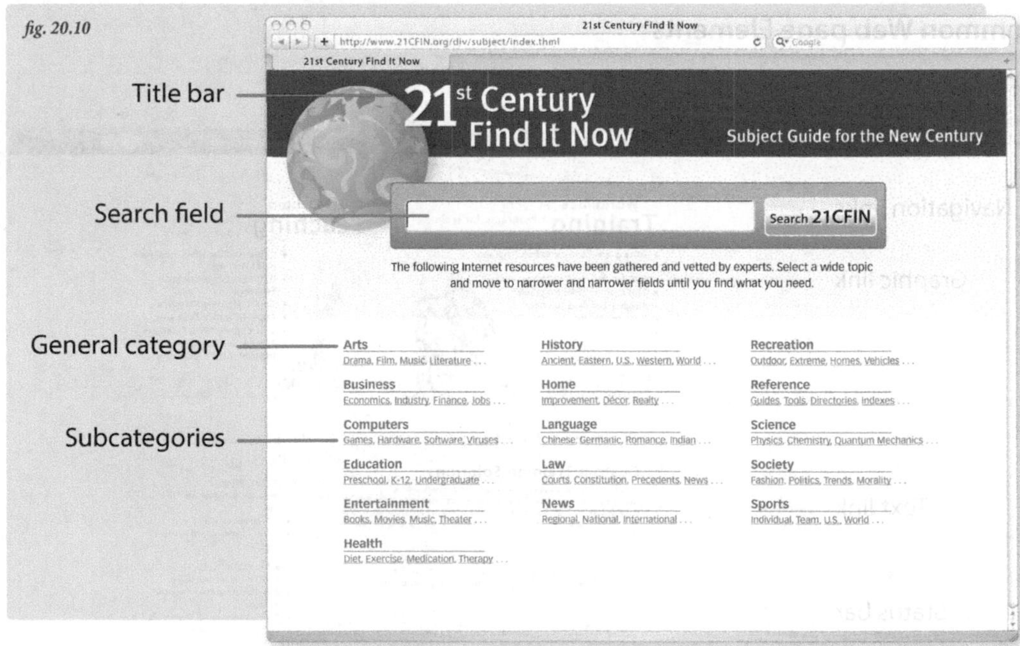

Using Search and Metasearch

Search and metasearch engines provide quick and powerful access to much of the content of the Web. They are invaluable tools for researchers. This page gives tips for getting the most out of your searches, and the next two pages look at Web searching in depth.

1. **Select effective keywords:** Keywords are words or phrases that the search engine looks for across the Web. The more specific a keyword or phrase is, the more tightly a search will be focused. Here are a set of keywords for the research topic of "games used to simulate real-world scenarios":

	Keyword	Result
General	**game**	**This general term will produce a very unfocused list of millions of Web sites, ranging from stores selling games to recipes for cooking game.**
	simulation	**This more-specific term will narrow the search considerably, but will show off-topic sites such as suppliers of simulated wood products.**
	simulation game	**This set of keywords is much more specific, but the engine will also find sites using both words but not in combination.**
Specific	**"simulation game"**	**The quotation marks around this search will turn up only sites that use the exact phrase "simulation game."**

2. **Use Boolean operators:** In addition to using quotation marks, you can use words and symbols to make your search specific. (See also page 383.)

game and **war**	*and* indicates sites with both terms
game + war	+ indicates sites with both terms
game not **war**	*not* indicates sites with the first term but not the second
game – war	– indicates sites with the first term but not the second
game or **simulation**	*or* indicates sites with either term

3. **Act on search results:** Once a search engine has generated a list of possible sites, you need to survey the results and act on them.
   - Read the name of the site and determine how the term is used.
   - Review the domain and extension to decide if you will click it.
   - Look for information and links.

Using Search Engines as Research Tools

Like millions of people, you probably "Google it" when you have a question. But how should you use search engines for college research projects? A search engine is a program that automatically scours a large amount of Web material using keywords and commands that you submit. In that respect, the search is only as productive as the terms you use, the quality of the search program, and the amount and areas of the Web that the engine searches. When you use search engines, be aware of the issues below, and use the tips on the following page to work around the limitations discussed.

- **Web Coverage:** Even though the largest search engines search billions of Web resources, those pages represent just a portion of the Web—as little as 20 percent. The point to keep in mind is that any given search engine is not searching the entire Web for you and may be focusing on particular kinds of pages and documents. Moreover, a given engine may not be searching each resource in its entirety but only certain portions (e.g., citations) or up to a certain size of the document.
- **Resource Ranking:** A search engine returns results in a ranking of resources based on complex mathematical algorithms—a weighing of a variety of criteria that differ from one engine to the next. One criterion used is the number of times your keywords appear in a given resource. A second criterion might be the number and type of links to a given page—a measure, in other words, of the site's importance or popularity on the Web. A third criterion relates to your search history: given sites that you have looked at in the past, what types of sites do you prefer? Algorithms answer this question by *personalizing* your search, potentially creating what Eli Pariser calls a "filter bubble"—results restricted to your interests and biases. One more point: organizations on the Web work very hard to make sure that their pages get ranked near the top of searches; some companies hire consultants to help achieve this result or even try to fool the programs. In other words, what you are getting in your search is not necessarily an objective listing of the most relevant and reliable resources for an academic research project.
- **Search Habits:** Using search engines is complicated not just by algorithms but by the habits of users themselves. Studies suggest, for example, that very few users look past the first three hits returned by a search; in fact, only one percent of searchers go past the first ten hits. (You can understand, then, why some organizations work so hard to get into that top-ten list for specific keyword searches.) Moreover, very few users go on to refine their search after the initial results, supposedly satisfied with what they have found, although studies also suggest that few users can effectively evaluate the returned resources in terms of their quality, authority, objectivity, and timeliness (currency of information). The implications for your college research projects are clear: such search habits rarely lead to quality resources that you can use in an academic project.

Use Search Engines Well

Given how search engines work, what practices should you follow in using them for an academic research project? Obviously, start by following the assignment's restrictions about using free-Web resources. But here are four additional guidelines:

1. **Restrict search-engine use to specific purposes.** Generally, a search engine is useful for college research projects in these circumstances:
    - You have a very narrow topic in mind or an exact question you need answered.
    - You have a highly specific word or phrase to use in your search.
    - You want a large number of results.
    - You are looking for a specific type of Internet file.
    - You have the time to sort the material for reliability.
2. **Learn to do advanced searches.** Basic searches tend to lead to basic results. Most search engines actually allow you to do quite complex searches through advanced-search screens. With these, you can employ Boolean logic to a degree, use limiters and expanders, and refine your results in other ways. Study the search engine's help pages for instructions on how to benefit from these advanced-searching techniques.
3. **Approach results with suspicion.** Given the wide-ranging quality and reliability of material on the free Web, it is imperative that you evaluate resources that you find through search engines. See "Evaluating Online Sources" on pages 426–429.
4. **Use search engines that seem to give you more quality results.** Conduct the same search using a variety of search engines and compare the results. While you generally want to choose search engines that cover a large portion of the Web, offer quality indexing, and give you high-powered search capabilities, you also want to consider a search-engine's information focus: try out search engines whose goals seem more obviously focused on academics. Consider, for example, Google Scholar. While it indexes just a small portion of all published articles, Google Scholar can help you build citations from a variety of sources, citations you can then find in your library's subscription databases. Moreover, it ranks articles by weighing the full text, the author, the publication, and frequency of citation in other sources.

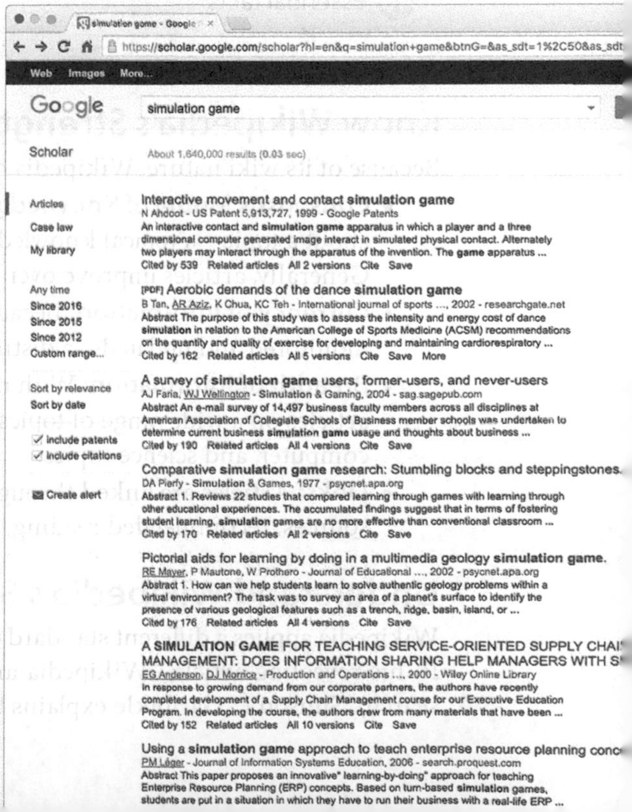

Google and the Google logo are registered trademarks of Google Inc., used with permission.

Understanding the Uses and Limits of Wikipedia

You likely recognize Figure 20.11—an article from Wikipedia. From Wikipedia's beginning in 2001 to today, a large population of volunteer writers and editors has made it a top-ten Internet-traffic site. But is Wikipedia acceptable for college-level research? Put simply, Wikipedia is a controversial resource for academic research.

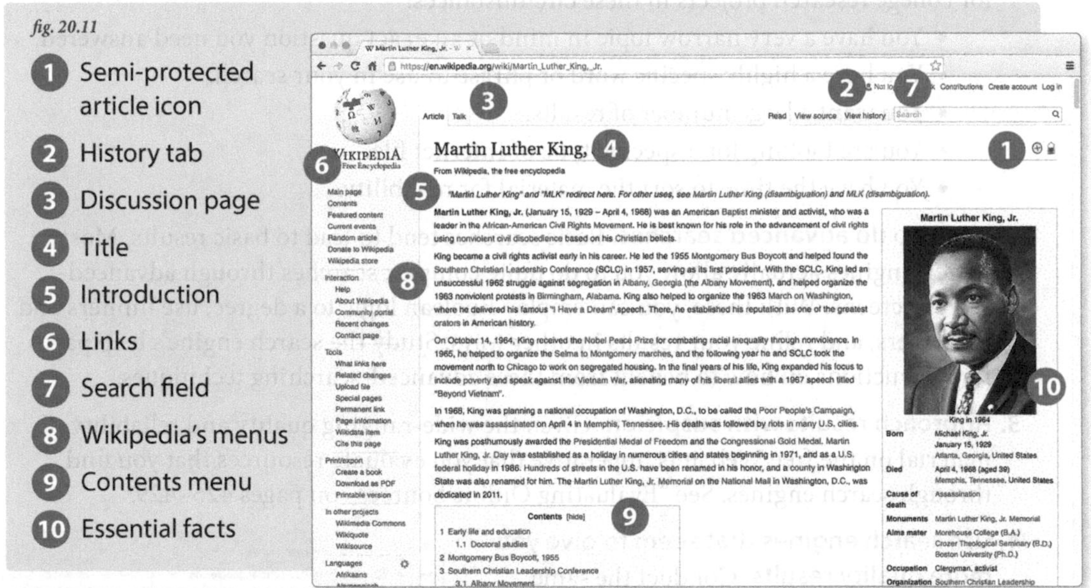

fig. 20.11

Image courtesy of Wikipedia

Know Wikipedia's Strengths

Because of its wiki nature, Wikipedia offers researchers a number of advantages.

- **Consensus Model of Knowledge:** Articles represent a collaborative agreement about a topic—a topical knowledge base that is fair and fairly comprehensive. Generally, articles improve over time, offering "open-source" knowledge.
- **Currency of Information:** Because they are Web-based, articles are regularly monitored and updated—a distinct advantage over print encyclopedias.
- **Breadth of Information:** With its size and global community, Wikipedia offers articles on a wide range of topics—especially strong in pop culture, current events, computer, and science topics.
- **Links:** Articles are linked throughout so that readers can pursue associated topics, sources, recommended reading, and related categories.

Understand Wikipedia's Standards for Truth

Wikipedia applies a different standard of truth than more traditional sources of information. In his revealing article, "Wikipedia and the Meaning of *Truth*" (available through a Web search), Simson L. Garfinkle explains this standard of truth.

Know Wikipedia's Weaknesses

In some ways, Wikipedia's strengths are closely related to its weaknesses for college-level research. Consider these issues:

- **Popularity Model of Knowledge:** The dynamics of popularity can lead to bias, imbalance, and errors. In some ways, this approach minimizes the value of training, education, and expertise while promoting a kind of democracy of knowledge.
- **Anonymity of Authorship:** Wikipedia allows contributors to remain anonymous. Researchers thus have little way of checking credentials and credibility.
- **Variable Quality of Content:** While many well-established articles are quite stable, balanced, and comprehensive, other articles can be partial, driven by a biased perspective, erroneous, and poorly sourced.
- **Variable Coverage:** Wikipedia's strength in some content areas is matched by gaps and incompleteness in other content areas.
- **Vulnerability to Vandalism:** Wikipedia has a number of processes in place to limit people from harming articles with misinformation, with the result that most vandalism is corrected within hours, but some errors have persisted for months.
- **Tertiary Nature of Information:** For most research projects, Wikipedia articles function as tertiary sources—reports of reports of research. As such, Wikipedia articles are not substantial enough for academic projects.

Use Wikipedia Cautiously

Based on Wikipedia's strengths and weaknesses, follow these guidelines:

1. **Respect your assignment.** Instructors may give you varied instruction about using Wikipedia. Respect their guidelines.
2. **Verify Wikipedia information.** If you use information from Wikipedia, also use other more traditional sources to verify that information.
3. **Use Wikipedia as a semi-authoritative reference source.** Generally, the more academic your research assignment, the less you should rely on Wikipedia articles, which are essentially sources of basic and background information.
4. **Use Wikipedia as one starting point.** From a Wikipedia article, you can learn what is considered "open-source" knowledge on your topic, gather ideas for developing a topic, find links to related topics and other resources, and begin to build a bibliography.
5. **Study individual articles to get a sense of their reliability.** When you find a Wikipedia article relevant to your research project, check the article for quality and stability. Use the evaluation criteria on the following pages, but also check the article's history, its discussion page, any tags or icons indicating the article's state, and the "what links here" link in the toolbox at the left of the screen.

Evaluating Online Sources

The Internet contains a wealth of information, but much of it is not suitable for college-level research writing. The information may be incorrect, biased, outdated, plagiarized, or otherwise unreliable. These pages discuss issues to watch for.

Assignment Restrictions

Before engaging any Web resources, carefully review your assignment and note any restrictions on what type of sources may be used. If Web resources are allowed, abide by the number or percentage indicated in the assignment.

Author/Organization

When using Web resources, make sure the sites are sponsored by legitimate, recognizable organizations: government agencies, nonprofit groups, and educational institutions. For most projects, avoid relying on personal or special-interest sites, as well as chat rooms, blogs, news groups, or wikis. (These sources may help you explore a topic, but they do not provide scholarly material suitable for most research writing.)

Balance or Bias

Be aware of the purpose of a site or an article. Editorials and reviews, for example, express the point of view of a given author but are not sources for unbiased information. Unless your purpose is to show the author's point of view or point out two sides of an argument, avoid sources that show a bias toward or against a specific region, country, political party, industry, gender, race, ethnic group, or religion. Also, avoid sites that promote a specific cause, product, service, or belief.

Quality of Information

Test the quality of information on a site. Note whether the information is current (when was it posted/updated last) and check it against other sources for corroboration. Also, favor sites with a depth of information and those that show they truly engage their topic rather than treating it superficially.

Quality of Writing and Design

Avoid sites that show sloppy editing and poor design. These surface flaws can reveal a lack of scholarly rigor or serious commitment on the part of the site's creators. At the same time, don't be fooled by flashy sites where the design masks problems with the content.

Evaluation Checklist

Use this checklist to assess the reliability of Web sources. The more items you check off, the more reliable the source is.

Assignment Restrictions

_____ **1.** Does the source fit with the type and number allowed in the assignment?

Author/Organization

_____ **2.** Is the person or organization behind the site reliable?

_____ **3.** Is contact information for the person or organization provided?

_____ **4.** Is the site well known and well connected in the field?

_____ **5.** Does the site have a clear "About Us" page and mission statement?

Balance or Bias

_____ **6.** Is the material on the site balanced and unbiased?

_____ **7.** Does the site avoid unfair and inflammatory language?

_____ **8.** Does the site avoid pushing a particular product, cause, service, or belief?

_____ **9.** Does the site provide ample support for its claims?

_____ **10.** Does the site avoid logical fallacies and twisted statistics? (See pages 323–326.)

Quality of Information

_____ **11.** Is the material current?

_____ **12.** Is the Web site often updated?

_____ **13.** Is the Web site information-rich?

_____ **14.** Is the information backed up by other reputable print and online sources?

Quality of Writing and Design

_____ **15.** Is the text free of errors in punctuation, spelling, and grammar?

_____ **16.** Is the site effectively and clearly designed?

Gts / Shutterstock.com

Sample Evaluations

Assignment Restrictions

- The site shown in Figure 20.12 would be appropriate for most assignments about the life and work of William Faulkner, as long as free-Web sources are allowed.

Author/ Organization

- This site is sponsored by the University of Mississippi, a scholarly source for information, and the article's author, Dr. John B. Padgett, is an authority on Faulkner.

Balance or Bias

- The site clearly extols Faulkner as a great writer but does not shy from showing his shortcomings. The claims are fair and amply supported, without logical fallacies.

Quality of Information

- The Web site is current, often updated, and information-rich. It is also connected to many other Faulkner resources available on the Web.

Quality of Writing and Design

- The site is well designed, with easy navigation, readable text, informative headings, helpful photos, and strong links. The text is well written and well edited.

fig. 20.12

MWP: William Faulkner (1897–1962)

http://www.olemiss.edu/mwp/dir/faulkner_william/

▸ Publications
▸ Other Features
▸ Writer Listings

Go to

- Gallery
- Publications
- Bibliography
- Media Adaptations
- Internet Resources

See also:

▶ **Book Info:**

Faulkner in the Twenty-first Century (February 2003)
William Faulkner: Six Decades of Criticism (October 2002)
Absalom, Absalom! (September 2002)
Faulkner and the Politics of Reading, by Karl Zender (August 2002)
Faulkner and Postmodernism, edited by John Duvall and Ann Abadie (July 2002)
New Orleans Sketches (June 2002)
The

William Faulkner

© The Cofield Collection
William Faulkner

The man himself never stood taller than five feet, six inches tall, but in the realm of American literature, William Faulkner is a giant. More than simply a renowned Mississippi writer, the Nobel Prize-winning novelist and short story writer is acclaimed throughout the world as one of the twentieth century's greatest writers, one who transformed his "postage stamp" of native soil into an apocryphal setting in which he explored, articulated, and challenged "the old verities and truths of the heart." During what is generally considered his period of greatest artistic achievement, from *The Sound and the Fury* in 1929 to *Go Down, Moses* in 1942, Faulkner accomplished in a little over a decade more artistically than most writers accomplish over a lifetime of writing. It is one of the more remarkable feats of American literature, how a young man who never graduated from high school, never received a college degree, living in a small town in the poorest state in the nation, all the while balancing a growing family of dependents and impending financial ruin, could during the Great Depression write a series of novels all set in the same small Southern county — novels that include *As I Lay Dying*, *Light in August*, and above all, *Absalom, Absalom!* — that would one day be recognized as among the greatest novels ever written by an American.

The Early Years

Related Links & Info

© The Cofield Collection
William Clark Falkner

William Cuthbert Falkner (as his name was then spelled) was born on September 25, 1897, in New Albany, Mississippi, the first of four sons born to Murry and Maud Butler Falkner. He was named after his great-grandfather, William Clark Falkner, the "Old Colonel," who had been killed eight years earlier in a duel with his former business partner in the streets of Ripley, Mississippi. A lawyer, politician, planter, businessman, Civil War colonel, railroad financier, and finally a best-selling writer (of the novel *The White Rose of Memphis*), the Old Colonel, even in death, loomed as a larger-than-life model of personal and professional success for his male descendants.

A few days before William's fifth birthday, the Falkners moved to Oxford, Mississippi, at the urging of Murry's father, John Wesley Thompson Falkner. Called the "Young Colonel" out of homage to his father rather than to actual military service, the younger

Courtesy of Dr. John B. Padgett/Brevard College

- As a blog, the site shown in Figure 20.13 would not be appropriate for an assignment about the life and work of William Faulkner. A site such as this should be recognized as reflective only of the writer's opinion, not of reliable information or fact.

- There is no author or organization listed for this Web site. The domain name—myviewsonliterature.wordpress.com—shows that this is a personal opinion blog. Its lack of connection to other Web sites shows it represents an isolated opinion.

- This blog post shows a strong bias against William Faulkner. The few facts cited inadequately support the writer's main point, and logical fallacies are apparent. The tone of the post is unscholarly, with inflammatory language.

- Though this Web site is frequently updated, the blog post does not represent current scholarship about William Faulkner. The Web site is information-poor and is not backed up by any reputable print or online sources.

- The site has an amateurish design and numerous errors, including the persistent misspelling of William Faulkner's name. The writing is slipshod, and the editing is poor.

fig. 20.13

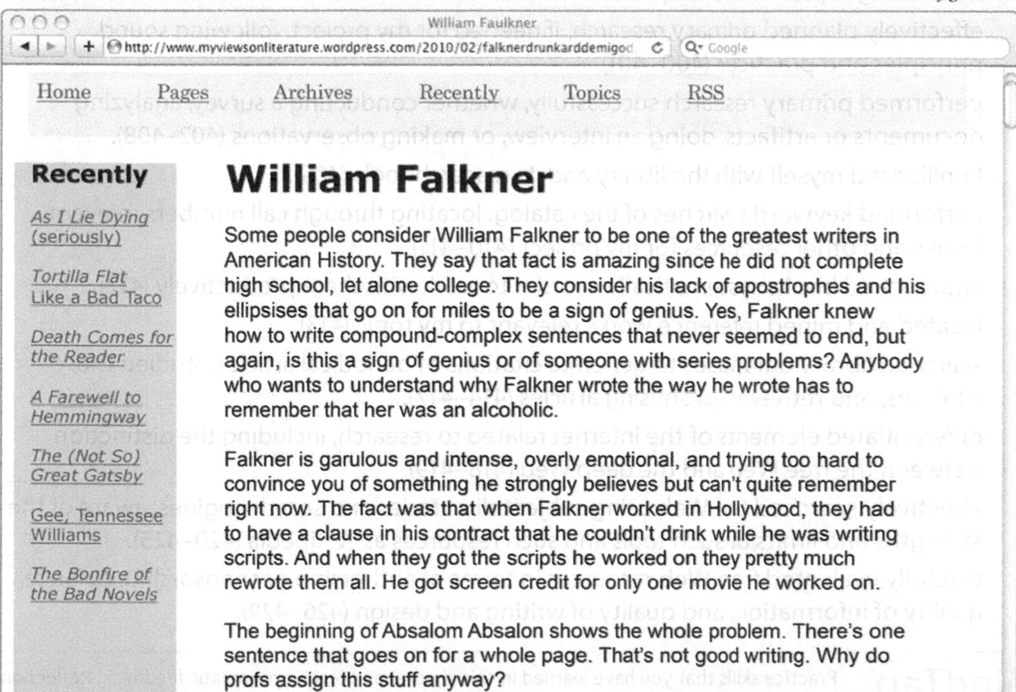

Critical Thinking and Writing: Applications

Once you have studied the research methods in this chapter, you might apply what you have learned through a number of activities.

1. **Research Map:** Think about a research project that you have done or are doing now. How might primary research and library research (scholarly books and journals) strengthen your writing? Why not do all your research on the free Web?
2. **Information Orientation:** Working with your library's Web site and its orientation tools, identify where you can physically and/or digitally locate books, reference resources, and journals. Then explore your library's handouts and Web site for information about Internet research. What services, support, and access does the library provide?
3. **Living Today:** Brainstorm issues related to food production, consumption, or culture. Choosing one issue, use your library's tools to find and evaluate print books and periodical articles. Then do a Web search of the topic, comparing the results.
4. **Public Texts:** Using the variety of methods outlined in this chapter, work with classmates to search the Internet for information on a controversial topic, event, person, or place. Analyze and evaluate the range of Web information you find.

Learning-Objectives Checklist ✓

Have you achieved this chapter's learning objectives? Check your progress with the items below, revisiting topics in the chapter as needed. I have . . .

____ effectively planned primary research, if needed for my project, following sound principles and practices (400–401).

____ performed primary research successfully, whether conducting a survey, analyzing documents or artifacts, doing an interview, or making observations (402–408).

____ familiarized myself with the library and its research tools (409).

____ performed keyword searches of the catalog, locating through call numbers relevant books and other resources for my project (410–411).

____ approached books systematically in order to work with them productively (412).

____ located and mined reference works relevant to my topic (413).

____ searched library databases to generate citations of periodical articles, studied those citations, and retrieved promising articles (414–417).

____ differentiated elements of the Internet related to research, including the distinction between the free Web and the deep Web (418–419).

____ effectively searched the Web using subject directories and search engines, aware of the strengths and limits of such tools and such resources as Wikipedia (420–425).

____ carefully evaluated free-Web resources in terms of authorship or sponsorship, balance, quality of information, and quality of writing and design (426–429).

MindTap® Practice skills that you have learned in this chapter and receive automatic feedback. Reflect on your writing process.

Chapter 21

Building Credibility: Avoiding Plagiarism

MindTap®

Understand the goals of the chapter and complete a warm-up activity online.

Learning Objectives

By working through this chapter, you will be able to

- differentiate between poor and effective uses of sources in your writing.
- define and recognize plagiarism.
- explain why plagiarism is a serious academic offense.
- prevent plagiarism within your own writing.
- distinguish other source abuses and avoid them in your writing.

"That's incredible!" is normally a positive exclamation of amazement. But maybe it's an exclamation that you do not want to hear about your research writing, if "incredible" means "unbelievable." If your paper is unbelievable, your credibility as a researcher and a writer is seriously damaged.

Obviously, you want to draft a strong, well-documented paper—a credible discussion of your carefully researched topic. While the next chapter focuses on drafting such a paper, this chapter prepares you for drafting by explaining how to build and maintain credibility. It starts with these principles:

1. Write the paper yourself. Take ownership of your thinking, research, and writing.
2. Be honest, accurate, and measured.
3. Show respect to your reader, the topic, and opposing viewpoints.
4. Establish your credentials by showing that you have done careful research.

Visually Speaking Copying—what's wrong with it? Using Figure 21.1 as a starting point, reflect on the nature of copying as an issue in life and in research.

Jason Benz Bennee / Shutterstock.com

fig. 21.1

Developing Credibility through Source Use

Your credibility—how fully readers trust and believe you—is partly rooted in how well you treat your sources. While abuses such as distorting a source's ideas damage your credibility, good practices enhance it. Contrast the passages below and on the next page.

Writing with Poor Use of Sources

A poor paper might read like a recitation of unconnected facts, unsupported opinions, or undigested quotations. It may contain contradictory information or illogical conclusions. A source's ideas may be distorted or taken out of context. At its worst, poor source use involves plagiarism.

The writing offers weak generalizations in several spots.

Material from sources is clearly borrowed but not referenced through in-text citation.

A passage from an online source is copy-and-pasted into the paper without credit.

The writer uses a visual without indicating the source or effectively discussing its meaning.

It goes without saying that cell phone usage has really increased a lot, from the 1
beginning of the cell phone's history until now. How many people still don't have a cell—basically, no one! The advantages of cell phones are obvious, but has anyone really thought about the downside of this technological innovation? For example, there's "rinxiety," where people believe that their cell phones are ringing but they're not. Two-thirds of cell users have reported this feeling, which some experts believe to be a rewiring of the nervous system similar to phantom limb pain, while other experts thinks it's about the pitch of cell rings. It's not good.

But the most serious problem with cell phones is without a doubt driving 2
while talking or texting. Due to the increasing complexity of mobile phones -often more like mobile computers in their available uses– it has introduced additional difficulties for law enforcement officials in being able to tell one usage from another as drivers use their devices. This is more apparent in those countries who ban both hand-held and hands-free usage, rather than those who have banned hand-held use only, as officials cannot easily tell which function of the mobile phone is being used simply by visually looking at the driver. This can mean that drivers may be stopped for using their device illegally on a phone call, when in fact they were not; instead using the device for a legal purpose such as the phones' incorporated controls for car stereo or satnav usage – either as part of the cars' own device or directly on the mobile phone itself.

The question arises, is the cell 3
phone even being used as a phone? And are these other uses legitimate or just gimmicks? This chart makes the point.

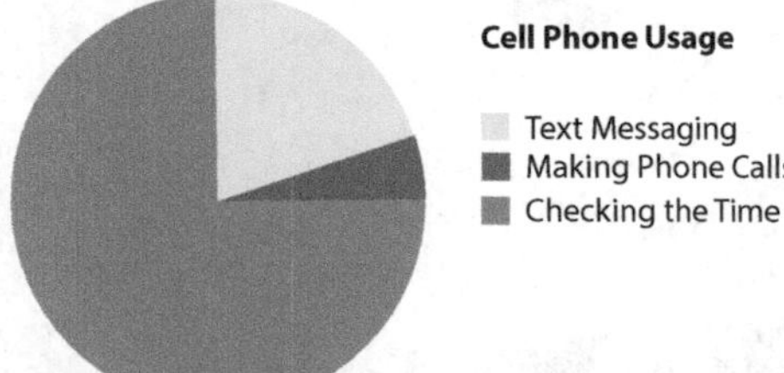

Writing with Strong Use of Sources

A strong paper centers on the writer's ideas—ideas advanced through thoughtful engagement with and crediting of sources. It offers logical analysis or a persuasive argument built on reliable information from quality sources that have been treated with intellectual respect. Note these features at work in the excerpt below from student writer Brandon Jorritsma's essay on cell-phone dependency.

> Facts and ideas are credited through in-text citations, which are linked to full source information on a works-cited page.

> The writer builds on and reasons with source material.

This dependency on cells is reflected in the phenomenon that has come to be 1
termed "rinxiety." Frequent cell phone users are reporting numerous instances of either hearing their phones ring or feeling them vibrate, even if their phones are not around. Two thirds of cell phone users in a recent survey report having experienced this phenomenon ("Phantom Ringing"), which is thought by some to be a rewiring of the nervous system similar to phantom limb pain (Lynch). Others theorize that rinxiety is a result of the pitch of typical cell rings being similar to elements of commonplace sounds, such as running water, music, traffic, and television (Lynch, Goodman). Regardless of the particular explanation, the experience of rinxiety is more common among young, frequent users of cell phones, which seems to indicate a constant expectation of calls ("Phantom Ringing"). This expectation is damaging to relationships because someone expecting a phone call, email, or text to arrive at any moment is not mentally present in other interactions he or she may be involved in. We've all experienced being around someone who was waiting for a phone call. How much more distracted would that person be if he or she subconsciously expected a phone call every hour of the day?

> Direct quotations from sources are indicated with quotation marks.

> A case study from a source makes a concept concrete through cause-effect reasoning.

The corollary of constantly expecting incoming cell communication is the 2
constant impulse to send out messages. Fifty-two percent of respondents to an informal survey at CSU, Fresno, admitted to being "preoccupied with the next time they could text message," and forty-six percent of students "reported irritability when unable to use their cell phones" (Lui). In a study of an international sample of cell phone users, some respondents recounted how they felt anxiety if they forgot to take their phone out of the house with them (Jarvenpaa 12). Even when the phone was not anywhere near them, they couldn't escape its demands on their attention. The phone has transformed from being an object of utility to being one of psychological necessity, which constantly demands attention from its user regardless of its proximity or restrictions on its use. Lauren Hawn, a student at Pennsylvania State University, reports that when she is near her cell, she does the following: "I seem to look at it a lot and check the time [on the phone's digital display] even when I don't need to" (qtd. in Lynch). Hawn does not consciously think that there is a phone call or text message . . . .

Recognizing Plagiarism

The road to plagiarism may be paved with the best intentions—or the worst. Either way, the result is still a serious academic offense. As you write your research paper, do everything you can to stay off that road! Start by studying your school's and your instructor's guidelines on plagiarism and other academic offenses. Then study the following pages.

What Is Plagiarism?

Plagiarism is using someone else's words, ideas, or images (what's called intellectual property) so they appear to be your own. When you plagiarize, you use source material—whether published in print or online—without acknowledging the source. In this sense, plagiarism refers to a range of thefts:

- Submitting a paper you didn't write yourself
- Pasting large chunks of a source into your paper and passing it off as your own work
- Using summaries, paraphrases, or quotations without documentation
- Using the exact phrasing of a source without quotation marks
- Mixing up source material and your own ideas—failing to distinguish between the two

Plagiarism refers to more than "word theft." Because plagiarism is really about failing to credit ideas and information, the rules also apply to visual images, tables, graphs, charts, maps, music, videos, and so on.

What Does Plagiarism Look Like?

Plagiarism refers to a range of source abuses. What exactly do these violations look like? Read the passage below, and then review the five types of plagiarism that follow, noting how each example misuses the source.

The passage below is from page 87 of "Some Stories Have to Be Told by Me: A Literary History of Alice Munro," by Marcela Valdes, published in the *Virginia Quarterly Review*, vol. 82, no. 3, 2006.

What makes Munro's characters so enthralling is their inconsistency; like real people, at one moment they declare they will cover the house in new siding, at the next, they vomit on their way to the hospital. They fight against and seek refuge in the people they love. The technique that Munro has forged to get at such contradictions is a sort of pointillism, the setting of one bright scene against another, with little regard for chronology.

Sielan / Shutterstock.com

Submitting Another Writer's Paper

The most blatant plagiarism is taking an entire piece of writing and claiming it as your own work. Examples:

- Downloading, reformatting, and submitting an article as your own work
- Buying a paper from a "paper mill" or taking a "free" paper off the Internet
- Turning in another student's work as your own (see "Falstaffing" on page 439)

Using Copy and Paste

It is unethical to take chunks of material from another source and splice them into your paper without acknowledgment. In the example below, the writer pastes in a sentence from the original article (boldfaced red text) without using quotation marks or a citation. Even if the writer changed some words, it would still be plagiarism.

> Life typically unfolds mysteriously for Munro's characters, with unexplained events and choices. **Like real people, at one moment they declare they will cover the house in new siding, at the next, they vomit on their way to the hospital.**

Failing to Cite a Source

Borrowed material must be documented. Even if you use information accurately and fairly, don't neglect to cite the source. Below, the writer correctly summarizes the passage's idea but offers no citation.

> For the reader, the characters in Munro's stories are interesting because they are so changeable. Munro shows these changes by using a method of placing scenes side by side for contrast, without worrying about the chronological connections.

Neglecting Necessary Quotation Marks

Whether it's a paragraph or a phrase, if you use the exact wording of a source, that material must be enclosed in quotation marks. In the example below, the writer cites the source but doesn't use quotation marks around a phrase taken from the original (boldfaced red text).

> What makes Munro's characters so typically human is that they **fight against and seek refuge in the people they love** (Valdes 87).

Confusing Borrowed Material with Your Own Ideas

Through carelessness (often in note taking), you may confuse source material with your own thinking. Below, the writer indicates that he borrowed material in the first sentence, but fails to indicate that he also borrowed the next sentence.

> As Marcela Valdes explains, "[w]hat makes Munro's characters so enthralling is their inconsistency" (87). **To achieve this sense of inconsistency, Munro places brightly lit scenes beside each other in a kind of pointillist technique.**

fyi Just as it's easy to plagiarize using the Internet, it's also easy for your professors to recognize and track down plagiarism using Internet tools.

Understanding Why Plagiarism Is Serious

Perhaps the answer is obvious. But some people operate with the notion that material on the Internet is "free" and, therefore, fairly used in research writing. After all, a lot of stuff on the Web doesn't even list an author, so what's the harm? Here's some food for thought:

Academic Dishonesty

At its heart, plagiarism is cheating—stealing intellectual property and passing it off as one's own work. Colleges take such dishonesty seriously. Plagiarism, whether intentional or unintentional, will likely be punished in one or more ways:

- A failing grade for the assignment
- A failing grade for the course
- A note on your academic transcript (often seen by potential employers) that failure resulted from academic dishonesty
- Expulsion from college

Theft from the Academic Community

The research paper represents your dialogue with other members of the academic community—classmates, the instructor, others in your major, others who have researched the topics, and so on. When you plagiarize, you short-circuit the dialogue:

- You gain an unfair advantage over your classmates who follow the rules and earn their grades.
- You disrespect other writers, researchers, and scholars.
- You disrespect your readers by passing off others' ideas as your own.
- You insult your instructor, a person whose respect you need.
- You harm your college by risking its reputation and its academic integrity.

Present and Future Harm

Because research projects help you master course-related concepts and writing skills, plagiarism robs you of an opportunity to learn. Moreover, you rob yourself of your integrity and reputation. After all, as a student you are seeking to build your credibility within the broader academic community, your major, and your future profession.

In addition, research projects often train you for your future work in terms of research, thinking, and writing skills—skills that you will need to succeed in the workplace. If you do not learn the skills now, you will enter the workplace without them—a situation that your employer will, at some point, find out.

One tool to deter plagiarism is Turnitin.com. Students submit their papers for comparison against millions of Web pages and other student papers. Students and instructors get reports about originality and matching text.

Avoiding Plagiarism

Preventing plagiarism begins the moment you get an assignment. Essentially, prevention requires your commitment and diligence throughout the project. Follow these tips:

1. **Resist temptation.** With the Internet, plagiarism is a mouse click away. Avoid last-minute all-nighters that make you desperate; start research projects early. Note: It's better to ask for an extension or accept a penalty for lateness than to plagiarize.
2. **Play by the rules.** Become familiar with your college's definition, guidelines, and policies regarding plagiarism so that you don't unknowingly violate them. When in doubt, ask your instructor for clarification.
3. **Take orderly, accurate notes.** From the start, carefully keep track of source material and distinguish it from your own thinking. Specifically, do the following:
   - Maintain an accurate working bibliography (pages 388–389).
   - Adopt an effective note-taking system (pages 390–393).
   - Accurately summarize, paraphrase, and quote sources (pages 394–396).
4. **Document borrowed material.** Credit information that you have summarized, paraphrased, or quoted from any source, whether that information is statistics, facts, graphics, phrases, or ideas. Readers can then see what's borrowed and what's yours, understand your support, and do their own follow-up research.

   Common Knowledge Exception: Common knowledge is information—a basic fact, for instance—that is generally known to readers or easily found in several sources, particularly reference works. Such knowledge need not be cited. However, when you go beyond common knowledge into research findings, interpretations of the facts, theories, explanations, claims, arguments, and graphics, you must document the source. Study the examples below, but whenever you are in doubt, document.

   Examples:
   - The fact that automakers are developing hybrid-electric cars is common knowledge, whereas the details of GM's AUTOnomy project are not.
   - The fact that Shakespeare wrote *Hamlet* is common knowledge, whereas the details of his sources are not.

5. **Work carefully with source material in your paper.** See pages 448–551 for more on integrating and documenting sources, but here, briefly, are your responsibilities:
   - Distinguish borrowed material from your own thinking by signaling where source material begins and ends.
   - Indicate the source's origin with an attributive phrase and a citation (parenthetical reference or footnote).
   - Provide full source information in a works-cited or references page.

Avoiding Other Source Abuses

Plagiarism, though the most serious offense, is not the only source abuse to avoid when writing a paper with documented research. Consider these pitfalls, which refer again to the sample passage on page 434.

Sample Source Abuses

Using Sources Inaccurately

When you get a quotation wrong, botch a summary, paraphrase poorly, or misstate a statistic, you misrepresent the original. In this quotation, the writer carelessly uses several wrong words that change the meaning, as well as adding two words that are not in the original.

> As Marcela Valdes explains, "[w]hat makes Munro's characters so appalling is their consistency. . . . They fight against and seek refuse in the people they say they love" (87).

Using Source Material Out of Context

By ripping a statement out of its context and forcing it into yours, you can make a source seem to say something that it didn't really say. This writer uses part of a statement to say the opposite of the original.

> According to Marcela Valdes, while Munro's characters are interesting, Munro's weakness as a fiction writer is that she shows "little regard for chronology" (87).

Overusing Source Material

When your paper reads like a string of references, especially quotations, your own thinking disappears. The writer below takes the source passage, chops it up, and splices it together.

> Anyone who has read her stories knows that "[w]hat makes Munro's characters so enthralling is their inconsistency." That is to say, "like real people, at one moment they declare they will cover the house in new siding, at the next, they vomit on their way to the hospital." Moreover, "[t]hey fight against and seek refuge in the people they love." This method "that Munro has forged to get at such contradictions is a sort of pointillism," meaning "the setting of one bright scene against another, with little regard for chronology" (Valdes 87).

"Plunking" Quotations

When you "plunk" or "drop" quotations into your paper without preparing the reader for them and clearly transitioning out of them, the discussion becomes choppy and disconnected. The writer below interrupts the flow of ideas with a quotation "out of the blue." In addition, the quotation hangs at the end of a paragraph with no follow-up.

> Typically, characters such as Del Jordan, Louisa Doud, and Almeda Roth experience a crisis through contact with particular men. "They fight against and seek refuge in the people they love" (Valdes 87).

Using "Blanket" Citations

Your reader shouldn't have to guess where borrowed material begins and ends. For example, if you place a parenthetical citation at the end of a paragraph, does that citation cover the whole paragraph or just the final sentence?

Relying Too Heavily on One Source

If your writing is dominated by one source, readers may doubt the depth and integrity of your research. Instead, your writing should show your reliance on a balanced diversity of sources.

Failing to Match In-Text Citations to Bibliographic Entries

All in-text citations must clearly refer to accurate entries in the works-cited, references, or endnotes page. Mismatching occurs in the following circumstances:

- An in-text citation refers to a source that is not listed in the bibliography.
- A bibliographic resource is never actually referenced anywhere in the paper.

Related Academic Offenses

Beyond plagiarism and related source abuses, steer clear of these academic offenses:

Double-dipping: When you submit one paper in two different classes or otherwise turn in a paper you have turned in before without permission from both instructors, you take double credit for one project.

Falstaffing: This practice refers to a particular type of plagiarism in which one student submits another student's work. Know that you are guilty of Falstaffing if you let another student submit your paper.

Copyright violations: When you copy, distribute, and/or post in whole or in part any intellectual property without permission from or payment to the copyright holder, you commit a copyright infringement, especially when you profit from this use. To avoid copyright violations in your research projects, do the following:

- **Observe fair use guidelines:** Quote small portions of a document for limited purposes, such as education or research. Avoid copying large portions for your own gain.
- **Understand what's in the public domain:** You need not obtain permission to copy and use public domain materials—primarily documents created by the government, but also some material posted on the Internet as part of the "copy left" movement.
- **Observe intellectual property and copyright laws:** First, know your college's policies on copying documents. Second, realize that copyright protects the expression of ideas in a range of materials—writings, videos, songs, photographs, drawings, computer software, and so on. Always obtain permission to copy and distribute copyrighted materials.
- **Avoid changing a source** (e.g., a photo) without permission of the creator or copyright holder.

Critical Thinking and Writing: Applications

Now that you have learned strategies to avoid plagiarism and to build your credibility in your own writing, there may be more to consider. Apply your knowledge through the following activities:

1. **Photo Op:** The image on the chapter's opening page focuses on the concept of copying. Consider another key idea in this chapter and find or develop an image that suggests the concept.
2. **Living Today:** In the wider world, what happens when research is shoddy, involves deception, or contains plagiarized material? Research a story of unethical research and/or plagiarism. What were the circumstances, the nature of the offense, and the consequences?
3. **Public Texts:** Find three articles on the same topic, articles from different media (e.g., a news source, a magazine, a blog). How does each writer attempt to establish and build credibility? How well does each succeed?
4. **School Policy:** Research your school's academic-integrity policies. How does your school define plagiarism, and how does it address the problem in its policies and procedures? Similarly, explore your school's use or lack of use of Turnitin.com: what role does this program play in academic life where you are?
5. **Major Work:** What does credibility mean in your discipline? What ethical practices for treating sources are emphasized in your major? Research these questions by interviewing professors, examining publications in the field, and studying ethics statements from professional organizations (e.g., MLA, APA).

Learning-Objectives Checklist ✓

Have you achieved this chapter's learning objectives? Check your progress with the items below, revisiting topics in the chapter as needed. I have . . .

____ differentiated between writing that uses sources poorly and writing that uses sources effectively (432–433).

____ defined plagiarism and distinguished the various forms that it might take (434–435).

____ explained the seriousness of plagiarism as a form of academic dishonesty that harms the academic community, as well as my own integrity now and in the future (436).

____ prevented plagiarism in my own writing, following strategies that include knowing the difference between material that must be credited and material that is common knowledge (437).

____ distinguished other source abuses, from inaccurate use of a source to mismatched in-text citations and bibliographic entries, and avoided these abuses in my writing (438–439).

____ identified and avoided academic offenses such as double dipping, falstaffing, and copyright violations (439).

MindTap® Practice skills that you have learned in this chapter and receive automatic feedback. Reflect on your writing process.

Chapter 22

Drafting Papers with Documented Research

When you write a research paper, you enter a larger conversation about your topic. Because you are seeking to add your voice to the conversation, the paper should center on your own ideas while thoughtfully engaging with the ideas of others. Crediting sources ensures that each voice in the conversation is fairly represented.

This chapter explains how to make the shift from researching your topic to writing about it, focuses on effective and conscientious use of sources in your writing, and helps you write a first draft of your paper. The chapter then shows you good research-writing practices at work in a humanities essay and a science report.

Visually Speaking Scales like the one shown in Figure 22.1 are used for weighing and balancing. In what ways does drafting research-based writing involve mental versions of these activities?

MindTap®

Understand the goals of the chapter and complete a warm-up activity online.

By working through this chapter, you will be able to

- examine your research findings so as to deepen your thinking on a topic.
- assess and strengthen your working thesis.
- organize your writing with your research findings in mind.
- draft your essay so as to respect, smoothly integrate, and effectively document source material.
- compare and contrast research-writing practices in the humanities and the sciences.

vetre / Shutterstock.com

fig. 22.1

Reviewing Your Findings

With every research project, the time comes when you must transition from exploring your topic to sharing discoveries, from research to writing. To start this transition, take time to review your findings—to go over your notes as many times as necessary, using them to stimulate your thinking and planning. Try these strategies, in particular:

Conduct Q & A

Early in your project, you may have generated a set of research questions (see page 372). Now that you have completed the bulk of your research, you might do the following Q & A activity to clarify how your research has impacted your thinking:

- **Review your primary research question:** What answers has your research produced? Are the answers affirming, engaging, or unsettling?
- **Review your secondary research questions:** What information have you found to answer these questions? How do the answers enhance your thinking?

Deepen Your Thinking on the Topic

During note-taking, you focused on making sense of what individual sources said about your topic. Now, take these steps to deepen and expand your thinking:

- **Identify key discoveries.** What central ideas and new facts have you learned through research? What conclusions have you reached, and why?
- **Identify connections between sources.** How are your sources related to each other? Do they share similar points of view and similar conclusions? Do some sources build on other sources? Which one was published first, second, third, etc.?
- **Identify differences between sources.** In what ways and on what issues do sources disagree? Why? What sense do you make of the differences?
- **Identify limits and gaps.** What issues do your sources not cover? For what questions have you not found answers? How are these gaps important for your project?

Imagine Your Paper

As you review your findings, you can also prepare to write your paper by imagining what it might include. Consider these strategies:

1. **Look for organizational clues.** How do your sources organize their discussions of your topic? Are there particular patterns that make sense of the issues?
2. **Anticipate how you might use source material.** As you study your notes, imagine how different points could be used in your writing. Here are possibilities:
    - background, historical context, and definitions—foundational information
    - principles and theories—idea "tools" for exploring your topic
    - expert reasoning—the thinking of those most knowledgeable about the topic
    - examples and case studies—illustrations that vivify an idea
    - concrete evidence—the facts that support your claims

Sharpening Your Working Thesis

As you prepare to draft your research paper, you might refine your focus by revisiting and revising your working thesis (page 373).

Deepen Your Thesis

Review your working thesis. Given the research that you have completed, does this thesis stand up? It is possible, of course, that your research has led you to a conclusion quite different from your original working thesis. If so, rewrite your thesis accordingly. However, you might also retain your original thesis but strengthen it by using these strategies:

1. **Use richer, clearer terms.** Test your working thesis for vague, broad, or inappropriate terms or concepts. Replace them with terms that have rich meanings, are respected in discussions of your topic, and refine your original thinking.
2. **Introduce qualifying terms where needed.** With qualifying terms such as "normally," "often," and "usually," as well as with phrases that limit the reach of your thesis, you are paradoxically strengthening your thesis by making it more reasonable.
3. **Stress your idea through opposition.** You can deepen your working thesis by adding an opposing thought (usually phrased in a dependent clause).

Original Working Thesis: In Alice Munro's "An Ounce of Cure," infatuation messes with the narrator's head so her life gets turned upside down.

Revised Working Thesis: While Alice Munro's "An Ounce of Cure" tells a simple story of infatuation leading to confusion and trouble, the story is more importantly about the "plots of life"—the ways in which the narrator experiences life as a competing set of stories (romance, fairy tale, farce), none of which does justice to the complexity of real life.

Question Your Thesis

You can also sharpen your working thesis by questioning it—viewing it from your readers' point of view. What questions might readers have, given the phrasing of your thesis? Here, for example, are questions about the revised working thesis above:

- In what ways is the story primarily about infatuation? What kinds of trouble flow from the infatuation? What confusions?
- What do you mean by the phrase "plots of life" and where does it come from?
- What is the nature of the types of stories listed? In what ways are they "competing"?
- How is real life more complex than these fictional stories? Does the narrator experience real life? If so, where and how?

Probing your thesis in this way can help you (1) decide which questions you want to answer in your paper, and (2) imagine a question-answer structure for your paper.

Considering Methods of Organization

Before drafting, explore which methods of organization would work well for your paper. For help, see chapter 3, "Planning." The discussion on this page and the next will help you make choices, but start by avoiding these simplistic patterns:

- The five-paragraph essay: Popularly known as the high school hamburger, this structure is too basic and limiting for most college research projects.
- Information regurgitation: Generally, college-level research requires analytical thinking about information, not just the presentation of data.
- A series of source summaries: Your paper should not be structured simply as a summary of one source after another.

Organizational Practices That Consider Sources

Because the writing you are doing is research based, you want to factor your sources into your thinking about organization. Here are some ideas that may work with your project.

Consider Where to Position Primary and Secondary Sources

Different writing projects require different approaches to using, balancing, and integrating primary and secondary sources. Where and how should you work in primary sources—interview material, survey data, textual analysis, observation results? Where and how should you bring in secondary sources—scholarly books, journal articles, and the like? ***Example:*** In a literary analysis, you may rely on primary textual analysis of a novel throughout your paper but support that analysis with secondary-source information from biographical research.

Order Your Writing Around Key Sources

While you shouldn't organize your whole paper as a series of source summaries, sometimes your writing can take direction specifically from source material. Consider these options:

- **Make one of your key points a response to a specific source.** Did a particular source stand out as especially supportive of or especially contrary to your own thinking? Shape part of your paper as an affirmation or rebuttal of the source.
- **Structure your paper around a dialogue with sources.** Do your sources offer multiple, divergent, or even contradictory perspectives on your topic? If they do, consider organizing your paper around a dialogue with these sources.

Map Out Relationships Between Sources and Ideas

Having reviewed your findings and sharpened your working thesis, consider how your sources support that thesis. To visualize your options, create a diagram, map, or flowchart that shows where particular sources speak to particular points.

Put Your Discussion in Context

Often, the early part of your paper will involve establishing a context for exploring your topic. Consider, then, tapping your sources to present necessary background, explain key terms, describe the big picture, or establish a theoretical framework for your discussion.

Traditional Organizational Patterns

As shown in the "writing moves" chart on page 59, organizing your paper into an opening, middle, and closing can involve a variety of strategies. The traditional patterns below offer sound methods for developing your thinking. Each choice offers a basic structure for your paper, but several patterns may be useful within your paper's body. As indicated, full instruction for many of these patterns can be found elsewhere in this book.

- **Analysis** clarifies how something works by breaking the object or phenomenon into parts or phases and then showing how they work together. See pages 173–308.
- **Argumentation** asserts and supports a main claim with supporting claims, logical reasoning about each claim, and concrete evidence to back up the reasoning. This pattern also includes acknowledging and countering any opposition, as well as reasserting the main claim (perhaps in a modified form). See pages 309–330.
- **Cause-effect** can (1) explore the factors that led to an event or phenomenon, (2) explore the consequences of an event or phenomenon, or (3) do both. See pages 252–278.
- **Chronological order** arranges items in a temporal sequence (order of events, steps in a process). See pages 210–211.
- **Classification** places items within categories. Each category is characterized by what the items share with each other and by what makes them different from items in the other categories. See pages 193–208.
- **Comparison-contrast** examines two or more items for similarities, differences, or both. Such a study typically holds the items side by side, comparing or contrasting traits point by point. See pages 233–250.
- **Definition** clarifies a term's meaning through appropriate strategies: explaining the term's origin and history, offering examples and illustrations, elaborating key concepts at the heart of the term, and so on. See pages 173–192.
- **Description** orders details in terms of spatial relationships, sounds, components, color, form, texture, and so on. See pages 145–146.
- **Evaluation** measures the strength or quality of something against particular standards, standards that are already accepted or that are established prior to the evaluation.
- **Order of importance** arranges items from most to least important, or least to most.
- **Partitioning** breaks down an object, a space, or a location into ordered parts, or a process into steps or phases.
- **Problem-solution** describes a problem, explores its causes and effects, surveys possible solutions, proposes the best one, and defends it as desirable and doable. This pattern may also involve explaining how to implement the solution. See pages 335–336.
- **Question-answer** moves back and forth from questions to answers in a sequence that logically clarifies a topic.

Considering Drafting Strategies

With research writing, developing the first draft involves exploring your own thinking in relation to the ideas and information that you have discovered through research. Your goal is to develop and support your ideas—referring to and properly crediting sources, but not being dominated by them. Such drafting requires both creativity and care: the creativity to see connections and to trace lines of thinking, and the care to respect ideas and information that you are borrowing from sources. Consider the tips below.

Choose a Drafting Method

Before starting your draft, choose a drafting method that makes sense for your project (its complexity, formality, etc.) and your writing style. Here are two options:

Writing Systematically

1. Develop a detailed outline, including supporting evidence, such as the formal sentence outline on page 50.
2. Arrange all your research notes in the precise order of your outline.
3. Write methodically, following your thesis, outline, and notes. However, be open to taking your writing in an interesting direction and modifying your outline as you write.
4. Cite sources as you draft.

Writing Freely

1. Review your working thesis and notes. Then set them aside.
2. If you need to, jot down a brief outline (see the basic list on page 48).
3. Write away—get all your research-based thinking down without stressing about details and flow.
4. Going back to your notes, develop your draft further and carefully integrate and cite research material.

Respect Your Sources While Drafting

Research writing involves handling your sources with care, including during the first draft. While drafting, try to have source material at your fingertips so that you can integrate summaries, paraphrases, and quotations without disrupting the flow and energy of your drafting. Moreover, take care not to overwhelm your draft with source material. As you draft, keep the focus on your own ideas:

- **Avoid strings of references and chunks of source material** without your discussion, explanation, or interpretation in between.
- **Don't offer entire paragraphs of material from a source** (whether paraphrased or quoted) with a single in-text citation at the end: when you do so, your thinking disappears.
- **Be careful not to overload your draft with complex information** and dense data lacking explanation.
- **Resist the urge to copy-and-paste big chunks from sources.** Even if you document the sources, your paper will quickly become a patchwork of source material with a few stitches (your slim contribution) holding the paper together.

Reason with the Evidence

Your paper presents the weight of your research findings in the light of your best thinking. Here you support your thesis with a line of reasoning that is carefully thought out and backed up by evidence. That line of reasoning is typically carried by well-developed paragraphs. A typical body paragraph starts with a topic sentence that makes a point in support of your thesis, then elaborates that point with careful reasoning and detailed evidence, and finishes with a concluding sentence that reiterates and advances the idea.

Sample Body Paragraph Showing Reasoning with Evidence:

Topic Sentence: idea elaborating and supporting thesis

Development of idea through reasoning

Support of idea through reference to evidence from source material

Concluding statement of idea

Finally, Fairtrade consumers can misjudge producers. Whereas Fairtrade has been rightly criticized for inadvertently spreading a sort of neo-colonial attitude, consider, for instance, the problem of quality control that was explored earlier: that Fairtrade does not press producers to develop high-quality products. "Companies such as Green & Black's," on the other hand, "say they aid farmers more by helping them to improve quality and go organic rather than just guaranteeing a price" (Beattie 34). The Fairtrade model ensures that producers will never be able to grow beyond the need for a fixed minimum, while alternate models seek to empower producers. It is not hard to see which paradigm is rife with paternalistic, colonialist implications. Getting consumers in the right frame of mind is not an irrelevant need. As Ian Hussey puts it, "decolonization is not just a material process, but also a mental one" (17). Fair trade, he says, "serves to reinforce racist and colonial distinctions between the poor Global South farmer and the benevolent Global North consumer" (15). In the long run, this mindset is destructive in that it denigrates Fairtrade producers as charity cases rather than potential partners.

As your writing unfolds, make sure that your thinking is sound. To that end, consider these points:

- **Supporting Ideas:** Your topic sentence is essentially a claim—an idea that explains or argues a point. Clearly and logically tie your claim to your thesis.
- **Reasons:** These sentences develop and deepen the claim in the topic sentence. However, reasoning also functions to explain the evidence when you present it. Just remember that the evidence does not generally speak for itself: you will likely have to introduce it to your reader, who is seeing it for the first time.
- **Evidence:** This material is foundational to your thinking—the facts, statistics, quotations, artifacts, illustrations, case studies, and more that you have gathered through research. Always choose evidence that clarifies and convinces, and aim for providing a level of detail that makes your discussion concrete, clear, and convincing.

Using Source Material in Your Writing

After you've found good sources and taken good notes on them, you want to use that research effectively in your writing. Specifically, you want to show (1) what information you are borrowing and (2) where you got it. By doing so, you create credibility. This section shows you how to develop credibility by integrating and documenting sources so as to avoid plagiarism and other abuses (see chapter 21). ***Note:*** For a full treatment of documentation, see chapter 23 (MLA) and chapter 24 (APA).

Integrate Source Material Carefully

Source material—whether a summary, a paraphrase, or a quotation—should be integrated smoothly into your discussion. Follow these strategies:

The Right Reasons

Focus on what you want to say, not on all the source material you've collected. Use sources to do the following:

- **Deepen and develop your point** with the reasoning offered by a source.
- **Support your point and your thinking** about it with evidence—with facts, statistics, details, and so on.
- **Give credibility to your point** with an expert's supporting statement.
- **Bring your point to life** with an example, an observation, a case study, an anecdote, or an illustration.
- **Address a counterargument** or an alternative.

Quotation Restraint

In most research documents, restrict your quoting to nuggets:

- **Key statements by authorities** (e.g., the main point that a respected Shakespeare scholar makes about the role of Ophelia in *Hamlet*)
- **Well-phrased claims and conclusions** (e.g., a powerful conclusion by an ethicist about the problem with the media's coverage of cloning debates and technological developments)
- **Passages where careful word-by-word analysis and interpretation** are important to your argument (e.g., an excerpt from a speech made by a politician about the International Space Station—a passage that requires a careful analysis for the between-the-lines message)

Quotations, especially long ones, must pull their weight, so generally paraphrase or summarize source material instead.

Primary Document Exception: When a primary text (a novel, a piece of legislation, a speech) is a key piece of evidence or the actual focus of your project, careful analysis of quoted excerpts is required. See pages 404–405 for more.

Smooth Integration

When you use quotations, work them into your writing as smoothly as possible. To do so, you need to pay attention to style, punctuation, and syntax. (See pages 450–451.)

Use enough of the quotation to make your point without changing the meaning of the original. Use quotation marks around key phrases taken from the source.

> Ogden, Williams, and Larson also conclude that the hydrogen fuel-cell vehicle is "a strong candidate for becoming the Car of the Future," given the trend toward "tighter environmental constraints" and the "intense efforts underway" by automakers to develop commercially viable versions of such vehicles (25).

Integrate all sources thoughtfully. Fold source material into your discussion by relating it to your own thinking. Let your ideas guide the way, not your sources, by using this pattern:

1. **State and explain your idea,** creating a context for the source.
2. **Identify and introduce the source,** linking it to your discussion.
3. **Summarize, paraphrase, or quote the source,** providing a citation in an appropriate spot.
4. **Use the source by explaining, expanding, or refuting it.**
5. **When appropriate, refer back to a source** to further develop the ideas it contains.

Sample Passage: Note the integration of sources in the following paragraph.

Writer's ideas | Attributive phrase | Paraphrase, quotation, or summary | Citation | Commentary | Conclusion

The motivation and urgency to create and improve hybrid-electric technology comes from a range of complex forces. Some of these forces are economic, others environmental, and still others social. In "Societal Lifestyle Costs of Cars with Alternative Fuels/Engines," Joan Ogden, Robert Williams, and Eric Larson argue that "[c]ontinued reliance on current transportation fuels and technologies poses serious oil supply insecurity, climate change, and urban air pollution risks" (7). Because of the nonrenewable nature of fossil fuels as well as their negative side effects, the transportation industry is confronted with making the most radical changes since the introduction of the internal-combustion automobile more than 100 years ago. Hybrid-electric vehicles are onc response to this pressure.

Fabio Berti / Shutterstock.com

Effectively Document Your Sources

Just as you need to integrate source material carefully into your writing, so you must also carefully document where that source material comes from. Readers should recognize which material is yours and which material is not.

Identify Clearly Where Source Material Begins

Your discussion must offer a smooth transition to source material. Follow these guidelines:

- For first reference to a source, use an attributive statement that indicates some of the following: author's name and credentials, title of the source, nature of the study or research, and helpful background.

  > **Joan Ogden, Robert Williams, and Eric Larson, members of the Princeton Environmental Institute, explain** that modest improvements in energy efficiency and emissions reductions will not be enough over the next century because of anticipated transportation increases (7).

- For subsequent references to a source, use a simplified attributive phrase, such as the author's last name or a shortened version of the title.

  > **Ogden, Williams, and Larson go on to argue** that "[e]ffectively addressing environmental and oil supply concerns will probably require radical changes in automotive engine/fuel technologies" (7).

- In some situations, such as providing straightforward facts, simply skip the attributive phrase. The parenthetical citation supplies sufficient attribution.

  > Various types of transportation are by far the main consumers of oil (three fourths of world oil imports); moreover, these same technologies are responsible for one fourth of all greenhouse gas sources (Ogden, Williams, and Larson 7).

- The verb you use to introduce source material is key. Use fitting verbs, such as those in the table below—verbs indicating that the source informs, analyzes, or argues. Normally, use the present tense. Use the past tense only to stress the "pastness" of a source.

  > In their 2004 study, "Societal Lifecycle Costs of Cars with Alternative Fuels/Engines," Ogden, Williams, and Larson **present** a method for comparing and contrasting alternatives to internal-combustion engines. Earlier, these authors **made** preliminary steps . . .

Verbs for Signal Phrases

accepts	considers	explains	rejects	contrasts
contradicts	highlights	reminds	adds	insists
identifies	responds	affirms	criticizes	shows
shares	argues	declares	interprets	believes
asserts	defends	lists	states	describes
denies	maintains	stresses	cautions	points out
outlines	suggests	claims	disagrees	urges
supports	compares	discusses	praises	confirms
concludes	emphasizes	proposes	verifies	
enumerates	refutes	warns	acknowledges	

Indicate Where Source Material Ends

Closing quotation marks and a citation, as shown below, indicate the end of a source quotation. Generally, place the citation immediately after any quotation, paraphrase, or summary. However, you may also place the citation early in the sentence or at the end if the parenthetical note is obviously obtrusive. When you discuss several details from a page in a source, use an attributive phrase at the beginning of your discussion and a single citation at the end.

> As the "Lifestyle Costs" study concludes, when greenhouse gases, air pollution, and oil insecurity are factored into the analysis, alternative-fuel vehicles "offer lower LCCs than typical new cars" (Ogden, Williams, and Larson 25).

Set Off Longer Quotations

If a quotation is longer than four typed lines, set it off from the main text. Generally, introduce the quotation with a complete sentence and a colon. Indent the quotation a half inch (five spaces) and double-space it, but don't put quotation marks around it. Put the citation outside the final punctuation mark.

> Toward the end of the study, Ogden, Williams, and Larson argue that changes to the fuel-delivery system must be factored into planning:
>
> > In charting a course to the Car of the Future, societal LCC comparisons should be complemented by considerations of fuel infrastructure requirements. Because fuel infrastructure changes are costly, the number of major changes made over time should be minimized. The bifurcated strategy advanced here—of focusing on the H2 FCV for the long term and advanced liquid hydrocarbon-fueled ICEVs and ICE/HEVs for the near term—would reduce the number of such infrastructure changes to one (an eventual shift to H2). (25)

Mark Changes to Quotations

You may shorten or change a quotation so that it fits smoothly into your sentence—but don't alter the original meaning. Use an ellipsis to indicate that you have omitted words from the original. An ellipsis is three periods with spaces between them.

> In their projections of where fuel-cell vehicles are heading, Ogden, Williams, and Larson discuss GM's AUTOnomy vehicle, with its "radical redesign of the entire car. . . . In these cars, steering, braking, and other vehicle systems are controlled electronically rather than mechanically" (24).

Use square brackets to indicate a clarification or to change a pronoun or verb tense or to switch around uppercase and lowercase.

> As Ogden, Williams, and Larson explain, "[e]ven if such barriers [the high cost of fuel cells and the lack of an H2 fuel infrastructure] can be overcome, decades would be required before this embryonic technology could make major contributions in reducing the major externalities that characterize today's cars" (25).

To indicate a spelling error or typographical error in the original source, add [sic] immediately after the error.

Sample Research Paper: A Humanities Essay

MindTap®
Read, highlight, and take notes online.

As discussed on page 137, the humanities study aspects of human experience, as well as the ideas that grow out of that experience. Student writer Lucas Koomans does that in the humanities essay below: he explores the impact of a new surveillance technology on people's privacy and security. As you read Lucas's essay, explore how it is rooted in research and how he reasons with that research. Note: the sample essay shows source documentation according to the MLA style. However, the paper does not show MLA format rules (heading, margins, spacing, etc.). Those details are addressed in chapter 23.

Chipping Away at Our Privacy?

Ever since English novelist George Orwell explored possible threats to privacy in his dystopian novel *1984* (published in 1949), many people have responded by condemning advances in technology, particularly in surveillance. However, the dangers with these privacy threats are not the technology itself, but rather what its capabilities are, who controls it, and how it is used. These issues deserve special attention as they relate to *1984*, which describes how people's privacy is threatened when their every movement is monitored and every thought controlled by Big Brother, the representation of government in the novel. This monitoring is accomplished through two-way cameras known as "telescreens" and by "thoughtpolice." Though many examples of privacy breaches are evident in the novel (e.g. encouragement of spying on others), the main concern is Big Brother's use of telescreens and thoughtpolice to destroy citizens' privacy and to maintain control over them. Today, the VeriChip could represent a similar threat to personal privacy. To understand why this surveillance technology might be labeled Orwellian, it's helpful to explore the VeriChip's capabilities, uses, and potential abuses. While misuse of the device could be destructive, effective public policy guidelines and regulations could help ensure that the VeriChip remains a useful technology. 1

What exactly is the VeriChip? It is a "glass-encapsulated RFID [radio frequency identification] microchip designed for implantation in the human body" (Albrecht 2

1). Similar in size to a grain of rice, the device "holds an identification number, an electromagnetic coil for transmitting data, and a turning capacitor" (Barnea 1). Importantly, these RFID tags "do not contain an internal source of power, but instead receive transmission power from an interrogating reader"; as a result, they have "short read ranges" of approximately thirty feet (Halamka et al 603). The interrogating reader is a device that activates the information in the chip; at all other times, the chip is passive in that it does not transmit information. Although it is unknown how many people use the VeriChip today, the VeriChip corporation stated in 2007 that "several thousand people throughout the world have been implanted with its product" (Albrecht 1).

On the positive side, the VeriChip offers many useful services, including "identification of medical patients, physical access control, contactless retail payment, and even the tracing of kidnapping victims" (Halamka et al 1). The VeriChip's main function is to serve as an identification device for human beings. For example, in the healthcare industry, hospitals use this chip to track patients and maintain their medical records. Ann Marburger, Jim Coon, Kevin Fleck, and Treva Kremer explain how areas in the healthcare industry such as trauma centers, nursing homes, and physicians' offices are "main areas where VeriChips [are used]" (5). With patients bearing the VeriChip, doctors and nurses can have access to "implanted medical device identification [and] emergency access to patient-supplied health information" (6). The VeriChip is also useful as an identification device when patients' identities are "difficult to establish," if they happen to be "incapacitated or disoriented" (6). With the VeriChip, doctors and nurses are able to identify patients, access their medical records, and treat individuals effectively. In addition, the VeriChip provides medical personnel enhanced control. For example, in private facilities, it "permits automated identification of individuals and tracking of their movements in buildings" (Halamka et al 2). Lastly, the VeriChip is capable of tracking lost patients at a hospital or even kidnapped victims. In brief, as these examples illustrate, the VeriChip has proven to be what it was originally designed to be—an effective identification device that benefits the bearer by offering his or her trusted contacts ready access to the user's personal information.

Unfortunately, this ready-access feature also makes the personal information 4
recorded on the VeriChip vulnerable to exploitation. The danger exists if the VeriChip's nature were to shift from identification to authentication. Identification means "the action or process of identifying someone or something"; by contrast, authentication means "the process of determining whether someone or something is, in fact, who or what it is declared to be" (Halamka et al 602). Whereas identification is passive, authentication is active; for that reason, authentication makes users vulnerable to attack and abuse. This danger is illustrated by the story of a man whose thumb was severed by attackers so that they could use it to steal his Mercedes, a car whose starting mechanism required fingerprint recognition (Kent 1). Because the VeriChip as an authentication device would be like a fingerprint, this example indicates one reason that the VeriChip should not be used for authentication purposes: to physically protect the bearers of the chip. Similarly, the user's private information could become more vulnerable if the VeriChip were to become an active rather than a passive device. In addition, if the read range on these chips grows larger than its current distance of roughly thirty feet, the chips' information also becomes less secure. And if people are capable of accessing personal information from VeriChip users, what can be done with such information becomes troubling. The VeriChip itself "contains only a unique 16 digit identification number," something similar to an American's social security number. That number "can be used to look up a record in a database" (Albrecht 1). Abusing that record would begin with sharing it with others, a common privacy concern today, and would expand from there.

For these reasons, use of the VeriChip must be guided by sound policies and 5
regulations. The VeriChip must remain an identification device that receives its power only from "an interrogating reader" (Halamka et al 603). The chip must continue to be

designed with no internal source of power and a short reading range. Moreover, the VeriChip must also be equipped with a privacy protection plan (604). Emily Stewart, a policy analyst at the Health Privacy Project, argues that "to protect patient privacy, the devices should reveal only vital medical information, like blood type and allergic reactions, needed for healthcare workers to do their jobs" (qtd. in "FDA Approves" 1). Stewart agrees that to do their jobs, healthcare workers need access to some information from VeriChip bearers; however, such access becomes a concern when other information is accessible and the user's privacy is not protected in the process. In "Microchip Implants for Humans as Unique Identifiers: A Case Study on VeriChip," the authors ask readers to consider what it means for technology "to be embedded beneath the skin in a perfectly healthy human being for the purposes of 'easy' identification" (Michael et al 1). These authors believe that people should consider this question when implanting VeriChips, and when developing policies and regulations for devices such as these.

In *1984*, Orwell still speaks to the modern world by warning humans how 6
privacy is fragile, particularly because of surveillance technology. As a surveillance technology, the VeriChip may seem to be an Orwellian device for Big Brother. However, it was designed to be a technology that benefits humans, and it can remain so if it is used in accordance with its original purpose: to identify people. If the VeriChip is used for authentication, it becomes Orwellian and puts users in danger of having their privacy invaded and their lives threatened. For this reason, designers must develop a privacy-protection plan for the chip to prevent people from exploiting users' privacy. Ensuring that the VeriChip has no internal source of power is a start, but that is not enough to protect VeriChip users from being exploited. More safeguards are needed to keep the VeriChip a beneficial piece of technology.

Works Cited

Albrecht, Katherine. "Microchip Implants: Answers to Frequently Asked Questions." *CASPIAN Consumer Privacy,* 2008, www.antichips.com/faq/.

Barnea, Sivan. "VeriChip." *TechTarget*, contributed by Margaret Rouse, Sept. 2005, http://internetofthingsagenda.techtarget.com/definition/VeriChip.

"FDA Approves Computer Chip for Humans." *NBC News*, 13 Oct. 2004, nbcnews.com/id/6237364/ns/health-health_care/t/fda-approves-computer-chip-humans/#.V2gnYaIk3T8.

Halamka, J, et al. "The Security Implications of Verichip Cloning." *Journal of the American Medical Informatics Association*, vol. 13, no. 6, 2006, pp. 601-07.

Kent, Jonathan. "Malaysia Car Thieves Steal Finger." *BBC News*, 31 Mar. 2005, news.bbc.co.uk/2/hi/world/asiapacific/4396831.stm.

Marburger, Ann, et al. *VeriChip: Implantable RFID for the Health Industry*, 7 June 2005, docplayer.net/12920605-Verichip-implantable-rfid-for-the-health-industry-ann-marburger-jim-coon-kevin-fleck-treva-kremer.html.

Michael, Katina, et al. "Microchip implants for humans as unique identifiers: a case study on VeriChip." *Conference on Ethics, Technology, and Identity*, edited by N. Manders-Huits, Delft U of Technology, 2008, pp. 81-84.

Orwell, George. *1984*. Plume, 1983.

Reading for Better Writing

1. *Connections:* How has your own privacy been impacted by technology? In a digital age, how do you maintain your privacy—if at all?
2. *Comprehension:* Summarize the VeriChip's nature, its benefits, its potential dangers, and policies to safeguard its use.
3. *Writing Strategies:*
   a. In paragraphs 3 and 4, Lucas seeks to balance the benefits and dangers of the VeriChip. What strategies does he use to present each?
   b. Writers of Humanities essays aim to understand more deeply human experience and humanity's place in the world. Where and how does this essay present such big ideas?
   c. Review the essay's sources as listed in the Works Cited, but also as they are referred to and used in the paper itself. What does this review suggest to you about the nature of research in the Humanities?

Your Project: What other technologies—current or historical—have challenged and changed humanity's sense of itself? Choose a technology, consider its impact on your own life, research it carefully, and write about its effects on humans, past or present.

Sample Research Paper: Science IMRAD Report

As discussed on pages 138–139, a common form of research writing in the natural and social sciences is the experiment report, often called the IMRAD report because of its structure: an *introduction* establishing the problem, a *methods* section detailing experimental procedures, a *results* section providing the data, and a *discussion* that interprets the data. This structure is rooted in the scientific method, a procedure by which experiments are set up to test hypotheses about why things happen.

In the report below, student writers Dana Kleckner, Brittany Korver, Nicolette Storm, and Adam Verhoef share the results of an experiment in which they tested a hypothesis about the impact of an invasive plant species, Eastern Red Cedar, on Midwestern native species. Note: the sample essay shows source documentation according to the APA style. However, the paper does not show in detail APA format rules (running head, margins, spacing, etc.). Those details are addressed in chapter 24. Note, as well, that documentation in the natural sciences often follows CSE format: for more information, check councilscienceeditors.org.

The Effects of the Eastern Red Cedar on Seedlings and Implications for Allelopathy

Abstract

The Eastern Red Cedar *(Juniperus virginiana)* is an invasive species that threatens 1
native tall-grass prairies in much of the Midwest (Norris, Blair, Johnson, & McKane, 2001). In an effort to learn more about its invasive characteristics, we decided to test for possible allelopathic properties. Allelopathy refers to the growth inhibition of one species by another species releasing toxins from its tissues (Simberloff, 1995). In this study, the germination and survival of black-eyed Susans *(Rudbeckia hirta)* and poppies *(Papaver orientale)* were examined. Seeds were planted in soil gathered from under three eastern red cedar trees at Oak Grove State Park (Northwestern Iowa) and in soil from three non-cedar locations at this park. Germination and survival of the seedlings in controlled conditions were documented over thirty-two days. We found no significant difference between germination and survival proportions of the two seed types between the cedar and non-cedar soil. This led us to conclude that the eastern red cedar does not negatively affect the germination and survival of the selected seed types.

Introduction

Several factors can give a plant dominance in an area. One of these factors is 2
the production of allelopathic chemicals. Allelopathy is the secretion of chemicals by one plant that suppresses the growth of other nearby plants (Simberloff, 1995).

This phenomenon reduces competition for limited resources. One possible method of allelopathy is the secreting of chemicals through the roots, directly into the soil. The chemicals can also be stored in the leaves, flowers, fruits, and seeds, releasing chemicals into the soil as they decompose (Norris, Blair, & Johnson, 2007). These allelopathic properties are present in several invasive species, such as the Japanese Red Pine (Node et al., 2003).

The object in this experiment was to test for allelopathic capabilities of the 3
eastern red cedar *(Juniperus virginiana)*. The eastern red cedar is a pioneer invader in the Midwest, quickly populating disturbed land (Norris et al., 2001). This invasion is problematic in certain areas of the Midwest, as it often changes the native ecology of the area it invades, namely tall-grass prairies (Norris et al., 2001). In the effort to preserve native ecosystems, a correct understanding of the characteristics of invaders is useful. The knowledge of the allelopathic properties of this species could assist in preservation efforts.

We predicted that eastern red cedars are allelopathic and that the soil around 4
cedar trees would have a negative effect on the germination and lifespan of other plants. We hypothesized that seeds planted in cedar soil would germinate at a lower frequency and have shorter life spans than those planted in non-cedar soil under the same conditions.

Methods

The experiment took place from March 19 to April 20, 2009, in the Northwestern 5
College biology lab. Our professors collected soil from Oak Grove State Park near Hawarden, Iowa, several months in advance. They gathered soil from three different locations under three different cedars trees and from three nearby non-cedar locations. They placed the soils under sun lamps to dry, and then stored the soil in plastic ziplock bags.

To prepare for this experiment, two rows of evenly spaced holes were drilled into 6
18 potting trays for drainage. Each tray was labeled with the soil's location number and the soil type (cedar or non-cedar). From each specified location, soil was measured out equally and placed into the trays. In an effort to make the growing conditions realistic, any foreign plant roots, stems, etc. were left in the soil.

Black-eyed Susans *(Rudbeckia hirta)* and poppies *(Papaver orientale)* were chosen 7
because of their equal planting depth and equal time for seed germination. Two rows were planted in each tray with 10 evenly spaced black-eyed Susan seeds on one side and ten evenly spaced poppy seeds on the other side (both were planted according to the directions on the packages).

On March 19, each tray was placed approximately 35cm. under sun lamps that ran on a 12hrs. on/12hrs. off cycle. Each day, the trays were watered and rotated so that they received an equal amount of light and warmth. When a seed germinated, the date and the plant location in the tray were documented. If the plant died, the date of the death was recorded. Any foreign species that grew were left so as not to disturb the soil. On April 20, thirty-two days later, the data were compiled. The number of each species that germinated at each location and the number of days each plant survived were recorded. 8

Using Microsoft Excel, we first ran ANOVAs to see if there were any significant differences in germination rates among the three cedar soil sites or any significant difference in germination rates among the non-cedar sites. Then we ran paired t-tests on germination for each seed type between the cedar and non-cedar soils. To compare the percentage of surviving seedlings between cedar and non-cedar soils, we ran an ANOVA for each seed type. 9

Results

We found no significant differences related to location in germination of black-eyed Susan seeds (ANOVA: F=2.71, F-crit=5.14, df=8, p-value=0.14) (Fig.1) or poppy seeds (ANOVA: F=0.37, F-crit=5.14, df=8, p-value=0.7) (Fig. 1) among the three cedar sites. We also found that there were no significant differences related to location in the germination of black-eyed Susans (ANOVA: F=1.63, F-crit=5.14, df=8, p-value=0.27) (Fig. 2) or poppies (ANOVA: F=0.31, F-crit=5.14, df=8, p-value=0.74) (Fig. 2) among the three non-cedar sites. Knowing that there were no significant differences in germination among the sites, we condensed the data into four different groups: black-eyed Susan cedar, black-eyed Susan non-cedar, poppy cedar, and poppy non-cedar. 10

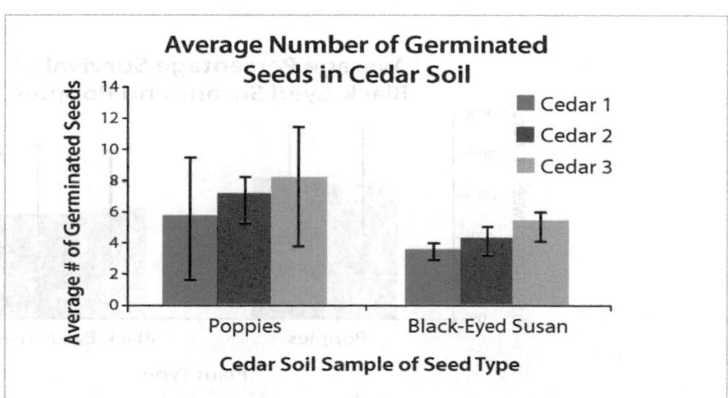

Figure 1. There is no significant difference in seed germination among the three cedar soils for poppies (p=.7) or black-eyed Susans (p=.14). Bars represent standard deviation.

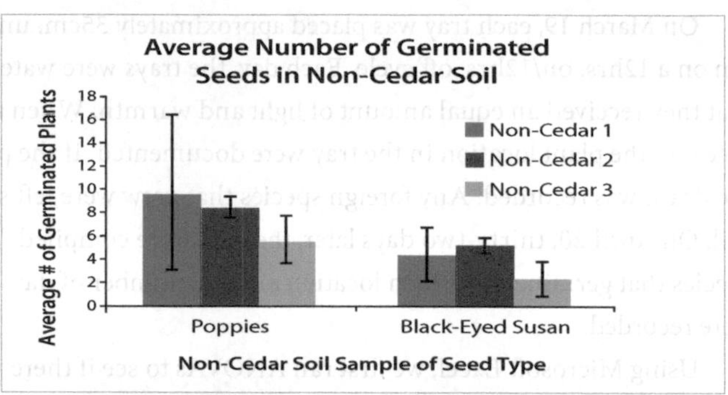

Figure 2. There is no significant difference in seed germination among the three non-cedar soils for poppies (p=.74) or black-eyed Susans (p=.27). Bars represent standard deviation.

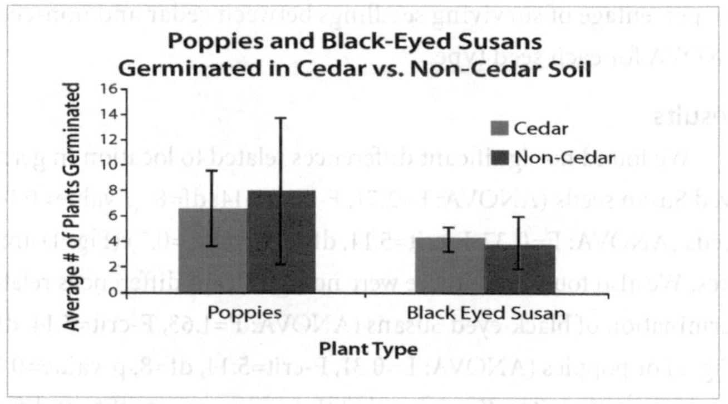

Figure 3. There is no significant difference in germination between cedar and non-cedar soil for poppies (p=.48) or black-eyed Susans (p=.77). Bars represent standard deviation.

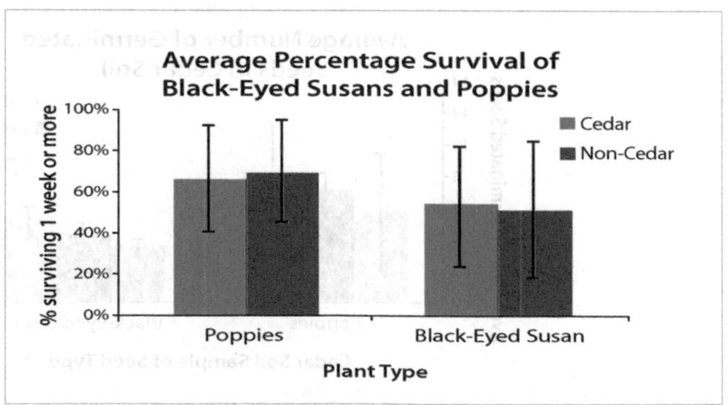

Figure 4. There is no significant difference in seedling survival between cedar and non-cedar soil for poppies (p=.82) or black-eyed Susans (p=.92). Bars represent standard deviation.

The two paired t-tests comparing seed germination in cedar soil versus non-cedar 11
soil showed no significant differences in black-eyed Susan germination between the two soil types (t=0.31, p=0.77) (Fig.3) or in poppy germination between the two soil types (t=-0.78, p=0.46) (Fig.3).

When comparing survivorship of the two seedling types in each soil, we defined 12
surviving plants as those that lived for seven days or more. We ran ANOVAs and found that there was no significant difference between the proportion of seedlings that survived in cedar versus non-cedar soil for black-eyed Susans (ANOVA: F=0.01, F-crit=4.49, df=1, p=0.92) (Fig. 4) or for poppies (ANOVA: F=0.06, F-crit=4.49, df=1, p=0.82) (Fig. 4).

Discussion

In this experiment, we sought to discover whether eastern red cedar soil is 13
allelopathic. We predicted that cedar soil was allelopathic and hypothesized that if our prediction were correct, seeds planted in non-cedar soil would show higher germination and higher survival. We tested for significant differences in soil sites, germination of the two seeds types between soil types, and survival percentages of the seed types between soil types. None of these tests yielded a significant difference.

If the black-eyed Susans and poppies are good representatives of typically affected 14
plants, then eastern red cedar soil appears not to reduce germination or survival. For those concerned with protecting native ecosystems from these invaders, the implications seem positive. An allelopathic invader would produce more damage than a non-allelopathic invader not only in the secretion of chemicals, but also in those chemicals remaining to harm desirable native species even if that invader is removed (Medley & Krisko, 2007).

However, even if cedars do not release allelopathic chemicals, a study conducted 15
in the tall grass prairies of Kansas found that the eastern red cedar increased the amount of above-ground biomass and surface-litter nitrogen pools that are linked to the conversion of grassland to forest (Norris et al., 2007). Though this is not allelopathy, the invasive eastern red cedar still changes the composition of the soil in a manner that could affect the growth of other plants (Norris et al., 2007).

Also, though the cedar soil appeared not to be allelopathic in our study, we are 16
hesitant to make an assessment of the eastern red cedar's affect on other plant types. Several factors may have confounded our non-allelopathic conclusion. The cedar's chemical may simply not be allelopathic to the types of plants we chose (Medley & Krisko, 2007). We purchased the seeds at a local Bomgaars store, and these seeds

are domesticated strains. Domesticated strains may be more resistant to allelopathic chemicals and selected for high germination (Node et al., 2003). If allelopathic chemicals are present, the chemicals may have been affected by the storage period and drying process and consequently have a different effect on seedlings (Norris et al., 2001).

Though we doubt that chemicals affected the outcome of our study, we had several 17
slight complications. In one of our planting boxes, more than ten poppies germinated. This was likely due to accidentally planting more than ten of the tiny seeds. In our statistics, we chose to count them all because excessive seeds were likely accidentally planted in other boxes as well. A recording complication occurred when some poppies germinated outside of their row in their container. The species type of some of the small seedlings was hard to distinguish as they were mixed together.

If we repeated this experiment, we would change both materials and methods. We 18
would grow separate seed types in separate containers so there would be no confusion as to the species. We would also be more attentive to the seeds during the planting process, so none would stick together and distort our data. To see if the drying process was a factor, in addition to planting in dried soil, we would plant in freshly gathered soil. Finally, we would use plant species that are actually threatened by possible cedar allelopathy instead of species to which this possibility is irrelevant in real life. A native tall grass may react much differently to cedar soil and would provide more interesting and relevant application.

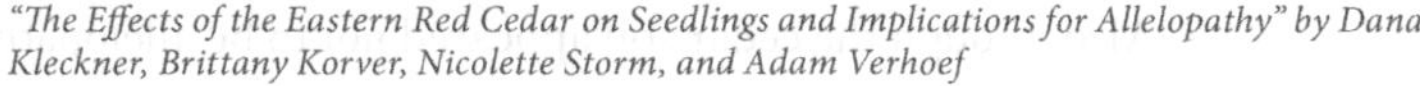

"The Effects of the Eastern Red Cedar on Seedlings and Implications for Allelopathy" by Dana Kleckner, Brittany Korver, Nicolette Storm, and Adam Verhoef

Smit / Shutterstock.com

References

Medley, K., & Krisko, B. (2007). Physical site conditions and land use history as factors influencing the conservation of regrowth forests in a southwest Ohio nature reserve. *Natural Areas Journal*, 27(1), 31-40. doi:10.3375/0885-8608

Node, M., Tomita-Yokotani, K., Suzuki, T., Kosemura, S., Hirata, H., Hirata, K., . . . Hasegawa, K. (2003). Allelopathy of pinecone in Japanese red pine tree *(Pinus densiflora Sieb. et Zucc.). Weed Biology & Management,* 3(2), 111-116. doi:10.1046/j.1445-6664.2003.00092.x

Norris, M. D., Blair, J.M., Johnson, L. C., & McKane, R. B. (2001). Assessing changes in biomass, productivity, and C and N stores following *Juniperus virginiana* forest expansion into tallgrass prairie. *Canadian Journal of Forest Research, 31*(11), 1940. doi:10.1139/x01-132

Norris, M. D., Blair, J. M., & Johnson, L. C. (2007). Altered ecosystem nitrogen dynamics as a consequence of land cover change in tallgrass prairie. *American Midland Naturalist, 158*(2), 432-445. doi:10.1674/0003-0031

Simberloff, D. (1995). Introduced species. In *Encyclopedia of environmental biology* (pp. 323-336). San Diego, CA: Academic Press.

Reading for Better Writing

1. *Connections:* This IMRAD report studies the possible impacts of an invasive species. Where you live or go to school, what invasive species—plant or animal—have impacted the environment? What have those impacts been? Can you sense or imagine how your own experience of this place has been shaped by this invasion?
2. *Comprehension:* The abstract in paragraph 1 summarizes the report. Choose one statement from the abstract and elaborate your understanding of it in more detail.
3. *Writing Strategies:*
   a. The IMRAD structure—introduction, methods, results, and discussion—reflects a pattern of scientific thinking. How would you characterize that pattern? What are the key principles behind it and features of it, based upon your reading?
   b. Select any one of the IMRAD parts in the report and study the writing strategies used in that section. What practices do the writers follow? What do those practices accomplish in dealing with the subject matter?

Your Project: If you have the time and resources, you might consider conducting an experiment related to an invasive species in your local environment. However, if that is not possible, consider writing a literature review—a survey and synthesis of the scientific studies that have been conducted and published about that invasive species.

Critical Thinking and Writing: Applications

Once you have applied the instruction in this chapter to your own research writing, there may be more to think about. Consider these applications:

1. **Photo Op:** The opening of this chapter includes an image of a scale to suggest the weighing and balancing of researched material that goes into drafting research writing. Based on the key concepts covered in this chapter, what other image might capture the head work involved?
2. **Public Texts:** This chapter focuses on deepening one's thinking through reflecting on sources and reasoning well with documented evidence. While news stories, Web pages from organizations, and speeches by prominent figures are not identical to research papers, we do have expectations that such statements be rooted in sound research. Look closely at a news story, a Web page from a nonprofit or business, or a speech by a politician or celebrity: how would you evaluate the use of reasoning and evidence?
3. **Writing Reset:** Review a research paper that you wrote in the past. Does that paper follow the principles for using, integrating, and documenting source material, as outlined in this chapter? How might you improve the treatment of sources in your paper?
4. **Major Work:** Compare and contrast the humanities essay on pages 452–456 and the IMRAD report on pages 457–463. What similarities do they share with respect to research and research writing? What differences stand out? What do these similarities and differences suggest about research writing in your own field of study?

Learning-Objectives Checklist ✓

Have you achieved this chapter's learning objectives? Check your progress with the following items, revisiting topics in the chapter as needed. I have . . .

____ carefully examined my research findings so as to deepen my thinking on the topic and imagine my paper (442).

____ assessed my working thesis and strengthened it in light of my research (443).

____ organized my thinking by considering what I discovered through research, along with traditional methods of organization (444–445).

____ drafted my paper either systematically or freely, but have focused on respecting my sources and reasoning with the evidence (446–447).

____ smoothly integrated and carefully documented source material into my writing (448–451).

____ compared and contrasted research-writing practices in a humanities essay and a sciences IMRAD report (452–463).

Chapter 23

MLA Style

In writing research papers, it is commonly said, "You are commanded to borrow but forbidden to steal." To borrow ideas while avoiding plagiarism (see pages 431–440), you must not only mention the sources you borrow from but also document them completely and accurately. You must follow the documentation principles for papers written in your area of study.

If you are composing a research paper in the humanities, your instructor will most likely require you to follow the conventions established in the style manual of the Modern Language Association (MLA). This chapter provides you with overarching guidelines, detailed explanations, and helpful examples for citing sources in MLA format.

Visually Speaking Library shelves organize a vast amount of knowledge (Figure 23.1). In what sense does a system such as MLA style make sense of and order knowledge in research writing?

MindTap®

Understand the goals of the chapter and complete a warm-up activity online.

Learning Objectives

By working through this chapter, you will be able to

- explain and implement MLA guidelines for documenting sources.
- produce research writing that adheres to MLA guidelines for formatting.
- evaluate MLA practices at work in a sample student research-based essay.

Amy Johansson / Shutterstock.com

fig. 23.1

MLA Documentation: Quick Guide

The MLA system aims, above all, to make documentation clear and useful to readers. To do so, the system involves two parts: (1) an in-text citation within your paper when you use a source and (2) a matching bibliographic entry at the end of your paper. Note these features:

- **It's minimalist.** In your paper, you provide the least amount of information needed for your reader to identify the source in the works-cited list.
- **It uses signal phrases and parenthetical references** to set off source material from your own thinking and discussion. A signal phrase names the author and places the material in context (e.g., "As Margaret Atwood argues in *Survival*").
- **It's smooth, unobtrusive, flexible, and orderly.** While in-text citations keep the paper readable, alphabetized entries in the works-cited list make locating source details easy. Moreover, instead of requiring writers to follow unique, "correct" formats for several different source types, MLA style offers a basic pattern that researchers can follow, allowing them to make judgements about what to include.

You can see these features at work in the example below. "Anna Hutchens" and "(449)" tell the reader the following things:

- The borrowed material came from a source written by Anna Hutchens.
- The specific material can be found on page 449 of the source.
- Full source details are in the works-cited list under the author's last name.

1. **In-Text Citation in Body of Paper**

> As Anna Hutchens puts it, there is an "absence of a policy framework and institutional mechanisms that promote women's empowerment as a rights-based rather than a culture-based issue" (449).

2. **Matching Works-Cited Entry at End of Paper**

> Hutchens, Anna. "Empowering Women Through Fair Trade? Lessons from Asia." *Third World Quarterly*, vol. 31, no. 3, 2010, pp. 449-67. *EBSCOhost*, doi:10.1080/01436597.2010.488477.

In-Text Citation: The Basics

In MLA, in-text citations typically follow these guidelines:

1. Refer to the author (plus the work's title, if helpful) and a page number by using one of these methods:

Last name and page number in parentheses:

last name only in citation

> Fair trade is not necessary for consumers to "exercise a moral choice" with their money (Chandler 256).

no "p." for "page"

no comma between name and page number

Name cited in sentence, page number in parentheses:

full name in first reference

> As Paul Chandler admits, fair trade is not necessary for consumers to "exercise a moral choice" with their money (256).

page number only in citation

2. Present and punctuate citations according to these rules:
    - Place the parenthetical reference after the source material.
    - Within the parentheses, normally give the author's last name only.
    - Do not put a comma between the author's last name and the page reference.
    - Cite the page number as a numeral, not a word.
    - Don't use *p.*, *pp.*, or *page(s)* before the page number(s).
    - Place any sentence punctuation after the closed parenthesis.

For many of these rules, exceptions exist. For example, many electronic sources have no stated authors and/or no pagination. See pages 468–475 for complete coverage of in-text citation practices.

Works Cited: Nine Core Elements

Essentially, all works-cited entries are built out of nine core elements typically shared across different sources. Here is a sample entry and an overview of the nine elements. Note: not all entries must contain all nine elements. (The example does not include a *version* or *number.*)

> [1] Beckerman, Bernard. [2] "The Uses and Management of the Elizabethan Stage." [3] *The Third Globe: Symposium for the Reconstruction of the Globe Playhouse, Wayne State University, 1979,* [4] edited by C. Walter Hodges, S. Schoenbaum, and Leonard Leone, [7] Wayne State UP, [8] 1981, [9] pp. 151-63.

1. **Author:** the person, people, or organization that created the source; or the person whose work on the source you choose to emphasize.
2. **Title of Source:** the full title of the specific source you are using—a whole book, an essay or other text within a book, an article in a periodical or reference work, a specific Web page, a film, an episode of a television show, and so on.
3. **Title of Container:** the larger source that contains or holds the source you are using—possibly a book, a journal or magazine, a database, or a Web site. Note: stand-alone sources have no containers.
4. **Other Contributors:** people whose contribution may be noteworthy—editors, translators, performers, and so on.
5. **Version:** when there is more than one version of a source (e.g., revised or numbered editions), a description of the version used.
6. **Number:** an indication of how the source fits into a sequence—volume and issue numbers for journals, season and episode numbers for televisions shows.
7. **Publisher:** the organization that produces or sponsors the source, responsible for delivering it—a book publisher, a production company, a Web site host.
8. **Publication Date:** when the source was made available to the public.
9. **Location:** where a source was and can be found—page numbers within print sources, DOI (digital object identifier) or URL (uniform resource locator) for online sources, the site for a lecture or performance.

Guidelines for In-Text Citations

The *MLA Handbook*, Eighth Edition (2016), suggests giving credit for your sources of information in the body of your research paper. One way to do so is by indicating the author and/or title in the text of your essay, and then putting a page reference in parentheses after the summary, paraphrase, or quotation, as needed. The simplest way to do so is to insert the appropriate information (usually the author and page number) in parentheses after the words or ideas taken from the source.

To avoid disrupting your writing, place citations where a pause would naturally occur (usually at the end of a sentence but sometimes within a sentence, before internal punctuation such as a comma or semicolon). These in-text citations (often called "parenthetical references") refer to sources listed on the "Works Cited" page at the end of your paper. (See page 500 for a sample works-cited list.) Essentially, each in-text citation must clearly point to a source in your works cited, and every source in the works-cited list must be referred to at least once within your paper.

Citations for Regular Sources

As you integrate citations into your paper, follow the guidelines below, referring to the sample citation as needed.

Sample In-Text Citation

> As James Cuno, director of the Harvard University Art Museums, points out, the public, which subsidizes museums either directly through donations or indirectly via their status as tax-free nonprofit organizations, expects them to "carry out their duties professionally on its behalf" (164).

- **Make sure each in-text citation clearly points to an entry in your list of works cited.** The identifying information provided (usually the author's last name) must be the word or words by which the entry is alphabetized in that list.
- **Keep citations brief, and integrate them smoothly** into your writing.
- **When paraphrasing or summarizing rather than quoting, make it clear where your borrowing begins and ends.** Use stylistic cues to distinguish the source's thoughts ("Kalmbach points out . . . ," "Some critics argue . . .") from your own ("I believe . . . ," "It seems obvious, however"). See pages 448–451 for more on integrating sources.
- **When using a shortened title of a work, begin with the word by which the work is alphabetized** in your list of works cited (e.g., "Egyptian, Classical," not "Middle Eastern Art," for "Egyptian, Classical, and Middle Eastern Art").
- **For inclusive page numbers larger than ninety-nine, give only the last two digits of the second number** (346–48, not 346–348).
- **When including a parenthetical citation at the end of a sentence, place it before the end punctuation.** (Citations for long, indented quotations are an exception. See page 451.)

Citations for Sources without Traditional Authorship and/or Pagination

Today many sources, especially electronic ones, have no stated authors and/or no pagination. For such sources, use these in-text citation strategies:

Source Without a Stated Author

In a signal phrase or in the parenthetical reference, identify the source as precisely as possible by indicating the sponsoring agency, the type of document, or the title (shortened in the parenthetical reference). See pages 470–471.

> While the Brooklyn Museum may be best known for the recent controversy over the Sensation exhibition, the museum does contain a strong collection of contemporary if less controversial art, "ranging from representational to abstract to conceptual" ("Contemporary Art").

Source with No Pagination

If no pagination exists within the document, use paragraph numbers (with the abbreviation *par.*), if the document provides them. If the document includes neither page nor paragraph numbers, cite the entire work. Do not create your own numbering system.

> The Museum's *Art of the Americas* collection includes extensive holdings of works by the aboriginal peoples of North, Central, and South America, many of these gathered by archaeologist Herbert Spinden during at least seven expeditions between 1929 and 1950 (*Art of the Americas*, par. 3).

Because parenthetical notations are used to signal the end of an attribution, sources with no pagination or paragraph numbers offer a special challenge. When no parenthetical notation is possible, signal a shift back to your own discussion with a source-reflective statement indicating your thinking about the source.

> . . . indicated by his recording the audio tour of the exhibit, his supporting the show financially, and his promoting *Sensation* at his Web site. As Welland's discussion of David Bowie's participation suggests, the controversy over the Brooklyn Museum of Art's *Sensation* exhibit . . .

Ilin Sergey / Shutterstock.com

INSIGHT Stable pagination for many digital resources is available when you use the ".pdf" rather than the ".html" version of the source. For instruction on smoothly integrating source material into your paper, see pages 448–451. For cautions about sources without identified authors, see pages 472 and 480.

Sample In-Text Citations

The following entries illustrate the most common in-text citations.

One Author: A Complete Work

You do not need a parenthetical citation if you identify the author in your text. (See the first entry below.) However, you must give the author's last name in a parenthetical citation if it is not mentioned in the text. (See the second entry.) When a source is listed in your works-cited page with an editor, a translator, a speaker, or an artist instead of the author, use that person's name in your citation.

With Author in Text: (This is the preferred way of citing a complete work.)

> In *No Need for Hunger,* Robert Spitzer recommends that the U.S. government develop a new foreign policy to help Third World countries overcome poverty and hunger.

Without Author in Text:

> *No Need for Hunger* recommends that the U.S. government develop a new foreign policy to help Third World countries overcome poverty and hunger (Spitzer).

Note: Do not offer page numbers when citing complete works, articles in alphabetized encyclopedias, one-page articles, and unpaginated sources.

One Author: Part of a Work

List the necessary page numbers in parentheses if you borrow words or ideas from a particular source. Leave a space between the author's last name and the page reference. No abbreviation or punctuation is needed.

With Author in Text:

> Bullough writes that genetic engineering was dubbed "eugenics" by a cousin of Darwin's, Sir Francis Galton, in 1885 (5).

Without Author in Text:

> Genetic engineering was dubbed "eugenics" by a cousin of Darwin's, Sir Francis Galton, in 1885 (Bullough 5).

A Work by Two Authors

Give the last names of both authors in the same order that they appear in the works-cited section. (The correct order of the authors' names can be found on the title page of the book.)

> Students learned more than a full year's Spanish in ten days using the complete supermemory method (Ostrander and Schroeder 51).

A Work by Three or More Authors

Give the first author's last name as it appears in the works-cited section followed by *et al.* (meaning "and others").

> Communication on the job is more than talking; it is "inseparable from your total behavior" (Culligan et al. 111).

Note: You may instead choose to list all of the authors' last names.

Two or More Works by the Same Author(s)

In addition to the author's last name(s) and page number(s), include a shortened version of the work's title when you cite two or more works by the same author(s).

With Author in Text:

> Wallerstein and Blakeslee claim that divorce creates an enduring identity for children of the marriage (*Unexpected Legacy* 62).

Without Author in Text:

> They are intensely lonely despite active social lives (Wallerstein and Blakeslee, *Second Chances* 51).

Note: When including both author(s) and title in a parenthetical reference, separate them with a comma, as shown above, but do not put a comma between the title and the page number.

Works by Authors with the Same Last Name

When citing different sources by authors with the same last name, it is best to use the authors' full names in the text to avoid confusion. However, if circumstances call for parenthetical references, add each author's first initial. If first initials are the same, use each author's full name.

> Some critics think *Titus Andronicus* too abysmally melodramatic to be a work of Shakespeare (A. Parker 73). Others suggest that Shakespeare meant it as black comedy (D. Parker 486).

A Work Authored by an Agency, a Committee, or an Organization

If a book or other work was created by an organization such as an agency, a committee, a studio, or a task force, it is said to have a corporate author. (See also page 480.) If the corporate name is long, include it in the text (rather than in parentheses) to avoid disrupting the flow of your writing. After the full name has been used at least once, use a shortened form of the name (including common abbreviations such as *Dept.*) in subsequent references. For example, *Task Force* may be used for *Task Force on Education for Economic Growth*.

> The thesis of the Task Force's report is that economic success depends on our ability to improve large-scale education and training as quickly as possible (113–14).

An Anonymous Work

When there is no author listed, give the title or a shortened version of the title as it appears in the works-cited section. (See page 480.)

> Statistics indicate that drinking water can make up 20 percent of a person's total exposure to lead (*Information* 572).

Two or More Works Included in One Citation

To cite multiple works within a single parenthetical reference, separate the references with a semicolon.

> In Medieval Europe, Latin translations of the works of Rhazes, a Persian scholar, were a primary source of medical knowledge (Albala 22; Lewis 266).

A Series of Citations from a Single Work

If no confusion is possible, it is not necessary to name a source repeatedly when making multiple parenthetical references to that source in a single paragraph. If all references are to the same page, identify that page in a parenthetical note after the last reference. If the references are to different pages within the same work, you need identify the work only once, and then use a parenthetical note with page number alone for the subsequent references.

> Domesticating science meant not only spreading scientific knowledge, but also promoting it as a topic of public conversation (Heilbron 2). One way to enhance its charm was by depicting cherubic putti as "angelic research assistants" in book illustrations (5).

A Work Referred to in Another Work

If you must cite an indirect source—that is, information in a source that is quoted from another source—use the abbreviation *qtd. in* (quoted in) before the indirect source in your reference.

> Paton improved the conditions in Diepkloof (a prison) by "removing all the more obvious aids to detention. The dormitories [were] open at night: the great barred gate [was] gone" (qtd. in Callan xviii).

A Work Without Page Numbers or Other Markers

If a work has no page numbers, paragraph numbers, or other markers included, treat it as you would a complete work. (See page 470.) This is commonly the case with some digital resources, for example. Do not count pages or paragraphs to create reference numbers of your own.

> Antibiotics become ineffective against such organisms through two natural processes: first, genetic mutation; and second, the subsequent transfer of this mutated genetic material to other organisms (Davies).

A Work in an Anthology or a Collection

When citing the entirety of a work that is part of an anthology or a collection, if it is identified by author in your list of works cited, treat the citation as you would for any other complete work. (See page 470.)

> In "The Canadian Postmodern," Linda Hutcheon offers a clear analysis of the self-reflexive nature of contemporary Canadian fiction.

Similarly, if you are citing particular pages of such a work, follow the directions for citing part of a work. (See page 470.)

> According to Hutcheon, "postmodernism seems to designate cultural practices that are fundamentally self-reflexive, in other words, art that is self-consciously artifice" (18).

(To format this sort of entry in your list of works cited, see pages 480–481.)

An Item from a Reference Work

An entry from a reference work such as an encyclopedia or a dictionary should be cited similarly to a work from an anthology or a collection (see above). For a dictionary definition, include the abbreviation *def.* followed by the particular entry designation.

> This message becomes a juggernaut in the truest sense, a belief that "elicits blind devotion or sacrifice" ("Juggernaut," def. 1).

Note: While many such entries are identified only by title (as above), some reference works include an author's name for each entry (as below). Others may identify the entry author by initials, with a list of full names elsewhere in the work.

> The decisions of the International Court of Justice are "based on principles of international law and cannot be appealed" (Pranger).

(See pages 482–483 for guidelines to formatting these entries in your works-cited list.)

A Part of a Multivolume Work

When citing only one volume of a multivolume work, if you identify the volume number in the works-cited list, there is no need to include it in your in-text citation. However, if you cite more than one volume of a work, each in-text reference must identify the appropriate volume. Give the volume number followed by page number, separated by a colon and a space.

> "A human being asleep," says Spengler, ". . . is leading only a plantlike existence" (2: 4).

When citing a whole volume, however, either identify the volume number in parentheses with the abbreviation *vol.* (using a comma to separate it from the author's name) or use the full word *volume* in your text.

> The land of Wisconsin has shaped its many inhabitants more significantly than they ever shaped that land (Stephens, vol. 1).

A One-Page Work

Cite a one-page work just as you would a complete work. (See page 470.)

> As Samantha Adams argues in her editorial, it is time for NASA "to fully reevaluate the possibility of a manned mission to Mars."

A Sacred Text or Famous Literary Work

Sacred texts and famous literary works are published in many different editions. For that reason, it is helpful to identify sections, parts, chapters, and such instead of or in addition to page numbers. If using page numbers, list them first, followed by a semicolon and then an abbreviation for the type of division and the division number.

> The more important a person's role in society—the more apparent power an individual has—the more that person is a slave to the forces of history (Tolstoy 690; bk. 9, ch. 1).

Books of the Bible and other well-known literary works may be abbreviated, if no confusion is possible. The first reference should indicate the edition being used; subsequent references need supply only the abbreviated citation.

> "A generation goes, and a generation comes, but the earth remains forever" (*The New Oxford Annotated Bible*, Eccles. 1.4).

> As Shakespeare's famous Danish prince observes, "One may smile, and smile, and be a villain" (Ham. 1.5.104).

Quoting Prose

To cite prose from fiction (novels, short stories), list more than the page number if the work is available in several editions. Give the page reference first, and then add a chapter, section, or book number in abbreviated form after a semicolon.

> In *The House of the Spirits,* Isabel Allende describes Marcos, "dressed in mechanic's overalls, with huge racer's goggles" (13; ch. 1).

When you are quoting any sort of prose that takes more than four typed lines, indent each line of the quotation a half inch (five spaces) and double-space it; do not add quotation marks. In this case, you put the parenthetical citation (the pages and chapter numbers) outside the end punctuation mark of the quotation itself.

> Allende describes the flying machine that Marcos has assembled:
>
> > The contraption lay with its stomach on terra firma, heavy and sluggish and looking more like a wounded duck than like one of those newfangled airplanes they were starting to produce in the United States. There was nothing in its appearance to suggest that it could move, much less take flight across the snowy peaks. (12; ch. 1)

Quoting Verse

Do not use page numbers when referencing classic verse plays and poems. Instead, cite them by division (act, scene, canto, book, part) and line, using Arabic numerals for the various divisions unless your instructor prefers Roman numerals. Use periods to separate the various numbers.

> In the first act, Hamlet comments, "How weary, stale, flat and unprofitable, / Seem to me all the uses of this world" (1.2.133–34).

Note: A slash, with a space on each side, shows where each line of verse ends and a new one begins. If a short poem's lines are numbered in the edition you are using, you may cite the poem using lines only, not page number. Use the word *line* or *lines* in your first reference and numbers only in additional references. If a short poem's lines are not numbered in the edition, simply cite the whole work; do not count lines yourself.

> At the beginning of the sestet in Robert Frost's "Design," the speaker asks this pointed question: "What had that flower to do with being white, / The wayside blue and innocent heal-all?" (lines 9–10).

Verse quotations of more than three lines should be indented one inch and double-spaced. Do not add quotation marks. Each line of the poem or play begins a new line of the quotation; do not run the lines together. If a line or lines of poetry are dropped from the quotation, ellipses that extend the width of the stanza should be used to indicate the omission.

> Bin Ramke's poem "A Little Ovid Late in the Day" tells of reading by the last light of a summer day:
>
> [T]ales of incest, corruption,
> any big, mythic vice
> against the color of the sun,
> the sweetness of the time of day—
> I know the story,
> it is the light I care about. (3–8)

Alina Poronik / Shutterstock.com

Guidelines for Works-Cited Entries

The works-cited section lists only those sources that you have cited in your paper. For guidelines on formatting your works-cited list, see pages 487–488, as well as the sample works-cited list on pages 501–502. In what follows, you will first find a template for works-cited entries, showing the essential pattern to follow. After the template, you will find guidelines for constructing any entry by drawing upon the nine core elements of source identification and arranging those elements in the order listed.

Works-Cited Template

Every works-cited entry will include some or all of nine elements, formatted and punctuated in the manner indicated.

> Author. Title of Source [normally italicized or in quotation marks]. *Title of Container,* Other Contributors, Version, Number, Publisher, Publication Date, Location.

Works-Cited Components

The following table provides you with guidelines for presenting each of the nine main components of works-cited entries. Review both the instructions and examples to understand the logic of each element.

1. The Author is the person, people, or organization that created the source. Note that for online sources, pseudonyms and handles may be used. In general, omit titles and degrees from names, but present the name accurately from the source. Follow the author with a period. • **One author:** Invert the author's name. • **Two authors:** Follow the order given in the source. Invert the first author's name, but put the second in traditional order. Separate the authors' names with a comma. • **Three or more authors:** Name only the first author listed, followed by *et al.* (meaning *and others).* • **Other contributors:** If appropriate, you may put another contributor in this first position to emphasize the focus in your writing: an editor, a director, a performer, and so on. Spell out the role after the name and a comma.	Jacob, Mira. King, Martin Luther, Jr. @PiradorUSA. Environmental Protection Agency. Pratchett, Terry, and Neil Gaiman. Raabe, William A., et al. Dunham, Lena, performer.

2. The Title of the Source is the full title of the specific source you are using—a whole book, an essay or other text within a book, an article within a periodical, a specific Web page, a film, an episode of a television show, and so on. Typically, titles of longer works and stand-alone works are italicized; titles of shorter works and those within longer works are placed within quotation marks; untitled sections of a work are neither italicized nor put in quotation marks. Follow standard capitalization practices, and separate a main title and a subtitle with a colon and a space. Conclude the full title with a period. (See page 601 for more on italics, page 599 for more on quotation marks, and page 607 for more on capitalization.)

Design for How People Learn.

The Martian.

"The Yellow Wallpaper."

"The One with Phoebe's Wedding."

Introduction.

3. The Title of the Container refers to the name of a larger whole that may contain or hold the specific source you are using. Information about containers is key for readers seeking to understand and/or find your source. The container may be a book containing an essay or short story, a journal or magazine issue containing a specific article, a television series containing an episode, a Web site containing a specific Web page or posting. Sometimes, a container may be nested inside a larger container. For example, an article may be contained in a journal that is itself contained within the database you used to access the article. In this case, your entry would list information for both containers, in order, with as much information from core elements 3-9 as you have for each container. Note that stand-alone sources have no container, so you would not list one in the entry. Italicize the title of a container; normally follow the title with a comma, as the entry supplies more information (elements 4-9) about the container.

The New Yorker,

African American Review,

The Concise Anthology of American Literature,

Game of Thrones,

EBSCOhost,

Netflix,

ACLS Humanities E-book,

Fairtrade International

Sergey Mironov / Shutterstock.com

4. Other Contributors are those people whose contribution is important to your use of the source or whose identity is valuable information for your readers. Introduce each name that you include in the entry with a description of the role. If a contributor follows element 2 (title of the source, punctuated with a period), capitalize the description; if listed after element 3 (title of container, punctuated with a comma), do not capitalize the description. Separate multiple roles with commas. Note that in scholarly books, editors and translators play important roles and should generally be included in the entry.

. Translated by David McLoghlin,

, adapted by Anne Carson,

. Directed by Mira Nair, performance by Naseeruddin Shah.

5. The Version refers to the form of the source you used, when there is more than one version available. Such a version may indicate a revised, expanded, updated, or numbered edition; or it may be a descriptive phrase. Use the abbreviations *ed.* (edition) and *rev.* (revised), but spell out other words; use ordinal numbers with arabic numerals for numbered editions. Write the edition description all lowercase, unless it is a proper noun phrase, which would be capitalized.

rev. ed.,

6th ed.,

updated ed.,

director's cut,

Authorized King James Version,

6. The Number indicates how the source fits into a sequence: volume and issue numbers for journals, volume number for a book in a numbered multivolume set, season and episode numbers for television shows, comic book numbers, and so on. Use abbreviations *vol.* (volume) and *no.* (issue), but spell out other descriptors, such as *episode*. Lowercase all words and use numerals; follow each number with a comma.

vol. 24, no. 2,

season 6, episode 11,

no. 77,

7. The Publisher is the organization that produces or sponsors the source, making it available to readers or viewers. These organizations include book publishers, production companies, Web site hosts (e.g., museums, libraries, businesses), and blog networks. If a source has more than one publisher, separate them with a slash (/). Omit the publisher's name for a periodical, a work published by an author, a Web site whose name is essentially the same as the organization, or a Web site such as YouTube that isn't involved in producing the source (but is essentially a container). The publication city is not required. Spell out most names, but omit initial articles (*a, an, the*) and corporate words (*Inc., Corp.*). Abbreviate *University* (U) and *Press* (P).

Vintage Books,

U of Virginia Library / Museum of Design,

Melville House,

Rutgers UP,

U of Michigan P,

Cengage Learning,

8. The Publication Date indicates when the source was made available to the public through publishing, republishing, updating, releasing, broadcasting, or performing. In some cases, the source may indicate more than one date (e.g., an original copyright date of a book's first edition, a print publication date for an online source, an original broadcast date for a television episode). When this happens, cite the date most meaningful to your use and discussion of the source; as a general rule for books, however, give the most recent date offered by the book's title or copyright page.

2017,

Jan.-Feb. 2014,

10 May 2016, 9:30 p.m.,

9. The Location indicates where a source was and can be found. For some sources, this detail typically includes page numbers, listed in numerals after the abbreviation *p.* (for a single page) or *pp.* (for multiple pages). For periodical articles printed on non-consecutive pages, use a plus sign (+) after the numeral for the first page. For online sources, provide a DOI (digital object identifier), if available, after *doi* plus a colon, with no space between. If a DOI is not available, use a direct URL (uniform resource locater), ideally a permalink. Do not use angle brackets or include prefixes such as http://.

p. 45.

pp. 185-89.

p. 13+

doi:10.1002/cplx.21590.

milkdelivers.org/about

Guthrie Theater, Minneapolis.

Optional Elements

Most details that you need to include in a works-cited entry will fit in core elements 1–9. Occasionally, you may choose to include one or more of the following details:

- **Date of original publication:** If the original publication date of a republished source is important to know, supply it right after the source's title.
- **Date of access:** If you believe that an online source might change or disappear (especially if the source itself provides no publication or posting date), supply the date you accessed it in this format: Accessed 26 April 2017. Place the access date at the end of the citation, after the location.
- **Publication city:** If the publisher is unfamiliar, if the version of the text is unexpected, or if a book was published before 1900, consider adding the publication city before the publisher's name, separated by a comma.
- **Type of work:** If the source's format is unclear from the rest of the entry, clarify the medium with a term such as *Transcript, Lecture,* or *Address*, placed at the end of the entry.
- **Name of series:** If a book is part of a publishing series, consider adding the name of the series (capitalized, but not in italics or quotation marks) and the book's number within the series (if applicable) at the end of the entry.
- **Prior publication information:** If the source was previously published in another form and that information is useful to your readers, add an "Originally published" statement at the end of the entry, supplying full publication details.

Sample Works-Cited Entries

Knowing the nine core elements of any works-cited entry should prove sufficient for building your works-cited list. You may find it useful, however, to develop your entries by following sample entries such as those that follow.

Books

A Print Book

Wagner-Martin, Linda. *Toni Morrison: A Literary Life*. Palgrave Macmillan, 2015.

A Book from an Online Database

Note that the first date in the entry, placed after the title, refers to the original publication date. The second date indicates when the book was published online.

Wells, H. G. *The Invisible Man: A Grotesque Romance*. 1897. *Bartleby.com*, 2000, bartleby.com/1003/.

An E-Reader Version of a Book (App or on Device)

Cadhain, Máirtín Ó. *The Dirty Dust*. Translated by Alan Titley, Kindle ed., Yale UP, 2015.

A Book by Two Authors

Naifeh, Steven, and Gregory White Smith. *Van Gogh: The Life*. Random House, 2011.

A Book by Three or More Authors

Baron, Cynthia, et al. *Appetites and Anxieties: Food, Film, and the Politics of Representation*. Wayne State UP, 2014.

A Work Authored by an Agency, a Committee, or an Organization

Exxon Mobil Corporation. *Great Plains 2000*. Publications International, 2001.

An Anonymous Book

Chase's Calendar of Events 2002. Contemporary, 2002.

A Complete Anthology, Collection, or Conference Proceedings

King, Lovalerie, and Shirley Moody-Turner, editors. *Contemporary African American Literature: The Living Canon*. Indiana UP, 2013.

A Single Work from an Anthology, Collection, or Conference Proceedings

Díaz, Junot. "Aurora." *The Ecco Anthology of Contemporary American Short Fiction*, edited by Joyce Carol Oates and Christopher R. Beha, Harper Perennial, 2008, pp. 213-26.

Two or More Works from an Anthology, Collection, or Conference Proceedings

To avoid unnecessary repetition when citing two or more entries from a larger collection, you may cite the collection once with complete publication information (see Rothfield, below). The individual entries (see Becker and Cuno, below) can then be cross-referenced by listing the author, title of the piece, editor of the collection, and page numbers.

Becker, Carol. "The Brooklyn Controversy: A View from the Bridge." Rothfield, pp. 15–21.

Cuno, James. "Sensation and the Ethics of Funding Exhibitions." Rothfield, pp. 162–70.

Rothfield, Lawrence, editor. *Unsettling Sensation: Arts-Policy Lessons from the Brooklyn Museum of Art Controversy.* Rutgers UP, 2001. Rutgers Series on the Public Life of the Arts.

One Volume of a Multivolume Work

Kennedy, David M., and Lizabeth Cohen. *The American Pageant: Since 1865,* 15th ed., vol. 2, Wadsworth, 2012.

An Introduction, a Preface, a Foreword, or an Afterword

Start with the author of the part, followed by the type of the part, with no quotation marks or italics. If the part has a distinct title, that title can go in quotation marks after the author's name. Follow the book's title with the book's author, publication details, and page numbers for the part, as shown in the examples below.

Barry, Anne. Afterword. *Making Room for Students,* by Celia Oyler, Teachers College, 1996, pp. 139–40.

Atwood, Margaret. Introduction. *Alice Munro's Best: Selected Stories,* by Alice Munro, McClelland and Stewart, 2006, pp. vii-xviii.

A Book with a Title within Its Title

If the book's title contains within it a title normally in quotation marks, keep the quotation marks and italicize the entire title. If the title contains within it another title that is normally italicized, do not italicize that title within the entry's title.

Stuckey-French, Elizabeth. *"The First Paper Girl in Red Oak, Iowa" and Other Stories.* Doubleday, 2000.

Beckwith, Charles E., editor. *Twentieth Century Interpretations of* A Tale of Two Cities: *A Collection of Critical Essays.* Prentice Hall, 1972.

Periodical Articles

A Print Journal Article

Give the original publication date after the title.

Parikka, Jussi. "Earth Forces: Contemporary Land Arts, Technology, and New Materialist Aesthetics." *Cultural Studies Review*, vol. 21, no. 2, 2015, pp. 47-75.

An Online Journal Article from a Database

This entry shows how to nest a container within a container. The article is contained within the journal (container 1), which is contained within the EBSCOhost database (container 2).

Pavlovic, R. Y., and A. M. Pavlovic. "Dostoevsky and Psychoanalysis: Psychiatry in 19th-Century Literature." *The British Journal of Psychiatry*, vol. 200, no. 3, 2012, p. 181. *EBSCOhost*, doi:10.1192/bjp.bp.111.093823.

A Print Magazine Article

Brennan, William. "TV's Fake-Language Master." *The Atlantic*, Apr. 2016, pp. 16-18.

An Online Magazine Article

The first example that follows is from the free Web; the second is from a database, which functions as the second container in the entry.

Kay, Jonathan. "Uber v. Taxi." *The Walrus*, Aug. 2015, thewalrus.ca/uber-v-taxi/.

Wood, Graeme. "Prison Without Walls." *The Atlantic*, Sept. 2010, pp. 86-96. *EBSCOhost*, eds.b.ebscohost.com.libproxy.redeemer.ca:2048/eds/detail/detail?sid=e2ff81a2-0421-4fa2-a646-86b4230f9119%40sessionmgr105&vid=7&hid=119&bdata=JnNpdGU9ZWRzLWxpdmU%3d#AN=53442640&db=rch.

A Print Newspaper Article

Simon, Lizzie. "The Art of Obsession." *The Wall Street Journal*, 19 Mar. 2012, pp. A24+.

An Online Newspaper Article

The first example that follows is from the free Web; the second is from a database, which functions as the second container in the entry.

Chen, Brian X. "Virtual Reality Is Here. Is Oculus Rift Worth It?" *The New York Times*, 28 Mar. 2016, nyti.ms/1XYcowB.

"Outsider Candidates Generating Buzz." *The Toronto Star*, 19 Mar. 2016, p. A16. *LexisNexis Academic*, www.lexisnexis.com.proxy.wexler.hunter.cuny.edu/ lnacui2api/api/version1/getDocCui?1ni=5JBB-WWG1-DY91-K4PR&csi =237924&hl=t&hv=t&hnsd=f&hns=t&hgn=t&oc=00240&perma=true.

A Review

Buskey, Megan. "A Wealth of Insight." Review of *When I Was a Child I Read Books*, by Marilynne Robinson. *Wilson Quarterly*, vol. 36, no. 2, 2012, pp. 98-99.

An Editorial or Letter to the Editor

Sory, Forrest. Letter. *Milwaukee Journal Sentinel*, July 2001, p. 10.

An Article with a Title or Quotation Within Its Title

When an article title contains within it a title of a longer work (e.g., a novel or a film), italicize that title. If the article title contains within it a quotation or the title of a shorter work (e.g., a poem or a short story), then place that quotation or title within single quotation marks.

Petit, Susan. "Field of Deferred Dreams: Baseball and Historical Amnesia in Marilynne Robinson's *Gilead* and *Home*." *MELUS*, vol. 37, no. 4, 2012, pp. 119-37.

Melczarek, Nick. "Narrative Motivation in Faulkner's 'A Rose for Emily.'" *Explicator*, vol. 67, no. 4, 2009, pp. 237-43.

Interviews and Personal Correspondence

A Printed Interview

Begin with the name of the person interviewed if he or she is the person whom you are quoting. If the interview is untitled, use *Interview* (no italics) after the interviewee's name. Follow the title or description with a comma, *by*, and the interviewer's name.

Robinson, Marilynne. "Marilynne Robinson: The Art of Fiction No. 198," by Sarah Fay. *Paris Review*, no. 186, 2008, pp. 37-66.

A Personal Interview by You (the Author)

Place the name of the person you interviewed in the author position.

Jackson, Sha-Mena. Personal Interview. 7 Aug. 2016.

A Letter, Memo, Email, or Text

For correspondence of this nature, put the writer in the author position; use the subject line, if available, as the title; and offer a *Received* by statement for the recipient. If helpful, add the medium at the end of the entry.

Thomas, Bob. "Re: Research Plan." Received by author, 10 Jan. 2017. Email.

Multimedia Works

A Web Page or Blog Post

Wise, Hannah. "An American Mystery: Who or What Is Killing All These Bald Eagles?" *The Scoop Blog*, Dallas Morning News, 28 Mar. 2016, 4:31 p.m., thescoopblog. dallasnews. com/2016/03/an-american-mystery-who-or-what-is-killing-bald-eagles.html/.

A Podcast or Video Podcast

Kine, Starlee, narrator. "Belt Buckle." *The Mystery Show*, episode 3, Gimlet, 18 June 2015, gimletmedia.com/episode/case-3-belt-buckle/.

A Tweet or Similar Social Media Post

Untitled sources typically use a generic descriptive term in place of the title. For quite short posts, such as tweets, you may reproduce the entire post enclosed in quotation marks as the title. Indicate not only the date of posting but the time as well.

@susanorlean. "Write what you care about. Teach readers why you care about it." *Twitter*, 19 Apr. 2016, 11:27 a.m., twitter.com/susanorlean.

An Episode or Program (App, Streaming Service)

"Cops Redesign." *Portlandia*, directed by Jonathan Krisel, performances by Fred Armisen and Carrie Brownstein, season 2, episode 5, IFC, 3 Feb. 2012. *Netflix*, www.netflix.com/watch/70236274.

A Transcript of a Broadcast

Lehrer, Jim. "Character Above All." *Online NewsHour*, National Public Radio, 29 May 1996, www.pbs.org/newshour/spc/character/transcript/. Transcript.

A Recording (Music, Film, Etc.)

Beyoncé. "Flawless." *Beyoncé*, performance by Chimamanda Ngozi Adichie, Columbia Records, 12 Aug. 2014.

Lincoln. Directed by Steven Spielberg, performances by Daniel Day-Lewis and Sally Field, Dreamworks, 2012.

An Artwork

When referring to the work of art itself (not a reproduction of it in print or online), include the medium. Place the date of creation immediately after the title.

da Vinci, Leonardo. *Mona Lisa.* 1517, oil on canvas. Louvre Museum, Paris.

A Cartoon or Comic Strip

Chast, Roz. "Ed Revere, Spam Courier." Cartoon. *The New Yorker*, 22 Apr. 2013, p. 67.

A Map or Chart

West Virginia State Map. Folded ed. Rand McNally, 2011.

A Public Speech, Address, Lecture, or Performance

Gopnik, Adam. "Radical Winter." CBC Massey Lectures, 12 Oct. 2011, Dalhousie Arts Centre, Halifax, Nova Scotia. Address.

Sense and Sensibility. 10 Sept. 2016, Wurtele Thrust Stage, Guthrie Theater, Minneapolis. Performance.

An Advertisement

"Apple Watch—Dance." Advertisement. *YouTube*, 21 Oct. 2015, www.youtube.com/user/Apple?v=fHE5WDO515Y.

Government Publications, Reference Works, and Other Documents

A Document from a Government Agency

When a government agency is the author of a document, start with the name of the government; then follow with any organizational units, moving from larger to smaller, separating each unit with a comma.

United States, Department of Labor, Office of Disability Employment Policy. "Self-Employment for Artists with Disabilities." *Job Accommodation Network*, 17 Mar. 2015, askjan.org/media/occind.htm.

An Item from Congress

For U.S. congressional publications (reports, bills, etc.), you may include additional details about the session and the chamber, as well as publication type and number.

United States, Congress, House, House Administration Committee. National POW/ MIA Remembrance Act of 2015. Congress.gov, www.congress.gov/congressional-report/114th-congress/house-report/410/1. 114th Congress, 2nd session, House Report 114-410.

An Item from a Print Reference Source

Lum, P. Andrea. "Computed Tomography." *World Book*, 2000 edition.

"Macaroni." Def. 2b. *The American Heritage College Dictionary*, 4th edition, 2007.

An Item from an Online or Digital Reference Source

Hutchinson, George. "Harlem Renaissance." *Encyclopedia Britannica*, 8 Jan. 2016, www.britannica.com/event/Harlem-Renaissance-American-literature-and-art.

A Sacred Text

The Bible and other such sacred texts are treated as anonymous books. Documentation should read exactly as it is printed on the title page.

The Jerusalem Bible. Doubleday, 1966.

An Unpublished Manuscript or Historical Document

"The Work-for-All-Plan." 1933. Mildred Hicks Papers. Manuscript, Archives, and Rare Book Library, Emory U. *Online Manuscript Resources in Southern Women's History*, pid.emory.edu/ark:/25593/8zfd6.

Two or More Works by the Same Author

When your works-cited list includes two or more works by the same author, list the items alphabetically according to the titles. (Ignore *a*, *an*, or *the* if it is the first word in a title.) For second and subsequent items, substitute the author's name with three hyphens.

McCluhan, Marshall. *Counterblast*. Harcourt, 1969.

---. *The Gutenberg Galaxy: The Making of Typographic Man*. U of Toronto P, 1962.

MLA Format Guidelines

The eighth edition of the *MLA Handbook* is less explicit about paper format than past editions, partially because media and formats for research-based writing continue to expand. For traditional research papers, however, we recommend following accepted formatting guidelines. These are detailed in Figures 23.2–23.4 and on the following pages, as well as in the sample MLA paper on page 492.

MLA Format at a Glance

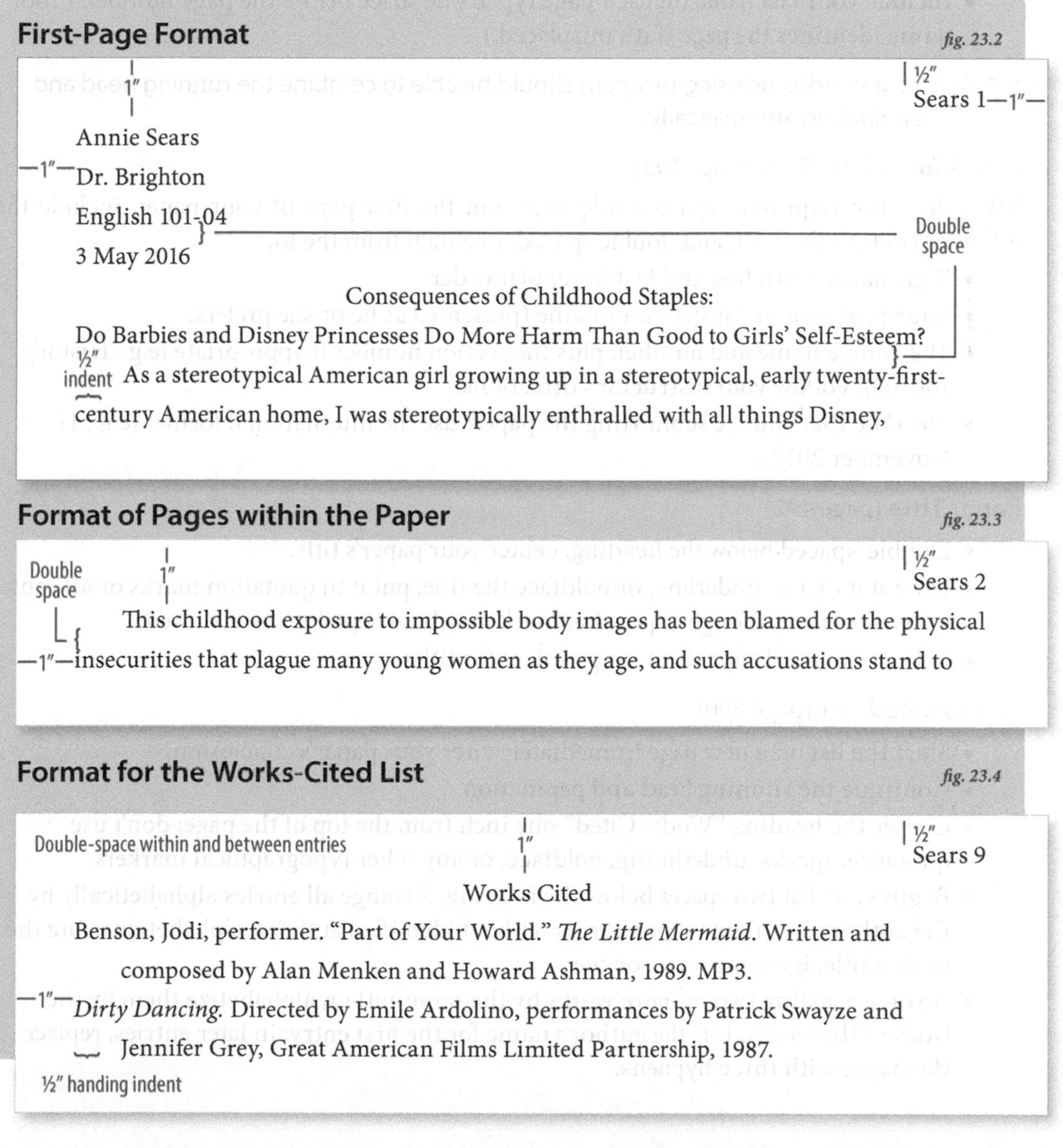

Whole-Paper Format and Printing Issues

The instructions below and on the next pages explain how to set up the parts of a traditional academic paper and print it for submission. Page references are to the sample MLA paper later in this chapter.

Running Head and Pagination (page 492)

- Number pages consecutively in the upper-right corner, one-half inch from the top and flush with the right margin (1 inch from the edge of the page).
- Use numerals only—without *p., page, #,* or any other symbol.
- Include your last name on each page typed one space before the page number. (Your name identifies the page if it's misplaced.)

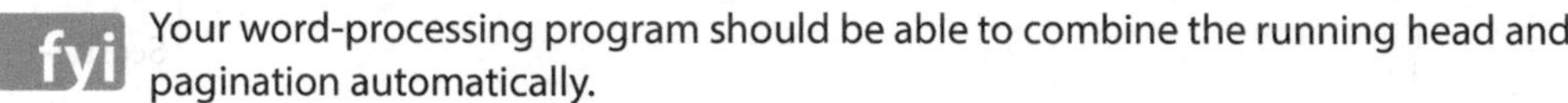

Your word-processing program should be able to combine the running head and pagination automatically.

Heading on First Page (page 492)

MLA does not require a separate title page. On the first page of your paper, include the following details flush left and double spaced, one inch from the top:

- Your name, both first and last in regular order
- Your professor's or instructor's name (presented as he or she prefers)
- The course name and number, plus the section number if appropriate (e.g., History 100-05). Follow your instructor's directions.
- The date that you are submitting the paper: use the international format (e.g., 11 November 2017).

Paper Title (page 492)

- Double-spaced below the heading, center your paper's title.
- Do not italicize, underline, or boldface the title; put it in quotation marks or all caps; or use a period (though a question mark may be acceptable if warranted).
- Follow standard capitalization practices for titles.

Works-Cited List (page 500)

- Start the list on a new page immediately after your paper's conclusion.
- Continue the running head and pagination.
- Center the heading "Works Cited" one inch from the top of the page; don't use quotation marks, underlining, boldface, or any other typographical markers.
- Begin your list two spaces below the heading. Arrange all entries alphabetically by the authors' last names; for sources without identified authors, alphabetize using the work's title, ignoring *a, an,* or *the.*
- If you are listing two or more works by the same author, alphabetize them by the titles of the works. Use the author's name for the first entry; in later entries, replace the name with three hyphens.

- Start each entry flush left; indent second and subsequent lines for specific entries one-half inch. Use your word-processing program's hanging indent feature.
- Double-space within and between all entries, and follow standard rules for capitalization, italics, quotation marks, and punctuation.
- Do not repeat the "Works Cited" heading if your list runs longer than one page.

Paper, Printing, and Binding

- Print on standard 8.5-by 11-inch paper.
- Use quality 20 pound bond paper. Avoid both thin, erasable paper and heavy card stock. Similarly, use only standard white or off-white paper—no neons, pastels, letterheads, or scents.
- Use a laser or inkjet printer to create a crisp, clean copy; avoid using nearly empty print cartridges.
- Avoid submitting a paper with handwritten corrections; however, if you must make a change, make a caret symbol (^), put a single clean line through words that must be dropped, and write additions above the line.
- As a first choice, use a paperclip. A single staple in the upper left corner may be acceptable. Avoid fancy covers or bindings, and never simply fold over the corners.
- Print your essay single-sided.

Typographical Issues

Typeface: Choose a standard serif typeface like Times New Roman. (Serif type, for example, the type you're reading, has finishes on each letter, as opposed to sans serif, like this.) Avoid unusual, hard-to-read typefaces.

Type Size: Use a readable type size, preferably 12 points, throughout the paper.

Type Styles (underlining, italics, bold, etc.):

- Use italics (not underlining) for titles of resources and individual words requiring this feature. An exception may be an online publication or posting; consult your instructor.
- Avoid using boldface, yellow highlighting, all caps, and so on.

rangizzz / Shutterstock.com

Page-Layout Issues

Spacing

- **Margins:** Set margins top and bottom, left and right at one inch, with the exception of the running head (one-half inch from top).
- **Line Spacing:** Double-space the entire paper—including the heading and works-cited entries, as well as tables, captions, and inset quotations.
- **Line Justification:** Use left justified throughout, except for the running head (right justified) and the title and works-cited heading (both centered). Leave the right margin ragged.
- **Word Hyphenation:** Avoid hyphenating words at the end of lines.
- **Spacing after Punctuation:** Use one space after most forms of punctuation, including end punctuation—but not before or after a dash or a hyphen.
- **Paragraph Indenting:** Indent all paragraphs one-half inch.

Longer (Inset) Quotations (see page 496)

- Indent one half inch any verse quotations longer than three lines and prose quotations longer than four typed lines.
- Use no quotation marks, and place the parenthetical citation after the closing punctuation.
- With a verse quotation, make each line of the poem or play a new line; do not run the lines together. Follow the indenting and spacing in the verse itself.
- To quote two or more paragraphs, indent the first line of each paragraph one-quarter inch in addition to the half inch for the whole passage. However, if the first sentence quoted does not begin a paragraph in the source, do not make the additional indent. Indent only the first lines of subsequent paragraphs.

Tables and Illustrations

Position tables, illustrations, and other visuals near your discussion of them—ideally, immediately after your first reference to the graphic, whether pasted in after a paragraph or positioned on a separate following page. Observe these rules:

- **Tables:** Identify all tables using "Table," an Arabic numeral, and a caption (descriptive title). Both the identifying headings and captions should be flush left, appropriately capitalized. Provide source information and explanatory notes below the table. Identify notes with superscript lowercase letters, not numerals. Double-space throughout the table.
- **Illustrations:** Number and label other visuals (graphs, charts, drawings, photos, maps, etc.) using "Figure" or "Fig.," an Arabic numeral (followed by a period), and a title or caption one space after the period—all flush left below the illustration, along with source information and notes.

Formatting Non-Print Media

The eighth edition of the *MLA Handbook* no longer stresses the traditional research paper and its formatting, acknowledging instead that today research writing may be published in many formats shared both in print and digitally. Whatever the format, however, when projects rely on research, they should still document their sources. In any research-based document, your goals should be to credit sources you relied upon and provide source details that allow readers to find those resources themselves. The MLA offers the following tips for different media:

- **Slide Presentations:** when using programs such as PowerPoint, include brief citations for borrowed material (quotations, paraphrases, images, etc.) on each slide. Then add a works-cited list at the end of your presentation. Consider, as well, including your works cited in any handout you share.
- **Videos:** Integrate acknowledgements and brief text overlays (e.g., title of a borrowed clip); offer full documentation in closing credits.
- **Web Pages and Postings:** Integrate links to online sources that you reference within your document, but also provide a works-cited list at the end of your project.

INSIGHT If traditional works-cited format and spacing are note possible or desirable, use other spacing techniques, typographical features, or color to separate and feature entries for easy reading.

Sample MLA Paper

Student writer Annie Sears wrote "Consequences of Childhood Staples" as a research paper for her composition class. In her paper, starting on the next page, she explores whether toys such as Barbie and characters such as Disney princesses harm or benefit girls as they grow up, documenting her research using MLA style. Strictly speaking, MLA format does not require or even recommend a title page or an outline. (For more on outlines, you can also see pages 49–52.) You can use Sears's paper in three ways:

MindTap®
Read, highlight, and take notes online.

1. To study how a well-written, major research paper develops careful thinking, builds a discussion, and orders supporting points and evidence.
2. To examine how source summaries, paraphrases, and quotations are carefully integrated into the writer's discussion to advance her thinking—a full-length example of the strategies addressed on pages 448–451.
3. To see in detail the format and documentation practices of MLA style, practices that allow the writer to share a professional-looking paper that fairly respects sources used.

Sample Paper: Format, In-Text Citation, and Works-Cited List

Note that a traditional research paper is double-spaced throughout.

The writer's last name and page number are placed in the upper right corner of every page.

Sears 1

No separate title page is required. The heading identifies the writer, the professor, the course, and the date—in the order and format shown, flush left.

Annie Sears

Dr. Brighton

English 101-04

3 May 2016

The title, indicating the paper's topic and theme, is centered, in regular typeface and type size—no special effects such as boldface.

Consequences of Childhood Staples:

Do Barbies and Disney Princesses Do More Harm Than Good to Girls' Self-Esteem?

As a stereotypical American girl growing up in a stereotypical, early twenty-first-century American home, I was stereotypically enthralled with all things Disney, especially where the princesses were concerned. I owned dozens of dresses, ranging from Cinderella's pale blue to Belle's vibrant yellow, from Aurora's modest neckline to Jasmine's belly-baring attire. I would watch the same films repeatedly, never growing weary of Snow White's humming or Ariel's "Part of Your World." I would imitate Cinderella in my chores or Belle in my bedtime stories. The magic I experienced as a child, the enchantment with the princesses who brought me innocent delight and taught me essential life lessons will forever linger. The same is true for millions of girls who had similar, Disney-focused childhood fixations.

From the start, in-text citations indicate borrowed material: summaries, paraphrases, and quotations.

Other girls, however, deemed their stereotypical childhood staple to be Barbie: the portable doll with brushable hair and hundreds of changeable outfits. Barbie has held many vocations, ranging from stay-at-home mom to astronaut, from professional basketball player to schoolteacher: a Barbie doll exists to appeal to every aspiring child, making her a universal role model over the years. In fact, Mattel released the first Barbie doll in 1959 (Do Rozario 38). Her sales reached a peak toward the end of the twentieth century, when "available in 150 countries, Barbie [sold] at the rate of two per second . . . racking up more than $1.9 billion a year" (Meyer). Those sales statistics are so remarkable that, "if you placed head to foot every doll ever sold, Barbie . . . would circle the globe 72 times" (Meyer). However, it was also at the height of her popularity that worldwide organizations began to attack Barbie: ridiculously thin, disproportionate, and, therefore, an unhealthy standard of beauty for all girls.

In 1992, researchers at a hospital in Helsinki released Barbie's first criticism: "If Barbie were real, she'd be too thin to menstruate" (Meyer). Since then, many studies have been done on the never-aging doll's body-type. (See figure 1 contrasting Barbie's

Sears 2

A visual is properly referenced, labeled, and documented with an in-text citation.

body proportions with an average woman's.) As stated in "Ken and Barbie at Life Size," Barbie's bust, which to scale would be 32 inches, is only 4 inches smaller than the average woman's (Norton et al. 291). However, her waist, a mere 16 inches, is *half* that of the average. Barbie's 29-inch hips are significantly smaller than the average 37-38 inches. Just as her 7-inch bicep and 6-inch forearm are much thinner than the average 11-inch bicep and 10-inch forearm, her 16-inch thighs and 11-inch calf are much thinner than the average 22-inch thigh and 15-inch calf. Her 3.5-inch wrist (half of the average value) would prevent all moderate lifting; in turn, her US size-3 feet would render walking impossible. In addition, her two-times-too-tall, six-inches-too-thin neck wouldn't be able to bolster the weight of her slightly enlarged head, just as her half-sized waist would not allow room for more than half a liver and a few inches of intestine (291). Ultimately, Barbie would not exist; she could not sustain life.

Figure 1. A computer-generated woman with Barbie's proportions is compared to a woman with average proportions ("Dying to Be Barbie")

The typeface is a traditional serif type, Times New Roman.

Barbie is not only unrealistic; she is also highly sexualized, sporting a hip 4
to waist ratio of 0.56: her waist circumference is exactly 56 percent of her hip circumference. Instead, a healthy woman's hip to waist ratio is closer to 0.80. Her bust to waist ratio (2.0) is almost twice that of a healthy woman's (Norton et al. 291).

A series of quotations and paraphrases from one source begin with a complete parenthetical citation but then follow with page numbers only, as the borrowed material clearly is from the same source.

This childhood exposure to impossible body images has been blamed for 5
the physical insecurities that plague many young women as they age, and such accusations stand to reason. However, recent studies have proven that such effects may not be as drastic as accusers insist. In 2006, a research team led by Helga Dittmar, a psychology professor at the University of Sussex, took 162 five-to-eight-year-old girls and divided them into three groups. The first group, serving as a control, was not exposed to any dolls during playtime. The second was exposed only to Barbie dolls, while the third was exposed only to Emme dolls: a US size 16 doll designed to combat Barbie's unrealistic body shape (286-87). After an allotted amount of playtime, these girls were asked to honestly complete a body-image survey.

Sears 3

Overall, the girls who had played with the Barbie dolls were more prone to desire thinner, curvier body shapes while the other two groups were more satisfied with their current state. Nonetheless, primarily the younger girls (ages five and six) were susceptible to Barbie's self-depreciating effects; the majority of the older girls (ages seven and eight) were content with their body shapes (290). Thus, the data gathered from this experiment supports a twofold conclusion: Barbie does indeed have an effect on girls' self-esteem, but this effect lessens with age. Girls are able to recognize Barbie as a flawed role model.

Lastly, all children involved in Kuther and McDonald's study engaged in 6
"imaginative play" (42), wherein Barbie would go to prom, have a family, seek adventure in outer space, and more. These girls would often reenact the same scenarios over and over, as if writing and perfecting a script. Kuther and McDonald explain, "Toys present messages about gender, adult roles, and values that children internalize" (39). Through repetitively enacting scenes with their dolls, children begin to understand how to interact with other people, what different roles exist within a culture, and what roles and interactions they long to emulate. It is precisely through imaginative play that these sorts of ideas become concrete, a part of each child's identity.

One-inch margins are used left and right, top and bottom, with the exception of the header, which is one-half inch from the top.

Another study, instead involving older, middle-school-aged girls, yielded similar 7
results. In 2004, Tara Kuther and Erin McDonald, psychology professors at Western Connecticut State University, took 20 sixth-grade girls from a typical, Connecticut middle school (primarily white, middle-class students) and had them participate in a weekly support group, discussing honest views on Barbie dolls, self-esteem, and correlations between the two. Each girl had played with Barbie as a child, but the manner of play differed from girl to girl (41).

Some girls engaged in "torture play" (42-43), in which Barbie was manipulated, 8
shaved, painted, thrown out windows, flushed down toilets, and so on for pure enjoyment; girls admitted that this type of play usually occurred when boys were around, in an attempt to impress them. Interestingly, though, one child openly stated that this type of play occurred solely with Barbie, not with other dolls, "because she is the only one that is perfect" (43). Even at a young age, when children are not cognizant of significant gender issues, they resent the body type placed before them, demanded of them. More important than any sort of resentment, though, is the fact

When an author is named in an attributive phrase, the parenthetical citation includes only a page number.

Sears 4

that the child recognized Barbie's unrealistic standard of perfection. These children were not unlike those from the 2006 study: aware of Barbie's physical abnormalities.

9 Other girls in Kuther and McDonald's study admitted to "anger play" (43), in which Barbie was thrown against the wall or abused repeatedly after an argument with parents, siblings, or classmates. One child explained, "I did [those things] to Barbie and said that [whoever I was angry at] got it back, but I would never really do that to a person" (43). In this case, Barbie play seems to be a healthy outlet for the inevitable emotions precipitated by social interactions; children are able to release their pent-up anger without causing harm to friends and family members. Therefore, children are able to ignore Barbie's unrealistic attributes and instead use her.

The text is double-spaced throughout, including inset quotations, tables, and visuals. No extra space or lines are added between paragraphs.

10 Thus, it would appear that Barbie's influence, though it may seem negative initially, proves positive: she helps children release strong emotions and internalize concepts pertaining to societal values, all without affecting self-esteem too detrimentally. In fact, one eighth-grade student responded eloquently when asked about Barbie-related experiences: "I think Barbie was a good role model for girls, even though she was fake. She was pretty, lovable, and could do any profession. Even though she was kind of anorexic, Barbie gave girls the chance to imagine things and to be anything they wanted to" (Kuther and McDonald 47-48).

The right margin is ragged, not justified.

11 Regarding Kuther and McDonald's research, if all three types of common Barbie play prove healthy, and if each type of activity is essential to a child's development in regard to societal understanding, social interaction, and identity formation, then shouldn't attacks on Barbie's body shape be muted? Regarding Dittmar's study, if, as they age, children realize that Barbie's image is unattainable, shouldn't the same attacks become even further irrelevant? Barbie's effect on young girls proves more beneficial than detrimental.

Strong topic sentences offer transitions between paragraphs and move the discussion forward.

12 The ongoing allegations about Barbie have recently shifted to another childhood staple: my personal favorite, the Disney princess. In May 2013, when Disney decided to make Merida an official princess, including her on princess merchandising and the princess Web page, she was redesigned for her coronation. The results sparked public outrage. Signatories of an online petition argued that the beloved Pixar princess, who refuses marriage, rides bareback through Medieval Scottish forests, and sports red, untamed hair to match her fiery personality, had been redesigned to mask her strongest characteristics: Merida proved "thinner with a bigger bust, more revealing

Ellipses indicate an omission from the original source; a shortened title in parentheses, with no page number, indicates a one-page source or one without pagination that also has no author.

Sears 5

dress, a face full of makeup, less wild hair, and . . . a sassy sash" in lieu of her "signature bow and arrows" ("PR Nightmare"). The free spirit who offered hope to anyone waiting for or uninterested in marriage, capturing hearts with her contrast to former princesses, was gone. At least 200,000 people who signed a Change.org petition wanted her back. Once the petition reached such great popularity, Disney did indeed replace sexualized-Merida with carefree-Merida on the princess homepage ("PR Nightmare").

While the extent of Merida's sexual nature in the new design may have been too 13
much, the changes did not warrant such a large outcry. In her essay on the function of Disney princesses, Rebecca Anne Do Rozario, a professor at Monash University, explains Disney's design philosophy this way:

A quotation longer than four typed lines is inset—indented 5 spaces (about a half inch) and double-spaced throughout; end punctuation is placed before the parenthetical citation.

> The princess has always thus been rendered in the cinematic trends occurring at her original release. Disney actually maintains her contemporaneity in its dual aspects: maintaining the original design, while successfully renewing its appeal by re-rendering her in new releases, marketing, and merchandising. Disney does not precisely erase her original quality, so much as create continuity between that quality and her contemporary audiences. (36-37)

Snow White, the original Disney princess, is a prime example. The technology used to produce *Snow White and the Seven Dwarfs* is long outdated; thus, Snow White needed to be redesigned so that her animation was cohesive with that of the newer princesses (Do Rozario 37). When this change happened, there were no petitions, no discontented fans. Yet, when Merida's computer animation was altered to match the simpler animation of her fellow princesses, many people were upset. It seems that the effective attacks on Barbie's body have made an impact on American society; the concept that media sources are entirely to blame for personal insecurities has permeated popular thinking. Therefore, even the Disney princesses, who are redesigned for practical purposes, are subject to unjust criticism.

Because Barbie's body shape is so drastically unreal, it is difficult to argue that 14
her effects on children are solely beneficial; some of the false ideas girls have about their own bodies are rooted in the images ingrained in their minds while growing up, and, despite all of the positive impacts she does make, Barbie undoubtedly plays a role in a child's negative self-image development. The same, however, is not true of Disney princesses. These young heroines' negative impacts are practically nonexistent

When the author of a source is not named in the sentence, his or her last name appears in the in-text citation.

Paragraphs and inset quotations are indented 5 spaces.

In the parenthetical citation, "qtd. in" indicates that the source was quoted in another source (an indirect quotation).

Sears 6

in light of all the good they do for a child's development, beginning with the fact that a princess is a "relevant anachronism over centuries, through revolutions, wars, and globalization. Some have sought to reveal her beauty as a stereotype, her good nature as submissiveness, but still she prevails" (Do Rozario 34). The princess is a timeless classic, a character that never ages, never loses popularity, and perfectly represents the cultural aspects of her story's historical time period.

15 However, the princess represents not only the society her story takes place in but also the society her movie was released into. Snow White, yet again, offers a perfect example. *Snow White and the Seven Dwarfs*, released in 1937, opens with Snow White as a formal princess, living in the castle with her jealous stepmother; in this scene, Snow White is still a "1920's starlet with a flapper's haircut, rosebud mouth, and high-pitched warble" (Do Rozario 38). When the queen attempts to kill Snow White, forcing her to flee into the woods, the 1920s beauty finds herself in poverty, a Great Depression of sorts. She lives with the working-class dwarves, cooks and cleans and engages in all activities not suited for a princess or the glamour of the Roaring Twenties. At the end of the film, though, she is restored from her peasant state, rescued by her prince; similarly, America came out of the Great Depression, rescued by the president (39). Snow White exemplifies not only the women of her medieval day and age but also the women who survived the Great Depression: willing to help, able to overcome, and lady-like through all adverse circumstances.

16 The second Disney princess offers no less a complete example. Princess Aurora from *Sleeping Beauty*, released in 1959, is a "prototype Baby Boomer. She wanders barefoot in the woods and is uninterested in the affairs of kings, devastated when she learns she is a princess and will not be able to make her date with the boy she met in the woods" (Do Rozario 38). Like other young people of her era, the Baby Boomer generation, Princess Aurora resents responsibility and the nagging of her parents. Prince Phillip, her male counterpart, goes as far as to ridicule his father, the king: "Father, you're living in the past. This is the fourteenth century!" (qtd. in Do Rozario 38). These young royals exemplify the dominant character traits of 1950s-1960s youth.

17 Similarly, *The Little Mermaid*, released in 1989, features Princess Ariel: a rebellious young girl, dissatisfied with the customs of her people and the constraints of her own body. Ariel's father, naturally, wishes her to fall in love with a merman

Brackets indicate changes to the original quotation.

and live happily, as Sebastian's song boasts, "under the sea," but Ariel's heart lies elsewhere (Wright). She "[wants] to be where the people are," to "[walk] around on those—what do they call 'em?—feet" (Benson). This desire for a world beyond her own runs so deep that Princess Ariel falls in love with a two-legged, land-loving man.

18 Ariel's unruly nature is similar to that of other media icons of her day: Sandy from *Grease* (1978) and Baby from *Dirty Dancing* (1987). Just as Sandy falls in love with a bad boy, of sorts, Ariel goes for the unattainable Erik; neither girl's father approves of her romance. Just as Ariel is "sick of swimming, ready to stand," Baby feels awkward, dissatisfied with her developing body (Benson; Do Rozario 50). Additionally, both girls mimic Busby Berkeley's burlesque dance moves (Do Rozario 48), and Ariel and Ursula both dance somewhat suggestively during "Poor Unfortunate Souls"; Ursula even advises, "Don't underestimate the power of body language" (qtd. in Do Rozario 49). The same lesson is applied in both *Grease* and *Dirty Dancing*, highly successful teen-movie-musicals. These similarities simply reinforce the parallels between Ariel and the young women of the world *The Little Mermaid* was released into.

19 Furthermore, each early princess living within a patriarchal society was incredibly dependent upon her prince. Neither Snow White nor Sleeping Beauty could reawaken from eternal sleep, nor could Ariel speak without true love's kiss. Cinderella was powerless to escape her stepmother's tyranny until her prince identified her foot. Belle was literally the Beast's prisoner. Jasmine could only claim her throne through marriage to a prince, but, much like Ariel, she fell in love with an unsuitable, forbidden "street rat" (Kane). Each early princess does not have a functioning story without a prince to complete the picture.

Throughout the paper, authors' names, titles of works, and page references create clear, accurate citations for borrowed material—summaries, paraphrases, and quotations.

20 The later princesses, however, initially live independently of flirtation; their romance enhances the story rather than serving as the primary focus. Pocahontas (1995), though she falls in love with a white man, teaches him more about "things [he] never knew [he] never knew" and, ultimately, saves her tribe before giving up romance to remain with her family (Kuhn). Mulan (1998) pretends to be a man to protect her father and eventually saves all of China before dating General Shang. Tiana (2009) places her restaurant before love, belittling the concept while singing, "That's just gonna have to wait a while. I ain't got time for messin' around, and that's not my style" (Rose). Merida (2011) refuses marriage entirely; instead, her story chronicles a conflict with her mother. Also more family-focused, Ana's relationship

An online report without pagination is identified in an attributive phrase by the sponsoring organization and the title, as well as in the parenthetical citation by the author.

Sears 8

with Hans in *Frozen* (2013) proves an act, whereas her relationship with her sister, fellow princess Elsa, proves true. As time progresses, each princess becomes more and more independent of her prince—resulting in nonexistent princes in the most recent princess films.

This shift into more independent, family-focused, feminist princesses runs 21
parallel to the progression of feminism within America. As stated in the Pew Research Center's study "Breadwinner Moms," the number of American families with children under 18 years of age utilizing both maternal and paternal income to provide for their family increased from 25 percent in 1960 to 65 percent in 2011. In addition, nearly 50 percent of all college degrees are earned by women, resulting in nearly 50 percent of America's workforce being composed of women (Wang). American feminism has advanced toward gender equality quickly over the last 50 years, and the Disney Princesses have clearly joined the movement.

If each princess is a representation of the culture her movie was released into, 22
then she must teach young viewers about the society they were born into, about how to behave and interact within that cultural context; therefore, a princess's influence on children is primarily beneficial, enabling each child to develop his or her own societal identity. Any sort of visual presentation or animation alteration becomes irrelevant in light of the learning potential each princess's story exemplifies.

All childhood fixations have great impact on children's development, including 23
their body-image-related self-esteem, personal identity, and concept of social interactions. For American girls, the most significant toys are likely Barbie and Disney princesses. These characters have received a great deal of criticism for the influence they have on girls' body-image-related self-esteem, but the benefits of these childhood fascinations far outweigh any negative effects that may come later in life. Barbie's body image is skewed, but even at a young age, children are able to recognize her impossibility; therefore, her encouragement of childhood aspirations holds more weight than her body shape. Disney princesses undergo constant redesign, but their stories ultimately reflect the society their movie was released into; therefore, children are able to better understand their world and, in turn, themselves through princess obsession. Ultimately, the childhood staples that permeate current American culture do much more good than harm for upcoming generations. Disney princesses—and even Barbie!—should be shown immense gratitude for the impact they have on child development.

The paper's works cited lists a range of scholarly resources as well as reliable Web sites on the topic.

Sources are listed in alphabetical order by author (or by title if no author is given).

The list is double-spaced throughout—both between and within entries.

Second and subsequent lines of entries are indented one half inch (hanging indent).

Sears 9

Works Cited

Benson, Jodi, performer. "Part of Your World." *The Little Mermaid.* Written and composed by Alan Menken and Howard Ashman, 1989. MP3.

Dirty Dancing. Directed by Emile Ardolino, performances by Patrick Swayze and Jennifer Grey, Great American Films Limited Partnership, 1987.

Dittmar, Helga, et al. "Does Barbie Make Girls Want to be Thin? The Effect of Experimental Exposure to Images of Dolls on the Body Image of 5-to-8-Year-Old Girls." *Developmental Psychology,* vol. 42, no.2, March 2006, pp. 283-92. ProQuest, doi:10.1037/0012-1649.42.2.283.

Do Rozario, Rebecca-Anne C. "The Princess and the Magic Kingdom: Beyond Nostalgia, the Function of the Disney Princess." *Women's Studies in Communication*, vol. 27, no. 1, Spring 2004, pp. 34-59. ProQuest, doi:10.1080/07491409.2004.10162465.

"Dying to Be Barbie: Eating Disorders in Pursuit of the Impossible." *Rehabs.com*, 2012, rehabs.com/explore/dying-to-be-barbie/.

Grease. Directed by Randal Kleiser, performances by John Travolta and Olivia Newton-John, Paramount Pictures, 1978.

Kane, Brad, performer. "One Jump Ahead." *Aladdin*. Written and composed by Alan Menken and Tim Rice, 1992. MP3.

Kuhn, Judy, performer. "Colors of the Wind." *Pocahontas*. Written by Stephen Schwartz, composed by Alan Menken, 1995. MP3.

Kuther, Tara L., and Erin McDonald. "Early Adolescents' Experiences with and Views of Barbie." *Adolescence*, vol. 39, no. 153, Spring 2004, pp. 39-51. ProQuest, proxy1. aims.edu:2080/docview/195942979/BF73B52E053E4F19PQ/3?accountid=35907.

Meyer, Michele. "Barbie Hits 40." *Parenting*, vol. 13, no. 2, March 1999, p. 31. ProQuest, proxy1.aims.edu:2080/docview/203323009/92A6745C7C404442PQ/1?accountid=35907.

Norton, Kevin I., et al. "Ken and Barbie at Life Size." *Sex Roles: A Journal of Research*, vol. 34, no. 3-4, Feb. 1996, pp. 287-94.

Sears 10

"PR Nightmare for Disney Princess." *Advertising Age*, vol. 84, no. 20 (2013), p. 5. ProQuest, proxy1.aims.edu:2080/docview/1354351849/F7D80244F83B43D9PQ/1?accountid= 35907.

Rose, Anika Noni, performer. "Almost There." *The Princess and the Frog*. Composed by Randy Newman, 2009. MP3.

Wang, Wendy, et al. "Breadwinner Moms: Mothers Are the Sole or Primary Provider in Four-in-Ten Households with Children; Public Conflicted about the Growing Trend." *Pew Research Center*, 29 May 2013, pewsocialtrends.org/2013/05/29/breadwinner-moms/.

Wright, Samuel E., performer. "Under the Sea." *The Little Mermaid*. Written by Howard Ashman, composed by Alan Melken, 1989. MP3.

Titles are properly italicized or placed in quotation marks.

Correct abbreviations are used throughout.

Reading for Better Writing

1. *Connections:* In her essay, Annie Sears examines the effects of childhood toys and entertainment on girls. Whether you are female or male, how do you relate to Sears's discussion? What toys and activities engaged you as a child? What influence have those had on who you are as an adult?
2. *Comprehension:* Sears's essay offers an extended discussion of both Barbies and Disney princesses. Condense that discussion by developing your own one-paragraph summary of the essay.
3. *Writing Strategies:*
   a. In her argument, what types of evidence does Sears use? Where has she gotten her evidence? Are her sources reliable? Does she have a balanced range of sources?
   b. How does Sears distinguish her own thinking from source material? Why are these strategies necessary?

Your Project: In addition to toys and movie characters, many childhood influences shape us into the adults we become: environment (e.g., urban vs. rural), religious institutions, friendships, sports and leisure activities, family dynamics, and so on. For your own paper, consider researching and writing about a particular influence that matters to you.

Critical Thinking and Writing: Applications

Once you have used the instruction in this chapter to format and document your paper according to MLA style, extend what you have learned by doing the following activities:

1. **System Check:** The MLA style involves many guidelines and rules about documentation. To make some sense of these rules, answer these questions: What is the essential logic of the MLA system? In other words, what does the MLA hope to accomplish with these rules?
2. **Works-Cited Practice:** Create MLA works-cited entries for the following publications:
   a. An article in the summer 2009 issue (volume 34, no. 2) of the periodical *MELUS,* by Joni Adamson and Scott Slovic: "The Shoulders We Stand On: An Introduction to Ethnicity and Ecocriticism" (pages 5-24)
   b. Ernest Hemingway's novel *A Farewell to Arms,* published in 1986 by Collier Books, located in New York City
   c. The Web page "Vaccines for Children Program (VCP)," part of the Vaccines and Immunizations section of the Centers for Disease Control and Prevention (CDC) Web site, sponsored by the U.S. government's Department of Health and Human Services. No author or publication date is listed. The site was last accessed April 26, 2016, at http://www.cdc.gov/vaccines/programs/vfc/index.html

Learning-Objectives Checklist ✓

Have you achieved this chapter's learning objectives? Check your progress with the following items, revisiting topics in the chapter as needed. I have . . .

___ gained an overview of the MLA system of documentation—the basic logic of in-text citations in relation to works-cited entries (466–467).

___ applied rules of in-text citation, whether for regular sources or for sources without traditional authorship and/or pagination (468–475).

___ developed a works-cited list that is properly formatted and that correctly and fully identifies sources, whether books, journal articles, or other resources (476–486).

___ correctly implemented MLA format guidelines for whole-paper issues (e.g., header, heading on the first page, pagination), typography, and page layout (487–491).

___ examined MLA style at work in "Consequences of Childhood Staples" by Annie Sears, learning how the system is practiced concretely in a research-based argumentative essay (492–501).

Chapter 24

APA Style

Those who write papers in the social sciences—psychology, sociology, political science, and education, for example—usually follow the research-writing guidelines of the American Psychological Association (APA). This chapter summarizes these guidelines and helps you use APA format and documentation.

APA format is similar to MLA format in two ways: Both require (1) parenthetical citations within the text and (2) a final listing of all references cited in the paper. But in the social sciences, the date of publication is often much more crucial than it is in the humanities, so the date is highlighted in in-text citations. APA format also requires a cover page and an abstract.

Visually Speaking Figure 24.1 suggests something about humans and their societies. Consider the possibilities, and explore what social-science research and research writing in particular seek to contribute to an understanding of people and the societies they build.

MindTap®

Understand the goals of the chapter and complete a warm-up activity online.

Learning Objectives

By working through this chapter, you will be able to

- explain and implement APA guidelines for documenting sources.
- produce research writing that adheres to APA guidelines for format.
- identify and critique APA practices at work in a sample student research report.

Scott Norsworthy / Shutterstock.com

fig. 24.1

APA Documentation: Quick Guide

The APA system involves two parts: (1) an in-text citation within your paper when you use a source and (2) a matching bibliographic entry at the end of your paper. Note these features of the APA author-date system:

- **It uses signal phrases and parenthetical references** to set off source material from your own thinking and discussion. A signal phrase names the author and places the material in context (e.g., "As Jung described it, the collective unconscious . . .").
- **It's date-sensitive.** Because the publication dates of resources are especially important in social science research, the publication year is included in the parenthetical reference and after the authors' names in the reference entry.
- **It's smooth, unobtrusive, and orderly.** APA in-text citations identify borrowed material while keeping the paper readable. Moreover, alphabetized reference entries at the end of the paper make locating source details easy.

You can see these features at work in the example below. The parenthetical material "Pascopella, 2011, p. 32" tells the reader these things:

- The borrowed material came from a source authored by Pascopella.
- The source was published in 2011.
- The specific material can be found on page 32 of the source.
- Full source details are in the reference list under the surname Pascopella.

1. In-Text Citation in Body of Paper

> In newcomer programs, "separate, relatively self-contained educational interventions" (Pascopella, 2011, p. 32) are implemented to meet the academic and transitional needs of recent immigrants before they enter a mainstream English Language Development.

2. Matching Reference Entry at End of Paper

> Pascopella, A. (2011). Successful strategies for English language learners. *District Administration, 47*(2), 29-44.

In-Text Citation: The Basics

See pages 506–509 for complete details on in-text citation.

1. Refer to the author(s) and date of publication by using one of these methods:

Last name(s), publication date in parentheses:

> ELLs normally spend just three years in 30-minute "pull-out" English language development programs (Calderón et al., 2011).

Last name(s) cited in text with publication date in parentheses:

> In "Key Issues for Teaching English Learners in Academic Classrooms," Carrier (2005) explained that it takes an average of one to three years to reach conversational proficiency in a second language, but five to seven years to reach academic proficiency.

2. Present and punctuate citations according to these rules:
   - Keep authors and publication dates as close together as possible in the sentence.
   - Separate the author's last name, the date, and any locating detail with commas.
   - If referencing part of a source, use an appropriate abbreviation: *p.* (page), *para.* (paragraph)—but do not abbreviate *chapter.*

Note: When citing previous research, use past tense or present perfect tense—Smith (2003) found *or* Smith (2003) has found.

References: The Basics

Complete coverage of reference issues is offered on pages 510–520, and a sample references list is shown on page 530. Here, however, are templates for the most common entries:

Template for Book:

Author's Last Name, Initials. (Publication Year). *Title of book.* Publication City, State or Country: Publisher. [Other publication details are integrated as needed.]

author's name, followed by period — publication year in parentheses, followed by period — exact and full title in italics, first word and proper nouns capitalized, followed by period

Pandya, J. Z. (2011). *Overtested: How high-stakes accountability fails English Language Learners.* New York, NY: Teachers College Press.

publication location from title page, followed by colon — publisher name from title page, followed by period

Template for Periodical Article:

Author's Last Name, Initials. (Publication Year). Title of article. *Journal Title, volume*(issue), page numbers. [Other publication details are integrated as needed. For online periodical articles, add the digital object identifier (see page 516).]

author's name, followed by period — article title, no quotation marks, first word and proper nouns capitalized

Slama, R. B. (2012). A longitudinal analysis of academic English proficiency outcomes for adolescent English Language Learners in the United States. *Journal of Educational Psychology, 104*(2), 265-285. doi: 10.1037/a0025861

page numbers followed by period — journal title and volume number italicized

Template for Online Document:

Author's Last Name, Initials. (Publication Date). *Title of work* OR Title of entry. DOI (digital object identifier) OR Retrieval statement including URL

author's name, followed by period — publication date in parentheses, followed by period — document title

U.S. Department of Education. (2013, January). *Projection of education statistics to 2021.* Retrieved from http://nces.ed.gov/programs/projections/projections2021/

retrieval statement

Guidelines for In-Text Citations

The Form of an Entry

The APA documentation style is sometimes called the "author-date" system because both the author and the date of the publication must be mentioned in the text when citing a source. Both might appear in the flow of the sentence, like this:

> Children in India are being trafficked for adoption, organ transplants, and labor such as prostitution, according to a 2016 article by Nilanjana Ray.

If either name or date does not appear in the text, it must be mentioned within parentheses at the most convenient place, like this:

> According to an article by Nilanjana Ray (2016), children in India . . .
>
> According to a recent article (Ray, 2016), children in India . . .

Points to Remember

1. When paraphrasing rather than quoting, make it clear where your borrowing begins and ends. Use stylistic cues to distinguish the source's thoughts ("Sacks points out . . . ," "Some critics argue . . .") from your own ("I believe . . . ," "It seems obvious, however . . .").
2. When using a shortened title of a work, begin with the word by which the work is alphabetized in your references list (for example, for "Measurement of Stress in Fasting Man," use "Measurement of Stress," not "Fasting Man").
3. When including a parenthetical citation at the end of a sentence, place it before the end punctuation: (Sacks, 2009).

Sample In-Text Citations

One Author: A Complete Work

The correct form for a parenthetical reference to a single source by a single author is parenthesis, last name, comma, space, year of publication, parenthesis. Also note that final punctuation should be placed outside the parentheses.

> . . . in this way, the public began to connect certain childhood vaccinations with an autism epidemic (Baker, 2008).

One Author: Part of a Work

When you cite a specific part of a source, give the page number, chapter, or section, using the appropriate abbreviations (p. or pp. or sec. For others, see page 510). Always give the page number for a direct quotation.

> . . . while a variety of political and scientific forces were at work in the developing crisis, it was parents who pressed the case "that autism had become epidemic and that vaccines were its cause" (Baker, 2008, p. 251).

One Author: Several Publications in the Same Year

If the same author has published two or more articles in the same year, avoid confusion by placing a small letter *a* after the first work listed in the references list, *b* after the next one, and so on. Determine the order alphabetically by title.

Parenthetical Citation:

- Reefs harbor life forms heretofore unknown (Milius, 2001a, 2001b).

References:

> Milius, D. (2001a). Another world hides inside coral reefs. *Science News, 160*(16), 244.
>
> Milius, D. (2001b). Unknown squids—with elbows—tease science. *Science News, 160*(24), 390.

Works by Authors with the Same Last Name

When citing different sources by authors with the same last name, add the authors' initials to avoid confusion, even if the publication dates are different.

> While J. D. Wallace (2011) argued that privatizing social security would benefit only the wealthiest citizens, others such as E. S. Wallace (2013) supported greater control for individuals.

Two to Five Authors

In APA style, all authors—up to as many as five—must be mentioned in the first text citation, like this:

> Love changes not just who we are, but who we can become, as well (Lewis, Amini, & Lannon, 2000).

Note: The last two authors' names are always separated by a comma and an ampersand (&) when enclosed in parentheses.

For works with two authors, list both in every citation. For works with three to five authors, list all names only the first time; after that, use only the name of the first author followed by "et al.," like this:

> These discoveries lead to the hypothesis that love actually alters the brain's structure (Lewis et al., 2000).

Six or More Authors

If your source has six or more authors, refer to the work by the first author's name followed by "et al.," both for the first reference in the text and all references after that. However, be sure to list all the authors (up to seven) in your references list.

> According to a recent study, post-traumatic stress disorder (PTSD) continues to dominate the lives of Vietnam veterans, though in modified forms (Trembley et al., 2016).

A Work Authored by an Agency, a Committee, or Other Organization

Treat the name of the group as if it were the last name of the author. If the name is long and easily abbreviated, provide the abbreviation in square brackets. Use the abbreviation without brackets in subsequent references, as follows:

First Text Citation:

> A problem for many veterans continues to be heightened sensitivity to noise (National Institute of Mental Health [NIMH], 2016).

Subsequent Citations:

> In addition, veterans suffering from PTSD continue to have difficulty discussing their experiences (NIMH, 2016).

A Work with No Author Indicated

If your source lists no author, treat the first few words of the title (capitalized normally) as you would an author's last name. A title of an article or a chapter belongs in quotation marks; the titles of books or reports should be italicized:

> . . . including a guide to low-stress postures ("How to Do It," 2015).

A Work Referred to in Another Work

If you need to cite a source that you have found referred to in another source (a "secondary" source), mention the original source in your text. Then, in your parenthetical citation, cite the secondary source, using the words "as cited in."

> . . . theorem given by Ullman (as cited in Hoffman, 2008).

Note: In your references list at the end of the paper, you would write out a full citation for Hoffman (not Ullman).

A Work in an Anthology

When citing an article or a chapter in an anthology or a collection, use the authors' names for the specific article, not the names of the anthology's editors. (Similarly, the article should be listed by its authors' names in the references section. See page 511.)

> Phonological changes can be understood from a variationist perspective (Guy, 2005).

An Electronic or Other Internet Source

As with print sources, cite an electronic source by the author (or by shortened title if the author is unknown) and the publication date (not the date you accessed the source).

> One study compared and contrasted the use of Web and touch screen transaction log files in a hospital setting (Nicholas, Huntington, & Williams, 2014).

A Web Site

Whenever possible, cite a Web site by its author and posting date. In addition, refer to a specific page or document rather than to a home page or a menu page. If you are referring to a specific part of a Web page that does not have page numbers, direct your reader, if possible, with a section heading and a paragraph number.

> According to the National Multiple Sclerosis Society (2015, "Complexities" section, para. 2), understanding of MS could not begin until scientists began to research nerve transmission in the 1920s.

Two or More Works in a Parenthetical Reference

Sometimes it is necessary to lump several citations into one parenthetical reference. In that case, cite the sources as you usually would, separating the citations with semicolons. Place the citations in alphabetical order, just as they would be ordered in the references list.

> Others report near-death experiences (Rommer, 2013; Sabom, 2016).

A Sacred Text or Famous Literary Work

Sacred texts and famous literary works are published in many different editions. For that reason, the original date of publication may be unavailable or not pertinent. In these cases, use your edition's year of translation (for example, *trans.* 2003) or indicate your edition's year of publication (2003 *version*). When you are referring to specific sections of the work, it is best to identify parts, chapters, or other divisions instead of your version's page numbers.

> An interesting literary case of such dysfunctional family behavior can be found in Franz Kafka's *The Metamorphosis,* where it becomes the commandment of family duty for Gregor's parents and sister to swallow their disgust and endure him (trans. 1972, part 3).

Books of the Bible and other well-known literary works may be abbreviated, if no confusion is possible.

> "Generations come and generations go, but the earth remains forever" (*The New International Version Study Bible,* 1985 version, Eccles. 1.4).

Personal Communications

If you do the kind of personal research recommended elsewhere in *The College Writer,* you may have to cite personal communications that have provided you with some of your knowledge. Personal communications may include personal letters, phone calls, emails, and so forth. Because they are not published in a permanent form, APA style does not place them among the citations in your references list. Instead, cite them only in the text of your paper in parentheses, like this:

> . . . according to M. T. Cann (personal communication, April 1, 2016).
>
> . . . by today (M. T. Cann, personal communication, April 1, 2016).

Guidelines for APA References

The references section lists all the sources you have cited in your text (with the exception of personal communications such as phone calls and emails). Begin your references list on a new page after the last page of your paper. Number each references page, continuing the numbering from the text. Then format your references list by following the guidelines that follow. (See also page 530 for a sample references page.)

1. Type the running head in the upper-left corner and the page number in the upper-right corner, approximately one-half inch from the top of the page.
2. Center the title, *References,* approximately one inch from the top; then double-space before the first entry.
3. Begin each entry flush with the left margin. If the entry runs more than one line, indent additional lines approximately one-half inch (five to seven spaces) using a hanging indent.
4. Adhere to the following conventions about spacing, capitalization, and italics:
   - Double-space between all lines on the references page.
   - Use one space following each word and punctuation mark.
   - With book and article titles, capitalize only the first letter of the title (and subtitle) and proper nouns. (Note that this practice differs from the presentation of titles in the body of the essay.) ***Example:*** The impact of the cold war on Asia.
   - Use italics for titles of books and periodicals, not underlining.
5. List each entry alphabetically by the last name of the author, or, if no author is given, by the title (disregarding *A, An,* or *The*). For works with multiple authors, use the first author listed in the publication.
6. Follow these conventions with respect to abbreviations:
   - With authors' names, generally shorten first and middle names to initials, leaving a space after the period. For a work with more than one author, use an ampersand (&) before the last author's name.
   - For publisher locations, use the full city name plus the two-letter U.S. Postal Service abbreviation for the state. For international publishers, include a province and country name.
   - Spell out "Press" in full, but for other publishing information, use the abbreviations in Figure 24.2.

Abbreviation	Meaning	Abbreviation	Meaning
Comp.	compiler, compiled, compiled by	Pt.	Part
Ed.	editor(s)	Sec. (sect.)	section(s)
N.d.	no date given	2nd ed.	Second edition
N.p.	no place of publication, no publisher given	Suppl.	Supplement
p., pp.	page(s) (if necessary for clarity)	Tech. Rep.	Technical Report
		Trans. (tr.)	translator, translation

fig. 24.2

Sample Reference Entries

The guidelines for references on page 510 and the templates for books, journal articles, and online material on page 516 should help you develop reference entries for most resources. However, the following pages offer detailed instructions and sample entries for specific types of sources. These samples are divided into print books and other documents (pages 511–513); print periodical articles (pages 514–515); online sources, including articles and ebooks from databases (pages 516–518); and other sources, including primary, personal, and multimedia (pages 519–520).

Books and Other Documents

The general form for a book or brochure entry is this:

Author, A. (year). *Title.* Location: Publisher.

The entries that follow illustrate the information needed to cite books, sections of a book, brochures, and government publications.

A Book by One Author

Horstmann, A. (2015). *Building Noah's ark for migrants, refugees, and religious communities.* New York, NY: Palgrave Macmillan.

A Book by Two or More Authors

List up to seven authors by last name and first initial, separating them by commas, with an ampersand (&) before the last.

Hooyman, N., & Kramer, B. (2006). *Living through loss: Interventions across the life span.* New York, NY: Columbia University Press.

For eight or more authors, list the first six followed by an ellipsis, and then the last.

An Anonymous Book

If an author is listed as "Anonymous," treat it as the author's name. Otherwise, follow this format:

Publication manual of the American Psychological Association (6th ed.). (2010). Washington, DC: American Psychological Association.

A Chapter from a Book

List the chapter title after the date of publication, followed by a period or appropriate end punctuation. Use *In* before the book title, and follow the book title with the inclusive page numbers of the chapter.

Tattersall, I. (2002). How did we achieve humanity? In *The monkey in the mirror* (pp. 138–168). New York, NY: Harcourt.

A Single Work from an Anthology

Start with information about the individual work, followed by details about the collection in which it appears, including the page span. For editors' names in the middle of an entry, follow the usual order: initial first, surname last. Note the placement of Eds. in parentheses.

> Guy, G. R. (2005). Variationist approaches to phonological change. In B. D. Joseph & R. D. Janda (Eds.), *The handbook of historical linguistics* (pp. 369–400). Malden, MA: Blackwell.

One Volume of a Multivolume Edited Work

Indicate the volume in parentheses after the work's title.

> Salzman, J., Smith, D. L., & West, C. (Eds.). (1996). *Encyclopedia of African-American culture and history* (Vol. 4). New York, NY: Simon & Schuster Macmillan.

A Separately Titled Volume in a Multivolume Work

> The Associated Press. (1995). *Twentieth-century America: Vol. 8. The crisis of national confidence: 1974–1980.* Danbury, CT: Grolier Educational Corp.

Note: When a work is part of a larger series or collection, as with this example, make a two-part title with the series and the particular volume you are citing.

An Edited Work, One in a Series

Start the entry with the work's author, publication date, and title. Then follow with publication details about the series.

> Marshall, P. G. (2002). The impact of the cold war on Asia. In T. O'Neill (Ed.), *World history by era: Vol. 9. The nuclear age* (pp. 162–166). San Diego, CA: Greenhaven Press.

A Group Author as Publisher

When the author is also the publisher, simply put Author in the spot where you would list the publisher's name.

> Amnesty International. (2007). *Maze of injustice: The failure to protect indigenous women from sexual violence in the USA*. London, England: Author.

Note: If the publication is a brochure, identify it as such in brackets after the title.

An Edition Other Than the First

> Baylis, J., Smith, S., & Owens, P. (2011). *The globalization of world politics: An introduction to international relations* (5th ed.). Oxford, England: Oxford University Press.

Two or More Books by the Same Author

When you are listing multiple works by the same author, arrange them by the year of publication, earliest first.

Sacks, O. (1995). *An anthropologist on Mars: Seven paradoxical tales*. New York, NY: Alfred A. Knopf.

Sacks, O. (2015). *On the move: A life*. New York, NY: Alfred A. Knopf.

An English Translation

Setha, R. (1998). *Unarmed* (R. Narasimhan, Trans.). Chennai, India: Macmillan. (Original work published 1995).

Note: If you use the original work, cite the original version; the non-English title is followed by its English translation, not italicized, in square brackets.

An Article in a Reference Book

Start the entry with the author of the article, if identified. If no author is listed, begin the entry with the title of the article.

Lewer, N. (1999). Non-lethal weapons. In *World encyclopedia of peace* (pp. 279–280). Oxford, England: Pergamon Press.

A Reprint, Different Form

Albanov, V. (2000). *In the land of white death: An epic story of survival in the Siberian Arctic*. New York, NY: Modern Library. (Original work published 1917).

Note: This work was originally published in Russia in 1917; the 2000 reprint is the first English version. If you are citing a reprint from another source, the parentheses would contain "Reprinted from Title, pp. xx–xx, by A. Author, year, Location: Publisher."

A Technical or Research Report

Taylor, B. G., Fitzgerald, N., Hunt, D., Reardon, J. A., & Brownstein, H. H. (2001). *ADAM preliminary 2000 findings on drug use and drug markets: Adult male arrestees*. Washington, DC: National Institute of Justice.

A Government Publication

Generally, refer to the government agency as the author. When possible, provide an identification number for the document after the title in parentheses.

National Institute on Drug Abuse. (2000). *Inhalant abuse* (NIH Publication No. 00–3818). Rockville, MD: National Clearinghouse on Alcohol and Drug Information.

For reports obtained from the U.S. Government Printing Office, list location and publisher as "Washington, DC: Government Printing Office."

Print Periodical Articles

The general form for a periodical entry is this:

> Author, A. (year). Article title. *Periodical Title, volume number*(issue number), page numbers.

If the periodical does not use volume and issue numbers, include some other designation with the year, such as a date, a month, or a season. The entries that follow illustrate the information and arrangement needed to cite most types of print periodicals. For instructions on reference entries for periodical articles from databases or other online resources, see pages 516–518.

Note: Issue number is required only for journals that paginate each issue separately.

An Article in a Scholarly Journal

> Dunn, E. C. (2016). Refugee protection and resettlement problems. *Science, 352*(6287), 772-773

Pay attention to the features of this basic reference to a scholarly journal:

1. Provide the authors' last names and initials, as for a book reference.
2. Place the year of publication in parentheses, followed by a period.
3. Format the article's title in lowercase, except for the first word of the main title and of a subtitle and except for proper nouns, acronyms, or initialisms; do not italicize the article title or place it in quotation marks.
4. Capitalize the first and all main words in the journal title; italicize it.
5. Italicize the volume number but not the issue number; place the issue in parentheses, without a space after the volume number. No issue number is needed if the journal is paginated consecutively throughout a volume.
6. Provide inclusive page numbers, without "pp." or "pages."

An Abstract of a Scholarly Article (from a Secondary Source)

When referencing an abstract published separately from an article, provide publication details of the article followed by information about where the abstract was published.

> Shlipak, M. G., Simon, J. A., Grady, O., Lin, F., Wenger, N. K., & Furberg, C. D. (2001, September). Renal insufficiency and cardiovascular events in postmenopausal women with coronary heart disease. *Journal of the American College of Cardiology, 38*, 705–711. Abstract obtained from *Geriatrics, 2001, 56*(12). (Abstract No. 5645351.)

A Journal Article, More Than Seven Authors

Yamada, A., Suzuki, M., Kato, M., Suzuki, M., Tanaka, S., Shindo, . . . Furkawa, TA. (2007). Emotional distress and its correlates among parents of children with persuasive developmental disorders. *Psychiatry & Clinical Neurosciences, 61*(6), 651–657.

Note: In the text, abbreviate the parenthetical citation: (Yamada et al., 2007).

A Review

To reference a book review or a review of another medium (film, exhibit, and so on), indicate the review and the medium in brackets, along with the title of the work being reviewed by the author listed.

Hutcheon, L., & Hutcheon, M. (2008). Turning into the mind. [Review of the book *Musicophilia: Tales of music and the brain,* by O. Sacks]. *Canadian Medical Association Journal, 178*(4), 441.

A Magazine Article

Pincott, J. (2016, May-June). Acting a fool: Why is female intelligence a turnoff for some men—even those who profess otherwise? *Psychology Today, 49*(3), 35, 39.

Note: If the article is unsigned, begin the entry with the title of the article.

Tomatoes target toughest cancer. (2002, February). *Prevention, 54*(2), 53.

A Newspaper Article

For newspaper articles, include the full publication date, year first followed by a comma, the month (spelled out) and the day. Identify the article's location in the newspaper using page numbers and section letters, as appropriate. If the article is a letter to the editor, identify it as such in brackets following the title. For newspapers, use *p.* or *pp.* before the page numbers; if the article is not on continuous pages, give all the page numbers, separated by commas.

Schmitt, E., & Shanker, T. (2008, March 18). U.S. adapts cold-war idea to fight terrorists. *The New York Times*, pp. 1A, 14A–15A.

Knaub, M. (2013, August 12). Area men recall their time as 'braceros.' *Yuma Times,* pp. 1A, 5A.

A Newsletter Article

Newsletter article entries are similar to newspaper article entries; only a volume number is added.

Teaching mainstreamed special education students. (2002, February). *The Council Chronicle,* 11, pp. 6–8.

Online Sources

When it comes to references for online sources, follow these guidelines:

1. **Whenever possible, use the final version of an electronic resource.** Typically, this is called the archival copy or the version of record, as opposed to a prepublished version. Right now, that final version is likely the same as the printed version of an article, though there is some movement toward the online publication being the final version (complete with additional data, graphics, and so on).
2. **In the reference entry for an electronic source, start with the same elements in the same order as for print or other fixed-media resources** (author, title, and so on). Then add the most reliable electronic retrieval information that will (a) clarify what version of the source you used and (b) help your reader find the source him- or herself. Determine what you need to include based on these guidelines:
   - **Whenever possible, use the electronic document's digital object identifier (DOI).** More and more, electronic publishers are using this registration code for the content of journal articles and other documents so that the document can be located on the Internet, even if the URL changes. The DOI will usually be published at the beginning of the article or be available in the article's citation.

     Author, A. A. (year). Title of article. *Title of Periodical, volume number*(issue number), pages. doi: code

   - **If a DOI is not available for the electronic document,** give the complete URL (without a period at the end). Generally, a database name is no longer needed, except for hard-to-find documents and those accessed through subscription-only databases. Use the home- or menu-page URL for subscription-only databases and online reference works.

     Author, A. A. (year). Title of article. *Title of Periodical, volume number*(issue number), pages. Retrieved from URL

   - **If the content of the document is stable** (e.g., archival copy or copy of record with DOI), do not include a retrieval date in your reference entry. However, if the content is likely to change or be updated, as is the case with a lot of the material on the free Web, then offer a retrieval date. This would be the case with open-Web material with no fixed publication date, edition, or version, or material that is prepublished (in preparation, in press).

     Author, A. A. (year). *Title of document.* Retrieved date from Web site: URL

A Journal Article with DOI

Grinker, R. R. (2015). Reframing the science and anthropology of autism. *Culture, Medicine and Psychiatry, 39*(2), 345-350. doi: 10.1007/s11013-015-9444-9

Note: Because the DOI references the final version of the article, the retrieval date, URL, and database name are not needed. If the online article is a preprint version, add "Advance online publication" and your retrieval date before the DOI.

A Journal Article Without DOI

Bell, J. B., & Nye, E. C. (2007). Specific symptoms predict suicidal ideation in Vietnam combat veterans with post-traumatic stress disorder. *Military Medicine, 172*(11), 1144–1147. Retrieved from http://www.ebscohost.com

Note: Because this article has no DOI, the complete URL is provided for the subscription database search service. If you retrieved the article from the open Web, you would supply the exact URL. If the version of the article you access is in press and you have retrieved it from the author's personal or institutional Web site, place "in press" in parentheses after the author's name and add a retrieval date before the URL.

A Newspaper Article

Zernike, K. (2016, June 28). For Detroit's children, more school choice but not better schools. *The New York Times*. Retrieved from http://www.nytimes.com

An Article in an Online Magazine (Ezine) not Published in Print

Grossman, A. (2016, April 5). Why didn't you tell me that I love you? Asexuality, polymorphous perversity, and the liberation of the cinematic clown. *Bright Lights Film Journal*. Retrieved June 28, 2016, from http://brightlightsfilm.com/didnt-tell-love-chaplin-tati-keaton-lloyd-langdon-silent-comedy-asexuality-polymorphous-perversity-liberation-cinematic-clown/#.V3KkxaIk3T8p

A Book Review

Shapiro, K. (2007). Mystic chords. [Review of the book *Musicophilia: Tales of music and the brain,* by O. Sacks]. Commentary, *124*(5), 73–77. Retrieved from http://web.ebscohost.com

An Electronic Book

Kafka, F. (2002). *Metamorphosis*. D. Wylie (Trans.). Available from http://www.gutenberg.org/etext/5200

Note: If the URL goes directly to the ebook, use "Retrieved from."

Material from an Online Reference Work

Agonism. (2008). In *Encyclopaedia Britannica.* Retrieved from http://search.eb.com

Note: See pages 424–425 for advice on using Wikipedia.

Online Course Material

Roderiguez, N. Unit 3, *Lecture 3: Sociological Theories of Deviance.* Retrieved from University of Houston Web site: http://www.uh.edu/~nestor/lecturenotes /unit3lecture3.html

A Workplace Document or Other "Gray Literature"

"Gray Literature" refers to informative documents (e.g., brochures, fact sheets, white papers) produced by government agencies, corporations, and nonprofit groups. If possible, give a document number or identify the type of document in brackets.

Foehr, U. G. (2006). *Media multitasking among American youth: Prevalance, predictors and pairings* (Publication No. 7592). Retrieved from the Kaiser Family Foundation: http://www.kff.org/entmedia/upload/7592.pdf

Undated Content on Web site

National Institute of Allergy and Infectious Diseases. (n.d.). *Antimicrobial (drug) resistance.* Retrieved from http://www3.niaid.nih.gov/topics /AntimicrobialResistance/default.htm

A Podcast

Byrd, D., & Block, J. (Producers). (2008, February 5). Antonio Rangel: This is your brain on wine. *Earth & Sky: A Clear Voice for Science* [Audio podcast]. Retrieved from http://www.earthsky.org/clear-voices/52199

Message on a Newsgroup, an Online Forum, or a Discussion Group

Avnish, J. (2008, March 18). Sex education especially vital to teens nowadays. [Online forum post]. Retrieved from http://groups.google.ca/group/AIDS-Beyond -Borders/topics

A Blog Post

Koyzis, D. (2007, June 27). Conservative environmentalists. [Web log post]. Retrieved from http://byzantinecalvinist.blogspot.com/2007_06_01_archive.html

Note about URLs: When necessary, break a URL before a slash or other punctuation mark or after a double slash. Do not underline or italicize the URL, place it in angle brackets, or end it with a period.

Other Sources (Primary, Personal, and Multimedia)

Cite audiovisual media sources and electronic sources as follows.

Specialized Computer Software with Limited Distribution

Standard nonspecialized computer software does not require a reference entry. Treat software as an unauthored work unless an individual has property rights to it.

> Carreau, S. (2001). Champfoot (Version 3.3) [Computer software]. Saint Mandé, France: Author.

Show the software version in parentheses after the title and the medium in brackets.

A Television or Radio Broadcast

Indicate the episode by writers, if possible. Then follow with the airing date, the episode title, and the type of series in brackets. Add the producer(s) as you would the editors(s) of a print medium, and complete the entry with details about the series itself.

> Berger, C. (Writer). (2001, December 19). Feederwatch [Radio series program]. In D. Byrd & J. Block (Producers), *Earth & Sky*. Austin, TX: The Production Block.

An Audio Recording

Begin the entry with the speaker's or writer's name, not the producer. Indicate the type of recording in brackets.

> Kim, E. (Author, speaker). (2000). *Ten thousand sorrows* [CD]. New York, NY: Random House.

A Music Recording

Give the name and function of the originators or primary contributors. Indicate the recording medium in brackets immediately following the title.

> ARS Femina Ensemble. (Performers). (1998). *Musica de la puebla de Los Angeles: Music by women of baroque Mexico, Cuba, & Europe* [CD]. Louisville, KY: Nannerl Recordings.

A Motion Picture

Give the name and function of the director, producer, or both.

> Lee, A. (Director). (2012). *Life of Pi* [Motion picture]. United States: Twentieth-Century Fox.

A Published Interview, Titled, No Author

Start the entry with the interview's title, followed by publication details.

> Stephen Harper: The Report interview. (2002, January 7). *The Report* (Alberta, BC), 29, 10–11.

A Published Interview, Titled, Single Author

Start the entry with the interviewee's name, followed by the date and the title. Place the interviewer's name in brackets before other publication details.

> Fussman, C. (2002, January). What I've learned. [Interview by Robert McNamara.] Esquire, 137, 85.

An Unpublished Paper Presented at a Meeting

Indicate when the paper was presented, at what meeting, in what location.

> Sifferd, K., & Hirstein, W. (2012, June). *On the criminal culpability of successful and unsuccessful psychopaths.* Paper presented at the meeting of the Society for Philosophy and Psychology, Boulder, CO.

An Unpublished Doctoral Dissertation

Place the dissertation's title in italics, even though the work is unpublished. Indicate the school at which the writer completed the dissertation.

> Roberts, W. (2001). *Crime amidst suburban wealth* (Unpublished doctoral dissertation). Bowling Green State University, Bowling Green, OH.

mikeledray / Shutterstock.com

APA Format Guidelines

To submit a polished academic paper in APA format, follow the rules below and refer to the sample APA paper on pages 522–531.

- **Title Page:** On the first page, include your paper's title, your name, and your institution's name on three separate lines, double-spaced, centered, and positioned in the top half of the page. Flush left at the top, type *Running head:* (no italics) followed by your abbreviated title in all uppercase letters; and flush right at the top, type the page number 1.
- **Abstract:** On the second page, include an abstract—a 150- to 250-word paragraph summarizing your paper. Place the title *Abstract* (no italics) approximately one inch from the top of the page and center it. Place the running head and page number 2 at the top of the page.
- **Body:** Format the body (which begins on the third page) as follows:
  - **Margins:** Leave a one-inch margin on all four sides of each page (one and one-half inches on the left if the paper will be bound). Do not justify lines, but rather leave a ragged right margin and do not break words at the ends of lines.
  - **Line Spacing:** Double-space your entire paper, unless your instructor allows single spacing for tables and figures.
  - **Page Numbers:** Place your running head and the page number flush left and flush right respectively, at the top of each page, beginning with the title page.
  - **Headings:** Like an outline, headings show the organization of your paper and the importance of each topic. All topics of equal importance should have headings of the same level, or style. Figure 24.3 shows the levels of headings used in APA papers.

Level 1: **Centered, Boldface, Uppercase and Lowercase Heading**
Level 2: **Flush Left, Boldface, Uppercase and Lowercase Side Heading**
Level 3: **Indented, boldface, lowercase paragraph heading ending with a period.**
Level 4: ***Indented, boldface, italicized, lowercase paragraph heading with a period.***
Level 5: *Indented, italicized, lowercase paragraph heading with a period.*

Example:

Teaching K-12 English Language Learners in the Mainstream Classroom
The English Language Learner Landscape
Myths and misconceptions.
Myth 1: Exposure will lead to learning.
The need for explicit morphological instruction.

fig. 24.3

- **Appendix:** Tables and figures (graphs, charts, maps, etc.) already appear on separate pages following the reference list. If necessary, one or more appendices may also supplement your text, following any tables or figures.

Sample APA Paper

In her Writing in Psychology and Human Development course, Julia Sweigert wrote the following report on siblings of children with autism. Inspired by her own experience as the sibling of a sister with Down syndrome and by interactions with other siblings of children with disabilities, Julia researched this topic with the goal of advancing family support in a household where a sibling has autism.

MindTap®
Read, highlight, and take notes online.

You can use Julia's paper in three ways:

1. To study how a well-written research paper uses a range of resources to build a discussion or line of reasoning that answers a research question.
2. To examine how sources are used and integrated into social-sciences research writing—a full-length discussion of the strategies addressed on pages 448–451.
3. To see in detail the format and documentation practices of APA style.

Note: Often, a social-sciences research paper takes the form of an experiment report. For an example of such a report, see pages 457–463.

Sample Title Page

Note that APA format requires that the paper be double-spaced throughout, with a one-inch margin on all sides.

Type running head (abbreviated title in uppercase letters) flush left.

Running Head: THE SILENT SIBLING 1

Full title, author(s), and school name are centered on the page, typed in uppercase and lowercase.

The Silent Sibling:

How Current Autism Intervention Neglects Typically-Developing Siblings

Julia Sweigert

University of California Davis

Sample Abstract

The abstract summarizes the paper's central issue, its main conclusion, the key reasoning and evidence presented, and the study's significance.

THE SILENT SIBLING 2

Abstract

This paper explores the experience of siblings of individuals with autism and the failure of current systems to understand and support that experience. With current rates of autism, more and more siblings are playing an instrumental role in the care and support of their affected brothers and sisters, including as playmates, translators, and caregivers. However, current research and services rarely provide opportunities for siblings to participate in the conversation on autism. To achieve a better understanding of autism spectrum disorders and to create more effective intervention and treatment programs, the sibling experience should be heard. Siblings need the opportunity to voice their stories and to reach out for help as they face the unique realities of providing long-term care for brothers and sisters with autism.

A running head and page number top each page.

THE SILENT SIBLING 3

The title is centered one inch from the top, and the paper is double-spaced throughout.

The Silent Sibling:

How Current Autism Intervention Neglects Typically Developing Siblings

The Centers for Disease Control and Prevention (2014) recently reported that 1
1 in 68 children is diagnosed with an autism spectrum disorder. Autism spectrum disorders, or ASD, include a variety of developmental disabilities characterized by communication deficits and repetitive interests or behaviors. Because American families average approximately two children per family (U.S. Census Bureau, 2013), the reported autism rate means that about 1 in 68 children is also growing up as the sibling to someone with autism spectrum disorder. From a young age, these typically-developing siblings experience firsthand the full impact of autism, as they help their parents with the extensive care required of some people with this disability. Yet, siblings rarely receive any external help as they endure the challenges and responsibilities that autism can bring to a family. Despite the growing number of autism research and treatment centers in the United States, very few of these organizations offer programs geared towards siblings. By neglecting the siblings, current autism intervention services leave these children isolated and struggling to process their unique experiences, a situation that can be detrimental later in life as siblings prepare to take on the increasing responsibilities of caregiving for their brothers and sisters with autism.

A heading identifies the first section.

What Makes a Sibling?

In the disabilities community, siblings include any typically developing 2
children in the family of a person with autism or other physical and developmental disabilities. Siblings can be young children living at home or older adults with children of their own. Because autism can affect individuals across many different regions, cultures, and socioeconomic groups, siblings come from various backgrounds as well. Regardless of these differences, siblings share many common experiences and emotional struggles. Research has found that most siblings report some level of frustration, embarrassment, and isolation as a result of their situation (Orsmond & Seltzer, 2007b). These shared experiences result from the stress brought on by disabilities themselves, as well as a failure on the part of disability treatment centers to provide intervention services just for siblings.

The "b" after the date in the parenthetical citation distinguishes this source from another one published by the same authors in the same year.

While siblings can have brothers or sisters with a number of different 3
disabilities, the recently reported rise in autism rates (Centers for Disease Control and Prevention [CDC], 2014) coupled with the unique and diverse behavioral

THE SILENT SIBLING 4

profiles seen in individuals with autism makes siblings of children with autism an important group in need of support. In order to be diagnosed with autism spectrum disorder, a child must show two key behavioral traits: a deficit in social communication and interactions, and some form of restricted, repetitive behaviors and interests (American Psychiatric Association [APA], 2013). Commonly, children with autism meet the diagnostic criteria with behaviors that include limited to absent verbal communication, increased sensory sensitivity, a strong preference for predictable schedules, and compulsive actions, such as hand-flapping or full-body rocking. Day-to-day experiences that conflict with these behaviors can often trigger a sort of "fight or flight" response from people with autism; they may become aggressive or attempt to escape the situation. Additionally, as a result of these pervasive behavioral deficits, people with autism might have very limited ability to self-care, including both the personal hygiene and life skills that allow for independent living. The complexities and magnitudes of these behaviors associated with autism transform the sibling relationship.

Siblings of people with autism grow up experiencing life in a manner distinctly different from members of a neurotypical sibling pair. Children diagnosed with the disability can be very dependent on family members for care and behavioral mediation. While most of this caregiving burden falls on parents, siblings take on a significant portion of the responsibility too. On a daily basis, siblings help feed their affected brothers or sisters, supervise them in public settings, and help to interpret their limited communication. Because of their close proximity, siblings can also become the target of aggression when the child with autism is upset or over-stimulated (Orsmond & Seltzer, 2007b). Thus, on a daily basis, these siblings become caregivers and emotional buffers, a distinct difference when compared to the playmate relationship of typical sibling pairs.

A heading identifies the second main section of the essay.

Why Do Siblings Matter?

Siblings witness most things that their families go through as a result of the disability and serve as life-long friends and caregivers. In addition to dealing with typical autism behaviors and providing personal care, siblings know their brothers and sisters intimately, including what they like, what they dislike, how to annoy them, and how to make them smile. Thus, the sibling perspective is an invaluable and underappreciated one that can enhance our understanding of disabilities such as autism.

When authors are not identified within the sentence, both the authors and the date, separated by a comma, are listed in the in-text citation.

A direct quotation is cited by page number.

"Et al." indicates a subsequent reference to a source with three or more authors.

THE SILENT SIBLING 5

Siblings Are Playmates

6 Siblings of children with autism spend a significant portion of their day interacting directly with their affected brother or sister. For example, researchers conducting in-home observations found that siblings, age 2-12, spend as much as 40 minutes of every hour in shared activities with the child with autism (Orsmond & Seltzer, 2007b). The siblings' frequent and close proximity commonly enables them to understand the wants and needs of the child with autism better than the child's caregiving adults, including parents and teachers. As one 13-year-old sibling said, "I can understand my brother—a lot of other people don't—even my dad doesn't always understand him—then he's asking me: what does he mean? And I always know what my brother means" (Moyson & Roeyers, 2012, p. 93). While parents pay close attention to the care and therapies a child with autism needs, many siblings better understand what their brother or sister wants and needs. Siblings' perspective on the disability may differ significantly from their parents' perspective, as these children do not yet have to bear the added stress of being primary caregivers. Sibling perspectives could supplement parent and therapist perspectives in autism intervention to create a more accurate picture of how autistic behavior transpires at home.

Siblings Become Caregivers

7 As parents age and their ability to provide care declines, the sibling transitions from companion to caregiver. In addition to normal aging, parents of people with intellectual and developmental disabilities, including autism, experience significantly more health problems by their early sixties (Seltzer, Floyd, Song, Greenberg, & Hong, 2011), which can interfere with their ability to provide care to their dependent child. Consequently, during this time parents must find an alternate living situation for their child. A longitudinal study of parents found that between their mid-fifties and mid-sixties, approximately 20% of parents saw their children with intellectual and developmental disabilities move out of the parents' home into a different residential living situation (Seltzer et al., 2011). As parents experience a diminishing ability to provide care for their children with autism, the adult siblings begin to take on a greater caregiving and support role.

8 Siblings may simultaneously have to offer additional support for both their brother or sister with autism and for their aging parents; in addition, as they enter adulthood, these siblings commonly have careers and families of their own. Such

siblings increasingly take on the responsibilities of their affected brother or sister's well-being (Burke, Taylor, Urgano, & Hodapp, 2012). While typical sibling pairs may develop close friendships as they move into adulthood, siblings of people with autism must adjust their future to include the realities of providing care and making decisions regarding their brother or sister. In some instances, the person with autism is moved into a residential facility, but the siblings still provide significant emotional support (Orsmond & Seltser, 2007a). Thus, siblings play an important and lifelong role in maintaining a stable and enriching environment for their brothers and sisters with autism.

When Are Siblings Absent?

Autism takes center-stage in the life of these siblings; even so, siblings are 9
often left out of the research and services aimed at improving autism outcomes. For example, as parents take their child with autism to a number of behavior therapies and life skills classes each week, siblings are often lost in the shuffle. During the various appointments, neurotypical siblings play in the waiting room or spend the afternoon at a friend or relative's house. This accidental exclusion can leave the siblings uninformed. They might have a basic understanding of what autism looks like because they see it daily at home, but they miss the opportunity to learn fully how autism affects people, and why their brother or sister has such distinct behaviors. Additionally, because young siblings do not get to see the interventions in action, they may not understand the benefits of constant therapy and fail to see all the hard work that goes into little moments of progress seen in the children with autism.

Sibling Absence in Research

When authors are identified in the sentence, only the date is required in the in-text citation.

Research into the effects of autism on families relies primarily on assessments 10
of the affected child and reports made by the parents, with minimal to no input from school-age siblings. For example, D. E. Gray (2002) conducted a longitudinal study of families having a child diagnosed with autism, but only surveyed the parents from each family. While he did give some attention to the topic of autism's impact on other children in the family, he based these results entirely on parental reports, without providing the siblings an opportunity to share their perspectives. Thus, his conclusions about the sibling experience came only from parents inferring what their other children might be experiencing, a filtering that introduces significant bias to the results. More recently, researchers have begun to consider the sibling's

THE SILENT SIBLING 7

perspective but often rely on retrospective accounts by adult siblings (Arnold, Heller, & Kramer, 2012), rather than allowing younger siblings to report for themselves. By omitting narratives made directly by school-age siblings, current research does not adequately present or address the needs of neurotypically developing children.

Sibling Absence in Support Services

Because therapy providers base autism interventions on current research 11
findings, the absence of young siblings in research leads to a lack of services geared specifically toward their needs. Children with autism receive intervention services to improve behavioral problems and develop life skills, while parents have access to support groups that help them to endure the challenges of raising a child with autism. Siblings have begun expressing a need for help in coping with their unique experiences. In 2012, to more thoroughly assess the needs of siblings, researchers conducted a survey of adult siblings of people with developmental disabilities. Over half of these individuals cited the need for better sibling inclusion, both with services geared directly towards sibling support and also with a definition of "family" that includes the neurotypical siblings, in addition to the parents and child with autism (Arnold et al., 2012). Siblings need a safe space to process their experiences and work through challenges, away from their parents and brother or sister.

Sibling Absence in Awareness

While they have a general idea of the day-to-day needs of their brother or 12
sister with autism, siblings do not necessarily know the full scope of autism across the lifetime and may not be aware of the services and programs available to support individuals with autism (Arnold et al., 2012). As children, siblings might have a general idea of the services their brother or sister is receiving, but they are uninformed regarding the process involved in procuring such services. This lack of information can become problematic. As siblings mature and begin to take on an instrumental role in supporting their loved one with autism, they must quickly learn to navigate the complicated system of accessing the necessary autism-support programs. The failure to involve siblings earlier in the therapy process can lead to a more stressful transition of care-giving responsibilities as the siblings enter adulthood.

What Do Siblings Need?

The emotional impact of autism on siblings' lives raises the question of how 13

THE SILENT SIBLING 8

such emotions, particularly the stresses and isolation, can be better mediated during the earlier years to produce more favorable outcomes. Support groups are being developed that allow siblings a forum to share their stories and connect with people who share those experiences. The efficacy of these programs has not been fully confirmed, but preliminary analysis of participant outcomes in one such program showed a positive and persistent effect on the well-being of siblings (Conway & Meyer, 2008).

Unfortunately, such programs are not widespread and need to be made more 14
readily accessible. Sibshop, one such sibling support program that is starting to gain momentum, has only 57 programs within the United States listed in their online database (Sibling Support Project, 2015), meaning that many states have only one such program available to families in need. Incorporating sibling-support programs into currently existing autism intervention services could quickly increase availability and access. For example, Easter Seals already provides a variety of services and resources to individuals with autism and their parents (Easter Seals, 2014) and could serve as excellent facilitators for sibling-support therapy. These organizations already see the families of autism frequently and could partner with Sibshop to connect siblings and form a support network. By providing these new programs, service providers can engage the siblings more effectively in the autism treatments and also allow them to gain a better understanding of their sibling experiences and identity.

Conclusion

School-age siblings hold a unique position in the discussion of autism treatment 15
and intervention. While therapies frequently address the needs of the diagnosed child and of parents, these intervention programs often overlook the siblings. These typically developing children have their own unique set of needs and play a significant role in providing care and company to their brother or sister with autism. Siblings experience frequent frustrations and isolation, which can lead to significant stress later in adulthood as they transition into becoming the primary caregivers for their brothers and sisters with autism. By developing programs that meet the emotional and peer needs of siblings, service providers can create a more holistic family-based approach to autism and move towards improved outcomes for people with autism and their entire family.

References

All works referred to in the paper appear on the references page, listed alphabetically by author (or title).

Each entry follows APA guidelines for listing authors, dates, titles, and publishing information.

Capitalization, punctuation, and hanging indentation are consistent with APA format.

American Psychiatric Association. (2013). *Diagnostic and statistical manual of mental disorders.* 5th ed. Arlington, VA: Author.

Arnold, C., Heller, T., & Kramer, J. (2012). Support needs of siblings of people with developmental disabilities. *Intellectual and Developmental Disabilities, 50*(5), 373-382.

Burke, M., Taylor, J., Urbano, R., & Hodapp, R. (2012). Predictors of future caregiving by adult siblings of individuals with intellectual and developmental disabilities. *Journal on Intellectual and Developmental Disabilities, 117*(1), 33-47.

Centers for Disease Control and Prevention. (2014). Prevalence of autism spectrum disorder among children aged 8 years. *MMWR Surveillance Summaries Publication, 63*(2), 1-21.

Conway, S. & Meyer, D. (2008). Developing support for siblings of young people with disabilities. *Support for Learning, 23*(3), 113-117. doi: 10.1111/j.1467-9604.2008.00381.x

Easter Seals Inc. (2014). *Autism Spectrum Disorder Services.* Retrieved November 22, 2015 from http://www.easterseals.com/our-programs/autism-services/

Gray, D. E. (2002). Ten years on: A longitudinal study of families of children with autism. *Journal of Intellectual and Developmental Disability, 27*(3), 215-222. doi: 10.1080/1366825021000008639

Moyson, T. & Roeyers, H. (2012). "The overall quality of my life as a sibling is all right, but of course it could always be better." Quality of life of siblings of children with intellectual disability: the siblings' perspective. *Journal of Intellectual Disability Research, 56*(1), 87-101. doi: 10.1111/j.1365-2788.2011.01393.x

Orsmond, G. & Seltzer, M. (2007a). Siblings of individuals with autism or Down syndrome: effects on adult lives. *Journal of Intellectual Disability Research, 51*(9), 682-696. doi: 10.1111/j.1365-2788.2007.00954.x

Orsmond, G. & Seltzer, M. (2007b). Siblings of individuals with autism spectrum disorder across the lifetime. *Mental Retardation & Developmental Disabilities Research Review, 13*, 313-320.

Seltzer, M., Floyd, F., Song, J., Greenberg, J., & Hong, J. (2011). Midlife and aging parents of adults with intellectual and developmental disabilities: Impacts of lifelong parenting. *American Journal on Intellectual and Developmental Disabilities, 116*(6), 479-499.

Sibling Support Project. (2015). *Sibshops.* Retrieved November 19, 2015 from https://www.siblingsupport.org/about-sibshops

U.S. Census Bureau. (2013). FM-3: Average number of own children under 18, for families with children under 18. *Current Population Survey.* Retrieved November 23, 2015 from https://www.census.gov/hhes/families/data/families.html

Reading for Better Writing

1. *Connections:* In your extended family and acquaintances, do you know of someone with autism or another disability? How would you describe that person's experience and the experience of his or her family?
2. *Comprehension:* What did you learn from Julia's paper about the experiences and needs of siblings of autistic children? List all the points that you can remember.
3. *Writing Strategies:*
   a. Julia uses questions as headings to organize her paper. What is the effect of using questions? How do the questions create a logical structure or flow for the paper?
   b. Study Julia's list of sources and her use of those sources within her paper. How would you characterize the research she has done? How does she use sources within her own writing, while also distinguishing source material from her own thinking?

Your Project: What sibling issues interest you? The phenomenon of only-children? Brother-sister dynamics? Birth order of siblings? Twins? Grandparent-grandchild relationships? The impact of divorce on sibling relationships? The impact of culture, gender identity, and/or race on sibling dynamics? Consider a phenomenon like these for your own research and writing.

Critical Thinking and Writing: Applications

Once you have used the instruction in this chapter to format and document your paper according to APA style, extend what you have learned by doing the following activities:

1. **System Check:** To make sense of APA guidelines and rules, answer these questions: What is the essential logic of the APA system? How does this logic reflect research practices and values in the Social Sciences?
2. **Reference Practice:** Create references list entries in correct APA style for the following sources:
   - An article in the summer 2009 issue (volume 34, no. 2) of the periodical *MELUS*, by Joni Adamson and Scott Slovic: "The Shoulders We Stand On: An Introduction to Ethnicity and Ecocriticism" (pages 5–24)
   - The book *The Playful World: How Technology Is Transforming Our Imagination*, by Mark Pesce, published in 2000 by Ballantine Books, located in New York City
   - The Web page "Vaccines for Children Program (VCP)," part of the Vaccines and Immunizations section of the Centers for Disease Control and Prevention (CDC) Web site, sponsored by the U.S. government's Department of Health and Human Services. No author or publication date is listed. The site was last accessed April 26, 2016, at http://www.cdc.gov/vaccines/programs/vfc/index.html

Learning-Objectives Checklist ✓

Have you achieved this chapter's learning objectives? Check your progress with the following items, revisiting topics in the chapter as needed. I have . . .

____ gained an overview of the APA system of documentation—the basic logic of in-text citations in relation to reference entries (504–505).

____ applied rules of in-text citation for a whole range of sources (506–509).

____ developed a references list that is properly formatted and that correctly and fully identifies sources, whether books or journal articles or online documents (510–520).

____ correctly implemented APA format guidelines (e.g., title page, abstract, running head, pagination, heading system, references page) (521).

____ examined APA style at work in Julia Sweigert's "The Silent Sibling: How Current Autism Intervention Neglects Typically-Developing Siblings," learning how the system is practiced effectively in her literature review (522–531).

MindTap® Practice skills that you have learned in this chapter and receive automatic feedback. Reflect on your writing process.

IV. Handbook

STILLFX / Shutterstock.com

Chapter 25

Understanding Grammar

Grammar is the study of the structure and features of the language, consisting of rules and standards that are to be followed to produce acceptable writing and speaking. **Parts of speech** refers to the eight different categories that indicate how words are used in the English language—as *nouns, pronouns, verbs, adjectives, adverbs, prepositions, conjunctions,* or *interjections.*

Noun 535.1

A **noun** is a word that names something: a person, a place, a thing, or an idea.

Toni Morrison/author ***The Revenant*/film** **Renaissance/era**
UC-Davis/university ***A Congress of Wonders*/book**

ESL Note: See 645.1–646.2 for information on count and noncount nouns.

Classes of Nouns

All nouns are either proper nouns or common nouns. Nouns may also be classified as *individual* or *collective,* or *concrete* or *abstract.*

Proper Nouns 535.2

A **proper noun,** which is always capitalized, names a specific person, place, thing, or idea.

Rembrandt, Bertrand Russell (people)
Stratford-upon-Avon, Tower of London (places)
***The Night Watch,* Rosetta stone** (things)
New Deal, Christianity (ideas)

Common Nouns 535.3

A **common noun** is a general name for a person, a place, a thing, or an idea. Common nouns are not capitalized.

optimist, instructor (people) **cafeteria, park** (places)
computer, chair (things) **freedom, love** (ideas)

536.1 Collective Nouns

A **collective noun** names a group or a unit.

family audience crowd committee team class

536.2 Concrete Nouns

A **concrete noun** names a thing that is tangible (can be seen, touched, heard, smelled, or tasted).

child The White Stripes gym village microwave oven pizza

536.3 Abstract Nouns

An **abstract noun** names an idea, a condition, or a feeling—in other words, something that cannot be seen, touched, heard, smelled, or tasted.

beauty Jungian psychology anxiety agoraphobia trust

Forms of Nouns

Nouns are grouped according to their *number, gender,* and *case.*

536.4 Number of Nouns

Number indicates whether a noun is singular or plural.

A singular noun refers to one person, place, thing, or idea.

student laboratory lecture note grade result

A plural noun refers to more than one person, place, thing, or idea.

students laboratories lectures notes grades results

536.5 Gender of Nouns

Gender indicates whether a noun is masculine, feminine, neuter, or indefinite.

Masculine:

father king brother men colt rooster

Feminine:

mother queen sister women filly hen

Neuter (without sex):

notebook monitor car printer

Indefinite or common (masculine or feminine):

professor customer children doctor people

Case of Nouns 537.1

The **case** of a noun tells what role the noun plays in a sentence. There are three cases: *nominative, possessive,* and *objective.*

A noun in the **nominative case** is used as a subject. The subject of a sentence tells who or what the sentence is about.

Dean Henning manages the College of Arts and Communication.

Note: A noun is also in the nominative case when it is used as a predicate noun (or predicate nominative). A predicate noun follows a linking verb, usually a form of the *be* verb (such as *am, is, are, was, were, be, being, been*), and repeats or renames the subject.

Ms. Yokum is the **person** to talk to about the college's impact in our community.

A noun in the **possessive case** shows possession or ownership. In this form, it acts as an adjective.

Our **president's** willingness to discuss concerns with students has boosted campus morale.

A noun in the **objective case** serves as an object of the preposition, a direct object, an indirect object, or an object complement.

To survive, institutions of higher **learning** sometimes cut **budgets** in spite of **protests** from **students** and **instructors.** (*Learning* is the object of the preposition *of, protests* is the object of the preposition *in spite of, budgets* is the direct object of the verb *cut,* and *students* and *instructors* are the objects of the preposition *from.*)

A Closer Look 537.2

Direct and Indirect Objects

A **direct object** is a noun (or pronoun) that identifies what or who receives the action of the verb.

Budget cutbacks reduced class **choices.** (*Choices* is the direct object of the active verb *reduced.*)

An **indirect object** is a noun (or pronoun) that identifies the person *to whom* or *for whom* something is done, or the thing *to which* or *for which* something is done. An indirect object is always accompanied by a direct object.

Recent budget cuts have given **students** fewer class choices. (*Choices* is the direct object of *have given; students* is the indirect object.)

ESL Note: Not every transitive verb is followed by *both* a direct object and an indirect object. Both can, however, follow *give, send, show, tell, teach, find, sell, ask, offer, pay, pass,* and *hand.*

Grammar Exercises:

Nouns

A. Classes of Nouns

Identify the class or classes that correctly describe the underlined noun in each sentence.

1. Jenna used a pencil to sketch a design for the new recreational center.
   a. proper noun   b. common noun   c. concrete noun
2. My team won a regional debate championship.
   a. collective noun   b. common noun   c. abstract noun
3. The end of the movie left me with deep disappointment.
   a. common noun   b. concrete noun   c. abstract noun
4. Tomorrow night I'm going to the Arizona Diamondbacks game.
   a. proper noun   b. abstract noun   c. common noun
5. Can someone buy me a soda at the store?
   a. collective noun   b. concrete noun   c. abstract noun
6. I'm trying to work up the motivation to go to the gym.
   a. proper noun   b. common noun   c. abstract noun

B. Case of Nouns

For each sentence identify the case of the underlined noun.

1. Social media Web sites have changed the way we receive news.
   a. nominative case   b. possessive case   c. objective case
2. Kings of Leon play rock music.
   a. nominative case   b. possessive case   c. objective case
3. Justin's favorite restaurant is on LaGrange Avenue.
   a. nominative case   b. possessive case   c. objective case

C. Gender of Nouns

Write down the feminine nouns from the list below.

desk   writer   princess   child   pilot   tree   waitress

Pronoun 539.1

A **pronoun** is a word that is used in place of a noun.

> Roger was the most interesting 10-year-old **I** ever taught. **He** was a good thinker and thus a good writer. **I** remember **his** paragraph about the cowboy hat **he** received from **his** grandparents. **It** was "too new looking." The brim was not rolled properly. But the hat's imperfections were not the main idea in Roger's writing. No, the main idea was how **he** was fixing the hat **himself** by wearing it when **he** showered.

Antecedents 539.2

An **antecedent** is the noun or pronoun that the pronoun refers to or replaces. Most pronouns have antecedents, but not all do. (See 540.4.)

> As the wellness **counselor** checked *her* chart, several **students** *who* were waiting *their* turns shifted uncomfortably. (*Counselor* is the antecedent of *her; students* is the antecedent of *who* and *their.*)

Note: Each pronoun must agree with its antecedent in number, person, and gender. (See pages 541–542 and 571.)

Classes of Pronouns 539.3

Personal

I, me, my, mine / we, us, our, ours / you, your, yours
they, them, their, theirs / he, him, his, she, her, hers, it, its

Reflexive and Intensive

myself, yourself, himself, herself, itself, ourselves, yourselves, themselves

Relative

who, whose, whom, which, that

Indefinite

all	anything	everybody	most	no one	some
another	both	everyone	much	nothing	somebody
any	each	everything	neither	one	someone
anybody	each one	few	nobody	other	something
anyone	either	many	none	several	such

Interrogative

who, whose, whom, which, what

Demonstrative

this, that, these, those

Reciprocal

each other, one another

Classes of Pronouns

There are several classes of pronouns: *personal, reflexive and intensive, relative, indefinite, interrogative,* and *demonstrative.*

540.1 ### Personal Pronouns

A **personal pronoun** refers to a specific person or thing.

> *Marge* started **her** car; **she** drove the antique *convertible* to Monterey, where **she** hoped to sell **it** at an auction.

540.2 ### Reflexive and Intensive Pronouns

A **reflexive pronoun** is formed by adding *-self* or *-selves* to a personal pronoun. A reflexive pronoun can act as a direct object or an indirect object of a verb, an object of a preposition, or a predicate nominative.

> Charles loves **himself**. (direct object of *loves*)
>
> Charles gives **himself** A's for fashion sense. (indirect object of *gives*)
>
> Charles smiles at **himself** in store windows. (object of preposition *at*)
>
> Charles can be **himself** anywhere. (predicate nominative)

An **intensive pronoun** intensifies, or emphasizes, the noun or pronoun it refers to.

> Leo **himself** taught his children to invest their lives in others.
>
> The lesson was sometimes painful—but they learned it **themselves**.

540.3 ### Relative Pronouns

A **relative pronoun** relates an adjective dependent (relative) clause to the noun or pronoun it modifies. (The noun is italicized in each example below; the relative pronoun is in bold.)

> *Freshmen* **who** believe they have a lot to learn are absolutely right.
>
> Just navigating this *campus,* **which** is huge, can be challenging.

Make sure you know when to use the relative pronouns *who* or *whom* and *that* or *which.* (See 589.3, 643.7, and 643.8.)

540.4 ### Indefinite Pronouns

An **indefinite pronoun** refers to unnamed or unknown people, places, or things.

> **Everyone** seemed amused when I was searching for my classroom in the student center. (The antecedent of *everyone* is unnamed.)
>
> **Nothing** is more unnerving than rushing at the last minute into the wrong room for the wrong class. (The antecedent of *nothing* is unknown.)

Most indefinite pronouns are singular, so when they are used as subjects, they should have singular verbs. (See pages 567–570.)

Interrogative Pronouns 541.1

An **interrogative pronoun** asks a question.

So **which** will it be—highlighting and attaching a campus map to the inside of your backpack, or being lost and late for the first two weeks?

Note: When an interrogative pronoun modifies a noun, it functions as an adjective.

Demonstrative Pronouns 541.2

A **demonstrative pronoun** points out people, places, or things.

We advise **this:** Bring along as many maps and schedules as you need.
Those are useful tools. **That** is the solution.

Note: When a demonstrative pronoun modifies a noun, it functions as an adjective.

Forms of Personal Pronouns

The **form** of a personal pronoun indicates its *number* (singular or plural), its *person* (first, second, or third), its *case* (nominative, possessive, or objective), and its *gender* (masculine, feminine, neuter, or indefinite).

Number of Pronouns 541.3

A **personal pronoun** is either singular *(I, you, he, she, it)* or plural *(we, you, they).*

He should have a budget and stick to it. (singular)

We can help new students learn about budgeting. (plural)

Person of Pronouns 541.4

The **person** of a pronoun indicates whether the person is speaking (first person), is spoken to (second person), or is spoken about (third person).

First person is used to name the speaker(s).

I know **I** need to handle **my** stress in a healthful way, especially during exam week; **my** usual chips-and-doughnuts binge isn't helping. (singular)

We all decided to bike to the tennis court. (plural)

Second person is used to name the person(s) spoken to.

Maria, **you** grab the rackets, okay? (singular)

John and Tanya, would **you** find the water bottles? (plural)

Third person is used to name the person(s) or thing(s) spoken about.

Today's students are interested in wellness issues. **They** are concerned about **their** health, fitness, and nutrition. (plural)

Maria practices yoga and feels **she** is calmer for **her** choice. (singular)

One of the advantages of regular exercise is that **it** raises one's energy level. (singular)

542.1 **Case of Pronouns**

The **case** of each pronoun tells what role it plays in a sentence. There are three cases: *nominative, possessive,* and *objective.*

A pronoun in the **nominative case** is used as a subject. The following are nominative forms: *I, you, he, she, it, we, they.*

He found an old map in the trunk.

My friend and **I** went biking. (not *me*)

A pronoun is also in the nominative case when it is used as a predicate nominative, following a linking verb *(am, is, are, was, were, seems)* and renaming the subject.

It was **he** who discovered electricity. (not *him*)

A pronoun in the **possessive case** shows possession or ownership: *my, mine, our, ours, his, her, hers, their, theirs, its, your, yours.* A possessive pronoun before a noun acts as an adjective: *your* coat.

That coat is **hers**. This coat is **mine**. **Your** coat is lost.

A pronoun in the **objective case** can be used as the direct object, indirect object, object of a preposition, or object complement: *me, you, him, her, it, us, them.*

Professor Adler hired **her**. (*Her* is the direct object of the verb *hired.*)

He showed Mary and **me** the language lab. (*Me* is the indirect object of the verb *showed.*)

He introduced the three of **us**—Mary, Shavonn, and **me**—to the faculty. (*Us* is the object of the preposition of; *me* is part of the appositive renaming *us.*)

542.2 **Gender of Pronouns**

The **gender** of a pronoun indicates whether the pronoun is masculine, feminine, neuter, or indefinite.

Masculine:
he, him, his

Feminine:
she, her, hers

Neuter (without gender):
it, its

Indefinite (masculine or feminine):
they, them, their

542.3

Number, Person, and Case of Personal Pronouns

	Nominative Case	Possessive Case	Objective Case
First Person Singular	I	my, mine	me
Second Person Singular	you	your, yours	you
Third Person Singular	he, she, it	his, her, hers, its	him, her, it
First Person Plural	we	our, ours	us
Second Person Plural	you	your, yours	you
Third Person Plural	they	their, theirs	them

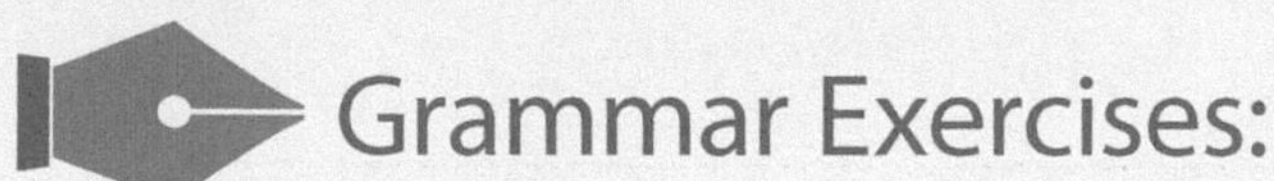

Pronouns

A. Classes of Pronouns

Identify the class of the underlined pronoun in each sentence.

1. Krunal asked himself if he should reprioritize his responsibilities.
a. personal b. reflexive c. relative

2. Who is coming to the pep rally?
a. demonstrative b. relative c. interrogative

3. That is quite possibly the most worthless product I've ever used.
a. demonstrative b. reflexive c. interrogative

4. Victoria washed her car on the way home from work.
a. personal b. intensive c. indefinite

5. Some of the hamburgers were undercooked.
a. personal b. intensive c. indefinite

6. The new fitness center, which is awesome, is open until 10:00 p.m.
a. personal b. relative c. reflexive

B. Person of Pronouns

For each sentence, indicate whether the underlined pronoun is written in the first, second, or third person.

1. Russell is excited for his new opportunity at the sailing club.
a. first person b. second person c. third person

2. Hey Britney, can you pass me the salt and pepper?
a. first person b. second person c. third person

3. I was hoping I could make the start of the play, but my class schedule interfered with my plans.
a. first person b. second person c. third person

C. Case of Pronouns

Write down the objective-case pronouns from the list below.

his me your us he they them him

544.1 # Verb

A **verb** shows action *(pondered, grins)*, links words *(is, seemed)*, or accompanies another action verb as an auxiliary or helping verb *(can, does)*.

Harry **honked** the horn. (shows action)

Harry **is** impatient. (links words)

Harry **was** honking the truck's horn. (accompanies the verb *honking*)

Classes of Verbs

Verbs are classified as *action*, *auxiliary (helping)*, or *linking (state of being)*.

544.2 ### Action Verbs: Transitive and Intransitive

As its name implies, an **action verb** shows action. Some action verbs are *transitive*; others are *intransitive*. (The term *action* does not always refer to a physical activity.)

Rain **splashed** the windshield. (transitive verb)

Josie **drove** off the road. (intransitive verb)

Transitive verbs have direct objects that receive the action (537.2).

The health care industry **employs** more than 7 million **workers** in the United States. (*Workers* is the direct object of the action verb *employs*.)

Intransitive verbs communicate action that is complete in itself. They do not need an object to receive the action.

My new college roommate **smiles** and **laughs** a lot.

Note: Some verbs can be either transitive or intransitive.

Ms. Hull **teaches** physiology and microbiology. (transitive)

She **teaches** well. (intransitive)

544.3 ### Auxiliary (Helping) Verbs

Auxiliary verbs (helping verbs) help to form some of the *tenses* (546.1), the *mood* (547.2), and the *voice* (547.1) of the main verb. In the following example, the auxiliary verbs are in **bold**, and the main verbs are in *italics*.

I *believe*, I **have** always *believed*, and I **will** always *believe* in private enterprise as the backbone of economic well-being in America. —Franklin D. Roosevelt

Common Auxiliary Verbs

am	been	could	does	have	might	should	will
are	being	did	had	is	must	was	would
be	can	do	has	may	shall	were	

ESL Note: "Be" auxiliary verbs are always followed by either a verb ending in *ing* or a past participle. Also see "Common Modal Auxiliary Verbs" (651.2).

Linking (State of Being) Verbs 545.1

A **linking verb** is a special form of intransitive verb that links the subject of a sentence to a noun, a pronoun, or an adjective in the predicate.

The streets **are** flooded. (adjective) The streets **are** rivers! (noun)

Common Linking Verbs

am are be become been being is was were

Additional Linking Verbs

appear feel look seem sound grow remain smell taste

Note: The verbs listed as "additional linking verbs" above function as linking verbs when they do not show actual action. An adjective usually follows these linking verbs.

The thunder **sounded** ominous. (adjective)

My little brother **grew** frightened. (adjective)

Note: When these same words are used as action verbs, an adverb or a direct object may follow them.

I **looked** *carefully* at him. (adverb)

My little brother **grew** *corn* for a science project. (direct object)

Forms of Verbs

A verb's **form** differs depending on its *number* (singular, plural), *person* (first, second, third), *tense* (present, past, future, present perfect, past perfect, future perfect), *voice* (active, passive), and *mood* (indicative, imperative, subjunctive).

Number of a Verb 545.2

Number indicates whether a verb is singular or plural. The verb and its subject both must be singular, or they both must be plural. (See "Subject–Verb Agreement," pages 567–570.)

My college **enrolls** high schoolers in summer programs. (singular)

Many colleges **enroll** high schoolers in summer courses. (plural)

Person of a Verb 545.3

Person indicates whether the subject of the verb is *first, second,* or *third person.* The verb and its subject must be in the same person. Verbs usually have a different form only in **third person singular of the present tense.**

	First Person	Second Person	Third Person
Singular	I think	you think	he/she/it thinks
Plural	we think	you think	they think

546.1 **Tense of a Verb**

Tense indicates the time of an action or state of being. There are three basic tenses *(past, present,* and *future)* and three verbal aspects *(progressive, perfect,* and *perfect progressive).*

546.2 **Present Tense**

Present tense expresses action happening at the present time or regularly.

In the United States, more than 75 percent of workers **hold** service jobs.

Present progressive tense also expresses action that is happening continually, in an ongoing fashion at the present time, but it is formed by combining *am, are,* or *is* and the present participle (ending in *ing*) of the main verb.

More women than ever before **are working** outside the home.

Present perfect tense expresses action that began in the past and has recently been completed or that continues up to the present time.

My sister **has taken** four years of swimming lessons.

Present perfect progressive tense also expresses an action that began in the past but stresses the continuing nature of the action. Like the present progressive tense, it is formed by combining auxiliary verbs (*have been* or *has been*) and present participles.

She **has been taking** them since she was six years old.

546.3 **Past Tense**

Past tense expresses action that was completed at a particular time in the past.

A hundred years ago, more than 75 percent of laborers **worked** in agriculture.

Past progressive tense expresses past action that continued over an interval of time. It is formed by combining *was* or *were* with the present participle of the main verb.

A century ago, my great-grandparents **were farming.**

Past perfect tense expresses an action in the past that was completed at a specific time before another past action occurred.

By the time we sat down for dinner, my cousins **had eaten** all the olives.

Past perfect progressive tense expresses a past action but stresses the continuing nature of the action. It is formed by using *had been* along with the present participle.

They **had been eating** the olives all afternoon.

546.4 **Future Tense**

Future tense expresses action that will take place in the future.

Next summer I **will work** as a lifeguard.

Future progressive tense expresses an action that will be continuous in the future.

I **will be working** for the park district at North Beach.

Future perfect tense expresses future action that will be completed by a specific time.

By 10:00 p.m., I **will have completed** my research project.

Future perfect progressive tense also expresses future action that will be completed by a specific time but (as with other perfect progressive tenses) stresses the action's continuous nature. It is formed using *will have been* along with the present participle.

I **will have been researching** the project for three weeks by the time it's due.

Voice of a Verb 547.1

Voice indicates whether the subject is acting or being acted upon.

Active voice indicates that the subject of the verb is performing the action.

People **update** their resumés on a regular basis. (The subject, *People,* is acting; *resumés* is the direct object.)

Passive voice indicates that the subject of the verb is being acted upon or is receiving the action. A passive verb is formed by combining a *be* verb with a past participle.

Your resumé **should be updated** on a regular basis. (The subject, *resumé,* is receiving the action.)

Using Active Voice

Generally, use active voice rather than passive voice for more direct, energetic writing. To change your passive sentences to active ones, do the following: First, find the noun that is doing the action and make it the subject. Then find the word that had been the subject and use it as the direct object.

Passive: The winning goal **was scored** by Eva. (The subject, *goal,* is not acting.)

Active: Eva **scored** the winning goal. (The subject, *Eva,* is acting.)

Note: When you want to emphasize the receiver more than the doer—or when the doer is unknown—use the passive voice (see page 81). (Much technical and scientific writing regularly uses the passive voice.)

Mood of a Verb 547.2

The mood of a verb indicates the tone or attitude with which a statement is made.

Indicative mood, the most common, is used to state a fact or to ask a question.

Can any theme **capture** the essence of the complex 1960s culture? President John F. Kennedy's directive [stated below] **represents** one ideal popular during that decade.

Imperative mood is used to give a command. (The subject of an imperative sentence is *you,* which is usually understood and not stated in the sentence.)

Ask not what your country can do for you—**ask** what you can do for your country.

—John F. Kennedy

Subjunctive mood is used to express a wish, an impossibility or unlikely condition, a necessity, or a motion in a formal business meeting. The subjunctive mood is often used with *if* or *that.* The verb forms below create an atypical subject–verb agreement, forming the subjunctive mood.

If I **were** rich, I would travel for the rest of my life. (a wish)

If each of your brain cells **were** one person, there would be enough people to populate 25 planets. (an impossibility)

The English Department requires that every student **pass** a proficiency test. I move that the motion **be adopted.** (a necessity)

Verbals

A **verbal** is a word that is made from a verb, but it functions as a noun, an adjective, or an adverb. There are three types of verbals: *gerunds, infinitives,* and *participles.*

548.1 ### Gerunds

A **gerund** ends in *ing* and is used as a noun.

Waking each morning is the first challenge. (subject)

I start **moving** at about seven o'clock. (direct object)

I work at **jump-starting** my weary system. (object of the preposition)

As Woody Allen once said, "Eighty percent of life is **showing up**." (predicate nominative)

548.2 ### Infinitives

An **infinitive** is *to* and the base form of the verb. The infinitive may be used as a noun, an adjective, or an adverb.

To succeed is not easy. (noun)

That is the most important thing **to remember**. (adjective)

Students are wise **to work** hard. (adverb)

ESL Note: It can be difficult to know whether a gerund or an infinitive should follow a verb. It's helpful to become familiar with lists of specific verbs that can be followed by one but not the other. (See 650.2–651.1.)

548.3 ### Participles

A **present participle** ends in *ing* and functions as an adjective. A **past participle** ends in *ed* (or another past tense form) and also functions as an adjective.

The **studying** students were annoyed by the **partying** ones.

The students **playing** loud music were **annoying**.
(These participles function as adjectives: *studying* students and *partying* students. Notice, however, that *playing* has a direct object: *music*. All three types of verbals may have direct objects. See 561.3.)

Using Verbals

Make sure that you use verbals correctly; look carefully at the examples below.

Verbal: **Diving** is a popular Olympic sport.
(*Diving* is a gerund used as a subject.)

Diving gracefully, the Olympian hoped to get high marks.
(*Diving* is a participle modifying *Olympian*.)

Verb: The next competitor was **diving** in the practice pool.
(Here, *diving* is a verb, not a verbal.)

Irregular Verbs

Irregular verbs can often be confusing. That's because the past tense and past participle of irregular verbs are formed by changing the word itself, not merely by adding *d* or *ed*. The following list contains the most troublesome irregular verbs.

549.1

Common Irregular Verbs and Their Principal Parts

Present Tense	Past Tense	Past Participle
am, be	was, were	been
arise	arose	arisen
awake	awoke, awaked	awoken, awaked
beat	beat	beaten
become	became	become
begin	began	begun
bite	bit	bitten, bit
blow	blew	blown
break	broke	broken
bring	brought	brought
build	built	built
burn	burnt, burned	burnt, burned
burst	burst	burst
buy	bought	bought
catch	caught	caught
choose	chose	chosen
come	came	come
cost	cost	cost
cut	cut	cut
dig	dug	dug
dive	dived, dove	dived
do	did	done
draw	drew	drawn
dream	dreamed, dreamt	dreamed, dreamt
drink	drank	drunk
drive	drove	driven
eat	ate	eaten
fall	fell	fallen
feel	felt	felt
fight	fought	fought
find	found	found
flee	fled	fled

Present Tense	Past Tense	Past Participle
fly	flew	flown
forget	forgot	forgotten, forgot
freeze	froze	frozen
get	got	gotten
give	gave	given
go	went	gone
grow	grew	grown
hang (execute)	hanged	hanged
hang (suspend)	hung	hung
have	had	had
hear	heard	heard
hide	hid	hidden
hit	hit	hit
keep	kept	kept
know	knew	known
lay	laid	laid
lead	led	led
leave	left	left
lend	lent	lent
let	let	let
lie (deceive)	lied	lied
lie (recline)	lay	lain
make	made	made
mean	meant	meant
meet	met	met
pay	paid	paid
prove	proved	proved, proven
put	put	put
read	read	read
ride	rode	ridden
ring	rang	rung
rise	rose	risen
run	ran	run

Present Tense	Past Tense	Past Participle
see	saw	seen
set	set	set
shake	shook	shaken
shine (light)	shone	shone
shine (polish)	shined	shined
show	showed	shown
shrink	shrank	shrunk
sing	sang	sung
sink	sank	sunk
sit	sat	sat
sleep	slept	slept
speak	spoke	spoken
spend	spent	spent
spring	sprang	sprung
stand	stood	stood
steal	stole	stolen
strike	struck	struck, stricken
strive	strove	striven
swear	swore	sworn
swim	swam	swum
swing	swung	swung
take	took	taken
teach	taught	taught
tear	tore	torn
tell	told	told
think	thought	thought
throw	threw	thrown
wake	woke, waked	woken, waked
wear	wore	worn
weave	wove	woven
wind	wound	wound
wring	wrung	wrung
write	wrote	written

Grammar Exercises:

Verbs

A. Classes of Verbs

Identify the class of the underlined verb in each sentence.

1. Shawn sprinted back to his apartment to retrieve his homework.
a. action verb b. auxiliary verb c. linking verb

2. The streets were teeming with partygoers.
a. action verb b. auxiliary verb c. linking verb

3. Niki's gaze remained fixed on the ice-cream cone.
a. action verb b. auxiliary verb c. linking verb

4. I think I should take time to study the new material.
a. action verb b. auxiliary verb c. linking verb

B. Forms of Verbs

For each sentence, identify the tense of the underlined verb.

1. Before we even got to the concert, the band had played my favorite song.
a. past tense b. past progressive tense c. past perfect tense

2. On Sunday I will finish my manuscript.
a. future tense b. future progressive tense c. future perfect tense

3. The mechanics have been working for ten straight hours.
a. present progressive tense b. present perfect tense
c. past progressive tense

4. Yesterday at this time I was relaxing on the beach.
a. past tense b. past progressive tense c. past perfect tense

C. Irregular Verbs

Write the past tense of the following irregular verbs.

1. buy
2. prove
3. swim
4. lead
5. pay
6. lay
7. wear
8. fly
9. give
10. sleep

Adjective 551.1

An **adjective** describes or modifies a noun or pronoun. The articles *a, an,* and *the* are adjectives.

> Advertising is **a big** and **powerful** industry. (*A, big,* and *powerful* modify the noun *industry.*)

Numbers are also adjectives.

> **Fifty-three** relatives came to my party.

Note: Many demonstrative, indefinite, and interrogative forms may be used as either adjectives or pronouns (*that, these, many, some, whose,* and so on). These words are adjectives if they come before a noun and modify it; they are pronouns if they stand alone.

> **Some** advertisements are less than truthful. (*Some* modifies *advertisements* and is an adjective.)
>
> **Many** cause us to chuckle at their outrageous claims. (*Many* stands alone; it is a pronoun and replaces the noun *advertisements.*)

Proper Adjectives 551.2

Proper adjectives are created from proper nouns and are capitalized.

> **English** has been influenced by advertising slogans. (proper noun)
>
> The **English** language is constantly changing. (proper adjective)

Predicate Adjectives 551.3

A **predicate adjective** follows a form of the *be* verb (or other linking verb) and describes the subject. (See 545.1.)

> At its best, advertising is **useful**; at its worst, **deceptive.** (*Useful* and *deceptive* modify the noun *advertising.*)

Forms of Adjectives 551.4

Adjectives have three forms: *positive, comparative,* and *superlative.*

The **positive form** is the adjective in its regular form. It describes a noun or a pronoun without comparing it to anyone or anything else.

> Joysport walking shoes are **strong** and **comfortable**.

The **comparative form** (*-er, more,* or *less*) compares two things. (*More* and *less* are used generally with adjectives of two or more syllables.)

> Air soles make Mile Eaters **stronger** and **more comfortable** than Joysports.

The **superlative form** (*-est, most,* or *least*) compares three or more things. (*Most* and *least* are used most often with adjectives of two or more syllables.)

> My old Canvas Wonders are the **strongest, most comfortable** shoes of all!

ESL Note: Two or more adjectives before a noun should have a certain order when they do not modify the noun equally. (See 587.3.)

552.1 # Adverb

An **adverb** describes or modifies a verb, an adjective, another adverb, or a whole sentence. An adverb answers questions such as *how, when, where, why, how often,* or *how much.*

The temperature fell **sharply**. (*Sharply* modifies the verb *fell.*)

The temperature was **quite** low. (*Quite* modifies the adjective *low.*)

The temperature dropped **very quickly**. (*Very* modifies the adverb *quickly,* which modifies the verb *dropped.*)

Unfortunately, the temperature stayed cool. (*Unfortunately* modifies the whole sentence.)

552.2 ## Types of Adverbs

Adverbs can be grouped in four ways: *time, place, manner,* and *degree.*

Time (These adverbs tell *when, how often,* and *how long.*)

today, yesterday **daily, weekly** **briefly, eternally**

Place (These adverbs tell *where, to where,* and *from where.*)

here, there **nearby, beyond** **backward, forward**

Manner (These adverbs often end in *ly* and tell *how* something is done.)

precisely **regularly** **regally** **smoothly** **well**

Degree (These adverbs tell *how much* or *how little.*)

substantially **greatly** **entirely** **partly** **too**

552.3 ## Forms of Adverbs

Adverbs have three forms: *positive, comparative,* and *superlative.*

The **positive form** is the adverb in its regular form. It describes a verb, an adjective, or another adverb without comparing it to anyone or anything else.

With Joysport shoes, you'll walk **fast**. They support your feet **well**.

The **comparative form** *(-er, more,* or *less)* compares two things. (*More* and *less* are used generally with adverbs of two or more syllables.)

Wear Jockos instead of Joysports, and you'll walk **faster**. Jockos' special soles support your feet **better** than the Joysports do.

The **superlative form** *(-est, most,* or *least)* compares three or more things. (*Most* and *least* are used most often with adverbs of two or more syllables.)

Really, I walk **fastest** wearing my old Canvas Wonders. They seem to support my feet, my knees, and my wallet **best** of all.

Regular Adverbs

positive	comparative	superlative
fast	faster	fastest
effectively	more effectively	most effectively

Irregular Adverbs

positive	comparative	superlative
well	better	best
badly	worse	worst

Preposition 553.1

A **preposition** is a word (or group of words) that shows the relationship between its object (a noun or pronoun following the preposition) and another word in the sentence.

> **Regarding** your reasons **for** going **to** college, do they all hinge **on** getting a good job **after** graduation? (In this sentence, *reasons, going, college, getting,* and *graduation* are objects of their preceding prepositions *regarding, for, to, on,* and *after.*)

Prepositional Phrases 553.2

A **prepositional phrase** includes the preposition, the object of the preposition, and the modifiers of the object. A prepositional phrase may function as an adverb or an adjective.

> A broader knowledge **of the world** is one benefit **of higher education**. (The two phrases function as adjectives modifying the nouns *knowledge* and *benefit* respectively.)

> He placed the flower **in the window**. (The phrase functions as an adverb modifying the verb *placed*.)

553.3

Prepositions

aboard	back of	excepting	notwithstanding	save
about	because of	for	of	since
above	before	from	off	subsequent to
according to	behind	from among	on	through
across	below	from between	on account of	throughout
across from	beneath	from under	on behalf of	'til
after	beside	in	onto	to
against	besides	in addition to	on top of	together with
along	between	in behalf of	opposite	toward
alongside	beyond	in front of	out	under
alongside of	by	in place of	out of	underneath
along with	by means of	in regard to	outside	until
amid	concerning	inside	outside of	unto
among	considering	inside of	over	up
apart from	despite	in spite of	over to	upon
around	down	instead of	owing to	up to
as far as	down from	into	past	with
aside from	during	like	prior to	within
at	except	near	regarding	without
away from	except for	near to	round	

ESL Note: Prepositions often pair up with a verb and become part of an idiom, a slang expression, or a two-word verb. (See pages 652 and 667–670.)

554.1 # Conjunction

A **conjunction** connects individual words or groups of words.

When we came back to Paris, it was clear **and** cold **and** lovely.
—Ernest Hemingway

554.2 ## Coordinating Conjunctions

Coordinating conjunctions usually connect a word to a word, a phrase to a phrase, or a clause to a clause. The words, phrases, or clauses joined by a coordinating conjunction are equal in importance or are of the same type.

Civilization is a race between education **and** catastrophe.
—H. G. Wells

554.3 ## Correlative Conjunctions

Correlative conjunctions are a type of coordinating conjunction used in pairs.

There are two inadvisable ways to think: **either** believe everything **or** doubt everything.

554.4 ## Subordinating Conjunctions

Subordinating conjunctions connect two clauses that are not equally important. A subordinating conjunction connects a dependent clause to an independent clause. The conjunction is part of the dependent clause.

Experience is the worst teacher; it gives the test **before** it presents the lesson. (The clause *before it presents the lesson* is dependent. It connects to the independent clause *it gives the test.*)

554.5 ### Conjunctions

Coordinating: and, but, or, nor, for, so, yet

Correlative: either, or; neither, nor; not only, but (but also); both, and; whether, or

Subordinating: after, although, as, as if, as long as, because, before, even though, if, in order that, provided that, since, so that, though, unless, until, when, whenever, where, while

Note: Relative pronouns (540.3) can also connect clauses.

554.6 # Interjection

An **interjection** communicates strong emotion or surprise (*oh, ouch, hey,* and so on). Punctuation (often a comma or an exclamation point) is used to set off an interjection.

Hey! Wait! Well, so much for catching the bus.

Adjectives, Adverbs, Prepositions, Conjunctions, and Injections

A. Forms of Adjectives

Write the correct form (positive, comparative, or superlative) of the adjective shown in parentheses for each sentence.

1. I ate the __________ chicken wings I had ever tasted in my life. (*spicy*)
2. The Internet connection at the coffeehouse is __________ than the connection at the library. (*fast*)
3. Arizona is known for its _________ and dry climate. (*hot*)
4. Online shopping is _________ than mall shopping. (*efficient*)

B. Types of Adverbs

Indicate whether the adverb reveals time, place, manner, or degree.

1. completely
2. smartly
3. easily
4. briefly
5. everywhere
6. tomorrow

C. Conjunctions

Create a three-column table and label the columns "Coordinating," "Subordinating," and "Correlative." Then sort out the conjunctions below into their appropriate columns.

after
although
and
as
as if
as long as
because
before
both/and
but
either/or
even though
for
if
in order that
neither/nor
nor
not only/but also
or
provided that
since
so
so that
that
though
unless
until
when
whenever
where
while
yet

MindTap® Practice skills that you have learned in this section and receive automatic feedback.

A Closer Look
Parts of Speech

Noun A **noun** is a word that names something: a person, a place, a thing, or an idea.

Toni Morrison/author ***The Revenant*/film**
UC–Davis/university **Renaissance/era**
***A Congress of Wonders*/book**

Pronoun A **pronoun** is a word used in place of a noun.

I my that themselves which
it ours they everybody you

Verb A **verb** is a word that expresses action, links words, or acts as an auxiliary verb to the main verb.

are break drag fly run sit was
bite catch eat is see tear were

Adjective An **adjective** describes or modifies a noun or pronoun. (The articles *a, an,* and *the* are adjectives.)

The carbonated drink went down easily on **that hot, dry** day.
(*The* and *carbonated* modify *drink; that, hot,* and *dry* modify *day.*)

Adverb An **adverb** describes or modifies a verb, an adjective, another adverb, or a whole sentence. An adverb generally answers questions such as *how, when, where, how often,* or *how much.*

greatly precisely regularly there
here today partly quickly
slowly yesterday nearly loudly

Preposition A **preposition** is a word (or group of words) that shows the relationship between its object (a noun or pronoun that follows the preposition) and another word in the sentence. Prepositions introduce prepositional phrases, which are modifiers.

across for with out to of

Conjunction A **conjunction** connects individual words or groups of words.

and because but for or since so yet

Interjection An **interjection** is a word that communicates strong emotion or surprise. Punctuation (often a comma or an exclamation point) is used to set off an interjection from the rest of the sentence.

Stop! No! What, am I invisible?

Chapter 26

Constructing Sentences 557.1

A **sentence** is made up of at least a subject (sometimes understood) and a verb and expresses a complete thought. Sentences can make statements, ask questions, give commands, or express feelings.

The Web delivers the universe in a box.

Using Subjects and Predicates 557.2

Sentences have two main parts: a **subject** and a **predicate**.

Technology frustrates many people.

Note: In the sentence above, *technology* is the subject—the sentence talks about technology. *Frustrates many people* is the complete predicate—it tells what the subject is doing.

The Subject 557.3

The **subject** names the person or thing either performing the action, receiving the action, or being described or renamed. The subject is most often a noun or a pronoun.

Technology is an integral part of almost every business.
Manufacturers need technology to compete in the world market.
They could not go far without it.

A verbal phrase or a noun dependent clause may also function as a subject.

To survive without technology is difficult. (infinitive phrase)

Downloading information from the Web is easy. (gerund phrase)

That the information age would arrive was inevitable. (noun dependent clause)

Note: To determine the subject of a sentence, ask yourself *who* or *what* performs or receives the action or is described. In most sentences, the subject comes before the verb; however, in many questions and some other instances, that order is reversed. (See 564.2, 564.3, 568.1, and 660.)

ESL Note: Some languages permit the omission of a subject in a sentence; English does not. A subject must be included in every sentence. (The only exception is an "understood subject," which is discussed at 558.4.)

558.1 Simple Subject

A **simple subject** is the subject without the words that describe or modify it.

Thirty years ago, reasonably well-trained **mechanics** could fix any car on the road.

558.2 Complete Subject

A **complete subject** is the simple subject *and* the words that describe or modify it.

Thirty years ago, **reasonably well-trained mechanics** could fix any car on the road.

558.3 Compound Subject

A **compound subject** is composed of two or more simple subjects joined by a conjunction and sharing the same predicate(s).

Today, **mechanics** and **technicians** would need to master a half million manual pages to fix every car on the road.

Dealerships and their service **departments** must sometimes explain that situation to the customers.

558.4 Understood Subject

Sometimes a subject is **understood**. This means it is not stated in the sentence, but a reader clearly understands what the subject is. An understood subject occurs in a command (imperative sentence). (See 564.3.)

(You) Park on this side of the street. (The subject *you* is understood.)

Put your smart phone in the glove box.

558.5 Delayed Subject

In sentences that begin with *There is, There was,* or *Here is,* the subject follows the verb.

There are 70,000 **fans** in the stadium. (The subject is *fans; are* is the verb. *There* is an expletive, an empty word.)

Here is a **problem** for stadium security. (*Problem* is the subject. *Here* is an adverb.)

The subject is also delayed in questions.

Where was the **event**? (*Event* is the subject.)

Was **Dave Matthews** playing? (*Dave Matthews* is the subject.)

Common Sentence Patterns

Working together, subjects and predicates make sentences. But what are the most common patterns that subject-predicate combinations take? See page 660 for five basic patterns of simple sentences:

- Subject + Verb
- Subject + Verb + Direct Object
- Subject + Verb + Indirect Object + Direct Object
- Subject + Verb + Direct Object + Object Complement
- Subject + Linking Verb + Predicate Nominative (or Predicate Adjective)

The Predicate (Verb) 559.1

The **predicate**, which contains the verb, is the part of the sentence that either tells what the subject is doing, tells what is being done to the subject, or describes or renames the subject.

Students **need technical skills as well as basic academic skills.**

Simple Predicate 559.2

A **simple predicate** is the complete verb without the words that describe or modify it. (The complete verb can consist of more that one word.)

Today's workplace **requires** employees to have a range of skills.

Complete Predicate 559.3

A **complete predicate** is the verb, all the words that modify or explain it, and any objects or complements.

Today's workplace **requires employees to have a range of skills.**

Compound Predicate 559.4

A **compound predicate** is composed of two or more verbs, all the words that modify or explain them, and any objects or complements.

Engineers **analyze problems** and **calculate solutions.**

Direct Object 559.5

A **direct object** is the part of the predicate that receives the action of an active transitive verb. A direct object makes the meaning of the verb complete.

Marcos visited several **campuses.** (The direct object *campuses* receives the action of the verb *visited* by answering the question "Marcos visited what?")

Note: A direct object may be compound.

A counselor explained the academic **programs** and the application **process.**

Indirect Object 559.6

An **indirect object** is the word(s) that tells *to whom/to what* or *for whom/for what* something is done. A sentence must have a direct object before it can have an indirect object.

I showed our **children** my new school.

Use these questions to find an indirect object:

- What is the verb? *showed*
- *Showed* what? *school* (direct object)
- Showed *school* to whom? *children* (indirect object)

I wrote **them** a note.

Note: An indirect object may be compound.

I gave the **instructor** and a few **classmates** my email address.

Constructing Sentences Exercises:

Subjects and Predicates

A. Subjects

1. Write the complete subject of each numbered sentence in the following paragraph. Then underline the simple subjects. (You will find one compound subject.)

(1) Every modern war seems to have its own terrible illness for soldiers. (2) In World War I, blistered skin and ravaged lungs resulted from exposure to mustard gas. (3) World War II saw the problem of "shell shock." (4) Agent Orange was blamed for causing cancer in Vietnam War veterans. (5) The Gulf War saw the rise of "post-traumatic stress disorder." (6) And many veterans of combat in Iraq and Iran return with "mild traumatic brain injury" due to improvised explosive devices.

2. Create your own sentence with an understood subject.
3. Create your own sentence with a delayed subject.

B. Predicates

1. Write the complete predicate of each numbered sentence in the following paragraph. Then underline the simple predicates. (You will find one compound predicate.)

(1) Women today have more than one choice for professional assistance with childbirth. (2) The obstetrician of your parents' era is trained to diagnose abnormalities and is prepared to deal with emergencies. (3) Today's midwife practitioner, on the other hand, is focused upon normal deliveries. (4) This makes the two occupations quite complementary.

2. List the direct objects in the numbered sentences of the following paragraph. If a sentence also includes an indirect object, list that in parentheses after the direct object.

(1) Different situations bring you happiness. (2) Various pursuits deliver satisfaction. (3) And many agree that parents pass along their values and goals to their children. (4) So your own offspring will also receive this intangible inheritance.

Using Phrases 561.1

A **phrase** is a group of related words that functions as a single part of speech. A phrase lacks a subject, a predicate, or both. There are three phrases in the following sentence:

Examples of technology can be found in ancient civilizations.

of technology
(prepositional phrase that functions as an adjective; no subject or predicate)

can be found
(verb phrase—all of the words of the verb; no subject)

in ancient civilizations
(prepositional phrase that functions as an adverb; no subject or predicate)

Types of Phrases

There are several types of phrases: *verb, verbal, prepositional, appositive,* and *absolute.*

Verb Phrase 561.2

A **verb phrase** consists of a main verb and its helping verbs.

Students, worried about exams, **have camped** at the library all week.

Verbal Phrase 561.3

A **verbal phrase** is a phrase that expands on one of the three types of verbals: *gerund, infinitive,* or *participle.* (See Figure 26.1 on the next page.)

A **gerund phrase** consists of a gerund and its modifiers and objects. The whole phrase functions as a noun. (See 548.1.)

Becoming a marine biologist is Rashanda's dream. (The gerund phrase is used as the subject of the sentence.)

She has acquainted herself with the various methods for **collecting sea-life samples.** (The gerund phrase is the object of the preposition *for.*)

An **infinitive phrase** consists of an infinitive and its modifiers and objects. The whole phrase functions as a noun, an adjective, or an adverb. (See 548.2.)

To dream is the first step in any endeavor. (The infinitive phrase functions as a noun used as the subject.)

Remember **to make a plan to realize your dream.** (The infinitive phrase *to make a plan* functions as a noun used as a direct object; *to realize your dream* functions as an adjective modifying plan.)

Finally, apply all of your talents and skills **to achieve your goals.** (The infinitive phrase functions as an adverb modifying *apply.*)

A **participial phrase** consists of a present or past participle (a verb form ending in *ing* or *ed*) and its modifiers. The phrase functions as an adjective. (See 548.3.)

Doing poorly in biology, Theo signed up for a tutor. (The participial phrase modifies the noun *Theo.*)

Some students **frustrated by difficult course work** don't seek help.
(The participial phrase modifies the noun *students.*)

562.1

Functions of Verbal Phrases

fig. 26.1

	Noun	Adjective	Adverb
Gerund	■		
Infinitive	■	■	■
Participial		■	

562.2

Prepositional Phrase

A **prepositional phrase** is a group of words beginning with a preposition and ending with its object, a noun or a pronoun. Prepositional phrases are used mainly as adjectives and adverbs. See 553.3 for a list of prepositions.

> Denying the existence **of exam week** hasn't worked **for anyone** yet.
> (The prepositional phrase *of exam week* is used as an adjective modifying the noun *existence; for anyone* is used as an adverb modifying the verb *has worked.*)
>
> Test days still dawn and GPAs still plummet **for the unprepared student.**
> (The prepositional phrase *for the unprepared student* is used as an adverb modifying the verbs *dawn* and *plummet.*)

ESL Note: Do not mistake the following adverbs for nouns and incorrectly use them as objects of prepositions: *here, there, everywhere.*

562.3

Appositive Phrase

An **appositive phrase**, which follows a noun or a pronoun and renames it, consists of a noun and its modifiers. An appositive adds new information about the noun or pronoun it follows.

> The Olympic-size pool, **a prized addition to the physical education building,** gets plenty of use. (The appositive phrase renames *pool.*)

562.4

Absolute Phrase

An **absolute phrase** consists of a noun and a participle (plus the participle's object, if there is one, and any modifiers). It usually modifies the entire sentence.

> **Their enthusiasm sometimes waning,** the students who cannot swim are required to take lessons. (The noun *enthusiasm* is modified by the present participle *waning;* the entire phrase modifies *students.*)

fyi Phrases can add valuable information to sentences, but some phrases add nothing but "fat" to your writing. For a list of phrases to avoid, see page 104.

Using Clauses

A **clause** is a group of related words that has both a subject and a verb.

Independent/Dependent Clauses 563.1

An **independent clause** contains at least one subject and one verb, presents a complete thought, and can stand alone as a sentence; a **dependent clause** (also called a subordinate clause) does not present a complete thought and cannot stand alone (make sense) as a sentence.

> Though airplanes are twentieth-century inventions (dependent clause), people have always dreamed of flying (independent clause).

Types of Clauses

There are three basic types of dependent, or subordinate, clauses: *adverb, adjective,* and *noun.* These dependent clauses are combined with independent clauses to form complex and compound-complex sentences.

Adverb Clause 563.2

An **adverb clause** is used like an adverb to modify a verb, an adjective, or an adverb. All adverb clauses begin with subordinating conjunctions. (See 554.4.)

> **Because Orville won a coin toss,** he got to fly the power-driven air machine first. (The adverb clause modifies the verb *got.*)

Adjective Clause 563.3

An **adjective clause** is used like an adjective to modify a noun or a pronoun. Adjective clauses begin with relative pronouns *(which, that, who).* (See 540.3.)

> The men **who invented the first airplane** were brothers, Orville and Wilbur Wright. (The adjective clause modifies the noun *men. Who* is the subject of the adjective clause.)
>
> The first flight, **which took place December 17, 1903,** was made by Orville. (The adjective clause modifies the noun *flight. Which* is the subject of the adjective clause.)

Noun Clause 563.4

A **noun clause** is used in place of a noun. Noun clauses can appear as subjects, as direct or indirect objects, as predicate nominatives, or as objects of prepositions. Noun clauses can also play a role in the independent clause. They are introduced by subordinating words such as *what, that, when, why, how, whatever, who, whom, whoever,* and *whomever.*

> He wants to know **what made modern aviation possible**. (The noun clause functions as the object of the infinitive.)
>
> **Whoever invents an airplane with vertical takeoff ability** will be a hero. (The noun clause functions as the subject.)

Note: If you can replace a whole clause with the pronoun *something* or *someone,* it is a noun clause.

Using Sentence Variety

A sentence can be classified according to the kind of statement it makes and according to the way it is constructed.

Kinds of Sentences

Sentences can make five basic kinds of statements: *declarative, interrogative, imperative, exclamatory,* or *conditional.*

564.1

Declarative Sentence

Declarative sentences make statements. They tell us something about a person, a place, a thing, or an idea.

In 1955, Rosa Parks refused to follow segregation rules on a bus in Montgomery, Alabama.

564.2

Interrogative Sentence

Interrogative sentences ask questions.

Do you think Ms. Parks knew she was making history?

Would you have had the courage to do what she did?

564.3

Imperative Sentence

Imperative sentences give commands. They often contain an understood subject (*you*). (See 558.4.)

Read chapters 6 through 10 for tomorrow.

ESL Note: Imperative sentences with an understood subject are the only sentences in which it is acceptable to have no subject stated.

564.4

Exclamatory Sentence

Exclamatory sentences communicate strong emotion or surprise. They are punctuated with exclamation points.

I simply can't keep up with these long reading assignments!

Oh my gosh, you scared me!

564.5

Conditional Sentence

Conditional sentences express two circumstances. One of the circumstances depends on the other circumstance. The words *if, when,* or *unless* are often used in the dependent clause in conditional sentences.

If you practice a few study-reading techniques, college reading loads will be manageable.

When I manage my time, it seems I have more of it.

Don't ask me to help you **unless** you are willing to do the reading first.

Structure of Sentences

A sentence may be *simple, compound, complex,* or *compound-complex,* depending on how the independent and dependent clauses are combined.

Simple Sentence 565.1

A **simple sentence** contains one independent clause. The independent clause may have compound subjects and verbs, and it may also contain phrases.

My **back aches.**
(single subject: *back;* single verb: *aches*)

My **teeth** and my **eyes hurt.**
(compound subject: *teeth* and *eyes;* single verb: *hurt*)

My **memory** and my **logic come** and **go.**
(compound subject: *memory* and *logic;* compound verb: *come* and *go*)

I must need a vacation.
(single subject: *I;* single verb: *must need;* direct object: *vacation*)

Compound Sentence 565.2

A **compound sentence** consists of two independent clauses. The clauses must be joined by a semicolon, by a comma and a coordinating conjunction *(and, but, or, nor, so, for, yet)*, or by a semicolon followed by a conjunctive adverb *(besides, however, instead, meanwhile, then, therefore)* and a comma.

I had eight hours of sleep**, so** why am I so exhausted?

I take good care of myself; I get enough sleep.

I still feel fatigued**; therefore,** I must need more exercise.

Complex Sentence 565.3

A **complex sentence** contains one independent clause (in bold) and one or more dependent clauses (underlined).

When I can, **I get eight hours of sleep.** (dependent clause; independent clause)

When I get up on time, and if someone hasn't used up all the milk,
I eat breakfast. (two dependent clauses; independent clause)

When the dependent clause comes before the independent clause, use a comma.

Compound-Complex Sentence 565.4

A **compound-complex sentence** contains two or more independent clauses (in bold type) and one or more dependent clauses (underlined).

If I'm not in a hurry, **I take leisurely walks,** and **I try to spot some wildlife.**
(dependent clause; two independent clauses)

I saw a hawk when I was walking, and **other smaller birds were chasing it.**
(independent clause; dependent clause; independent clause)

Constructing Sentences Exercises:

Phrases, Clauses, and Sentence Variety

A. Phrases and Clauses

Identify the numbered phrases (gerund, infinitive, participial, prepositional, appositive, or absolute), and clauses (adverb, adjective, or noun). Note that not every type is represented.

The marionette, (1) a type of puppet manipulated by strings or rods, has been around for millennia. Stringed puppets have been found in Egyptian tombs from around 2000 B.C. Greek philosophers such as Xenophon wrote about these articulated puppets as early as 422 B.C. (2) To control their marionettes, the ancient Romans used rods from above, and Italy retains a strong tradition of articulated puppetry from these Roman roots. (3) Employed in religious performances during ancient times, marionettes found similar use in morality plays during the Renaissance. Most likely, the term "marionette" originated as a diminutive form (4) of the Virgin Mary's name in these plays. Starting in the eighteenth century, entire operas were performed by marionettes in theaters such as the Salzburg Marionette Theatre in Austria, (5) which continues performances to this day. Of course, marionettes have also starred in television and film, and (6) since puppetry is still a valued storytelling art, chances are you've seen them perform at your local grade school.

B. Sentence Variety

Identify each sentence in the following paragraph by kind (declarative, interrogative, imperative, exclamatory, or conditional).

(1) Do you realize how far personal computers have come since their early days? (2) Understand that the first examples were marketed to scientists and researchers. (3) After that came kits for hobbyists to build and program their own machines. (4) The introduction of the microprocessor chip allowed PCs to proliferate after 1975. (5) If blinkenlights.com is correct, the HP 9830, originally sold in 1972, qualifies as the very first personal computer, being a fully built desktop machine with a keyboard and display. (6) Other people argue that the Commodore PET in 1977 better suited that designation because it was commercially available to everyone. (7) In any case, the popular Apple II and the IBM-PC then solidified the personal computer's role in business and at home.

Chapter 27

Avoiding Sentence Errors

Subject–Verb Agreement 567.1

The subject and verb of any clause must agree in both *person* and *number.* Person indicates whether the subject of the verb is *first, second,* or *third person. Number* indicates whether the subject and verb are *singular* or *plural.* (See 545.2 and 545.3.)

	Singular	Plural
First Person	I think	we think
Second Person	you think	you think
Third Person	he/she/it thinks	they think

Agreement in Number 567.2

A verb must agree in number (singular or plural) with its subject.

The **student was** rewarded for her hard work. (Both the subject *student* and the verb *was* are singular; they agree in number.)

Note: Do not be confused by phrases that come between the subject and the verb. Such phrases may begin with words like *in addition to, as well as,* or *together with.*

The **instructor**, as well as the students, **is** expected to attend the orientation. (*Instructor,* not *students,* is the subject.)

Compound Subjects 567.3

Compound subjects connected with *and* usually require a plural verb.

Dedication and creativity are trademarks of successful students.

Note: If a compound subject joined by *and* is thought of as a unit, use a singular verb.

Macaroni and cheese is always available in the cafeteria.

(Also see 568.3 and 568.4.)

568.1 **Delayed Subjects**

Delayed subjects occur when the verb comes *before* the subject in a sentence. In these inverted sentences, the true (delayed) subject must still agree with the verb.

There **are** many nontraditional **students** on our campus.
Here **is** the **syllabus** you need.
(*Students* and *syllabus* are the subjects of these sentences, not the adverbs *there* and *here.*)

Note: Using an inverted sentence, on occasion, will lend variety to your writing style. Simply remember to make the delayed subjects agree with the verbs.

However, included among the list's topmost items **was "revise research paper."**
(Because the true subject here is singular—one item—the singular verb *was* is correct.)

568.2 **Titles as Subjects**

When the subject of a sentence is the title of a work of art, literature, or music, the verb should be singular. This is also true of a word (or phrase) being used as a word (or phrase).

***Lyrical Ballads* was** published in 1798 by two of England's greatest poets, Wordsworth and Coleridge. (Even though the title of the book, *Lyrical Ballads,* is plural in form, it is still a single title being used as the subject, correctly taking the singular verb *was.*)

"Over-the-counter drugs" is a phrase that means nonprescription medications. (Even though the phrase is plural in form, it is still a single phrase being used as the subject, correctly taking the singular verb *is.*)

568.3 **Singular Subjects with *Or* or *Nor***

Singular subjects joined by *or* or *nor* take a singular verb.

Neither a **textbook** nor a **notebook is required** for this class.

Note: When the subject nearer a present-tense verb is the singular pronoun *I* or *you,* the correct singular verb does not end in *s.*

Neither **Marcus** nor **I feel** (not *feels*) right about this.
Either **Rosa** or **you have** (not *has*) to take notes for me.
Either **you** or **Rosa has** to take notes for me.

568.4 **Singular/Plural Subjects**

When one of the subjects joined by *or* or *nor* is singular and one is plural, the verb must agree with the subject nearer the verb.

Neither the **professor** nor her **students were** in the lab. (The plural subject *students* is nearer the verb; therefore, the plural verb *were* agrees with *students.*)

Neither the **students** nor the **professor was** in the lab. (The singular subject *professor* is nearer the verb; therefore, the singular verb *was* is used to agree with *professor.*)

Collective Nouns 569.1

Generally, **collective nouns** (*faculty, pair, crew, assembly, congress, species, crowd, army, team, committee,* and so on) take a singular verb. However, if you want to emphasize differences among individuals in the group or are referring to the group as individuals, you may use a plural verb.

My lab **team takes** its work very seriously. (*Team* refers to the group as a unit; it requires a singular verb, *takes*.)

The **team assume** separate responsibilities for each study they undertake. (In this example, *team* refers to individuals within the group; it requires a plural verb, *assume*.)

Note: Collective nouns such as (the) *police, poor, elderly,* and *young* use plural verbs.

The police direct traffic here between 7:00 and 9:00 a.m.

Plural Nouns with Singular Meaning 569.2

Some nouns that are plural in form but singular in meaning take a singular verb: *mumps, measles, news, mathematics, economics, robotics,* and so on.

Economics is sometimes called "the dismal science."

The economic **news is** not very good.

Note: The most common exceptions are *scissors, trousers, tidings,* and *pliers*.

The **scissors are** missing again.

Are these **trousers** prewashed?

With Linking Verbs 569.3

When a sentence contains a linking verb (usually a form of *be*)—and a noun or pronoun comes before and after that verb—the verb must agree with the subject, not the predicate nominative (the noun or pronoun coming after the verb).

The cause of his problem **was** poor study habits. (*Cause* requires a singular verb, even though the predicate nominative, *habits*, is plural.)

His poor study habits **were** the cause of his problem. (*Habits* requires a plural verb, even though the predicate nominative, *cause*, is singular.)

Nouns Showing Measurement, Time, and Money 569.4

Mathematical phrases and phrases that name a period of time, a unit of measurement, or an amount of money take a singular verb.

Three and three **is** six.

Eight pages **is** a long paper on this topic.

In my opinion, two dollars **is** a high price for a cup of coffee.

570.1 **Relative Pronouns**

When a **relative pronoun** *(who, which, that)* is used as the subject of a dependent clause, the number of the verb is determined by that pronoun's antecedent. (The *antecedent* is the word to which the pronoun refers.)

This is one of the **books that are** required for English class. (The relative pronoun *that* requires the plural verb *are* because its antecedent is *books*, not the word *one*. To test this type of sentence for agreement, read the *of* phrase first: *Of the books that are . . .*)

Note: Generally, the antecedent is the nearest noun or pronoun to the relative pronoun and is often the object of a preposition. Sometimes, however, the antecedent is not the nearest noun or pronoun, especially in sentences with the phrase "the only one of."

Dr. Graciosa wondered why Claire was the only **one** of her students **who was** not attending lectures regularly. (In this case, the addition of the modifiers *the only* changes the meaning of the sentence. The antecedent of *who* is *one*, not *students*. Only one student was not attending.)

570.2 **Indefinite Pronoun with Singular Verb**

Many indefinite pronouns *(someone, somebody, something; anyone, anybody, anything; no one, nobody, nothing; everyone, everybody, everything; each, either, neither, one, this)* serving as subjects require a singular verb.

Everybody is welcome to attend the chancellor's reception.

No one was sent an invitation.

Note: Although it may seem to indicate more than one, *each* is a singular pronoun and requires a singular verb. Do not be confused by words or phrases that come between the indefinite pronoun and the verb.

Each of the new students **is** (not *are*) **encouraged** to attend the reception.

570.3 **Indefinite Pronoun with Plural Verb**

Some indefinite pronouns (*both, few, many, most,* and *several*) are plural; they require a plural verb.

Few are offered the opportunity to study abroad.

Most take advantage of opportunities closer to home.

570.4 **Indefinite Pronoun or Quantity Word with Singular/Plural Verb**

Some indefinite pronouns or quantity words (*all, any, most, part, half, none,* and *some*) may be either singular or plural, depending on the nouns they refer to. Look inside the prepositional phrase to see what the antecedent is.

Some of the students **were** missing. (*Students,* the noun that *some* refers to, is plural; therefore, the pronoun *some* is considered plural, and the plural verb *were* is used to agree with it.)

Most of the lecture **was** over by the time we arrived. (Because *lecture* is singular, *most* is also singular, requiring the singular verb *was.*)

Pronoun–Antecedent Agreement 571.1

A pronoun must agree in number, person, and gender (sex) with its *antecedent*. The antecedent is the word to which the pronoun refers.

Yoshi brought **his** laptop computer and e-book to school. (The pronoun *his* refers to the antecedent *Yoshi*. Both the pronoun and its antecedent are singular, third person, and masculine; therefore, the pronoun is said to agree with its antecedent.)

Singular Pronoun 571.2

Use a singular pronoun to refer to such antecedents as *each, either, neither, one, anyone, anybody, everyone, everybody, somebody, another, nobody,* and *a person.*

Each of the maintenance vehicles has **their** doors locked at night. (Incorrect)

Each of the maintenance vehicles has **its** doors locked at night. (Correct: Both *Each* and *its* are singular.)

Somebody left **his or her** (not *their*) vehicle unlocked. (Correct)

Plural Pronoun 571.3

When a plural pronoun *(they, their)* is mistakenly used with a singular indefinite pronoun (such as *everyone* or *everybody*), you may correct the sentence by replacing *their* or *they* with optional pronouns *(her or his* or *he or she)*, or make the antecedent plural.

Everyone must learn to wait **their** turn. (Incorrect)

Everyone must learn to wait **her or his** turn. (Correct: Optional pronouns *her* or *his* are used.)

People must learn to wait **their** turns. (Correct: The singular antecedent, *Everyone,* is changed to the plural antecedent, *People*. In addition, *turn* is changed to *turns*.)

Two or More Antecedents 571.4

When two or more antecedents are joined by *and,* they are considered plural.

Tomas and **Jamal** are finishing **their** assignments.

When two or more singular antecedents are joined by *or* or *nor,* they are considered singular.

Connie or **Shavonn** left **her** headset in the library.

Note: If one of the antecedents is masculine and one feminine, likewise one pronoun should be masculine and one should be feminine.

Is **Ahmad** or **Phyllis** bringing **his or her** laptop computer?

Note: If one of the antecedents joined by *or* or *nor* is singular and one is plural, the pronoun is made to agree with the nearer antecedent.

Neither **Ravi** nor **his friends** want to spend **their** time studying.

Neither **his friends** nor **Ravi** wants to spend **his** time studying.

Avoiding Sentence Errors Exercises:

Agreement

A. Subject-Verb Agreement

Correct the agreement errors in the following paragraph by writing down the line number and any incorrect verb, crossed out, with the correct form beside it.

There is in beautiful Barcelona, Spain, many surprises to be found. Barcelona, Spain's second-largest city, and Madrid, the country's capital, has a traditional rivalry. At one time, the population of Barcelona were forbidden to speak the city's native tongue, Catalan, by a royal decree from Madrid. Today, however, neither Spanish nor Catalan are discriminated against in the region. One of the sites that belongs on every tour, the outlandish cathedral La Sagrada Familia ("The Sacred Family"), was designed by Antoni Gaudi. Everyone using the word "gaudy" actually has Gaudi's name on his or her tongue. A series of thirteenth- to fifteenth-century palaces now house the Museo Picasso, which display a history of Picasso's work and his many years living in Barcelona. *Les Demoiselles d'Avignon,* or *The Young Ladies of Avignon,* are one example of a painting inspired by his time in Barcelona. Whether you prefer cobblestone streets with centuries-old buildings or asphalt streets with modern shops and taverns, each are found in Barcelona. At night, every one of the streets seem to have a festive air, reflecting the vivacity of Spanish culture.

B. Pronoun-Antecedent and Subject-Verb Agreement

Provide the correct pronoun or verb for each blank in the following sentences. Use the directions or choices in parentheses.

1. Some people ___________ math with an abacus. (*do/does*)
2. This counting device has been used for thousands of years, and ___________ is still very popular in Eastern nations. (pronoun for "device")
3. The earliest examples ___________ employed between 2700 and 2300 B.C. in Sumeria. (*was/were*)
4. As recently as the 1990s, school children in the Soviet Union were taught to use ___________. (pronoun for "examples" in the previous sentence)
5. Pocket-sized abacuses ___________ still popular in Japan, despite the availability of portable calculators. (*is/are*)
6. Expert abacus users ___________ able to add, subtract, multiply, divide, and even calculate square roots and cube roots very quickly. (*is/are*)

MindTap® Practice skills that you have learned in this section and receive automatic feedback.

Shifts in Sentence Construction

A shift is an improper change in structure midway through a sentence. The following examples will help you identify and fix several different kinds of shifts.

Shift in Person 573.1

Shift in person is mixing first, second, or third person within a sentence. (See 541.4 and 545.3.)

Shift: **One** may get spring fever unless **you** live in California or Florida. (The sentence shifts from third person, *one,* to second person, *you.*)

Corrected: **You** may get spring fever unless **you** live in California or Florida. (Stays in second person)

Corrected: **People** may get spring fever unless **they** live in California or Florida. (*People,* a third person plural noun, requires a third person plural pronoun, *they.*)

Shift in Tense 573.2

Shift in tense is using more than one tense in a sentence when only one is needed.

Shift: Sheila **looked** at nine apartments in one weekend before she **had chosen** one. (Tense shifts from past to past perfect for no reason.)

Corrected: Sheila **looked** at nine apartments in one weekend before she **chose** one. (Tense stays in past.)

Shift in Voice 573.3

Shift in voice is mixing active with passive voice. Usually, a sentence beginning in active voice should remain so to the end.

Shift: As you look (active voice) for just the right place, many interesting apartments **will probably be seen.** (passive voice)

Corrected: As you look (active voice) for just the right place, **you will probably see** (active voice) many interesting apartments.

Unparallel Construction 573.4

Unparallel construction occurs when the kind of words or phrases being used shifts or changes in the middle of a sentence.

Shift: In my hometown, people pass the time shooting pool, pitching horseshoes, and at softball games. (Sentence shifts from a series of general phrases, *shooting pool* and *pitching horseshoes,* to the prepositional phrase *at softball games.*)

Parallel: In my hometown, people pass the time **shooting pool, pitching horseshoes, and playing softball.** (Now all three activities are gerund phrases—they are consistent, or parallel.)

Fragments, Comma Splices, and Run-Ons

Except in a few special situations, you should use complete sentences when you write. By definition, a complete sentence expresses a complete thought. However, a sentence may actually contain several ideas, not just one. The trick is getting those ideas to work together to form a clear, interesting sentence that expresses your exact meaning. Among the most common sentence errors that writers make are fragments, comma splices, and run-ons.

574.1 Fragments

A **fragment** is a phrase or dependent clause used as a sentence. It is not a sentence, however, because a phrase lacks a subject, a verb, or some other essential part, and a dependent clause must be connected to an independent clause to complete its meaning.

Fragment: Pete gunned the engine. Forgetting that the boat was hooked to the truck. (This is a sentence followed by a fragment. This error can be corrected by combining the fragment with the sentence.)

Corrected: Pete gunned the engine, forgetting that the boat was hooked to the truck.

Fragment: Even though my best friend had a little boy last year. (This clause does not convey a complete thought. We need to know what is happening despite the birth of the little boy.)

Corrected: Even though my best friend had a little boy last year, **I do not comprehend the full meaning of "motherhood."**

574.2 Comma Splices

A **comma splice** is a mistake made when two independent clauses are connected ("spliced") with only a comma. The comma is not enough: A period, semicolon, or conjunction is needed.

Splice: People say that being a stay-at-home mom or dad is an important job, their actions tell a different story.

Corrected: People say that being a stay-at-home mom or dad is an important job, **but** their actions tell a different story. (The coordinating conjunction *but,* added after the comma, corrects the splice.)

Corrected: People say that being a stay-at-home mom or dad is an important job; their actions tell a different story. (A semicolon—rather than just a comma—makes the sentence correct.)

Corrected: People say that being a stay-at-home mom or dad is an important job; however, their actions tell a different story. (A semicolon and a conjunction—or conjunctive adverb—also make the sentence correct.)

Corrected: People say that being a stay-at-home mom or dad is an important job. **Their** actions tell a different story. (A period creates two sentences and corrects the splice.)

Run-Ons 575.1

A run-on sentence is actually two sentences (two independent clauses) joined without adequate punctuation or a connecting word.

Run-on: The Alamo holds a special place in American history it was the site of an important battle between the United States and Mexico.

Corrected: **The Alamo holds a special place in American history because it was the site of an important battle between the United States and Mexico.** (A subordinating conjunction is added to fix the run-on by making the second clause dependent.)

Run-on: Antonio de Santa Anna, the president of Mexico who once held a funeral for his amputated leg, is the same Santa Anna who stormed the Alamo he led his troops to victory over the Texan rebels defending that fort. Two famous American frontiersmen died they were James Bowie and Davy Crockett. Santa Anna enjoyed fame, power, and respect among his followers. He died in 1876 he was poor, blind, and ignored.

Corrected: Antonio de Santa Anna, the president of Mexico who once held a funeral for his amputated leg, is the same Santa Anna who stormed the Alamo. He led his troops to victory over the Texan rebels defending that fort. Two famous American frontiersmen were killed in the battle; they were James Bowie and Davy Crockett. Santa Anna enjoyed fame, power, and respect among his followers. When he died in 1876, he was poor, blind, and ignored.

The writer corrected the run-on sentences in the paragraph above by adding punctuation and making one sentence a dependent clause. While doing so, the writer also made a few changes to improve the ideas. The writer makes further improvements in the paragraph below by revising one sentence and by combining two sets of short sentences into one stronger sentence. 575.2

Improved: Antonio de Santa Anna, the president of Mexico who once held a funeral for his amputated leg, is the same Santa Anna who stormed the Alamo. He led his troops to victory over Texan rebels defending that fort. Two famous American frontiersmen, **James Bowie and Davy Crockett, were killed in the battle.** Santa Anna enjoyed fame, power, and respect among his followers; **but when** he died in 1876, he was poor, blind, and ignored.

fyi Once you make a correction, you may see an opportunity to add, cut, or improve something else. Correcting and editing sentences can be frustrating at times, but with practice, these processes can become some of the more enjoyable parts of the writing process.

Avoiding Sentence Errors Exercises:

Shifts in Construction, Fragments, Comma Splices, and Run-Ons

A. Identifying Errors

Identify the type of sentence error illustrated by each example below. If the error is a shift in construction, tell which type. (See page 573.)

1. Much music in the Western world is based upon a "diatonic scale" of seven notes, five half steps separate all but two notes in a complete diatonic scale.
2. A quick look at the piano keyboard to understand this scale.
3. From C to B, for example, you can count seven white keys and five black keys, and one can see that each black key is a half step between the white keys on either side.
4. There is no black key between E and F, nor between B and C, so these notes were understood to be only a half step apart.
5. One advantage of this arrangement of black and white keys is that pianists can easily tell the difference between notes as they touch the keyboard imagine if there were nothing but white keys all a half step apart!

B. Correcting Errors

In the following paragraph, locate each sentence error (fragment, comma splice, run-on, and unparallel construction). Identify each with the sentence number and name of the error. Then write the sentence correctly.

(1) When you're listening to jazz, you're hearing a uniquely American style of music. (2) From the American South, a fusion of African and European traditions. (3) As Art Blakely, an originator of bebop drumming, is quoted saying, "No America, no jazz." (4) The earliest jazz bands emerged in New Orleans around the turn of the twentieth century here black gospel music and Latin American brass met, and Dixieland was spawned in the 1910s. (5) During the 1920s, many popular and influential jazz musicians found their way to Chicago clubs, recordings in the Windy City began to spread the sound to other parts of the country. (6) New York City also played an important role in jazz history by adding piano, incorporating jazz into swing music, and through sales of jazz records. (7) During the late 1920s and the 1930s, local jazz bands formed all around the country, establishing the style firmly in American culture.

Misplaced and Dangling Modifiers

Writing is thinking. Before you can write clearly, you must think clearly. Nothing is more frustrating for the reader than having to reread writing just to understand its basic meaning. Look carefully at the common errors that follow. Then use this section as a checklist when you revise. Always avoid leaving misplaced or dangling modifiers in your finished work.

Misplaced Modifiers 577.1

Misplaced modifiers are descriptive words or phrases so separated from what they are describing that the reader is confused.

Misplaced: The neighbor's dog has nearly been barking nonstop for two hours. (*Nearly* been barking?)

Corrected: The neighbor's dog has been barking nonstop **for nearly two hours**. (Watch your placement of *only, just, nearly, barely,* and so on.)

Misplaced: The commercial advertised an assortment of combs for active people with unbreakable teeth. (*People* with unbreakable teeth?)

Corrected: For active people, the commercial advertised an assortment of combs with unbreakable teeth. (*Combs* with unbreakable teeth)

Misplaced: The pool staff gave large beach towels to the students marked with chlorine-resistant ID numbers. (*Students* marked with chlorine-resistant ID numbers?)

Corrected: The pool staff gave the students large beach towels marked with chlorine-resistant ID numbers. (*Towels* marked with chlorine-resistant ID numbers)

Dangling Modifiers 577.2

Dangling modifiers are descriptive phrases that tell about a subject that isn't stated in the sentence. These often occur as participial phrases containing *ing* or *ed* words.

Dangling: After standing in line all afternoon, the manager informed us that all the tickets had been sold. (It sounds as if the manager has been *standing in line all afternoon.*)

Corrected: **After we had stood in line all afternoon,** the manager informed us that all the tickets had been sold.

Dangling: After living in the house for one month, the electrician recommended we update all the wiring. (It sounds as if the electrician has been *living in the house.*)

Corrected: After living in the house for one month, **we hired an electrician, who recommended that we update all the wiring.**

Ambiguous Wording

Sloppy sentences confuse readers. No one should have to wonder, "What does this writer mean?" When you revise and edit, check for indefinite pronoun references, incomplete comparisons, and unclear wording.

578.1 Indefinite Pronoun References

An **indefinite reference** is a problem caused by careless use of pronouns. There must always be a word or phrase nearby (its antecedent) that a pronoun clearly replaces.

Indefinite: When Tonya attempted to put her dictionary on the shelf, it fell to the floor. (The pronoun *it* could refer to either the dictionary or the shelf since both are singular nouns.)

Corrected: When Tonya attempted to put her dictionary on the shelf, **the shelf** fell to the floor.

Indefinite: Juanita reminded Kerri that she needed to photocopy her resumé before going to her interview. (Who *needed to photocopy her resumé*—Juanita or Kerri?)

Corrected: Juanita reminded Kerri **to photocopy her resumé before going to her interview.**

578.2 Incomplete Comparisons

Incomplete comparisons—leaving out words that show exactly what is being compared to what—can confuse readers.

Incomplete: After completing our lab experiment, we concluded that helium is lighter. (*Lighter* than what?)

Corrected: After completing our lab experiment, we concluded that helium is lighter **than oxygen.**

578.3 Unclear Wording

One type of ambiguous writing is wording that has two or more possible meanings due to an unclear reference to something elsewhere in the sentence. (See 578.1.)

Unclear: I couldn't believe that my sister bought a cat with all those allergy problems. (Who has the *allergy problems*—the cat or the sister?)

Corrected: I couldn't believe that my sister, **who is very allergic, bought a cat.**

Unclear: Dao intended to wash the car when he finished his homework, but he never did. (It is unclear which he *never did*—wash the car or finish his homework.)

Corrected: Dao intended to wash the car when he finished his homework, **but he never did manage to wash the car.**

Avoiding Sentence Errors Exercises:

Misplaced and Dangling Modifiers and Ambiguous Wording

A. Correcting Sentences

Rewrite the following sentences to correct misplaced and dangling modifiers and ambiguous wording.

1. When it touched down on the moon in 1969, the onboard guidance computer of the *Apollo 11's Eagle* lander contained less than 80 kilobytes of memory.
2. The cheapest mp3 player today at least has 1 gigabyte.
3. That's equivalent to 14,000 *Apollo 11* computers roughly in one device.
4. Even a typical smartphone or handheld computer could theoretically control about 5,000 lunar landers at once, properly programmed!
5. Imagine using your phone or pocket game to land 5,000 *Apollo* craft in your car or bedroom.
6. Of course, you couldn't see all the lunar-lander controls at once because of their tiny screens.
7. After spending almost a day on the moon's surface, NASA had the crew launch back into orbit and return to Earth.
8. The *Eagle's* journey to the moon had made it a sensation around the world.
9. The crew were all heroes, but they certainly liked the Earth better.
10. Today the Science Museum in London displays a lunar-lander replica for visitors in full size.

B. Correcting Errors in Context

Locate a misplaced modifier and several indefinite-pronoun-reference errors in the following paragraph. For each error, write the sentence number, identify the error type, and rewrite the sentences correctly.,

(1) One famous Russian joke lampoons the *nouveau-riche* Russians, known as "New Russians," by comparing cars. (2) In this joke, unexpectedly, a New Russian and an old man wake up in an emergency room. (3) The New Russian asks the old man how he ended up there. (4) The old man replies, "I put my war-trophy Messerschmitt jet engine on my old Zaporozhets car to make it go faster. (5) But after a couple of miles I lost control and crashed into a tree. (6) How about you?" (7) He answers that when an old Zaporozhets passed his new Ferrari on the highway, he thought it had stalled. (8) So he opened the door and stepped out.

Nonstandard Language

Nonstandard language is language that does not conform to the standards set by schools, media, and public institutions. It is often acceptable in everyday conversation and in fictional writing but seldom is used in formal speech or other forms of writing.

580.1

Colloquial Language

Colloquial language is wording used in informal conversation that is unacceptable in formal writing.

Colloquial: Hey, wait up! Cal wants to go with.

Standard: **Hey, wait!** Cal wants to go with us.

580.2

Double Preposition

The use of certain **double prepositions**—*off of, off to, from off*—is unacceptable.

Double Preposition: Pick up the dirty clothes from off the floor.

Standard: Pick up the dirty clothes **from the floor.**

580.3

Substitution

Avoid substituting *and* for *to.*

Substitution: Try and get to class on time.

Standard: **Try to** get to class on time.

Avoid substituting *of* for *have* when combining with *could, would, should,* or *might.*

Substitution: I should of studied for that exam.

Standard: **I should have** studied for that exam.

580.4

Double Negative

A **double negative** is a sentence that contains two negative words used to express a single negative idea. Double negatives are unacceptable in academic writing.

Double Negative: After paying for essentials, I haven't got no money left.

Standard: **I haven't got** any money left. / **I have no** money left.

Note: Because a double negative makes a positive statement, "I haven't got no money left" means "I have money left."

580.5

Slang

Avoid the use of **slang** or any "in" words in formal writing.

Slang: The way the stadium roof opened was way cool.

Standard: The way the stadium roof opened **was remarkable.**

Avoiding Sentence Errors Exercises:

Nonstandard Language

A. Correcting Sentences

Identify the type of error exhibited in each sentence below (colloquialism, double preposition, substitution, double negative, or slang). Then correct it.

1. Would you of guessed that soccer is the world's most popular sport?
2. The word "soccer" is Oxford slang for "association," 'cause officially the game is "Association Football."
3. In most countries the sport's called "football," or some variation like *fútbol* or *fußball.*
4. The World Cup is a wicked awesome competition played every four years.
5. Soccer rules were set up in England in 1863, and they haven't hardly changed since then.
6. The point of the game is to try and kick the ball into the other team's goal area.
7. Normally play continues until someone commits a foul or kicks a ball off of the field.
8. Most players aren't not allowed to touch the ball with their hands.
9. If you've ever watched soccer, though, you might of seen the goalie engage the ball that way.
10. The other players don't have no official titles.
11. Most times, though, there are forwards, defenders, and midfielders.
12. According to the rules, games needn't never go into overtime; they can end in a tie.
13. But some games can just keep agoin' in overtime till somebody scores.
14. The U.S. team did pretty good for itself in the 2010 games.
15. Some folks say that Europeans feel closer to us since our team rocked big time and stayed in the competition so long.
16. I wonder what they would of thought if the U.S. had won!
17. Personally, though, I was rooting for Spain from the get go.
18. If you're interested, it doesn't hardly take much equipment to play soccer.
19. All's you really need's a ball and maybe some markers for the goals.
20. Well, you also gotta have two teams with eleven players each.

B. Correcting Your Own Writing

Write freely about a sport you find interesting. Imagine describing that sport to someone unfamiliar with it, or simply explain your own interest in it. When you have finished, review your writing for nonstandard language and make any necessary corrections.

MindTap® Practice skills that you have learned in this section and receive automatic feedback.

Avoiding Sentence Problems Review

Does every subject agree with its verb? (See pages 567–570.)

- In person and number?
- When a word or phrase comes between the subject and the verb?
- When the subject is delayed?
- When the subject is a title?
- When a compound subject is connected with *or*?
- When the subject is a collective noun (*faculty, team,* or *crowd*)?
- When the subject is a relative pronoun (*who, which, that*)?
- When the subject is an indefinite pronoun (*everyone, anybody,* or *many*)?

Does every pronoun agree with its antecedent? (See page 571.)

- When the pronoun is a singular indefinite pronoun such as *each, either,* or *another*?
- When two antecedents are joined with *and*?
- When two antecedents are joined with *or*?

Did you unintentionally create inappropriate shifts? (See page 573.)

- In person?
- In tense?
- From active voice to passive voice?
- In another unparallel construction?

Are all your sentences complete? (See pages 574–575.)

- Have you used sentence fragments?
- Are some sentences "spliced" or run together?

Did you use any misplaced modifiers or ambiguous wording? (See pages 577–578.)

- Have you used misplaced or dangling modifiers?
- Have you used incomplete comparisons or indefinite references?

Did you use any nonstandard language? (See page 580.)

- Have you used slang or colloquial language?
- Have you used double negatives or double prepositions?

Chapter 28

Marking Punctuation

Period

After Sentences 583.1

Use a **period** to end a sentence that makes a statement, requests something, or gives a mild command.

Statement: By 2013, women made up 56 percent of undergraduate students and 59 percent of graduate students.

Request: Please read the instructions carefully.

Mild command: If your topic sentence isn't clear, rewrite it.

Indirect question: The professor asked if we had completed the test.

Note: It is not necessary to place a period after a statement that has parentheses around it and is part of another sentence.

Think about joining a club **(the student affairs office has a list of organizations)** for fun and for leadership experience.

After Initials and Abbreviations 583.2

Use a period after an initial, after some abbreviations, and between a Bible chapter and verse.

Mr.	**Mrs.**	**Dr.**	**John 3.16**	**i.e.**	**Booker T. Washington**
Sr.	**U.S.**	**p.m.**	**Rev. 21.3**	**e.g.**	**Sen. Joni Ernst**

Use no periods after academic degrees (e.g., *BA, PhD, MD*), acronyms (e.g., *radar, CARE, NASA*), and initialisms (e.g., *CIA, DVD, ROTC*). See also "Abbreviations" (pages 617–618) and "Acronyms and Initialisms" (page 619).

When an abbreviation is the last word in a sentence, use only one period at thc end of the sentence.

Mikhail promptly locked the door at 10:00 p.m.

As Decimal Points 583.3

Use a period as a decimal point.

The government spends approximately **$15.5** million each year just to process student loan forms.

Ellipsis

584.1 To Show Omitted Words

Use an **ellipsis** (three periods) to show that one or more words have been omitted in a quotation. When typing, leave one space before and after each period.

(Original) We the people of the United States, in order to form a more perfect Union, establish justice, insure domestic tranquility, provide for the common defense, promote the general welfare, and secure the blessings of liberty to ourselves and our posterity, do ordain and establish this Constitution for the United States of America.

—Preamble, U.S. Constitution

(Quotation) "We the people . . . in order to form a more perfect Union . . . establish this Constitution for the United States of America."

Note: Omit internal punctuation (a comma, a semicolon, a colon, or a dash) on either side of the ellipsis marks unless it is needed for clarity.

584.2 To Use After Sentences

If words from a quotation are omitted at the end of a sentence, place the ellipsis after the period or other end punctuation.

(Quotation) "Five score years ago, a great American, in whose symbolic shadow we stand, signed the Emancipation Proclamation. . . . But one hundred years later, we must face the tragic fact that the Negro is still not free."

—Martin Luther King, Jr., "I Have a Dream"

The first word of a sentence following a period and an ellipsis may be capitalized, even though it was not capitalized in the original.

(Quotation) "Five score years ago, a great American . . . signed the Emancipation Proclamation. . . . One hundred years later, . . . the Negro is still not free."

Note: If the quoted material forms a complete sentence (even if it was not in the original), use a period, then an ellipsis.

(Original) I am tired; my heart is sick and sad. From where the sun now stands I will fight no more forever. —Chief Joseph of the Nez Percé

(Quotation) "I am tired. . . . I will fight no more forever."

584.3 To Show Pauses

Use an ellipsis to indicate a pause or to show unfinished thoughts.

Listen . . . did you hear that?

I can't figure out . . . this number doesn't . . . just how do I apply the equation in this case?

Question Mark

After Direct Questions 585.1

Use a **question mark** at the end of a direct question.

What can I know? What ought I to do? What may I hope? —Immanuel Kant

Since when do you have to agree with people to defend them from injustice? —Lillian Hellman

Not After Indirect Questions 585.2

No question mark is used after an indirect question.

After listening to Edgar sing, Mr. Noteworthy asked him if he had ever had formal voice training.

Note: When a single-word question like *how, when,* or *why* is woven into the flow of a sentence, capitalization and special punctuation are not usually required.

The questions we need to address at our next board meeting are not *why* or *whether,* but *how* and *when.*

After Quotations That Are Questions 585.3

When a question ends with a quotation that is also a question, use only one question mark, and place it within the quotation marks. (Also see 599.4.)

Do you often ask yourself, "What should I be?"

To Show Uncertainty 585.4

Use a question mark within parentheses to show uncertainty about a word or phrase within a sentence.

This July will be the forty-seventh (?) anniversary of the first moon walk.

Note: Do *not* use a question mark in this manner for formal writing.

For Questions in Parentheses or Dashes 585.5

A question within parentheses—or a question set off by dashes—is punctuated with a question mark unless the sentence ends with a question mark.

You must consult your handbook **(what choice do you have?)** when you need to know a punctuation rule.

Should I use your charge card (you have one, don't you), or should I pay cash?

Maybe somewhere in the pasts of these humbled people, there were cases of bad mothering or absent fathering or emotional neglect—**what family surviving the '50s was exempt?**—but I couldn't believe these human errors brought the physical changes in Frank.

—Mary Kay Blakely, *Wake Me When It's Over*

Punctuation Exercises:

Periods, Ellipses, Question Marks

A. End Punctuation

Indicate the correct form of end punctuation for each sentence—a period or a question mark.

1. Have you heard of the Ring of Fire
2. It is a volcanically active area
3. The Ring of Fire circles the Pacific
4. How many people has it killed
5. Over 300,000 died from one tsunami
6. Where did the tsunami take place
7. The tsunami ravaged India
8. An earthquake rocked Chile
9. The Ring of Fire is restless
10. How can we predict its catastrophes

B. Ellipses

Shorten each sentence by removing the bold words and inserting an ellipsis.

1. "Now we are engaged in a great civil war, testing whether that nation, **or any nation so conceived and so dedicated,** can long endure."
2. "We have come to dedicate a portion of that field, as a final resting place for those who here gave their lives **that that nation might live.**"
3. "But, in a larger sense, we can not dedicate—**we can not consecrate—we can not hallow**—this ground."
4. "The brave men, **living and dead,** who struggled here, have consecrated it, **far above our poor power to add or detract.**"
5. "The world will little note, **nor long remember** what we say here, but it can never forget what they did here."

C. Punctuation Practice

Indicate where periods and question marks are needed in the following paragraph by writing the word and the mark after it, and by writing any initials or abbreviations correctly.

Music is the universal language At least that's what people say But have you ever noticed how hard it is to get people to agree on music Play a song by BB King, and some people will be in heaven and others in dread Why would that be Dr Jim Fredericks indicates that the reason may be music's power to reach to our very hearts "Music is intensely personal, and the type of music that makes one person excited and happy may make another person very uncomfortable" Jill Davis, PhD, disagrees She says music is primarily cultural What does music do except make us feel "at home" or feel like a stranger When music alienates us, we dislike it, but when it makes us feel welcome, we like it So, what music makes you feel at home

Comma

Between Independent Clauses 587.1

Use a **comma** between independent clauses that are joined by a coordinating conjunction (*and, but, or, nor, for, yet, so*). (See 565.2.)

Heath Ledger completed his brilliant portrayal as the Joker in *The Dark Knight,* **but** he died before the film was released.

Note: Do not confuse a compound verb with a compound sentence.

Ledger's Joker became instantly iconic and won him the Oscar for best supporting actor. (compound verb)

His death resulted from the abuse of prescription drugs, but it was ruled an accident. (compound sentence)

Between Items in a Series 587.2

Use commas to separate individual words, phrases, or clauses in a series. (A series contains at least three items.)

Many college students must balance studying with **taking care of a family, working a job, getting exercise, and finding time to relax.**

Note: Do *not* use commas when all the items in a series are connected with *or, nor,* or *and.*

Hmm . . . should I study **or** do laundry **or** go out?

To Separate Adjectives 587.3

Use commas to separate adjectives that *equally* modify the same noun. Notice in the examples below that no comma separates the last adjective from the noun.

You should exercise regularly and follow a **sensible, healthful** diet.

A good diet is one that includes lots of **high-protein, low-fat** foods.

To Determine Equal Modifiers

To determine whether the adjectives in a sentence modify a noun *equally,* use these two tests.

1. Reverse the order of the adjectives; if the sentence is clear, the adjectives modify equally. (In the example below, *hot* and *crowded* can be reversed, and the sentence is still clear; *short* and *coffee* cannot.)

   Matt was tired of working in the **hot, crowded** lab and decided to take a **short coffee** break.

2. Insert *and* between the adjectives; if the sentence reads well, use a comma when *and* is omitted. (The word *and* can be inserted between *hot* and *crowded,* but *and* does not make sense between *short* and *coffee.*)

588.1 **To Set Off Nonrestrictive Appositives**

A specific kind of explanatory word or phrase called an **appositive** identifies or renames a preceding noun or pronoun. (See "A Closer Look," page 589.)

Albert Einstein, **the famous mathematician and physicist,** developed the theory of relativity.

Note: Do *not* use commas with *restrictive appositives.* A restrictive appositive is essential to the basic meaning of the sentence.

The famous mathematician and physicist **Albert Einstein** developed the theory of relativity.

588.2 **To Set Off Adverb Dependent Clauses**

Use a comma after most introductory dependent clauses functioning as adverbs.

Although Charlemagne was a great patron of learning, he never learned to write properly. (adverb dependent clause)

You may use a comma if the adverb dependent clause following the independent clause is not essential. Adverb clauses beginning with *even though, although, while,* or another conjunction expressing a contrast are usually not needed to complete the meaning of a sentence.

Charlemagne never learned to write properly, **even though he continued to practice.**

Note: A comma is *not* used if the dependent clause following the independent clause is needed to complete the meaning of the sentence.

Maybe Charlemagne didn't learn **because he had an empire to run.**

588.3 **After Introductory Phrases**

Use a comma after introductory phrases.

In spite of his practicing, Charlemagne's handwriting remained poor.

Note: A comma is usually omitted if the phrase follows an independent clause.

Charlemagne's handwriting remained poor **in spite of his practicing.**

Also Note: You may omit the comma after a short (four or fewer words) introductory phrase unless it is needed to ensure clarity.

At 6:00 a.m. he would rise and practice his penmanship.

588.4 **To Set Off Transitional Expressions**

Use a comma to set off conjunctive adverbs and transitional phrases. (See 593.2–593.3.)

Handwriting is not, **as a matter of fact,** easy to improve upon later in life; **however,** it can be done if you are determined enough.

Note: If a transitional expression blends smoothly with the rest of the sentence, it does not need to be set off. ***Example:*** If you are in fact coming, I'll see you there.

A Closer Look
Nonrestrictive and Restrictive Clauses and Phrases

Use Commas with Nonrestrictive Clauses and Phrases 589.1

Use commas to enclose **nonrestrictive** (unnecessary) phrases or dependent (adjective) clauses. A nonrestrictive phrase or dependent clause adds information that is not necessary to the basic meaning of the sentence. For example, if the clause or phrase (in **boldface**) were left out of the two examples below, the meaning of the sentences would remain clear. Therefore, commas are used to set off the nonrestrictive information.

The locker rooms in Swain Hall, **which were painted and updated last summer**, give professors a place to shower. (nonrestrictive clause)

Work-study programs, **offered on many campuses,** give students the opportunity to earn tuition money. (nonrestrictive phrase)

Don't Use Commas with Restrictive Clauses and Phrases 589.2

Do *not* use commas to set off **restrictive** (necessary) adjective clauses and phrases. A restrictive clause or phrase adds information that the reader needs to understand the sentence. For example, if the adjective clause and phrase (in **boldface**) were dropped from the examples below, the meaning would be unclear.

Only the professors **who run at noon** use the locker rooms in Swain Hall to shower. (restrictive clause)

Using tuition money **earned through work-study programs** is the only way some students can afford to go to college. (restrictive phrase)

Using "That" or "Which" 589.3

Use *that* to introduce restrictive (necessary) adjective clauses; use *which* to introduce nonrestrictive (unnecessary) adjective clauses. When the two words are used in this way, the reader can quickly distinguish the necessary information from the unnecessary.

Campus jobs **that are funded by the university** are awarded to students only. (restrictive)

The cafeteria, **which is run by an independent contractor**, can hire nonstudents. (nonrestrictive)

Note: Clauses beginning with *who* can be either restrictive or nonrestrictive.

Students **who pay for their own education** are highly motivated. (restrictive)

The admissions counselor, **who has studied student records,** said that many returning students earn high GPAs in spite of demanding family obligations. (nonrestrictive)

590.1 **To Set Off Items in Addresses and Dates**

Use commas to set off items in an address and the year in a date.

Send your letter to **1600 Pennsylvania Avenue, Washington, DC 20006, before January 1, 2017,** or send an email to president@whitehouse.gov.

Note: No comma is placed between the state and ZIP code. Also, no comma separates the items if only the month and year are given: January 2017.

590.2 **To Separate Numbers**

Use commas to separate a series of numbers to distinguish hundreds, thousands, millions, and so on.

Do you know how to write the amount **$2,025** on a check?

25,000 **973,240** **18,620,197**

590.3 **To Set Off the Speaker from Dialogue**

Use commas to set off the words of the speaker from the rest of the sentence.

"Never be afraid to ask for help," advised Ms. Kane.

"With the evidence that we now have," Professor Thom said, **"many scientists believe there is life on Mars."**

590.4 **To Separate the Person Named in Direct Address**

Use a comma to separate a noun of direct address from the rest of the sentence.

Jamie, would you please stop whistling while I'm trying to work?

590.5 **Before Tags**

Use a comma before tags, which are short statements or questions at the ends of sentences.

You studied for the test, **right?**

590.6 **To Separate Interjections**

Use a comma to separate a mild interjection from the rest of the sentence.

Okay, so now what do I do?

Note: Exclamation points are used after strong interjections: Wow! You're kidding!

590.7 **To Set Off Interruptions**

Use commas to set off a word, phrase, or clause that interrupts the movement of a sentence. Such expressions usually can be identified through the following tests: (1) They may be omitted without changing the meaning of a sentence; and (2) they may be placed nearly anywhere in the sentence without changing its meaning.

For me, **well,** it was just a good job gone! —Langston Hughes, "A Good Job Gone"

Lela, **as a general rule,** always comes to class ready for a pop quiz.

To Enclose Explanatory Words 591.1

Use commas to enclose an explanatory word or phrase.

> Time management**, according to many professionals,** is such an important skill that it should be taught in college.

To Separate Contrasted Elements 591.2

Use commas to separate contrasted elements within a sentence.

> We work to become**, not to acquire.** —Eugene Delacroix
>
> Where all think alike**, no one thinks very much.** —Walter Lippmann

To Enclose Titles or Initials 591.3

Use commas to enclose a title or initials and given names that follow a surname.

> Until Martin**, Sr.,** was 15, he never had more than three months of schooling in any one year.
>
> —Ed Clayton, *Martin Luther King: The Peaceful Warrior*
>
> The genealogical files included the names Sanders**, L. H.,** and Sanders**, Lucy Hale.**

Note: Some style manuals no longer require commas around titles.

For Clarity or Emphasis 591.4

Use a comma for clarity or for emphasis. There will be times when none of the traditional rules call for a comma, but one will be needed to prevent misreading or to emphasize an important idea.

> What she does**,** does matter to us. (clarity)
>
> It may be those who do most**,** dream most. (emphasis) —Stephen Leacock

Avoid Overusing Commas

The commas (in **red**) below are used incorrectly. Do *not* use a comma between the subject and its verb or the verb and its object.

> Current periodicals on the subject of psychology**,** are available at nearly all bookstores.
>
> I think she should read**,** *Psychology Today.*

Do *not* use a comma before an indirect quotation.

> My roommate said**,** that she doesn't understand the notes I took.

Punctuation Exercises:

Commas

A. Basic Comma Use

Indicate correct comma placement in each sentence below. Some sentences have multiple commas.

1. To succeed in college you need focus dedication and hard work.
2. A compatible amiable roommate helps and you will want access to a computer.
3. To keep your sanity a balanced workable schedule is also a must.
4. You should consult with family friends and counselors about course schedules.
5. Between classes jobs and the social scene many students are stretched.
6. College prepares people for life and one way is by teaching them to juggle priorities.
7. Students also must afford books supplies and food.
8. A manageable realistic budget keeps money matters in order.
9. Students should work hard think deeply and enjoy their time in college.
10. With goals such as these students can get the most out of college.

B. Restrictive and Nonrestrictive Clauses and Phrases

For each sentence, indicate correct comma placement. If a sentence needs no commas, write "correct."

1. Author Lauren Beukes who lives in South Africa wrote *Moxyland.*
2. *Moxyland* a dystopian thriller focuses on a world overrun by governmental and corporate domination of technology.
3. Gareth L. Powell who is an author in his own right said the book "gives us a dystopia to rival *1984.*"
4. Another reviewer said *Moxyland* is a book that changed science fiction.
5. Lauren Beukes an avid user of social media released a *Moxyland* soundtrack and a plush doll which gave two-thirds of its proceeds to a women's charity.

C. Advanced Comma Use

For each sentence, indicate correct comma placement.

1. I live at 3415 West Kane Drive Chicago Illinois.
2. Jamar where do you live?
3. All right who turned out the lights?
4. If you think I turned them out well you're mistaken.
5. I sure would like to receive a check for $5000.

Semicolon

To Join Two Independent Clauses 593.1

Use a **semicolon** to join two or more closely related independent clauses that are not connected with a coordinating conjunction. In other words, each of the clauses could stand alone as a separate sentence.

I was thrown out of college for cheating on the metaphysics exam; I looked into the soul of the boy next to me.

—Woody Allen

Before Conjunctive Adverbs 593.2

Use a semicolon before a conjunctive adverb when the word clarifies the relationship between two independent clauses in a compound sentence. A comma often follows the conjunctive adverb. Common conjunctive adverbs include *also, besides, however, instead, meanwhile, then,* and *therefore.*

Many college freshmen are on their own for the first time; **however,** others are already independent and even have families.

Before Transitional Phrases 593.3

Use a semicolon before a transitional phrase when the phrase clarifies the relationship between two independent clauses in a compound sentence. A comma usually follows the transitional phrase.

Pablo was born in the Andes; **as a result,** he loves mountains.

Transitional Phrases

after all	at the same time	in addition	in the first place
as a matter of fact	even so	in conclusion	on the contrary
as a result	for example	in fact	on the other hand
at any rate	for instance	in other words	

To Separate Independent Clauses Containing Commas 593.4

Use a semicolon to separate independent clauses that contain internal commas, even when the independent clauses are connected by a coordinating conjunction.

Your iPad, computer, bike, and other valuables are expensive to replace; so include these items in your homeowner's insurance policy and remember to use the locks on your door, bike, and storage area.

To Separate Items in a Series That Contains Commas 593.5

Use a semicolon to separate items in a series that already contain commas.

My favorite foods are pizza with pepperoni, onions, and olives; peanut butter and banana sandwiches; and liver with bacon, peppers, and onions.

Colon

594.1 **After Salutations**

Use a **colon** after the salutation of a business letter.

Dear Mr. Spielberg: Dear Professor Higgins: Dear Members:

594.2 **Between Numbers Indicating Time or Ratios**

Use a colon between the hours, minutes, and seconds of a number indicating time.

8:30 p.m. 9:45 a.m. 10:24:55

Use a colon between two numbers in a ratio.

The ratio of computers to students is 1:20. (one to twenty)

594.3 **For Emphasis**

Use a colon to emphasize a word, a phrase, a clause, or a sentence that explains or adds impact to the main clause.

I have one goal for myself: to become the first person in my family to graduate from college.

594.4 **To Distinguish Parts of Publications**

Use a colon between a title and a subtitle and between a volume and a page.

Ron Brown: An Uncommon Life *Britannica* 4: 211

594.5 **To Introduce Quotations**

Use a colon to introduce a quotation following a complete sentence.

John Locke is credited with this prescription for a good life: "A sound mind in a sound body."

Lou Gottlieb, however, offered this version: "A sound mind or a sound body—take your pick."

594.6 **To Introduce a List**

Use a colon to introduce a list following a complete sentence.

A college student needs a number of things to succeed: basic skills, creativity, and determination.

Avoid Colon Errors

Do *not* use a colon between a verb and its object or complement.

Dave likes: comfortable space and time to think. **(Incorrect)**

Dave likes two things: comfortable space and time to think. **(Correct)**

Hyphen

In Compound Words 595.1

Use a **hyphen** to make some compound words.

great-great-grandfather (noun) starry-eyed (adjective)
mother-in-law (noun) three-year-old (adjective)

Writers sometimes combine words in new and unexpected ways. Such combinations are usually hyphenated.

> And they pried pieces of **baked-too-fast** sunshine cake from the roofs of their mouths and looked once more into the boy's eyes.
>
> —Toni Morrison, *Song of Solomon*

Note: Consult a dictionary to find how it lists a particular compound word. Some compound words (*living room*) do not use a hyphen and are written separately. Some are written solid (*bedroom*). Some do not use a hyphen when the word is a noun (*ice cream*) but do use a hyphen when it is a verb or an adjective (*ice-cream sundae*).

To Join Letters and Words 595.2

Use a hyphen to join a capital letter or a lowercase letter to a noun or a participle.

T-shirt U-turn V-shaped x-ray

To Join Words in Compound Numbers 595.3

Use a hyphen to join the words in compound numbers from twenty-one to ninety-nine when it is necessary to write them out. (See 614.1.)

Forty-two people found seats in the cramped classroom.

Between Numbers in Fractions 595.4

Use a hyphen between the numerator and the denominator of a fraction, but not when one or both of these elements are already hyphenated.

four-tenths five-sixteenths seven thirty-seconds (7/32)

In a Special Series 595.5

Use a hyphen when two or more words have a common element that is omitted in all but the last term.

We have cedar posts in **four-**, **six-**, and **eight-**inch widths.

To Create New Words 595.6

Use a hyphen to form new words beginning with the prefixes *self, ex, all,* and *half.* Also use a hyphen to join any prefix to a proper noun, a proper adjective, or the official name of an office.

post-Depression mid-May ex-mayor

596.1 **To Prevent Confusion**

Use a hyphen with prefixes or suffixes to avoid confusion or awkward spelling.

re-cover (not *recover*) the sofa **shell-like** (not *shelllike*) shape

596.2 **To Join Numbers**

Use a hyphen to join numbers indicating a range, a score, or a vote.

Students study **30-40** hours a week. The final score was **84-82.**

596.3 **To Divide Words**

Use a hyphen to divide a word between syllables at the end of a line of print.

Guidelines for Word Division

1. Leave enough of the word at the end of the line to identify the word.
2. Never divide a one-syllable word: **rained, skills, through.**
3. Avoid dividing a word of five or fewer letters: **paper, study, July.**
4. Never divide a one-letter syllable from the rest of the word: **omit-ted,** not **o-mitted.**
5. Always divide a compound word between its basic units: **sister-in-law,** not **sis-ter-in-law.**
6. Never divide abbreviations or contractions: **shouldn't,** not **should-n't.**
7. When a vowel is a syllable by itself, divide the word after the vowel: **epi-sode,** not **ep-isode.**
8. Avoid dividing a numeral: **1,000,000,** not **1,000,-000.**
9. Avoid dividing the last word in a paragraph.
10. Never divide the last word in more than two lines in a row.
11. Check a dictionary for acceptable word divisions.

596.4 **To Form Adjectives**

Use a hyphen to join two or more words that serve as a single-thought adjective before a noun.

In real life I am a large, **big-boned** woman with rough, **man-working** hands.

—Alice Walker, "Everyday Use"

Most single-thought adjectives are not hyphenated when they come after the noun. (Check the dictionary to be sure.)

In real life, I am large and **big boned.**

Note: When the first of these words is an adverb ending in *ly,* do not use a hyphen. Also, do not use a hyphen when a number or a letter is the final element in a single-thought adjective.

fresh**ly** painted barn grade **A** milk (letter is the final element)

Dash

To Set Off Nonessential Elements 597.1

Use a **dash** to set off nonessential elements—explanations, examples, or definitions—when you want to emphasize them.

Near the semester's end—**and this is not always due to poor planning**—some students may find themselves in academic trouble.

The term *caveat emptor*—**let the buyer beware**—is especially appropriate to Internet shopping.

Note: A dash is indicated by two hyphens--with no spacing before or after--in typewriter-generated material and in handwritten material. Don't use a single hyphen when a dash (two hyphens) is required.

To Set Off an Introductory Series 597.2

Use a dash to set off an introductory series from the clause that explains the series.

Cereal, coffee, and Facebook—without these I can't get going in the morning.

To Show Missing Text 597.3

Use a dash to show that words or letters are missing.

Mr. — won't let us marry. —Alice Walker, *The Color Purple*

To Show Interrupted Speech 597.4

Use a dash (or an ellipsis) to show interrupted or faltering speech in dialogue. (Also see 584.3.)

Well, **I—ah—had** this terrible case of the flu, **and—then—ah—the** library closed because of that flash flood, **and—well—the** high humidity jammed my printer.

—Excuse No. 101

"If you *think* you can—"

"Oh, I *know*—"

"Don't interrupt!"

For Emphasis 597.5

Use a dash in place of a colon to introduce or to emphasize a word, a series, a phrase, or a clause.

Jogging—that's what he lives for.

Life is like a grindstone—whether it grinds you down or polishes you up depends on what you're made of.

This is how the world moves—not like an arrow, but a boomerang.

—Ralph Ellison

Punctuation Exercises:

Semicolons, Colons, Hyphens, and Dashes

A. Semicolons and Colons

Indicate correct placement of semicolons or colons in each sentence.

1. Aaron Copland revolutionized music Leonard Bernstein called him "Moses."
2. Copland wrote ballets such as *Appalachian Spring, Billy the Kid,* and *Rodeo* music for films such as *Our Town* and *The Red Pony* and symphonies such as the *Organ Symphony,* the *Short Symphony,* and his *Third Symphony.*
3. Copland also founded ASCAP the American Society of Composers, Authors, and Publishers.
4. ASCAP made it possible to be a composer it set up royalty standards.
5. Copland was trained in Paris despite that fact, he was all-American.
6. Copland is well known for one piece "Fanfare for the Common Man."
7. Unlike Bernstein, Copland wrote slowly he composed at the piano.
8. At first, Copland composed atonal music he changed his style during the Great Depression.
9. In the '50s, Copland and Bernstein ran up against an antagonist McCarthy.
10. Copland showed the way for young composers he was a kind of "Moses."

B. Hyphens

For each item, insert hyphens correctly. If an item needs no hyphen, write "correct."

1. forty five
2. midMarch
3. nine thirty seconds
4. father in law
5. recreate (meaning "to create again")
6. a 36 38 score
7. hard working people
8. grade A meat
9. U shaped valley
10. two year old

C. Dashes

For each sentence, indicate correct dash placement.

1. The expression *carpe diem* seize the day was written on the classroom wall.
2. "Faith, hope, and love these three, but the greatest of these is love."
3. He stuttered, "I um well wanted to ask you on a date."
4. Performing before a live audience that's what I love.
5. I will caution you this is what I tell everyone don't give up your dreams.

Quotation Marks

To Punctuate Titles 599.1

Use **quotation marks** to punctuate some titles. (Also see 601.2.)

"Two Friends" (short story)
"New Car Designs" (newspaper article)
"Sparks" (song)
"Multiculturalism and the Language Battle" (lecture title)
"The New Admissions Game" (magazine article)
"Reflections on Advertising" (chapter in a book)
"Blink" (television episode from *Doctor Who*)
"Annabel Lee" (short poem)

For Special Words 599.2

Use quotation marks (1) to show that a word is being discussed as a word, (2) to indicate that a word or phrase is directly quoted, (3) to indicate that a word is slang, or (4) to point out that a word is being used in a humorous or ironic way.

1. A commentary on the times is that the word **"honesty"** is now preceded by **"old-fashioned."**
2. She said she was **"incensed."**
3. I drank a Dixie and ate bar peanuts and asked the bartender where I could hear **"chanky-chank,"** as Cajuns call their music. —William Least Heat-Moon, *Blue Highways*
4. In an attempt to be popular, he works very hard at being **"cute."**

Note: A word used as a word can also be set off with italics.

Placement of Periods or Commas 599.3

Always place periods and commas inside quotation marks.

"Dr. Slaughter wants you to have liquids, Will," Mama said anxiously. "He said not to give you any solid food tonight." —Olive Ann Burns, *Cold Sassy Tree*

Placement of Exclamation Points or Question Marks 599.4

Place an exclamation point or a question mark inside quotation marks when it punctuates both the main sentence and the quotation *or* just the quotation; place it outside when it punctuates the main sentence.

Do you often ask yourself, "What should I be?"

I almost croaked when he asked, "That won't be a problem, will it?"

Did he really say, "Finish this by tomorrow"?

Placement of Semicolons or Colons 599.5

Always place semicolons or colons outside quotation marks.

I just read "Computers and Creativity"; I now have some different ideas about the role of computers in the arts.

A Closer Look
Marking Quoted Material

600.1 **For Direct Quotations**

Use quotation marks before and after a direct quotation—a person's exact words.

Sitting in my one-room apartment, I remember Mom saying, **"Don't go to the party with him."**

Note: Do *not* use quotation marks for *indirect* quotations.

I remember Mom saying **that I should not date him.** (These are not the speaker's exact words.)

600.2 **For Quoted Passages**

Use quotation marks before and after a quoted passage. Any word that is not part of the original quotation must be placed inside brackets.

(Original) First of all, it must accept responsibility for providing shelter for the homeless.

(Quotation) "First of all, it **[the federal government]** must accept responsibility for providing shelter for the homeless."

Note: If you quote only part of the original passage, be sure to construct a sentence that is both accurate and grammatically correct.

The report goes on to say that the federal government **"must accept responsibility for providing shelter for the homeless."**

600.3 **For Long Quotations**

If more than one paragraph is quoted, quotation marks are placed before each paragraph and at the end of the last paragraph **(Example A).** Quotations that are five or more lines (MLA style) or forty words or more (APA style) are usually set off from the text by indenting one-half inch from the left margin (a style called "block form"). Do not use quotation marks before or after a block-form quotation **(Example B),** except in cases where quotation marks appear in the original passage **(Example C).**

Example A	Example B	Example C
"______	______.	______.
______.	______	______
"______	______	______
______.	______	______
"______	______	"______
______."	______.	______."

600.4 **For Quoting Quotations**

Use single quotation marks to punctuate quoted material within a quotation.

"I was lucky," said Jane. "The proctor announced, **'Put your pencils down,'** just as I was filling in the last answer."

Italics (Underlining)

In Handwritten and Printed Material 601.1

Italics is a printer's term for a style of type that is slightly slanted. In this sentence, the word *happiness* is printed in italics. In material that is handwritten or typed on a machine that cannot print in italics, underline each word or letter that should be in italics.

In The Road to Memphis, racism is a contagious disease. (typed or handwritten)

Mildred Taylor's *The Road to Memphis* exposes racism. (printed)

In Titles 601.2

Use italics to indicate the titles of magazines, newspapers, books, pamphlets, full-length plays, films, videos, radio and television programs, book-length poems, ballets, operas, lengthy musical compositions, CDs, paintings and sculptures, legal cases, Web sites, and the names of ships and aircraft. (Also see 599.1)

The Week (magazine)
The Lost Symbol (book)
Enola Gay (airplane)
ACLU v. State of Ohio (legal case)
Avatar (film)
Castle (television program)
College Loans (pamphlet)
The New York Times (newspaper)
Yankee Tavern (play)
The Fame (album)
Billy the Kid (ballet)
The Thinker (sculpture)
The Ringer (Web site)

When one title appears within another title, punctuate as follows:

I read an article entitled "The Making of *Up*." (title of movie in an article title)

He wants to watch *Inside* The New York Times on PBS tonight. (title of newspaper in title of TV program)

For Key Terms 601.3

Italics are often used for a key term in a discussion or for a technical term, especially when it is accompanied by its definition. Italicize the term the first time it is used. Thereafter, put the term in roman type.

This flower has a ***zygomorphic*** (bilateral symmetry) structure.

For Foreign Words and Scientific Names 601.4

Use italics for foreign words that have not been adopted into the English language; italics are also used to denote scientific names.

Say ***arrivederci*** to your fears and try new activities. (foreign word)

The voyageurs discovered the shy ***Castor canadensis,*** or North American beaver. (scientific name)

Parentheses

602.1 **To Enclose Explanatory or Supplementary Material**

Use **parentheses** to enclose explanatory or supplementary material that interrupts the normal sentence structure.

> Students use *The College Writer* (*TCW*) in this class.

602.2 **To Set Off Numbers in a List**

Use parentheses to set off numbers used with a series of words or phrases.

> Dr. Beck told us **(1)** plan ahead, **(2)** stay flexible, and **(3)** follow through.

602.3 **For Parenthetical Sentences**

When using a full "sentence" within another sentence, do not capitalize it or use a period inside the parentheses.

> Your friend doesn't have the assignment **(he was just thinking about calling you),** so you'll have to make a few more calls.

When the parenthetical sentence comes after the main sentence, capitalize and punctuate it the same way you would any other complete sentence.

> But Mom doesn't say boo to Dad; she's always sweet to him. **(Actually she's sort of sweet to everybody.)**
> —Norma Fox Mazer, *Up on Fong Mountain*

602.4 **To Set Off References**

Use parentheses to set off references to authors, titles, pages, and years.

> The statistics are alarming **(see page 9)** and demand action.

Note: For unavoidable parentheses within parentheses (. . . [. . .] . . .), use brackets. Avoid overuse of parentheses by using commas instead.

Diagonal

602.5 **To Form Fractions or Show Choices**

Use a **diagonal** (also called a *slash*) to form a fraction. Also place a diagonal between two words to indicate that either is acceptable.

> My **walking/running** shoe size is **5 1/2**; my dress shoes are **6 1/2**.

602.6 **When Quoting Poetry**

When quoting poetry, use a diagonal (with one space before and after) to show where each line ends in the actual poem.

> A dryness is upon the house / My father loved and tended. / Beyond his firm and sculptured door / His light and lease have ended.
> —Gwendolyn Brooks, "In Honor of David Anderson Brooks, My Father"

Brackets

With Words That Clarify 603.1

Use **brackets** before and after words that are added to clarify what another person has said or written.

> "They'd **[the sweat bees]** get into your mouth, ears, eyes, nose. You'd feel them all over you."
> —Marilyn Johnson and Sasha Nyary, "Roosevelts in the Amazon"

Note: The brackets indicate that the words *the sweat bees* are not part of the original quotation but were added for clarification. (See 600.2.)

Around Comments by Someone Other Than the Author 603.2

Place brackets around comments that have been added by someone other than the author or speaker.

> "In conclusion, *docendo discimus*. Let the school year begin!" **[Huh?]**

Around Editorial Corrections 603.3

Place brackets around an editorial correction or addition.

> "Brooklyn alone has 8 percent of lead poisoning **[victims]** nationwide," said Marjorie Moore.
> —Donna Actie, student writer

Around the Word *Sic* 603.4

Brackets should be placed around the word *sic* (Latin for "so" or "thus") in quoted material; the word indicates that an error appearing in the quoted material was made by the original speaker or writer.

> "There is a higher principal **[sic]** at stake here: Is the school administration aware of the situation?"

Exclamation Point

To Express Strong Feeling 603.5

Use an **exclamation point** to express strong feeling. It may be placed at the end of a sentence (or an elliptical expression that stands for a sentence). Use exclamation points sparingly.

> "That's not the point," said Wangero. "These are all pieces of dresses Grandma used to wear. She did all this stitching by hand. **Imagine!**"
> —Alice Walker, "Everyday Use"

> Su-su-something's crawling up the back of my neck!
> —Mark Twain, Roughing It

> She was on tiptoe, stretching for an orange, when they heard, "**HEY YOU!**"
> —Beverley Naidoo, *Journey to Jo'burg*

Apostrophe

604.1 **In Contractions**

Use an **apostrophe** to show that one or more letters have been left out of two words joined to form a contraction.

don't → **o** is left out **she'd** → **woul** is left out **it's** → **i** is left out

Note: An apostrophe is also used to show that one or more numerals or letters have been left out of numbers or words.

class of **'02** → **20** is left out good **mornin'** → **g** is left out

604.2 **To Form Plurals**

Use an apostrophe and an *s* to form the plural of a letter, a number, a sign, or a word discussed as a word.

A → **A's** t → **t's** + → **+'s**
You use too many ***and*'s** in your writing.

Use only an *s* to form the plural of a number or an abbreviation.

1950s 2s and 3s $10s and $20s BAs MFAs PhDs TVs

Note: If two apostrophes are called for in the same word, omit the second one.

Follow closely the **do's** and **don'ts** (not **don't's**) on the checklist.

604.3 **To Form Singular Possessives**

The possessive form of singular nouns is usually made by adding an apostrophe and an *s*.

Spock's ears my **computer's** memory

Note: When a singular noun of more than one syllable ends with an *s* or a *z* sound, the possessive may be formed by adding just an apostrophe—or an apostrophe and an *s*.

When the singular noun is a one-syllable word, however, the possessive is usually formed by adding both an apostrophe and an *s*.

Dallas' sports teams *or* **Dallas's** sports teams (two-syllable word)

Kiss's last concert my **boss's** generosity (one-syllable words)

604.4 **To Form Plural Possessives**

The possessive form of plural nouns ending in *s* is made by adding just an apostrophe.

the **Joneses'** great-grandfather **bosses'** offices

Note: For plural nouns not ending in *s*, add an apostrophe and *s*.

women's health issues **children's** program

To Determine Ownership

You will punctuate possessives correctly if you remember that the word that comes immediately before the apostrophe is the owner.

girl's guitar (*girl* is the owner) **girls'** guitar (*girls* are the owners)

To Show Shared Possession 605.1

When possession is shared by more than one noun, use the possessive form for the last noun in the series.

Jason, Kamil, and **Elana's** sound system
(All three own the same system.)

Jason's, Kamil's, and Elana's sound systems
(Each owns a separate system.)

In Compound Nouns 605.2

The possessive of a compound noun is formed by placing the possessive ending after the last word.

his **mother-in-law's** name (singular)
the **secretary of state's** career (singular)

their **mothers-in-law's** names (plural)
the **secretaries of state's** careers (plural)

With Indefinite Pronouns 605.3

The possessive form of an indefinite pronoun is made by adding an apostrophe and an *s* to the pronoun. (See 540.4.)

everybody's grades   **no one's** mistake   **one's** choice

In expressions using *else,* add the apostrophe and *s* after the last word.

anyone else's   **somebody else's**

To Show Time or Amount 605.4

Use an apostrophe and an *s* with an adjective that is part of an expression indicating time or amount.

yesterday's news   a **day's** wage   a **month's** pay

Punctuation Marks 605.5

´ (é)	Accent, acute	:	Colon	¶	Paragraph
` (è)	Accent, grave	,	Comma	( )	Parentheses
< >	Angle brackets	†	Dagger	.	Period
’	Apostrophe	—	Dash	?	Question mark
*	Asterisk	/	Diagonal/slash	“ ”	Quotation marks
{ }	Braces	¨ (ä)	Dieresis	§	Section
[ ]	Brackets	. . .	Ellipsis	;	Semicolon
^	Caret	!	Exclamation point	˜ (ñ)	Tilde
ç	Cedilla	-	Hyphen	____	Underscore
^ (â)	Circumflex	.....	Leaders		

Punctuation Exercises:

Quotation Marks, Apostrophes, and Other Marks

A. Quotation Marks and Italics (Underlining)

For each sentence, indicate the correct use of quotation marks or italics (underlining).

1. I read the article Five Cures for Writer's Block in the magazine Writer's Digest.
2. When I used the word interesting, I really meant the word bizarre.
3. The receptionist said, The doctor will be available shortly. While you wait, why don't you read the article New Vaccine in Time magazine?
4. Did the judge just say, Apolo Ohno is disqualified?
5. The music on the album Solar Plexus is what people call jazz fusion.
6. Where is Bill? asked Jacob. Didn't he say he'd be right back?
7. The short story Coffee appeared in the anthology Wake Up.
8. I played The Llama Song; my roommate objected.
9. My roommate said that he had heard that song enough.
10. Doesn't the law state, Any male 18 or over needs to sign up for the draft?

B. Parentheses, Brackets, Diagonals, Exclamation Points

For each sentence, indicate the correct use of these marks.

1. The TA teaching assistant in my psychology class is great.
2. "I think that I shall never see A poem lovely as a tree." Joyce Kilmer
3. He signed the letter "Your fiend sic Fred."
4. This is not an either or proposition.
5. I want to 1 finish the paper, 2 revise the paper, and 3 be done with the paper.

C. Apostrophes

For each item, write the word or words, inserting apostrophes correctly.

1. didnt
2. dos and donts
3. Daves thumb drive
4. Jane and Jills room
5. anyones folder
6. mother-in-laws hat
7. Lynnes job
8. wouldve
9. two *ands* and three *ors*
10. mens magazine

Chapter 29

Checking Mechanics

Capitalization

Proper Nouns and Adjectives 607.1

Capitalize all proper nouns and all proper adjectives (adjectives derived from proper nouns). The chart below provides a quick overview of capitalization rules. The pages following explain specific or special uses of capitalization.

Capitalization at a Glance

Days of the week	Sunday, Monday, Tuesday
Months	June, July, August
Holidays, holy days	Thanksgiving, Easter, Hanukkah
Periods, events in history	Middle Ages, World War I
Special events	Tate Memorial Dedication Ceremony
Political parties	Republican Party, Socialist Party
Official documents	the Declaration of Independence
Trade names	Oscar Mayer hot dogs, Mazda Miata
Formal epithets	Alexander the Great
Official titles	Mayor John Spitzer, Senator Tim Scott
Official state nicknames	the Badger State, the Aloha State
Geographical names	
Planets, heavenly bodies	Earth, Jupiter, the Milky Way
Continents	Australia, South America
Countries	Ireland, Grenada, Sri Lanka
States, provinces	Ohio, Utah, Nova Scotia
Cities, towns, villages	El Paso, Burlington, Sioux Center
Streets, roads, highways	Park Avenue, Route 66, Interstate 90
Sections of the United States and the world	the Southwest, the Far East
Landforms	the Rocky Mountains, the Kalahari Desert
Bodies of water	the Nile River, Lake Superior, Bee Creek
Public areas	Central Park, Yellowstone National Park

608.1 **First Words**

Capitalize the first word in every sentence and the first word in a full-sentence direct quotation. (Also see 600.1.)

> **Attending** the orientation for new students is a good idea.
>
> Max suggested, **"Let's** take the guided tour of the campus first."

608.2 **Sentences in Parentheses**

Capitalize the first word in a sentence that is enclosed in parentheses if that sentence is not contained within another complete sentence.

> The bookstore has the software. (**Now** all I need is my MacBook Pro.)

Note: Do *not* capitalize a sentence that is enclosed in parentheses and is located in the middle of another sentence. (Also see 602.3.)

> Your college will probably offer everything (**this** includes general access to a printer) that you'll need for a successful year.

608.3 **Sentences Following Colons**

Capitalize a complete sentence that follows a colon when that sentence is a formal statement, a quotation, or a sentence that you want to emphasize. (Also see 594.5.)

> Sydney Harris had this to say about computers: "**The** real danger is not that computers will begin to think like people, but that people will begin to think like computers."

608.4 **Salutation and Complimentary Closing**

In a letter, capitalize the first and all major words of the salutation. Capitalize only the first word of the complimentary closing.

> **Dear Personnel Director:** **Sincerely** yours,

608.5 **Sections of the Country**

Words that indicate sections of the country are proper nouns and should be capitalized; words that simply indicate direction are not proper nouns.

> Many businesses move to the **South.** (section of the country)
>
> They move **south** to cut fuel costs and other expenses. (direction)

608.6 **Languages, Ethnic Groups, Nationalities, and Religions**

Capitalize languages, ethnic groups, nationalities, and religions.

> **African American** **Latino** **Navajo** **French** **Islam**

Nouns that refer to the Supreme Being and holy books are capitalized.

> **God** **Allah** **Jehovah** **the Koran** **Exodus** **the Bible** **Christ**

Titles 609.1

Capitalize the first word of a title, the last word, and every word in between except articles (*a, an, the*), short prepositions, *to* in an infinitive, and coordinating conjunctions. Follow this rule for titles of books, newspapers, magazines, poems, plays, songs, articles, films, works of art, and stories.

Going to Meet the Man — ***The New York Times***
"Nothing Gold Can Stay" — **"Jobs in the Cyber Arena"**
A Midsummer Night's Dream — ***The War of the Roses***

Note: When citing titles in a bibliography, check the style manual you've been asked to follow. For example, in APA style, only the first word of a title is capitalized.

Organizations 609.2

Capitalize the name of an organization or a team and its members.

American Indian Movement — **Democratic Party**
Tampa Bay Buccaneers — **Tucson Drama Club**

Abbreviations 609.3

Capitalize abbreviations of titles and organizations. (Some other abbreviations are also capitalized. See pages 617–618.)

MD PhD NAACP CE BCE GPA AD 2017 TV CST

Letters 609.4

Capitalize letters used to indicate a form or shape.

U-turn I-beam S-curve V-shaped T-shirt

Words Used as Names 609.5

Capitalize words like *father, mother, uncle, senator,* and *professor* when they are parts of titles that include a personal name or when they are substituted for proper nouns (especially in direct address). (Also see 590.3.)

Hello, **Senator Tim Scott.** (*Senator* is part of the name.)
Our **senator** is an environmentalist.
Who was your chemistry **professor** last quarter?
I had **Professor** Williams for Chemistry 101.

Note: To test whether a word is being substituted for a proper noun, simply read the sentence with a proper noun in place of the word. If the proper noun fits in the sentence, the word being tested should be capitalized. Usually the word is not capitalized if it follows a possessive—*my, his, our, your,* and so on.

Did **Dad (Brad)** pack my bluetooth speakers in the trailer? (Brad works in this sentence.)

Did your **dad (Brad)** pack the bluetooth speakers in the trailer? (*Brad* does not work in this sentence; the word *dad* follows the possessive your.)

610.1 Titles of Courses

Words such as *technology, history,* and *science* are proper nouns when they are included in the titles of specific courses; they are common nouns when they name a field of study.

Who teaches **Art History 202?** (title of a specific course)

Professor Bunker loves teaching **history.** (a field of study)

Note: The words *freshman, sophomore, junior,* and *senior* are not capitalized unless they are part of an official title.

The **seniors** who maintained high GPAs were honored at the **Mount Mary Senior Honors Banquet.**

610.2 Internet and Email

The words *Internet* and *World Wide Web* are always capitalized because they are considered proper nouns. When your writing includes a web address (URL), capitalize any letters that the site's owner does (on printed materials or on the site itself). Not only is it respectful to reprint a web address exactly as it appears elsewhere, but, in fact, some web addresses are case-sensitive and must be entered into a browser's address bar exactly as presented.

When doing research on the **Internet,** be sure to record each site's **Web** address (**URL**) and each contact's **email** address.

Note: Some people include capital letters in their email addresses to make certain features evident. Although email addresses are not case-sensitive, repeat each letter in print just as its owner uses it.

Avoid Capitalization Errors

Do not capitalize any of the following:

- A prefix attached to a proper noun
- Seasons of the year
- Words used to indicate direction or position
- Common nouns and titles that appear near, but are not part of, a proper noun

Capitalize	Do Not Capitalize
American	un-American
January, February	winter, spring
The South is quite conservative.	Turn south at the stop sign.
Duluth City College	a Duluth college
Prime Minister Justin Trudeau	the prime minister of Canada
President Obama	the president of the United States
Earth (the planet)	earthmover
Internet	email

Mechanics Exercises:

Capitalization

A. Capitalization Practice

For each sentence, write the correct form of any incorrectly capitalized or lowercased words.

1. Vice president Joe Biden will speak in topeka, Kansas, on thursday.
2. What Jarrod meant to say is this: the dallas cowboys have enough talent to win the Super bowl.
3. The beautiful double rainbow in Yellowstone national park seemed like an act of god.
4. Does starbucks have a wireless internet connection?
5. The vehicle in question was driving North along interstate 55 before making a u-turn.
6. are you taking introduction to mass communication 101 with professor Williams next semester?
7. I'm going to the south to visit my brother in the peach state.
8. A story in the *San Francisco chronicle* quoted the Secretary of Agriculture saying, "we are concerned with the development of our farmland."
9. Shoot me an email if you want to go with me to the civil war reenactment.
10. The french restaurant serves an amazing aged Cheese platter.

B. Using Capitalization

For each line of the following email message, write the correct form of any incorrectly capitalized or lowercased words.

dear Dr. Cruz,

Thank You for letting me shadow you for a day at St. Vincent Hospital. I very much enjoyed observing the arthroscopic surgery and was impressed with the expertise of the hospital's Staff! I hope we can meet up soon to discuss questions about my Human functional anatomy 410 course.

Best Wishes,
Kimbra Jenson

C. Capitalization Errors

Write the correct form of any incorrectly capitalized or lowercased words.

summer	prime minister	David Cameron	md
Vice President	the bible	spanish	

Plurals

612.1 Nouns Ending in a Consonant

Some nouns remain unchanged when used as plurals (*species, moose, halibut,* and so on), but the plurals of most nouns are formed by adding an *s* to the singular form.

dorm—**dorms** credit—**credits** midterm—**midterms**

The plurals of nouns ending in *sh, ch, x, s,* and *z* are made by adding *es* to the singular form.

lunch—**lunches** wish—**wishes** class—**classes**

612.2 Nouns Ending in *y*

The plurals of common nouns that end in *y* (preceded by a consonant) are formed by changing the *y* to *i* and adding *es.*

dormitory—**dormitories** sorority—**sororities** duty—**duties**

The plurals of common nouns that end in *y* (preceded by a vowel) are formed by adding only an s.

attorney—**attorneys** monkey—**monkeys** toy—**toys**

The plurals of all proper nouns ending in *y* (whether preceded by a consonant or a vowel) are formed by adding an *s.*

the three **Kathys** the five **Faheys**

612.3 Nouns Ending in *o*

The plurals of words ending in *o* (preceded by a vowel) are formed by adding an *s.*

radio—**radios** cameo—**cameos** studio—**studios**

The plurals of most nouns ending in *o* (preceded by a consonant) are formed by adding *es.*

echo—**echoes** hero—**heroes** tomato—**tomatoes**

Musical terms always form plurals by adding an *s;* check a dictionary for other words of this type.

alto—**altos** banjo—**banjos** solo—**solos** piano—**pianos**

612.4 Nouns Ending in *f* or *fe*

The plurals of nouns that end in *f* or *fe* are formed in one of two ways: If the final *f* sound is still heard in the plural form of the word, simply add *s;* if the final sound is a *v* sound, change the *f* to *ve* and add an *s.*

Plural ends with *f* sound: roof—**roofs** chief—**chiefs**

Plural ends with *v* sound: wife—**wives** loaf—**loaves**

Note: The plurals of some nouns that end in *f* or *fe* can be formed by either adding *s* or changing the *f* to *ve* and adding an *s.*

Plural ends with either sound: hoof—**hoofs, hooves**

Irregular Spelling 613.1

Many foreign words (as well as some of English origin) form a plural by taking on an irregular spelling; others are now acceptable with the commonly used *s* or *es* ending. Take time to check a dictionary.

child—**children** alumnus—**alumni** syllabus—**syllabi, syllabuses**
goose—**geese** datum—**data** radius—**radii, radiuses**

Words Discussed as Words 613.2

The plurals of symbols, letters, figures, and words discussed as words are formed by adding an apostrophe and an *s*.

Many colleges have now added **A/B's** and **B/C's** as standard grades.

Note: Omit the apostrophe when the omission does not cause confusion.

YMCAs **CDs** **TVs** **MDs** **fours**

Nouns Ending in *ful* 613.3

The plurals of nouns that end with *ful* are formed by adding an *s* at the end of the word.

three **teaspoonfuls** two **tankfuls** four **bagfuls**

Compound Nouns 613.4

The plurals of compound nouns are usually formed by adding an *s* or an *es* to the important word in the compound. (Also see 595.1.)

brothers-in-law **maids** of honor **secretaries** of state

Collective Nouns 613.5

Collective nouns do not change in form when they are used as plurals.

class (a unit—singular form)
class (individual members—plural form)

Because the spelling of the collective noun does not change, it is often the pronoun used in place of the collective noun that indicates whether the noun is singular or plural. Use a singular pronoun (**its**) to show that the collective noun is singular. Use a plural pronoun (**their**) to show that the collective noun is plural.

The class needs to change **its** motto.
(The writer is thinking of the group as a unit.)

The class brainstormed with **their** professor.
(The writer is thinking of the group as individuals.)

ESL Note: To determine whether a plural requires the article *the*, you must first determine whether it is definite or indefinite. Definite plurals use *the*, whereas indefinite plurals do not require any article. (See 646.3–647.1.)

Numbers

614.1 ### Numerals or Words

Numbers from one to one hundred are usually written as words; numbers 101 and greater are usually written as numerals. (APA style uses numerals for numbers 10 and higher.) Hyphenate numbers written as two words if less than one hundred.

two seven ten twenty-five 106 1,079

The same rule applies to the use of ordinal numbers.

second tenth twenty-fifth ninety-eighth 106th 333rd

If numbers greater than 101 are used infrequently in a piece of writing, you may spell out those that can be written in one or two words.

two hundred fifty thousand six billion

You may use a combination of numerals and words for very large numbers.

1.5 million 3 billion to 3.2 billion 6 trillion

Numbers being compared or contrasted should be kept in the same style.

8 to **11** years old *or* **eight** to **eleven** years old

Particular decades may be spelled out or written as numerals.

the **'80s** and **'90s** *or* the **eighties** and **nineties**

614.2 ### Numerals Only

Use numerals for the following forms: decimals, percentages, pages, chapters (and other parts of a book), addresses, dates, telephone numbers, identification numbers, and statistics.

26.2	**8** percent	chapter **7**	**8 May 2017**
pages **287–289**	Highway **36**	**(212) 555–1234**	**Joshua 1: 9**
398-55-0000	a vote of **23** to **4**	May **8, 2007**	**315 Burr Oak Road**

Note: Abbreviations and symbols are often used in charts, graphs, footnotes, and so forth, but typically they are not used in texts.

He is **five feet one inch** tall and **ten years old.**

She walked **three and one-half miles** through **twelve inches** of snow.

However, abbreviations and symbols may be used in scientific, mathematical, statistical, and technical texts (APA style).

Between **20%** and **23%** of the cultures yielded positive results.

Your **245B** model requires **220V.**

Always use numerals with abbreviations and symbols.

5'4" 8% 10 in. **3** tbsp. **6** lb. **8** oz. **90**°F

Use numerals after the name of local branches of labor unions.

The Office and Professional Employees International Union, Local **8**

Hyphenated Numbers 615.1

Hyphens are used to form compound modifiers indicating measurement. They are also used for inclusive numbers and written-out fractions.

a **three-mile** trip
a **2,500-mile** road trip
one-sixth of the pie
a **thirteen-foot** clearance
three-eighths of the book

Time and Money 615.2

If time is expressed with an abbreviation, use numerals; if it is expressed in words, spell out the number.

4:00 a.m. *or* **four** o'clock (not 4 o'clock)
the **5:15** p.m. train
a **seven o'clock** wake-up call

If money is expressed with a symbol, use numerals; if the currency is expressed in words, spell out the number.

$20 or **twenty** dollars (not 20 dollars)

Abbreviations of time and of money may be used in text.

The concert begins at **7:00** p.m., and tickets cost **$30.**

Words Only 615.3

Use words to express numbers that begin a sentence.

Fourteen students "forgot" their assignments.
Three hundred contest entries were received.

Note: Change the sentence structure if this rule creates a clumsy construction.

Six hundred thirty-nine students are new to the campus this fall. (Clumsy)
This fall, **639** students are new to the campus. (Better)

Use words for numbers that precede a compound modifier that includes a numeral. (If the compound modifier uses a spelled-out number, use numerals in front of it.)

She sold **twenty 35-millimeter** cameras in one day.
The chef prepared **24 eight-ounce** filets.

Use words for the names of numbered streets of one hundred or fewer.

Ninth Avenue
123 **Forty-fourth** Street

Use words for the names of buildings if that name is also its address.

One Thousand State Street
Two Fifty Park Avenue

Use words for references to particular centuries.

the twenty-first century
the fourth century BCE

Mechanics Exercises:

Plurals and Numbers

A. Plurals

For each of the following words, write the correct plural form.

1. team
2. party
3. ratio
4. shelf
5. child
6. sister-in-law
7. video
8. bucketful
9. choir
10. serf

B. Numbers

For each sentence below, write the correct form of any incorrectly used numbers.

1. 4 tiny ducklings crossed a driveway near Six Hundred and Nine Lewis Street.
2. Out of all my friends, Alex woke up 1st around 6 o'clock.
3. The 6 cheeseburgers cost 12 dollars.
4. I read only fifty % of chapter three.
5. At half past 2 the temperature was still seventy degrees Fahrenheit.
6. The recipe calls for two tsp. salt and three oz. butter.

C. Mechanics Practice

In the following paragraph, correct any number errors by writing the line number and the correct form. Also write the plural of each underlined word.

Let me tell you how to grill some wonderful steak. First, consider buying your meat from a butcher rather than from local grocery. The ideal steak cut is between one and a half to 2 inches thick. Next, you will need to prepare the steaks for grilling. Start by trimming excess fat to about one-quarter of an inch thick and seasoning the meat with two tsp. of salt and cracked pepper. Then, when the grill has preheated, grill the steaks for 16 to twenty minutes. If you so choose, rotate the steaks forty-five degrees on both sides for nice diamond grill mark. When the steaks are done, turn off the grill and enjoy. And remember, steak goes great with potato and fresh mushroom.

Abbreviations 617.1

An **abbreviation** is the shortened form of a word or a phrase. These abbreviations are always acceptable in both formal and informal writing:

Mr. Mrs. Ms. Dr. Jr. a.m. (A.M.) p.m. (P.M.) BS MFA PhD

Note: In formal writing, do not abbreviate the names of states, countries, months, days, units of measure, or courses of study. Do not abbreviate the words *Street, Road, Avenue, Company,* and similar words when they are part of a proper name. Also, do not use signs or symbols (%, &, #, @) in place of words. (The dollar sign, however, is appropriate when numerals are used to express an amount of money. See 615.2.)

Also Note: When abbreviations are called for (in charts, lists, bibliographies, notes, and indexes, for example), standard abbreviations are preferred. Reserve the postal abbreviations for ZIP code addresses.

Correspondence Abbreviations 617.2

States/Territories

	Standard	Postal
Alabama	**Ala.**	**AL**
Alaska	**Alaska**	**AK**
Arizona	**Ariz.**	**AZ**
Arkansas	**Ark.**	**AR**
California	**Cal.**	**CA**
Colorado	**Colo.**	**CO**
Connecticut	**Conn.**	**CT**
Delaware	**Del.**	**DE**
District of Columbia	**D.C.**	**DC**
Florida	**Fla.**	**FL**
Georgia	**Ga.**	**GA**
Guam	**Guam**	**GU**
Hawaii	**Hawaii**	**HI**
Idaho	**Idaho**	**ID**
Illinois	**Ill.**	**IL**
Indiana	**Ind.**	**IN**
Iowa	**Ia.**	**IA**
Kansas	**Kans.**	**KS**
Kentucky	**Ky.**	**KY**
Louisiana	**La.**	**LA**
Maine	**Me.**	**ME**
Maryland	**Md.**	**MD**
Massachusetts	**Mass.**	**MA**
Michigan	**Mich.**	**MI**
Minnesota	**Minn.**	**MN**
Mississippi	**Miss.**	**MS**
Missouri	**Mo.**	**MO**
Montana	**Mont.**	**MT**
Nebraska	**Neb.**	**NE**
Nevada	**Nev.**	**NV**
New Hampshire	**N.H.**	**NH**
New Jersey	**N.J.**	**NJ**
New Mexico	**N. Mex.**	**NM**
New York	**N.Y.**	**NY**
North Carolina	**N.C.**	**NC**
North Dakota	**N. Dak.**	**ND**
Ohio	**Ohio**	**OH**
Oklahoma	**Okla.**	**OK**
Oregon	**Ore.**	**OR**
Pennsylvania	**Pa.**	**PA**
Puerto Rico	**P.R.**	**PR**
Rhode Island	**R.I.**	**RI**
South Carolina	**S.C.**	**SC**
South Dakota	**S. Dak.**	**SD**
Tennessee	**Tenn.**	**TN**
Texas	**Tex.**	**TX**
Utah	**Utah**	**UT**
Vermont	**Vt.**	**VT**
Virginia	**Va.**	**VA**
Virgin Islands	**V.I.**	**VI**
Washington	**Wash.**	**WA**
West Virginia	**W. Va.**	**WV**
Wisconsin	**Wis.**	**WI**
Wyoming	**Wyo.**	**WY**

Canadian Provinces

	Standard	Postal
Alberta	**Alta.**	**AB**
British Columbia	**B.C.**	**BC**
Manitoba	**Man.**	**MB**
New Brunswick	**N.B.**	**NB**
Newfoundland and Labrador	**N.F. Lab.**	**NL**
Northwest Territories	**N.W.T.**	**NT**
Nova Scotia	**N.S.**	**NS**
Nunavut		**NU**
Ontario	**Ont.**	**ON**
Prince Edward Island	**P.E.I.**	**PE**
Quebec	**Que.**	**QC**
Saskatchewan	**Sask.**	**SK**
Yukon Territory	**Y.T.**	**YT**

Address Abbreviations

	Standard	Postal
Apartment	**Apt.**	**APT**
Avenue	**Ave.**	**AVE**
Boulevard	**Blvd.**	**BLVD**
Circle	**Cir.**	**CIR**
Court	**Ct.**	**CT**
Drive	**Dr.**	**DR**
East	**E.**	**E**
Expressway	**Expy.**	**EXPY**
Freeway	**Frwy.**	**FWY**
Heights	**Hts.**	**HTS**
Highway	**Hwy.**	**HWY**
Hospital	**Hosp.**	**HOSP**
Junction	**Junc.**	**JCT**
Lake	**L.**	**LK**
Lakes	**Ls.**	**LKS**
Lane	**Ln.**	**LN**
Meadows	**Mdws.**	**MDWS**
North	**N.**	**N**
Palms	**Palms**	**PLMS**
Park	**Pk.**	**PK**
Parkway	**Pky.**	**PKY**
Place	**Pl.**	**PL**
Plaza	**Plaza**	**PLZ**
Post Office Box	**P.O. Box**	**PO BOX**
Ridge	**Rdg.**	**RDG**
River	**R.**	**RV**
Road	**Rd.**	**RD**
Room	**Rm.**	**RM**
Rural	**R.**	**R**
Rural Route	**R.R.**	**RR**
Shore	**Sh.**	**SH**
South	**S.**	**S**
Square	**Sq.**	**SQ**
Station	**Sta.**	**STA**
Street	**St.**	**ST**
Suite	**Ste.**	**STE**
Terrace	**Ter.**	**TER**
Turnpike	**Tpke.**	**TPKE**
Union	**Un.**	**UN**
View	**View**	**VW**
Village	**Vil.**	**VLG**
West	**W.**	**W**

Common Abbreviations

abr. abridged, abridgment
AC, ac alternating current, air-conditioning
ack. acknowledgment
AM amplitude modulation
A.M., a.m. before noon (Latin *ante meridiem*)
AP advanced placement
ASAP as soon as possible
avg., av. average
BA bachelor of arts degree
BBB Better Business Bureau
BCE before common era
bibliog. bibliography
biog. biographer, biographical, biography
BS bachelor of science degree
C 1. Celsius **2.** centigrade **3.** coulomb
c. 1. circa (about) **2.** cup(s)
cc 1. cubic centimeter **2.** carbon copy **3.** community college
CDT, C.D.T. central daylight time
CE common era
CEEB College Entrance Examination Board
chap. chapter(s)
cm centimeter(s)
c/o care of
COD, c.o.d. 1. cash on delivery **2.** collect on delivery
co-op cooperative
CPA CPA Certified Public Accountant
CST, C.S.T. central standard time
cu 1. cubic **2.** cumulative
D.A. district attorney
d.b.a., d/b/a doing business as
DC, dc direct current
DDS Doctor of Dental Surgery
dec. deceased
dept. department
disc. discount
DST daylight saving time
dup. duplicate
ed. edition, editor
EDT eastern daylight time
EdD Doctor of Education
e.g. for example (Latin *exempli gratia*)
EST eastern standard time
etc. and so forth (Latin *et cetera*)
F Fahrenheit, French, Friday
FM frequency modulation
F.O.B., f.o.b. free on board
FYI for your information
g 1. gravity **2.** gram(s)
gal. gallon(s)
gds. goods
gloss. glossary
GNP gross national product
GPA grade point average
hdqrs. headquarters
HIV human immunodeficiency virus
hp horsepower
Hz hertz
ibid. in the same place (Latin *ibidem*)
id. the same (Latin *idem*)
i.e. that is (Latin *id est*)
illus. illustration
inc. incorporated
IQ, I.Q. intelligence quotient
IRS Internal Revenue Service
ISBN International Standard Book Number
JD Juris Doctor
JP, J.P. justice of the peace
K 1. kelvin (temperature unit) **2.** Kelvin (temperature scale)
kc kilocycle(s)
kg kilogram(s)
km kilometer(s)
kn knot(s)
kw kilowatt(s)
L liter(s), lake
lat. latitude
l.c. lowercase
lit. literary; literature
log logarithm, logic
long. longitude
Ltd., ltd. limited
m meter(s)
MA master of arts degree
man. manual
MBA Master of Business Administration
MC master of ceremonies
MD doctor of medicine (Latin *medicinae doctor*)
mdse. merchandise
MDT mountain daylight time
mfg. manufacture, manufacturing
mg milligram(s)
mi. 1. mile(s) **2.** mill(s) (monetary unit)
misc. miscellaneous
mL milliliter(s)
mm millimeter(s)
mpg, m.p.g. miles per gallon
mph, m.p.h. miles per hour
MS 1. manuscript **2.** multiple sclerosis
Ms. title of courtesy for a woman
MS master of science degree
MST mountain standard time
NE northeast
neg. negative
N.S.F., n.s.f. not sufficient funds
NW northwest
oz, oz. ounce(s)
PA public-address system
pct. percent
pd. paid
PDT Pacific daylight time
PFC, Pfc. private first class
pg., p. page
PhD doctor of philosophy
P.M., p.m. after noon (Latin *post meridiem*)
POW, P.O.W. prisoner of war
pp. pages
ppd. 1. postpaid **2.** prepaid
PR, P.R. public relations
PSAT Preliminary Scholastic Aptitude Test
psi, p.s.i. pounds per square inch
PST, Pacific standard time
PTA, P.T.A. Parent-Teacher Association
R.A. residence assistant
RF radio frequency
R.P.M., rpm revolutions per minute
R.S.V.P., r.s.v.p. please reply (French *répondez s'il vous plaît*)
SAT Scholastic Aptitude Test
SE southeast
SOS 1. international distress signal **2.** any call for help
Sr. 1. senior (after surname) **2.** sister (religious)
SRO, S.R.O. standing room only
std. standard
SW southwest
syn. synonymous, synonym
tbs., tbsp. tablespoon(s)
TM trademark
UHF, uhf ultrahigh frequency
v 1. physics: velocity **2.** volume
V electricity: volt
VA Veterans Administration
VHF, vhf very high frequency
VIP informal: very important person
vol. 1. volume **2.** volunteer
vs. versus, verse
W 1. electricity: watt(s) **2.** physics: (also **w**) work **3.** west
whse., whs. warehouse
whsle. wholesale
wkly. weekly
w/o without
wt. weight
www World Wide Web

Acronyms and Initialisms

Acronyms 619.1

An **acronym** is a word formed from the first (or first few) letters of words in a set phrase. Even though acronyms are abbreviations, they require no periods.

radar	radio detecting and ranging
CARE	Cooperative for Assistance and Relief Everywhere
NASA	National Aeronautics and Space Administration
VISTA	Volunteers in Service to America
FICA	Federal Insurance Contributions Act

Initialisms 619.2

An **initialism** is similar to an acronym except that the initials used to form this abbreviation are pronounced individually.

CIA	Central Intelligence Agency
FBI	Federal Bureau of Investigation
FHA	Federal Housing Administration

Common Acronyms and Initialisms 619.3

AIDS	acquired immune deficiency syndrome
APR	annual percentage rate
CAD	computer-aided design
CAM	computer-aided manufacturing
CETA	Comprehensive Employment and Training Act
FAA	Federal Aviation Administration
FCC	Federal Communications Commission
FDA	Food and Drug Administration
FDIC	Federal Deposit Insurance Corporation
FEMA	Federal Emergency Management Agency
FHA	Federal Housing Administration
FTC	Federal Trade Commission
IRS	Internal Revenue Service
MADD	Mothers Against Drunk Driving
NAFTA	North American Free Trade Agreement
NATO	North Atlantic Treaty Organization
OEO	Office of Economic Opportunity
ORV	off-road vehicle
OSHA	Occupational Safety and Health Administration
PAC	political action committee
PIN	personal identification number
POP	point of purchase
PSA	public service announcement
REA	Rural Electrification Administration
RICO	Racketeer Influenced and Corrupt Organizations (Act)
ROTC	Reserve Officers' Training Corps
SADD	Students Against Destructive Decisions
SASE	self-addressed stamped envelope
SPOT	satellite positioning and tracking
SSA	Social Security Administration
SUV	sport-utility vehicle
SWAT	Special Weapons and Tactics
TDD	telecommunications device for the deaf
TMJ	temporomandibular joint
TVA	Tennessee Valley Authority
VA	Veterans Administration
WHO	World Health Organization

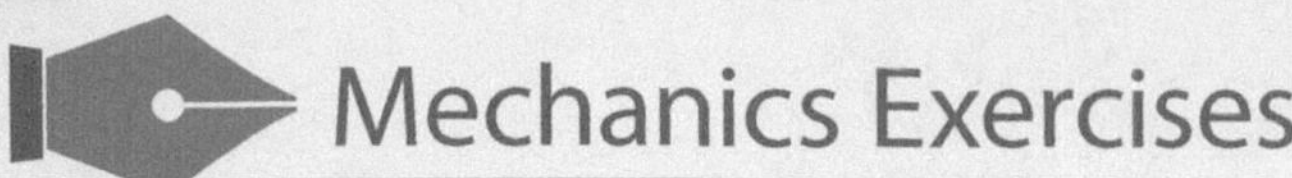

Mechanics Exercises:

Abbreviations, Acronyms, and Initialisms

A. Abbreviations

Indicate whether the following abbreviations would be acceptable in a formal piece of writing. Write "yes" for appropriate and "no" for inappropriate.

1. MN
2. Sask.
3. Dr.
4. R.A.
5. P.M.
6. Jr.
7. Ave.
8. Misc.
9. Mrs.
10. $5.25

B. Acronyms and Initialisms

Indicate whether each term is an acronym or an initialism.

1. PSA
2. FDA
3. MADD
4. NATO
5. NASA
6. TMJ
7. VA
8. SWAT
9. IRS
10. FAA

C. Mechanics Practice

For each sentence, write the correct abbreviation, acronym, or initialism of the underlined word or words.

1. <u>Mister</u> Anderson of the <u>Federal Deposit Insurance Corporation</u> called today regarding the bank's membership status.
2. We cruised south on Falcon <u>Drive</u> in our new <u>sport-utility vehicle</u>.
3. The student's low <u>grade point average</u> negated a high score on the <u>Scholastic Aptitude Test</u>.
4. Do you know the <u>latitude</u> and <u>longitude</u> of Key West, <u>Florida</u>?
5. You can add two <u>teaspoons</u> salt and one <u>tablespoon</u> basil for extra flavor.

MindTap® Practice skills that you have learned in this section and receive automatic feedback.

Basic Spelling Rules

Write *i* Before *e* 621.1

Write *i* before *e* except after *c*, or when sounded like *a* as in *neighbor* and *weigh*.

believe relief receive eight

Note: This sentence contains eight exceptions:

Neither sheik dared leisurely seize either weird species of financiers.

Words with Consonant Endings 621.2

When a one-syllable word (*bat*) ends in a consonant (*t*) preceded by one vowel (*a*), double the final consonant before adding a suffix that begins with a vowel (*batting*).

sum—**summary** god—**goddess**

Note: When a multisyllable word (*control*) ends in a consonant (*l*) preceded by one vowel (*o*), the accent is on the last syllable (*con trol´*), and the suffix begins with a vowel (*ing*)—the same rule holds true: Double the final consonant (*controlling*).

prefer—**preferred** begin—**beginning**
forget—**forgettable** admit—**admittance**

Words with a Final Silent *e* 621.3

If a word ends with a silent *e*, drop the *e* before adding a suffix that begins with a vowel. Do *not* drop the *e* when the suffix begins with a consonant.

state—**stating—statement** like—**liking—likeness**
use—**using—useful** nine—**ninety—nineteen**

Note: Exceptions are **judgment, truly, argument, ninth.**

Words Ending in *y* 621.4

When *y* is the last letter in a word and the *y* is preceded by a consonant, change the *y* to *i* before adding any suffix except those beginning with *i*.

fry—**fries, frying** hurry—**hurried, hurrying**
lady—**ladies** ply—**pliable**
happy—**happiness** beauty—**beautiful**

Note: When forming the plural of a word that ends with a *y* that is preceded by a vowel, add *s*.

toy—**toys** play—**plays** monkey—**monkeys**

Tip: Never trust your spelling to even the best spell checker. Carefully proofread and use a dictionary for words you know your spell checker does not cover.

Commonly Misspelled Words

The commonly misspelled words that follow are hyphenated to show where they would logically be broken at the end of a line.

A

ab-bre-vi-ate
abrupt
ab-scess
ab-sence
ab-so-lute (-ly)
ab-sorb-ent
ab-surd
abun-dance
ac-a-dem-ic
ac-cede
ac-cel-er-ate
ac-cept (-ance)
ac-ces-si-ble
ac-ces-so-ry
ac-ci-den-tal-ly
ac-com-mo-date
ac-com-pa-ny
ac-com-plice
ac-com-plish
ac-cor-dance
ac-cord-ing
ac-count
ac-crued
ac-cu-mu-late
ac-cu-rate
ac-cus-tom (-ed)
ache
achieve (-ment)
ac-knowl-edge
ac-quaint-ance
ac-qui-esce
ac-quired
ac-tu-al
adapt
ad-di-tion (-al)
ad-dress
ad-e-quate
ad-journed
ad-just-ment
ad-mi-ra-ble
ad-mis-si-ble
ad-mit-tance
ad-van-ta-geous
ad-ver-tise-ment
ad-ver-tis-ing
ad-vice (n.)
ad-vis-able
ad-vise (v.)
ad-vis-er
ae-ri-al
af-fect
af-fi-da-vit
a-gainst
ag-gra-vate
ag-gres-sion
a-gree-able
a-gree-ment
aisle
al-co-hol
a-lign-ment
al-ley
al-lot-ted
al-low-ance
all right
al-most
al-ready
al-though
al-to-geth-er
a-lu-mi-num
al-um-nus
al-ways
am-a-teur
a-mend-ment
a-mong
a-mount
a-nal-y-sis
an-a-lyze
an-cient
an-ec-dote
an-es-thet-ic
an-gle
an-ni-hi-late
an-ni-ver-sa-ry
an-nounce
an-noy-ance
an-nu-al
a-noint
a-non-y-mous
an-swer
ant-arc-tic
an-tic-i-pate
anx-i-ety
anx-ious
a-part-ment
a-pol-o-gize
ap-pa-ra-tus
ap-par-ent (-ly)
ap-peal
ap-pear-ance
ap-pe-tite
ap-pli-ance
ap-pli-ca-ble
ap-pli-ca-tion
ap-point-ment
ap-prais-al
ap-pre-ci-ate
ap-proach
ap-pro-pri-ate
ap-prov-al
ap-prox-i-mate-ly
ap-ti-tude
ar-chi-tect
arc-tic
ar-gu-ment
a-rith-me-tic
a-rouse
ar-range-ment
ar-riv-al
ar-ti-cle
ar-ti-fi-cial
as-cend
as-cer-tain
as-i-nine
as-sas-sin
as-sess (-ment)
as-sign-ment
as-sist-ance
as-so-ci-ate
as-so-ci-a-tion
as-sume
as-sur-ance
as-ter-isk
ath-lete
ath-let-ic
at-tach
at-tack (-ed)
at-tempt
at-tend-ance
at-ten-tion
at-ti-tude
at-tor-ney
at-trac-tive
au-di-ble
au-di-ence
au-dit
au-thor-i-ty
au-to-mo-bile
au-tumn
aux-il-ia-ry
a-vail-a-ble
av-er-age
aw-ful
aw-ful-ly
awk-ward

B

bac-ca-lau-re-ate
bach-e-lor
bag-gage
bal-ance
bal-loon
bal-lot
ba-nan-a
ban-dage
bank-rupt
bar-gain
bar-rel
base-ment
ba-sis
bat-tery
beau-ti-ful
beau-ty
be-com-ing
beg-gar
be-gin-ning
be-hav-ior
be-ing
be-lief
be-lieve
ben-e-fi-cial
ben-e-fit (-ed)
be-tween
bi-cy-cle
bis-cuit
bliz-zard
book-keep-er
bought
bouil-lon
bound-a-ry
break-fast
breath (n.)
breathe (v.)
brief
bril-liant
Brit-ain
bro-chure
brought
bruise
bud-get
bul-le-tin
buoy-ant
bu-reau
bur-glar
bury
busi-ness
busy

C

caf-e-te-ria
caf-feine
cal-en-dar
cam-paign
can-celed
can-di-date
can-is-ter
ca-noe
ca-pac-i-ty
cap-i-tal
cap-i-tol
cap-tain
car-bu-ret-or
ca-reer
car-i-ca-ture
car-riage
cash-ier
cas-se-role
cas-u-al-ty
cat-a-log
ca-tas-tro-phe
caught
cav-al-ry
cel-e-bra-tion

cem-e-ter-y
cen-sus
cen-tu-ry
cer-tain
cer-tif-i-cate
ces-sa-tion
chal-lenge
chan-cel-lor
change-a-ble
char-ac-ter (-is-tic)
chauf-feur
chief
chim-ney
choc-o-late
choice
choose
Chris-tian
cir-cuit
cir-cu-lar
cir-cum-stance
civ-i-li-za-tion
cli-en-tele
cli-mate
climb
clothes
coach
co-coa
co-er-cion
col-lar
col-lat-er-al
col-lege
col-le-giate
col-lo-qui-al
colo-nel
col-or
co-los-sal
col-umn
com-e-dy
com-ing
com-mence
com-mer-cial
com-mis-sion
com-mit
com-mit-ment
com-mit-ted
com-mit-tee
com-mu-ni-cate
com-mu-ni-ty
com-par-a-tive
com-par-i-son
com-pel
com-pe-tent
com-pe-ti-tion
com-pet-i-tive-ly
com-plain
com-ple-ment
com-plete-ly
com-plex-ion
com-pli-ment
com-pro-mise
con-cede
con-ceive
con-cern-ing
con-cert
con-ces-sion
con-clude
con-crete
con-curred
con-cur-rence
con-demn
con-de-scend
con-di-tion
con-fer-ence
con-ferred
con-fi-dence
con-fi-den-tial
con-grat-u-late
con-science
con-sci-en-tious
con-scious
con-sen-sus
con-se-quence
con-ser-va-tive
con-sid-er-ably
con-sign-ment
con-sis-tent
con-sti-tu-tion
con-tempt-ible
con-tin-u-al-ly
con-tin-ue
con-tin-u-ous
con-trol
con-tro-ver-sy
con-ven-ience
con-vince
cool-ly
co-op-er-ate
cor-dial
cor-po-ra-tion
cor-re-late
cor-re-spond
cor-re-spond-ence
cor-rob-o-rate
cough
coun-cil
coun-sel
coun-ter-feit
coun-try
cour-age
cou-ra-geous
cour-te-ous
cour-te-sy
cous-in
cov-er-age
cred-i-tor
cri-sis
crit-i-cism
crit-i-cize
cru-el
cu-ri-os-i-ty
cu-ri-ous
cur-rent
cur-ric-u-lum
cus-tom
cus-tom-ary
cus-tom-er
cyl-in-der

D

dai-ly
dair-y
dealt
debt-or
de-ceased
de-ceit-ful
de-ceive
de-cid-ed
de-ci-sion
dec-la-ra-tion
dec-o-rate
de-duct-i-ble
de-fend-ant
de-fense
de-ferred
def-i-cit
def-i-nite (-ly)
def-i-ni-tion
del-e-gate
de-li-cious
de-pend-ent
de-pos-i-tor
de-pot
de-scend
de-scribe
de-scrip-tion
de-sert
de-serve
de-sign
de-sir-able
de-sir-ous
de-spair
des-per-ate
de-spise
des-sert
de-te-ri-o-rate
de-ter-mine
de-vel-op
de-vel-op-ment
de-vice
de-vise
di-a-mond
di-a-phragm
di-ar-rhe-a
dic-tio-nary
dif-fer-ence
dif-fer-ent
dif-fi-cul-ty
di-lap-i-dat-ed
di-lem-ma
din-ing
di-plo-ma
di-rec-tor
dis-agree-able
dis-ap-pear
dis-ap-point
dis-ap-prove
dis-as-trous
dis-ci-pline
dis-cov-er
dis-crep-an-cy
dis-cuss
dis-cus-sion
dis-ease
dis-sat-is-fied
dis-si-pate
dis-tin-guish
dis-trib-ute
di-vide
di-vis-i-ble
di-vi-sion
doc-tor
doesn't
dom-i-nant
dor-mi-to-ry
doubt
drudg-ery
du-pli-cate
dye-ing
dy-ing

E

ea-ger-ly
ear-nest
eco-nom-i-cal
econ-o-my
ec-sta-sy
e-di-tion
ef-fer-ves-cent
ef-fi-ca-cy
ef-fi-cien-cy
eighth
ei-ther
e-lab-o-rate
e-lec-tric-i-ty
el-e-phant
el-i-gi-ble
e-lim-i-nate
el-lipse
em-bar-rass
e-mer-gen-cy
em-i-nent
em-pha-size
em-ploy-ee
em-ploy-ment
e-mul-sion
en-close
en-cour-age
en-deav-or
en-dorse-ment
en-gi-neer
En-glish
e-nor-mous
e-nough
en-ter-prise
en-ter-tain
en-thu-si-as-tic
en-tire-ly
en-trance
en-vel-op (v.)
en-ve-lope (n.)
en-vi-ron-ment
equip-ment
equipped
e-quiv-a-lent
es-pe-cial-ly
es-sen-tial
es-tab-lish
es-teemed
et-i-quette
ev-i-dence
ex-ag-ger-ate
ex-ceed
ex-cel-lent

ex-cept
ex-cep-tion-al-ly
ex-ces-sive
ex-cite
ex-ec-u-tive
ex-er-cise
ex-haust (-ed)
ex-hi-bi-tion
ex-hil-a-ra-tion
ex-is-tence
ex-or-bi-tant
ex-pect
ex-pe-di-tion
ex-pend-i-ture
ex-pen-sive
ex-pe-ri-ence
ex-plain
ex-pla-na-tion
ex-pres-sion
ex-qui-site
ex-ten-sion
ex-tinct
ex-traor-di-nar-y
ex-treme-ly

F

fa-cil-i-ties
fal-la-cy
fa-mil-iar
fa-mous
fas-ci-nate
fash-ion
fa-tigue (-d)
fau-cet
fa-vor-ite
fea-si-ble
fea-ture
Feb-ru-ar-y
fed-er-al
fem-i-nine
fer-tile
fic-ti-tious
field
fierce
fi-ery
fi-nal-ly
fi-nan-cial-ly
fo-li-age
for-ci-ble
for-eign
for-feit
for-go
for-mal-ly
for-mer-ly
for-tu-nate
for-ty
for-ward
foun-tain
fourth
frag-ile
fran-ti-cal-ly
freight
friend
ful-fill
fun-da-men-tal
fur-ther-more
fu-tile

G

gad-get
gan-grene
ga-rage
gas-o-line
gauge
ge-ne-al-o-gy
gen-er-al-ly
gen-er-ous
ge-nius
gen-u-ine
ge-og-ra-phy
ghet-to
ghost
glo-ri-ous
gnaw
go-ril-la
gov-ern-ment
gov-er-nor
gra-cious
grad-u-a-tion
gram-mar
grate-ful
grat-i-tude
grease
grief
griev-ous
gro-cery
grudge
grue-some
guar-an-tee
guard
guard-i-an
guer-ril-la
guess
guid-ance
guide
guilty
gym-na-si-um
gyp-sy
gy-ro-scope

H

hab-i-tat
ham-mer
hand-ker-chief
han-dle (-d)
hand-some
hap-haz-ard
hap-pen
hap-pi-ness
ha-rass
har-bor
hast-i-ly
hav-ing
haz-ard-ous
height
hem-or-rhage
hes-i-tate
hin-drance
his-to-ry
hoarse
hol-i-day
hon-or
hop-ing
hop-ping
horde
hor-ri-ble
hos-pi-tal
hu-mor-ous
hur-ried-ly
hy-drau-lic
hy-giene

I

i-am-bic
i-ci-cle
i-den-ti-cal
id-io-syn-cra-sy
il-leg-i-ble
il-lit-er-ate
il-lus-trate
im-ag-i-nary
im-ag-i-na-tive
im-ag-ine
im-i-ta-tion
im-me-di-ate-ly
im-mense
im-mi-grant
im-mor-tal
im-pa-tient
im-per-a-tive
im-por-tance
im-pos-si-ble
im-promp-tu
im-prove-ment
in-al-ien-able
in-ci-den-tal-ly
in-con-ve-nience
in-cred-i-ble
in-curred
in-def-i-nite-ly
in-del-ible
in-de-pend-ence
in-de-pend-ent
in-dict-ment
in-dis-pens-able
in-di-vid-u-al
in-duce-ment
in-dus-tri-al
in-dus-tri-ous
in-ev-i-ta-ble
in-fe-ri-or
in-ferred
in-fi-nite
in-flam-ma-ble
in-flu-en-tial
in-ge-nious
in-gen-u-ous
in-im-i-ta-ble
in-i-tial
ini-ti-a-tion
in-no-cence
in-no-cent
in-oc-u-la-tion
in-quir-y
in-stal-la-tion
in-stance
in-stead
in-sti-tute
in-struc-tor
in-sur-ance
in-tel-lec-tu-al
in-tel-li-gence
in-ten-tion
in-ter-cede
in-ter-est-ing
in-ter-fere
in-ter-mit-tent
in-ter-pret (-ed)
in-ter-rupt
in-ter-view
in-ti-mate
in-va-lid
in-ves-ti-gate
in-ves-tor
in-vi-ta-tion
ir-i-des-cent
ir-rel-e-vant
ir-re-sis-ti-ble
ir-rev-er-ent
ir-ri-gate
is-land
is-sue
i-tem-ized
i-tin-er-ar-y

J

jan-i-tor
jeal-ous (-y)
jeop-ar-dize
jew-el-ry
jour-nal
jour-ney
judg-ment
jus-tice
jus-ti-fi-able

K

kitch-en
knowl-edge
knuck-le

L

la-bel
lab-o-ra-to-ry
lac-quer
lan-guage
laugh
laun-dry
law-yer
league
lec-ture
le-gal
leg-i-ble
leg-is-la-ture
le-git-i-mate
lei-sure
length

let-ter-head
li-a-bil-i-ty
li-a-ble
li-ai-son
lib-er-al
li-brar-y
li-cense
lieu-ten-ant
light-ning
lik-able
like-ly
lin-eage
liq-ue-fy
liq-uid
lis-ten
lit-er-ary
lit-er-a-ture
live-li-hood
log-a-rithm
lone-li-ness
loose
lose
los-ing
lov-able
love-ly
lun-cheon
lux-u-ry

M

ma-chine
mag-a-zine
mag-nif-i-cent
main-tain
main-te-nance
ma-jor-i-ty
mak-ing
man-age-ment
ma-neu-ver
man-u-al
man-u-fac-ture
man-u-script
mar-riage
mar-shal
ma-te-ri-al
math-e-mat-ics
max-i-mum
may-or
mean-ness
meant
mea-sure
med-i-cine
me-di-eval
me-di-o-cre
me-di-um
mem-o-ran-dum
men-us
mer-chan-dise
mer-it
mes-sage
mile-age
mil-lion-aire
min-i-a-ture
min-i-mum
min-ute
mir-ror
mis-cel-la-neous
mis-chief
mis-chie-vous
mis-er-a-ble
mis-ery
mis-sile
mis-sion-ary
mis-spell
mois-ture
mol-e-cule
mo-men-tous
mo-not-o-nous
mon-u-ment
mort-gage
mu-nic-i-pal
mus-cle
mu-si-cian
mus-tache
mys-te-ri-ous

N

na-ive
nat-u-ral-ly
nec-es-sary
ne-ces-si-ty
neg-li-gi-ble
ne-go-ti-ate
neigh-bor-hood
nev-er-the-less
nick-el
niece
nine-teenth
nine-ty
no-tice-able
no-to-ri-ety
nu-cle-ar
nui-sance

O

o-be-di-ence
o-bey
o-blige
ob-sta-cle
oc-ca-sion
oc-ca-sion-al-ly
oc-cu-pant
oc-cur
oc-curred
oc-cur-rence
of-fense
of-fi-cial
of-ten
o-mis-sion
o-mit-ted
op-er-ate
o-pin-ion
op-po-nent
op-por-tu-ni-ty
op-po-site
op-ti-mism
or-di-nance
or-di-nar-i-ly
orig-i-nal
out-ra-geous

P

pag-eant
pam-phlet
par-a-dise
para-graph
par-al-lel
par-a-lyze
pa-ren-the-ses
pa-ren-the-sis
par-lia-ment
par-tial
par-tic-i-pant
par-tic-i-pate
par-tic-u-lar-ly
pas-time
pa-tience
pa-tron-age
pe-cu-liar
per-ceive
per-haps
per-il
per-ma-nent
per-mis-si-ble
per-pen-dic-u-lar
per-se-ver-ance
per-sis-tent
per-son-al (-ly)
per-son-nel
per-spi-ra-tion
per-suade
phase
phe-nom-e-non
phi-los-o-phy
phy-si-cian
piece
planned
pla-teau
plau-si-ble
play-wright
pleas-ant
plea-sure
pneu-mo-nia
pol-i-ti-cian
pos-sess
pos-ses-sion
pos-si-ble
prac-ti-cal-ly
prai-rie
pre-cede
pre-ce-dence
pre-ced-ing
pre-cious
pre-cise-ly
pre-ci-sion
pre-de-ces-sor
pref-er-a-ble
pref-er-ence
pre-ferred
prej-u-dice
pre-lim-i-nar-y
pre-mi-um
prep-a-ra-tion
pres-ence
prev-a-lent
pre-vi-ous
prim-i-tive
prin-ci-pal
prin-ci-ple
pri-or-i-ty
pris-on-er
priv-i-lege
prob-a-bly
pro-ce-dure
pro-ceed
pro-fes-sor
prom-i-nent
pro-nounce
pro-nun-ci-a-tion
pro-pa-gan-da
pros-e-cute
pro-tein
psy-chol-o-gy
pub-lic-ly
pump-kin
pur-chase
pur-sue
pur-su-ing
pur-suit

Q

qual-i-fied
qual-i-ty
quan-ti-ty
quar-ter
ques-tion-naire
quite
quo-tient

R

raise
rap-port
re-al-ize
re-al-ly
re-cede
re-ceipt
re-ceive
re-ceived
rec-i-pe
re-cip-i-ent
rec-og-ni-tion
rec-og-nize
rec-om-mend
re-cur-rence
ref-er-ence
re-ferred
reg-is-tra-tion
re-hearse
reign
re-im-burse
rel-e-vant
re-lieve
re-li-gious
re-mem-ber
re-mem-brance
rem-i-nisce
ren-dez-vous
re-new-al
rep-e-ti-tion

rep-re-sen-ta-tive
req-ui-si-tion
res-er-voir
re-sis-tance
re-spect-a-bly
re-spect-ful-ly
re-spec-tive-ly
re-spon-si-bil-i-ty
res-tau-rant
rheu-ma-tism
rhyme
rhythm
ri-dic-u-lous
route

S

sac-ri-le-gious
safe-ty
sal-a-ry
sand-wich
sat-is-fac-to-ry
Sat-ur-day
scarce-ly
scene
scen-er-y
sched-ule
schol-ar-ship
sci-ence
scis-sors
sec-re-tary
seize
sen-si-ble
sen-tence
sen-ti-nel
sep-a-rate
ser-geant
sev-er-al
se-vere-ly
shep-herd
sher-iff
shin-ing
siege
sig-nif-i-cance
sim-i-lar
si-mul-ta-ne-ous
since
sin-cere-ly
ski-ing
sol-dier
sol-emn
so-phis-ti-cat-ed
soph-o-more
so-ror-i-ty
source
sou-ve-nir
spa-ghet-ti
spe-cif-ic
spec-i-men
speech
sphere
spon-sor
spon-ta-ne-ous
sta-tion-ary
sta-tion-ery
sta-tis-tic
stat-ue
stat-ure
stat-ute
stom-ach
stopped
straight
strat-e-gy
strength
stretched
study-ing
sub-si-dize
sub-stan-tial
sub-sti-tute
sub-tle
suc-ceed
suc-cess
suf-fi-cient
sum-ma-rize
su-per-fi-cial
su-per-in-tend-ent
su-pe-ri-or-i-ty
su-per-sede
sup-ple-ment
sup-pose
sure-ly
sur-prise
sur-veil-lance
sur-vey
sus-cep-ti-ble
sus-pi-cious
sus-te-nance
syl-la-ble
sym-met-ri-cal
sym-pa-thy
sym-pho-ny
symp-tom
syn-chro-nous

T

tar-iff
tech-nique
tele-gram
tem-per-a-ment
tem-per-a-ture
tem-po-rary
ten-den-cy
ten-ta-tive
ter-res-tri-al
ter-ri-ble
ter-ri-to-ry
the-ater
their
there-fore
thief
thor-ough (-ly)
though
through-out
tired
to-bac-co
to-geth-er
to-mor-row
tongue
to-night
touch
tour-na-ment
tour-ni-quet
to-ward
trag-e-dy
trai-tor
tran-quil-iz-er
trans-ferred
trea-sur-er
tru-ly
Tues-day
tu-i-tion
typ-i-cal
typ-ing

U

unan-i-mous
un-con-scious
un-doubt-ed-ly
un-for-tu-nate-ly
unique
u-ni-son
uni-ver-si-ty
un-nec-es-sary
un-prec-e-dent-ed
un-til
up-per
ur-gent
us-able
use-ful
using
usu-al-ly
u-ten-sil
u-til-ize

V

va-can-cies
va-ca-tion
vac-u-um
vague
valu-able
va-ri-ety
var-i-ous
veg-e-ta-ble
ve-hi-cle
veil
ve-loc-i-ty
ven-geance
vi-cin-i-ty
view
vig-i-lance
vil-lain
vi-o-lence
vis-i-bil-i-ty
vis-i-ble
vis-i-tor
voice
vol-ume
vol-un-tary
vol-un-teer

W

wan-der
war-rant
weath-er
Wednes-day
weird
wel-come
wel-fare
where
wheth-er
which
whole
whol-ly
whose
width
wom-en
worth-while
wor-thy
wreck-age
wres-tler
writ-ing
writ-ten
wrought

Y

yel-low
yes-ter-day
yield

Steps to Becoming a Better Speller

1. **Be patient.** Becoming a good speller takes time.
2. **Check the correct pronunciation of each word you are attempting to spell.**
   Knowing the correct pronunciation of each word can help you to remember its spelling.
3. **Note the meaning and history of each word as you are checking the dictionary for the pronunciation.**
   Knowing the meaning and history of a word provides you with a better notion of how the word is properly used, and it can help you remember the word's spelling.
4. **Before you close the dictionary, practice spelling the word.**
   You can do so by looking away from the page and trying to "see" the word in your "mind's eye." Write the word on a piece of paper. Check the spelling in the dictionary and repeat the process until you are able to spell the word correctly.
5. **Learn some spelling rules.**
   The four rules in this handbook (page 621) are four of the most useful—although there are others.
6. **Make a list of the words that you misspell.**
   Select the first ten words and practice spelling them.
   First: Read each word carefully; then write it on a piece of paper. Look at the written word to see that it's spelled correctly. Repeat the process for those words that you misspelled.
   Then: Ask someone to read the words to you so you can write them again. Then check for misspellings. Repeat both steps with your next ten words.
7. **Write often.**
   As noted educator Frank Smith said,

> *"There is little point in learning to spell if you have little intention of writing."*

Mechanics Exercises:

Spelling

Correct any spelling errors in the following letter by writing the line number and the correct spelling of the word(s).

Dear Dr. Hanson: 1

I wanted to pass along an updat regarding my project for the Undergraduate 2
Recerach Conference. I'm makin great progress, but I have a few questions. 3
I'll start with my progress: 4

- As of Febuary 21, my primary and secondary research is in excelent 5
order. 6
- I've completed writng, revising, and editing my literature review. 7
- I beleive I will finish a first draft by the end of the week. 8

Here are my questions for you: 9

- Should I make a PowerPoint version for my presentation? 10
- Who is in charge of advertiseing for the event? 11
- How soon from now will room asignments be announced? 12

I've really enjoyed researching the relatinship between stress and eating 13
habits among college students. You'll find the introduction to my 14
presentation in the enclosed pamflet. 15

Thanks for takin the time to read over these materials. 16

Sinserely, 17
Jim White 18

Chapter 30

Using the Right Word

The following glossary contains words that are commonly confused.

a, an Use *a* as the article before words that begin with consonant sounds and before words that begin with the long vowel sound *u* (yü). Use *an* before words that begin with other vowel sounds. 629.1

An older student showed Kris **an** easier way to get to class.

A uniform is required attire for **a** cafeteria worker.

a lot, alot, allot *Alot* is not a word; *a lot* (two words) is a vague descriptive phrase that should be used sparingly, especially in formal writing. *Allot* means to give someone a share. 629.2

Prof Dubi **allots** each of us five spelling errors per semester, and he thinks that's **a lot**.

accept, except The verb *accept* means "to receive or believe"; the preposition *except* means "other than." 629.3

The instructor **accepted** Mike's story about being late, but she wondered why no one **except** Mike had forgotten about the change to daylight saving time.

adapt, adopt, adept *Adapt* means "to adjust or change to fit"; *adopt* means "to choose and treat as your own" (a child, an idea). *Adept* is an adjective meaning "proficient or well trained." 629.4

After much thought and deliberation, we agreed to **adopt** the black Lab from the shelter. Now we have to agree on how to **adapt** our lifestyle to fit our new roommate, who is quite **adept** at getting food off the kitchen counter.

adverse, averse *Adverse* means "hostile, unfavorable, or harmful." *Averse* means "to have a definite feeling of distaste—disinclined." 629.5

Groans and other **adverse** reactions were noted as the new students, **averse** to strenuous exercise, were ushered past the X-5000 pump-and-crunch machine.

advice, advise *Advice* is a noun meaning "information or recommendation"; *advise* is a verb meaning "to recommend." 629.6

Successful people will often give you sound **advice**, so I **advise** you to listen.

affect, effect *Affect* means "to influence"; the noun *effect* means "the result." 629.7

The employment growth in a field will **affect** your chances of getting a job. The **effect** may be a new career choice.

630.1 **aid, aide** As a verb, *aid* means "to help"; as a noun, *aid* means "the help given." An *aide* is a person who acts as an assistant.

630.2 **all, of** *Of* is seldom needed after *all.*

All the reports had an error in them.

All the speakers spoke English.

All of us voted to reschedule the meeting.
(Here *of* is needed for the sentence to make sense.)

630.3 **all right, alright** *Alright* is the incorrect form of *all right.* (***Note:*** The following are spelled correctly: *always, altogether, already, almost.*)

630.4 **allude, elude** *Allude* means "to indirectly refer to or hint at something"; *elude* means "to escape attention or understanding altogether."

Ravi often **alluded** to wanting a supper invitation by mentioning the "awfully good" smells from the kitchen. These hints never **eluded** Ma's good heart.

630.5 **allusion, illusion** *Allusion* is an indirect reference to something or someone, especially in literature; *illusion* is a false picture or idea.

Did you recognize the **allusion** to David in the reading assignment? Until I read that part, I was under the **illusion** that the young boy would run away from the bully.

630.6 **already, all ready** *Already* is an adverb meaning "before this time" or "by this time." *All ready* is an adjective form meaning "fully prepared." (***Note:*** Use *all ready* if you can substitute *ready* alone in the sentence.)

By the time I was a junior in high school, I had **already** taken my SATs. That way, I was **all ready** to apply early to college.

630.7 **altogether, all together** *Altogether* means "entirely." *All together* means "in a group" or "all at once." (***Note:*** Use *all together* if you can substitute *together* alone in the sentence.)

All together there are 35,000 job titles to choose from. That's **altogether** too many to even think about.

630.8 **among, between** *Among* is used when emphasizing distribution throughout a body or a group of three or more; *between* is used when emphasizing distribution to two individuals.

There was discontent **among** the relatives after learning that their aunt had divided her entire fortune **between** a canary and a favorite waitress at the local cafe.

630.9 **amoral, immoral** *Amoral* means "neither moral (right) nor immoral (wrong)"; *immoral* means "wrong, or in conflict with traditional values."

Carnivores are **amoral** in their hunt; poachers are **immoral** in theirs.

630.10 **amount, number** *Amount* is used for bulk measurement. *Number* is used to count separate units. (See also fewer.)

The **number** of new instructors hired next year will depend on the **amount** of revenue raised by the new sales tax.

and etc. Don't use *and* before *etc.* since *et cetera* means "and the rest." 631.1

Did you remember your textbook, notebook, handout, **etc.**?

annual, biannual, semiannual, biennial, perennial An *annual* event happens once every year. A *biannual* event happens twice a year (*semiannual* is the same as *biannual*). A *biennial* event happens every two years. A *perennial* event happens throughout the year, every year. 631.2

anxious, eager Both words mean "looking forward to," but *anxious* also connotes fear or concern. 631.3

The professor is **eager** to move into the new building, but she's a little **anxious** that students won't be able to find her new office.

anymore, any more *Anymore* (an adverb) means "any longer"; *any more* means "any additional." 631.4

We won't use that textbook **anymore**; call if you have **any more** questions.

any one (of), anyone *Any one* means "any one of a number of people, places, or things"; *anyone* is a pronoun meaning "any person." 631.5

Choose **any one** of the proposed weekend schedules. **Anyone** wishing to work on Saturday instead of Sunday may do so.

appraise, apprise *Appraise* means "to determine value." *Apprise* means "to inform." 631.6

Because of the tax assessor's recent **appraisal** of our home, we were **apprised** of an increase in our property tax.

as Don't use *as* in place of *whether* or *if.* 631.7

I don't know **as** I'll accept the offer. (Incorrect)

I don't know **whether** I'll accept the offer. (Correct)

Don't use *as* when it is unclear whether it means *because* or *when.*

We rowed toward shore **as** it started raining. (Unclear)

We rowed toward shore **because** it started raining. (Correct)

assure, ensure, insure (See insure.)

bad, badly *Bad* is an adjective, used both before nouns and as a predicate adjective after linking verbs. *Badly* is an adverb. 631.8

Christina felt **bad** about serving us **bad** food.

Larisa played **badly** today.

beside, besides *Beside* means "by the side of." *Besides* means "in addition to." 631.9

Besides the two suitcases you've already loaded into the trunk, remember the smaller one **beside** the van.

between, among (See among.)

bring, take *Bring* suggests the action is directed toward the speaker; *take* suggests the action is directed away from the speaker. 631.10

If you're not going to **bring** the video to class, **take** it back to the resource center.

Using the Right Word Exercises:

Using the Right Word: I

A. Selecting the Right Word

Choose the correct word from those in parentheses for each sentence.

1. Hunter was *(accepted, excepted)* into a summer internship program at an accounting firm.
2. The celebrity was unable to (*allude, elude*) the paparazzi outside of the night club.
3. Juan is quite (*adapt, adopt, adept*) at playing the electric guitar.
4. Does (*anyone, any one*) know of a scenic location for a Sunday picnic?
5. I feel (*anxious, eager*) around people who are loud and outgoing.
6. Today was a good day because it did not go as (*bad, badly*) as yesterday.
7. (*Altogether, All together*) thirty-five people waited outside of the movie theater for the premiere of the new movie.
8. Are you under the (*allusion, illusion*) that the young businesswoman will abandon her friends?
9. The new round of layoffs may (*affect, effect*) my position with the company.
10. What (*amount, number*) of money will it take to purchase a plane ticket to France?

B. Replacing Incorrect Words

For each sentence below, identify the misused words and correct them.

1. Phil appraised his buddy about the affects of pushing a car more than 3,000 miles without a oil change.
2. Do you mean to elude that I'm in need of some fashion advise?
3. A strong friendship among Cary and Nyssa helped get them through an averse situation.

can, may In formal contexts, *can* is used to mean "being able to do"; *may* is used to mean "having permission to do." 633.1

May I borrow your bicycle to get to the library? Then I **can** start working on our group project.

capital, capitol The noun *capital* refers to a city or to money. The adjective *capital* means "major or important" or "seat of government." *Capitol* refers to a building. 633.2

The **capitol** is in the **capital** city for a **capital** reason. The city government contributed **capital** for the building expense.

cent, sent, scent *Cent* is a coin; *sent* is the past tense of the verb "send"; *scent* is an odor or a smell. 633.3

For forty-nine **cents**, I **sent** my friend a love poem in a perfumed envelope. She adored the **scent** but hated the poem.

chord, cord *Chord* may mean "an emotion or a feeling," but it also may mean "the combination of three or more tones sounded at the same time," as with a guitar *chord*. A *cord* is a string or a rope. 633.4

The guitar player strummed the opening **chord**, which struck a responsive **chord** with the audience.

chose, choose *Chose* (choz) is the past tense of the verb *choose* (chüz). 633.5

For generations, people **chose** their careers based on their parents' careers; now people **choose** their careers based on the job market.

climactic, climatic *Climactic* refers to the climax, or high point, of an event; *climatic* refers to the climate, or weather conditions. 633.6

Because we are using the open-air amphitheater, **climatic** conditions will just about guarantee the wind gusts we need for the **climactic** third act.

coarse, course *Coarse* means "of inferior quality, rough, or crude"; *course* means "a direction or a path taken." *Course* also means "a class or a series of studies." 633.7

A basic writing **course** is required of all students.

Due to years of woodworking, the instructor's hands are rather **coarse**.

compare with, compare to Things in the same category are *compared with* each other; things in different categories are *compared to* each other. 633.8

Compare Christopher Marlowe's plays **with** William Shakespeare's plays.

My brother **compared** reading *The Tempest* **to** visiting another country.

complement, compliment *Complement* means "to complete or go well with." *Compliment* means "to offer an expression of admiration or praise." 633.9

We wanted to **compliment** Zach on his decorating efforts; the bright yellow walls **complement** the purple carpet.

comprehensible, comprehensive *Comprehensible* means "capable of being understood"; *comprehensive* means "covering a broad range, or inclusive." 633.10

The theory is **comprehensible** only to those who have a **comprehensive** knowledge of physics.

634.1 **comprise, compose** *Comprise* means "to contain or consist of"; *compose* means "to create or form by bringing parts together."

Fruitcake **comprises** a variety of nuts, candied fruit, and spice.

Fruitcake is **composed of** (not *comprised of*) a variety of ingredients.

634.2 **conscience, conscious** A *conscience* gives one the capacity to know right from wrong. *Conscious* means "awake or alert, not sleeping or comatose."

Your **conscience** will guide you, but you have to be **conscious** to hear what it's "saying."

634.3 **continual, continuous** *Continual* often implies that something is happening often, recurring; *continuous* usually implies that something keeps happening, uninterrupted.

The **continuous** loud music during the night gave the building manager not only a headache but also **continual** phone calls.

634.4 **counsel, council, consul** When used as a noun, *counsel* means "advice"; when used as a verb, *counsel* means "to advise." *Council* refers to a group that advises. A *consul* is a government official appointed to reside in a foreign country.

The city **council** was asked to **counsel** our student **council** on running an efficient meeting. Their **counsel** was very helpful.

634.5 **decent, descent, dissent** *Decent* means "good." *Descent* is the process of going or stepping downward. *Dissent* means "disagreement."

The food was **decent**.

The elevator's fast **descent** clogged my ears.

Their **dissent** over the decisions was obvious in their sullen expressions.

634.6 **desert, dessert** *Desert* is barren wilderness. *Dessert* is food served at the end of a meal. The verb *desert* means "to abandon."

634.7 **different from, different than** Use *different from* in formal writing; use either form in informal or colloquial settings.

Rafael's interpretation was **different from** Andrea's.

634.8 **discreet, discrete** *Discreet* means "showing good judgment, unobtrusive, modest"; *discrete* means "distinct, separate."

The essay question had three **discrete** parts.

Her roommate had apparently never heard of quiet, **discreet** conversation.

634.9 **disinterested, uninterested** Both words mean "not interested." However, *disinterested* is also used to mean "unbiased or impartial."

A person chosen as an arbitrator must be a **disinterested** party.

Professor Eldridge was **uninterested** in our complaints about the assignment.

effect, affect (See affect.)

634.10 **elicit, illicit** *Elicit* is a verb meaning "to bring out." *Illicit* is an adjective meaning "unlawful."

It took a hand signal to **elicit** the **illicit** exchange of cash for drugs.

eminent, imminent *Eminent* means "prominent, conspicuous, or famous"; *imminent* means "ready or threatening to happen." 635.1

With the island's government about to collapse, assassination attempts on several **eminent** officials seemed **imminent**.

ensure, insure, assure (See insure.)

except, accept (See accept.)

explicit, implicit *Explicit* means "expressed directly or clearly defined"; *implicit* means "implied or unstated." 635.2

The professor **explicitly** asked that the experiment be wrapped up on Monday, **implicitly** demanding that her lab assistants work on the weekend.

farther, further *Farther* refers to a physical distance; *further* refers to additional time, quantity, or degree. 635.3

Further research showed that walking **farther** rather than faster would improve his health.

fewer, less *Fewer* refers to the number of separate units; *less* refers to bulk quantity. 635.4

Because of spell checkers, students can produce papers containing **fewer** errors in **less** time.

figuratively, literally *Figuratively* means "in a metaphorical or analogous way—describing something by comparing it to something else"; *literally* means "actually." 635.5

The lab was **literally** filled with sulfurous gases—**figuratively** speaking, dragon's breath.

first, firstly Both words are adverbs meaning "before another in time" or "in the first place." However, do not use *firstly,* which is stiff and unnatural sounding. 635.6

Firstly I want to see the manager. (Incorrect)

First I want to see the manager. (Correct)

Note: When enumerating, use the forms *first, second, third, next, last*—without the *ly.*

fiscal, physical *Fiscal* means "related to financial matters"; *physical* means "related to material things." 635.7

The school's **fiscal** work is handled by its accounting staff.

The **physical** work is handled by its maintenance staff.

for, fore, four *For* is a conjunction meaning "because" or is a preposition used to indicate the object or recipient of something; *fore* means "earlier" or "the front"; *four* is the word for the number 4. 635.8

The crew brought treats **for** the barge's **four** dogs, who always enjoy the breeze at the **fore** of the vessel.

former, latter When two things are being discussed, *former* refers to the first thing, and *latter* to the second. 635.9

Our choices are going to a movie or eating at the Pizza Palace: The **former** is too expensive, and the **latter** too fattening.

Using the Right Word Exercises:

Using the Right Word: II

A. Selecting the Right Word

Choose the correct word from those in parentheses for each sentence.

1. The (*capital, capitol*) building looked radiant with the fall sunshine beaming on its white dome.
2. That jacket would (*complement, compliment*) the colors of your dress.
3. The museum had three (*discreet, discrete*) levels, each with a different theme.
4. Darren took (*counsel, council, consul*) from his internship coordinator regarding his career path.
5. Would you (*comprise, compose*) an updated report on our position in the New York power and electric industry?
6. Our destination along Interstate 43 was (*farther, further*) than we expected.
7. The (*climactic, climatic*) point of the baseball game occurred when Vicki caught a foul ball.
8. Our (*decent, descent, dissent*) of Pike's Peak Mountain was a scary experience.
9. I was so sleepy that I felt barely (*conscience, conscious*).
10. The (*cent, sent, scent*) coming from the garbage left us all gagging for fresh air.

B. Replacing Incorrect Words

For each sentence below, identify the misused words and correct them.

1. Our second coarse was descent, but the desert was the real winner.
2. The farther we delay restructuring our finances, the worse our physical situation will be.
3. My aunt is firstly a good judge of character and second an imminent authority on all things Milwaukee.

good, well *Good* is an adjective; *well* is nearly always an adverb. (When used to indicate state of health, *well* is an adjective.) 637.1

A **good** job offers opportunities for advancement, especially for those who do their jobs **well**.

heal, heel *Heal* (a verb) means "to mend or restore to health"; a *heel* (noun) is the back part of a human foot. 637.2

healthful, healthy *Healthful* means "causing or improving health"; *healthy* means "possessing health." 637.3

Healthful foods and regular exercise build **healthy** bodies.

I, me *I* is a subject pronoun; *me* is used as an object of a preposition, a direct object, or an indirect object. (See 542.1.) (A good way to know if *I* or *me* should be used in a compound subject is to eliminate the other subject; the sentence should make sense with the pronoun—*I* or *me*—alone.) 637.4

My roommate and **me** went to the library last night. (Incorrect)

My roommate and **I** went to the library last night. (Correct: Eliminate "my roommate and"; the sentence still makes sense.)

Rasheed gave the concert tickets to Erick and **I**. (Incorrect)

Rasheed gave the concert tickets to Erick and **me**. (Correct: Eliminate "Erick and"; the sentence still makes sense.)

illusion, allusion (See allusion.)

immigrate (to), emigrate (from) *Immigrate* means "to come into a new country or environment." *Emigrate* means "to go out of one country to live in another." 637.5

Immigrating to a new country is a challenging experience.

People **emigrating** from their homelands face unknown challenges.

imminent, eminent (See eminent.)

imply, infer *Imply* means "to suggest without saying outright"; *infer* means "to draw a conclusion from facts." (A writer or a speaker *implies;* a reader or a listener *infers.*) 637.6

Dr. Rufus **implied** I should study more; I **inferred** he meant my grades had to improve, or I'd be repeating the class.

ingenious, ingenuous *Ingenious* means "intelligent, discerning, clever"; *ingenuous* means "unassuming, natural, showing childlike innocence and candidness." 637.7

Gretchen devised an **ingenious** plan to work and receive college credit for it.

Ramón displays an **ingenuous** quality that attracts others.

insure, ensure, assure *Insure* means "to secure from financial harm or loss," *ensure* means "to make certain of something," and *assure* means "to put someone's mind at rest." 637.8

Plenty of studying generally **ensures** academic success.

Nicole **assured** her father that she had **insured** her new car.

interstate, intrastate *Interstate* means "existing between two or more states"; *intrastate* means "existing within a state." 637.9

638.1 **irregardless, regardless** *Irregardless* is a nonstandard synonym for *regardless.*

Irregardless of his circumstance, José is cheerful. (Incorrect)

Regardless of his circumstance, José is cheerful. (Correct)

638.2 **it's, its** *It's* is the contraction of "it is." *Its* is the possessive form of "it."

It's not hard to see why my husband feeds that alley cat; **its** pitiful limp and mournful mewing would melt any heart.

638.3 **later, latter** *Later* means "after a period of time." *Latter* refers to the second of two things mentioned.

The **latter** of the two restaurants you mentioned sounds good.
Let's meet there **later.**

638.4 **lay, lie** *Lay* means "to place." *Lay* is a transitive verb. (See 544.2.) Its principal parts are *lay, laid, laid.* (See 549.)

If you **lay** another book on my table, I won't have room for anything else.

Yesterday, you **laid** two books on the table.

Over the last few days, you must have **laid** at least twenty books there.

Lie means "to recline." *Lie* is an intransitive verb. (See 544.2.) Its principal parts are *lie, lay, lain.*

The cat **lies** down anywhere it pleases.

It **lay** down yesterday on my tax forms.

It has **lain** down many times on the kitchen table.

638.5 **learn, teach** *Learn* means "to acquire information"; *teach* means "to give information."

Sometimes it's easier to **teach** someone else a lesson than it is to **learn** one yourself.

638.6 **leave, let** *Leave* means "to allow something to remain behind." *Let* means "to permit."

Please **let** me help you carry that chair; otherwise, **leave** it for the movers to pick up.

638.7 **lend, borrow** *Lend* means "to give for temporary use"; *borrow* means "to receive for temporary use."

I asked Haddad to **lend** me $15 for an ink cartridge, but he said I'd have to find someone else to **borrow** the money from.

less, fewer (See fewer.)

638.8 **liable, libel** *Liable* is an adjective meaning "responsible according to the law" or "exposed to an adverse action"; the noun *libel* is a written defamatory statement about someone, and the verb *libel* means "to publish or make such a statement."

Supermarket tabloids, **liable** for ruining many a reputation, make a practice of **libeling** the rich and the famous.

638.9 **liable, likely** *Liable* means "responsible according to the law" or "exposed to an adverse action"; *likely* means "in all probability."

Rain seems **likely** today, but if we cancel the game, we are still **liable** for paying the referees.

like, as *Like* should not be used in place of *as. Like* is a preposition, which is followed by its object (a noun, a pronoun, or a noun phrase). *As* is a subordinating conjunction, which introduces a clause. Do not use *like* as a subordinating conjunction. Use *as* instead. 639.1

You don't know her **like** I do. (Incorrect)

You don't know her **as** I do. (Correct)

Like the others in my study group, I do my work as any serious student would—carefully and thoroughly. (Correct)

literally, figuratively (See figuratively.)

loose, lose, loss The adjective *loose* (lüs) means "free, untied, unrestricted"; the verb *lose* (lüz) means "to misplace or fail to find or control"; the noun *loss* (los) means "something that is misplaced and cannot be found." 639.2

Her sadness at the **loss** of her longtime companion caused her to **lose** weight, and her clothes felt uncomfortably **loose**.

may, can (See can.)

maybe, may be Use *maybe* as an adverb meaning "perhaps;" use *may be* as a verb phrase. 639.3

She **may be** the computer technician we've been looking for. **Maybe** she will upgrade the software and memory.

miner, minor A *miner* digs in the ground for ore. A *minor* is a person who is not legally an adult. The adjective *minor* means "of no great importance." 639.4

The use of **minors** as coal **miners** is no **minor** problem.

number, amount (See amount.)

OK, okay This expression, spelled either way, is appropriate in informal writing; however, avoid using it in papers, reports, or formal correspondence of any kind. 639.5

Your proposal is satisfactory [not okay] on most levels.

oral, verbal *Oral* means "uttered with the mouth"; *verbal* means "relating to or consisting of words and the comprehension of words." 639.6

The actor's **oral** abilities were outstanding, her pronunciation and intonation impeccable, but I doubted the playwright's **verbal** skills after trying to decipher the play's meaning.

passed, past *Passed* is a verb. *Past* can be used as a noun, an adjective, or a preposition. 639.7

That little pickup truck **passed** my 'Vette! (verb)

My stepchildren hold on dearly to the **past**. (noun)

I'm sorry, but my **past** life is not your business. (adjective)

The officer drove **past** us, not noticing our flat tire. (preposition)

peace, piece *Peace* means "tranquility or freedom from war." A *piece* is a part or fragment. 639.8

Someone once observed that **peace** is not a condition, but a process—a process of building goodwill one **piece** at a time.

Using the Right Word Exercises:

Using the Right Word: III

A. Selecting the Right Word

Choose the correct word from those in parentheses for each sentence.

1. Raphael injured his (*heal, heel*) when he took out the trash shoeless.
2. (*Irregardless, Regardless*) of how you feel about the assignment, you have to get it done by Friday.
3. Could you (*borrow, lend*) me three quarters for laundry?
4. My car suffered (*miner, minor*) damages from last night's hailstorm.
5. You (*maybe, may be*) upset with me, but I hope you will soon forgive me.
6. Before you look to the future, you should recognize lessons from the (*passed, past*).
7. Can you (*insure, ensure, assure*) me that I will receive an annual review?
8. Andrew (*immigrated, emigrated*) from Australia.
9. The offender was found (*liable, libel*) for all medical expenses.
10. The Taj Mahal was incredible; I was most impressed by (*it's, its*) majesty.

B. Replacing Incorrect Words

For each sentence below, identify the misused words and correct them.

1. Despite feeling under the weather, Andre was good enough to give a verbal presentation at a company meeting.
2. Teresa inferred I should look for a new job, while I implied she meant I had no chance for a promotion.
3. Before you lie down another box, make sure the shelf is sturdy enough; otherwise it is liable to collapse.

MindTap® Practice skills that you have learned in this section and receive automatic feedback.

people, person Use *people* to refer to human populations, races, or groups; use *person* to refer to an individual or the physical body. 641.1

What the American **people** need is a good insect repellent.

The forest ranger recommends that we check our **persons** for wood ticks when we leave the woods.

percent, percentage *Percent* means "per hundred"; for example, 60 percent of 100 jelly beans would be 60 jelly beans. *Percentage* refers to a portion of the whole. Generally, use the word *percent* when it is preceded by a number. Use *percentage* when no number is used. 641.2

Each person's **percentage** of the reward amounted to $125—25 **percent** of the $500 offered by Crime Stoppers.

personal, personnel *Personal* (an adjective) means "private." *Personnel* (a noun) are people working at a particular job. 641.3

Although choosing a major is a **personal** decision, it can be helpful to consult with guidance **personnel**.

perspective, prospective *Perspective* (a noun) is a point of view or the capacity to view things realistically; *prospective* is an adjective meaning "expected in or related to the future." 641.4

From my immigrant neighbor's **perspective**, any job is a good job.

Prospective students wandered the campus on visitors' day.

pore, pour, poor The noun *pore* is an opening in the skin; the verb *pore* means "to gaze intently." *Pour* means "to move with a continuous flow." *Poor* means "needy or pitiable." 641.5

Pour hot water into a bowl, put your face over it, and let the steam open your **pores**. Your **poor** skin will thank you.

precede, proceed To *precede* means "to go or come before"; *proceed* means "to move on after having stopped" or "go ahead." 641.6

Our biology instructor often **preceded** his lecture with these words:

"OK, sponges, **proceed** to soak up more fascinating facts!"

principal, principle As an adjective, *principal* means "primary." As a noun, it can mean "a school administrator" or "a sum of money." A *principle* (noun) is an idea or a doctrine. 641.7

His **principal** gripe is lack of freedom. (adjective)

My son's **principal** expressed his concerns to the teachers. (noun)

After 20 years, the amount of interest was higher than the **principal**. (noun)

The **principle** of *caveat emptor* guides most consumer groups. (noun)

quiet, quit, quite *Quiet* is the opposite of noisy. *Quit* means "to stop or give up." *Quite* (an adverb) means "completely" or "to a considerable extent." 641.8

The meeting remained **quite quiet** when the boss told us he'd **quit**.

quote, quotation *Quote* is a verb; *quotation* is a noun. 641.9

The **quotation** I used was from Woody Allen. You may **quote** me on that.

real, very, really Do not use the adjective *real* in place of the adverbs *very* or *really*. 641.10

My friend's cake is usually **very** [not *real*] fresh, but this cake is **really** stale.

642.1 **right, write, wright, rite** *Right* means "correct or proper"; it also refers to that which a person has a legal claim to, as in *copyright*. *Write* means "to inscribe or record." A *wright* is a person who makes or builds something. *Rite* is a ritual or ceremonial act.

Did you **write** that it is the **right** of the **shipwright** to perform the **rite** of christening—breaking a bottle of champagne on the bow of the ship?

642.2 **scene, seen** *Scene* refers to the setting or location where something happens; it also may mean "sight or spectacle." *Seen* is the past participle of the verb "see."

An exhibitionist likes to be **seen** making a **scene**.

642.3 **set, sit** *Set* means "to place." *Sit* means "to put the body in a seated position." *Set* is a transitive verb; *sit* is an intransitive verb (See 544.2.).

How can you just **sit** there and watch as I **set** the table?

642.4 **sight, cite, site** *Sight* means "the act of seeing" (a verb) or "something that is seen" (a noun). *Cite* (a verb) means "to quote" or "to summon to court." *Site* means "a place or location" (noun) or "to place on a site" (verb).

After **sighting** the faulty wiring, the inspector **cited** the building contractor for breaking two city codes at a downtown work **site**.

642.5 **some, sum** *Some* refers to an unknown thing, an unspecified number, or a part of something. *Sum* is a certain amount of money or the result of adding numbers together.

Some of the students answered too quickly and came up with the wrong **sum**.

642.6 **stationary, stationery** *Stationary* means "not movable"; *stationery* refers to the paper and envelopes used to write letters.

Odina uses **stationery** that she can feed through her portable printer. Then she drops the mail into a **stationary** mail receptacle at the mall.

take, bring (See bring.)

teach, learn (See learn.)

642.7 **than, then** *Than* is used in a comparison; *then* is an adverb that tells when.

Study more **than** you think you need to. **Then** you will probably be satisfied with your grades.

642.8 **their, there, they're** *Their* is a possessive personal pronoun. *There* is an adverb used as a filler word or to point out location. *They're* is the contraction for "they are."

Look over **there**. **There** is a comfortable place for students to study for **their** exams, so **they're** more likely to do a good job.

642.9 **threw, through** *Threw* is the past tense of "throw." *Through* (a preposition) means "from one side of something to the other."

In a fit of frustration, Sachiko **threw** his cell phone right **through** the window.

642.10 **to, too, two** *To* is a preposition that can mean "in the direction of." *To* is also used to form an infinitive. *Too* (an adverb) means "also" or "very." *Two* is the number 2.

Two causes of eye problems among students are lights that fail **to** illuminate properly and computer screens with **too** much glare.

vain, vane, vein *Vain* means "valueless or fruitless"; it may also mean "holding a high regard for oneself." *Vane* is a flat piece of material set up to show which way the wind blows. *Vein* refers to a blood vessel or a mineral deposit. 643.1

The weather **vane** indicates the direction of the wind; the blood **vein** determines the direction of flowing blood; and the **vain** mind moves in no particular direction, content to think only about itself.

vary, very The verb *vary* means "to change"; the adverb *very* means "to a high degree." 643.2

To ensure the **very** best employee relations, the workloads should not **vary** greatly from worker to worker.

verbal, oral (See oral.)

waist, waste The noun *waist* refers to the part of the body just above the hips. The verb *waste* means "to squander" or "to wear away, decay"; the noun *waste* refers to material that is unused or useless. 643.3

His **waist** is small because he **wastes** no opportunity to exercise.

wait, weight *Wait* means "to stay somewhere expecting something." *Weight* refers to a degree or unit of heaviness. 643.4

The **weight** of sadness eventually lessens; one must simply **wait** for the pain to dissipate.

ware, wear, where The noun *ware* refers to a product that is sold; the verb *wear* means "to have on or to carry on one's body"; the adverb *where* asks the question "In what place?" or "In what situation?" 643.5

The designer boasted, "**Where** can one **wear** my **wares**? Anywhere."

weather, whether *Weather* refers to the condition of the atmosphere. *Whether* refers to a possibility. 643.6

Weather conditions affect all of us, **whether** we are farmers or plumbers.

well, good (See good.)

which, that (See 589.3.)

who, which, that *Who* refers to people. *Which* refers to nonliving objects or to animals. (*Which* should never refer to people.) *That* may refer to animals, people, or nonliving objects. (See also 589.3.) 643.7

who, whom *Who* is used as the subject of a verb; *whom* is used as the object of a preposition or as a direct object. 643.8

Captain Mather, to **whom** the survivors owe their lives, is the man **who** is being honored today.

who's, whose *Who's* is the contraction for "who is." *Whose* is a possessive pronoun. 643.9

Whose car are we using, and **who's** going to pay for the gas?

your, you're *Your* is a possessive pronoun. *You're* is the contraction for "you are." 643.10

If **you're** like most Americans, you will have held eight jobs by **your** fortieth birthday.

Using the Right Word Exercises:

Using the Right Word: IV

A. Selecting the Right Word

Choose the correct word from those in parentheses for each sentence.

1. The (*principal, principle*) of relativity applies to any scientific investigation.
2. Vince gave an interesting (*perspective, prospective*) on the importance of workplace writing proficiency.
3. The large piece of rock that fell from the cliff face remained (*stationary, stationery*) near the entrance to the hiking trail.
4. Have you decided (*weather, whether*) to take your boyfriend to your Thanksgiving dinner?
5. If (*your, you're*) planning to begin work on Monday, we'll have the training materials ready for you.
6. Latoya tried in (*vain, vane, vein*) to find her missing car keys.
7. I think Christopher Nolan's *Inception* is even better (*than, then*) *The Dark Knight*.
8. The professor reminded her students to (*sight, cite, site*) any sources they use in their papers.
9. Mack and Gordon discussed (*who's, whose*) car they should take to the mall.
10. Although not recommended, pulling an all-night study session is considered a (*right, write, wright, rite*) of passage among college students.

B. Replacing Incorrect Words

For each sentence below, identify the misused words and correct them.

1. The company began making personal changes by interviewing perspective suitors.
2. Students whom wish to proceed with the medical mission trip will need to bring there applications to the volunteer office.
3. Hopefully the some of my two checks will not go to waist at the casino.

Chapter 31

Multilingual and ESL Guidelines

English may be your second, third, or fifth language. As a multilingual learner, you bring to your writing the culture and knowledge of the languages you use. This broader perspective enables you to draw on many experiences and greater knowledge as you write and speak. Whether you are an international student or someone who has lived in North America a long time and is now learning more about English, this chapter provides you with important information about writing in English.

Five Parts of Speech

Noun

Count Nouns 645.1

Count nouns refer to things that can be counted. They can have *a, an, the,* or *one* in front of them. One or more adjectives can come between the articles *a, an, the,* or *one* and the singular count noun.

an apple, one orange, a plum, a purple plum

Count nouns can be singular, as in the examples above, or plural, as in the examples below.

plums, apples, oranges

Note: When count nouns are plural, they can have the article *the,* a number, or a demonstrative adjective in front of them. (See 647.1 and 647.3.)

I used **the** plums to make a pie.

He placed **five** apples on my desk.

These oranges are so juicy!

The *number* of a noun refers to whether it names a single thing (*book*), in which case its number is *singular,* or whether it names more than one thing (*books*), in which case the number of the noun is *plural.*

Note: There are different ways in which the plural form of nouns is created. For more information, see pages 612–613.

646.1 **Noncount Nouns**

Noncount nouns refer to things that cannot be counted. Do not use *a, an,* or *one* in front of them. They have no plural form, so they always take a singular verb. Some nouns that end in *s* are not plural; they are noncount nouns.

fruit, furniture, rain, thunder, advice, mathematics, news

Abstract nouns name ideas or conditions rather than people, places, or objects. Many abstract nouns are noncount nouns.

The students had **fun** at the party. Good **health** is a wonderful gift.

Collective nouns name a whole category or group and are often noncount nouns.

homework, furniture, money

Note: The parts or components of a group or category named by a noncount noun are often count nouns. For example, *report* and *assignment* are count nouns that are parts of the collective, noncount noun *homework.*

646.2 **Two-Way Nouns**

Some nouns can be used as either count or noncount nouns, depending on what they refer to.

I would like a **glass** of water. (count noun)

Glass is used to make windows. (noncount noun)

Articles and Other Noun Markers

646.3 **Specific Articles**

Use articles and other noun markers or modifiers to give more information about nouns. The **specific** (or **definite**) **article** *the* is used to refer to a specific noun.

I found **the** book I misplaced yesterday.

646.4 **Indefinite Articles and Indefinite Adjectives**

Use the **indefinite article** *a* or *an* to refer to a nonspecific noun. Use *an* before singular nouns beginning with the vowels *a, e, i, o,* and *u.* Use *a* before nouns beginning with all other letters of the alphabet, the consonants. Exceptions do occur: *a* unit; *a* university.

I always take **an** apple to work.

It is good to have **a** book with you when you travel.

Indefinite adjectives can also mark nonspecific nouns—*all, any, each, either, every, few, many, more, most, neither, several, some* (for singular and plural count nouns); *all, any, more, most, much, some* (for noncount nouns).

Every student is encouraged to register early.

Most classes fill quickly.

Determining Whether to Use Articles 647.1

Listed below are a number of guidelines to help you determine whether to use an article and which one to use.

Use *a* or *an* with singular count nouns that do not refer to one specific item.

A zebra has black and white stripes. **An apple** is good for you.

Do not use *a* or *an* with plural count nouns.

Zebras have black and white stripes. **Apples** are good for you.

Do not use *a* or *an* with noncount nouns.

Homework needs to be done promptly.

Use *the* with singular count nouns that refer to one specific item.

The apple you gave me was delicious.

Use *the* with plural count nouns.

The zebras at Brookfield Zoo were healthy.

Use *the* with noncount nouns.

The money from my uncle is a gift.

Do not use *the* with most singular proper nouns.

Mother Theresa loved the poor and downcast.

Note: There are many exceptions: *the* Sahara Desert, *the* University of Minnesota, *the* Fourth of July, *The New York Times*

Use *the* with plural nouns.

the Joneses (both Mr. and Mrs. Jones), **the Rocky Mountains, the United States**

Possessive Adjectives 647.2

The possessive case of nouns and pronouns can be used as adjectives to mark nouns.

possessive nouns: *Tanya's, father's, store's*

The car is **Tanya's,** not her **father's.**

possessive pronouns: *my, your, his, her, its, our*

My hat is purple.

Demonstrative Adjectives 647.3

Demonstrative pronouns can be used as adjectives to mark nouns.

Demonstrative adjectives: *this, that, these, those* (for singular and plural count nouns); *this, that* (for noncount nouns)

Those chairs are lovely. Where did you buy **that** furniture?

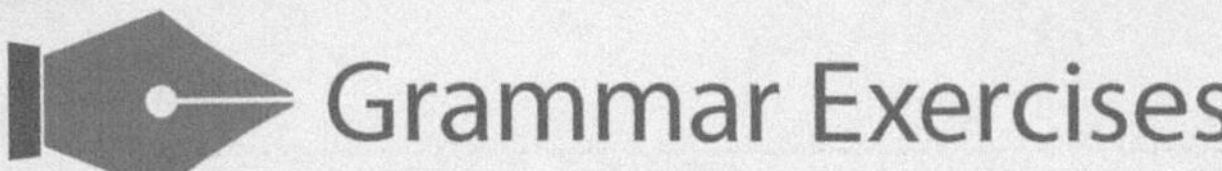

Grammar Exercises:

Nouns, Articles, and Other Noun Markers

A. Count and Noncount Nouns

Make a list of count nouns from the following paragraph. Next make a list of noncount nouns.

We live in a time of confusing economics. On the one hand, it is necessary to spend money to keep the economy stimulated. Manufacturers use every psychological trick they can identify to coax consumers to buy more products. As a matter of fact, advertisers work to make the public want things it doesn't actually need. On the other hand, citizens are expected to invest and save for emergencies and for their retirement. Shame is used as a motivator to accomplish this. Unfortunately, in a world where citizens have been relabeled as consumers, the psychology of sales too often outweighs the shadow of shame.

B. Articles and Other Noun Markers

For each numbered blank, write an appropriate article or noun marker as needed. (If none is needed, write "none needed.") Then identify each added article or adjective by type (specific article, indefinite article, indefinite adjective, possessive adjective, demonstrative adjective, or quantifier).

Does (1)______ family own a dog? If so, what made you choose (2)______ breed instead of a different one? In (3)______ house, we have (4) ______ dogs. (5)______ dog is a Chihuahua and (6)______ other is (7)______ Bichon Frise. The Chihuahua barks at (8)______ people but not at others. Well, to be truthful, he always barks at (9)______ strangers, but seldom at a family member or (10)______ friend. (11)______ Bichon Frise is too friendly and excited to bark. He jumps on each and (12)______ person who visits us. Scientists say that (13)______ dogs originally descended from (14)______ wolf. From my observation of (15)______ Chihuaha and Bichon Frise, it is obvious that different dogs descended differently.

Quantifiers 649.1

Expressions of quantity and measure are often used with nouns. Below are some of these expressions and guidelines for using them.

The following expressions of quantity can be used with count nouns: *each, every, both, a couple of, a few, several, many, a number of.*

We enjoyed **both** concerts we attended. **A couple of** songs performed were familiar to us.

Use a number to indicate a specific quantity of a continuum.

I saw **fifteen** cardinals in the park.

To indicate a specific quantity of a noncount noun, use *a* + quantity (such as *bag, bottle, bowl, carton, glass,* or *piece*) + *of* + noun.

I bought **a carton of milk, a head of lettuce, a piece of cheese,** and **a bag of flour** at the grocery store.

The following expressions can be used with noncount nouns: *a little, much, a great deal of.*

We had **much** wind and **a little** rain as the storm passed through yesterday.

The following expressions of quantity can be used with both count and noncount nouns: *no/not any, some, a lot of, lots of, plenty of, most, all, this, that.*

I would like **some** apples *(count noun)* and **some** rice *(noncount noun),* please.

Verb

As the main part of the predicate, a verb conveys much of a sentence's meaning. Using verb tenses and forms correctly ensures that your readers will understand your sentences as you intend them to. For a more thorough review of verbs, see pages 544–547.

Progressive (Continuous) Tenses 649.2

Progressive or continuous tense verbs express action in progress (see page 546).

To form the **present progressive** tense, use the helping verb *am, is,* or *are* with the *ing* form of the main verb.

He **is washing** the car right now.
Kent and Chen **are studying** for a test.

To form the **past progressive** tense, use the helping verb *was* or *were* with the *ing* form of the main verb.

Yesterday he **was working** in the garden all day.
Julia and Juan **were watching** a movie.

To form the future progressive tense, use *will* or a phrase that indicates the future, the helping verb *be,* and the *ing* form of the main verb.

Next week he **will be painting** the house.
He **plans to be painting** the house soon.

650.1 Note that some verbs are generally not used in the progressive tenses, such as the following groups of frequently used verbs:

- Verbs that express thoughts, attitudes, and desires: *know, understand, want, prefer*
- Verbs that describe appearances: *seem, resemble*
- Verbs that indicate possession: *belong, have, own, possess*
- Verbs that signify inclusion: *contain, hold*

Kala **knows** how to ride a motorcycle.

NOT THIS: Kala is **knowing** how to ride a motorcycle.

650.2 Objects and Complements of Verbs

Active transitive verbs take objects. These can be direct objects, indirect objects, or object complements. Linking verbs take subject complements—predicate nominatives or predicate adjectives—that rename or describe the subject.

650.3 Infinitives as Objects

Infinitives can follow many verbs, including these: *agree, appear, attempt, consent, decide, demand, deserve, endeavor, fail, hesitate, hope, intend, need, offer, plan, prepare, promise, refuse, seem, tend, volunteer, wish.* (See 548.2 for more on infinitives.)

He **promised to bring** some samples.

The following verbs are among those that can be followed by a noun or pronoun plus the infinitive: *ask, beg, choose, expect, intend, need, prepare, promise, want.*

I **expect you to be** there on time.

Note: Except in the passive voice, the following verbs must have a noun or pronoun before the infinitive: *advise, allow, appoint, authorize, cause, challenge, command, convince, encourage, forbid, force, hire, instruct, invite, order, permit, remind, require, select, teach, tell, tempt, trust.*

I will **authorize Emily to use** my credit card.

Unmarked infinitives (no *to*) can follow these verbs: *have, help, let, make.*

These glasses **help me see** the board.

650.4 Gerunds as Objects

Gerunds can follow these verbs: *admit, avoid, consider, deny, discuss, dislike, enjoy, finish, imagine, miss, postpone, quit, recall, recommend, regret.* (Also see 548.1.)

I **recommended hiring** Ian for the job.

Here *hiring* is the direct object of the active verb *recommended,* and *Ian* is the object of the gerund.

Infinitives or Gerunds as Objects 651.1

Either **gerunds** or **infinitives** can follow these verbs: *begin, continue, hate, like, love, prefer, remember, start, stop, try.*

I **hate having** cold feet. I **hate to have** cold feet. (In either form, the verbal phrase is the direct object of the verb hate.)

Note: Sometimes the meaning of a sentence will change depending on whether you use a gerund or an infinitive.

I stopped to smoke. (I *stopped* weeding the garden *to smoke* a cigarette.)

I stopped smoking. (I no longer smoke.)

Common Modal Auxiliary Verbs 651.2

Modal auxiliary verbs are a kind of auxiliary verb. (See 544.3.) They help the main verb express meaning. Modals are sometimes grouped with other helping or auxiliary verbs.

Modal verbs must be followed by the base form of a verb without *to* (not by a gerund or an infinitive). Also, modal verbs do not change form; they are always used as they appear in the following chart.

Modal	Expresses	Sample Sentence
can	ability	I ***can*** make tamales.
could	ability	I ***could*** babysit Tuesday.
	possibility	He ***could*** be sick.
might	possibility	I ***might*** be early.
may, might	possibility	I ***may*** sleep late Saturday.
	request	***May*** I be excused?
must	strong need	I ***must*** study more.
have to	strong need	I ***have to*** (have got to) exercise.
ought to	feeling of duty	I ***ought to*** (should) help Dad.
should	advisability	She ***should*** retire.
	expectation	I ***should*** have caught that train.
shall	intent	***Shall*** I stay longer?
will	intent	I ***will*** visit my grandma soon.
would	intent	I ***would*** live to regret my offer.
	repeated action	He ***would*** walk in the meadow.
would + you	polite request	***Would you*** help me?
could + you	polite request	***Could you*** type this letter?
will + you	polite request	***Will you*** give me a ride?
can + you	polite request	***Can you*** make supper tonight?

Common Two-Word Verbs

This chart lists some common verbs in which two words—a verb and a preposition—work together to express a specific action. A noun or pronoun is often inserted between the parts of the two-word verb when it is used in a sentence: *break it down, call it off.*

break down .... to take apart or fall apart
call off .... cancel
call up .... make a phone call
clear out .... leave a place quickly
cross out .... draw a line through
do over .... repeat
figure out .... find a solution
fill in/out .... complete a form or an application
fill up .... fill a container or tank
* **find out** .... discover
* **get in** .... enter a vehicle or building
* **get out of** .... leave a car, a house, or a situation
* **get over** .... recover from a sickness or a problem
give back .... return something
give in/up .... surrender or quit
hand in .... give homework to a teacher
hand out .... give someone something
hang up .... put down a phone receiver
leave out .... omit or don't use
let in/out .... allow someone or something to enter or go out
look up .... find information
mix up .... confuse
pay back .... return money or a favor
pick out .... choose
point out .... call attention to
put away .... return something to its proper place
put down .... place something on a table, the floor, and so on.
put off .... delay doing something
shut off .... turn off a machine or light
* **take part** .... participate
talk over .... discuss
think over .... consider carefully
try on .... put on clothing to see if it fits
turn down .... lower the volume
turn up .... raise the volume
write down .... write on a piece of paper

* These two-word verbs should not have a noun or pronoun inserted between their parts.

Spelling Guidelines for Verb Forms

The same spelling rules that apply when adding a suffix to other words apply to verbs as well. Most verbs need a suffix to indicate tense or form. The third-person singular form of a verb, for example, usually ends in *s*, but it can also end in *es*. Formation of *ing* and *ed* forms of verbs and verbals needs careful attention, too. Consult the rules below to determine which spelling is correct for each verb. (For general spelling guidelines, see page 621.)

There may be exceptions to these rules when forming the past tense of irregular verbs because the verbs are formed by changing the word itself, not merely by adding *d* or *ed*. (See the chart of irregular verbs on page 549.)

Past Tense: Adding *ed* 653.1

Add *ed* . . .

- When a verb ends with two consonants:
  touch—**touched** ask—**asked** pass—**passed**
- When a verb ends with a consonant preceded by two vowels:
  heal—**healed** gain—**gained**
- When a verb ends in *y* preceded by a vowel:
  annoy—**annoyed** flay—**flayed**
- When a multisyllable verb's last syllable is not stressed (even when the last syllable ends with a consonant preceded by a vowel):
  budget—**budgeted** enter—**entered** interpret—**interpreted**

Change *y* to *i* and add *ed* when a verb ends in a consonant followed by *y:*
liquefy—**liquefied** worry—**worried**

Double the final consonant and add *ed* . . .

- When a verb has one syllable and ends with a consonant preceded by a vowel:
  wrap—**wrapped** drop—**dropped**
- When a multisyllable verb's last syllable (ending in a consonant preceded by a vowel) is stressed:
  admit—**admitted** confer—**conferred** abut—**abutted**

Past Tense: Adding *d* 653.2

Add *d* . . .

- When a verb ends with *e:*
  chime—**chimed** tape—**taped**
- When a verb ends with *ie:*
  tie—**tied** die—**died** lie—**lied**

654.1 Present Tense: Adding *s* or *es*

Add *es* . . .

- When a verb ends in *ch, sh, s, x,* or *z:*
  watch—**watches** fix—**fixes**
- To *do* and *go:*
  do—**does** go—**goes**

Change *y* to *i* and add *es* when the verb ends in a consonant followed by *y:*

liquefy—**liquefies** quantify—**quantifies**

Add *s* to most other verbs, including those already ending in *e* and those that end in a vowel followed by *y:*

write—**writes** buy—**buys**

654.2 Present Tense: Adding *ing*

Drop the *e* and add *ing* when the verb ends in *e:*

drive—**driving** rise—**rising**

Double the final consonant and add *ing* . . .

- When a verb has one syllable and ends with a consonant preceded by a single vowel:
  wrap—wrapping sit—sitting
- When a multisyllable verb's last syllable (ending in a consonant preceded by a single vowel) is stressed:
  forget—forgetting begin—beginning abut—abutting

Change *ie* to *y* and add *ing* when a verb ends with *ie:*

tie—**tying** die—**dying** lie—**lying**

Add *ing* . . .

- When a verb ends with two consonants:
  touch—**touching** ask—**asking** pass—**passing**
- When a verb ends with a consonant preceded by two vowels:
  heal—**healing** gain—**gaining**
- When a verb ends in *y:*
  buy—**buying** study—**studying** cry—**crying**
- When a multisyllable verb's last syllable is not stressed (even when the last syllable ends with a consonant preceded by a vowel):
  budget—**budgeting** enter—**entering** interpret—**interpreting**

Note: Never trust your spelling to even the best computer spell checker. Carefully proofread. Use a dictionary for questionable words your spell checker may miss.

Verbs, Objects, and Complements

A. Errors in Context

Correct any verb, object, and complement errors in the sentences below. Write down the error, crossed out, with the correction beside it.

(1) Evolutionary psychologist Robert Dunbar suggest that brain size directly affects behavior in terms of how many individuals a mammal can to care about. (2) A chimpanzee is possessing an emotional connection with about 50 other chimpanzees. (3) If a tribe's size grow beyond that, the group tends fighting. (4) Studies of human brain size predict that humans are having the ability to care for roughly 150 other people, and Dunbar says research bears that out. (5) Fortunately, humans decide building hierarchies to support larger societies. (6) Also, people can conceiving of a universal family of humanity. (7) Can you to think that way?

B. Forming Tenses

Write the correct past tense for each of the verbs listed below. (Note that some of these verbs have irregular past-tense forms.)

1. say ______
2. go ______
3. derive ______
4. maintain ______

Write the correct present tense form (adding *s* or *es*) for each of these verbs.

1. will ______
2. come ______
3. wonder ______
4. verify ______

Write the correct present tense form (adding *ing*) for each of these verbs.

1. activate ______
2. portray ______
3. begin ______
4. start ______

MindTap® Practice skills that you have learned in this section and receive automatic feedback.

Adjective

656.1 **Placing Adjectives**

You probably know that an adjective often comes before the noun it modifies. When several adjectives are used in a row to modify a single noun, it is important to arrange the adjectives in the well-established sequence used in English writing and speaking. The following list shows the usual order of adjectives. (Also see 587.3.)

First, place . . .

1. articles . . . . **a, an, the**
   demonstrative adjectives . . . . **that, those**
   possessives . . . . **my, her, Misha's**

Then place words that . . .

2. indicate time . . . . **first, next, final**
3. tell how many . . . . **one, few, some**
4. evaluate . . . . **beautiful, dignified, graceful**
5. tell what size . . . . **big, small, short, tall**
6. tell what shape . . . . **round, square**
7. describe a condition . . . . **messy, clean, dark**
8. tell what age . . . . **old, young, new, antique**
9. tell what color . . . . **blue, red, yellow**
10. tell what nationality . . . . **English, Chinese, Mexican**
11. tell what religion . . . . **Buddhist, Jewish, Protestant**
12. tell what material . . . . **satin, velvet, wooden**

Finally, place nouns . . .

13. used as adjectives . . . . **computer [monitor], spice [rack]**

my second try (1 + 2 + noun)
gorgeous young white swans (4 + 8 + 9 + noun)

656.2 **Present and Past Participles as Adjectives**

Both the **present participle** and the **past participle** can be used as adjectives. (Also see 548.3.) Exercise care in choosing whether to use the present participle or the past participle. A participle can come either before a noun or after a linking verb.

A **present participle** used as an adjective should describe a person or thing that is causing a feeling or situation.

His **annoying** comments made me angry.

A **past participle** should describe a person or thing that experiences a feeling or situation.

He was **annoyed** because he had to wait so long.

Note: Within each of the following pairs, the present (*ing* form) and past (*ed* form) participles have different meanings.

annoying/annoyed
boring/bored
confusing/confused
depressing/depressed
exciting/excited
exhausting/exhausted
fascinating/fascinated
surprising/surprised

Nouns as Adjectives 657.1

Nouns sometimes function as adjectives by modifying another noun. When a noun is used as an adjective, it is always singular.

Many European cities have **rose** gardens.

Marta recently joined a **book** club.

Note: Try to avoid using more than two nouns as adjectives for another noun. These "noun compounds" can get confusing. Prepositional phrases may get the meaning across better than long noun strings.

Correct: Omar is a **crew** member in the **restaurant** kitchen during **second** shift.

Not correct: Omar is a **second-shift restaurant kitchen crew** member.

Adverb

Placing Adverbs 657.2

Consider the following guidelines for placing adverbs correctly. See page 552 for more information about adverbs.

Place adverbs that tell how often (*frequently, seldom, never, always, sometimes*) after a helping (auxiliary) verb and before the main verb. In a sentence without a helping verb, adverbs that tell *how often* are placed before an action verb but after a linking verb.

The salesclerk will **usually** help me.

Place adverbs that tell when (*yesterday, now, at five o'clock*) at the end of a sentence.

Auntie El came home **yesterday.**

Adverbs that tell where (*upside-down, around, downstairs*) usually follow the verb they modify. Many prepositional phrases (*at the beach, under the stairs, below the water*) function as adverbs that tell where.

We waited **on the porch.**

Adverbs that tell how (*quickly, slowly, loudly*) can be placed either at the beginning, in the middle, or at the end of a sentence—but not between a verb and its direct object.

Softly he called my name. He **softly** called my name. He called my name **softly.**

Place adverbs that modify adjectives directly before the adjective.

That is a **most** unusual dress.

Adverbs that modify clauses are most often placed in front of the clause, but they can also go inside or at the end of the clause.

Fortunately, we were not involved in the accident.
We were not involved, **fortunately,** in the accident.
We were not involved in the accident, **fortunately.**

Note: Adverbs that are used with verbs that have direct objects must *not* be placed between the verb and its object.

Correct: Luis **usually** catches the most fish. **Usually,** Luis catches the most fish.

Not correct: Luis catches **usually** the most fish.

Preposition

A **preposition** combines with a noun to form a prepositional phrase, which acts as a modifier—an adverb or an adjective. See pages 553 and 556 for a list of common prepositions and for more information about prepositions.

658.1 Using *in, on, at,* and *by*

In, on, at, and *by* are four common prepositions that refer to time and place. Here are some examples of how these prepositions are used in each case.

To show time

on a specific day or date: ***on*** June 7, ***on*** Wednesday
in part of a day: ***in*** the afternoon
in a year or month: ***in*** 2016, ***in*** April
in a period of time: completed ***in*** an hour
by a specific time or date: ***by*** noon, ***by*** the fifth of May
at a specific time of day or night: ***at*** 3:30 this afternoon

To show place

at a meeting place or location: ***at*** school, ***at*** the park
at the edge of something: standing ***at*** the bar
at the corner of something: turning ***at*** the intersection
at a target: throwing a dart ***at*** the target
on a surface: left ***on*** the floor
on an electronic medium: ***on*** the Internet, ***on*** television
in an enclosed space: ***in*** the box, ***in*** the room
in a geographic location: ***in*** New York City, ***in*** Germany
in a print medium: ***in*** a journal
by a landmark: ***by*** the fountain

Note: Do not insert a preposition between a transitive verb and its direct object. Intransitive verbs, however, are often followed by a prepositional phrase (a phrase that begins with a preposition).

I **cooked** hot dogs on the grill. (transitive verb)

I **ate** in the park. (intransitive verb)

658.2 Phrasal Prepositions

Some prepositional phrases begin with more than one preposition. These **phrasal prepositions** are commonly used in both written and spoken communication. A list of common phrasal prepositions follows:

according to	because of	in case of	on the side of
across from	by way of	in spite of	up to
along with	except for	instead of	with respect to

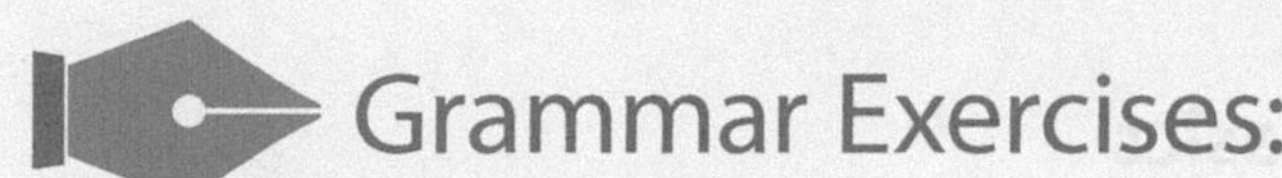

Grammar Exercises:

Adjectives, Adverbs, Prepositions

A. Adjective Order

Rewrite the following phrases to place the adjectives in the proper order.

1. sandstone first square several red gigantic the blocks
2. a sticky brown few last delicious figs
3. rough-barked old some round huge trees

B. Present and Past Participles

Choose the correct adjective form (present or past participle) in each case below.

1. Deborah was annoying/annoyed that her wedding dress was not finished.
2. The exciting/excited day was quickly approaching, but the preparation was making her exhausting/exhausted.
3. Then surprising/surprised news arrived: An old high school friend was coming to help!
4. Her fiancé Trevor was confusing/confused at first that her old friend, Michael, was willing to be a "bridesmaid."
5. Trevor figured that Michael must be a fascinating/fascinated fellow.

C. *At, By, In,* or *On*

Write the best preposition—*at, by, in,* or *on*—for each blank in the sentences below.

1. _______ what time do you get up most mornings?
2. Do you come to school _______ car, _______ bike, _______ bus, or do you walk?
3. After school, I have to work _______ a pizza parlor most evenings.
4. The pizza restaurant is _______ the downtown area, _______ the public library.
5. I like pizza with mushrooms _______ it.
6. The place I work posts free coupons _______ its Web site.
7. The current coupon expires _______ June 8.
8. We have tables, so you can eat _______ the store if you like.
9. Our pizzas are cooked _______ a wood-burning oven.
10. Once, I cooked a pizza _______ my grill at home, over charcoal.

MindTap® Practice skills that you have learned in this section and receive automatic feedback.

660.1 Understanding Sentence Basics

Simple sentences in the English language follow the five basic patterns shown below. (See pages 557–566 for more information.)

Subject + Verb

S V

Naomie winked.

Some verbs like *winked* are intransitive. Intransitive verbs do not need a direct object to express a complete thought. (See 544.2.)

Subject + Verb + Direct Object

S V DO

Harris grinds his teeth.

Some verbs like *grinds* are transitive. Transitive verbs *do* need a direct object to express a complete thought. (See 544.2.)

Subject + Verb + Indirect Object + Direct Object

S V IO DO

Elena offered her friend an anchovy.

The direct object names who or what receives the action; the indirect object names to whom or for whom the action was done.

Subject + Verb + Direct Object + Object Complement

S V DO OC

The chancellor named Ravi the outstanding student of 2016.

The object complement renames or describes the direct object.

Subject + Linking Verb + Predicate Nominative (or Predicate Adjective)

S LV PN — S LV PA

Paula is a computer programmer. — Paula is very intelligent.

A linking verb connects the subject to the predicate noun or predicate adjective. The predicate noun renames the subject; the predicate adjective describes the subject.

660.2 Inverted Order

In the sentence patterns above, the subject comes before the verb. In a few types of sentences, such as those below, the subject comes *after* the verb.

LV S PN — LV S

Is Larisa a poet? — **There was a meeting.**

(A question) — (A sentence beginning with "there")

Sentence Problems

This section looks at potential trouble spots and sentence problems. For more information about English sentences, their parts, and how to construct them, see pages 557–566 in the handbook. Pages 567–582 cover the types of problems and errors found in English writing. The guide to avoiding sentence problems found on page 582 is an excellent editing tool.

Double Negatives 661.1

When making a sentence negative, use *not* or another negative adverb (*never, rarely, hardly, seldom,* and so on), but not both. Using both results in a double negative (see 580.4).

Subject–Verb Agreement 661.2

Be sure the subject and verb in every clause agree in person and number. (See pages 567–570.)

The **student was** rewarded for her hard work.

The **students were** rewarded for their hard work.

The **instructor,** as well as the students, **is** expected to attend the orientation.

The **students,** as well as the instructor, **are** expected to attend the orientation.

Omitted Words 661.3

Do not omit subjects or the expletives *there* or *here.* In all English clauses and sentences (except imperatives in which the subject *you* is understood), there must be a subject.

Correct: Your mother was very quiet; **she** seemed to be upset.
Not correct: Your mother was very quiet; seemed to be upset.

Correct: **There** is not much time left.
Not correct: Not much time left.

Repeated Words 661.4

Do not repeat the subject of a clause or sentence.

Correct: The doctor prescribed an antibiotic.
Not correct: The doctor, **she** prescribed an antibiotic.

Do not repeat an object in an adjective dependent clause.

Correct: I forgot the flowers that I intended to give to my hosts.
Not correct: I forgot the flowers that I intended to give **them** to my hosts.

Note: Sometimes the relative pronoun that begins the adjective dependent clause is omitted but understood.

I forgot the flowers I intended to give to my hosts.
(The relative pronoun *that* is omitted.)

662.1 Conditional Sentences

Conditional sentences express a situation requiring that a condition be met in order to be true. Selecting the correct verb tense for use in the two clauses of a conditional sentence can be problematic. Below you will find an explanation of the three types of conditional sentences and the verb tenses that are needed to form them.

1. **Factual conditionals:** The conditional clause begins with *if, when, whenever,* or a similar expression. Furthermore, the verbs in the conditional clause and the main clause should be in the same tense.

   Whenever we **had** time, we **took** a break and **went** for a swim.

2. **Predictive conditionals** express future conditions and possible results. The conditional clause begins with *if* or *unless* and has a present tense verb. The main clause uses a modal (*will, can, should, may, might*) plus the base form of the verb.

   Unless we **find** a better deal, we **will buy** this sound system.

3. **Hypothetical past conditionals** describe a situation that is unlikely to happen or that is contrary to fact. To describe situations in the past, the verb in the conditional clause is in the past perfect tense, and the verb in the main clause is formed from *would have, could have,* or *might have* plus the past participle.

   If we **had started out** earlier, we **would have arrived** on time.

Note: If the hypothetical situation is a present or future one, the verb in the conditional clause is in the past tense, and the verb in the main clause is formed from *would, could,* or *might* plus the base form of the verb.

If we **bought** groceries once a week, we **would** not **go** to the store so often.

662.2 Quoted and Reported Speech

Quoted speech is the use of exact words from another source in your own writing; you must enclose these words in quotation marks. It is also possible to report nearly exact words without quotation marks. This is called **reported speech,** or indirect quotation. (See pages 599–600 for a review of the use of quotation marks.)

Direct quotation: Felicia said, "Don't worry about tomorrow."

Indirect quotation: Felicia said that you don't have to worry about tomorrow.

In the case of a question, when a direct quotation is changed to an indirect quotation, the question mark is not needed.

Direct quotation: Ahmad asked, "Who of you will give me a hand?"

Indirect quotation: Ahmad asked who of us would give him a hand.

Notice how pronouns are often changed in indirect quotations.

Direct quotation: My friends said, "**You**'re crazy."

Indirect quotation: My friends said that **I** was crazy.

Note: In academic writing, the use of another source's spoken or written words in one's own writing without proper acknowledgment is called *plagiarism.* Plagiarism is severely penalized in academic situations. (See pages 431–440.)

Grammar Exercises:

Sentence Problems

A. Errors in Context

Correct the error(s) in each sentence below. Write down the error, crossed out, with the correction beside it.

(1) Flying by commercial jet can be a great way to travel if you have a long way to go and needs to get there quickly. (2) You can't never ignore, however, that the convenience comes with a price. (3) Security checks is becoming more intrusive every year. (4) Also, airlines they are reducing flights, crowding planes, and charging for services like meals. (5) If you wanted a leisurely vacation, you do better to choose different transportation. (6) An ocean voyage it takes longer but doesn't cause no jet lag. (7) People makes the same mistake with their road trips. (8) They gets in a car and rushes down the highway to a destination. (9) If they took a train instead, they relax and watch the countryside. (10) A jeep or a motorcycle are another great way to make a road trip. (11) Because these vehicles are open to the air, can feel in touch with the terrain. (12) If you were to travel back roads, you enjoy the journey as much as the arrival.

B. Quoted and Reported Speech

Rewrite direct quotations as indirect quotations and vice versa.

1. Kimi told Hal, "I pay my bills with income from my online writing."
2. "How did you get started?" he asked.
3. She answered that their friend Toi had introduced her to a site for essayists.
4. She told him, "I had to fill out an application and submit a sample of work."
5. She said they made her revise her biography several times before accepting it.

C. Defining Problems

In your own words, define each of the following sentence problems or types.

1. Double negatives
2. Omitted words
3. Repeated words
4. Conditional sentences
5. Quoted speech
6. Reported speech

Numbers, Word Parts, and Idioms

Numbers

As a multilingual/ESL learner, you may be accustomed to a way of writing numbers that is different from the way it is done in North America. Become familiar with the North American conventions for writing numbers. Pages 614–615 show you how numbers are written and punctuated in both word and numeral forms.

664.1 Using Punctuation with Numerals

Note that the **period** is used to express percentages (5.5%, 75.9%) and the **comma** is used to organize large numbers into units (7,000; 23,100; 231,990,000). Commas are not used, however, in writing the year (2016).

664.2 Cardinal Numbers

Cardinal numbers (such as *one, two, three)* are used when counting a number of parts or objects. Cardinal numbers can be used as nouns (she counted to **ten**), pronouns (I invited many guests, but only **three** came), or adjectives (there are **ten** boys here).

Write out in words the numbers one through one hundred. Numbers 101 and greater are often written as numerals. (See 614.1.)

664.3 Ordinal Numbers

Ordinal numbers show place or succession in a series: the fourth row, the twenty-first century, the tenth time, and so on. Ordinal numbers are used to talk about the parts into which a whole can be divided, such as a fourth or a tenth, and as the denominator in fractions, such as one-fourth or three-fifths. Written fractions can also be used as nouns (I gave him **four-fifths**) or as adjectives (a **four-fifths** majority).

Note: See the list that follows for names and symbols of the first twenty-five ordinal numbers. Consult a college dictionary for a complete list of cardinal and ordinal numbers.

First	1st	Tenth	10th	Nineteenth	19th
Second	2nd	Eleventh	11th	Twentieth	20th
Third	3rd	Twelfth	12th	Twenty-first	21st
Fourth	4th	Thirteenth	13th	Twenty-second	22nd
Fifth	5th	Fourteenth	14th	Twenty-third	23rd
Sixth	6th	Fifteenth	15th	Twenty-fourth	24th
Seventh	7th	Sixteenth	16th	Twenty-fifth	25th
Eighth	8th	Seventeenth	17th		
Ninth	9th	Eighteenth	18th		

Prefixes, Suffixes, and Roots

Following is a list of many common word parts and their meanings. Learning them can help you determine the meaning of unfamiliar words as you come across them in your reading. For instance, if you know that *hemi* means "half," you can conclude that *hemisphere* means "half of a sphere."

Prefixes	Meaning
a, an	not, without
anti, ant	against
co, con, com	together, with
di	two, twice
dis, dif	apart, away
ex, e, ec, ef	out
hemi, semi	half
il, ir, in, im	not
inter	between
intra	within
multi	many
non	not
ob, of, op, oc	toward, against
per	throughout
post	after
super, supr	above, more
trans, tra	across, beyond
tri	three
uni	one

Suffixes	Meaning
able, ible	able, can do
age	act of, state of
al	relating to
ate	cause, make
en	made of
ence, ency	action, quality
esis, osis	action, process
ice	condition, quality
ile	relating to
ish	resembling
ment	act of, state of
ology	study, theory
ous	full of, having
sion, tion	act of, state of
some	like, tending to
tude	state of
ward	in the direction of

Roots	Meaning
acu	sharp
am, amor	love, liking
anthrop	man
aster, astr	star
auto	self
biblio	book
bio	life
capit, capt	head
chron	time
cit	to call, start
cred	believe
dem	people
dict	say, speak
erg	work
fid, feder	faith, trust
fract, frag	break
graph, gram	write, written
ject	throw
log, ology	word, study, speech
man	hand
micro	small
mit, miss	send
nom	law, order
onym	name
path, pathy	feeling, suffering
rupt	break
scrib, script	write
spec, spect, spic	look
tele	far
tempo	time
tox	poison
vac	empty
ver, veri	true
zo	animal

Grammar Exercises: Numbers and Word Parts

A. Punctuating Numerals

For the following numbers, add or correct punctuation as necessary to suit North American style. (Some of the numbers are already correct, and two items need to be punctuated correctly as percentages.)

A. 3000
B. 44
C. 9.400.207,33
D. 200,000,01
E. 600000009
F. 23,7%
G. Dec. 21 2012
H. 100
I. 1.877,14
J. 17,7%

B. Numbers in Text

Write each number below as it should appear in text.

A. 900
B. 4/5
C. 99
D. 24
E. 101
F. 42
G. 17
H. 1/3
I. 70
J. 1,001

C. Prefixes, Suffixes, and Roots

Break each of the following terms into its component parts (prefix, root, and/or suffix) and define it in your own words.

1. semiserious
2. pseudonym
3. toxicology
4. bibliography
5. verified
6. coauthor
7. westward
8. microfinance
9. antipathy
10. international
11. infantile
12. postponement
13. astrophysics
14. ticklish
15. multihued
16. incredulous

MindTap® Practice skills that you have learned in this section and receive automatic feedback.

Idioms

Idioms are phrases that are used in a special way. An idiom can't be understood just by knowing the meaning of each word in the phrase. It must be learned as a whole. For example, the idiom to *bury the hatchet* means to "settle an argument," even though the individual words in the phrase mean something much different. These pages list some of the common idioms in American English.

a bad apple — • One troublemaker on a team may be called **a bad apple.** *(a bad influence)*

an axe to grind — • Mom has **an axe to grind** with the owners of the dog that dug up her flower garden. *(a problem to settle)*

as the crow flies — • She lives only two miles from here **as the crow flies.** *(in a straight line)*

beat around the bush — • Dad said, "Where were you? Don't **beat around the bush.**" *(avoid getting to the point)*

benefit of the doubt — • Ms. Hy gave Henri the **benefit of the doubt** when he explained why he fell asleep in class. (*another chance*)

beyond the shadow of a doubt — • Salvatore won the 50-yard dash **beyond the shadow of a doubt.** *(for certain)*

blew my top — • When my money was stolen, I **blew my top.** *(showed great anger)*

bone to pick — • Nick had a **bone to pick** with Adrian when Nick learned they both liked the same girl. *(problem to settle)*

break the ice — • Shanta was the first to **break the ice** in the room full of new students. *(start a conversation)*

burn the midnight oil — • Carmen had to **burn the midnight oil** the day before the big test. *(work late into the night)*

chomping at the bit — • Dwayne was **chomping at the bit** when it was his turn to bat. *(eager, excited)*

cold shoulder — • Alicia always gives me the **cold shoulder** after our disagreements. *(ignores me)*

cry wolf — • If you **cry wolf** too often, no one will come when you really need help. *(say you are in trouble when you aren't)*

drop in the bucket — • My donation was a **drop in the bucket.** *(a small amount compared with what's needed)*

face the music — • José had to **face the music** when he got caught cheating on the test. *(deal with the punishment)*

flew off the handle — • Tramayne **flew off the handle** when he saw his little brother playing with matches. *(became very angry)*

floating on air — • Teresa was **floating on air** when she read the letter. *(feeling very happy)*

food for thought • The coach gave us some **food for thought** when she said that winning isn't everything. *(something to think about)*

get down to business • In five minutes you need to **get down to business** on this assignment. *(start working)*

get the upper hand • The other team will **get the upper hand** if we don't play better in the second half. *(probably win)*

go overboard • The teacher told us not **to go overboard** with fancy lettering on our posters. *(do too much)*

hit the ceiling • Rosa **hit the ceiling** when she saw her sister painting the television. *(was very angry)*

hit the hay • Patrice **hit the hay** early because she was tired. *(went to bed)*

in a nutshell • **In a nutshell,** Coach Roby told us to play our best. *(to summarize)*

in the nick of time • Zong grabbed his little brother's hand **in the nick of time** before he touched the hot pan. *(just in time)*

in the same boat • My friend and I are **in the same boat** when it comes to doing Saturday chores. *(have the same problem)*

iron out • Jamil and his brother were told to **iron out** their differences about cleaning their room. *(solve, work out)*

it stands to reason • **It stands to reason** that if you keep lifting weights, you will get stronger. *(it makes sense)*

knuckle down • Grandpa told me to **knuckle down** at school if I want to be a doctor. *(work hard)*

learn the ropes • Being new in school, I knew it would take some time to **learn the ropes.** *(get to know how things are done)*

let's face it • "**Let's face it!**" said Mr. Sills. "You're a better long distance runner than you are a sprinter." *(let's admit it)*

let the cat out of the bag • Tia **let the cat out of the bag** and got her sister in trouble. *(told a secret)*

lose face • If I strike out again, I will **lose face.** *(be embarrassed)*

nose to the grindstone • If I keep my **nose to the grindstone,** I will finish my homework in one hour. *(working hard)*

on cloud nine • Walking home from the party, I was **on cloud nine.** *(feeling very happy)*

on pins and needles • I was **on pins and needles** as I waited to see the doctor. *(feeling nervous)*

over and above • **Over and above** the assigned reading, I read two library books. *(in addition to)*

put his foot in his mouth	• Chivas **put his foot in his mouth** when he called his teacher by the wrong name. *(said something embarrassing)*
put your best foot forward	• Grandpa said that whenever you do something, you should **put your best foot forward.** *(do the best that you can do)*
rock the boat	• The coach said, "Don't **rock the boat** if you want to stay on the team." *(cause trouble)*
rude awakening	• I had a **rude awakening** when I saw the letter *F* at the top of my Spanish quiz. *(sudden, unpleasant surprise)*
save face	• Grant tried to **save face** when he said he was sorry for making fun of me in class. *(fix an embarrassing situation)*
see eye to eye	• My sister and I finally **see eye to eye** about who gets to use the phone first after school. *(are in agreement)*
sight unseen	• Grandma bought the television **sight unseen.** *(without seeing it first)*
take a dim view	• My brother will **take a dim view** if I don't help him at the store. *(disapprove)*
take it with a grain of salt	• If my sister tells you she has no homework, **take it with a grain of salt.** *(don't believe everything you're told)*
take the bull by the horns	• This team needs to **take the bull by the horns** to win the game. *(take control)*
through thick and thin	• Max and I will be friends **through thick and thin.** *(in good times and in bad times)*
time flies	• When you're having fun, **time flies.** *(time passes quickly)*
time to kill	• We had **time to kill** before the ballpark gates would open. *(extra time)*
under the weather	• I was feeling **under the weather,** so I didn't go to school. *(sick)*
word of mouth	• We found out who the new teacher was by **word of mouth.** *(talking to other people)*

Note: Like idioms, collocations are groups of words that often appear together. They may help you identify different senses of a word; for example, *old* means slightly different things in these collocations: *old man, old friends.* You will find sentence construction easier if you check for collocations.

Grammar Exercises:

Idioms

A. Using Idioms

Replace the underlined words with appropriate idioms.

Here's (1) something to think about. In order for a democracy to succeed, its citizens must participate. That just (2) makes sense. But (3) let's admit it, far too many U.S. citizens just don't vote. What excuse do they give? Many say, "My vote doesn't matter; it's just (4) a small amount compared to what's needed." I (5) disapprove of this excuse. It's time for these people to (6) deal with the negative effects concerning this abdication of responsibility. Notice that word "abdication." In a democracy, every person is a king. We are all (7) facing the same problem. I'm not saying we need (8) to do too much with our political involvement. However, we should at least vote, and that means researching the issues to avoid (9) being embarrassed because of our choices.

B. Defining Idioms

Using your own words, define the following idioms.

1. benefit of the doubt
2. burn the midnight oil
3. floating on air
4. get down to business
5. let's face it
6. over and above
7. see eye to eye
8. a bad apple
9. flew off the handle
10. break the ice
11. food for thought
12. iron out
13. lose face
14. hit the ceiling
15. on cloud nine
16. learn the ropes
17. bone to pick
18. cold shoulder
19. as the crow flies
20. in a nutshell

MindTap® Practice skills that you have learned in this section and receive automatic feedback.

Targeting Trouble Spots

A sentence that is perfectly acceptable in one language may be unacceptable when directly translated into English. For example, many East Asian languages do not use articles, so using these words can be a challenge to learners of English. The following pages will help you target trouble spots for your general language group.

Help for Speakers of Latin Languages

Advice	DO NOT Write . . .	DO Write . . .
Study the use of count and noncount nouns (645.1–645.2).	I have three homeworks.	I have three homework assignments. *or* I have three types of homework.
Do not omit the subject, *it* as subject, or *there* with delayed subjects (567.1, 568.1).	Is hot sitting in this room. Are people in the theater.	It is hot sitting in this room. There are people in the theater.
Place most subjects before the verb (567).	Gave I the tutor my thanks.	I gave the tutor my thanks.
Avoid using *the* with certain generalizations (647.1).	The business is a difficult major.	Business is a difficult major.
Avoid using *the* with singular proper nouns (647.1).	The April is the cruelest month.	April is the cruelest month.
Avoid double subjects (661.4).	My mother she is a nurse.	My mother is a nurse.
Learn whether to use a gerund or an infinitive after a verb (650.2–651.1).	The professor wants finishing the paperwork. She regrets to wait until the last minute.	The professor wants to finish the paperwork. She regrets waiting until the last minute.
Do not use *which* to refer to people (643.7).	The professors which teach English are here.	The professors who teach English are here. *or* The professors that teach English are here.
Avoid double negatives (661.1).	I never got no assignment.	I never got the assignment. *or* I received no assignment.

Help for Speakers of European Languages

Advice	DO NOT Write . . .	DO Write . . .
Do not omit the subject, *it* as a subject, or *there* with delayed subjects (567.1, 568.1).	Are thousands of books in the library. Is okay to talk.	There are thousands of books in the library. It is okay to talk.
Avoid using *the* with certain generalizations and singular proper nouns (647.1).	I excel at the physics. The Professor Smith marks grammar errors.	I excel at physics. Professor Smith marks grammar errors.
Learn to use progressive verb tenses (649.2).	I still work on my term paper.	I am working on my term paper.
Learn whether to use a gerund or an infinitive after a verb (650.2–651.1).	The students need finishing their projects. The professors finished to grade the papers.	The students need to finish their projects. The professors finished grading the papers.
Avoid placing adverbs between verbs and direct objects (657.2).	I wrote very quickly the first draft.	I wrote the first draft very quickly.
Do not use *which* to refer to people (643.7).	I am one of the students which sing in the choir.	I am one of the students who sing in the choir.

Help for Speakers of African and Caribbean Languages

Advice	DO NOT Write . . .	DO Write . . .
Avoid double subjects (661.4).	The professor she gave us an assignment.	The professor gave us an assignment.
Use plural nouns after plural numbers (649.1).	The class has two professor.	The class has two professors.
Use the correct form of the *be* verb (545.1).	The union be having a blood drive. We be going.	The union is having a blood drive. We are going.
Make subjects and verbs agree in number (567).	She have her own notes. They finishes on time.	She has her own notes. They finish on time.
Use past tense verbs correctly (546).	When the semester began, I study hard.	When the semester began, I studied hard.
Study the rules for article use (646.3–647.1).	I need to buy computer. Entrance exam is required.	I need to buy a computer. An entrance exam is required.

Help for Speakers of East Asian Languages

Advice	DO NOT Write . . .	DO Write . . .
Use plural forms of nouns (649.1).	I have three difficult class.	I have three difficult classes.
Learn to use adjectival forms (656.1–657.1).	He is a very intelligence professor.	He is a very intelligent professor.
Use the objective case of pronouns (542.1).	The tutor helps I with homework.	The tutor helps me with homework.
Include a subject (or *there*) (567.1, 568.1).	Is good to be here. Are many parts.	It is good to be here. There are many parts.
Study subject–verb agreement (567.2).	The course have a long reading list.	The course has a long reading list.
Study past tenses (546).	We study yesterday. At first, I don't get it.	We studied yesterday. At first, I didn't get it.
Use articles—*a, an,* and *the* (646.3–647.1).	I want to be nurse.	I want to be a nurse.
Study conjunction use (554.1–554.5).	Though she studies, but she struggles.	Though she studies, she struggles.
Learn whether to use a gerund or an infinitive (650.2–651.1).	The students need helping each other study.	The students need to help each other study.

Help for Speakers of Middle Eastern Languages

Advice	DO NOT Write . . .	DO Write . . .
Study pronoun gender and case (542).	My mother works hard at his job. Give she credit.	My mother works hard at her job. Give her credit.
Don't include a pronoun after a relative clause (563.3, 661.4).	The study space that I share with two others it is too small.	The study space that I share with two others is too small.
Place most subjects before the verb (567).	Received the freshmen the assignment.	The freshmen received the assignment.
Don't overuse progressive verb tenses (649.2).	I am needing a nap. I am wanting food.	I need a nap. I want food.
Use the definite article *the* correctly (647.1).	Union is closed during the July.	The union is closed during July.

Grammar Exercises:

A. Period, Comma, Quotation Marks, Question Mark, Apostrophe

Rewrite each of the following sentences, inserting punctuation where needed.

1. I asked Could I have an extension on my paper Professor Rubel
2. He responded Well Rob all the other papers have been turned in
3. Yes thats true I replied but no one elses paper will be as good as mine
4. Youd better be right said Professor Rubel How many days better will it be
5. I cringed and asked How about five days better
6. Professor Rubels eyebrows shot up Five days better will have to be phenomenal
7. Three days I asked sheepishly
8. Thats still very much better than everyone else Professor Rubel pointed out.
9. Okay what about one day better I responded
10. I think thats the level of better that you can do Rob One day it is

B. Title Capitalization, Quotation Marks, Italics

For each sentence, rewrite titles, correctly capitalizing them and using quotation marks or italics (underlining) as needed.

1. In the New york times, I read the article, Four representatives Charged In ethics Probe.
2. The music album Sea of cowards by the band The Dead Weather includes the song I'm mad.
3. I read the chapter An empire Crumbles in the novel The shadow of Reichenbach falls, which was reviewed well in the library journal.
4. Have you read the poem the Fiddler Of Dooney in the collection W.b. Yeats: selected Poems?
5. In John Steinbeck's book The acts of King Arthur And his noble Knights, I most enjoyed the chapter the Noble tale of Sir Lancelot Of The Lake.
6. A chapter entitled Management writing has been added to the second edition of the handbook Write For Business.
7. We went to the Riverside Theater to see Adam Lambert sing his song For your entertainment.
8. The radio show Performance today stars Fred Child.
9. The song Joyful, Joyful comes from Beethoven's symphony Ode to joy.
10. We'll sail to Mexico aboard a boat called The lark Of The sea.

MindTap® Practice skills that you have learned in this section and receive automatic feedback.

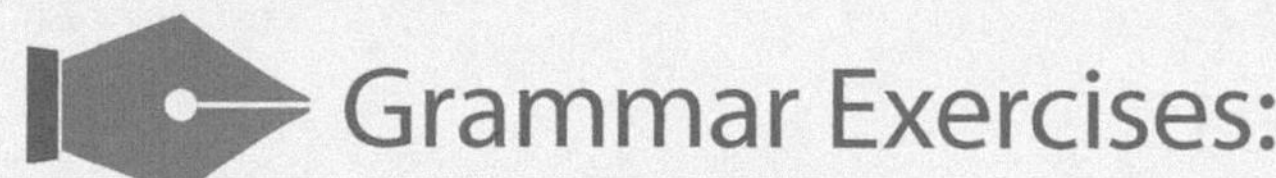

Grammar Exercises:

A. Capitalization, Plurals

Correct the capitalization and plural errors in each sentence by writing the correct word or words.

1. Some Holidays fall on different daies of the week.
2. A holiday like the fourth of july or halloween can fall on only one Date but on any day.
3. Holidaies such as Memorial day or Labor day always fall on a Monday.
4. In the badger state, christmas is often white, but in the aloha state, it never is.
5. Festivals such as taste of chicago or milwaukee's summerfest stretch out over weekes.
6. In that way, these celebrationes are similar to chinese new year, which lasts for many daies.
7. On new year's eve in the west, husbands dance with their wifes and leave their childs with babysitters.
8. Reveleres often have a few glassesful of wine or champagne to celebrate New year's eve.
9. It's funny how most Americanes don't know when columbus day is, which celebrates Columbus's discovery of the new world.
10. It's also strange how many earthlings don't know if earth day is in march, april, or may.

B. Numbers and Spelling

Correct the number and spelling errors in each sentence by writing the correct form or words.

1. Do monkies and other great aps like to eat French frys?
2. 300 million Americans seem to like frys, as do many of the 6,000,000,000 others in the world.
3. Fries and a 4- or eight-ounce burger is a common meal for Americans.
4. If you drive through before eleven a.m., you'll get hashes brown instead of frys at most fast-food places.
5. One eight-ounce burger can pack a whopping four hundred fifty calories.
6. The local fast-food restaurant employs 43 people, with 2 Steve's and 3 Jacob's.
7. They cut about three hundred tomatos every day.
8. In addition to 11 fry cooks, they employ 3 cheves.
9. They advertise over 1,000,000,000 served.
10. On each burger, they squirt one teaspoon of ketchup and one half teaspoon of mustard.

Grammar Exercises:

Spelling

Write the correct spelling of each word below.

1. abundence
2. acommodate
3. aquiesce
4. advize
5. althrough
6. annoint
7. biscut
8. celibration
9. comission
10. concieve
11. confidencial
12. consientous
13. deseased
14. dependant
15. disipline
16. eficeincy
17. essencial
18. exhorbitant
19. extreem
20. Feberary
21. freind
22. harrass
23. interupt
24. irigate
25. judgement
26. laundary
27. licence
28. ofen
29. opperate
30. parlament
31. personell
32. preferrance
33. previlant
34. procede
35. pumkin
36. questionaire
37. reccurrence
38. rehersal
39. restaraunt
40. reumatism
41. sceen
42. seperate
43. simmilar
44. speciman
45. stomache
46. sumerize
47. surveylance
48. unneccessary
49. useable
50. vegtable
51. villian
52. volunter
53. wether
54. wholely
55. writen
56. yeild

MindTap® Practice skills that you have learned in this section and receive automatic feedback.

Grammar Exercises:

Usage

Correct the usage in the following document by writing down the line number and the usage errors, crossed out, with the correct words beside them.

When I sat down to eat at Leon's Texas Grill, I remembered a friend's advise: "Alright, get ready for allot of food." His prediction was all together accurate. When I smelled the delicious aroma of beef brisket on the barbecue, I was anxious to get some of my own. I wanted it bad. But the brisket was complimented by beans, potato salad, and other sides. Leon's also offered spicy sausage, steaks, and more meats than I could chose from. I decided that the first coarse would be brisket with beans. I had a guilty conscious as I ate fore hunks of brisket and went back for more. Everything tasted so well. I was under no allusion that I would be loosing wait tonight.

Brisket would normally be vary tough, but slow grilling assures its tenderness. Brisket often cooks for hours and is only latter served to customers. What an ingenuous way to make tough meat flavorful and delicious! I was liable to literally eat everything in the restaurant, and then loose conscienceness.

I was in the midst of my third helping when one of the restaurant's personal past me with a cart that had peaces of cake and pie and other types of desert. My pour stomach was already quiet full, and I felt real sleepy, but from my prospective, I wasn't going to be getting back here anytime soon. Those were sum of the most delicious sweets I'd ever scene. I looked threw all the options their and picked too cupcakes. I was being vary gluttonous, and my waste would reveal my indiscretions.

After my meal, I wished I could meet the man whom established this restaurant. I would have told him, "Leon, your my hero." Then, a second latter, I would've past out.

Grammar Exercises:

A. Noun, Pronoun, Verb, Adjective, Adverb

Identify each underlined word as a noun (n), a pronoun (pron), a verb (v), an adjective (adj), or an adverb (adv).

(1) You may not (2) think much about that (3) green stuff under your feet—yes, (4) grass—but it has conquered the world. Grass didn't exist at all until the (5) late Cretaceous period, but once it (6) arrived on the scene, (7) it took over. Whole animal (8) species grew up to graze upon this (9) hardy plant, eating both the leaves and the (10) heads of grain. Some types of grass, such as barley, (11) produce grains that humans (12) also eat. Farm kids (13) often pluck a long stalk of grass and chew on (14) it, but you wouldn't be able to chew on the (15) largest stalks from the grass family—the giant bamboo. Unlike its (16) tiny cousins, bamboo plants grow (17) so rapidly that they have been purported to be used to torture people. (18) Maybe they are just getting back at (19) us for (20) always walking on top of them.

B. Coordinating, Correlative, and Subordinating Conjunctions

Create a three-column table, labeling the columns "Coordinating," "Correlative," and "Subordinating." Then sort the following conjunctions, writing them in their correct columns.

as long as	so that	whenever
after	so	as
yet	or	whereas
both/and	even though	until
when	for	nor
because	where	not only/but also
either/or	as if	and
though	in order that	provided that
before	whether/or	
neither/nor	but	
while	since	
although	unless	

Grammar Exercises:

A. Fragments

Turn each fragment into a sentence by adding what is missing (a subject, a verb, a subject and a verb, or a complete thought).

1. During the big game.
2. When we scored the winning goal.
3. Shouted our fight song.
4. Just before the whistle blew.
5. Smiling from ear to ear.
6. The scoreboard overhead.
7. With looks of amazement.
8. In order to commemorate the win.
9. The college newspaper.
10. Whenever we win a big game.

B. Other Sentence Errors

Rewrite each sentence, fixing the comma splice, run-on, agreement error, or nonstandard language.

1. The team fought like never before they won in overtime.
2. Each team member gave their all.
3. Three touchdowns, three extra points, and a field goal sets the score at 24-21.
4. Tim, Jake, and Kurt, they played their best games ever.
5. Tim broke his passing record, Jake beat his rushing yards.
6. Kurt been kicking the ball through the goalposts every time.
7. You should of been there.
8. I'm gonna watch every game this year.
9. Coach Carlson say he's never had such a good team.
10. I is planning to try out next year.

C. Dangling/Misplaced Modifiers

Rewrite each sentence to correct the dangling or misplaced modifiers.

1. After watching from the stands for the whole game, the team scored the winning field goal.
2. I congratulated the linebacker for tackling the quarterback on his way to the locker room.
3. A kicker once punted the ball from our second string.
4. A cheerleader climbed to the top of the pyramid with red hair.
5. After kicking the winning field goal, the other team left looking dejected.

Index